THE ZOHAR: RECEPTION AND IMPACT

THE LITTMAN LIBRARY OF
JEWISH CIVILIZATION

Life Patron
COLETTE LITTMAN

Dedicated to the memory of
LOUIS THOMAS SIDNEY LITTMAN
who founded the Littman Library for the love of God
and as an act of charity in memory of his father
JOSEPH AARON LITTMAN
and to the memory of
ROBERT JOSEPH LITTMAN
who continued what his father Louis had begun
יהא זכרם ברוך

'Get wisdom, get understanding:
Forsake her not and she shall preserve thee'
PROV. 4:5

The Zohar
Reception and Impact

BOAZ HUSS

TRANSLATED BY YUDITH NAVE

London
The Littman Library of Jewish Civilization
in association with Liverpool University Press

The Littman Library of Jewish Civilization
Registered office: 14th Floor, 33 Cavendish Square, London W1G 0PW

in association with Liverpool University Press
4 Cambridge Street, Liverpool L69 7ZU, UK
www.liverpooluniversitypress.co.uk/littman

Managing Editor: Connie Webber

Distributed in North America by Longleaf Services
116 S Boundary St, Chapel Hill, NC 27514, USA

First published in Hebrew 2008

First published in English 2016
First published in paperback 2024

Catalogue records for this book are available from the
British Library and the Library of Congress

ISBN 978–1–802075–84–7

Publishing co-ordinator: Janet Moth
Copy-editing: Agnes Erdos
Proofreading: Ezra Margulies
Index: Meg Davies FSI
Designed and typeset by Pete Russell, Faringdon, Oxon.

Printed and bound by CPI Group (UK) Ltd, Croydon, CR0 4YY

Preface

THIS BOOK is dedicated to the study of the various modes of reception of the Zohar and the impact it has had on Jewish culture over the centuries. Rather than presenting an exhaustive chronological description, it focuses on key aspects of its reception and impact, such as its literary formation and canonization, its dispersal and veneration, as well as criticisms of the Zohar and the polemics surrounding it.

The volume was first published in Hebrew by the Ben-Zvi Institute and the Bialik Institute. This English translation, diligently prepared by Yudith Nave, contains only minor differences from the Hebrew edition: some of the more detailed bibliographical discussions have been omitted, and references to new studies which appeared after the publication of the Hebrew volume have been added.

It is a great honour and pleasure for me to publish the English edition with the Littman Library of Jewish Civilization. I am very grateful to Connie Webber, the managing editor of the Littman Library, who accompanied the translation project from its beginning, for her efficiency, patience, and support. I thank Yudith Nave and her team for the efforts they put into translating the text. I would also like to thank Janet Moth for her editorial work. I am especially indebted to Agi Erdos, whose wisdom and knowledge much enhanced the final text.

Beer Sheva
December 2015

BOAZ HUSS

Translator's Preface

THIS TRANSLATION is a collaborative effort by the Hebrew Institute of Boston. It was my pleasure to translate this book with Samuel Tarlin, Alix Ginsburg, and Aaron Dockser. I would like also to acknowledge and thank my friends, Phyllis Birnbaum, Larry Denenberg, Dan Deykin, Raya Dreben, and Bill Moran, who volunteered to proofread different parts of the translation and whose observations and remarks had a significant impact on the final work. Last but not least I would like to express my gratitude to Connie Webber, managing editor of the Littman Library of Jewish Civilization, and to Professor Boaz Huss of the University of Beersheba in Israel for entrusting this enormous project to me.

It is hard to imagine the amount of time and work required to complete a translation of an academic text saturated with biblical, talmudic, and cryptic zoharic quotations, as well as statements of *rishonim* and *aḥaronim*. When scholars support their arguments by quoting ancient sources, the sources speak for themselves. The translator of these sources, however, is responsible for conveying the allusions, metaphors, style, and meanings that are not always straightforward. This may explain why the most obscure segments of the Zohar were omitted from the Soncino translation.

Huss's narrative is very clear, and he was always available to answer our questions, but the cryptic zoharic quotations posed a real challenge. Our goal was to produce an intelligible translation of the basic meaning of these quotations without losing the biblical and talmudic allusions embedded within them. Towards that end we relied on the best-known and most commonly used translations of the Bible, the JPS New Translation of the Holy Scriptures (1985) and the New King James Version of the Old and New Testaments (1982). Whenever possible we used the Soncino translation of the Talmud and of the Zohar. We also consulted David Goldstein's translation of the Zohar and that of Daniel Matt.

Yet even after Professor Huss approved our interpretations of the zoharic quotations we were still left with the methodological and stylistic question—to what extent should we paraphrase cryptic passages to make them accessible to the reader? Although intelligibility was our primary goal, we also wanted to preserve some of the mystical and cryptic character of the original zoharic texts. We therefore avoided paraphrasing the text as much as possible.

As for the irony and satire in playful Hebrew rhyme used by maskilim and other opponents of Jewish mysticism, we attempted to preserve the same style in the English translation.

We would like to emphasize that we did not translate Bourdieu's quotations from the French and Geiger's and Scholem's from German. Professor Huss chose to quote these segments from the existing English version of each of these works.

We were challenged by this work and we learned much from it.

YUDITH NAVE

*

The Littman Library records with sorrow that
Yudith Nave died on 4 January 2016, while this book was
being prepared for press.
Her skills as a translator and her passionate concern for
each word will be much missed.

Contents

Note on Transliteration

THE TRANSLITERATION of Hebrew in this book reflects consideration of the type of book it is, in terms of its content, purpose, and readership. The system adopted therefore reflects a broad approach to transcription, rather than the narrower approaches found in the *Encyclopaedia Judaica* or other systems developed for text-based or linguistic studies. The aim has been to reflect the pronunciation prescribed for modern Hebrew, rather than the spelling or Hebrew word structure, and to do so using conventions that are generally familiar to the English-speaking reader.

In accordance with this approach, no attempt is made to indicate the distinctions between *alef* and *ayin*, *tet* and *taf*, *kaf* and *kuf*, *sin* and *samekh*, since these are not relevant to pronunciation; likewise, the *dagesh* is not indicated except where it affects pronunciation. Following the principle of using conventions familiar to the majority of readers, however, transcriptions that are well established have been retained even when they are not fully consistent with the transliteration system adopted. On similar grounds, the *tsadi* is rendered by 'tz' in such familiar words as barmitzvah. Likewise, the distinction between *ḥet* and *khaf* has been retained, using *ḥ* for the former and *kh* for the latter; the associated forms are generally familiar to readers, even if the distinction is not actually borne out in pronunciation, and for the same reason the final *heh* is indicated too. As in Hebrew, no capital letters are used, except that an initial capital has been retained in transliterating titles of published works (for example, *Shulḥan arukh*).

Since no distinction is made between *alef* and *ayin*, they are indicated by an apostrophe only in intervocalic positions where a failure to do so could lead an English-speaking reader to pronounce the vowel-cluster as a diphthong—as, for example, in *ha'ir*—or otherwise mispronounce the word.

The *sheva na* is indicated by an *e*—*perikat ol*, *reshut*—except, again, when established convention dictates otherwise.

The *yod* is represented by *i* when it occurs as a vowel (*bereshit*), by *y* when it occurs as a consonant (*yesodot*), and by *yi* when it occurs as both (*yisra'el*).

Names have generally been left in their familiar forms, even when this is inconsistent with the overall system.

Introduction

THE ZOHAR is one of the most sacred, authoritative, and influential books in Jewish culture, and it has also attracted the interest of many non-Jews. It is a collection of texts which were probably written by several Castilian authors in the late thirteenth and early fourteenth centuries. Soon after their first appearance, these texts came to be perceived as part of a literary work attributed to the *tana* R. Shimon bar Yohai (Rashbi) and called 'the Zohar'.

Many scholarly works have been dedicated to the ideas found in the Zohar, to its literary style, and to the question of its authorship. This book focuses on different questions: its purpose is to examine the ways in which the Zohar was received and the impact it had on Jewish culture, from its emergence in the thirteenth century to the present. In the chapters that follow I look at the fluctuations in the Zohar's status and value, and explore the various cultural practices linked to these changes. I also throw light on the fact that those who determined the Zohar's value often did so in an effort to strengthen their own cultural power.

From its earliest appearance, several kabbalistic circles invested the Zohar with a status of authority and holiness. Yet it only became widely accepted as a pre-eminent source of doctrines, laws, and customs after the finalization and printing of the zoharic corpus in the sixteenth century. Numerous commentaries have been written on it since, and Zohar exegesis has become one of the most prevalent genres of kabbalistic literature, if not *the* most prevalent. Several kabbalistic systems, especially the Lurianic one, were created to a large degree as an interpretation of the Zohar. Since the eighteenth century, customs and practices described in the Zohar, such as the night prayer on Shavuot, inviting *ushpizin* (guests) to the *sukah*, and the recitation of the 'Berikh shemeh' prayer, have been widely adopted.

Zoharic excerpts have been incorporated into the liturgy, and the practice of ritual reading of the Zohar has been established, based on the belief that its text is so sacred that its recital is beneficial even if one does not understand its content. From the sixteenth century on, Christian scholars, too, showed interest in the Zohar, and it was translated first into Latin and later into modern European languages.

Yet not everyone accepted the Zohar's sanctity; ever since its first appearance, there have been scholars who questioned or denied its divine provenance, authority, and antiquity, as well as R. Shimon's authorship. Up until the eighteenth century, though, such criticism was very rare. During the Haskalah (Jewish Enlightenment) Zohar criticism became more central, and in the nineteenth century many historical studies, polemical works, satires, and parodies were written by maskilim against kabbalah in general, and the Zohar in particular. However, in the late nineteenth and early twentieth centuries, under the influence of neo-Romantic trends and in the context of the rise of Jewish nationalism, a new approach to the Zohar emerged. While scholars continued to deny its ancient and sacred origins, they came to recognize its historical and literary importance. It was within this framework that the academic research of the Zohar was developed, primarily by Gershom Scholem, the founder of modern kabbalah scholarship.

Conflicting approaches to the Zohar have persisted to the present day. There are those who believe in its sanctity and authority, while others appreciate its literary and historical value. Interest in the Zohar has grown significantly in recent years, and its study, ritual reading, research, commentary, translation, and printing have proliferated.

In this study I explore different aspects of the Zohar's reception from its appearance to the present day. This reception history examines not only how readers responded to the Zohar over time, but also how the Zoharic texts themselves changed, how they were transmitted and translated, and, in general, how they were used. Below I present a short survey of previous research published on the reception history of the Zohar, but before doing so I would like to dedicate a few words to the textual complexity of this unparalleled work of kabbalah.

As mentioned above, the Zohar is a collection of texts. The scope of this collection as we know it today was defined, to a great extent, by its first printers in the second half of the sixteenth century. During that period three zoharic texts were printed: *Tikunei hazohar* (Mantua, 1557), two editions of Zohar on the Torah (Mantua, 1558–60; Cremona, 1559–60), and *Zohar ḥadash* (Salonica, 1597). Later printers relied on these editions, and notwithstanding some textual changes they introduced, the general format of the Zohar continued to follow the editions published in the sixteenth century.

The printed editions of the Zohar were, naturally, preceded by a number of manuscripts, which comprise a variety of textual units written in the late thirteenth and early fourteenth centuries. These manuscript collections differ from each other in the range of material they contain, but none of them compares in scope to the printed editions. Gershom Scholem has identified about twenty different textual units in the zoharic collections, including Zohar commentaries on the Torah portions (the so-called 'body of the Zohar'), *Midrash hane'elam*, *Tikunei hazohar*, *Ra'aya meheimna*, and *Sifra ditseniuta*.[1] Although there are resemblances in content and style between these units, they do not share a single common denominator.

Scholars disagree as to the authorship of these zoharic components. Scholem believed that most of them were written by the kabbalist R. Moses de León in Spain between 1280 and 1286. However, both Scholem and his followers have agreed that the texts known as *Tikunei hazohar* and *Ra'aya meheimna* were composed by a different, anonymous kabbalist in the early fourteenth century.[2] Yehuda Liebes has suggested, on the other hand, that the zoharic units were written by several kabbalists active in Castile in the late thirteenth and early fourteenth centuries, and that the Zohar also contains some earlier materials. Liebes's proposal, which was developed further in the research of Ronit Meroz, is accepted today by most kabbalah scholars.[3]

[1] Scholem, *Major Trends in Jewish Mysticism*, 159–62.

[2] Ibid. 156–204; Tishby and Lachower, *The Wisdom of the Zohar*, i. 92–4.

[3] Liebes, 'How the Zohar Was Written' (Heb.); id., *Studies in the Zohar*, 85–138. Ronit Meroz has developed the theory of multiple authors in many of her studies, including 'Zoharic Narratives', 'Der Aufbau des Buches Zohar', 'The Writing of the Zoharic *Sitrei torah*' (Heb.), and in her forthcoming book *Headwaters of the Zohar* (Heb.). On the possibility that parts of the zoharic texts were written as early as the 11th century see Oron, '*Midrash hane'elam*' (Heb.), 109–49; Meroz, 'The Middle Eastern Origins of the Kabbalah', 39–56.

Some aspects of the Zohar's reception, including its influence on custom, law, and liturgy, its printing and dissemination, as well as its commentaries, have been discussed in the scholarly literature.[4] Isaiah Tishby's introduction to *The Wisdom of the Zohar*, written in collaboration with Fischel Lachower, contains such a survey. In it Tishby discusses the zoharic manuscripts, the printed editions, the commentaries, and modern scholarship on the Zohar.[5] These topics have also been explored in the works of Arthur Green and Daniel Abrams.[6]

Some of the scholarship has focused on the question of the canonization of the Zohar. Scholem and Tishby have claimed that it was in the sixteenth century, in the wake of the expulsion from Spain, that it was accepted as a canonical text;[7] Moshe Idel, however, believes that its canonization had taken place in the fourteenth century, soon after its appearance.[8] Zeev Gries, who has set up his own criteria for a text to be accepted into the Jewish cultural canon, has argued that the Zohar was not canonized until the second half of the eighteenth century.[9]

Differences among scholars stem mainly from their different definitions of the term 'canon',[10] as well as from a lack of specification of the communities and periods in which the Zohar was accepted as a canonical text. If the adjective 'canonical' describes an important work to which sacredness and authority are attributed, then the Zohar, indeed, already had canonical status in some kabbalistic circles, mainly in Spain, in the fourteenth century. However, only in the sixteenth century was it granted such status by a wider range of cultural circles, at first by the intellectual elite of the Spanish exiles and later by the rabbinic elite in Italy, Ashkenaz, and other Jewish communities. Yet, if the term 'canon' denotes a closed literary

[4] The relevant studies will be mentioned in the following chapters.

[5] Tishby and Lachower, *The Wisdom of the Zohar*, i. 13–105.

[6] Green, *A Guide to the Zohar*, 178–87; Abrams, *Kabbalistic Manuscripts and Textual Theory*, 224–438.

[7] Scholem, *Major Trends in Jewish Mysticism*, 156; Tishby and Lachower, *The Wisdom of the Zohar*, i. 25; Green, *A Guide to the Zohar*, 181–2.

[8] Idel, *Kabbalah*, 216; id., 'On Symbolic Self-Interpretations' (Heb.), 95.

[9] Gries, 'The Copying and Printing of Kabbalistic Books' (Heb.), 208–10; id., *The Book in the Jewish World*, 76–80.

[10] For a survey of scholarly definitions of 'canon' and 'canonization' see Huss, '*Sefer Hazohar* as a Canonical, Sacred and Holy Text', 258–61.

corpus—that is, one to which nothing can be added and from which nothing can be taken away—then the (almost final) canonization of the Zohar occurred only in the second half of the sixteenth century, when its first editions were printed in Mantua, Cremona, and Salonica. Then again, if we employ Gries's definition, according to which a text becomes part of the Jewish cultural canon only when it is integrated into scheduled study and ritual order, the Zohar was not canonized until as late as the eighteenth century. The dating depends, then, on the meaning of 'canon' and on specifying the communities in which the Zohar obtained such status. In what follows, I use the term 'canon' in the sense of privileged texts that obtain a central status in a certain community or cultural system, with special reference to recognition of the Zohar as an authoritative source and to the formation of the printed zoharic corpus.

The chapters of this book examine various aspects of the reception and canonization of the Zohar, as well as of its criticism and rejection. An underlying assumption of these discussions is that the different values attributed to the Zohar—its being a source of authority, a sacred book, a mystical text, or a work of national and literary import—are not inherent or permanent qualities, but rather values that readers ascribed to it in different cultural contexts. As the scholar of comparative religion Wilfred Cantwell Smith has argued: 'Being scripture is not a quality inherent in a given text or type of text so much as an interactive relation between that text and a community of persons.'[11] I believe this is true regarding any object to which values are attributed, particularly literary texts. In the words of the literary critic Barbara Herrnstein Smith, 'all value is radically contingent, being neither a fixed attribute, an inherent quality, or an objective property of things, but, rather, an effect of multiple, continuously interacting variables, or to put it another way, the product of the dynamics of a system, specifically an economic system.'[12]

The French sociologist and philosopher Pierre Bourdieu claims, in relation to works of art, that they 'exist as symbolic objects only if they are

[11] W. C. Smith, *What Is Scripture?*, 9.

[12] B. H. Smith, *Contingencies of Value*, 30. Smith's position is very close to Bourdieu's, according to which aesthetic value is a variable of a complex system and is contingent upon social and institutional changes. See Randall Johnson's introduction to Bourdieu, *Cultural Production*, 10.

known and recognized, that is, socially instituted as works of art and received by spectators capable of knowing and recognizing them as such'.[13] In Bourdieu's view, it is necessary to investigate not only the material production of a work of art 'but also the symbolic production of the work, that is, the production of the value of the work, or, which amounts to the same thing, of belief in the value of the work'.[14] One must take into consideration not only the direct producers of cultural works but also those who establish their meaning and value, 'the whole set of agents whose combined effort produces consumers capable of knowing and recognizing the works of art as such'.[15]

Bourdieu's conclusions are true with regard to the values ascribed to any literary work, including the Zohar. Basing myself on his and Herrstein Smith's observations, I examine below the attribution of different qualities and values to the Zohar through time, such as 'sacred', 'authoritative', 'mystical', or 'poetic'. I also consider the people who were engaged in establishing these different qualities and values, as well as the social and cultural functions of the creation, re-creation, and rejection of those values, from the early appearance of the zoharic texts until now.

My discussion focuses on the factors that influenced the responses to the Zohar and its reproduction as a privileged text in different historical periods. I also show that it continued to maintain its revered status through the ages, in spite of cultural and social changes, due to the endurance of its value as a sacred and authoritative text. As Herrnstein Smith has pointed out, a literary text that successfully performs various cultural functions in a specific community is more likely to endure than other texts because its chances of being copied, quoted, printed, imitated, and translated are greater; and if a text has a strong presence within that culture, it will be readily available to perform the same functions or others later on.[16] The historical and social conditions that enabled and stimulated the preservation, reproduction, and veneration of the Zohar, as well as the functions it performed through its enduring privileged status, will be part of my analysis.

Another important area to be examined is criticism and rejection of the

[13] Bourdieu, *The Field of Cultural Production*, 37. [14] Ibid.
[15] Ibid. [16] B. H. Smith, *Contingencies of Value*, 48.

Zohar. Such rejection is likely to have occurred not only because the Zohar had ceased to fulfil its previous roles, but also because the criticism itself served a desired goal. Just as the attribution of positive values to the Zohar and its perception as a sacred and authoritative text had their own cultural functions in certain historical periods, so did its dismissal as a forged, degraded, and immoral work. And as its canonical status persisted so did the criticism endure; objections that were raised against it in earlier periods were reproduced in later generations.

In the first chapter of the book I examine the strategy of the Zohar to present itself to readers through a juxtaposition of the figures of R. Shimon bar Yohai and Moses. By means of this contrast the compilers of the work sought to create a canonical literature which was not only comparable to the Torah of Moses but was, they claimed, superior to it. The context for the comparison between R. Shimon and Moses, and for the portrayal of the rabbinic sage as greater than the biblical prophet, is the struggle between competing schools of kabbalah on the Iberian peninsula in the thirteenth century. In the second chapter I describe the emergence of the Zohar as an imagined book, that is, the idea that the zoharic texts are part of a unified work entitled *Sefer hazohar* (Book of the Zohar) and written by R. Shimon. The concept of the Zohar as an ancient and authoritative book was used by its distributors to subvert the dominance of the most prominent kabbalistic school of the period, that headed by Nahmanides and his disciples.

The third chapter discusses the formation of the zoharic manuscript collections, from the early fourteenth century until the first print editions in the second half of the sixteenth century. According to Bourdieu, cultural goods such as pictures, books, dictionaries, instruments, and the like are forms of 'cultural capital', that is, they are part of the knowledge and skills that give people cultural advantages which in turn enable them to attain or preserve a higher status in society.[17] Adopting Bourdieu's concept, I argue that the collectors and scribes of the zoharic manuscripts were accumulating cultural capital: possession of these texts, and the ability to quote from them, increased the power and influence of those who copied, collected, and edited them. As long as the scope of the zoharic canon remained undefined, that is, before the printing of the book, the collectors and editors

[17] Bourdieu, 'Forms of Capital', 243.

strove to compile collections as comprehensive as they could, and thus enhance their cultural capital. This process shaped, to a great extent, the scope of the zoharic canon, which was ultimately defined by the first printers of zoharic literature in the second half of the sixteenth century.

In Chapter 4 I look at the various manifestations of the Zohar's increasing authority and the historical and social contexts that finally led to its recognition by most Jewish communities in the early modern period. A further question I examine is how its perception as a sacred and authoritative work increased the cultural power of the elite circles of the Spanish exile and advanced Sephardi cultural dominance in their new settlements and beyond.

As I point out in Chapter 5, the value of the Zohar as a form of cultural capital was further reflected in the intensive engagement in its interpretation, which became a central practice of kabbalists in the second half of the sixteenth century. Following the rise of Zohar commentary, a struggle ensued in later generations to obtain primacy in this field. Before the formulation of the Zohar in its printed form, the possession of zoharic manuscripts, control over the collection and editing process, and the ability to quote zoharic texts were all a part of the cultural capital of the elite circles of the Iberian exiles. However, following its finalization, printing, and wide dissemination, the Zohar ceased to be a rare commodity; the value of manuscript collections diminished and one could no longer benefit from possessing or quoting the texts. The new way to derive cultural power from the work was to control its meaning. This was achieved through the commentator's ability to establish his interpretation as the authoritative one. Thus, when commentary became the principal genre of kabbalistic literature, the struggle for dominance shifted to the field of hermeneutics.

Chapter 6 focuses on the tension between the desire to disseminate the Zohar and the wish to limit access to it. This tension is inherent in the economic logic of cultural systems as described by Bourdieu: 'all the goods offered tend to lose some of their relative scarcity and their distinctive value as the number of consumers both inclined and able to appropriate them grows'.[18] To increase and maintain the value of cultural products, then, a fine balance must be struck between their circulation, on the one hand, and

[18] Bourdieu, *Sociology in Question*, 108.

restrictions on their accessibility on the other. In establishing the Zohar's image as a sacred and authoritative text, some circulation was necessary; yet uncontrolled access to the book was to diminish its value. In this chapter I discuss the tension that emerged in different periods between those who desired to disseminate the Zohar and those who wished to control its circulation. I pay special attention to eighteenth-century popularization attempts, mainly by Sabbatians, and the reactions that followed, leading to the imposition of restrictions on kabbalistic study.

In addition to the advocates and opponents of the proliferation of the Zohar, there were Jewish scholars who rejected its value altogether and did everything in their power to subvert its revered status. In Chapter 7 I survey the criticism of the Zohar, focusing on the measures the maskilim took against kabbalah in general, and against the Zohar in particular, in the late eighteenth and early nineteenth centuries. Such criticism was part of the maskilic struggle against traditional Jewish circles, especially the hasidic movement in eastern Europe. The rejection of the Zohar played an important role in their endeavour to create a modern European, enlightened Jewish identity, and to distinguish themselves from traditional east European Jewish culture, in which that work had gained canonical status.

The last chapter is dedicated to the re-evaluation of the Zohar at the turn of the nineteenth and twentieth centuries. Under the influence of Jewish national and neo-Romantic trends, the book regained somewhat its old status, although the scholars who called for its recanonization insisted on its purely historical importance, denying its sacredness or divine authority. Rather, they emphasized its unique literary value and the central role it had played in Jewish national history.

The various responses to the Zohar, the values attributed to it, and the scholars who took part in its reproduction and dissemination all played a major role in the shaping of the zoharic canon. It was these forces that established its study and ritual reading, and produced a rich literature of dictionaries, anthologies, commentaries, translations, and academic research. The complex modes of reception of the Zohar have had a decisive influence on the history of Jewish culture from the appearance of the early zoharic texts to the present day. Some aspects of this dynamic and multilayered history are the subject of this book.

CHAPTER ONE

The Depiction of R. Shimon bar Yohai and Moses in Zoharic Literature

A sage is superior to a prophet.
Bava batra 12a

ONE OF THE STRIKING FEATURES of zoharic literature is the frequent comparison between its central protagonist, R. Shimon bar Yohai (Rashbi), and Moses, and the depiction of the mishnaic rabbi as surpassing the biblical prophet. I believe that by means of this comparison the compilers of the Zohar sought to establish a canonical literature which did not only equal the Torah of Moses but which, they claimed, was superior to it. In the chapters that follow I explore the reception of zoharic literature through time; I wish to begin, however, by examining the way in which that literature presented itself to readers through the juxtaposition of R. Shimon and Moses.

The comparison of the two figures reflects the struggle over cultural capital between competing schools of kabbalah on the Iberian peninsula in the thirteenth century. As I show below, this competition was the framework in which the zoharic texts were created and in which their distribution and reception began.

The dominant school of kabbalah at the time was that of the followers of Nahmanides and R. Solomon ben Adret (Rashba). Centred in Catalonia, their school was characterized by an esoteric and conservative stance that opposed the public revelation and dissemination of kabbalistic knowledge. Members of this circle, the disciples of Nahmanides and their students, claimed to have exclusive authority in this field by virtue of the oral tradition that they had received directly from their masters. Nahmanides formulated the essence of this approach in the introduction to his commentary on the Torah. The only way to understand the secrets of kabbalah, he explained, was 'through oral transmission from a master transmitter [*mekubal*] to the ear of a capable recipient [*mekabel*], and any assumption [regarding these secrets] has no merit and is very harmful'.[1]

Nahmanides and his disciples were part of a social class that Moshe Idel has classified as the 'primary elite'. They were the spiritual leadership of the Jewish community in Catalonia and were occupied mainly with halakhah.[2] During the same period, in Castile, a different school of kabbalists was active, whose members, according to Idel's typology, were part of the 'secondary elite'. These kabbalists (Joseph Gikatilla, Isaac ibn Sahula, Moses de León, Joseph Angelet, Joseph of Hamadan, and others) did not hold any public positions and were engaged mainly in kabbalah and philosophy, not halakhah.[3] They developed a novel, creative, and exoteric approach to kabbalah, and it was among them that zoharic texts circulated for the first time. Quite probably some of these kabbalists were the authors of major segments of that literature.

The tensions between Nahmanides' Catalonian circle and the Castilian kabbalists stemmed from their different stance regarding modes of transmitting kabbalistic knowledge and the source of kabbalistic authority. In the context of this cultural struggle the Castilian kabbalists appear to have adopted a more open and innovative approach, which was also reflected in the Zohar. As Moshe Halbertal puts it, 'The Zohar presents a perfect alternative to the concept that the Kabbalah is a closed knowledge.'[4]

Both the attribution of the Zohar to R. Shimon and its promotion as an ancient and authoritative text were intended to subvert the esoteric and conservative approach of Nahmanides and his followers, and to undermine their authority. The pseudepigraphic nature of the Zohar enabled its writers to set their creative imagination free and voice their dissent from the Catalan kabbalists while avoiding direct confrontation with them.

1 *Commentary on the Torah*, ed. Chavel, i. 7.

2 Idel, 'Kabbalah and Elites'.

3 On the difference between kabbalists of the 'secondary' and 'primary' elites in Catalonia and Castile during this period see Idel, 'PaRDeS: Some Reflections on Kabbalistic Hermeneutics', 256; id., 'Transmission in Thirteenth-Century Kabbalah', 146–9.

4 Halbertal, *Concealment and Revelation*, 94. On the innovative and creative nature of the Zohar see Idel, *Kabbalah: New Perspectives*, 212; Liebes, 'Zohar and Eros' (Heb.), 71.

Their implicit criticism is expressed through contrasting depictions of Moses and R. Shimon. Moses, hesitant and modest, reflects the conservative character of Nahmanides, while the daring and confident R. Shimon represents the innovative approach of the Castilian authors of the Zohar.

R. Shimon is the central figure in a considerable part of the zoharic literature. Scholars and kabbalists have struggled with the question: why was this sage, who is not counted among the mystics of the Talmud, given such a major role in the Zohar?[5] Or, as R. Hayim Vital asks, why was it specifically R. Shimon who was given permission to compose the Zohar, and not his teachers or the earlier authorities, given that they would surely have been more knowledgeable about this wisdom?[6]

The choice of R. Shimon for this role was based principally on the talmudic tradition according to which he had been privileged to look through the 'speculum that shines' (*aspaklarya hame'irah*) and to attain the highest level of prophecy, which no one but Moses had attained. Relying on this tradition, the zoharic authors elevated R. Shimon to a mystical status equalling that of Moses. However, in light of the differences between the prophet, who is depicted in the sources as modest, hesitant, and unsure of himself, and the rabbinic sage, who displays unusual self-confidence and self-awareness, the latter actually appears superior to the former.[7]

We find many statements in the zoharic literature—primarily in the so-called 'body of the Zohar'—that draw a parallel between R. Shimon and Moses. For example, the biblical verse 'I will speak face to face with him, plainly and not in riddles' (Num. 12: 8), which is a reference to Moses, is applied to R. Shimon and his contemporaries,[8] as is the verse 'And he drew upon the spirit that was on him and put it upon the seventy elders' (Num. 11: 25):

R. Hezekiah said: it is written: 'And he drew upon the spirit that was on him and gave it to the seventy elders', just like this light, from which many lights are kindled and which yet retains its brightness. That is R. Shimon bar Yohai, the

[5] Liebes, *Studies in the Zohar*, 4.

[6] *Sha'ar ma'amrei rashbi*, 92.

[7] Although the Zohar does not use the talmudic expression 'the sage is superior to the prophet' in comparing R. Shimon to Moses, there is no doubt in my mind that it adopts this view. On the use of this expression in the Zohar see Wolfson, *Through a Speculum that Shines*, 377–8.

[8] Zohar iii. 61*a*, 79*a*.

master of lights who illuminates everyone and yet his light is not diminished but remains steadfast in its full splendour. (Zohar ii. 86*a*)[9]

Zohar 'Shemot' makes an explicit comparison between R. Shimon and Moses:

While R. Shimon was sitting and his son, R. Eleazar, was standing and explicating the mysteries of the words of wisdom, his face was shining like the sun, and the words were spreading and flying in the firmament. They sat for two days, during which they did not eat or drink and they were unaware if it was day or night. When they came out they realized that two days had passed, in which they had tasted nothing. R. Shimon applied to it [the following verse]: '"And he [Moses] was there with the Lord forty days and forty nights; he ate no bread" [Exod. 34: 28]. Thus, if we have experienced it for a short time, then Moses, who was there with the Lord for forty days and forty nights, as scripture attests, even more so.' (Zohar ii. 15*a*)

The comparison of R. Shimon and his son to Moses is apparent not only in the exegesis of Exodus 34: 28 quoted above, but also in the statement that R. Eleazar's face shone like the sun.[10] Furthermore, according to Zohar 'Terumah', a pillar of cloud appears when R. Shimon is expounding the Torah. R. Isaac, who is privileged to see it, links it to the pillar of cloud that stood at the entrance to the Tabernacle (Exod. 33: 10) and explicitly compares R. Shimon's status to that of Moses:

R. Isaac said: it must be so, because one day, while I was walking with him [R. Shimon], he opened his mouth to expound the Torah and I saw a pillar of cloud hanging down from above, and splendour was shining within the pillar. I was very frightened and I said: happy is the man who experienced it in this world. What is written about Moses? 'When all the people saw the pillar of cloud poised at the entrance of the tent, all the people stood and worshipped, each man at the entrance of his tent' [Exod. 33: 10]. It befits Moses, the faithful prophet, supreme over all the prophets of the universe, and the generation who received the Torah at Mount Sinai and observed many miracles and triumphs in Egypt and at the sea. But now, in this generation, it is because of R. Shimon's utmost merit that miracles are revealed by him.

9 In this passage the Zohar draws on a rabbinic commentary on Num. 15: 25: 'What does Moses resemble at that time? A candle that rests on a lamp and lights many candles and its light does not diminish.' *Sifrei devei rav*, ed. Horovitz, 94.

10 Cf. *BB* 75*a*.

Further comparisons between the Exodus generation and that of R. Shimon, as well as between him and Moses, appear in Zohar 'Vayikra':

Come and see: As long as Moses lived he would admonish Israel so they would not be found guilty of sinning against the Holy One, blessed be He. And because Moses had lived among them there shall not be a similar generation till the messiah comes, when they shall see the glory of the Holy One, blessed be He, as that generation did, since they perceived it in a manner that the latter generation did not. As we have learned: A handmaid saw at the sea what even the prophet Ezekiel had not seen.[11] If they perceived so much, how much more so the wives of Israel, and how much more so their children, and how much more so the men, and how much more so their leaders, and even more so Moses, the most faithful supernal prophet, who is above everyone. And now, when the donkey drivers of the desert pour forth such wisdom, how much more so the sages of this generation, and how much more so those who are standing before R. Shimon and learn from him every day, and how very much more so R. Shimon, who is above all. (Zohar iii. 22*b*–23*a*)

The text proceeds to compare the impact of R. Shimon's death to that of Moses: 'After Moses died, [the following] was written: "And the people will go astray, etc." [Deut. 31: 16]. Alas, in the same way, when R. Shimon departs the fountains of wisdom shall be closed and men shall seek wisdom and there will be none to impart it' (Zohar iii. 23*a*).

In the passage that follows and elsewhere,[12] the Zohar presents God's revelation to Moses at Mount Sinai as analogous to R. Shimon's revelation of secrets at the assembly of the companions, which is described in the section entitled *Idra raba* (Great Assembly).[13] Following the death of three sages at the end of the assembly, R. Shimon says: 'Perhaps, God forbid, we were doomed to be punished because we had revealed what has not been revealed since the day Moses stood on Mount Sinai, as it is written [Exod. 34: 28]: "And he was there forty days and forty nights etc."' (Zohar iii. 144*a*). At the same event R. Shimon describes his face as shining like the sun, alluding to the Torah's description of Moses' radiant countenance: 'I see now what no one has seen since Moses ascended Mount Sinai for the second time, because I see my face shining as the fierce sun shines, which is

[11] See *Mekhilta derabi yishma'el*, ed. Horowitz and Rabin, 126.
[12] Zohar i. 216*b*–217*a*.
[13] Liebes, *Studies in the Zohar*, 23; Wolfson, *Through a Speculum that Shines*, 378.

expected to rise and bring healing to the world, as it is written [Mal. 3: 20]: "And for you who revere My name a sun of victory shall rise with healing in its wings"' (Zohar iii. 132*b*).[14]

As previously mentioned, the comparison between Moses and R. Shimon in the zoharic literature is based on talmudic sources. According to a statement in tractate *Yevamot*, Moses was the only prophet to be granted clear and direct vision: 'All the prophets looked through a speculum that does not shine; Moses, our teacher, looked through the speculum that shines' (*Yev.* 49*b*).[15] However, elsewhere in the Talmud two other sages are mentioned who were also permitted to look through the speculum that shines—R. Shimon and his son. In *Sukah* 45*b* and *Sanhedrin* 97*b* the famous words of R. Shimon are quoted: 'I have seen exalted men and they are few. If a thousand, my son and I are among them; if a hundred, my son and I are among them; if two, my son and I are them.' The Talmud wonders whether this is the case: are there indeed so very few exalted men? Rava believed there were many more: 'Eighteen thousand *tsadikim* were standing in the first row in the presence of the Holy One, blessed be He, as it says [Ezek. 48: 35]: "All the way around shall be eighteen thousand."' The Talmud offers the following solution to the apparent contradiction: 'It is not difficult. These [i.e. the few exalted ones] are those looking through the speculum that shines and these [i.e. the 18,000 *tsadikim*] are those looking through the speculum that does not shine.' Subsequently the Talmud says that those who were looking through the speculum that shines were the *lamed vav tsadikim* (thirty-six righteous men), among whom R. Shimon and his son were paramount.

The implied analogy between R. Shimon and Moses based on *Sukah* and *Yevamot* caught the attention of the sages in various periods. R. Samuel Eliezer Edels (Maharsha), in *Ḥidushei ha'agadot* on *Sukah*, compares what

[14] Liebes suggests two additional parallels between Moses and R. Shimon. The first is the erotic description of their interactions with the Shekhinah. Just as Moses died with a kiss, R. Shimon died through sexual union with the Shekhinah. The second parallel noted by Liebes is the Zohar's assertion that Moses and R. Shimon, in contrast to Job, were well acquainted with the powers of evil (*sitra aḥra*). See Liebes, *Studies in the Zohar*, 15, 73, 165 n. 12.

[15] *Vayikra rabah* 1: 14: 'Our teachers said: All the prophets looked through an obscured speculum, as it is written: "When I spoke to the prophets, for I granted many visions etc." [Hos. 12: 11]; and Moses looked through a shining speculum, as it is written: "And he beholds the likeness of the Lord" [Num. 12: 8].' Wolfson, *Through a Speculum that Shines*, 26, 274 n. 11.

R. Shimon says there to the statement in *Yevamot* about Moses:

And we said in chapter 'Ḥaḥolets' [in *Yevamot*] that only Moses looked through the speculum that shines and none of the prophets looked through the speculum that shines. However, there it refers to prophets and here [i.e. in *Sukah*] it refers to righteous men [*tsadikim*] and sages like R. Shimon and his circle, and thus we say: 'A sage is superior to a prophet.'[16]

The first to connect the passages in *Sukah* and *Yevamot* was Nahmanides in *Sha'ar hagemul*:

And it is said in *Sukah*: 'I have seen that there are few exalted men' and interpret it as [follows]: 'Those are looking through the speculum that does not shine and these are looking through the speculum that does shine.' This looking refers to what was said [in *Yevamot*]: 'Moses looked through the speculum that did shine and the rest of the prophets looked through the speculum that did not shine.' They used the verb 'looked' [metaphorically] to indicate intellectual perception and exaltation [*iluy*] of understanding. Therefore he referred to them as exalted men [*benei aliyah*].[17]

Although Nahmanides links his interpretation of R. Shimon's statement in *Sukah* to what is said about Moses in *Yevamot*, it is noteworthy that he never mentions R. Shimon by name.

Moses de León, who played an important role in the authorship of the zoharic literature, also links these segments. Clearly influenced by Nahmanides' *Sha'ar hagemul*,[18] he writes in *Sefer hamishkal*:

And as for what the Sage said—'I have seen exalted men and they are few'—it must be so, because only a few ascend and enter without [needing] permission. And one knows that God, blessed and blessed be He, no one can come instantly before Him. Even a *tsadik* like Moses had to enter the supreme light gradually. At the beginning of his prophecy, [when he was still] unaccustomed to the splendour, only the speculum that does not shine was revealed to him, not the one that shines. Only after he adjusted to the light was the shining speculum revealed.[19]

[16] Moses Kunitz also alludes to this comparison in *Sefer ben yoḥai*, 18*a*.

[17] Nahmanides, *Collected Works*, ed. Chavel, ii. 297. Wolfson, *Through a Speculum that Shines*, 305.

[18] Compare Nahmanides, *Collected Works*, ed. Chavel, ii. 297 to Wijnhoven, '*Sefer hamishkal*: Text and Study', 59.

[19] Wijnhoven, '*Sefer hamishkal*: Text and Study', 58.

As we can see, de León not only compares the few exalted men to Moses, but even suggests their superiority. Like Nahmanides, he avoids mentioning R. Shimon by name and refers to him as 'the Sage'. Elsewhere in his writings de León quotes R. Shimon's statement in *Sukah* and once again avoids mentioning his name.[20] This avoidance is significant in this context as it clearly indicates an attempt to obscure the comparison between R. Shimon and Moses, which in the zoharic literature is explicit.[21]

The analogy between the two figures, then, originated in talmudic sources, according to which both men looked through the speculum that shines (*aspaklarya hame'irah*). The word *aspaklarya* denotes a glass window, transparent stone, or a mirror. In the zoharic literature it refers to a transparent or reflective medium through which Moses and R. Shimon and his son (as well as the rest of the *lamed vav tsadikim*, as stated in tractate *Sukah*) encounter God.[22] Furthermore, in kabbalistic literature the speculum is not only a medium through which one observes God but it is in itself a divine entity that constitutes the object of observation. In most cases the speculum that shines is identified with the *sefirah* Tiferet, and the speculum that does not shine with that of Malkhut.[23] A kabbalistic reading of the above talmudic passages would suggest, therefore, that Moses and R. Shimon had attained the same level in the divine system.

One who looks into a mirror sees his or her own image. Indeed, this is how some understood the passages of the Talmud regarding the speculum that shines. Abraham Abulafia writes:

[20] Wolfson, *The Book of the Pomegranate*, 373; Scholem, 'Two Booklets by Moses de León' (Heb.), 253.

[21] Such explicit comparison between Moses and R. Shimon, and the claim that the latter is superior, contradict the seventh principle of Maimonides' Thirteen Principles of Faith. It should be noted that, at the beginning of the 13th century, Samuel Benvenisti was vehemently attacked by Makhir bar Sheshet for arguing (on the basis of rabbinic teachings) that the prophet Samuel was greater than Moses. See Baer, *The History of the Jews* (Heb.), 483 n. 43; Septimus, 'Hasidism and Power', 199, 209–10.

[22] About the observation technique of a reflecting medium to attain a prophetic experience, and its relation to the 'speculum that shines', see Gruenwald, 'The Speculum and the Technique of Prophetic and Apocalyptic Vision' (Heb.); Idel, 'On the Medieval Development of an Ancient Technique' (Heb.).

[23] On the identification of the *aspaklarya* with the *sefirah* Malkhut in the history of kabbalah see Wolfson, *Through a Speculum that Shines*, 351–2; Goetschel, 'Conception of Prophecy' (Heb.), 223–6, and David ben Judah Hehasid, *Sefer marot hatsovot*, ed. Matt, 9–10.

And regarding this man [the perfect one] it is said: 'And upon this semblance of a throne there was the semblance of a human form' [Ezek. 1: 26]. It [the semblance] appeared to him [the perfect man] in his own image. And his appearance was the semblance of the Presence of the Lord, and he sees himself in the mirror that illuminates [*aspaklarya hame'irah*] the eyes and the heart, and it is called the inner *urim vetumim*.[24]

It is likely that the authors of the Zohar knew about the possible interpretation of the speculum as a mirror. They, too, may have understood R. Shimon's and Moses' ability to peer into the speculum as a testimony to their self-awareness. This does not contradict the conception that the two men were privileged to observe God—the zoharic literature teaches that both of them were the embodiments of divine *sefirot*.[25]

R. Shimon's shining face at the Great Assembly is an allusion to Moses' face at Mount Sinai. This similarity suggests that looking through the speculum that shines causes the face to shine. Ezra of Gerona links this interpretation to Judah Halevi's discussion of the radiance of Moses' face in the *Kuzari*.[26] Apparently this interpretation was applied in the Zohar and led to the conclusion that R. Shimon's face shone because he, too, must have gazed into the speculum that shines.

The idea that the divine light is reflected in the faces of those who are privileged to look into the speculum that shines underlies, I believe, the

[24] Abulafia, *Imrei shefer*, 104–5; Idel, *The Mystical Experience in Abraham Abulafia*, 107.

[25] Liebes, *Studies in the Zohar*, 15.

[26] In *The Kuzari*, pt. A, ch. 109, he says:

> And none of the prophets but Moses attained the light, which is the light of the speculum that shines, but [they attained] joy, which is the one that does not shine, by which they [the prophets] are distinguished from each other in gradation, and *Bava batra* refers to this in chapter *lo yaḥpor* and similarly in the case of 'You shall give some of your authority to him [Joshua]' [Num. 27: 20]. Some of your authority but not all of your authority. The elders of that generation said: The face of Moses was like the sun [but] the face of Joshua is like the moon. And one can discover that one of the intellectuals wrote in his book that the sensible light rested on his face and the intellectual light rested in his heart.

See also Almalikh, *Likutei shikheḥah ufe'ah*, 7a; Azriel of Gerona, *Perush ha'agadot*, ed. Tishby, 34 n. 15. Ibn Ezra, in his commentary on Exod. 34: 29, employs this verse to explain the luminous countenance of Moses: 'And Moses did not know that the skin of his face was radiant while He had spoken with him . . . because the glory was seen upon his face, therefore it shone like the brightness of the firmament.'

way in which the authors of the Zohar understood the key verse to their work: 'And the enlightened will shine like the bright expanse [*zohar*] of the firmament' (Dan. 12: 3). Hence the book's title—Zohar—may refer to the divine light that is reflected in the speculum that shines, and into which Moses and R. Shimon looked, causing their faces to shine like the 'bright expanse of the firmament'.

Moses' depiction as worthy to look into the speculum that shines and as superior to all other prophets recurs in the zoharic literature again and again.[27] Yet the Zohar also implies that R. Shimon is greater than Moses. For example, according to Zohar 'Ruth', he has the power to annul God's decree while visiting the city of Lod during the plague:

For once there was a plague in Lod. R. Shimon bar Yohai came to the city. They said to R. Shimon: What shall we do? He got up and walked through the city and saw people dying. He said: Is all this happening in the city while I am here? I decree it to stop. They heard a divine voice saying: Get out of here since R. Shimon bar Yohai is here and what the Blessed One decrees he annuls. (*Zohar ḥadash* 85*c*)

When R. Hanina told R. Meir what had happened, the latter compared R. Shimon to Moses, saying:

Then Moses said to Aaron: 'Take the fire pan and put on it fire from the altar and add incense' [Num. 17: 11], and it is written: 'And Aaron took etc.' [Num. 17: 12]. And it is written: 'And the plague had begun among the people' [Num. 17: 13]. And it is written: 'He stood between the dead and the living until the plague was checked' [ibid.]. Moses did it through labour while R. Shimon did it through speech. The Holy One, blessed be He, decrees, and R. Shimon annuls the plague. (*Zohar ḥadash* 85*d*)

According to R. Meir's exegesis, Moses needed to burn incense in order to stop the plague,[28] while R. Shimon was able to annul the decree of the Holy One by means of speech alone. The zoharic story about his power is based on statements in the Talmud regarding the *tsadik* who is able to annul God's decree:

The God of Israel has spoken, the Rock of Israel said concerning me: 'He who rules men justly, he who rules in awe of God' [2 Sam. 23: 3]. What does it mean?

[27] Wolfson, *Through a Speculum that Shines*, 351, 379.

[28] R. Meir was surely alluding to the talmudic tradition (*Shab.* 89*a*) according to which the angel of death had taught Moses how to fight the plague.

R. Abahu said: 'This is what it means: The God of Israel has spoken, the Rock of Israel said concerning me: I rule over men. Who rules over Me? A *tsadik*. For I decree and he annuls.' (*MK* 16*b*)

Zohar 'Vayikra' paraphrases the above passage, asserting that R. Shimon is an example of a *tsadik* who is able to annul the decrees of the Holy One:

Thus the sign that a virtuous man is a *tsadik* is that the rainbow does not appear in his days and the world does not need that sign while he lives. Who is he? He is the one who prays for the world and is found worthy to shield it, like R. Shimon, in whose days the world never required a sign,[29] for he himself was a sign,[30] for if ever a decree was ordained in heaven against the world, he annulled it, as it is written: 'He who rules men' [2 Sam. 23: 3]. The Holy One, blessed be He, rules men, and who rules the Holy One, blessed be He? As it were, a *tsadik*, for the Holy One decrees and he annuls. (Zohar iii. 15*a*)

R. Shimon subsequently learns of a decree and goes forth to annul it. He and his son enter a vineyard and face the powers of evil, represented by a snake. After he fights and subdues it, he says: '"Snake, snake, go and tell the supernal serpent that R. Shimon exists in the world." It put its head into a crevice in the ground and R. Shimon says: "I decree that just as the lowest returned to its crevice in the ground, so the supernal serpent shall be returned to the crevice of the great abyss"' (Zohar iii. 15*a*).

Similarly to R. Shimon annulling the plague in the city of Lod in Zohar 'Ruth', here, too, a divine voice announces that the forces of evil are leaving the world because of the sage's virtues. The divine voice then adds the following: 'Blessed are you, R. Shimon, that your Master delights in honouring you more than the rest of mankind. Of Moses it is written: "And Moses implored [*vayeḥal*] etc." [Exod. 32: 11], which means that he was seized by gout.[31] And you, R. Shimon, decree and the Holy One fulfils.[32] He decrees and you annul' (Zohar iii. 15*a*).

The words of the divine voice regarding the gout that seizes Moses are based on the discussion of the word *vayeḥal* in *Berakhot* 32*a*: '"And Moses implored the Lord". And [in a *baraita*] R. Eliezer the Great says: "It teaches

[29] Based on JT *Ber.* 9*b* (13*d*).
[30] Zohar i. 225*a*. For its source see *Pesikta derav kahana*, ed. Mandelbaum, i. 190 (11: 15).
[31] *Pargoda*, which probably should be read as *pudagra*, i.e. gout (see *San.* 48*b*; *Sot.* 10*a*).
[32] See also *Zohar ḥadash*, 'Ki tavo', 60*a*.

that Moses was engaged in praying before the Holy One, blessed be He, until he was seized by *aḥilu*. What is *aḥilu*? R. Eleazar said: "Fire of the bones."' The obscure term *aḥilu* is understood by R. Eleazar to mean fever. It seems that in the above passage the Zohar replaces 'seized by *aḥilu*' with 'seized by *pudagra* [gout]', which appears elsewhere in the Talmud.[33] In this passage R. Shimon's superiority to Moses lies in the nature of his interaction with God. Moses pleads with God on behalf of Israel until fever (or trembling) seizes him,[34] while R. Shimon decrees and the Holy One fulfils. The description of R. Shimon fighting the snake and subduing it, in contrast to Moses, who flees the rod that turns into a snake,[35] further supports the portrayal of R. Shimon as superior.

Moses' fear of the snake is adapted in a zoharic story on portion 'Bo'. It describes the struggles of Moses and R. Shimon with the supernal sea serpent, the head of the powers of evil (usually termed in the Zohar *sitra aḥra*, the other side—that is, the side opposite the holy powers).[36] Unlike R. Shimon, who wrestles with both the lowly serpent and the supernal one, Moses fears approaching the supernal sea serpent (identified here also with Pharaoh) and the Holy One is forced to fight him by himself:

One mighty supernal sea serpent from which many lesser serpents emanate, what is it? The secret of the big serpent. Moses was afraid of it, and he only approached its streams, which are its subsidiaries. He did not approach it [the serpent] for he saw it rooted above and he feared it. When the Holy one, blessed be He, saw that Moses was afraid, and none of the celestial emissaries was able to approach it, He proclaimed: 'Behold, I am against you Pharaoh, king of Egypt, the great serpent sprawling amidst his streams' [Ezek. 29: 30]. And the Lord Himself had to war against it and no one else. (Zohar ii. 34*a*)

[33] *San.* 48*b*; *Sot.* 10*a*.

[34] In *Midrash hane'elam* 'No'aḥ' there is an exposition that explains the word *vayeḥal* as *ḥalḥalah* (fear): '*Vayeḥal*, what does it mean? He prayed until he was seized by tremor' (*Zohar ḥadash*, 'No'aḥ', 23*a*).

[35] Exod. 4: 3; see also the story about a snake that was sent to swallow Moses because he had not circumcised his son (Zohar i. 93*b*); cf. Jellinek, *Beit hamidrash*, i. 43.

[36] Liebes has noted, in his discussion of this myth, the similarity between R. Shimon and Moses—both struggle with the powers of evil, in contrast to Job, who shunned evil (*sar mera*); see *Studies in the Zohar*, 17. In my reading the Zohar emphasizes here R. Shimon's superiority to Moses.

In contrast to Moses, R. Shimon does not fear the evil power and is able to struggle with it through study of its secrets.[37] The above passage is followed by R. Shimon's exposition of the verse 'God created the great sea monsters' (Gen. 1: 21), which concludes as follows: 'Though the companions have studied the story of the Creation and they know it, only few are able to decipher the mystery of the big sea serpent included in it. Therefore we have taught that the whole world is dependent solely on its fins' (Zohar ii. 34*b*). As Yehuda Liebes has shown, R. Shimon alludes here to himself, recalling his famous saying, 'I have seen exalted men and they are few.'[38] The Zohar seems to be emphasizing R. Shimon's supernal merits—he, unlike Moses, confronts (the secrets of) the great sea serpent and does not flee the snake.

Idra raba contains the best-known description of R. Shimon's superiority to Moses. At the gathering the declaration of his supremacy is conveyed not by a divine voice but by R. Shimon himself (his statement is reminiscent of the statements of the sages (*Suk.* 45*b*) in which they quote him proclaiming his exalted merit):

> R. Shimon said: All the luminaries, the companions of this holy circle, the highest of the high heavens and the supernal of the supernal holy earth are my witnesses that I see now what no one has seen since Moses ascended Mount Sinai for the second time, because I see my face shining as the fierce sun shines, which is expected to rise and bring healing to the world, as it says: 'And for you who revere My name a sun of victory shall rise with healing in its wings' [Mal. 3: 20]. And more, I know that my face shines and Moses did not know and did not look, as it is written: 'Moses was unaware that the skin of his face was radiant' [Exod. 34: 29]. And more, I also see with my eyes the thirteen attributes of [God's] mercy engraved before me, luminous like lights. (Zohar iii. 132*b*)

Here R. Shimon compares the Great Assembly to the revelation at Mount Sinai, and his radiant face to that of Moses. He alludes to the description of Moses in *Bava batra* 75*a*: 'The elders of that generation said: "The face of Moses was like the face of the sun, [but] the face of Joshua is like the

[37] Torah study is also depicted as a struggle in the Talmud and in the Zohar.

[38] Liebes, *Studies in the Zohar*, 16.

moon."' Moreover, he proclaims his superiority to Moses, because he, in contrast to the prophet, is aware of that radiance.[39]

In light of Liebes' suggestion, one can read the entire *Idra* literature, whose primary interest lies in the detailed description of God's countenance, as a declaration of R. Shimon's superiority to Moses. These writings explain that while R. Shimon perceived and described in detail the Divine Countenance, Moses had to be content with the sight of God's back.[40] Furthermore, as R. Shimon declares, Moses could only hear the thirteen attributes of God's mercy, while he was privileged to see them: 'Moreover, I saw them with my eyes.' The attributes of mercy revealed in the *Idra* were the attributes mentioned in Micah (7: 18–20), not those of Exodus 34: 6–7. According to the Zohar, the attributes in Micah are those of the highest divine configuration, Atika Kadisha (the Ancient One), and they are greater than those revealed to Moses, which are identified with the attributes of the lower divine configuration, Ze'er Anpin (the Small Countenance).[41]

[These] thirteen attributes of mercy are of Atika Kadisha: 'Who is a God like You' [Mic. 7: 18], while 'A God compassionate and gracious, etc.' [Exod. 34: 6] are lower [attributes]. And if one says: 'Moses, how is it possible [that] he did not utter those that are supernal?' [It is] because Moses had no need [for them] but for a place of judgment. And where judgment takes place those [attributes of the Ancient One] should not be uttered. (Zohar iii. 131*b*)

As we have seen, the source for the comparison between Moses and R. Shimon is the talmudic tradition according to which both of them were privileged to look through the speculum that shines. The view that R. Shimon is the greater of the two also stems from a talmudic tradition. Let us re-examine the passage in *Sukah* 45*b*. At first, the Talmud attempts to settle the discrepancy between R. Shimon's statement regarding the 'few' exalted men and Rava's opinion that '18,000 righteous men' stand before God by suggesting that R. Shimon's few are those who look through the speculum that shines, and the 18,000 are those who look through the speculum that does not shine. But then the Talmud challenges this opinion: 'And those who look through the speculum that shines, are they so very few? For

39 Liebes, *Studies in the Zohar*, 174 n. 93.

40 Liebes, 'Zohar and *Tikunei hazohar*' (Heb.), 259.

41 Liebes, *Studies in the Zohar*, 205 n. 95.

Abaye said: "There are no fewer than thirty-six righteous men in the world who greet the Shekhinah every day, as it says: *ashrei kol ḥokhei lo* ['Happy are all who wait for Him' (Isa. 30: 18); the *lamed* and *vav* of the word *lo* add up to thirty-six in *gematriya*].'"[42] The Talmud responds as follows: 'These [Abaye's thirty-six righteous] needed permission to enter and those [R. Shimon's few] could enter without permission.'[43] On the basis of the discussion here and in *Yevamot* regarding Moses' prophecy, one might wonder whether he, although among the few who looked through the speculum that shines, needed permission to enter (like the thirty-six righteous men) or entered without having to ask for permission (like R. Shimon and his son). A possible answer might be that Moses, in contrast to R. Shimon and his son, did need permission to look through the speculum that shines. Thus R. Shimon and his son have attained a higher status than Moses. Rabbenu Hananel's commentary on the passage in *Sukah* supports this possibility:

And there are those who say: 'Those righteous men may enter the heavenly *yeshivah* without permission. That is to say, they are not stopped outside while ministering angels ask the Shekhinah whether permission can be granted. Rather, they are permitted to enter because they are highly regarded by the Shekhinah, and there is no one to stop them, and they enter instantly without waiting for permission. These men are very few and the other righteous men are unlike them.

R. Hananel's commentary alludes to stories in which the angels opposed Moses' ascent to the firmament to receive the Torah.[44] In *Pesikta rabati* the angel Hadraniel allows him to pass through the firmaments only after confirming that he has obtained permission from God to do so: 'When Hadraniel confirmed it, this is what he said to God: "It is well known to You that I did not know that he [Moses] came with Your permission. Now I will be his emissary and I will walk before him like a disciple before his teacher."'[45]

[42] In the Hebrew verse the word 'him' corresponds to *lo*, spelled *lamed–vav*, the numerical value (*gematriya*) of which is 36.

[43] The standard translation of the Aramaic word *bar* (in this context) is 'permission'. See Rabbenu Hananel's and Rashi's commentary on *Suk.* 45*a*, as well as Nathan ben Yehiel, *Arukh hashalem*, ii. 164.

[44] *Shab.* 88*b*; *Pesikta rabati*, 20 (96*b*–98*b*); Jellinek, *Beit hamidrash*, i. 58–61; Zohar ii. 58*a*.

[45] *Pesikta rabati*, 20 (97*a*).

From these sources the reader is led to conclude that R. Shimon and his son, the 'few' exalted men who are permitted to look through the speculum that shines without permission, have attained a higher status than Moses, who must overcome the angels' opposition by obtaining God's permission. Indeed, this is Moses de León's insight in *Sefer hamishkal*: 'With regard to what the Sage said—"I have seen exalted men and they are few"—it must be so because only a few ascend and enter without permission. And one knows that God, blessed and blessed be He, no one can come instantly before Him, not even a righteous one like Moses.'[46]

The superiority of R. Shimon can also be deduced by comparing the depiction of Moses in the Torah and in the rabbinic commentaries to R. Shimon's portrayal throughout talmudic literature. This comparison displays the two as polar opposites. In contrast to Moses, who is modest, hesitant, and unsure of himself, R. Shimon is presented as determined, self-aware, confident, and quick to proclaim his powers. Moses humbly says to God, 'Who am I that I should go to Pharaoh and free the Israelites from Egypt?' (Exod. 3: 11). He displeases God by insisting that he is unfit for this mission: 'I have never been a man of words' (Exod. 4: 10). In the following talmudic story, God rewards him for having underrated his own importance and names the Torah after him:

Satan went to Moses and said to him: 'The Torah that the Holy One, blessed be He, gave you, where is it?' He said to him: 'Who am I to be worthy of being given the Torah by the Holy One, blessed be He?' The Holy One, blessed be He, said to Moses: 'Moses, are you a fibber?' He said before Him: 'Master of the universe, You have this coveted and treasured [Torah] that You enjoy every day and I should take credit for it?' The Holy One said to Moses: 'Because you belittled yourself it will be called after you', as it says: 'The Torah of my servant Moses etc.' (*Shab.* 89*a*)

R. Shimon, on the other hand, not only does not underrate his own importance, but declares himself one of the exalted men, perhaps the only one: 'The world is not lacking thirty righteous men like Abraham. If there are thirty, my son and I are two of them. If there are twenty, my son and I are two of them. If there is one, I am the one' (*Bereshit rabah* 35*b*). He makes a similar comment to his son upon exiting the cave in which they hid from

[46] Wijnhoven, '*Sefer hamishkal*: Text and Study', 58.

the Romans for twelve years: 'My son, you and I are sufficient for the world' (*Shab.* 33*b*).

The contrast between Moses and R. Shimon is further highlighted in stories pertaining to their self-awareness. According to a passage in *Pirkei derabi eli'ezer*, when Moses pleaded with God to forgive the people for the sin of the Golden Calf, he was unaware of his own ability to atone for all the sins of Israel to the end of all generations: 'Moses began to cry aloud and said: "The Lord, the Lord, a God compassionate and gracious" [Exod. 34: 6]. Moses said before Him: "Pardon please the iniquities of Israel, the sin of the Golden Calf." Had Moses said "Pardon please the iniquities of Israel to the end of all generations", He would have done so because it was a propitious hour.'[47]

R. Shimon, on the other hand, proclaims the following: 'I am able to pardon the whole world from judgment [for the period starting] from the day I was born until this day; and were Eleazar my son here with me, from the day of the creation of the world to the present time; and were Yotam the son of Uziyahu with us, from the creation of the world to its final end' (*Suk.* 45*a*).

The consecutive reading of these passages reveals that, whereas Moses missed the opportunity to atone for Israel's iniquities to the end of all generations because he was humble and underestimated his power, R. Shimon was aware of his ability to atone not only for Israel but for the entire world, from its creation to its end. Moses' inability to correctly evaluate his power to influence God is also underlined in *Berakhot* 32*a*:

'The Lord said to Moses: Hurry down' [Exod. 32: 7]. 'Hurry down'—what does it mean? R. Eleazar said: The Holy One said to Moses: 'Hurry down, Moses, descend from your greatness. Didn't I grant you greatness but for the sake of Israel? But now Israel has sinned. What need have I for you?' Immediately Moses' strength ebbed and he was unable to speak. However, as soon as He said, 'Release Me and I shall destroy them' [Exod. 32: 10], Moses said [to himself]: 'This matter depends on me.' Immediately he arose and strengthened himself in prayer and pleaded for mercy.[48]

It is true that Moses' humility and lack of self-confidence could be viewed

47 *Pirkei derabi eli'ezer*, 111–12, ch. 45.

48 *Shab.* 89*a*.

favourably,[49] and R. Shimon's lack of humility and extreme self-confidence may provoke discomfort. Nevertheless, these specific traits are the very reason the zoharic literature regards the latter to be on a higher plane than the former. R. Shimon's self-awareness is his greatest virtue and it is expressed in his declaration in *Idra raba*: 'I am aware that my face shines but Moses was unaware and he did not look' (Zohar iii. 132*b*).

The contrast between the two figures seems to have been the primary reason for choosing R. Shimon for the lead role in the zoharic literature. The compilers of the Zohar identified themselves with him, their choice reflecting a confident self-awareness as well as their attempt to assign their work a place in the sacred Jewish canon. Suggesting that R. Shimon is superior to Moses induces a comparison between the Zohar and the Torah, implying that the former supplements, and might even be greater than, the latter. A similar interpretation has been offered by Elliot Wolfson:

> This classic of Jewish mysticism conveys in so many different ways the presumption that its authorial voice (R. Shimon bar Yohai) had reached the symbolic level of Moses in the Divine world and had thus identified with the historic Moses. By interpreting the Torah that the ancient Moses had revealed, this new Moses was in effect revealing a new Torah.[50]

This strategy is not unique to the Zohar. Because of the reverence in which Moses was held, the compilers of both early Christian and rabbinic literature compared their protagonists to him in an attempt to gain sacred and canonical status for their work.[51]

The Zohar's comparison between R. Shimon and Moses resembles that between Jesus and Moses in the New Testament: 'Now after six days Jesus took Peter, James, and John his brother, led them up on a high mountain by themselves, and He was transfigured before them. His face shone like the sun and his clothes became as white as the light. And behold, Moses and Elijah appeared to them talking with Him' (Matt. 17: 1–4).[52]

Alan Segal has argued that the idea that Jesus is greater than Moses appears in the Gospel of John (6: 46): 'Not that anyone has seen the Father

[49] See e.g. *Ber.* 7*a*.

[50] Wolfson, *Through a Speculum that Shines*, 390–1.

[51] As Idel has noted, the 13th-century kabbalist R. Abraham Abulafia, who identified himself as the messiah, compared himself to Moses and argued that he was superior to the prophet. See Idel, 'Abulafia on the Jewish Messiah', 72.

[52] Cf. Mark 9: 2–7; Luke 9: 28–35.

except he who is from God—he has seen the Father'.[53] Segal sees this statement as a commentary on Exodus 33: 20, suggesting that Jesus, unlike Moses, was able to see God because he is 'from God'. Jesus' superiority is made explicit in the Epistle to the Hebrews:

Therefore, holy brethren, partakers of the heavenly calling, consider the Apostle and High Priest of our confession, Jesus, who was faithful to Him, who appointed Him, as Moses also was in all His house. For this One has been counted worthy of more glory than Moses, inasmuch as He who built the house has more honour than the house. For every house is built by someone, but He who built all things is God. And Moses indeed was faithful in all His house as a servant, for a testimony of those things which would be spoken afterwards, but the messiah is as a Son over His own house. (Heb. 3: 1–6)

The author of the Epistle to the Hebrews alludes to Numbers 12: 7, which says: 'Not so with My servant Moses; he is trusted throughout My household.' Jesus, the 'son' of God, is ascribed a more exalted status in the household than is Moses, the 'faithful servant'. The Zohar, too, distinguishes between these two levels, with the son enjoying priority over the servant.[54] Elsewhere in the work R. Shimon is called 'the son of the Almighty'.[55] Abraham Elkayam has proposed that the Zohar's distinction between the status of the son and that of the servant is based on the above quotation from the Epistle to the Hebrews; he has further claimed that it is possible to interpret the Zohar as implying that Moses was on the level of servant whereas R. Shimon was the beloved son, perhaps even the son of God.[56]

The comparison between the messiah and Moses, and the conception that the former is greater than the latter, are also present in Jewish literature.[57] The superiority of R. Shimon to Moses as depicted in the Zohar surely stems from the conception of R. Shimon as a messianic figure.

[53] Segal, *Two Powers in Heaven*, 213–14; Wolfson, *Through a Speculum that Shines*, 27 n. 69.

[54] *Pikudin*, Zohar iii. 111*b*; Liebes, 'Zohar and Eros' (Heb.), 74; Elkayam, 'The Secret of Faith in Nathan of Gaza's Writings' (Heb.), 215.

[55] Zohar iii. 61*b*. Liebes, *Studies in the Zohar*, 155.

[56] Elkayam, 'The Secret of Faith in Nathan of Gaza's Writings' (Heb.), 365 n. 173.

[57] *Ruth rabah* 5: 6 and *Kohelet rabah* 1: 28: 'As the first saviour, so the last'. In *Midrash tanḥuma* (ed. Buber), 'Toledot', 20, p. 139, it is written: 'This is the king messiah . . . superior to Abraham, more exalted than Moses above the ministering angels.' See also Idel, 'Abulafia on the Jewish Messiah', 72.

Like Jesus in the New Testament, R. Akiva, the main protagonist of rabbinic lore, is granted supernal status through a comparison between him and Moses. Both were famous for their modesty,[58] were privileged to ascend to heaven, and were poorly treated by the angels.[59] But Akiva is depicted as even greater than Moses: 'Things that were not revealed to Moses were revealed to R. Akiva and his companions.'[60] The Talmud conveys this view in the famous description of Moses ascending to heaven and witnessing God affixing coronets to the letters of the Torah. In response to his enquiry God explains that R. Akiva is expected to expound on every tip of every letter of the Torah. Moses asks to see R. Akiva and his request is granted:

He went and sat behind eight rows [of Akiva's students] and could not understand what they were saying. His strength ebbed. When he [Akiva] came to a certain issue, his students said to him: 'Rabbi, how do you know?' He said to them: 'It is a halakhah given to Moses at Sinai.' His [Moses'] mind was relieved. He returned and came before the Holy One, blessed be He, and said to Him: 'You have a man like this and you give the Torah through me?' God said to him: 'Be quiet! Thus has it arisen in My thoughts.' (*Men.* 29*b*)

In his discussion of this passage, Yehuda Liebes has noted:

[Moses] is presented as a slightly inadequate man: he not only fails to understand the meaning of the coronets, needing to be 'telescoped' into the future, but he also fails to understand the discussion between R. Akiva and his students, and it weakens him. . . . Moses is 'comforted' when hearing the argument quoted in his name, but his sense of justice compels him to return to God to argue and request that the Torah be given through R. Akiva, who is more knowledgeable.[61]

Similarly to early Christian and rabbinic sources, the Zohar also has a protagonist evocative of Moses yet superior to him. We have seen that by utilizing existing motifs in rabbinic literature, R. Shimon's image is presented in close comparison to that of Moses and reflects the desire to

[58] *Ket.* 62*b*–63*a*; *Ned.* 50*a*; Liebes, *Elisha's Sin* (Heb.), 100–1.

[59] *Ḥag.* 15*b*. Liebes, *Elisha's Sin* (Heb.), 98–101.

[60] *Bamidbar rabah* 19: 6; *Tanḥuma*, 'Ḥukat', 8; *Pesikta rabati*, 14 (64*b*); Hellner-Eshed, *A River Flows from Eden*, 52.

[61] Liebes, *Studies in Jewish Myth*, 20.

achieve canonical status for the Zohar. In addition, his portrayal reveals the intent to subvert the dominant kabbalistic circles of the thirteenth century. As I suggested above, R. Shimon's persona mirrors either the self-perception of the compilers of the Zohar or the personality of a particular member of the zoharic circle.[62]

Furthermore, Moses' character as depicted in the Zohar may well reflect the image of a 'contemporary Moses'—R. Moses ben Nahman, Nahmanides,[63] who was the source of authority for the Catalan school of kabbalah in the thirteenth century. It was owing to their differing approaches to conveying kabbalistic knowledge, as well as differences regarding the source of kabbalistic authority, that tension arose between the followers of Nahmanides and the Castilian kabbalists who compiled the Zohar.[64] This tension is the setting for the composition of the zoharic literature and its distribution in the late thirteenth and early fourteenth centuries.

As I demonstrate in the next chapter, the kabbalists who were the first to declare the Zohar authoritative juxtaposed the zoharic kabbalah with that of Nahmanides and claimed that the former had greater authority. A passage found in an early collection of kabbalistic texts, *Likutei kabalah* ,[65] illustrates the point: 'And these matters are profound, unlike what R. Moses ben Nahman, of blessed memory, says. One should seek [answers] to questions from R. Shimon ben Yohai, of blessed memory.'[66] Joseph Angelet, in

[62] Liebes has raised the possibility that R. Shimon's figure in the Zohar is based on the personality of R. Todros Abulafia; see *Studies in the Zohar*, 131–8. Previously he suggested that R. Shimon represents Moses de León or another member of the circle; ibid. 18.

[63] My suggestion applies to the earlier layers of the Zohar, and not to *Ra'aya meheimna* or *Tikunei hazohar*. As one can learn from Amos Goldreich's article, Moses' image reflects the author of both works: Goldreich, 'Examinations of the Self-Image of the Author of *Tikunei hazohar*' (Heb.), 460, 471, 481–93.

[64] Idel, *Kabbalah: New Perspectives*, 212–18; id., 'We Have No Kabbalistic Tradition on This', 70–2; regarding the differences between the kabbalists of the secondary elite and those of the primary elite (in Catalonia and Castile) during this period, see id., 'PaRDeS': Some Reflections on Kabbalistic Hermeneutics', 256. On the tension between R. Isaac of Acre (also a member of the secondary elite) and the disciples of Nahmanides, see Huss, 'NiSAN, the Wife of the Infinite', 171–81.

[65] Jewish Theological Seminary, New York, MS 1768. For descriptions of the manuscript and its contents see Wolfson, *The Book of the Pomegranate*, 56–7; Danzig, 'Geonic Responsa' (Heb.), 23–6.

[66] *Likutei kabalah*, 105*b*; Wolfson, 'Hai Gaon's Letter', 369–70 n. 19.

his commentary on *Sha'arei orah*, explicitly contrasts the wisdom of the Zohar to the wisdom of Nahmanides, and grants the Zohar primacy: 'And this follows *Midrash hane'elam* [the term he uses to refer to his Zohar collection] in the *Idra*, even though Nahmanides, of blessed memory, did not write so, nor did the rest of the kabbalists. And we have nothing to rely on but the words of the *tana'im*, the eternal pillars of the world [i.e. R. Shimon and his companions].'[67] Moshe Idel has shown that, having weighed the Zohar against Nahmanides' teachings, R. Menahem Recanati also held the former in higher esteem.[68]

It seems reasonable to assume that the image of a modest and cautious Moses in the Zohar represents Nahmanides, the humble,[69] conservative kabbalist, who advocated a prudent and careful transferral of the secrets of the kabbalah, and opposed, as Idel emphasizes, innovations in the field.[70] It is possible that he himself was aware of the similarities between him and Moses. Hananel Mack, who claims that Nahmanides regarded James I, King of Aragon and Catalonia, as the living image of Pharaoh, has raised the possibility that Moses ben Nahman saw himself in the role of Moses ben Amram.[71]

Haviva Pedaya notes that Nahmanides, in his introduction to the commentary on the Torah, described Moses in his own image—a kabbalist appointed to preserve and transmit the kabbalistic tradition.[72] The attribute that R. Isaac of Acre attached to Nahmanides—'the faithful teacher'[73] —attests to the fact that he was perceived by his contemporaries as the semblance of Moses, 'the faithful shepherd'. In contrast to the authoritative and self-confident tone of R. Shimon's zoharic homilies, Nahmanides' writings display hesitation and humility. In *Sha'ar hagemul* he says: 'Because

[67] Angelet, *Perush sha'arei orah*, 43a.

[68] Idel, *R. Menahem Recanati the Kabbalist* (Heb.), 92, 117–18.

[69] It should be noted that humility is the principal trait discussed in the famous 'Letter for the Ages', ascribed to Nahmanides. See Nahmanides, *Collected Works*, ed. Chavel, i. 374–7.

[70] Idel, 'We Have No Kabbalistic Tradition on This', 70–2; Abrams, 'Orality in the Kabbalistic School', 88; Pedaya, *Nahmanides: Cyclical Time and Holy Text* (Heb.), 73–5; Halbertal, *By Way of Truth* (Heb.), 311–21; Wolfson, 'Beautiful Maiden without Eyes: *Peshat* and *Sod*', 161. On the reservations pertaining to this characterization of Nahmanides see Wolfson, 'By Way of Truth', 176.

[71] Mack, 'The Image of Pharaoh' (Heb.), 46.

[72] Pedaya, *Nahmanides: Cyclical Time and Holy Text* (Heb.), 134.

[73] Gottlieb, *Studies in Kabbalistic Literature* (Heb.), 232.

we are discussing the end of days, and since we are not prophets, I am hesitant and unable to say anything definite or to make an absolute statement with regard to the divine secrets.'[74] In his commentary on *Sefer yetsirah* he plainly admits, 'I do not understand this *bava* [section]'.[75] This approach stands in sharp contrast to the zoharic kabbalah, which Idel characterizes as the 'creative or innovative Kabbalah'.[76]

Moses' description in Zohar 'Bo' supports my view that his image in the zoharic literature reflects that of Nahmanides. As previously discussed, Moses, unlike R. Shimon, is portrayed as afraid to confront the supernal sea serpent, which represents the powers of evil. R. Shimon's statement regarding 'the few' who are able to interpret the biblical creation story in accordance with the secret of the great sea serpent[77] signifies the Castilian kabbalistic approach. Castilian scholars boasted that they were the only ones knowledgeable enough to understand both the secrets of the divine emanation (the *sefirot*) and those of the 'left emanation', the powers of evil.[78] Through this knowledge the authors of the Zohar, similar to other Castilian kabbalists, implied their superiority over their Catalan colleagues, who shied away from the secrets of the world of evil. R. Isaac of Acre explicitly argues that expertise in understanding the secrets of evil is what distinguishes the Castilian sages from the Catalans:

In contrast to the kabbalists of Spain [i.e. Castile], who were privileged to receive the kabbalah of the external grades, the kabbalists of Catalonia only have a true kabbalah with regard to the ten *sefirot belimah*, but they did not receive anything concerning the external grades. Thus R. Todros Halevi, of blessed memory, author of *Sefer haḥayim* [should be *harazim*] and *Otsar hakavod*,[79] says about them [the Catalans] that they did not descend below the Ten [i.e. did not understand the secrets of the powers below the ten *sefirot*].[80]

74 Nahmanides, *Collected Works*, ed. Chavel, i. 290; Idel, 'We Have No Kabbalistic Tradition on This', 70 n. 69.

75 Scholem, 'Nahmanides' Real Commentary' (Heb.), 407; Idel, 'Moses ben Nahman' (Heb.), 540.

76 Idel, *Kabbalah: New Perspectives*, 212; id., 'PaRDes': Some Reflections on Kabbalistic Hermeneutics', 255–6.

77 Zohar ii. 34*b*.

78 Liebes, *Studies in the Zohar*, 16–17.

79 Abulafia, *Sha'ar harazim*, ed. Oron, 81.

80 Isaac of Acre, *Otsar haḥayim*, Moscow MS, 12*a*; Gottlieb, *Studies in Kabbalistic Literature* (Heb.), 341–2; Liebes, *Studies in the Zohar*, 16–17; Huss, 'NiSAN, the Wife of the Infinite', 176.

Just as R. Shimon's engagement with the sea serpent alludes to the engagement of the Castilian kabbalists with the secrets of the powers of evil, Moses' fear of the serpent represents the reluctance of the Catalan kabbalists in general, and of Nahmanides in particular, to study the secrets of the *sitra aḥra*.

The zoharic circle's rejection of the esoteric approach of the Nahmanidean school is further expressed in Zohar 'Vayeḥi', where R. Shimon criticizes the Babylonian sages for concealing his public teachings and for being afraid to repeat them:

R. Shimon said: 'When I visit the companions in Babylon, they assemble to hear me, and I discourse with them openly, but they have sealed my teachings under iron padlock which is blocked on all sides. How often have I taught them the ways of the King's garden and the ways of the King? How often have I taught them all the different ranks of the righteous in the world to come? But all of them are scared to say those things and all they do is stutter, and therefore they are called *psilusin* [stammerers].[81] (Zohar i. 225*a*)

The 'stuttering companions of Babylonia' connotes Moses' impediment and alludes to the followers of Nahmanides. This passage possibly refers to Catalan kabbalists who joined the zoharic circle in Castile, listened to their discussions, and yet maintained their conservative and esoteric approach.[82]

The juxtaposition of R. Shimon and the sages of Babylonia, just like his description as greater than Moses, may well reflect the conviction of the zoharic circle that their creative kabbalistic interpretation and confident self-awareness granted them an advantage over the conservative kabbalistic position of Nahmanides and his followers. In contrast to the Nahmanidean approach, which called for the concealment of secrets, the Zohar extols the freedom to reveal and to interpret:

[81] Based on *Vayikra rabah*, 10: 2 (ed. M. Margalioth, 198). For this work and the origin of the word *psilusa* in Greek, see Margalioth's notes there. See also Liebes, 'The Zohar's Relation to the Land of Israel' (Heb.), 36.

[82] R. David Hakohen, a disciple of Nahmanides and of R. Solomon ben Adret, resided in Castile in the late 13th and early 14th centuries; see Goldreich, '*Sefer me'irat einayim*' (Heb.), 361–4, 389–90. Another kabbalist who was affiliated to the disciples of R. Solomon ben Adret, visited Castile, and was in contact with the zoharic circle was R. Isaac of Acre.

Happy is the generation in which R. Shimon lives. Blessed is its portion in the upper and lower realms. Scripture says about it: 'Happy are you, O land, for your king is a free man' [Eccles. 10: 17]. A free man, what does it mean? A man who lifts his head to reveal and interpret things without any fear—that is a free man. He says what he pleases and does not fear. (Zohar iii. 79*b*)

CHAPTER TWO

The Zohar as an Imagined Book

The ancient book that Rabbi Shimon wrote.
Isaac of Acre, *Sefer divrei hayamim*[1]

IN THE PREVIOUS CHAPTER I argued that the choice of R. Shimon as the protagonist of the zoharic literature, his comparison to Moses, and his alleged superiority all reflect the self-perception of the authors of the Zohar and their aspiration to subvert the dominant status of the kabbalistic circles of Nahmanides and R. Solomon ben Adret (Rashba). Initially the compilers of the zoharic literature (excepting *Tikunei hazohar* and *Ra'aya meheimna*) did not regard their work as a clearly defined literary unit, use the term *Sefer hazohar* (Book of the Zohar), or name R. Shimon as the author of the zoharic texts. In addition, early zoharic quotations at the end of the thirteenth century were not presented as part of a book called Zohar; nor did they contain any references to a work of supreme authority and holiness written by R. Shimon. We can assume, therefore, that the name *Sefer hazohar* (and others, such as 'R. Shimon's *midrash*' and *Midrash hane'elam*), along with the view that these names denoted an ancient kabbalistic book ascribed to R. Shimon, came into being only after most of the zoharic literature had been created and the first quotations from this literature had appeared.

How was the idea of the Zohar as a book conceived? What was the significance of the change in the way the zoharic literature was presented and distributed? Why did that change occur? In what follows I examine the initial reception of the zoharic literature, the nascence of the term *Sefer hazohar*, and the idea that it refers to a unified, sacred, and authoritative literary corpus. I further discuss the social forces that brought about the

[1] *Sefer divrei hayamim* is the lost book of Isaac of Acre; however, a small part of it has come down to us through Abraham Zacuto, who quoted from it in his book *Sefer yuḥasin*.

formation of the concept of the Zohar as a book and contributed to its spread.

Originally the zoharic literature did not emerge as a unified and structured literary corpus. In the introduction to his monumental book *The Wisdom of the Zohar*, Isaiah Tishby argues that the Zohar 'is not a single unified work, but a great literary anthology consisting of sections from various sources'.[2] Yehuda Liebes similarly points out that it is 'not really "a book" but a whole literature composed of various layers'.[3] According to Abraham Elkayam, the Zohar did not exist before it was first bound in Byzantium in the early fifteenth century,[4] and Daniel Abrams argues that it was 'neither written, nor edited, nor distributed as a book by the various figures who produced the literary units that were later known by the name "Zohar"'.[5]

The idea of the existence of a book written by R. Shimon and known as the Zohar (or *Midrash hane'elam* or 'R. Shimon's *midrash*') only crystallized after a significant number of zoharic texts had been written and circulated. That is to say, the Zohar as a book is an imagined text, an idea of a unified literary work the scope and nature of which were perceived and described in a variety of ways. Its emergence as such influenced the formation of zoharic collections, which differed significantly from one another yet came to be collectively referred to by that name. At least until the printing of the zoharic collections in the sixteenth century, and to a great extent even later, no agreement had been reached regarding the precise scope of the Zohar, and the name was used by kabbalists and scholars to denote varying literary entities.

As mentioned in the Introduction, the texts which later came to be perceived as belonging to the Zohar were written by different Castilian authors in the late thirteenth and early fourteenth centuries. Some of these

[2] Tishby and Lachower, *The Wisdom of the Zohar*, i. 1.

[3] Liebes, '*Shekel hakodesh* by Moses de León' (Heb.), 273.

[4] Elkayam, 'The Holy Zohar of Sabbatai Zevi' (Heb.), 350.

[5] Abrams, *Kabbalistic Manuscripts and Textual Theory*, 227; he discusses at length the 'invention of the Zohar' as a book (ibid. 224–438). In his earlier publications he has suggested that the Zohar was not initially produced as a book; see 'When Was the Introduction to the Zohar Written?' (Heb.), 221–6; 'The Zohar as a Book' (Heb.), 201–32, and 'Critical and Post-Critical Textual Scholarship', 17–71.

texts were cited for the first time in the writings of kabbalists (mainly from Castile) during the last two decades of the thirteenth century. The first scholars whose writings included texts similar or identical to those that later appeared in zoharic collections were Moses de León, who probably had a significant role in the writing of the zoharic texts; Isaac Ibn Sahula, Todros Halevi Abulafia, Joseph Gikatilla, Bahya ben Asher, Joseph of Hamadan, and Isaac of Acre.

Some zoharic texts are integrated into the works of the above-mentioned kabbalists without any specific reference. This is the case in some of the writings of Joseph Gikatilla, Bahya ben Asher, and Joseph of Hamadan, in a significant portion of parallel versions of the zoharic literature in the writings of Moses de León, and in *Me'irat einayim* by R. Isaac of Acre.[6]

Scholarship has struggled to explain why explicit references are absent in these cases. Those who believe that the above kabbalists had in their possession an edition of the Zohar (or one of its parts) view the absence of such references as indicative of the authors' scepticism regarding the book's antiquity.[7] Yet the form of the zoharic sources that these kabbalists had at their disposal, or whether they had any such sources in front of them at all, is unknown. Yehuda Liebes has suggested two other possibilities for the missing references: (*a*) some of the sources (written or oral) from which these texts were drawn did not have the characteristics of a zoharic *midrash* (i.e. they were not entitled Zohar, or attributed to R. Shimon), thus the compilers refrained from citing them as such; (*b*) these texts had been composed by the kabbalists themselves and the compilers derived them from their own writings and not the other way around[8]—hence their significance for the history of the Zohar's reception cannot be determined unequivocally.

Other zoharic texts appear as explicit quotations in kabbalistic writings from the late thirteenth and early fourteenth centuries. Most are simply

[6] Gikatilla, *Commentary on Ezekiel's Chariot*, ed. Farber-Ginat, 31; Gottlieb, *Kabbalah in the Writings of Rabbenu Bahya ben Asher* (Heb.), 169; Liebes, *Studies in the Zohar*, 90–1, 103–4; Scholem, *Major Trends in Jewish Mysticism*, 198; Wolfson, *The Book of the Pomegranate*, 49; Goldreich, '*Sefer me'irat einayim*' (Heb.), 61–8, 414–15.

[7] See Gikatilla, *Commentary on Ezekiel's Chariot*, ed. Farber-Ginat, 31; Gottlieb, *Kabbalah in the Writings of Rabbenu Bahya ben Asher* (Heb.), 171.

[8] See Liebes, *Studies in the Zohar*, 90–1, 99–103.

attributed to the sages, using the terms *razal* ('our rabbis of blessed memory'), 'our sages', *hagadah, midrash,* and the like. Such is the case in *Meshal hakadmoni* and in Isaac Ibn Sahula's commentary on Song of Songs;[9] in the writings of Todros Abulafia and Joseph Gikatilla;[10] in Isaac of Acre's *Me'irat einayim;*[11] in the anonymous text referred to by scholars as *Ta'amei hamitsvot,* second version;[12] and in the writings of Moses de León.[13] Joseph of Hamadan uses the term *tanina;* Isaac Ibn Sahula and de León use 'Yerushalmi';[14] de León further quotes zoharic texts citing *hamefarshim* ('the commentators'), *midrashot hapenimiyim* ('the inner exegeses'), *sitrei torah* ('secrets of the Torah'), *sitrei hayiḥud* ('secrets of the Union'), *ḥakhmei elyon hakadmonim* ('ancient supernal sages'), and others.[15]

In general, one cannot distinguish between the ways that these kabbalists quoted zoharic and other midrashic sources. Occasionally, however, there are indications that they were aware of the uniqueness of the zoharic texts. As Gershom Scholem points out, Ibn Sahula used the term 'Yerushalmi' exclusively for *Midrash hane'elam.*[16] In the writings of de León 'Yerushalmi' usually indicates zoharic texts. Arthur Green shows that on four occasions Ibn Sahula started a quote from *Midrash hane'elam* with the phrase 'I found', something he did not do with other sources. Thus, according to Green, one may assume that those texts were not widely known.[17]

[9] See Scholem, 'The First Quotation of *Midrash hane'elam*' (Heb.); id., 'The Kabbalah of Isaac ben Solomon ben Sahula' (Heb.), 111–16; Baer, *History of the Jews in Christian Spain* (Heb.), 509 n. 61*a*; Green, 'Isaac Ibn Sahula's Commentary on the Song of Songs' (Heb.), 400–1.

[10] For Abulafia see his *Otsar hakavod,* 17*a*; Scholem, 'Two Booklets by Moses de León' (Heb.), 27; Liebes, *Studies in the Zohar,* 93. For Gikatilla see *Sha'arei orah,* ed. Ben Shlomo (Heb.), 162; Liebes, *Studies in the Zohar,* 99–102.

[11] Goldreich, '*Sefer me'irat einayim*' (Heb.), 90, 157–8.

[12] Gottlieb, *Kabbalah in the Writings of Rabbenu Bahya ben Asher* (Heb.), 194; Liebes, *Studies in the Zohar,* 93, 204–5 n. 88.

[13] Wolfson, *The Book of the Pomegranate,* 48–9 nn. 194–5.

[14] Scholem, 'The Kabbalah of Isaac ben Solomon ben Sahula' (Heb.), 117; Wolfson, *The Book of the Pomegranate,* 6 n. 18, 49 n. 199; Farber-Ginat, 'A New Fragment' (Heb.), 169 n. 43; de León, *Sefer shekel hakodesh,* ed. Mopsik, 42, 84; Liebes, '*Shekel hakodesh* by Moses de León' (Heb.), 277.

[15] Scholem, 'Two Booklets by Moses de León' (Heb.), 23–4; Tishby and Lachower, *The Wisdom of the Zohar,* i. 22–3; Wolfson, *The Book of the Pomegranate,* 48–9; de León, *Commentary on Ezekiel's Chariot,* ed. Farber-Ginat, 23 n. 42.

[16] Scholem, 'The Kabbalah of Isaac ben Solomon ben Sahula' (Heb.), 117; Green, 'Isaac Ibn Sahula's Commentary on the Song of Songs' (Heb.), 400.

[17] Green, 'Isaac Ibn Sahula's Commentary on the Song of Songs' (Heb.), 401.

As mentioned earlier, de León introduces zoharic texts with phrases such as *midrashot hapenimiyim* and *sitrei torah*. However, he uses similar expressions when quoting rabbinic exegeses, *Sefer habahir*, and the writings of kabbalists of the thirteenth century.[18]

While neither the name 'Zohar' nor the attribution of zoharic texts to R. Shimon appear in thirteenth-century kabbalistic works, some writings of that period contain references to 'R. Shimon's *midrash*'. Bahya ben Asher, for example, mentions it twice in his commentary on the Torah. Yet Yehuda Liebes has argued that Bahya's references were not to the Zohar but rather to an angelological *midrash* that was ascribed to R. Shimon and which Bahya, as well as the writers of the zoharic texts, had in their possession.[19] Similarly, Joshua Ibn Shuaib cited 'R. Shimon's *midrash*' several times in his sermons. All of the quotes are in Hebrew (not Aramaic, the language of the majority of zoharic texts) and for the most part they do not deal with kabbalistic subjects or have a parallel in the zoharic literature.[20] Ibn Shuaib, then, did not quote zoharic texts but rather a *midrash* that was attributed to R. Shimon (perhaps the same *midrash* quoted by Bahya ben Asher) and which we do not have today.

It appears from this survey that the Castilian kabbalists had access to zoharic as well as midrashic or pseudo-midrashic sources that were also used by the authors of the zoharic literature. Sometimes they identified these texts as *midrashim* of the sages and at other times they distinguished them from other midrashic sources. Nevertheless, the idea of the Zohar as a book did not appear in their writings. They did not view the zoharic sources as part of a discrete literary work, and even if they used specific expressions to cite zoharic texts, elsewhere they quoted similar texts under different names. There is no indication that they treated the zoharic texts as parts of a larger literary unit, attributed them to R. Shimon, or referred to them by the name 'Zohar'.

In addition to the quotation of zoharic texts in the writings of thir-

[18] Scholem, 'Two Booklets by Moses de León' (Heb.), 329; Farber-Ginat, 'On the Sources of Moses de León's Early Kabbalistic System' (Heb.), 81–2 n. 32; de León, *Commentary on Ezekiel's Chariot*, ed. Farber-Ginat, 42 n. 128; Wolfson, *The Book of the Pomegranate*, 39.

[19] Liebes, *Studies in the Zohar*, 91–2.

[20] *The Sermons of Rabbi Joshua Ibn Shuaib*, ed. Metsger, i. 52, 91, 177, ii. 366–7, 376, 387, 412.

teenth- and fourteenth-century kabbalists, scholars have discovered other evidence that may attest to the emergence of the zoharic literature around that time. One example is a poem by Todros ben Judah Abulafia, an author living in Castile when the zoharic texts were first being distributed. He was a relative of two people instrumental in the appearance of the Zohar—Todros Halevi Abulafia (mentioned above) and his son Joseph. In one of Todros ben Judah's poems Joseph Weiss finds hints at the appearance of the Zohar:

> Listen, brother, and accept sayings more precious than pearls in the
> eye of the Lord.
> The knowledgeable delivered them from sage to sage as if they were
> words given at Sinai.
> Listen to the companions and the companions will listen to you.
> Do not spurn them because you are unfamiliar with them.
> There are secrets and there are an infinite number of books.
> They seem ancient in the eyes of the sages yet they are renewed
> every morning.[21]

In Weiss's interpretation the words of Todros ben Judah refer to the kabbalah in general and to the zoharic texts in particular.[22] He suggests that the phrases 'Do not spurn them because you are unfamiliar with them' and 'They seem ancient in the eyes of the sages yet are renewed every morning'[23] attest to the suspicion regarding the antiquity of those texts.[24] If indeed the poem refers to zoharic texts, it indicates that they were distributed as ancient *midrash*. Yet Todros ben Judah, like other kabbalists of his time, does not make any reference to the conception that these writings belong to a book that has been rediscovered, nor does he attribute the texts to R. Shimon or refer to them as the Zohar.

[21] Abulafia, *Gan hameshalim vehaḥidot*, ed. Yellin, i. 147, poem 797.

[22] J. G. Weiss, 'A Contemporary Poem on the Appearance of the Zohar', 219–21.

[23] See Lam. 3: 23: 'They are renewed every morning—ample is Your grace'. Yellin, followed by J. G. Weiss, interpreted *bekarim* as being based on *bakar* (cattle), in contempt of those who thought the texts were new; see Abulafia, *Gan hameshalim vehaḥidot*, ed. Yellin, i. 147, poem 797; J. G. Weiss, 'A Contemporary Poem on the Appearance of the Zohar', 220. Daniel Matt, on the other hand, has pointed out the parallel between the poem and the expression *milin ḥadatin atikin* ('new ancient words'), which recurs in the zoharic literature; see '*Matnita dilan*: A Technique of Innovation' (Heb.), 123 n. 1.

[24] J. G. Weiss, 'A Contemporary Poem on the Appearance of the Zohar', 220.

Other allusions to the zoharic literature seem to exist in the work of Moses de León. In *Sefer mishkan ha'edut*, composed in 1293, he relates:

And when I saw that human beings were engaged in alien thoughts and worthless opinions on these issues, and generations were coming and going, and the worthless ideas remained unchanged forever, 'and no one saw it nor heard it, neither did any awake, for they were all asleep, because a deep sleep from the Lord had fallen upon them' [1 Sam. 26: 12], so that they could neither enquire nor read nor explore, I felt it necessary to write and to conceal, to explore and to disclose to any enlightened person, and to inform [him] of all these matters that the holy ancient sages investigated throughout their lives, and which are scattered in the Talmud and in their sayings, concealed and hidden in their secrets and precious more than pearls. They locked them behind closed gates, and they hid their profound books [because they] realized that it would be inappropriate to reveal and publish them.[25]

In Scholem's reading de León refers here to the Zohar, and even implies that he is the author: '[The objective] of someone to refer to a work written shortly before in this manner and in so many ambiguous terms must be to reveal his own authorship. . . . Moses de León could hardly do more to proclaim himself author of these "words of the wise" as his own excellent phrase puts it.'[26]

Yehuda Liebes has argued that the following passage in de León's *Sefer harimon* also alludes to the Zohar and the group that compiled it:

Those engaged with the Torah concealed themselves behind their words and did not dare to say anything, particularly in matters related to antiquity, which have been included in the Kabbalah of the elders since ancient times. They neither dared to refer to them nor to utter them. Therefore, the Torah was much forgotten by Israel until a different spirit was roused by God, and men were given good counsel to return to the true knowledge of God, blessed be He. And through that gentle arousal they understood what our sages, of blessed memory, meant.[27]

It is reasonable to assume that in the above passages de León is hinting at zoharic texts, the zoharic circle, and his personal role in composing and distributing those texts. Nevertheless, one should note that whenever he refers to the words of the ancient sages, their secrets, and their ancient books, he uses plural forms; he does not talk about a distinct literary unit—

25 De León, *Mishkan ha'edut*, 51*a*–*b*.

26 Scholem, *Major Trends in Jewish Mysticism*, 202.

27 Liebes, *Studies in the Zohar*, 89; see also Wolfson, *The Book of the Pomegranate*, 392.

a *midrash* or a specific book. As previously said, nowhere in his writings does he ascribe the words of the sages to R. Shimon, or associate them with a book called 'the Zohar'.

Even though the concept of the Zohar as a book was not formulated until the beginning of the fourteenth century, we are justified in asking whether the individual zoharic texts reflect any awareness of being parts of some unified literary entity, and whether the seeds of the idea of a book were sown in them. True, the term *Sefer hazohar* does not appear at all in the zoharic texts (except in *Tikunei hazohar* and *Ra'aya meheimna*). Furthermore, the sections as they have come down to us do not present themselves as parts of a single comprehensive literary body, and they lack a defined beginning[28] and end.[29] Yet some of the units (such as the *Idrot*, *Yanuka*, *Saba demishpatim*, and *Midrash eikhah*) have a distinct literary framework, and earlier elements are occasionally referred to in the later strata. In addition to *Sifra ditseniuta*, which is mentioned and quoted principally in the *Idrot*,[30] there are a few places where the existence of different textual layers and zoharic literary units is alluded to, and reference is made to texts that were written by R. Shimon and his companions. According to Yehuda Liebes, for example, the term 'Jerusalem Talmud' as used in the below passage from the zoharic *Midrash eikhah* indicates sections that had been composed earlier:[31]

'Before the sun grows dark' [Eccles. 12: 2]: This is the visage of the Shekhinah from above and from below. [Those] below, who are they? [They are] the masters of the Mishnah who lived in the Land of Israel, the iron hammers who crushed rocks and moved high mountains. 'The light' [ibid.]: This is the Jerusalem Talmud, which illuminates the light of the Torah. (*Zohar ḥadash* 93*a*)

Matnita dilan ('our *mishnah*') is another example of an expression found in the literature that sometimes refers to earlier strata of zoharic texts, as Daniel Matt has shown.[32]

[28] The manuscript and print versions of the zoharic corpus begin differently; see Tishby and Lachower, *The Wisdom of the Zohar*, i. 99–100; Abrams, 'When Was the Introduction to the Zohar Written?' (Heb.), 218–22.

[29] Although the description of R. Shimon's death at the end of *Idra zuta* would have been a suitable conclusion to the book, the narrative of the zoharic literature continues beyond his death. See e.g. Zohar i. 4*a*–*b*, 216*b*–217*a*, ii. 123*b*.

[30] Liebes, *Studies in the Zohar*, 96.

[31] Liebes, '*Shekel hakodesh* by Moses de León' (Heb.), 277.

[32] Matt, '*Matnita dilan*: A Technique of Innovation' (Heb.), 140–4.

In Zohar 'Vayeḥi' a dream of R. Judah's is described in which he witnesses the passing of R. Shimon, along with all the books of supernal secrets and legends. When he tells his dream to R. Aba, the latter bursts into tears and says:

R. Shimon was the hand-mill out of which fine manna was ground daily, and it was gathered, as it is written: 'even he who gathered least had ten *ḥomarim*' [Num. 11: 32]. Now the mill and the manna have departed and nothing is left of them in the world except what is written: 'Take a jar, put one *omer* of manna in it, and place it before God to be stored throughout the ages' [Exod. 16: 33]. And it does not say 'revealed' but 'stored throughout the ages' [*lemishmeret*]; that is, kept in a private place [*le'atsniuta*]. Who is now able to reveal mysteries and who will understand them? (Zohar i. 217*a*)

It is possible that the books of secrets and legends that ascended to the heavens with R. Shimon were books that he himself had written. R. Aba states that, although R. Shimon's wisdom departed from the world upon his death, a memory of it was preserved, like the *omer* of manna that was kept throughout the ages. Perhaps this alludes to written teachings that R. Shimon had left behind, that is, to one of the sections of the Zohar.[33] R. Aba translates the word *lemishmeret* as *le'atsniuta* and Liebes suggests that it might be a reference to *Sifra ditseniuta*.[34]

R. Aba is mentioned in a few places in the Zohar as the scribe who sets down R. Shimon's words when the latter is on his deathbed. *Idra zuta* begins with the following:

R. Shimon said: It is a propitious hour and I am seeking to enter the world to come without shame. I wish to reveal in the presence of the Shekhinah sacred matters that have not been revealed up till now, so it should not be said that I departed from the world deficient. Until now these matters have been concealed in my heart, so I might enter the world to come with them. And now I command you—R. Aba will write, R. Eleazar will read, and the other companions will contemplate in their hearts. (Zohar iii. 287*b*)

At the end of *Idra zuta*, following R. Shimon's death, R. Aba himself speaks: 'The holy candle had not finished uttering the word "life" when his

[33] Hellner-Eshed, *A River Flows from Eden*, 429–31.

[34] Liebes, *Studies in the Zohar*, 200–1 n. 58.

words faded. And I had been writing and intended to continue to write but I heard nothing. And I did not raise my head because the light was strong and I could not look at it' (Zohar iii. 295*b*).

What R. Aba wrote down at the time of R. Shimon's death is also mentioned in *Idra raza derazin* (the title of which is *Idra demishkana* in the printed editions) in portion 'Mishpatim':

R. Eleazar said: 'All these *tikunim* [my] father revealed so that he would not enter the world to come in shame. Why was there a need to reveal them now?' R. Aba said to him: 'All I wrote from the holy candle [R. Shimon's mouth] I told the companions because they understand those things, and they should be known, as it is written: "And you shall know that I am the Lord" [Exod. 10: 2]; "And they shall know that I am the Lord" [Exod. 29: 46], so that the words shall settle in our heart. But from now on the words will remain concealed within us. Blessed is our portion in this world and in the world to come for the holy candle has been crowned until now with these words that are [concealed] within us.'

These descriptions indicate the existence of a text of R. Shimon's teachings, written by R. Aba at his master's deathbed and kept secret by the companions. However, *Idra zuta* does not present itself as the text written by R. Aba.

According to a famous tradition that emerged in the early fourteenth century, and which I discuss below, R. Shimon himself wrote the Zohar. This tradition, however, is not evident in the zoharic literature (except in *Tikunei hazohar* and *Ra'aya meheimna*), although some parts include descriptions of R. Shimon writing down his teachings. Such is the case in the section *Rav metivta* in Zohar 'Shelaḥ lekha', which says:

While sitting they said: 'Night has come.' The teacher of the academy [*rav metivta*] said to R. Shimon: 'You are a holy and righteous man, the light of the universe; take this secret notebook [*pinkasa de'aḥmeta*] and a candle and write down these words because the time has come for each one of us to visit his grave. [Our time will run out] at midnight, when the Holy One, blessed be He, enters the garden to enjoy these *tsadikim*, for at that time they will all fly away to be there.' . . . He cried and put his head between his knees and kissed the ground. While doing so he beheld a few silhouettes of the companions around him. They said to him: 'Fear not, son of Yohai, fear not, holy candle, write and take joy in the happiness of your Master.' He wrote all the words he heard that night, and read them and studied them, not missing a word. His candle did not burn out throughout that night, until morning came. (Zohar iii. 166*b*)[35]

R. Shimon, then, is said to have recorded the secrets that were revealed to him by the teacher of the celestial academy. However, what he noted down were only the secrets revealed to him on that particular night and not the larger zoharic sections. As in R. Aba's case, a distinction must be made between what R. Shimon wrote on that particular night and the text of *Rav metivta*. The above passage says that he wrote in a *pinkasa de'aḥmeta*. The word *aḥmeta* appears in Ezra 6: 2, and probably means a closet for storing books.[36] The choice of words in the zoharic text conveys the concealment of all that had been written that night. Similarly in *Idra raza derazin* R. Aba asserts that everything he wrote was concealed among the companions.

Texts written by R. Shimon are also mentioned in Zohar 'Song of Songs':

Elijah said to him: 'Rabbi, say your words and I will say mine after you, because [only] through you and me will it be completed. We have been granted permission by the Ancient of All to reveal these secrets—from below and from above. You correspond to those below and I to those above. And you, Rabbi, have an advantage on me, because all your words will be written above before the Ancient of Days, and my words will not be written above; they will be written only in this world by you. Your words will be written above and mine will be written below. And you, the righteous ones, are worthy in this world and in the world to come.'[37] (*Zohar ḥadash* 62*b*)

This passage is extremely interesting and, to my knowledge, has no parallel in any other layer of the zoharic literature. According to Elijah's statement, although R. Shimon's words were written down they do not exist in this world—they were written above, before the Ancient of Days. In contrast, Elijah's words were recorded in this world by R. Shimon. It seems that this is the first time that a manuscript written by R. Shimon is mentioned. Some reservation is conveyed regarding this text as it contains secrets revealed

35 Hellner-Eshed, *A River Flows from Eden*, 436–7.

36 See Rashi's and Abraham ibn Ezra's commentary ad loc. Regarding *aḥmeta* in the Zohar see Liebes, 'The Use of Words in the Zohar' (Heb.); id., 'Sections of a Zohar Lexicon' (Heb.), 346; Huss, 'Dictionary of Foreign Words in the Zohar', 173 n. 3.

37 See also *Zohar ḥadash*, 63*b*, 70*b*.

by Elijah to R. Shimon, which are seen as inferior to R. Shimon's secrets recorded in the world above.

As I have previously shown, kabbalists at the end of the thirteenth century did not identify zoharic texts in their writings by the name *Sefer ha-zohar*. The zoharic literature itself, however, contains a few passages that expound the word *zohar* and indicate the importance that the authors assigned to it.[38] Such is the case in *Sitrei torah*, included in Zohar 'Vayetse', where the splendour (*zohar*) of the speculum that shines is identified as the merging of two lights:

From within the hidden mystery, by means of a secret unification, the splendour [*zohar*] of a speculum that shines emerges consisting of two colours that have united. Once these [colours] have merged into one, all the colours can be seen within it. Purple is any vision in which the lights within are dashing to and fro. These lights do not pause to be seen; they unite [*ḥibura ḥad*] with that splendour [*zohar*]. Within this splendour dwells the one who dwells. It is a name for the concealed one, who is unknown. (Zohar i. 147*a*–*b*)

In Yehuda Liebes's interpretation the above passage alludes to the Zohar, as the Aramaic word *ḥibura* can be understood to mean a written work (*ḥibur* in Hebrew).[39] Daniel Matt, on the other hand, has suggested that the sentences 'Within this splendour dwells the one who dwells. It is a name for the concealed one, who is unknown' may be a hint at Moses de León's concealed role as the author of the Zohar.[40] Possibly, one may also find the word *zohar*, alluding to a literary creation, in portion 'Va'era'. Here the key verse of the zoharic literature is expounded—'And the enlightened will shine like the splendour [*zohar*] of the firmament' (Dan. 12: 3):

'And the enlightened will shine'—who are the 'enlightened'? It is the sage who from within himself perceives words that others cannot express; they are called the enlightened. 'Will shine like the splendour [*zohar*] of the firmament'—what is the 'firmament'? It is the firmament of Moses, who is set in the middle. This splendour of his is veiled, unrevealed by its own colour. It stands above this firmament, which is not illuminated, where the shades of colours can be seen. And these colours, even though they can be seen in it, do not shine like splendour

[38] Regarding the term *zohar* (splendour) in *Sefer hazohar* itself see Liebes, 'Zohar and Eros' (Heb.), 73–6, 85–6; Hellner-Eshed, *A River Flows from Eden*, 437–9.

[39] Liebes, 'Zohar and Eros' (Heb.), 85.

[40] *Zohar, the Book of Enlightenment*, trans. Matt, 30.

because they are concealed . . . Therefore we say that Moses was allowed [to look through the] speculum that shines, which is above the one that does not shine. (Zohar ii. *23a–b*)

It could be that this homily identifies the splendour of the speculum that shines with the work of the enlightened, the composers of the Zohar. Matt suggests that the words 'this splendour of his is veiled, unrevealed by its own colour' denote the Zohar and its pseudepigraphic nature.[41] The reference to the sage who is able to perceive what others cannot express certainly alludes to R. Shimon,[42] and reflects the self-image of the compilers.

The important role of R. Shimon and the companions, the description of the written record of his teachings, and the significance attributed to the term 'splendour' in some zoharic texts all contributed to the development of the concept of the Zohar as a unified work. However, this concept does not appear in the actual zoharic texts. On the contrary, they present themselves in a way that essentially negates the notion of a literary entity entitled *Sefer hazohar*. Furthermore, the fact that they refer to R. Shimon in the third person and describe his death and the events thereafter undermines the suggestion that he is the author of these writings.

As previously said, the term *Sefer hazohar*, as well as the idea that it denotes a sacred and authoritative literary body written by R. Shimon through supernatural revelations, appear for the first time in some early fourteenth-century sources. Yet even during this period there were kabbalists who continued to incorporate zoharic texts into their writings in the same manner as it had been done in the late thirteenth century. For example David ben Judah Hehasid, who frequently cited zoharic texts, mostly in Hebrew translation, never presented them as quotations from the Zohar.[43] R. Shem Tov Ibn Gaon, the disciple of R. Solomon ben Adret, includes zoharic passages in his book *Badei ha'aron umigdal ḥananel*, completed in Safed in 1324/5,[44] but he, too, fails to mention the Zohar by name.[45] A zoharic text, incorporated in a Torah commentary written at approximately the same time by an anonymous member of R. Solomon ben

[41] *Zohar, the Book of Enlightenment*, 243.

[42] Wolfson, *Through a Speculum that Shines*, 379 n. 190.

[43] Scholem, 'Rabbi David ben Judah Hehasid' (Heb.), 302, 309; Goldreich, '*Sefer hagevul* by David ben Judah Hehasid' (Heb.), 96–101.

[44] Dan, 'The Worms Epistle and the Pseudepigraphy Problem' (Heb.), 120–1.

[45] Ibid.

Adret's circle, also appears without any reference to its source.[46] Even in later periods there were sages who quoted zoharic texts as *midrash*, not as parts of the Zohar, and did not attribute them to R. Shimon.[47]

A famous testimony from the first decade of the fourteenth century regarding the appearance of the Zohar is found in *Sefer divrei hayamim*, the lost book of Isaac of Acre, quoted in Abraham Zacuto's *Sefer yuḥasin*.[48] In it, Isaac of Acre claims to have heard of the Zohar while staying in Navarre in 1304/5. That year, following his investigations, he arrived in Castile and met (in the cities of Valladolid, Avila, Talavera, and Toledo) several people, including Moses de León, Joseph ben Todros Abulafia, and de León's student R. Jacob, who had already heard of the Zohar and seen parts of it.[49]

The first kabbalist who regularly used the term *Sefer hazohar* in his writings was Menahem Recanati. He quoted a number of zoharic texts under this title in his *Perush hatefilot*, *Ta'amei hamitsvot*, and *Perush hatorah*,[50] all of which were probably written in the first decade of the fourteenth century.[51] R. Shemayah ben Isaac Halevi, who might have preceded Recanati, mentioned *Sefer hazohar* in his book *Tseror haḥayim*.[52] The name also occurs in *Tikunei hazohar* and *Ra'aya meheimna*, as well as in the Hebrew writings

46 Idel, 'Anonymous Commentary on the Pentateuch' (Heb.), 20.

47 R. Samuel Ibn Zarza quotes zoharic passages (from *Midrash hane'elam* on Genesis) several times as *Bereshit rabah* in his book *Mikhlal yofi*, written in 1369; see Holzman, 'The Introduction to Samuel Zarza's *Mikhlal yofi*' (Heb.), 23. R. Israel Al-Nakawa, who lived in the second half of the 14th century (and died as a martyr in the anti-Jewish riots of 1391/2) included in his book *Sefer menorat hamaor* a number of zoharic passages in Hebrew, cited as *Midrash vayehi or*; see *Sefer menorat hamaor*, ed. Enelow, i. 21–2, ii. 26–8, iii. 29–34.

48 Zacuto, *Sefer yuḥasin hashalem*, 88–9. Tishby and Lachower, *The Wisdom of the Zohar*, i. 13–15. Abrams, *Kabbalistic Manuscripts and Textual Theory*, 257–8.

49 Isaac of Acre states that Moses de León died that year (1304/5); however, another source, *Kitsur zekher tsadik* by Joseph ben Tsadik, says that he died in 1292/3; see David, *Two Chronicles* (Heb.), 14. Abraham Zacuto also mentioned this information; see his *Sefer yuḥasin hashalem*, 222. If indeed the testimony of Joseph ben Tsadik is more reliable (and I do not think one can unequivocally determine whether it is), the appearance of the Zohar must be dated to 1292/3 or earlier.

50 On Recanati's quotations from the Zohar see Ch. 3.

51 Recanati was acquainted with R. Shem Tov Ibn Gaon's *Keter shem tov*, written in 1297/8. His commentary *Perush hatorah* (written after *Sefer ta'amei hamitsvot*) is quoted for the first time by Joseph Angelet in *Kupat harokhlin*, written in Saragossa in 1311; see Idel, *Menahem Recanati the Kabbalist* (Heb.), 57, 62.

52 Shemayah ben Isaac Halevi, *Tseror haḥayim*, Leiden MS, 191*a*–*b*; see also the expanded version, Oxford MS, 61*b*–62*a*. I have not found a parallel to it in the zoharic corpus. When the

of their anonymous author,[53] likewise composed in the early fourteenth century.[54] Joseph Angelet used the same title in his book *Kupat harokhlin* (1310/11),[55] and the term *midrash hazohar* appears in his *Livnat hasapir* (1324/5).[56]

The name *Sefer hazohar* reappears in other works written in the first half of the fourteenth century, among them *Otsar haḥayim* by Isaac of Acre,[57] an untitled kabbalistic work by R. Hayim ben Samuel,[58] and the anthology *Sefer hane'elam*.[59] By the second half of the century it had become widespread, although occasionally zoharic texts continued to be quoted without reference to a book thus entitled.

book was written is unknown, but according to Idel, R. Shemayah lived at the end of the 13th century; see *Kabbalah: New Perspectives*, 247; 'The Kabbalah's "Window of Opportunities"', 172 n. 9, 181 n. 43. The earliest appearance of the term *Sefer hazohar* may be in *Tseror haḥayim*, if indeed it was written at the end of the 13th century.

[53] On zoharic quotations in the author's Hebrew writings see Liebes, 'Zohar and *Tikunei zohar*' (Heb.), 253.

[54] See Tishby, *Messianism in the Time of the Expulsion* (Heb.), 91 n. 284. See also Goldreich, 'Iberian Phrase in an Unknown Fragment' (Heb.), 91 n. 5; id., 'Examinations of the Self-Image of the Author of *Tikunei hazohar*' (Heb.), 477 n. 74; Gottlieb, *The Hebrew Writings of the Author of* Tikunei hazohar (Heb.), 40. In Idel's view, the composition of *Tikunei hazohar* should be dated to the end of the 13th century or no later than the very beginning of the 14th; see his introduction to Gottlieb, *The Hebrew Writings of the Author of Tikunei hazohar* (Heb.), 29, where he argues that the Hebrew writings of the author of *Tikunei hazohar* preceded *Tikunei hazohar* and *Ra'aya meheimna* (ibid. 29–30). Liebes, on the other hand, is of the opinion that the Hebrew writings were composed later. He even raises the possibility that they were not written by the same author but by a disciple of his; see Liebes, 'Zohar and *Tikunei hazohar*' (Heb.), 255.

[55] See Liebes, *Studies in the Zohar*, 224–5 n. 298. The term *sefer hazohar* does not occur in *Esrim ve'arba'ah sodot*, which is probably Angelet's first work.

[56] In his book *Livnat hasapir*, Angelet uses the name *Midrash hazohar* several times (London MS, 292*a*, 325*a*, 348*a*). At the beginning of *Perush sha'arei orah* he writes about 'the column of splendour [*zohar*] that is called the *midrash* of R. Shimon ben Yohai'; see *Perush sha'arei orah*, 1*a*. However, most of the time he uses the name *Midrash hane'elam* in these works.

[57] Moscow MS, 94*a*–95*a*, 183*a*, and New York MS, 123*b*. The references to the Zohar and the long quotations from it in Moscow MS, 65*a*–70*a* do not belong to the text of *Otsar haḥayim*—some of them were taken from Abraham Tsabah's commentary on the liturgy. The pages in the Moscow manuscript are out of order. See Huss, '*Sefer hazohar* as a Canonical, Sacred and Holy Text', 178. Regarding the dating of *Otsar haḥayim* (after 1313 and perhaps 1331 or 1336) see Goldreich, '*Sefer me'irat einayim*' (Heb.), 364.

[58] For the use of the term *zohar* in this work, see Bar Ilan, MS 1039 (previously Moussaieff 64) (F 22889); Goldreich, '*Sefer me'irat einayim*' (Heb.), 389.

[59] Farber-Ginat, 'On the Sources of Moses de León's Early Kabbalistic System' (Heb.), 71 n. 13.

The idea of the Zohar as a book surfaced concurrently with the notion that its authors were R. Shimon and his companions. As mentioned above, quotations from a *midrash* attributed to R. Shimon had appeared earlier in the writings of Bahya ben Asher and Joshua Ibn Shuaib. However, they made no reference to *Sefer hazohar*. Furthermore, the texts that they quote as 'R. Shimon's *midrash*' do not have zoharic characteristics—they are not written in Aramaic and do not contain kabbalistic themes. *Berit menuḥah*, a work that was probably written in the same period,[60] has many Aramaic quotations attributed to R. Shimon,[61] but only one of them has a parallel in the zoharic literature,[62] and the term *Sefer hazohar* is never mentioned.[63]

The attribution of the Zohar to R. Shimon appears in several early fourteenth-century sources. Isaac of Acre quotes de León as having said, 'I have transcribed for you these words from the book composed by R. Shimon ben Yohai and his son, R. Eleazar.'[64] De León added: 'May God do so to me and more, if at this moment the ancient book written by R. Shimon ben Yohai is not in my house, where I live in Avila.'[65] Abraham Zacuto quotes Isaac of Acre as saying that he had investigated *Sefer hazohar*, which R. Shimon had written together with his son in a cave while hiding from the Romans.[66] In his book *Otsar haḥayim*, Isaac of Acre reiterates his statement regarding R. Shimon's authorship: 'He [R. Shimon] and the ten great ones who were with him in the cave assembled and wrote *Sefer hazohar*.'[67]

[60] Scholem argues that the book was written in the second half of the 14th century (*Kabbalah*, 65, 105). Tishby, however, points out calculations in *Berit menuḥah* for an apocalypse to take place in the year 1332; see his *Messianism in the Time of the Expulsion* (Heb.), 137 n. 14.

[61] *Berit menuḥah*, 1*b*, 3*a*, 4*a*–*b*, 23*b*–24*a* (in the name of 'the Sage'), 25*a*–*b*, 27*a*–*b*, 31*b*. See also Tishby and Lachower, *Wisdom of the Zohar*, i. 39–40; Tishby, *Messianism in the Time of the Expulsion* (Heb.), 138.

[62] *Berit menuḥah*, 41*b*; cf. Zohar i. 219*a*. See also Liebes, 'God's Attributes' (Heb.), 72–4.

[63] Another work that is ascribed to R. Shimon, and which was possibly written in the early 14th century, is *Perush eser hasefirot* (London British Library, MS Add. 26929 (F. 5454), 108*b*–112*a*; also in the New York MS, JTS 2203 (F. 11301), 106*b*–10*a*). See too *Sefer habahir*, ed. Abrams, 94.

[64] Tishby and Lachower, *The Wisdom of the Zohar*, i. 14.

[65] Ibid. The same source records Joseph ben Todros Abulafia as having said to Isaac of Acre: 'Take it for a fact that the Zohar that R. Shimon ben Yohai wrote was in the possession of R. Moses [de León].' R. Jacob, de León's disciple, furthermore 'called heaven and earth to witness that the Book of the Zohar that R. Shimon ben Yohai had written . . .' (ibid. 15).

[66] Ibid.

[67] Moscow MS, 95*a*. In another place he speaks about '*Sefer hazohar* by R. Shimon, of blessed memory' (ibid. 183*a*). *Otsar haḥayim*, New York MS, 126*a* contains a quotation from

Tikunei hazohar and *Ra'aya meheimna* also mention that the Zohar was composed by R. Shimon and his companions. The introduction to *Tikunei hazohar* says:

It is written, 'And the enlightened will shine like the splendour of the firmament' [Dan. 12: 3]. These are R. Shimon bar Yohai and his companions, R. Eleazar his son, R. Aba, R. Jose, R. Hiya, R. Isaac, and other companions who illuminated a splendour above, 'like the splendour of the firmament'. What is the meaning of 'like the splendour'? When they wrote this work, it was accepted above and was named *Sefer hazohar*. (*Tikunei hazohar* 17*a*)

Joseph Angelet introduces zoharic texts in his writings as '*midrash* of R. Shimon, may he rest in peace' or 'R. Shimon's *midrash*'.[68] In *Livnat hasapir* and in his commentary on *Sha'arei orah*, he records a tradition that implicitly attributes the Zohar to R. Shimon. According to this tradition (which I discuss further below), R. Shimon had learned his wisdom in the cave of Moses and Elijah.[69] At the beginning of his commentary on *Sha'arei orah*, Angelet identifies 'R. Shimon's *midrash*' as the Zohar, saying, 'The pillar of splendour [*zohar*] called the *midrash* of R. Shimon ben Yohai.'[70]

Yet not all the sources in which the name *Sefer hazohar* appears ascribe the book to R. Shimon. This is particularly evident in the writings of Menahem Recanati, who frequently quotes from *Sefer hazohar* but never attributes it to R. Shimon.[71]

Some kabbalists further asserted that R. Shimon had written the Zohar following a divine revelation—Moses de León, for example, distributed the

what he calls Rabbi Shimon's *midrash*. I have not found an exact parallel version of it in the zoharic literature; it may refer to Zohar iii. 100*b*.

[68] Angelet, *Kupat harokhlin*, 39*a*, 111*b*, 130*a*. Rabbi Shimon's *midrash* is also mentioned by Angelet in *Livnat hasapir*, 13*a*, 21*b*, 21*c*, and in *Perush sha'arei orah*, 23*a*. Yehuda Liebes has drawn my attention to Angelet's comment in *Kupat harokhlin*, 157*b*: 'I have heard from R. Shimon'. In the same book Angelet mentions words that have been transmitted 'by R. Shimon' (ibid. 82*b*).

[69] Angelet, *Livnat hasapir* (printed edn.), 3*a*; London MS, 429*a*; id., *Perush sha'arei orah*, 1*a*. For the identification of R. Shimon's cave with that of Moses and Elijah, see n. 79 below.

[70] Angelet, *Perush sha'arei orah*, 1*a*.

[71] Idel, *R. Menahem Recanati the Kabbalist* (Heb.), 103; Abrams, *Kabbalistic Manuscripts and Textual Theory*, 261. *Sefer hane'elam*, *Tseror haḥayim* by Shemayah ben Isaac Halevi, and R. Hayim ben Samuel's untitled kabbalistic work are further sources where R. Shimon is not mentioned as the author of the Zohar.

book making such claims, as we learn from his wife's testimony.[72] Isaac of Acre argued that the source of the Zohar was the height of the divine world, the Infinite itself: 'and since I saw that its words were wonderful, drawn from the celestial source, the fountain that pours forth without being replenished (blessed be His glorious kingdom for ever and ever)'.[73] The holiness of the Zohar and its divine source are frequently emphasized in *Tikunei hazohar* and *Ra'aya meheimna*. In the introduction to the former work, a *midrash* on Daniel 12: 3 states that the secrets of the Zohar were revealed to R. Shimon and his companions by Elijah, the souls of the supernal academy, the angels, the attributes, and the ten *sefirot*:

'The enlightened' are R. Shimon and the companions. 'Will shine': when they assembled to write this book, permission was given to them and to Elijah, who was with them, and to all the souls of the heavenly academies, to descend and mingle among them. And the concealed angels were allowed to mingle with them by means of intellectual perception. And the Primary Cause of everything gave permission to all the sacred names, all the combinations of the Tetragrammaton and attributes, to reveal hidden secrets to them, each name in its own grade. And permission was given to the *sefirot* to reveal to them the concealed secrets that were not permitted to be revealed until the generation of the king messiah.

The supernatural provenance of the Zohar is emphasized in a homily in *Ra'aya meheimna* on the same verse; here the Zohar is called the 'tree of life' and its source of wisdom is the splendour of the *sefirah* Binah (understanding), also referred to as 'supernal mother' and 'repentance':

The enlightened will understand through the attribute Binah, which is the Tree of Life, as it says: 'And the enlightened will shine like the splendour of the firmament' in this work of yours, which is *Sefer hazohar*, from the *zohar* of a supernal mother, repentance . . . And since Israel will taste from the Tree of Life, which is this *Sefer hazohar*, they will emerge from exile through mercy, and the verse 'the Lord alone will guide him, no alien god [is] at His side' [Deut. 32: 12] will be fulfilled in them. (Zohar iii. 124*b*)

In these two passages (and others in *Tikunei hazohar* and *Ra'aya meheimna*) the 'revelation' of the Zohar has a messianic significance. As I show in Chapter 4 below, this idea became widespread in the fifteenth century and played an important role in the dissemination of the work.

[72] Tishby and Lachower, *The Wisdom of the Zohar*, i. 14–15.

[73] Ibid. i. 13.

In a previously quoted passage from *Tikunei hazohar*, Elijah reveals secrets to R. Shimon and his companions. The *Introduction to the Zohar* (which, despite its name, is not an introduction but an alternative exegesis of portion 'Bereshit') recounts an incident in which Elijah appears to R. Shimon by the sea, reveals a kabbalistic secret to him, and disappears.[74] Zohar 'Song of Songs' (discussed above) describes R. Shimon as recording the prophet's words. Traditions of this kind are rare in the early strata of zoharic literature; in most cases it is Elijah who comes to learn secrets from R. Shimon.[75] However, while the idea that Elijah revealed secrets to R. Shimon rarely appears in the early literature, it comes up frequently in *Tikunei hazohar* and *Ra'aya meheimna*.[76] It can also be found in the following text, which, according to Yehuda Liebes, was probably written by Joseph Angelet or a member of his circle: 'R. Shimon escaped to the desert of Lod and hid in a cave, he and Eleazar his son. A miracle happened and a carob tree grew for them and a spring of water sprang forth. They ate from that tree and drank from that water. Elijah, of blessed memory, came twice a day and taught them, and no one knew' (*Zohar ḥadash* 59*b*).[77]

This passage states that it was Elijah who taught R. Shimon and his son while they were hiding in the cave,[78] whereas in the version of Isaac of Acre R. Shimon wrote the Zohar by himself while in hiding. In *Livnat hasapir* (as well as in other writings) Angelet identifies R. Shimon's cave as that of Moses and Elijah:[79] 'Let a palanquin be put up for R. Shimon and he shall

[74] Zohar i. 1*b*–2*a*. I am grateful to Zeev Gries for pointing the passage out to me.

[75] See e.g. Zohar iii. 241*b*. R. Shimon's words at the end of *Idra raba* (Zohar iii. 144*b*) also suggest that Elijah is expected to come and listen to the secrets that he and his companions have revealed.

[76] See references collected by Ish Shalom (Friedmann) in the introduction to *Seder eliyahu raba veseder eliyahu zuta*, 40 n. 1.

[77] Cf. Angelet, *Livnat hasapir*, 100*a*; *Tikunei hazohar*, 1*a*. See also Goldreich, 'Iberian Phrase in an Unknown Fragment' (Heb.), 97 n. 28; Liebes, 'Two Young Does of a Roe' (Heb.), 151 n. 335.

[78] The above quotation is based on a story in *Shab*. 33*b*, in which Elijah revealed himself to R. Shimon and his son only after they had been hiding in the cave for twelve years (he came to announce Caesar's death to them). However, according to R. Hananel's commentary on *Suk*. 45*b*, R. Shimon could commune with the divine throughout his period of hiding. See also Nathan ben Yehiel, *Arukh hashalem*, vi. 317–18.

[79] The identification of Elijah's cave in Mount Horeb with the cleft of the rock in Moses' story in Exod. 33: 22 appears in a *beraita* (*Pes*. 54*a*), in which the 'cave where Elijah and Moses stood' is one of the things that were created on the eve of the first sabbath at dusk; see also

receive grace from above,[80] and so shall everyone who engages in his teachings. This is the wisdom that he obtained in the cave of Moses and Elijah.'[81] The tradition that links R. Shimon's cave to that of Moses and Elijah is based on similarities between the talmudic tales of R. Shimon's adventures and the biblical stories about the two prophets.[82] By identifying the cave in which secrets were revealed to R. Shimon with the cleft of rock where God places Moses as he passes by (Exod. 33: 23) and with Elijah's cave in Mount Horeb (1 Kgs 19: 9), the authors of the Zohar accentuate its sanctity and divine origins.

The Zohar's supernatural and holy character is emphasized in the writings of Angelet, Isaac of Acre, and the anonymous author of *Tikunei hazohar* and *Ra'aya meheimna*, but it is absent from the works of other kabbalists of that period who mention *Sefer hazohar*. Recanati, Shemayah ben Isaac Halevi's *Tseror haḥayim*, *Sefer hane'elam*, and the kabbalistic works of Hayim ben Samuel do not attribute zoharic texts to R. Shimon or accentuate their holiness.

Meg. 19*a*. The identification of the cave in which R. Shimon hid with that of Moses and Elijah can be found in the Munich manuscript of the Babylonian Talmud; see Strack, *Talmud Babylonicum*; Munich MS, 13*a*.

80 Based on *BM* 119*a* and Rashi's commentary on it.

81 *Livnat hasapir*, London MS, 429*a* (3*a* in the printed edn.); id., *Perush sha'arei orah*, 1*a*, and see Liebes, 'Two Young Roes of a Doe' (Heb.), 151 n. 335.

82 There is a parallel between the forty days and forty nights of Moses' first ascent of Mount Sinai and the twelve-year seclusion of R. Shimon and his son. This parallel had been developed in the apocalyptic writings ascribed to R. Shimon. In a text called 'The Prayer of R. Shimon bar Yohai', for example, he has a divine revelation at the cave after he has fasted for forty days and forty nights (a motif also connecting him to Elijah, who had walked for forty days and forty nights until he reached a cave in Mount Horeb); see Even-Shemuel, *Midreshei ge'ulah*, 269–70. One version of 'The Secrets of R. Shimon bar Yohai' starts with the words: 'These are the secrets that were revealed to R. Shimon bar Yohai when he was hiding in the cave from the emperor of Rome, and he stood and prayed continually for forty days and forty nights' (ibid. 401).

There is a further similarity between R. Shimon hiding in the cave for fear of being killed by the Romans and Elijah fleeing from Jezebel, as well as between Elijah being sustained by the miraculous appearance of a stone-baked cake and a jar of water and R. Shimon and his son being sustained by a carob tree and water that spring up. In *Shab.* 33*b* the story is recounted of Elijah bringing R. Shimon the news of Caesar's death and of the annulment of his decree—a further connection between Elijah, R. Shimon, and the cave. On the link between the zoharic R. Shimon and Elijah see Elkayam, 'The Holy Zohar of Sabbatai Zevi' (Heb.), 385–6.

By highlighting the supernatural source of the Zohar the authors meant to imbue it with authority. This is particularly apparent in the following excerpt from the introduction to *Tikunei hazohar*, which reiterates that R. Shimon and his companions had been granted permission to reveal the secrets:

When they assembled to write this book, they were given permission . . . and the Primary Cause of Everything gave permission to all the sacred names to reveal hidden secrets to them, each name in its own grade. And permission was granted to the ten *sefirot* to reveal hidden secrets to them that were not permitted to be revealed until the generation of the king messiah. (*Tikunei hazohar*, 1*a*)[83]

As we shall see below, declarations regarding the supremacy of the kabbalistic teachings of R. Shimon and the Zohar also appear in other sources from that period.

In order to further clarify the context of the emergence of the idea of the Zohar as a book, I wish now to discuss the distinguishing characteristics of the first kabbalists who coined the term *Sefer hazohar* and developed the concepts regarding its authority and sanctity. Although these scholars did not belong to a specific kabbalistic circle, they were biographically, bibliographically, and ideologically affiliated. Three of the figures mentioned in the testimony of Isaac of Acre regarding the discovery of the Zohar were Castilians close to one another—Moses de León, Joseph ben Todros Abulafia, and R. Jacob, de León's disciple.[84] When Isaac of Acre arrived in Castile he met all of them. Menahem Recanati, who lived in Italy, was also acquainted with a number of Castilian kabbalistic works. Moshe Idel has suggested that Recanati may have visited Castile (and Catalonia) in the first decade of the fourteenth century and written his commentary on the Torah there.[85] The Castilian kabbalah also influenced Joseph Angelet, who lived in Saragossa in the kingdom of Aragon and was familiar with the writings of de León and Recanati,[86] although he probably never met them. The domicile of the author of *Tikunei hazohar* is unknown but, as Amos

[83] See also *Tikunei hazohar*, 17*a*–*b*.

[84] De León dedicated his books to Joseph ben Todros and R. Jacob.

[85] See Idel, *Menahem Recanati the Kabbalist* (Heb.), 67.

[86] Ibid.; see also Felix, 'Joseph Angelet' (Heb.), 33.

Goldreich has argued, he had spent a significant number of years on the Iberian peninsula and it cannot be ruled out that he, too, lived in Castile.[87]

In addition to the personal relationships between some of the authors affiliated with the circle of the Zohar and their ties to the Castilian kabbalah, they were also linked by ideology and literature. Liebes and Goldreich have noted similarities between the kabbalah of Angelet and that of the author of *Tikunei hazohar*.[88] Idel has pointed out parallels between the kabbalah of Recanati, Isaac of Acre, and the author of *Tikunei hazohar*, and has raised the possibility that they were members of the same circle.[89] Idel focuses on the clear distinction these kabbalists made between the Cause of all causes and the *sefirot*—a distinction that also characterizes the kabbalah of Angelet.[90]

The first kabbalists who used the term *Sefer hazohar* have been classified by Idel as the 'secondary elite'. This sociocultural group included intellectuals who were primarily interested in kabbalah and philosophy and did not engage in halakhah or serve as communal rabbis. In contrast, the primary elite, the spiritual leadership of the Jewish community, were mainly engaged in halakhah.[91] In light of this typology almost all of the kabbalists in whose writings the concept of *Sefer hazohar* first appeared were of the secondary elite. The term is absent from the writings of the primary elite—those affiliated with the Catalan circle of Nahmanides and R. Solomon ben Adret.

The novelty of the idea of the Zohar as a book is highlighted by the shift in attitude towards zoharic texts among some of the aforementioned

[87] Goldreich, 'Iberian Phrase in an Unknown Fragment' (Heb.), 89–121; see also Baer, *Studies and Essays in the History of the Jewish People* (Heb.), ii. 342–5.

[88] See Liebes, *Studies in the Zohar*, 225 n. 293. Goldreich, 'Iberian Phrase in an Unknown Fragment' (Heb.), 95–7; Idel, *Menahem Recanati the Kabbalist* (Heb.), 107. Goldreich points out the similarities between the author of *Tikunei hazohar* and Isaac of Acre; see 'Examinations of the Self-Image of the Author of *Tikunei hazohar*' (Heb.), 468–9 n. 41.

[89] Idel, *Menahem Recanati the Kabbalist* (Heb.), 106–8.

[90] See Felix, 'Joseph Angelet' (Heb.), 34–44. On the similarities between *Tikunei hazohar* and Angelet's writings see Meroz, 'R. Joseph Angelet and his "Zoharic Writings"' (Heb.), 334–40.

[91] See Idel, 'Kabbalah and Elites in Thirteenth-Century Spain'. On the difference between kabbalists who belonged to the primary and secondary elites see id., 'PaRDeS': Some Reflections on Kabbalistic Hermeneutics', 246; id., 'Transmission in Thirteenth-Century Kabbalah', 146–9.

kabbalists. The most compelling example is the change that took place in the way Moses de León promoted the Zohar. As I have pointed out, the zoharic texts, some of which were probably written or edited by de León, do not mention *Sefer hazohar*. In his kabbalistic writings between 1286 and 1293 he quoted zoharic passages as if they were ancient exegeses but never mentioned the Zohar as a book; nor did he ascribe the texts to R. Shimon or to his companions. In a later period, according to Isaac of Acre, de León started to distribute pamphlets under the title *Sefer hazohar*, which he claimed had been written by R. Shimon. Thus, in the early fourteenth century (or in the last years of the thirteenth) de León changed the way in which he referred to and publicized the zoharic texts.

A similar phenomenon is discernible in the writings of Isaac of Acre. In his first work, *Me'irat einayim*, a few zoharic excerpts are quoted but the existence of *Sefer hazohar* is not mentioned. In the passage from *Divrei hayamim* cited by Zacuto, and in *Otsar haḥayim*, however, Isaac of Acre asserts that he is acquainted with *Sefer hazohar*, ascribes it to R. Shimon, and notes the book's supernatural source. Such a change in attitude also finds expression in the works of Joseph Angelet, whose first book, *Khaf dalet sodot*, contains no reference to *Sefer hazohar* or R. Shimon (although he was familiar with the names *Midrash hane'elam* and *Sifra ditseniuta*). Later, however, in his *Kupat harokhlin* (1311), he quotes zoharic texts as parts of the Zohar.

What, then, brought about the formation of the concept of the Zohar as a book, and what caused the change in the way zoharic texts were defined at the beginning of the fourteenth century?

It is not impossible that a new, cohesive collection of zoharic writings had come into the possession of the kabbalists who first made reference to *Sefer hazohar*, resulting in their emphasis on the literary unity of the texts and in the establishment of R. Shimon as their protagonist. However, while we can reasonably assume that in the last decade of the thirteenth century new zoharic texts were indeed produced and edited,[92] it seems that the emergence of the idea of the Zohar as a book cannot be explained purely

[92] About the fact that part of the zoharic literature was created after de León had finished writing his Hebrew works, see Liebes, 'How the Zohar Was Written' (Heb.), 2. On the adaptation of zoharic texts see Meroz, 'Zoharic Narratives'.

by textual changes that took place at that time. As I show in the next chapter, testimonies of kabbalists from the early fourteenth century (and even later) indicate that there was no comprehensive corpus of zoharic literature. Even in later periods, after the editing of larger zoharic collections, there were still sages who quoted zoharic sources as if they were midrashic texts, without attributing them to R. Shimon or treating them as parts of the Zohar, which shows that the concept of a single unified work continued to be surrounded by much ambiguity. The appearance of the name *Sefer hazohar* thus does not attest to the creation of a new literary unit, but rather to a new mode in which these texts were viewed, distributed, and received.

Pierre Bourdieu has argued that 'there is a need to investigate the specific forms of struggle that take place in every field between the newcomer, who tries to break through the entry barrier, and those who control it and try to protect their monopoly and prevent completion'.[93] Using Bourdieu's terminology we may say that the impetus for the development of the idea of *Sefer hazohar* was the desire of the Castilian kabbalists of the secondary elite, the 'newcomers', to break through the entry barriers of the kabbalistic production field—the barriers that had been raised by Nahmanides' and R. Solomon ben Adret's disciples, who enjoyed a monopoly in the field in the late thirteenth and early fourteenth centuries. Specifically, the zoharic concept seems to have crystallized in response to the canonization of Nahmanides' commentary on the Torah, which gave rise to a new genre of interpretation of the secrets in his text. The new idea provided a means to subvert the authority of Nahmanides and the dominant status of the kabbalists within R. Solomon ben Adret's circle.

Criticism of Nahmanides had been brewing among Castilian kabbalists before the appearance of the Zohar. As Asi Farber-Ginat shows, Moses de León engaged in sharp polemics with Nahmanides but refrained from mentioning him by name because of his prominent status.[94] In general, discontent with the sage and his circle was expressed only indirectly. It is

[93] Bourdieu, *Sociology in Question*, 72.

[94] Farber-Ginat, 'On the Sources of Moses de León's Early Kabbalistic System' (Heb.), 41 n. 118, 34 n. 106, 81–2 n. 32; de León, *Sefer shekel hakodesh*, ed. Mopsik, 28 n. 238; Pedaya, *Nahmanides: Cyclical Time and Holy Text* (Heb.), 452.

possible that de León's words, 'Those engaged in the Torah concealed themselves behind their words and did not dare to say anything',[95] were directed at the Nahmanidean circle and its approach to kabbalah. Moshe Idel has argued that the zoharic literature expresses a new and creative attitude, contrary to the conservative and esoteric trend that characterized Nahmanides and his disciples.[96]

As I demonstrated in the previous chapter, the pseudepigraphic setting of the Zohar, and the choice of R. Shimon as the protagonist of a significant part of it, enabled the authors of the Zohar to voice their opposition to the conservative character of the Nahmanidean kabbalah and to set their creative imagination free. Their criticism was expressed through contrasting depictions of Moses and R. Shimon. Moses, hesitant and modest, reflected Nahmanides the traditionalist, who believed in a cautious and restricted transmission of the secrets of kabbalah, and who opposed innovation in the field. Conversely, R. Shimon, who was portrayed as superior to Moses, represented the innovative and confident self-image of the Castilian authors of the Zohar. His disapproval of the 'stuttering sages of Babylon', who openly pursued new teachings but sealed them under an iron padlock and were afraid to disclose them to anyone, might also reflect the zoharic kabbalists' rejection of the esoteric approach of Nahmanides and his circle.[97]

Since the pseudepigraphic nature of the zoharic narratives prevented a direct confrontation with the Nahmanidean kabbalah, its criticism was only expressed indirectly in these texts. But once the concept of a unified, sacred, and authoritative literary work 'written' by R. Shimon was born, it could be employed by the distributors of the zoharic texts as a tool for open opposition. In all probability the idea of *Sefer hazohar* was formulated for precisely that purpose: to enable the distributors of the zoharic literature to confront the circle of conservatives with an alternative literary unit, placing R. Shimon and his book above Nahmanides and his commentary on the Torah. Indeed, the Zohar ultimately came to be accepted as

[95] Wolfson, *The Book of the Pomegranate*, 392.

[96] See Idel, *Kabbalah: New Perspectives*, 213–16; Mopsik, in the introduction to his edition of *Sefer shekel hakodesh*, suggests that 'the kabbalah of the "Zohar circle" is a response to the interpretative and speculative approach of the Nahmanidean circle and to that of the kabbalists of Gerona' (p. 6).

[97] Zohar i. 225*a*.

the most important kabbalistic text, undermining Nahmanides' dominant status.[98]

The showdown between the Zohar and Nahmanides, the principal sources of authority, respectively, of the Castilian and Catalan kabbalists, is recorded in *Otsar haḥayim*, in which Isaac of Acre describes the renaissance of Jewish theology at the turn of the thirteenth century:

I considered the words of the prophets and sages regarding the harshness of the Jewish exile, to which the late prophet refers: 'There was a long period during which Israel lived without Torah, without a priest, and without a true God' [2 Chron. 15: 3]. And our sages, of blessed memory, said: 'The Torah will eventually be forgotten by Israel' [*Shab.* 138*b*]. And indeed, I saw it was happening, until the arrival of the believing teacher . . . in Egypt [Maimonides], and R. Jacob the Nazirite, and R. Abraham ben David of Provence [Rabad], and the faithful teacher . . . in Catalonia [Nahmanides], and R. Jacob Cohen and R. Joseph Gikatilla in Segovia, and *Sefer hazohar* by R. Shimon, of blessed memory, in Spain.[99]

In this passage Isaac of Acre attributes the religious revival and the restoration of the Torah to its central role in the life of Israel to the activities of pivotal figures—Maimonides in Egypt, Nahmanides in Catalonia, and other figures in Provence and Segovia. In contrast, he does not link the Castilian revival to the activity of sages, but rather to an ancient text, the Zohar. This fact seems to throw some light on the background of the appearance of the Zohar: in the absence of a dominant figure among the Castilian kabbalists, a book was created to offset the primacy of Nahmanides and to serve as their source of authority.[100]

[98] See Gottlieb, *Studies in Kabbalistic Literature* (Heb.), 570. Idel has addressed the question why the conservative school of Nahmanides, whose representatives were central figures of the Jewish community, was defeated by innovative kabbalistic trends that were supported by less influential, sometimes even controversial, scholars. Idel argues that the failure of the school of Nahmanides was inherent: because of its conservative and esoteric nature it could not compete with the novel and creative approach of people like Joseph Gikatilla, Abraham Abulafia, and Moses de León, despite their marginal status in the field of halakhah. See Idel, 'We Have no Kabbalistic Tradition on This', 64–71. I believe that the appearance of the concept of *Sefer hazohar*, and the affirmation of its sacred and authoritative status, played an important role in the prevalence of the innovative trend over that of Nahmanides and his followers.

[99] *Otsar haḥayim*, Moscow MS, 183*a*.

[100] R. Isaac of Acre described the status and authority of the Zohar among the Castilian kabbalists in the following passage in *Otsar haḥayim*: 'The sages of Catalonia rely on *Sefer habahir*, which is a firm foundation, and the sages of Spain [Castile] rely on the Zohar, which

Several texts from the late thirteenth and early fourteenth centuries utilized the Zohar to subvert the position of Nahmanides. For instance, in a kabbalistic compilation that contains zoharic texts ascribed to R. Shimon and his son (without mentioning *Sefer hazohar*, however),[101] Nahmanides' opinion is juxtaposed with that of R. Shimon in the context of a discussion of Moses' sin at 'the waters of strife' (Num. 20: 7–8).[102] The author urges readers to defer to R. Shimon, for his stature exceeds that of Nahmanides: 'Unlike what Nahmanides says, these matters are profound, and one should seek answers from the saint, R. Shimon ben Yohai, of blessed memory.'[103] An unequivocal statement of the supremacy of the Zohar (referred to as *Midrash hane'elam*) appears in Joseph Angelet's commentary on *Sha'arei orah*. In discussing the thirteen attributes of God's mercy (Exod. 36: 6) and their symbolism, Angelet bases himself on *Idra raba* and rules that one should accord more weight to the opinions of the sages of the Zohar than to those of Nahmanides and other kabbalists:

> It seems that the order of the grades goes from lower to higher. 'Lord' [Exod. 36: 6] [stands] for Tiferet and Atarah; 'Lord' [ibid.] for Hokhmah Elyonah [supernal wisdom]; 'God' [ibid.]—'who is a God like You' [Mic. 7: 18], the Ancient of Days; and 'merciful' [Exod. 36: 6] for Tiferet, which is called mercy; and 'compassionate' [ibid.] for Hesed, an undeserved gift that is drawing from Hokhmah; 'slow to anger' [ibid.] for the Ancient of Days, who is called 'slow to anger'. And this follows *Midrash hane'elam* in the *Idra*,[104] even though Nahmanides, of blessed memory, did not write so, nor did the rest of the kabbalists. And we have nothing to rely on but the words of the *tana'im*, the eternal pillars of the world.[105]

An additional attempt to establish the authority of the Zohar against that of Nahmanides and his circle can be detected in the tradition which

is a strong foundation, and the enlightened will decide and make peace between them because "both go to the same place" [Eccles. 3: 20].'

101 New York, JTS, MS 1768. On this manuscript see Ta-Shma, 'Responsa from Heaven' (Heb.), 55; Danzig, 'The Geonic Responsa *Sha'arei teshuvah* and *Responsa from Heaven*' (Heb.), 23–6; Wolfson, *The Book of the Pomegranate*, 56–7; id., 'Hai Gaon's Letter', 368 n. 19. Wolfson thinks that this 'collection' was written by de León.

102 *Likutei kabalah*, 105*b*.

103 Ibid. Deference to the Zohar's rather than to Nahmanides' exegesis is also expressed in the commentary on Nadav and Avihu's sin in *Likutei kabalah*, 102*b*–106*a*. See too Wolfson, 'Hai Gaon's Letter', 368 n. 19.

104 Cf. Zohar iii. 138*a* (*Idra raba*) and 289*b* (*Idra zuta*).

105 Angelet, *Perush sha'arei orah*, 33*b*–34*a*; Felix, *Joseph Angelet* (Heb.), 83–4 n. 84; Huss, '*Sefer hazohar* as a Canonical, Sacred and Holy Text', 271.

says that the secrets of the Zohar were revealed to R. Shimon by the prophet Elijah. This statement was most probably directed at R. Solomon ben Adret's disciples, whose claim to power was based on their being links in a kabbalistic chain of transmission going back to Elijah's revelation to the kabbalists of Provence.[106] R. Shem Tov Ibn Gaon, in his book *Keter shem tov*, writes that he had received the secrets of the liturgy from his teachers, and they, in turn, from R. Isaac Sagi-Nahor, who was the third to receive them from Elijah: 'The principal blessings and prayers that were transmitted to me from mouth to ear go back to R. Isaac, the son of the rabbi of blessed memory . . . who was said to be third to Elijah, of blessed memory.'[107] In the same way R. Meir Ibn Sahulah claims to have received the tradition from Solomon ben Adret, the original source being, again, Elijah's revelation: 'Therefore, I have been trying to reveal the glory of God as it was transmitted to me and as I understood it through my teachers: R. Joshua Ibn Shuaib and R. Solomon of Barcelona, who received it from Nahmanides, who received it from R. Isaac Sagi-Nahor, who received it from the prophet Elijah, may he come to us swiftly and soon.'[108]

It should be noted that these traditions, together with that in which Elijah transmitted secrets directly to R. Shimon, are foreign to both Nahmanides and the early zoharic literature; neither needed Elijah to assert its supremacy. Nahmanides traces the chain of kabbalistic transmission all the way back to Moses,[109] while some stories found in the zoharic literature claim that it was Elijah who learned secrets from R. Shimon, not the other way around.

[106] Regarding the tradition of Elijah's revelation to the kabbalists of Provence see Scholem, *Origins of the Kabbalah*, 35–7, 238–48; Wolfson, 'Beyond the Spoken Word', 190–2. It should be noted that this tradition appears for the first time at the turn of the thirteenth and fourteenth centuries, particularly in the writings of R. Solomon ben Adret's disciples; thus it probably reveals more about the period in which it was written than about the beginnings of kabbalah in Provence. See Hames, 'Elijah and a Shepherd', 101 n. 27.

[107] Kuriat, *Maor vashemesh*, 35*b*.

[108] *Sefer habahir*, ed. R. Margaliot, 94*a*.

[109] In his commentary on the first verse of Genesis, Nahmanides writes: 'The story of the Creation is a profound secret which cannot be comprehended from the biblical text and can only be fully understood through oral transmission [*kabalah*] starting from Moses, who received it from the mouth of God. Those who know it must conceal it' (*Commentary on the Torah*, ed. Chavel, i. 9). See also Idel, 'We Have No Kabbalistic Tradition on This', 58, and id., 'Transmission in Thirteenth-Century Kabbalah', 144–6.

As we have seen, one of the distinctive characteristics of the Nahmanidean school was its conservative, esoteric approach to the body of kabbalistic knowledge. This outlook is reflected in Nahmanides' famous statement in the introduction to his Torah commentary:

I am bringing the reader of this book into a reliable covenant that offers honest advice not to make assumptions and develop thoughts based on the allusions that I make regarding the secrets of the Torah, because I honestly inform him [the reader] that my words [regarding those secrets] cannot be intellectually perceived in any way but through oral transmission from a master kabbalist to the ear of a kabbalistic sage, and any assumption [regarding these secrets] is without merit and is very harmful.[110]

An extension of this stance appears in *Badei ha'aron* by R. Solomon ben Adret's disciple R. Shem Tov Ibn Gaon, who legitimizes himself by linking his pedigree to the kabbalistic dynasty of Nahmanides:

These are the matters of paramount concern in the concealed order as they, of blessed memory, said: 'In ten utterances the world was created', and the wise one cannot obtain them through his wisdom, and the intelligent one cannot perceive them intellectually, nor the investigator through his investigation, nor the seeker through his quest; only the kabbalist according to what he has received, a man from a man who belongs to the dynasty of the greatest in all the generations, the famous ones who received from their teachers and the ancestors of their ancestors back to Moses, may he rest in peace, the Torah from Sinai. And in my *Keter shem tov* I wrote [things] as I had received them orally from my teachers, the great R. Solomon ben Abraham, of blessed memory, son of Adret, and R. Isaac ben Todros, may he rest in peace, who had received them orally from R. Moses ben Nahman, of blessed memory, and the righteous R. Isaac Sagi-Nahor, of

110 Nahmanides, *Commentary on the Torah*, ed. Chavel, i. 7. See also the quote in the previous note and Nahmanides' comment in his homily on Ecclesiastes: 'These words and others like them one cannot comprehend by oneself but through transmission [*kabalah*]. And this is explained in the Torah to everyone who understands properly the reason for the *mitsvot* according to the kabbalah, which is the oral transmission from a recipient going back to Moses, who received [it] orally from the Gevurah [God]' (*Collected Works*, ed. Chavel, i. 190). See also Nahmanides' introduction to his commentary on the book of Job: 'It is true that this matter conceals one of the great secrets of the Torah, which one cannot conceive intellectually, rather it must be received from the mouth of a teacher, back to our teacher Moses, may he rest in peace, who [received it] from God, blessed be He' (ibid. 23).

blessed memory, son of the great R. Abraham ben David, of blessed memory, who were famous for their wisdom and their virtue.[111]

This quotation aptly demonstrates how Nahmanides and his disciples strove to bar entrance to the kabbalistic field. The production of zoharic texts and the formation of the idea of *Sefer hazohar* helped kabbalists unaffiliated with the school of Nahmanides and R. Solomon ben Adret circumvent the obstacles that had been placed in their way and establish an innovative, creative, and open kabbalistic approach. In his testimony, R. Isaac of Acre describes the way in which the Zohar broke through the barriers of esotericism, and the impact it had on him:

And because I saw that its words were wonderful and that they drew from the supernal source, the well that emanates without receiving, blessed be the name of His kingdom for ever and ever, I pursued it [the Zohar] and asked the students [*talmidim*], who had large portions of it in their possession, how they had obtained these wondrous secrets, previously transmitted only orally and not meant to be set in writing, and which are explained in this book so that they can be comprehended by anyone who is able to read a book.[112]

The reference to those in possession of the zoharic texts as students (*talmidim*) supports the claim that the early distributors of the Zohar were members of the secondary elite—students as opposed to teachers. R. Isaac, a kabbalist previously affiliated with the circle of R. Solomon ben Adret, was surprised to discover texts containing explicit explanations of secrets that were to be transmitted only orally. His enquiry into the source of these writings led him to the Zohar—a book allegedly written by R. Shimon in the Land of Israel and which had surfaced in Spain in the hands of Moses de León. The claim that R. Shimon's ancient book was the source of the zoharic texts 'available for anyone who is able to read' legitimized the exoteric approach and subverted the authority of Nahmanides and R. Solomon ben Adret, who opposed the open, written distribution of kabbalistic knowledge.

In contrast to the secrets of kabbalah planted by Nahmanides in his commentary on the Torah, and which were presented as obscure teachings

[111] *Badei ha'aron umigdal ḥananel*, ed. Levinger, 27.

[112] Zacuto, *Sefer yuḥasin hashalem*, 88, and Tishby and Lachower, *The Wisdom of the Zohar*, i. 13.

that one should not attempt to understand outside the authorized oral tradition, the zoharic texts did not impose such limitations on the reader, and any kabbalist was able to offer his own understanding of them. While only a small elite circle held the key to Nahmanides' secrets, the Zohar was free of an interpretative tradition and of the restraints of an exegetical school. The idea of an ancient literary work composed by R. Shimon thus enabled the kabbalists who were not affiliated with the school of Nahmanides to break through the entrance barriers of the kabbalistic production field, base their authority on the sacred 'book' they had in their possession, and thereby weaken the monopoly of Nahmanides and R. Solomon ben Adret.

CHAPTER THREE

The Formation of the Zoharic Canon

I have found more from the book of the Zohar, gleanings after gleanings.
Recanati, *Perush hatorah*

AROUND THE TURN of the thirteenth and fourteenth centuries the writing of zoharic texts became a principal activity among kabbalists of the secondary elite of Iberian Jewish culture, particularly in the region of Castile. The creation of the zoharic literature allowed these scholars to express their kabbalistic ideas and subvert the authority of Nahmanides and his followers. The idea of *Sefer hazohar* was formulated, as I suggested in the previous chapter, within the framework of this struggle for dominance and as a response to the canonization of Nahmanides' kabbalistic commentary on the Torah.

The emergence of the Zohar as an imagined book marked a new stage in its reception—the texts were presented, edited, and circulated as segments of a sacred, authoritative, and complete work. This dynamic and complex process began with the assembling of texts and their arrangement into collections, to be promoted by the editors as *Sefer hazohar*. It is this undertaking of assembly and compilation, which commenced at the beginning of the fourteenth century and was completed (although not fully) with the printing of the first editions of the Zohar in the second half of the sixteenth, that the present chapter discusses.

The two major sources from which the consolidation process of the zoharic literature may be reconstructed are the manuscripts themselves and the many works in which those texts are quoted or their circulation is described. The existence of dozens of manuscripts and thousands of quotations, however, makes their exploration a difficult and arduous task.

We have seen that kabbalists possessed zoharic texts before the idea of *Sefer hazohar* took shape, which meant that these texts were not identified as parts of a cohesive literary entity (at least they were not presented to readers as such). The perception of the Zohar as a single unit, together with the first pamphlets containing zoharic collections, emerged in the early fourteenth century. As one can learn from the previously quoted testimony of Isaac of Acre, he had seen pamphlets, distributed by Moses de León and circulated among 'students', which de León claimed to have copied from the complete *Sefer hazohar*.[1] Isaac of Acre, despite his interest in the Zohar, rarely quoted from it in his writings; however, two of his contemporaries, Menahem Recanati and Joseph Angelet, did. On the basis of their works it is possible to estimate the scope of the zoharic collections, and to infer the way in which they were compiled and edited.

Recanati, who cited zoharic texts extensively, was the first to refer to some of them as segments of *Sefer hazohar*, and to declare their authoritative status. His quotations included zoharic passages on the Torah, a few portions from *Midrash hane'elam*, Zohar 'Ruth',[2] and some texts that were omitted from the printed corpus of the Zohar.[3] However, many sections of the Zohar and *Midrash hane'elam* on the Torah are not quoted by Recanati at all, for example the *Introduction to the Zohar*, *Sifra ditseniuta*, *Pikudin*, *Sava demishpatim*, Zohar 'Lamentations', and Zohar 'Song of Songs'. Nor does he cite later layers of that literature, such as *Tikunei hazohar* or *Ra'aya meheimna*. Although one might assume that he did not quote all the zoharic material that he had in his possession,[4] the complete absence of quotations from certain sections indicates with a high degree of certainty that he did not have those. At the same time one must remember that a quotation from a specific zoharic section does not prove that the author had the full text as it was later published in the printed editions.

Recanati identified as 'the Zohar' some sections on the Torah, *Midrash hane'elam* (portions 'No'aḥ', 'Lekh lekha', and 'Ḥayei sarah'), as well as parts of *Idra raba* and *Idra zuta*. At the same time, he referred to the

[1] Zacuto, *Sefer yuḥasin hashalem*, 88–9; Tishby and Lachower, *The Wisdom of the Zohar*, i. 13–15; Abrams, *Kabbalistic Manuscripts and Textual Theory*, 257–8.

[2] Rubin, *Citations from the Zohar* (Heb.), 36–7.

[3] Ibid. 34–5; Idel, *Menahem Recanati the Kabbalist* (Heb.), 250 n. 138.

[4] Idel, *Menahem Recanati the Kabbalist* (Heb.), 104.

Heikhalot section, printed as part of Zohar 'Bereshit', as *Sefer shivat haheikhalot*,[5] and to Zohar 'Ruth' as *Midrash ruth*,[6] and not as parts of the Zohar. The latter distinction is clearly reflected in the following statement: 'And the same was said in *Midrash ruth* and in the Zohar.'[7]

In the introduction to his book *Ta'amei hamitsvot*, Recanati distinguishes between what he calls 'the wondrous book of the Zohar' and 'the great book of the Zohar': 'Although most of what I refer to are matters suggested in *Sefer habahir* and in the wondrous book of the Zohar, in the great book of the Zohar, in *Bereshit rabah*, and also in the *midrashim* of our teachers of blessed memory, I will use these books to support me.'[8] A study of the sources quoted in *Ta'amei hamitsvot* reveals that what Recanati calls 'the great book of the Zohar' is the *Idra raba*, and the 'wondrous book of the Zohar' is a miscellaneous collection of zoharic sections.

The above distinction, however, only appears in *Ta'amei hamitsvot*. In his *Perush hatefilot* and *Perush hatorah*, which, according to Moshe Idel, are later works,[9] Recanati quotes from *Idra raba* and refers to it as the 'book of the Zohar'. This fact reflects a change that had taken place in the way he perceived the zoharic literature and compiled his own collection. His treatment of 'the great book of the Zohar' and 'the wondrous book of the Zohar' as separate entities suggests that *Idra raba* came into his hands as a section independent of other zoharic segments already known to him. Initially he might have thought that they were two separate collections. Later, however, possibly after becoming acquainted with more zoharic texts, he added *Idra raba* to his collection and no longer considered it a separate work. It is thus obvious that he was familiar with *Idra raba* as a distinct piece independent of other sections of the Zohar that he knew.[10] Yet, in contrast to *Midrash ruth* and *Sefer shivat haheikhalot*, he viewed it as part of the Zohar.

Over time Recanati collected zoharic texts from different sources and incorporated them into his collection. Passages from *Midrash hane'elam*, for example, are quoted only in his *Perush hatorah*, which was written after

[5] Rubin, *Citations from the Zohar* (Heb.), 3 n. 4, 23.

[6] Ibid. 32–4; Idel, *Menahem Recanati the Kabbalist* (Heb.), 247 n. 116.

[7] Idel, *Menahem Recanati the Kabbalist* (Heb.), 102.

[8] Recanati, *Sefer ta'amei hamitsvot*, 19*a*, 11*b*. Idel, *Menahem Recanati the Kabbalist* (Heb.), 31–2.

[9] Idel, *Menahem Recanati the Kabbalist* (Heb.), 71–2.

[10] Ibid. 104.

Ta'amei hamitsvot. One might assume, therefore, that only after he had completed the earlier work did he obtain sections of *Midrash hane'elam* on the Torah and add them to his zoharic collection. Other texts that are not mentioned in *Ta'amei hamitsvot*, including *Idra zuta*, are quoted in his *Perush hatorah* and *Perush hatefilot*, suggesting that they were not in his possession while writing *Ta'amei hamitsvot*. Recanati alludes to the process of collection in his introduction to a quotation from *Midrash hane'elam*, 'Ḥayei sarah', in the following words: 'I have found more from the book of the Zohar, gleanings after gleanings [*likutei betar likutei*].'[11]

The writings of Joseph Angelet of Saragossa, Spain, also provide clues to the formation of zoharic collections in the early fourteenth century. Angelet, who was active after Recanati (and was the first to quote him),[12] frequently incorporated zoharic texts into his pieces, identified them as quotations from the Zohar or *Midrash hane'elam*, attributed them to R. Shimon, and declared them authoritative. Following the zoharic model in some of his own works, he wrote texts that were later included in the printed editions of the Zohar.[13]

A study of Angelet's works reveals that his zoharic collection was more comprehensive than Recanati's and several other collections from later periods. He quoted a significant number of zoharic portions on the Torah, including ones that Recanati did not quote.[14] His texts further contain many segments of *Midrash hane'elam*, *Sitrei torah*, *Sitrei otiyot*, *Heikhalot* 'Pekudei', Zohar 'Ruth', and Zohar 'Lamentations', but, like Recanati, he was not acquainted with *Tikunei hazohar* or *Ra'aya meheimna*.

Angelet, like Recanati, viewed the Zohar and the Torah homilies of *Midrash hane'elam* as parts of a single literary entity. In his book *Livnat hasapir*, written in 1324/5, he refers to these texts as *Midrash hane'elam* (or as *Midrash hazohar* or *Midrasho shel rashbi*), sometimes in conjunction with the name of the Torah portion. He quotes segments from *Sitrei ha'otiyot*,

[11] Recanati, *Perush hatorah*, 'Bo', 42*c*. Idel, *Menahem Recanati the Kabbalist* (Heb.), 103. Abrams, 'The Zohar as a Book', 210; id., *Kabbalistic Manuscripts and Textual Theory*, 261.

[12] Angelet, *Kupat harokhlin*, 84*a*, 139*a*.

[13] Liebes, 'How the Zohar Was Written' (Heb.), 1–70; Meroz, 'R. Joseph Angelet and His "Zoharic Writings"' (Heb.), 303–404.

[14] *Livnat hasapir* has quotations from all zoharic portions on Genesis and Leviticus (except 'Behar', on which there is very little in the body of the Zohar) and from many on Exodus, Numbers, and Deuteronomy.

Zohar 'Ruth', *Idra raba*, *Idra zuta*, and the section he calls *Idra debei mishkana*, all under the title *Midrash hane'elam*. There is no evidence, at the same time, that he viewed *Sifra ditseniuta*, from which he quoted on several occasions, as part of *Midrash hane'elam*. In his commentary on *Sha'arei orah*, which he probably penned after *Livnat hasapir*, he again used the name *Midrash hane'elam* to identify quotations from various zoharic portions.[15]

Although it is impossible to determine the exact scope of Angelet's zoharic collection, it is clear that he had at his disposal texts from most zoharic sections. At the time of writing *Livnat hasapir* he considered all of them (except *Sifra ditseniuta*) parts of a single literary unit. He quoted a number of texts that Recanati did not have and, unlike the latter, he treated Zohar 'Ruth' as part of the Zohar. We may thus assume that, at the beginning of the fourteenth century, the zoharic collections used by the individual kabbalists differed significantly from each other.

As previously mentioned, Recanati claimed to have assembled his zoharic collection from different sources. Although Angelet did not discuss the constitution of his collection, his acquisition process may be reconstructed by comparing *Livnat hasapir*, written in 1324/5, to *Kupat harokhlin*, written fourteen years earlier, in 1310/11.[16] In *Livnat hasapir* and the *Commentary on Sha'arei orah*, he usually quotes zoharic texts under the name *Midrash hane'elam*. In *Kupat harokhlin*, on the other hand, in most cases he uses the term 'Zohar' to identify zoharic texts.[17] Yet his quotations from *Midrash hane'elam* 'Ruth' and the *Idra* do not indicate any awareness of a connection between these texts and the Zohar. The same is true regarding *Sifra ditseniuta*, which he also quotes in *Livnat hasapir* as a work distinct from *Midrash hane'elam*.[18]

[15] Goldreich, 'Iberian Phrase in an Unknown Fragment' (Heb.), 96 n. 26. Based on a reference to *Livnat hasapir* and the calculation that the 'end of days' was to occur in 1327/8, Iris Felix has concluded that *Perush sha'arei orah* was written after *Livnat hasapir*, and no later than 1327/8; see 'Chapters in the Kabbalistic Thought of Joseph Angelet' (Heb.), 10.

[16] See the colophon at the end of *Kupat harokhlin*, 239*a*.

[17] The quoted portions are: 'Lekh lekha', 'Vayera', 'Ḥayei sarah', 'Toledot', 'Vayeḥi', 'Tazria', and 'Naso'; Angelet, *Kupat harokhlin*, 78*b*, 80*b*, 81*b*, 82*a*, 99*a*, 107*b*, 114*b*, 116*a*, 119*a*, 121*a*, 135*b*, 137*b*, 205*a*. Page 134*a* has a quotation from *Sitrei torah*, Zohar i. 147*b*.

[18] Angelet also makes references, in *Kupat harokhlin*, to the *midrash* of R. Shimon and to the *midrash* of Shimon bar Yohai, which recur in *Livnat hasapir* and in his *Perush sha'arei orah*. *Sifra ditseniuta* is also quoted in *Livnat hasapir* as a work separate from *Midrash hane'elam*.

The fact that many zoharic units which Angelet cited in his later books, *Livnat hasapir* and the *Commentary on Sha'arei orah*, are not mentioned at all in the earlier *Kupat harokhlin* reflects the expansion of his zoharic collection over time. *Kupat harokhlin* contains significantly less zoharic material than *Livnat hasapir*; for example, it does not include any passages from *Midrash hane'elam* or *Sitrei otiyot*, both of which are cited in *Livnat hasapir*, or from Zohar 'Pinḥas', a portion quoted extensively in both *Livnat hasapir* and his *Commentary on Sha'arei orah*.

Although it is difficult to base an argument on what is absent, it is reasonable to assume that Angelet did not mention those sections in his early book because he did not have access to them at the time, and that they probably came into his possession and were added to his compilation at a later date. In *Livnat hasapir*, for example, Angelet quotes from both Zohar 'Bereshit' and Zohar 'No'aḥ', as well as from *Midrash hane'elam* 'Bereshit' and *Sitrei otiyot*. In the earlier *Kupat harokhlin*, however, these texts are absent from his commentary on the same biblical portions, even though they are directly connected to the subject matter. It is likely that he did not obtain those sections until after completing his commentary on 'Bereshit' and 'No'aḥ' in *Kupat harokhlin*. Angelet's zoharic collection, then, was also the product of 'gleanings after gleanings' (*likutei betar likutei*).

In addition to commentary on the Torah portions that had not been discussed in *Kupat harokhlin*, a new commentary on portions of Genesis was included in *Livnat hasapir*. It seems that, while writing *Kupat harokhlin*, Angelet had a relatively limited anthology of zoharic texts that he called 'the Zohar' (perhaps influenced by Recanati). His subsequent discovery of new texts might have inspired his new commentary and would explain the renaming of his collection. As previously noted, in *Kupat harokhlin* he refers to zoharic texts as 'the Zohar'; later, however, in *Livnat hasapir* and the *Commentary on Sha'arei orah*, he prefers the title *Midrash hane'elam*. This modification indicates that the term 'Zohar' had not yet been established as the standard name for zoharic collections. Furthermore, while writing *Kupat harokhlin*, Angelet did not consider other zoharic texts with which he was familiar (such as *Idra raba*, Zohar 'Ruth', and *Sifra ditseniuta*) to be part of the collection. After *Kupat harokhlin* had been completed, he came across a number of other zoharic texts, including segments of the body of the

Zohar, *Midrash hane'elam*, *Sitrei otiyot*, *Heikhalot*, Zohar 'Lamentations', and a zoharic *midrash* on the Song of Songs. They were later added to what he viewed as a broad corpus of esoteric midrashic literature (parallel to the classical midrashic literature), and to which he referred by the name *Midrash hane'elam*. This *midrash*, according to Angelet, included all of the zoharic sections that he had assembled, except *Sifra ditseniuta*.

In the second half of the fourteenth century and in the fifteenth, zoharic texts were quoted with far less frequency. R. Israel Al-Nakawa, a Spanish sage who was killed during the riots of 1390/1, owned a zoharic collection of unknown size from that period. His monumental book *Menorat hamaor* includes forty zoharic quotations in Hebrew translation (except for a few segments in Aramaic), referred to as *Midrash vayehi or*.[19] The quotations are from different portions of the Zohar on the Torah. There is no evidence, however, that the author was familiar with the portions of *Midrash hane'elam* or with the zoharic exegeses on the five *megilot*, *Tikunei hazohar*, or *Ra'aya meheimna*. The fact that he used *Midrash vayehi or* as a reference for his quotations indicates that the title 'Zohar' had not yet been established in his time. It seems that Al-Nakawa's zoharic collection began with the exegesis of the words *vayehi or* ('and there was light', Gen. 1: 3), printed in Zohar 'Bereshit' 45*b*.[20]

Another kabbalist who quoted from the zoharic literature, incorporating for the first time texts from *Tikunei hazohar*, was R. Menahem Tsiyon, who lived in Germany, Palestine, and Italy during the second half of the fourteenth century. He cited many zoharic sections in his Torah commentary *Sefer tsiyoni*, which was completed in 1383/4 in Cologne, and in *Tsefunei tsiyoni*, probably written later.[21] In some of his frequently used quotations

[19] *Sefer menorat hamaor*, ed. Enelow, i. 21–2, ii. 26–8, iii. 29–34. See also Tishby and Lachower, *The Wisdom of the Zohar*, i. 101.

[20] Tishby and Lachower, *The Wisdom of the Zohar*, i. 23.

[21] About R. Menahem Tsiyon's life and writings see Yuval, *Scholars in Their Time* (Heb.), 282–92. According to Goldreich, Tsiyon received all the kabbalistic material, including the zoharic texts, while staying in Jerusalem at the R. Isaac Asir Hatikvah Academy in the mid-14th century; see 'Iberian Phrase in an Unknown Fragment' (Heb.), 97. Israel Ta-Shma suggests that the texts may have come into his hands when he travelled through Candia in Crete, a way station for German Jews en route to and from the Land of Israel; *The Revealed in the Concealed* (Heb.), 81.

Tsiyon relied on Recanati's works, without mentioning his source.[22] He additionally cited passages from the body of the Zohar, *Idra raba*, *Idra zuta*, and Zohar 'Ruth', not found in Recanati's writings. As I have mentioned, Tsiyon was the first to quote from *Tikunei hazohar*, to which he referred as *Sefer hazohar*, and there is no evidence that he saw this work as separate from the rest of the zoharic literature with which he was acquainted.[23]

Shem Tov ibn Shem Tov, a near-contemporary of Tsiyon, was one of the few kabbalists active in Spain in the first half of the fifteenth century.[24] He quotes a number of texts from which we can draw important information about the zoharic collection he used, as well as about his concept of the Zohar as a book. As Asi Farber-Ginat has shown, Ibn Shem Tov quotes segments from several zoharic portions under the names *Sefer hazohar* or *Sitrei hazohar*, or simply in the name of R. Shimon. He also uses material from *Idra raba* (which he calls *Idra*), *Idra zuta* (referring to it as 'R. Shimon's Testament'), and *Heikhalot* 'Pekudei'.[25] While he usually makes reference to *Sefer hazohar*, in his commentary on the ten *sefirot* he talks about the 'books of R. Shimon', in the plural: 'And truly, as I found in his [i.e. R. Shimon's] testaments and in his *Idra* and a few of his books'.[26] To my knowledge, this is the first explicit reference to the zoharic literature as a 'library' of the writings of R. Shimon, an idea that was to become widespread in the sixteenth century.

In contrast to the texts mentioned above, Ibn Shem Tov did not identify the passages he quoted from *Midrash hane'elam* as parts of the Zohar or attribute them to R. Shimon, as Farber-Ginat has shown.[27] This is apparent,

22 This is the case in his *Commentary on the Torah*, 25*b*, where he borrows from Recanati's *Perush hatorah*, 40*b*; likewise, his *Commentary on the Torah*, 23*d*–24*b* was taken from Recanati's 39*a*–*c*. In his book *Tsefunei tsiyoni* Tsiyon mentions the 'Great Book of the Zohar' and the 'Wondrous Book of the Zohar'. As I have previously shown, the source for these expressions was Recanati's *Sefer ta'amei hamitsvot*.

23 Tsiyon, *Commentary on the Torah*, 4*c*, 6*d*, 33*b*, 65*c*, 67*d*.

24 See Zacuto, *Sefer yuḥasin hashalem*, 226.

25 Farber-Ginat, 'The Concept of the Merkavah' (Heb.), i. 156–8; Ariel, 'Shem-Tov ibn Shem-Tov's Kabbalistic Critique of Jewish Philosophy', 21, 86: Scholem, 'The Remnants of Shem Tov Ibn Gaon's Book' (Heb.), 129.

26 Ariel, 'Shem-Tov ibn Shem-Tov's Kabbalistic Critique of Jewish Philosophy', 88; see also pp. 5, 20, 48, 57. Ibn Shem Tov, *Sefer ha'emunot*, 82*b*.

27 'The Concept of the Merkavah' (Heb.), i. 156–7.

for example, in his citations from *Midrash hane'elam* on 'Bereshit'. Nor did he regard Zohar 'Ruth' or Zohar 'Lamentations' as belonging to the Zohar.[28] When quoting from *Tikunei hazohar*, however, like Tsiyon, he treated that work as part of the zoharic collection, referring to it in his *Sefer ha'emunot* as *Sefer hazohar* or *Sitrei zohar*.[29] *Sefer ha'emunot* was, in fact, the only book in which Ibn Shem Tov used segments of *Tikunei hazohar*; Gershom Scholem and Ephraim Gottlieb have argued that he did not own a copy of that text when he wrote his earlier works.[30] Like Recanati and Angelet, then, he also gathered zoharic texts piece by piece, continually expanding his collection. Some of the body of the Zohar, the *Idrot*, and *Heikhalot* 'Pekudei' he considered part of the Zohar, while other sections, such as *Midrash hane'elam* on Genesis, Zohar 'Ruth', and Zohar 'Lamentations', he viewed as separate entities. Eventually he obtained sections of *Tikunei hazohar*, added them to his collection, and treated them either as elements of 'the Zohar' or as one of 'R. Shimon's books'.

Tikunei hazohar is also mentioned in *Sefer poke'aḥ ivrim*, written in 1438/9 by an anonymous kabbalist in Medina de Pomar. This book has citations from portions of the body of the Zohar, from *Midrash hane'elam* on 'Bereshit' and 'Lekh lekha', as well as from Zohar 'Ruth'.[31] The author describes *Tikunei hazohar* as 'a book that R. Shimon wrote on the word *bereshit*'. Elsewhere, consistent with Ibn Shem Tov, he refers to the 'books' of R. Shimon bar Yohai in the plural.[32]

[28] Ariel, 'Shem-Tov ibn Shem-Tov's Kabbalistic Critique of Jewish Philosophy', 5; Farber-Ginat, 'The Concept of the Merkavah' (Heb.), i. 158. For Ibn Shem Tov's reference to Zohar 'Ruth' see his *Sefer ha'emunot*, 83*a*. See also his reference to *Midrash hane'elam* 'Lamentations', ibid. 78*a*.

[29] In *Sefer ha'emunot*, 29*a* he refers to it as 'another book by R. Shimon ben Yohai'. In most cases the name *Sitrei torah* signifies texts from *Tikunei hazohar*, but sometimes Ibn Shem Tov uses it as a reference to other zoharic units.

[30] Scholem, 'The Remnants of Shem Tov Ibn Gaon's Book' (Heb.), 399; Gottlieb, *Studies in Kabbalistic Literature* (Heb.), 353–4.

[31] On *Sefer poke'aḥ ivrim* see Huss, '*Sefer poke'aḥ ivrim*' (Heb.), 490–3. On quotations from the zoharic literature see ibid. 496–7. The author of *Poke'aḥ ivrim* quoted from portions 'Shemot', 'Beshalaḥ, and 'Naso'. From the way the quotations were used it seems that he did not consider *Midrash hane'elam* on portions 'Bereshit', 'Lekh lekha', and Zohar 'Ruth' to be parts of the Zohar.

[32] See Huss, '*Sefer poke'aḥ ivrim*' (Heb.), 496. The author of *Poke'aḥ ivrim* claims that in the time of Maimonides 'there were no books to be found of the holy R. Shimon, of blessed

During the same period R. Yohanan ben Reuben of Ohrid (today in Macedonia) referred to *Tikunei hazohar* as *Sefer hazohar* in his annotations to R. Ahai Gaon's *Sefer hashe'iltot*. He also quoted other zoharic sections, some of which he knew from Recanati's *Perush hatorah*.[33] As far as I know, no parts of *Tikunei hazohar* can be found among the sparse zoharic quotations that appear in other works written in the late fourteenth and early fifteenth centuries.[34]

The same is the case in the second half of the fifteenth century—zoharic literature is seldom quoted. In his book *Akedat yitsḥak*, written in the 1480s in the town of Calatayud, R. Isaac Arama included about twenty excerpts from the body of the Zohar and from *Midrash hane'elam* 'Bereshit' and 'Vayera', under the names *Midrash hane'elam*, *Midrash hazohar*, or *ḥazal* ('our sages').[35] Similarly, at approximately the same time in Saragossa, Abraham Bibago, in his book *Derekh emunah*, quoted zoharic portions on

memory, in all of his kingdom until after his death, when they were discovered in those countries' (ibid. 169*a*).

[33] On the dating of R. Yohanan ben Reuben's work to the late 14th or early 15th century, see Ta-Shma, 'On Greek Byzantine Rabbinic Literature' (Heb.), 105. R. Yohanan also cited two consecutive passages from Zohar 'Ruth'; Mirsky, *She'iltot derav aḥai gaon* (Heb.), 1–5. Recanati's *Perush hatorah*, 34*c* is the source for both quotations and for what follows. It should be noted that in *Sefer hakanah* and *Sefer hapeliah*, which were probably written in Greece during that time, there are quotations from the Zohar, though without reference to its name, and they were all drawn from the writings of Recanati, as Oron has shown; see 'The *Peliah* and the *Kanah*' (Heb.), 80–1, 98.

[34] A few quotations from *Midrash hane'elam* on portion 'Bereshit', referred to as *Bereshit rabah*, are included in *Mikhlol yofi* by R. Samuel ibn Zarzah; see Holzman, 'The Introduction to Samuel Zarza's *Mikhlal yofi*' (Heb.), 23. R. Shem Tov Ibn Shaprut quoted from the Zohar a few times in *Tsafenat pane'aḥ* (Bodleian, Oxford, MS 2350 (F. 21414), 12*a*, 16*a*–17*b*); see too Frimer and Schwartz, *The Life and Thought of Shem Tov Ibn Shaprut* (Heb.), 164. Quotations from zoharic portions on the Torah—from 'Terumah', 'Tazria', 'Emor', 'Aḥarei mot', and 'Pinḥas'—and from *Midrash hane'elam* on 'Lekh lekha' (always under the titles 'Zohar' and 'Midrash') appear in the responsa of R. Shimon ben Tsemah Duran (Rashbats), who lived in Majorca and then in Algeria in the late 14th and early 15th centuries; see Kadosh, 'Kabbalistic Jewish Laws in Responsa' (Heb.), 74–84. On the zoharic quotations of Rashbats's grandson, R. Simeon Duran, see ibid. 89–95. R. Joseph Albo also cited from Zohar 'Vayakhel' (*Sefer ha'ikarim*, article 4, ch. 33, 176*b*). On his criticism of study of the Zohar see ibid., article 2, ch. 28, 94*b*. I will elaborate on it in Ch. 6.

[35] See Heller-Wilensky, *The Philosophy of Isaac Arama* (Heb.), 46. As Sarah Heller-Wilensky has noted, Arama referred to a text from Zohar 'Vayishlaḥ', iii. 170*b*, about which he had heard 'from many people' but which he had not seen himself; see Arama, *Akedat*

'Bereshit' from *Midrash hane'elam* under the names *Midrash hazohar* and *Sefer hazohar*.[36] Whereas the above scholars did not cite *Tikunei hazohar*, that work was known to the author of *Sefer hameshiv*, which Moshe Idel believes to have been written in Spain in the 1460s.[37] R. Judah Hayat and Joseph Elcastil, who discussed kabbalistic questions in a work probably written in 1481/2 in the Spanish city of Xativa, were also acquainted with *Tikunei hazohar*: both Hayat, in his questions, and Elcastil, in his answers, referred to it as *Sefer hatikunin*, and treated it as part of the Zohar.[38] These, to my knowledge, were the first instances in which quotations from *Tikunei hazohar* were mentioned under that name.

The Zohar is frequently cited by R. Elijah of Genazzano in his *Igeret ḥamudot*, written in Italy at the end of the fifteenth century.[39] However, Alexander Altmann has claimed that Genazzano did not have a zoharic collection and that he copied zoharic texts from Recanati's *Perush hatorah*.[40] Idel regards this phenomenon as characteristic of Italian kabbalists who were active before the printing of the Zohar.[41] R. Moses of Kiev, the author

yitsḥak, i, ch. 26, 225*b*. On one occasion he quoted as *Midrash hane'elam* a segment from *Sefer habahir*; see *Akedat yitsḥak*, iii, ch. 67, 135*b*. Maybe it is not a mistake and *Sefer habahir* (or portions of it) was part of the zoharic collection that he was using.

[36] Lazaroff, *Abraham Bibago*, 57 n. 71. It is worth mentioning that Bibago, in his book *Derekh emunah*, 54*b*, introduces under the title *Midrash hazohar* Hebrew quotations that have a parallel in the introduction to the Zohar; see Zohar i. 11*b*–12*a*. If indeed the introduction is their source then it is one of the few cases in which a quotation from this zoharic section appears before the 16th century. Passages from the Zohar are also included in Joseph ben Tsadik's book *Zekher tsadik*, written in Arevalo between 1467 and 1487; see pp. 30–1, 35–40. See also Bibago, *Derekh emunah*, 226.

[37] For the dating of *Sefer hameshiv* see Idel, 'Enquiries into the Doctrine of *Sefer hameshiv*' (Heb.), 196. The author of *Hameshiv* refers to *tikun* 69 in *Tikunei hazohar*, 103*b*–104*a*; see Scholem, 'The Magid of R. Joseph Taitatsak' (Heb.), 94.

[38] For the dating of the responsa see Scholem, 'On Knowledge of Kabbalah in Spain' (Heb.), 169. Regarding Hayat and Elcastil's knowledge of *Tikunei hazohar* see ibid. 175–6, 183, 187, 190, 204.

[39] References to zoharic texts are also included in *Sefer ha'agur* by R. Jacob ben Judah Landau (Naples, 1491); see sections 36, 84, pp. 22, 27–8.

[40] Altmann, 'Beyond the Border of Philosophy' (Heb.), 87.

[41] Idel has shown that before the 16th century the Zohar was hardly known in Italy, and the main source for zoharic quotations was Recanati's *Perush hatorah*; see 'The Rabbinate in Italy' (Heb.), 101. Indeed, even Pico della Mirandola, who studied kabbalah with Jews and apostates in Florence in the second half of the 15th century, became acquainted with the Zohar through Recanati's *Perush hatorah* and *Sefer ta'amei hamitsvot*, which were translated

of *Shoshan sodot* (completed in Crimea in 1499), also had access to the zoharic texts via Recanati's commentary,[42] and so did R. Menahem Tsiyon and R. Yohanan of Ohrid.

Interesting information regarding the formulation of zoharic collections in that period is found in the epistles of the Spanish kabbalist R. Isaac Mar Hayim, who had in his possession 'about four measures of *Sefer ha-zohar*'.[43] Mar Hayim sent his missives from Naples to R. Isaac of Pisa,[44] who had probably asked him for copies of kabbalistic works. In the first epistle he copied a chapter from *Idra zuta*, which he had apparently found in Lisbon. He further noted that Recanati had not been acquainted with this chapter because the Zohar 'could not be obtained in its entirety in a single district since it had been scattered all over'.[45]

Manuscripts, as I have noted, are an additional source for the study of the formulation of the zoharic corpus in the fourteenth and fifteenth centuries.[46] These compilations reflect how texts were gathered and assorted

for him by Flavius Mithridates; see Secret, *Le Zohar chez les kabbalistes chrétiens*, 25; Wirszubski, *Pico della Mirandola's Encounter with Jewish Mysticism*, 20–61. Judah Hayat, who owned a comprehensive zoharic collection that he had personally compiled, nonetheless quoted certain zoharic texts from Recanati's commentary. Benayahu has shown that the French sage Azriel Diena, active in Italy in the early 16th century, was also familiar with zoharic texts through Recanati's work; see 'The Dispute between Kabbalah and Halakhah' (Heb.), 87.

42 On Moses of Kiev and his book see Lieberman, *Ohel raḥel*, i. 93–9.

43 Nadav, 'An Epistle of the Kabbalist Isaac Mar Hayim' (Heb.), 458. See also Altmann, 'Beyond the Border of Philosophy' (Heb.), 87 n. 105. Altmann inferred the length of four *yadot* (measures) from Isaac Abrabanel's comparison between his own commentary on the Torah, which, Abrabanel noted, consisted of twelve *yadot* of paper, and his commentary on Joshua, Judges, and Samuel, which came to five *yadot*.

44 He spent some time in Italy on his way to the Land of Israel.

45 Nadav, 'An Epistle of the Kabbalist Isaac Mar Hayim' (Heb.), 456. In his second letter to Isaac of Pisa, Mar Hayim translated the chapter into Hebrew and added to it a commentary. See Greenup, 'A Kabbalistic Epistle by Isaac b. Samuel', 370–4.

46 For a partial survey of manuscripts see Tishby and Lachower, *The Wisdom of the Zohar*, i. 99–101. A letter of Malachi Beit-Arié, included in Ta-Shma's book *The Revealed in the Concealed* (Heb.), 82, addendum *c*, presents a short study of the manuscripts. See also *The Zohar, Pritzker Edition*, i. 16 n. 4. For zoharic manuscripts at the library of the Vatican see Bonfil, *The Rabbinate in Italy during the Renaissance* (Heb.), 179. Abrams, in 'When Was the Introduction to the Zohar Written?' (Heb.), 218–24, looks at the manuscript of portion 'Bereshit' and the introduction to the Zohar, while Sed-Rajna, 'Manuscrits du *Tiqquney ha-Zohar*', and Giller, *The Enlightened Will Shine*, 131–2 n. 9, focus on the manuscript of *Tikunei hazohar*. On manuscripts of Zohar 'Ruth' see Abrams's introduction in *Midrash hane'elam: ruth*, 9–11. On the

from various sources and presented as the 'book' of the Zohar. Unfortunately only a small number of fourteenth-century manuscripts have come down to us, and few have a colophon to allow accurate chronological and geographical placement. One such document is Cambridge, MS Add. 1023 (F. 17030), the oldest partial zoharic collection we have,[47] which was copied in the late fourteenth century in Byzantine script by several scribes, probably in Crete.[48] Although its copyists (or first owners) did not refer to this collection as *Sefer hazohar*, they incorporated in it excerpts from *Midrash hane'elam* and from the body of the Zohar. The portions are copied in order but many are missing, and most of those included are shorter than the ones we find in the printed edition. As is the case with Recanati and Angelet, there is no sign that the copyists distinguished between segments from *Midrash hane'elam* and those from the body of the Zohar.

From time to time the scribes make references to zoharic texts that they had collected in 'another book'. Their notes tell us, for example, that portion 'Vayetse', which was left out of our manuscript, had been copied into this 'other book'. The same is the case with the beginning of portion 'Lekh lekha' and the latter part of portions 'Vayeḥi' and 'Mishpatim'. It is plausible, therefore, that the Cambridge manuscript is the second volume of a zoharic collection, and contains portions and parts of portions not included in the first volume. Although it could be the case that different pamphlets were copied simultaneously from the same manuscript by

manuscript of *Sava demishpatim* see Yisra'eli, *The Interpretation of Secrets and the Secrets of Interpretation* (Heb.), 17–19. Photocopies of many zoharic manuscripts as well as a partial survey were published as part of Rivka Schatz Uffenheimer's project dedicated to the Zohar. These manuscripts are kept at the Gershom Scholem Library. About the project see Abrams, 'Textual Scholarship', 60–1; Rubin, 'The Zohar Project' (Heb.). Ronit Meroz has engaged in comprehensive research into zoharic manuscripts and has added, with her team, references and important notes to the photocopies of the manuscripts held at the Scholem Library. On the early findings of this research see Meroz, 'Ezekiel's Chariot—An Unknown Zoharic Commentary' (Heb.); 'Zoharic Narratives'; '"And I Was Not There?!"' (Heb.). Her 'Bibliographical Introduction' to *Headwaters of the Zohar* (Heb.) contains a detailed study of the manuscripts. I would like to express my gratitude to her for allowing me to use a copy of this study. My discussion of the zoharic manuscripts relies on those sources, the catalogue of the Institute of Photocopies of Manuscripts, and other sources, which will be mentioned later.

47 For a detailed description of the manuscript see Kaddari, *The Aramaic of the Zohar* (Heb.), 161–72. See also Reif, *Hebrew Manuscripts at Cambridge University*, 432–3.

48 See Scholem, *Major Trends in Jewish Mysticism*, 393 n. 106; Reif, *Hebrew Manuscripts at Cambridge University*, 432.

different scribes into two separate books without adhering to the order of the portions, it is more likely that the collection was a result of 'gleanings after gleanings'. In other words, after the scribes had finished copying the first volume, they added new texts that came into their hands to the manuscript that is in our possession.

Another interesting collection, partly based on the Cambridge manuscript, is Vatican, MS 208 (F. 267), copied probably in Byzantium in the fifteenth century.[49] Its first section primarily comprises texts from *Tikunei hazohar*, the body of the Zohar, and *Midrash hane'elam*, while the latter part contains the same texts that are found in Cambridge, MS 1023. One might think that the first part could be the missing first volume of the Cambridge manuscript, yet the texts that are absent from the latter, and which had apparently been copied into another book, are also missing from the Vatican manuscript. It must be the case, therefore, that the editor of the Vatican manuscript compiled his collection from the Cambridge manuscript (or a similar collection) and from texts that he had found in other sources, among them segments of *Tikunei hazohar*.

Toronto, MS Friedberg 5-015 (F. 70561), a compilation written in Byzantine script, was produced in Crete in the early fifteenth century. According to Malachi Beit-Arié, it was copied by R. Sabbatai ben Isaiah Kohen Balbo, who transcribed a few manuscripts in Candia (Crete) between 1400 and 1414.[50] The manuscript contains many portions from the body of the Zohar as well as texts from *Midrash hane'elam*, *Sitrei torah*, *Idra raba*, *Sifra ditseniuta*, and *Heikhalot* 'Bereshit'. Its beginning, like that of Vatican, MS 208, has lengthy quotations from *Tikunei hazohar*.[51]

A different collection, probably copied in the same period and also

[49] Ta-Shma, *The Revealed in the Concealed* (Heb.), 83; Bonfil, *The Rabbinate in Italy during the Renaissance* (Heb.), 179. Ronit Meroz has recently discovered that the manuscript contains zoharic texts that were printed in *Zohar ḥadash* and were written by Joseph Angelet; see 'R. Joseph Angelet and his "Zoharic Writings"' (Heb.).

[50] Ta-Shma, *The Revealed in the Concealed* (Heb.), 82; Ronit Meroz has graciously given me a detailed description of zoharic texts found in this manuscript. The name Sabbatai is mentioned twice, on pp. 79*b* and 85*a*. The beginning of the manuscript, 1*a*–12*a*, was copied by a different scribe. On Sabbatai Balbo and the manuscripts that he copied see T. Malachi, *Pleasant Words* (Heb.), 249–57.

[51] The manuscript also contains an unknown zoharic text; see Meroz, 'Ezekiel's Chariot —An Unknown Zoharic Commentary' (Heb.), 598 n. 1.

written in Byzantine script, forms part of Vatican, MS 206 (F. 264),[52] which includes portions from *Midrash hane'elam* and numerous texts from *Tikunei hazohar*. As Ronit Meroz has shown, it was obviously copied from the Toronto manuscript or one similar to it.[53] However, the scribe of the Vatican manuscript added further zoharic segments to the texts found in the Balbo collection, mainly from *Midrash hane'elam*, and stated that they had been acquired from a variety of sources.[54]

Comparison of two further Vatican manuscripts, MS 213 (F. 272) and MS 68 (F. 185), both written in a Sephardi script and copied in the fifteenth century,[55] reveals a similar process of gleaning and expanding zoharic collections. The first part of MS 213 contains texts drawn mainly from *Midrash hane'elam*, under the title 'Gleanings from the Zohar'. It begins by stating 'I have found this in the book of the Zohar', and concludes with the words 'I did not find any more'. MS 68 contains in its first part the same texts as MS 213; these are followed by texts from the body of the Zohar and from Zohar 'Ruth' that are missing from MS 213. The scribe of MS 68 must have, thus, based his collection on MS 213 (or a similar collection) and added to it zoharic texts that he had acquired from other sources.

A comprehensive compilation of zoharic literature from the second half of the fifteenth century, entitled *Sefer hazohar*, was edited in the Byzantine cultural periphery (perhaps in Crete) and is currently catalogued as Paris, MSS 778–9 (F. 12560). There is a clear link between this manuscript, Toronto, MS Friedberg 5-015, and Vatican, MS 206. The compilation begins with texts from *Tikunei hazohar* and continues with portions from the body of the Zohar and *Midrash hane'elam*. This suggests that the editors

[52] Ta-Shma, *The Revealed in the Concealed* (Heb.), 82; Tishby and Lachower, *The Wisdom of the Zohar*, i. 99. Bonfil, *The Rabbinate in Italy during the Renaissance* (Heb.), 179; Meroz, *Headwaters of the Zohar*.

[53] See Meroz, 'Ezekiel's Chariot—An Unknown Zoharic Commentary' (Heb.), 598 n. 1. The manuscript contains a zoharic commentary on Ezekiel's chariot (pp. 287*b*–289*a*) which can also be found in the Toronto MS; on pp. 377*b*–378*a* there is an unknown zoharic text, which is discussed by Meroz in her article 'The Path of Silence'.

[54] Vatican, MS 206 (F. 264), 15*a*, 182*b*, 201*a*, 411*a*, 424*a*.

[55] Vatican, MS 213 might have been written even earlier. Bonfil has shown that Vatican, MS 68 had arrived at the Vatican Library from the collection of a Christian humanist in Syracuse, Sicily, and Vatican, MS 213 had come from Candia; see Bonfil, *The Rabbinate in Italy during the Renaissance* (Heb.), 179.

considered *Tikunei hazohar*, the body of the Zohar, and *Midrash hane'elam* to be parts of a single literary unit.[56]

The process of gleaning and assembling collections extended to other geographical areas in this period. There are two zoharic anthologies in our possession from the end of the fifteenth century that were edited in Italy: Palatina Library, Parma, MS 2718 (F. 13654) was copied in Mantua in 1482,[57] and contains portions from the body of the Zohar on the book of Genesis; and Vatican, MS 207 (F. 265–6) is a comprehensive collection of zoharic commentary on Genesis and Leviticus. The latter manuscript was at least partially copied in 1489 in Syracuse, Sicily, under the title 'Gleanings of *Sefer hazohar* by R. Shimon of blessed memory'.[58] Another manuscript that might have been copied in Italy during the same period is British Library, London, MS Add. 17745 (F. 4952), which has texts from the body of the Zohar on Genesis.[59] It is interesting that none of the three manuscripts includes texts from *Midrash hane'elam*.

In addition to the manuscripts copied in Byzantium and Italy, there is a fifteenth-century compilation from Palestine.[60] Although we have additional zoharic collections from the same period, their provenance is

[56] Tishby and Lachower, *The Wisdom of the Zohar*, i. 99. Sed-Rajna, 'Manuscrits du *Tiqquney ha-Zohar*', 162, 175; Ta-Shma, *The Revealed in the Concealed* (Heb.), 83; Meroz, 'R. Joseph Angelet and his "Zoharic Writings"' (Heb.), 313; ead., *Headwaters of the Zohar* (Heb.). The manuscript also includes segments that were printed in *Zohar ḥadash* and were, according to Meroz, written by Angelet. These segments are also found in the Toronto MS and in Vatican, MS 206. See Meroz, 'R. Joseph Angelet and his "Zoharic Writings"' (Heb.), 314.

[57] The manuscript was produced by R. Isaiah Messarn for R. Barukh of Posquières; see the colophon, Parma, Palatina MS 2718, 266*b*. It is mentioned in Tishby and Lachower, *The Wisdom of the Zohar*, i. 99; Simonsohn, *History of the Jews* (Heb.), ii. 459 n. 127; *The Zohar: Pritzker Edition*, i. 16 n. 5. In their essay 'The Source of Guillaume Postel's 1553 Zohar Latin Translation', Meroz and Weiss have recently shown that Postel's translation was based on a Zohar manuscript very similar to Parma, Palatina, MS 2718.

[58] Vatican, MS 207, 35*b*. Tseviyah Rubin has provided a description of the zoharic portions on Genesis that are included in the manuscript. In her description, kept in the archives of the Zohar project at the Scholem Library, she shows that some parts of the texts in the collection are in Hebrew (parts of portions 'Vayera' and 'Ḥayei sarah': 119*b*–120*a*, 126*b*–127*a*, 132*b*–133*a*, etc.). For the version of *Tikunei hazohar* which was copied at the beginning of the manuscript, see Giller, *The Enlightened Will Shine*, 132. Four scribes copied the manuscript, one of them Sabbatai ben Zerah Sabatanello.

[59] Tishby and Lachower, *The Wisdom of the Zohar*, i. 99.

[60] JTS, New York, MS 1644 (F. 10742), copied in 1483/4 in Safed by Shalom Zeituni. On the version of *Tikunei hazohar* in the manuscript see Giller, *The Enlightened Will Shine*, 131.

unknown. One of them, Malachi Beit-Arié has argued, was probably copied in Spain,[61] and contains texts from the body of the Zohar in random order.

The above survey indicates that most of the zoharic manuscripts from the late fourteenth and the fifteenth centuries were copied outside Spain. The fact that the three oldest and largest ones are written in Byzantine script has led Beit-Arié to assume that 'most of the zoharic corpus was unified and edited in Byzantium around 1400, and from there it spread to other places'.[62] This fact, however, can probably be attributed to the expulsion from Spain, as a result of which the Spanish manuscripts were not preserved. As I have shown above, an analysis of the writings of Recanati and Angelet proves that comprehensive zoharic collections already existed in Spain in the first half of the fourteenth century. In the fourteenth and fifteenth centuries zoharic literature was quoted primarily in Spain, and at the beginning of the sixteenth century it mostly appeared in the writings of Spanish exiles. Thus, in spite of the findings based on zoharic manuscripts in our possession, the formulation of the zoharic collections and their circulation is likely to have taken place primarily in Spain. Nevertheless, the significant number of fifteenth-century zoharic collections that were produced in Candia in Byzantine script indicates that Candia was an important centre for the copying, editing, and distribution of the Zohar at the time.

The fifteenth-century manuscripts, as well as the quotations incorporated in writings from the century before, indicate that the collections edited during that period varied significantly, and each compiler defined the scope and essence of the Zohar differently. The aforementioned findings suggest that the cultural agents who copied and distributed zoharic literature assembled their collections using a variety of sources.[63] From Mar Hayim's letter of 1476/7 it is clear that the Zohar was still an imagined book at the time, and that the compilations were perceived as parts of this 'book': '*Sefer hazohar* could not be obtained in its entirety in a single district since it

[61] British Library, London, MS Or. 10527 (F. 7889).

[62] Cited in Ta-Shma, *The Revealed in the Concealed* (Heb.), 82.

[63] The compiler of the manuscript held at the British Library, London, MS Or. 10763 (F. 8078), 114*a* states: 'From the beginning of this book, starting with "And the enlightened will shine", up to here, [I used] what I had found in one book . . . from here on I started to copy from another book.'

had been scattered all over.'[64] In the early sixteenth century, for example, R. Judah Hayat, a Spanish exile living in Italy, explained in the preface to his commentary on the book *Ma'arekhet ha'elohut* that he had put together his zoharic collection from different sources while he was living in Spain:

> And I, Judah, the son of my master, the righteous sage R. Jacob Hayat, may he rest in peace, tasted some honey while living in Spain and my eyes lit up, and I made it my goal to seek and learn the wisdom. And I went from strength to strength collecting anything to be found from the said book, and I collected some here and some there until most of it was in my possession.[65]

As I have previously shown, comprehensive collections that included texts from the body of the Zohar and *Midrash hane'elam* had already been compiled in the early fourteenth century. *Tikunei hazohar*, however, was not incorporated into any collection until the end of that century. Surprisingly, it appears for the first time in non-Spanish sources, for example in R. Menahem Tsiyon's *Commentary on the Torah*, written in Germany; in the annotations to *Sefer hashe'iltot* by the Greek sage R. Yohanan ben Reuben of Ohrid; and in Toronto, MS Friedberg 5-015, which was copied in Crete. Nevertheless, one should not conclude that *Tikunei hazohar* only circulated outside Spain; we have seen that quotations from it were incorporated into Spanish texts of the first half of the fifteenth century,[66] as well as into later Spanish sources.

The zoharic literature, which had occupied centre stage in the late thirteenth and early fourteenth centuries, lost its importance a few decades later. By the end of the fifteenth century, however, the circulation, gathering, and editing of zoharic texts had intensified. Collection and distribution through copying and quoting became principal kabbalistic activities after the expulsion from Spain, when kabbalah started to play a more important role in Jewish culture.

In the early sixteenth century zoharic sources were quoted almost exclusively in the writings of Spanish exiles. The rich kabbalistic literature they produced is filled with such excerpts, some of them quite long. A good

[64] Nadav, 'An Epistle of the Kabbalist Isaac Mar Hayim' (Heb.), 456; Abrams, 'The Zohar as a Book', 216; id., *Kabbalistic Manuscripts and Textual Theory*, 259.

[65] *Ma'arekhet ha'elohut*, 2*b*; Abrams, 'The Zohar as a Book', 209; id., *Kabbalistic Manuscripts and Textual Theory*, 259.

[66] e.g. *Sefer poke'aḥ ivrim* and Ibn Shem Tov's *Sefer ha'emunot* were written in this period.

example is the commentary on *Ma'arekhet ha'elohut* written in Mantua by R. Judah Hayat, who had collected and edited zoharic texts even before the expulsion. Hayat cites extensively from the body of the Zohar and from *Tikunei hazohar*, treating both as parts of a single literary entity. He also quotes from Zohar 'Ruth', although it was probably not in his possession; rather, Recanati's *Perush hatorah* seems to have been his source. Like Recanati, Hayat did not consider Zohar 'Ruth' part of the Zohar.

R. Abraham Saba, a Spanish kabbalist who was exiled to Portugal and then to North Africa, lamented the loss of his gigantic library in the expulsions, mentioning the many zoharic books it had included: 'Because I had my sight with me | the tools of my trade by my side | Books beyond count | Beyond belief | Editions upon editions of Splendour [Zohar] and luminaries, more than I could count'.[67] In his works written in North Africa in the years 1498–1500, he frequently inserted paraphrases in Hebrew (probably from memory) from the body of the Zohar, *Midrash hane'elam*, and *Tikunei hazohar*, usually referring to them as *Midrash hane'elam*.[68] In *Tseror haḥayim*, his commentary on *Pirkei avot* (1499/1500), he included paraphrases of *Ra'aya meheimna*, which he claimed to have found 'in a very old copy of the Zohar'.[69] This is one of the first references to *Ra'aya meheimna*, which, to my knowledge, was not quoted before the sixteenth century.

R. Abraham ben Eli'ezer Halevi, another Spanish exile, moved to Italy, Greece, Turkey, and Egypt before settling in Jerusalem. While his book *Masoret haḥokhmah*, written before the expulsion, contains some zoharic quotations, these are much more abundant in his post-expulsion works.[70] He was also a compiler of zoharic texts and reported that *Ra'aya meheimna*, which he regarded as part of the Zohar, had come into his hands in 1518, while staying in Jerusalem: 'And now, at the beginning of 279 [the end of 1518], I obtained one part of the wondrous book of the Zohar called

67 Cited in Gross, *Iberian Jewry*, 69.

68 Ibid. 68, and Weichelder's introduction to *Tseror hamor*, i. 53.

69 Cited in Gross's essay 'R. Abraham Saba's Abbreviated Messianic Commentary', 401; see also id., *Iberian Jewry*, 88 n. 4; Tishby, *Messianism in the Time of the Expulsion* (Heb.), 95–6.

70 See Robinson, 'Abraham ben Eli'ezer Halevi', 223 n. 109. The first part of his book *Ma'amar mashrei kitrin* was written in Serres, Greece, in 1483, in the Aramaic style of the Zohar, and was printed in Constantinople in 1509/10; see Scholem and Beit-Arié, *Ma'amar mashrei kitrin*, 21. Abraham Halevi's *Sefer hayiḥud*, composed after *Ma'amar mashrei kitrin*, is a comprehensive commentary on Zohar 'Bamidbar', iii. 120*a*.

Ra'aya meheimna.'[71] That text is also mentioned in *Kaf haketoret*, written by a Spanish kabbalist who, according to Moshe Idel, was active in the European part of the Ottoman empire in the early sixteenth century.[72] The anonymous author of *Kaf haketoret* referred to 'the books of R. Shimon and his writings', and probably did not count *Ra'aya meheimna* among them: 'And this wisdom has been hidden [reserved] for those who are capable of [great] deeds mentioned by the early sages in the books of R. Shimon and in his writings, and by [*Sefer*] *Hakanah* . . . and in *Ra'aya meheimna*.'[73] It is worth noting that in his book *Agudat ezov*, written in Bursa, Turkey, during the first half of the sixteenth century, R. Isaac Ha'ezovi also distinguished between the Zohar and *Ra'aya meheimna*:

And in order that you do not stray from the path I will tell you of the fields in which I glean. First, from *Sefer hazohar*, ascribed to the holy light, R. Shimon, may he rest in peace, and from his homilies; second, [from the writings of] R. Hamnuna Saba, may he rest in peace; third, from *Ra'aya meheimna* and its teachings; and fourth, from *Sefer habahir*, written by the holy R. Nehunyah ben Hakanah.[74]

Another kabbalist who quoted extensively from the zoharic literature was R. Meir Ibn Gabai, a Spanish exile who settled in Turkey. He wrote his first book, *Tola'at ya'akov*, in 1507, at the age of 26.[75] Like Hayat, he quoted segments from both the Zohar and *Tikunei hazohar*, which he believed were parts of a single literary unit. In most cases he cited these sources as *Midrasho shel rabi shimon*.[76] He, too, regarded Zohar 'Ruth' as a separate work. *Ra'aya meheimna* is not mentioned in *Tola'at ya'akov*, nor in *Avodat hakodesh*, which he completed in 1531. It probably came into his possession later since he quoted it several times in his *Derekh ha'emunah*, written after *Avodat hakodesh*.[77]

Additional testimony that in the fifteenth century Spanish kabbalists continued to glean zoharic literature from different sources appears in the book *Avnei zikaron* by Abraham ben Solomon Adrotil, a Spanish exile in Fez. Adrotil mentions a text that was not included in the local zoharic collections, except in one very old book:

71 Scholem, 'The Kabbalist Abraham ben Eli'ezer Halevi' (Heb.), 271.

72 Idel, 'Neglected Writings of the Author of *Kaf haketoret*' (Heb.), 78.

73 Ibid. 81.

74 *Agudat ezov*, 3.

75 Ibn Gabai, *Tola'at ya'akov*, 47*b*.

76 See e.g. ibid. 4*b*, 15*b*, and more.

77 Ibn Gabai, *Derekh ha'emunah*, 4*a*, 16*a*, 20*a*, 20*b*.

And in portion 'Vayishma yitro', in [the discussion of the verse] 'The Lord your God', one can identify many supernal secrets that R. Shimon, may he rest in peace, wrote about it [the verse]. I considered inserting it here since it has not been included in the books of the Zohar that I have seen in this place. I found it in a very old book among the books of R. Khalaf, of blessed memory.[78]

Adrotil distinguishes between *Sefer hatikunim* (i.e. *Tikunei hazohar*) and *Sefer hazohar*: while the former was written by R. Shimon himself, he explains, the Zohar was composed by other sages; he therefore viewed *Tikunei hazohar* as a superior text. He also realized that the early kabbalists had not been acquainted with this source:

I wish to record awesome and wondrous things that support this argument from *Sefer hatikunim* [written] by the holy light . . . R. Shimon, of blessed memory. And one can see the agreement between the opinion of the holy sages mentioned above and that of the holy R. Shimon, of blessed memory, although *Sefer hatikunim* was unknown in their time . . . And although the Zohar was revealed to some sages, as can be seen from their writings, nonetheless *Sefer hatikunim*, which R. Shimon, of blessed memory, wrote by himself, was not in their possession, because the Zohar is the work of the sages who lived in his time and also of those who came after him. Therefore R. Shimon, of blessed memory, revealed in this book [*Tikunei hazohar*] what the sages of the Zohar did not reveal in other works.[79]

Zoharic quotations frequently appear in the writings of other exiled authors, among them R. Joseph Alashkar, who settled in Tlemcen, North

[78] See Scholem, '*Sefer avnei zikaron*' (Heb.), 273.

[79] Ibid. 265. The claim that the Zohar was not written by R. Shimon himself but by his son, his disciples, and the disciples of his disciples also appears in R. Abraham Zacuto's *Sefer yuḥasin*: 'The Zohar, which illuminates the whole world, is called *Midrash vayehi or* and is one of the secrets of the Torah and of kabbalah. It was named after him [R. Shimon] although he did not write it. His disciples and his son, and the disciples of his disciples wrote it on the basis of what they had received from him' (*Sefer yuḥasin hashalem*, 45). According to R. Abraham Galante, the Zohar was compiled by the geonim, who had edited the sayings recorded by R. Aba:

> What we have learned [Zohar i. 168*a*] are not R. Eleazar's words . . . but those of the author, who lived at the time of the geonim or of other sages, and who compiled the sayings of R. Aba, R. Shimon's scribe. They divided them into portions, each verse in its portion, and they said the words that we have learned. There are many examples of this in the Zohar and all of them can be explained in this manner. (A. Azulai, *Or haḥamah*, i. 159*a*)

Africa;[80] R. Joseph ibn Sheraga, who settled in Argenata, Italy;[81] and R. Isaac Karo (Joseph Karo's uncle), who moved from Portugal to Turkey, and at the end of his life probably went to Palestine.[82] By the third decade of the sixteenth century the different sections of the zoharic literature were generally known to kabbalists, particularly to those of Spanish descent. For example R. Solomon Alkabets, who was born after the expulsion, most probably in Salonica, and moved to Safed in 1534/5, often quoted from the Zohar, *Ra'aya meheimna*, and *Sefer hatikunim*, as well as from the *Introduction to the Zohar*, which was rarely mentioned in manuscripts before the printing of the Zohar.[83] R. Judah Haliwah moved from Fez to Safed, where he wrote his book *Tsafenat pane'aḥ* in 1544/5; he, too, was acquainted with all the zoharic sections and perceived them as interconnected.[84]

The Zohar is central to the activities of R. Solomon Alkabets's brother-in-law and disciple, R. Moses Cordovero, who published one of the earliest and most comprehensive commentaries on the Zohar entitled *Or yakar*. His book *Pardes rimonim*, which he completed in 1548, ten years before the first printing of the Zohar, contains abundant long zoharic quotations. We can thus infer that he had in his possession a comprehensive collection, was acquainted with most of the zoharic sections, and treated them as units of a single literary entity.[85] However, I have not found portions from *Midrash hane'elam* on the Torah in either of those books. Cordovero started composing *Or yakar* while writing *Pardes rimonim*, and continued to work on it for the rest of his life.[86] The book contains a very large and comprehensive zoharic collection that Cordovero had compiled from various manuscripts,

[80] Idel, 'Rabbi Judah Haliwah and His Book *Tsafenat pane'aḥ*' (Heb.), 26; ibid., index of sources, 5.

[81] Tishby, *Messianism in the Time of the Expulsion* (Heb.), 138. Ibn Sheraga's unpublished manuscripts also contain a number of zoharic quotations.

[82] About Karo's life and emigration to the Land of Israel see Regev's introduction to *The Sermons of R. Isaac Karo*, ed. Regev, 9–12, 14–17. On his quotations from zoharic literature in his book *Ḥasdei david* see ibid. 28–31.

[83] About zoharic quotations in the writing of Alkabets see Sack, 'The Mystical Theology of Solomon Alkabez', 267–72.

[84] Haliwah generally quoted the Zohar in Hebrew translation; see Idel, 'R. Judah Haliwah and His Book *Tsafenat pane'aḥ*' (Heb.), 126.

[85] Abrams, 'The Zohar as a Book', 205–8; id., *Kabbalistic Manuscripts and Textual Theory*, 247–56.

[86] Sack, *The Kabbalah of Rabbi Moses Cordovero* (Heb.), 25–6.

as well as his commentary on it. Apart from the manuscripts he used to create his own zoharic corpus, he mentions having included passages he had found only in the printed editions of the Zohar: 'I have interpreted this text according to the book's printed editions. I could not verify its correct version because I found it only in print.'[87]

In the introduction to *Perush or yakar*, Cordovero describes the Zohar as a work written by R. Shimon and his companions:

And he wrote the concealed book called *Sefer hazohar*, which is without any doubt a high and steep mountain, and its words are pure as 'silver purged in an earthen crucible' [Ps. 12: 7], and in it all the reasons of the Torah and its secrets are revealed, and the knowledge of His names, blessed be He, is seen. 'His head is finest gold' [S. of S. 5: 11]—*Hatikunim*; 'His locks'—the remaining books of the Zohar; 'are curled'—braids of pleasant laws.[88]

The identification of the 'head' with *Tikunei hazohar* and the 'locks' with the remaining zoharic sections indicates the significance Cordovero attributed to *Tikunei hazohar*. Elsewhere he noted that, together with *Ra'aya meheimna*, *Pikudin*, *Idra*, and Zohar 'Song of Songs', that book contained the most recondite sections of zoharic literature:

The writing of zoharic portions was done casually when they would break from studying the laws of the Torah. But the writing of this work [*Tikunei hazohar*] and the writing of *Ra'aya meheimna*, [Zohar] 'Song of Songs', *Pikudin*, and the *Idra* was carried out while leaving everything else and concentrating solely on the writing of these works.[89]

Another Sephardi kabbalist to produce a commentary on the Zohar was R. Simeon Ibn Lavi, a contemporary of Cordovero's who resided in North Africa. Like Cordovero, he was acquainted with the printed version of the Zohar, but his commentary (which he might have begun before the

[87] Cordovero, *Sefer hazohar im perush or yakar*, xii. 9.

[88] Ibid. i, Introduction; Sack, *The Kabbalah of Rabbi Moses Cordovero* (Heb.), 25–6; Abrams, 'The Zohar as a Book', 207–8; id., *Kabbalistic Manuscripts and Textual Theory*, 248–9.

[89] Cordovero, *Tikunei hazohar im perush or yakar*, i. 15. Abrams, *Kabbalistic Manuscripts and Textual Theory*, 250. Cordovero also proclaims the superiority of *Tikunei hazohar* to the rest of the zoharic books (ibid. 44); see also Sack, *The Kabbalah of Rabbi Moses Cordovero* (Heb.), 48–50. In his commentary on *Tikunei hazohar*, Cordovero distinguishes between the 'revealed secrets' discussed in the portions of the Zohar and the 'recondite secrets' discussed in *Tikunei hazohar* and the *Idrot*; see *Tikunei hazohar im perush or yakar*, iii. 148.

printing) was based on a few manuscripts in his possession.[90] He considered his zoharic library a small segment of the lost, original Zohar: 'Truly, this collection is made up of the gleanings, the forgotten sheaf, and the poor man's tithe. And it was gleaned from the first big work that was, as we have heard, a load to be carried by forty camels, and which we lost because of our many sins.'[91] His words reflect his awareness of the zoharic gathering and editing process described above: 'Their sons took their place. God inspired them to search and desire to compile the gleanings of the surviving books, bit by bit. They were collecting from here and from there, editing them as best they could, and by doing so produced this work.'[92]

Ibn Lavi's book contains commentaries only on zoharic portions on the book of Genesis (including *Introduction to the Zohar*); in it he quotes *Tikunei hazohar* and *Ra'aya meheimna*. Although he was aware of the link between these texts and what he perceived to be the Zohar, he distinguished between them and criticized the publishers of the Zohar for not doing so:

> And I saw that the publishers of the Zohar mixed texts, some from *Ra'aya meheimna* and some from the *Tikunim*, and some from other *midrashim*. And although their intentions were good, they interrupted the flow of topics that belong together, and they corrupted the order for us by placing unrelated texts in the midst of R. Shimon's words.[93]

It is possible that 'other *midrashim*' refers to *Midrash hane'elam*, which Ibn Lavi did not consider part of the Zohar. Indeed, he does not comment on, or make reference to, portions from *Midrash hane'elam* on Genesis.[94]

On the basis of the above, it is clear that in the first half of the sixteenth century, as kabbalists continued to compile their own collections from the various sources they had gathered, the circulation of zoharic literature increased significantly. The ruling of R. Isaac de Lattes (1558, Italy) in sup-

90 See Huss, *Sockets of Fine Gold* (Heb.), 67.

91 Ibn Lavi, *Ketem paz*, i. 95*a*.

92 'Because of our many sins *Sefer hazohar*, as it was arranged in the days following R. Shimon, was lost. We lost it together with many other ancient books as we wandered from place to place in the exile. [It could be] that its profundity also discouraged the later generations, until the books were worn out and nothing was left of them but two or three grains at the top of the tree. And they gathered them, sheaf by sheaf, one from here and one from there and that is what we have today' (ibid. 30*a*).

93 Ibid. 96*b*.

94 Huss, *Sockets of Fine Gold* (Heb.), 70.

port of printing the Zohar attests to the fact that such copying and editing were primary kabbalistic activities at the time:

Aren't you aware of the great awakening in this country as everyone is inspired to search for it [the Zohar] and is willing to pay a high price for it, and to labour over copying it [in spite of] the difficulties and the significant expense? This is a clear sign that the days of God's calling have arrived and 'the time of pruning has come'.[95]

Indeed, in addition to the zoharic quotations, we have a number of collections that were copied in that period, mostly in Italy. As Ronit Meroz has shown in her study of zoharic manuscripts on portion 'Shemot', Italy played a pivotal role in the production of such collections. She attributes this to Renaissance culture, which provided the infrastructure and support needed for the intensive copying process and for the dissemination of manuscripts that followed.[96]

In 1513 Isaac ben Abraham Balilah copied a comprehensive collection for Cardinal Egidio da Viterbo, which included segments from the Zohar and *Midrash hane'elam* on the first four books of the Torah.[97] Since the cardinal regarded it as a partial collection, he asked Gabriele della Volta soon after to acquire for him a complete manuscript in Damascus.[98] The fact that a cardinal ordered the copying of a zoharic collection indicates that Christian kabbalists, too, played a role in the formulation and reception of the zoharic corpus. It should be noted that Jewish converts to Christianity were also involved in the printing of the Zohar in the sixteenth century and later.

Extensive reproduction and distribution of zoharic manuscripts took place in the home of the well-known, erudite banker, R. Yehiel Nisim of Pisa.[99] Between 1525 and 1528 he copied a comprehensive collection entitled

[95] Lattes's ruling was printed on the first page of the Mantua Zohar as well as in many other editions; see Tishby, *Studies in Kabbalah* (Heb.), i. 105 n. 89.

[96] Meroz, *Headwaters of the Zohar* (Heb.).

[97] The translation of the Zohar into Latin (probably by R. Barukh of Benevento) is based on this collection. In the manuscript one can see annotations in Latin, written probably by the translator; see Meroz, *Headwaters of the Zohar* (Heb.). On Latin translations of the Zohar in the early 16th century see Huss, 'Translations of the Zohar' (Heb.), 36–8.

[98] Secret, *Le Zohar chez les kabbalistes chrétiens*, 38; Penkower, 'A Renewed Enquiry into *Masoret hamasoret*' (Heb.), 39 n. 98. O'Malley, *Giles of Viterbo on Church and Reform*, 87.

[99] On the copying of zoharic manuscripts for R. Yehiel and his family see Meroz, *Headwaters of the Zohar* (Heb.).

The Wondrous Book of the Zohar,[100] the first volume of which (Paris, MS 781) contained zoharic portions on Genesis and was based on British Library, London, MS Add. 17745 (or a similar manuscript). It was produced in Adar 5286 (March 1526), after the copying of the second volume (Paris, MS 783) had been completed in Kislev 5286 (December 1525). The third volume of the collection (Paris, MS 784) was copied two years later, in 5288 (1527/8), by R. Yehiel and others, and it contained additional zoharic portions, mainly on Leviticus, which had not been included in the second volume.[101] This discrepancy indicates that R. Yehiel did not base his collection on a single source. Rather, after copying the first two volumes from one or more sources he continued collecting texts from other sources.[102] Further zoharic portions from *Midrash hane'elam* were copied at his home in 5288 (1527/8) by R. Menahem dell' Atripalda.[103] About twenty years later, in 1549, R. Yehiel copied yet another zoharic collection on Exodus.[104] In the colophon he apologizes for the texts he had missed in his first edition and makes reference to the fact that, following the expulsion, the homilies needed to be gathered together from scattered sources:

And the reader should not wonder if he finds the language imperfect or lacking, since it is known that these *midrashim* were not all edited by the same person and the scribe could not avoid the embedded mistakes. Since the great expulsion, when the people of Israel were banished from Spain, a well of wisdom and a source of Torah, they have gone from bad to worse in the countries of their enemies. All their precious belongings and most of their books, which they carried from place to place, have been captured by their foes. As a result, those who were left with one pamphlet were left without the other one, for they [the books] are

[100] The collection, which includes portions of the body of the Zohar, can be found in Paris, MS 781 (F. 12562); Paris, MS 783 (F. 12564); Paris, MS 784 (F. 12565). See Beit-Arié et al., *Collection of Medieval Hebrew Manuscripts* (Heb.), iii. 83.

[101] See the colophons in Paris, MS 783, 224*a* and Paris, MS 784, 148*b*. See also Beit-Arié et al., *Collection of Medieval Hebrew Manuscripts* (Heb.), iii. 78.

[102] In Paris, MS 783, 104*a*, R. Yehiel indicates that he had used two copies of the Zohar in his possession. See Beit-Arié et al., *Collection of Medieval Hebrew Manuscripts* (Heb.), iii. 78.

[103] Vatican, MS 504 (F. 589). See also colophon, ibid. 36*a*. Meroz, *Headwaters of the Zohar* (Heb.).

[104] As I show below, R. Yehiel's son R. Samuel copied a zoharic collection based on the one that his father had edited during the same period. R. Samuel's copy is held at Moscow, MS Guenzburg 293 (F. 47618). For more on the manuscript see Meroz, *Headwaters of the Zohar* (Heb.).

scattered all over. And only through great difficulties and enormous effort is one able to collect those *midrashim*, and one must go to the end the world to search for them in North Africa, in a big city such as Fez, where many sages live, and in other countries in which great sages, experts in this divine wisdom, dwell.[105]

Another Italian sage who was engaged in the production of zoharic texts around the same time was R. Levi ben Perets Foa. In 1527/8 he copied Zohar 'Ruth' under the title 'A Zoharic Homily on the Scroll of Ruth'.[106] Later he produced a collection of zoharic portions on Genesis entitled 'The Wondrous Book of the Zohar' (Orvieto, 1531), which was probably copied from the first volume of R. Yehiel ben Nisim's collection mentioned above.[107]

In the same year R. Judah ben Solomon de Blanis copied two volumes of zoharic texts for R. Judah ben Moses de Blanis,[108] and after their completion he continued to copy other material: Zohar 'Song of Songs' in 1532,[109] and later *Tikunei hazohar* (Ancona, 1546).[110] R. Judah ben Moses de Blanis was among the initiators of the printing of the Zohar in Mantua, and his zoharic collection was probably one of the sources for the printed Mantua edition.

In 1536 the Italian Isaiah Gershoni Parnas, known by the name Franciscus Parnas after converting to Christianity, copied (probably in Capua) a comprehensive zoharic collection for Johann Albrecht Widmanstetter, who eventually became the rector of the University of Vienna.[111] In addition to segments from the Zohar and *Midrash hane'elam*, his collection included parts of *Tikunei hazohar*.[112] Parnas based his copy on the collection of

[105] Moscow, MS Guenzburg 293, 213*b*. I would like to thank Ronit Meroz for mentioning to me the colophon in this manuscript and for giving me a copy of it.

[106] Warsaw, MS 198 (F. 30159).

[107] Vatican, MS Neofiti 22 (F. 630). See also colophon, ibid. 228*a*.

[108] Vatican, MS Neofiti 24 (F. 632) and Vatican, MS Neofiti 25 (F. 633). R. Judah ben Solomon finished copying the first volume, which contained mainly zoharic portions on Leviticus, in the month of Adar (Vatican, MS Neofiti 24, 236*b*), and the second volume, containing sections on Exodus, Numbers, and Deuteronomy, in the month of Iyar (Vatican, MS Neofiti 25, 209*a*). In 1544 another collection was copied for R. Judah ben Moses—JTS, New York, MS 1927 (F. 11025).

[109] Milan, MS O 100 Sup. (cat. no. 58) (F. 14601).

[110] British Library, London, MS Add. 27003 (F. 5660).

[111] Secret, *Les Kabbalistes chrétiens de la Renaissance*, 121–3; Meroz, *Headwaters of the Zohar* (Heb.).

[112] Munich, MS 217 (F. 23122); Munich, MS 218 (F. 31425); see also the colophon in Munich, MS 217, 327*b*. For more details on the manuscript see Meroz, *Headwaters of the Zohar* (Heb.).

Egidio da Viterbo, but it seems he supplemented it with zoharic manuscripts borrowed from the famous sage R. Jacob Mantino (the personal physician of Pope Pius III).[113] In 1543 a collection entitled 'An Abridgement of Zoharic Sayings' was copied in Perugia for the physician R. Judah ben Moses de Blanis by the scribe R. Aaron ben Benjamin of Nola,[114] and R. Samuel ben Yehiel Nisim, the son of Yehiel of Pisa, copied a comprehensive collection in 1547/8 in Pisa.[115]

Between 1548 and 1551, about a decade before producing the printed Cremona edition of the Zohar, the Sephardi sage R. Hayim ben Samuel Ibn Gatinyo collected zoharic texts and arranged them in three manuscripts. The first, prepared in Rome in 1548, consisted of Zohar 'Mishpatim', 'Yitro', and 'Terumah'.[116] In 1551 he copied a collection containing, among other things, Zohar 'Bereshit'. The first part of this manuscript is very similar to that of R. Yehiel ben Nisim and is therefore likely to have been copied from it or from another manuscript owned by his family. It also shows similarities to the collections of R. Levi ben Perets and R. Samuel ben Yehiel, as well as to British Library, London, MS Add. 17745. The remainder of the manuscript includes texts from *Midrash hane'elam* and *Tikunei hazohar*, which R. Hayim added from other sources.[117] Later in the same year he copied a third manuscript, a version of *Tikunei hazohar* which carried the title *Sefer hazohar hagadol*.[118] Another comprehensive collection (of which we may only have a part) was edited by R. Joseph ben Zion of Correggio shortly before the printing of the Zohar, between 1552 and 1554, in Pieve di Cento, near the city of Ferrara.[119]

[113] Perles, *Beiträge zur Geschichte der hebräischen und aramäischen Studien*, 157; Secret, *Le Zohar chez les kabbalistes chrétiens*, 38; Roth, *The Jews in the Renaissance*, 141. Barukhson, *Books and Readers*, 49.

[114] JTS, New York, MS 1927 (F. 11025). For a description of the manuscript see Meroz, *Headwaters of the Zohar* (Heb.).

[115] The first part of R. Samuel's collection is in Modena, Estense, MS cat. no. 12 (F. 27777), and the rest is in Cambridge, MS Add. 523 (F. 16815).

[116] Milan, MS O 81 Sup. (F. 12917). See the colophon there, 89*a*.

[117] Munich, MS 203 (F. 12917). See the colophon at the end of the manuscript, 391*a*. See also Scholem, *Bibliographia Kabbalistica* (Ger.), 167; Benayahu, *Hebrew Printing in Cremona* (Heb.), 134; Abrams, 'When Was the Introduction to the Zohar Written?' (Heb.), 220, 225 n. 41.

[118] Vatican, MS 204 (F. 262).

[119] The first zoharic collection gathered by R. Joseph that has come down to us is included in Cambridge, MS Add. 389 (F. 16307); it was copied between Dec. 1552 and Jan. 1553. See Reif,

In addition to these comprehensive collections, many sixteenth-century kabbalistic manuscripts produced before the printing of the Zohar in Mantua and Cremona include zoharic texts. The *Idrot* and *Sifra ditseniuta* can be found in an anthology compiled, at least in part, by R. Jacob of Corinaldi (Ferrara, 1507/8).[120] *Zohar ḥadash* 'Ruth' was copied by R. Judah ben Samuel of Fermo in 1528/9, and again in 1538.[121] In 1535 Raphael Joseph Treves copied in Ferrara a manuscript that included some zoharic portions for the well-known physician and kabbalist R. Elijah Halfan.[122] In 1550 a collection containing *Tikunei hazohar*, Zohar 'Song of Songs', and *Heikhalot* was produced for R. Mordecai Roshlo in Ferrara.[123] In 1551 a version of *Ra'aya meheimna* was copied in Venice, probably for the famous printer Cornelius ben Barukh Adelkind.[124] Between the years 1549 and 1552 a compilation including portions from the body of the Zohar, *Midrash hane'elam*, and *Tikunei hazohar* was probably also copied for him.[125] In 1556 R. Elijah ben Samuel Ibn Gikatilla reproduced in Pesaro a manuscript containing *Ra'aya meheimna* and *Tikunei hazohar*.[126] In Urbino in 1557, the year in which the Zohar first appeared in print, R. Isaac ben Abraham Tsarfati copied a manuscript that included *Idra raba*, Zohar 'Vayelekh', *Heikhalot* 'Bereshit', and *Heikhalot* 'Pekudei'.[127]

Hebrew Manuscripts at Cambridge University, 433. Other zoharic segments, including Zohar 'Ruth', were copied by R. Joseph and are part of JTS, New York, MS 1929 (F. 11027) and of JTS, New York, MS 1930 (F. 11028).

[120] Lorenziana, Florence, MS Plut. II. 18 (F. 17663).

[121] Ambrosiana, Milan, MS P 12 Sup. (F. 14595), *4a–36b*; Paris, MS 796 (F. 12628), *1a–37a*.

[122] Budapest, MS Kaufmann A 179 (F. 4513). See the colophon ibid. 83.

[123] R. Abraham ben Meshulam indicates, at the end of the third volume of the Mantua edition, that the version of *Sava demishpatim* was faulty in all the copies he had, 'except for one that was perfect, complete, and purified sevenfold, which came into our hands from the most perfect and noble among the physicians, our teacher R. Elijah Halfan, may he be remembered in the world to come, who brought it from Egypt, from a city famous for its striving for Torah and its wells of wisdom' (Tishby, *Studies in Kabbalah* (Heb.), i. 92 n. 47). Halfan was involved in a controversy regarding the printing of the Zohar: see Tishby, *Studies in Kabbalah* (Heb.), i. 84, 85 n. 26, 119 n. 142; Assaf, 'The Controversy over the Printing of Kabbalistic Literature' (Heb.), 9 n. 37.

[124] Munich, MS 47 (F. 82674). For the manuscripts of the Munich library that, according to Benayahu, were copied for Adelkind, see Benayahu, 'R. Ezra of Fano' (Heb.), 788.

[125] Munich, MS 12 (F. 23107); see also Benayahu, 'R. Ezra of Fano' (Heb.), 788.

[126] Paris, MS 791 (F. 12623).

[127] Moscow, MS Guenzburg 83 (F. 6763).

As the above survey shows, most of the Zohar manuscripts that have come down to us from the period were copied in Italy, but we do have some from other locations. Hayim ben Sasi Helmi (and other scribes) produced a compilation containing *Tikunei hazohar*, Zohar 'Song of Songs', Zohar 'Naso', and *Idra raba* in Constantine and Algeria in 1505.[128] A manuscript of *Tikunei hazohar* was copied in North Africa in 1536 by Suliman ben Abraham Ibn Magera.[129] In 1537 the Jerusalemite sage R. Joseph Kolon ben Moses Latif copied a collection of texts, probably in Jerusalem.[130] A comprehensive zoharic collection comprising three manuscripts was copied in 1544 or 1549 for R. Meir ben Obadiah in El Farag by various scribes, one of whom was R. Eleazar ben Solomon Zeitun.[131] The anthology begins with an introduction to *Tikunei hazohar* which contains excerpts from the body of the Zohar. In 1553 in Safed R. Abraham ben Tobias ben Abraham Halevi also copied a collection that included *Tikunei hazohar*.[132]

The study of zoharic manuscripts from the first half of the sixteenth century indicates (as did the study of zoharic quotations) that the boundaries and scope of the zoharic corpus were not yet defined at the time. Scholars continued to glean texts from different sources, edit them, and conceive in a variety of ways the possible extent of *Sefer hazohar*. It is evident that, just as the frequent quotations in the writings of kabbalists from that period indicate a growing circulation of zoharic texts, so do the large number of contemporaneous manuscripts.

It also becomes clear through examination of these manuscripts that zoharic texts that had been less available in previous periods, such as *Ra'aya meheimna*, the *Introduction to the Zohar*, *Sava demishpatim*, Zohar 'Song of Songs', and Zohar 'Lamentations', were now being copied.[133] The survey

[128] JTS, New York, MS 2069 (F. 11167).

[129] Moscow, MS Guenzburg 130 (F. 6810).

[130] The Jewish Congregation, Mantua, MS 129 (F. 2257). Gottlieb, *Studies in Kabbalistic Literature* (Heb.), 399 n. 10.

[131] Municipal Library, Lyons, MS 10 (F. 5604). Ibid. 11 (F. 5605). Ibid. 12 (F. 5606). For a detailed discussion of Municipal Library, Lyons, MS 12, see Meroz, *Headwaters of the Zohar* (Heb.).

[132] Sassoon, MS 27 (F. 9126). It should be noted that, in addition to the manuscripts with colophons surveyed above, there are many without colophons that might have been copied in the first half of the 16th century (most of them probably in Italy).

[133] *Ra'aya meheimna* is included in Budapest, MS Kaufmann A 180 (F. 12650) (copied in Venice, 1542); Munich, MS 47 (Venice, 1551); Paris, MS 791 (F. 12623) (copied in 1556 by

of zoharic quotations further indicates that more copies of these texts were circulating. However, the relationship between texts such as Zohar 'Ruth', 'Song of Songs', and 'Lamentations', and *Ra'aya meheimna*, on the one hand, and commentaries on the Torah portions (from the body of the Zohar and from *Midrash hane'elam*) on the other, remained undetermined. The texts in the first group were occasionally identified as segments of the Zohar but they were not included in the comprehensive collections surveyed here. It is interesting, moreover, that, although *Tikunei hazohar* was well known in Italy at the time, it was not incorporated in the majority of those large compilations (in contrast to Byzantine collections from the fifteenth century).

As I have mentioned, some of the above collections had been copied from earlier ones, at times with supplements and expansions. These anthologies were the main source for the printed Zohar, which indicates that Italy had become a major centre for the formulation, revision, and distribution of zoharic literature. At the same time, the Italian scholars who took part in the production process tried to make their editions more comprehensive by using manuscripts from the east and from North Africa. Cardinal Egidio

R. Samuel Ibn Gikatilla in Pesaro); and in other manuscripts that were probably produced in the 16th century: Parma, MS 351 (F. 27566); Cambridge, MS Add. 1196 (F. 17061); Cambridge, MS Add. 521.1 (F. 16813). See also Gottlieb, *Studies in Kabbalistic Literature* (Heb.), 220–1; Reif, *Hebrew Manuscripts at Cambridge University*, 435, 437. Also Vatican, MS 606 (F. 8671); Palatina, Parma, MS 2774 (F. 13623). A short segment of *Ra'aya meheimna* appears in the following manuscripts: Florence, MS Plut. II 48 (F. 17809); Cambridge, MS Dd.10.14.5 (F. 15927), and Cambridge, MS Dd.4.2.1 (F. 15917). See Abrams, 'When Was the Introduction to the Zohar Written?' (Heb.), 221; Reif, *Hebrew Manuscripts at Cambridge University*, 430–1. Vatican, MS 606 (F. 8671) contains a copy of *Sava demishpatim*, *Ra'aya meheimna*, and *Pikudin* (these texts were not widely distributed before the printed editions). *Sava demishpatim* can also be found in JTS, New York, MS 2076 (F. 11174); partially in JTS, New York, MS 1918 (F. 11016), and in Bodleian, Oxford, MS Heb. C. 53 (F. 21204). See also Yisra'eli, *The Interpretation of Secrets and the Secrets of Interpretation*, 19 n. 11. Yisra'eli has pointed out the appearance of a section in the Zohar manuscript with Moses Cordovero's commentary *Or yakar*; see ibid. 18. Zoharic *midrashim* on Song of Songs are included in JTS, New York, MS 1644 (F. 10742), copied in Safed in 1487/8; in JTS, New York, MS 2069 (F. 11167), copied in Constantine (Algeria) in 1504/5; in Milan, MS O 100 Sup. (Catalogue 58) (F. 14601), copied by Judah de Blanis in 1532/3; and in Vatican, MS 210 (269), copied in Serres in 1549/50. Other manuscripts that contain zoharic texts on Song of Songs, probably copied in the 16th century, are: JTS, New York, MS 1578 (F. 10676); Cambridge, MS Dd.3.3 (F. 15914); Parma, MS 351 (F. 27566); Cambridge, MS Add. 1196 (F. 17061); and Munich, MS 20 (F. 23110). A copy of Zohar 'Lamentations' appears in Escorial, MS G-3-14, 16 (F. 8840), copied in 1531/2.

da Viterbo, mentioned previously, had requested a complete edition of the Zohar from Damascus, and R. Yehiel Nisim of Pisa noted, we may recall, that zoharic texts should be obtained from Fez. The printers of the Mantua Zohar stated that they had used manuscripts originating from Salonica, Egypt, and Safed.

We have seen that the writings richest in zoharic quotations were those of the first and second generations of exiled Sephardi kabbalists. However, the majority of the Zohar's copyists and readers, as well as its later printers, were Italian.[134] This fact is noteworthy because the Zohar was little known in Italy before the sixteenth century. Spanish exiles had probably exerted significant influence within Italian Jewish culture in general and on kabbalah in particular. This could explain the great interest in the Zohar at the beginning of the sixteenth century, as well as the efforts of the Italian sages to advance their cultural standing by controlling the compilation and distribution of zoharic literature.

One should also recognize the co-operation between Christians, converts, and Jews in the gathering, copying, and editing process. I have already mentioned that a comprehensive zoharic collection was copied for Cardinal Egidio da Viterbo by R. Isaac ben Abraham Balilah, and that the convert Franciscus Parnas (Isaiah Gershoni) produced one for Johann Albrecht Widmanstetter. The latter employed another convert, Paulus Aemilius, to copy Zohar 'Ruth' for him. The printing of the Zohar in Cremona, as in Mantua, was also a joint initiative of Jews, Christians, and Jewish converts to Christianity.[135] Interestingly, R. Emmanuel of Benevento, the editor of

[134] It should be mentioned, though, that some of the scribes in Italy were Spanish, such as R. Hayim ibn Samuel Ibn Gatinyo (who was also involved in the printing of the Zohar) and R. Samuel Ibn Gikatilla. Malachi Beit-Arié discusses the Spanish influence on R. Yehiel Nisim of Pisa, who went as far as adopting the Spanish script, and in whose house large-scale production of zoharic literature took place. See Beit-Arié et al., *Collection of Medieval Hebrew Manuscripts* (Heb.), iii. 78.

[135] See Amram, *The Makers of Hebrew Books in Italy*, 324; Busi, *Mantua and the Kabbalah*, 55. Interestingly, the Christian kabbalist Gaius Fustel, who was in contact with R. Moses Basola, was aware of the polemic surrounding the printing of the Zohar, and claimed to have been the one who had persuaded Basola to support the printing. See Secret, *Le Zohar chez les kabbalistes chrétiens*, 55; Tishby, *Studies in Kabbalah* (Heb.), i. 151. Sixtus of Siena, one of the initiators of the burning of the Talmud, supported the distribution of the Zohar for missionary reasons; see Benayahu, *Hebrew Printing in Cremona* (Heb.), 121; Raz-Krakotzkin, *The Censor, the Editor, and the Text* (Heb.), 215.

the Mantua Zohar, complained in one of his writings that most kabbalistic texts, 'copied by hand as well as printed', were in Christian possession.[136] The Italian Renaissance and the complex relations between Jews, Christians, and converts provided the context for the final formulation of zoharic collections and their eventual printing.[137]

The scope and boundaries of the Zohar remained undefined until the middle of the sixteenth century; its final format was determined primarily by printers in the following decades. The first collections were printed between 1557 and 1560 in Mantua and Cremona.[138] The moulding of these early editions was the continuation and, to a great extent, the completion of the zoharic canonization and editing process. Accompanied by fierce polemics, the printing dramatically altered the book's marketing, distribution, and reception, all of which are discussed at length in the following chapters.

On 15 November 1557 the printing of the first zoharic volume, *Tikunei hazohar*, was completed in Mantua. This work was the first to be published probably because it was considered the introductory section of the Zohar, as is evident from the order in which some of the manuscripts were copied. Between 1558 and 1560 two parallel editions of the Zohar were printed: one in Mantua in three volumes, and another in Cremona in one volume. The printers of both watched each other closely and amended their version in light of the work of their competitors.[139] The Mantua edition was printed

[136] See R. Emmanuel's introduction to *Ma'arekhet ha'elohut*, 4*a*; Tishby, *Studies in Kabbalah* (Heb.), i. 142 n. 45.

[137] On Italy as a copying centre of zoharic manuscripts see Meroz, *Headwaters of the Zohar* (Heb.). On the co-operation between Jews, Christians, and converts in the Hebrew printing houses in Italy during that period see Raz-Krakotzkin, *The Censor, the Editor, and the Text* (Heb.), 127–32.

[138] Other important kabbalistic works were also published at that time. In 1557/8, while R. Emmanuel of Benevento was preparing the Zohar for printing in Mantua, he put out *Ma'arekhet ha'elohut* with the commentary of R. Judah Hayat, which had appeared earlier that year in Ferrara. R. Menahem Tsiyon's commentary on the Torah was printed in Cremona in the same year as the Zohar. R. Joseph Gikatilla's *Sha'arei orah* appeared (together with *Sha'arei tsedek*) in Riva di Trento in 1558/9, and then again in Mantua in 1560/1. In 1560/1 *Sefer hamusar* by R. Judah Khalats, with many kabbalistic annotations by Moses Khalats, was printed in Mantua, and in 1561/2 *Sefer yetsirah* was published. Previously printed kabbalistic works included Recanati's *Perush hatorah* (Venice, 1522/3), and his *Sefer ta'amei hamitsvot* (Constantinople, 1543/4).

[139] On the competition among printers and on the different templates of the Mantua and Cremona editions see Tishby and Lachower, *The Wisdom of the Zohar*, 108–9; Tishby, *Studies*

by the partners R. Meir ben Ephraim of Padua and Jacob ben Naphtali Hakohen of Gazullo, and among the initiators of the publication were the head of the yeshiva of Pesaro, R. Isaac de Lattes, and R. Judah ben Moses de Blanis.[140] The central figures engaged in the preparation of the edition were R. Emmanuel of Benevento (who passed away before the printing was completed), R. Abraham ben Meshulam of Modena, and R. Emmanuel of Corropoli. The Cremona edition was produced in the printing house of the Christian printer Vincenzo Conti by R. Hayim ben Samuel Ibn Gatinyo and the convert Vittorio Eliano (the grandson of R. Elijah Bahur).[141] Both the Mantua and the Cremona editions were arranged according to the portions of the Torah and contained texts on most of the Torah portions from a variety of zoharic layers.

In preparation for their editions, the publishers collected zoharic texts from a variety of sources and consulted several manuscripts. In his book *Livyat ḥen*, printed about a year before *Tikunei hazohar*, R. Emmanuel of Benevento described the compilation of his edition of the Zohar in the following words:

> The words of the divine *tana*, R. Shimon, and his companions, of blessed memory, from which I, though very poor, prepared for you by sword and bow, with great difficulty and expense, all I could afford after the burning of my heart's treasure [the burning of the Talmud]. And with my companions I lost sleep editing them. I had seven manuscripts before me, which I received from the 'holy and mighty ones that are in the land' [Ps. 16: 3] to separate the dross from the silver, a vessel to emerge for the smith [based on Prov. 25: 4].[142]

At the back of the printed edition of *Tikunei hazohar*, R. Jacob of Gazullo states that R. Emmanuel of Benevento had worked from ten manuscripts, which included those he had received from R. Judah ben

in Kabbalah (Heb.), i. 95 n. 54; Benayahu, *Hebrew Printing in Cremona* (Heb.), 121–34; Gries, 'The Image of the Jewish Publishing Editor' (Heb.), 11 n. 63; Abrams, 'When Was the Introduction to the Zohar Written?' (Heb.), 211–18.

[140] On the printing of the Zohar in Mantua see Amram, *The Makers of Hebrew Books in Italy*, 325–7; Tishby and Lachower, *The Wisdom of the Zohar*, i. 97–8; Kupfer, 'New Documents Concerning the Polemic over the Printing of the Zohar' (Heb.), 304–6; Busi, *Mantua and the Kabbalah*, 54–5; *Letters of Jewish Teachers in Renaissance Italy* (Heb.), ed. Boksenboim, 270–2.

[141] On the printing of the Zohar in Cremona see Benayahu, *Hebrew Printing in Cremona* (Heb.), 134–6.

[142] Emmanuel of Benevento, *Livyat ḥen*, 3*a*.

Moses de Blanis and R. Elyakim of Macerata:

[R. Emmanuel was] A poor man of broken spirit, who, in spite of his poverty, took interest in collecting and curating, and spent money in search of anything he could find from the Zohar and the *Tikunim*. Even at night his mind did not rest, and he stood with his students, friends, and admirers to edit them [the zoharic texts] according to the ten manuscripts that he had at his disposal, and which he had been given by exceptional individuals, among them the sage, the renowned physician, a trustworthy person, may his offspring be powerful, the exalted one, our honourable master, R. Judah de Blanis, may God protect and preserve him; and the most exalted one, the pride and glory of the enlightened, a strong foundation and main support for the wisdom and the mission, our honourable master, R. Elyakim of Macerata, may God protect and preserve him.[143]

It seems that the printers of the Mantua edition relied mainly on the collections of Judah ben Moses de Blanis and Elyakim of Macerata, and on one copied by Emmanuel of Benevento himself.[144] R. Emmanuel of Corropoli, in his introduction to the Mantua edition, states that, in addition to these collections, the printers had used an ancient manuscript from Safed:[145]

And it is well known how it used to be, that only one in a town and two in a family [were able] to bring the blessing of the book to their home, and even they did not have all of its wealth in their possession [i.e. all of the five books], therefore we had to expend money to find valuable items, new and old copies of all kinds, because we thought that the more copies we had the more likely we were to publish the perfect version. Our master and teacher, the perfect one, R. Emmanuel of Benevento, edited and adjusted his version according to two clear and straightforward

[143] In Zohar iii. 300*a*, which was printed in 1559/60, Abraham of Modena mentions having used 'five or six copies' of the Zohar. R. Jacob Israel Finzi, who opposed the printing of the Zohar, relates that a manuscript of R. Elyakim of Macerata had been extracted from him under false pretences and against his will; see Assaf, 'The Controversy over the Printing of Kabbalistic Literature' (Heb.), 7.

[144] In his notes on R. Judah Hayat's commentary on *Ma'arekhet ha'elohut*, R. Emmanuel of Benevento mentions a collection he had edited: pp. 79*b*, 101*b*, 112*a*. At the end of the volume Abraham ben Meshulam describes the manuscript that R. Emmanuel had brought with him from Salonica (Zohar iii. 300*a*).

[145] Ronit Meroz has suggested that the 'ancient manuscript' might be Bodleian, Oxford, MS 2512 (F. 22226), which was copied in Safed in the 16th century. See *Headwaters of the Zohar* (Heb.).

copies befitting those who are knowledgeable. Today they are in the possession . . . of the great sage, our master Judah de Blanis, the most noble physician, may God protect and preserve him, the son of our master and teacher the honourable Moses, the most noble physician, of blessed memory; and of our exalted master and teacher R. Elyakim, may God protect and preserve him, the son of our honourable teacher R. Isaiah, of blessed memory, of Macerata, in addition to all the other copies scattered throughout the provinces of Italy. In spite of everything, we did not rest until we found a single old copy from Safed, may it be rebuilt and re-established speedily in our days, on which we relied extensively.[146]

The printers note the importance of the Safed manuscript in other instances, too.[147] The authority of this manuscript (or at least its declaration) was based on the perception that the Zohar had originated in the Upper Galilee, and the highly regarded kabbalistic centre in Safed added to its prestige. In addition to the manuscript from Safed, R. Abraham ben Meshulam mentioned one that R. Emmanuel of Benevento had brought from Salonica, and another given to the printers by R. Elijah Halfan. Halfan's manuscript originated in Egypt and included a complete edition of *Sava demishpatim*, a text that, Abraham ben Meshulam noted, was corrupt in all the other manuscripts he had seen.[148]

The effort involved in collecting and editing texts was also noted in the Cremona edition (146*a*): 'After all of our labour the sacred work has been completed. [This is] all we have found from the Zohar by the divine *tana*, the holy light, R. Shimon ben Yohai, of blessed memory.' In their introduction, the editors claim to have used six manuscripts (relying mainly on two): 'What we have found we saw in six copies, out of which two showed us the way, and many important books we turned into few.'

The Mantua and Cremona editions, like most zoharic manuscripts, follow the order of the Torah portions. The Mantua printers also incorpor-

[146] R. Emmanuel of Corropoli's introduction to the Zohar (i. 2*b*–3*a*).

[147] See the beginning of Zohar 'Vayeḥi', i. 211*b*, where the printers state that the section they produced (211*b*–216*a*) was a section of *Midrash hane'elam* in Hebrew translation, and that it had not been part of the copy that came from Safed. R. Abraham ben Meshulam recounts, at the end of Zohar iii. 300*a*, that in Zohar 'Pinḥas' he had included 'segments that were not found in any copy but the one that had been brought from the holy city of Safed, a city faithful to the wisdom and to the purpose and to anything sacred, and its atmosphere turns people wise'.

[148] Zohar iii. 300*a*.

ated *Tikunei hazohar*, while the printers of Cremona did not (although Ibn Gatinyo, its editor, had included it in his manuscript). The first volume of the Mantua edition began with a section that the printers called *Introduction to the Zohar*, and which appeared in the Cremona edition as part of Zohar 'Bereshit', without any specific marker.[149] Both editions contained sections from *Midrash hane'elam* and *Ra'aya meheimna*, broken up and printed within the different zoharic portions. The printers of Cremona further included parts of Zohar 'Ruth' and *Sefer habahir* in their publication, while the printers of Mantua did not hesitate to incorporate texts that they doubted were zoharic. For example, at the beginning of Zohar 'Vayeḥi' (i. 211*b*–216*a*) they inserted a segment which in their opinion was not part of the Zohar:

The editors say: on the basis of the language it is clear that this is not part of *Sefer hazohar*, as light can be distinguished from darkness. And we think it is from *Midrash hane'elam*. It was written originally in the holy tongue [i.e. Hebrew], and those pretending to be wise changed the original language, and because they did not understand the language and did not know how to use it properly they missed the meaning and the intention of the text, and it turned into an illegible book for those who tried to understand it. And we would have omitted it, since it was not included in the manuscript that came from Safed, may it be rebuilt and re-established speedily in our days, but because of those who would realize it had been omitted and would boast and say that our work was faulty, we printed it as it was, being unable to correct what had been distorted.

The editors allude, of course, to the competition with Cremona. This passage indicates that the printers of the Mantua edition did not consider *Midrash hane'elam* to be part of the Zohar, although they included it in their edition. A similar distinction between the body of the Zohar and other zoharic sections (referred to as *ḥidushim*—novelties) is made on the title page of the Cremona edition:

Sefer hazohar on the Torah, by the man of God, sacred and very awesome, the *tana* R. Shimon ben Yohai, with many innovations [*ḥidushim*], which include *Sitrei torah*, *Midrash hane'elam*, and *Tosefta* on a few portions. And we have added more

149 On the history of this section, its different manuscripts, and its printing, see Abrams, 'When Was the Introduction to the Zohar Written?' (Heb.), 218–26.

innovations than the others on Genesis, all of *Ra'aya meheimna*, the novelties of *Habahir, Midrash ruth, Midrash ḥazit,* and the texts of *Ma'amar ta ḥazei* and *Heikhalot*.[150]

The printers of Cremona explained that their inclusion of *ḥidushim* was a result of the competition with Mantua ('the others') and reflected the desire of both printing houses to produce the most comprehensive edition possible. This aspiration was in conflict with the conception that the Zohar was a *midrash* on the Torah portions, as many of the additional texts could not be seen as commentaries on the Torah. The printers resolved this conflict by incorporating the non-midrashic texts, which did not correspond directly to any Torah portion, into the portions of the Zohar. This tendency had characterized the formulation process of the zoharic collections from their inception, and it can explain why *Idra raba* and *Idra zuta* were placed in portions 'Naso' and 'Ha'azinu' at an early stage of the Zohar's evolution. *Sifra ditseniuta*, which was included in several manuscripts as an independent section, was inserted in the Mantua edition into 'Terumah', and in the Cremona edition into 'Bereshit'. In the case of *Ra'aya meheimna* and *Pikudin* the original literary units were divided up and printed in different Torah portions.

In spite of the aspiration of both the Cremona and Mantua publishers to print the most comprehensive zoharic collection possible, they did not include in their respective editions all of the existing zoharic texts, either because there were some they did not have in their possession, or because they found it impossible to incorporate certain texts into the format of their edition. For example Zohar 'Ruth', parts of which were published in the Cremona edition, was left out of the Mantua one. In 1560 it was printed in Tuhingen by Eli'ezer ben Naftali Treves under the name *Yesod shirim*, without any mention of its link to the zoharic corpus. In 1566/7 Abraham

150 These sections (as well as those that were not mentioned on the title page of this edition) are listed again in the preface and are described as 'supplements' to the 'essential part of the Zohar':

> The rest of the supplements are placed at its feet and are encamped around it . . . *Tosefta* and *Saba, Sifra ditseniuta, Yenuka, Pikuda* [*sic*], *Midrash hane'elam, Midrash ḥazit, Midrash ruth, Bahir, Ma'amar ta ḥazei, Ra'aya meheimna, Heikhalot* . . . and they are mentioned by name in order to distinguish between the essential part of the Zohar and the supplements.

ben Solomon Alon of Safed reprinted it in Venice under the title *Midrash hane'elam* 'Ruth'. Later it was included by R. Joseph Hamitz and R. Moses Zacuto in *Zohar ḥadash* (Venice, 1658/9).

Other zoharic texts that did not make it into the Cremona and Mantua editions, sections from the Torah portions of *Midrash hane'elam* in particular, were printed in Salonica (1597) by Joseph Abraham Bat-Sheva as part of the collection that was later reprinted as *Zohar ḥadash* by Hamitz and Zacuto. The editor of the original collection, R. Naphtali ben Joseph Ashkenazi of Safed, related that the texts had been collected in North Africa and Safed by R. Abraham Halevi, 'who had gathered handfuls [of texts], and sifted through hidden treasures as far as he could reach . . . and followed the reapers and gleaned words, the pure words of the Lord, gathering gleanings, forgotten sheaves, and corner sheaves, a little bit here and a little bit there. He searched, toiled, and found.'

Naphtali ben Joseph had apparently received the collection from Judah Poli, and he had prepared it for print with R. Solomon ben Isaac Hakohen Ashkenazi and R. Moses ben Judah Gedalyah.[151] According to the title page of the first section, the book contained *Midrash hane'elam*, *Tikunim*, and a selection of verses. The title page of the second section lists *Midrash shir hashirim*, Zohar 'Ruth', and part of Zohar 'Lamentations' as its contents.[152]

The printing of the Zohar in the sixteenth century in Cremona, Mantua, and Salonica concluded the formulation process of the zoharic collection and defined the book's scope and shape. Most of the editions published since then have followed the sixteenth-century editions and include three 'books'—*Tikunei hazohar*, Zohar on the Torah (*Zohar al ḥamishah ḥumshei torah*), and *Zohar ḥadash*. Almost all printed editions of Zohar on the Torah have been based on the Mantua edition, with identical

[151] About these sages and their involvement in the printing of *Zohar ḥadash* see Hacker, 'The History of the Study of Kabbalah' (Heb.), 169, 174.

[152] *Zohar ḥadash* (Salonica), 1*a*–4*b*. Printed in this edition under the title 'Verses' are segments that were entitled 'Zohar Song of Songs' in later editions. *Zohar ḥadash* included several sections written by Angelet; see Liebes, *Studies in the Zohar*, 204 n. 298; Meroz, 'R. Joseph Angelet and his "Zoharic Writings"' (Heb.), 304–9. Based on the Salonica edition, *Zohar ḥadash* was reprinted in Kraków in 1603/4—the first time the collection was published under that title. The third edition, which had several additions, such as Zohar 'Ruth', was printed by R. Joseph Hamitz and R. Moses Zacuto in Venice (1658/9). Most of the later editions of *Zohar ḥadash* were based on this one; see Scholem, *Bibliographia Kabbalistica* (Ger.), 175.

pagination—except two seventeenth-century editions, which followed the Cremona Zohar.[153] The seventeenth and eighteenth centuries, however, saw some changes to both the scope and the form of the Zohar. Beginning with the Amsterdam edition of 1715, the printers added to the Mantua-based editions those sections that up until then had only been included in the Cremona edition. Following the publication of the Constantinople edition of 1736–7, annotations and corrections were inserted based on the manuscripts of R. Isaac Luria's disciples.[154] In the 1719 Orta Koj edition of *Tikunei hazohar*, corrections and amendments attributed to R. Hayim Vital were added. Other amendments were made in the Constantinople edition of 1740 by the editor, R. Yeruham ben Jacob of Vilna.[155] Beginning with the publication of the third edition in 1648, produced in Venice by R. Joseph Hamitz and Moses Zacuto, texts were added to *Zohar ḥadash*, including Zohar 'Ruth' and 'Lamentations'.[156]

The zoharic corpus did not develop in a linear, consecutive manner; rather, its evolution was a complex process of editing and distributing manuscripts and printed texts. It took place in different periods and places, and was influenced by a variety of factors, all of which moulded the zoharic corpus into its present format.

As we have seen, the shaping of the zoharic collections started at the beginning of the fourteenth century with the suggestion of the existence of a work called *Sefer hazohar*. Different cultural agents—kabbalists, collectors, copyists, and printers—collected texts that they understood to be segments of this 'book'; from these texts they compiled collections, first in manuscript form and later in print. The compilation of any collection is guided by certain criteria that define which materials will be included and which rejected. The criteria for identifying texts as parts of the Zohar were based on conceptions I have discussed in the previous chapter. According to those conceptions, the Zohar was a kabbalistic homily on the Torah authored by R. Shimon or his disciples. Indeed, most of the texts that were included in the zoharic collections were kabbalistic homilies written in

[153] The Lublin edition of 1623/4–1624/5, and the Sulzbach edition of 1623/4–1624/5. In the latter changes were made according to the Mantua edition. For a list of printed editions of the Zohar see Scholem, *Bibliographia Kabbalistica* (Ger.), 166–82.

[154] See ibid. 168.

[155] Ibid. 177–8; Giller, *The Enlightened Will Shine*, 4.

[156] Scholem, *Bibliographia Kabbalistica* (Ger.), 175.

Aramaic, with R. Shimon and his companions as protagonists. However, the compilers did not strictly abide by these requirements and included texts that did not fit the above criteria yet resembled other zoharic texts, such as portions of *Midrash hane'elam*, the zoharic homilies on Ruth, Lamentations, and Song of Songs, *Tikunei zohar*, *Ra'aya meheimna*, and other sections.

In the formation process of the zoharic corpus exclusion choices were also made. Many additional texts that could have been included in the canon were rejected, such as pseudepigraphic pieces by the so-called *iyun* circle and the writings of thirteenth-century Castilian kabbalists. Works by R. David ben Judah Hehasid, R. Joseph Angelet, and R. Joseph of Hamadan were mostly left out, even though some of them were written in a zoharic style, because they did not meet the above criteria and, more importantly, because they were known to have been composed by their respective authors and not by R. Shimon.

While attempts were made to reject certain texts, ultimately some of them did make their way into the zoharic canon. In the early fourteenth century R. Isaac of Acre declared, for example, that texts written in Hebrew were not part of the Zohar: apparently he 'was taught that whatever was written in the language of the Jerusalem Talmud [Aramaic] were the words of R. Shimon, and anything written in the holy tongue were not his words, rather those of the forger, for the real book was written in the language of the Jerusalem Talmud, all of it.'[157] R. Isaac's view, then, was that in order for texts to be included in the Zohar they had to be attributed to R. Shimon and had to have been written in Aramaic. The forged texts to which he refers are probably the Hebrew segments of *Midrash hane'elam*. However, there is a possibility that he is alluding to other zoharic texts written in Hebrew, such as the Zohar translations of R. David ben Judah Hehasid. R. Isaac was not

[157] Zacuto, *Sefer yuḥasin hashalem*, 88. In his *Otsar haḥayim*, Isaac of Acre reiterates that the Zohar in its entirety was written in Aramaic: 'R. Shimon . . . with his son R. Eleazar and the ten great ones who stayed with him in the cave . . . wrote the whole book of the Zohar in Jerusalem in Aramaic and not in the holy tongue' (*Otsar haḥayim*, Moscow MS, 95*a*). For a discussion of this quote see Liebes, 'Hebrew and Aramaic as Languages of the Zohar', 50–1. Joseph Angelet, too, at the beginning of *Livnat hasapir* (London MS), identifies the language of *Midrash hane'elam* as 'Yerushalmi': 'And this was conveyed in the Jerusalem Aramaic, based on what I drew from the charitable water of *Midrash hane'elam*.'

the only one to doubt that *Midrash hane'elam* was part of the Zohar; the compilers of several other collections discussed above (including R. Moses Cordovero) excluded portions from *Midrash hane'elam* from their anthologies. The printers of both the Mantua and Cremona editions, and of *Zohar ḥadash*, on the other hand, did incorporate segments of *Midrash hane'elam*. As previously mentioned, R. Simeon Ibn Lavi, who did not interpret texts from *Midrash hane'elam* or refer to them in his Zohar commentary, criticized the printers for inserting 'other homilies' into their editions, by which he meant, I believe, segments of that work.

Contrary to the common perception that literary canons are formed through a series of selections and rejections, the zoharic canon was established through a process of multiple gleanings and expansions. Collectors, scribes, and printers gathered texts from different sources and tried to incorporate as many of them as possible into their compilations. The fifteenth-century concept that, rather than being a book, the Zohar was a collection of works referred to as 'the books of Zohar' or 'Rashbi's homilies' further facilitated this process and justified the inclusion of different kabbalistic texts even if they lacked the typical characteristics of the Zohar. As I have shown, sections that had initially been rejected by some editors were later accepted into the printed zoharic canon. Menahem Haran has pointed out that a similar process of collection, rather than selection, had characterized the canonization of biblical books.[158]

This process can be explained by the symbolic value ascribed to the Zohar as an authoritative and sacred text, and by the power it bestowed upon the scholars who collected and compiled the zoharic anthologies. As Pierre Bourdieu has argued, the possession of cultural goods such as paintings, books and dictionaries, instruments, and the like is a form of capital.[159] Books carried a particularly high cultural and economic value before the age of printing, when each manuscript had its unique character and access to books was very limited. The collecting of zoharic texts can thus be viewed as the stockpiling of cultural capital (as well as of goods of significant financial value). The compilers and owners of the zoharic collections saw the possession of texts and the ability to quote from them as a

[158] Haran, *The Biblical Canon* (Heb.), 7, 30–1.

[159] See Bourdieu, 'The Forms of Capital', 243–8.

form of empowerment. Since the scope of the zoharic corpus had not yet been defined, these individuals tried to increase their cultural power by producing editions that were as comprehensive as possible.[160]

Awareness of the cultural power granted by access to the Zohar was expressed by R. Elijah Hayim ben Benjamin of Genazzano (who was acquainted with zoharic texts only through secondary sources): 'And you can trust me when I tell you that none of the later kabbalists is superior to our great teacher R. Menahem [Recanati], because he had obtained a great part of the Zohar and based all his teaching on it.'[161] In R. Elijah's view, Recanati's prominence stemmed from his ability to rely on a more comprehensive zoharic collection than other kabbalists could. His statement, written at the end of the fifteenth century in Italy, explains the trend among kabbalists of the next hundred years to produce comprehensive zoharic collections and to quote from them extensively in their writings.

Since the exalted status of the Zohar increased its power as a source of cultural capital, collectors and compilers naturally made efforts to reaffirm that status. In the early fourteenth century Recanati and Angelet were among the first to produce zoharic collections and to proclaim the Zohar's supremacy. Likewise R. Judah Hayat, a Spanish exile, in recounting the process by which he had collected zoharic material, formulated the most powerful and influential statements about the authority and sacred character of that book (to be discussed in Chapter 4). Similar statements were included in the writings of other kabbalists, as well as in the comments of editors and printers of the Zohar in the first half of the sixteenth century. From the early fourteenth to the second half of the sixteenth century, when Lurianic kabbalah became a prominent force, the Zohar re-

[160] Before the print era the act of copying kabbalistic literature and the possession of these texts, even without any comprehension of their content, carried a symbolic value. This was expressed in R. Isaac Polkar's criticism of kabbalists in his book *Ezer hadat*, written in Burgos in the early 14th century: 'They boast that they perceive such matters without any effort and labour, just by copying books they deem important, which were hidden and concealed in the homes of distinguished sages until God placed them in their hands to be copied' (*Ezer hadat*, rev. Levinger, 156–7). Even if Polkar does not refer to zoharic literature (and I have not found any evidence that he was acquainted with it), his words convey the value ascribed at the time to the copying and owning of 'important' books of kabbalah.

[161] Genazzano, *Igeret ḥamudot*, 5.

mained the kabbalists' main source of authority. Other factors, such as oral transmission (*kabalah*) and supernatural revelation, which had traditionally carried much weight, were hardly mentioned during that period.

The printing of the Zohar brought the book's formulation process to an end. The scope and shape of the canon were all but finalized in the Mantua and Cremona editions, although new texts were included in various editions of *Zohar ḥadash* in the hundred years that followed. Further additions and amendments were made in the eighteenth century. While it was the appearance of the first printed volumes that solidified the zoharic canon, a study of citations and manuscripts reveals that a general consensus regarding the scope of the Zohar had largely been reached before its printing, by the first half of the sixteenth century.

Scholars have discussed the relationship between the authoritative status of canonized texts and their closure. Albert Sundberg, for instance, has defined a canon as a closed, authoritative, and sacred collection of writings from which nothing can be omitted and to which nothing can be added.[162] As I have claimed elsewhere,[163] the closure of canons is linked to their function as sources of authority: when a text is accepted as authoritative, a need arises to delineate its boundaries. The more a text is promulgated as a source of authority, the more urgent it becomes to define its shape and scope. This is especially true when the canonized work had not been created from the start as a unified literary entity but was moulded into one through an editing process. Indeed, the history of the Zohar shows a link between its acceptance as authoritative and sacred and the formation of a general agreement regarding its scope.

The canonization of comprehensive zoharic collections and their distribution later in printed editions diminished the cultural power derived from the possession of such collections. As the Zohar became more readily available and its contents more defined, the practice of collecting, editing, and quoting zoharic texts lost its value; kabbalists could no longer assert their elite status and cultural dominance by possessing and citing such texts. Although the Zohar remained a source of cultural power, new ways

[162] Sundberg, 'Towards a Revised History of the New Testament', 454; Huss, '*Sefer Hazohar* as a Canonical, Sacred and Holy Text', 259 n. 6.

[163] Huss, '*Sefer Hazohar* as a Canonical, Sacred and Holy Text', 259.

were needed to utilize it—by controlling the meaning of its texts through interpretation. Indeed, not long after the printing of the first editions, Zohar commentary became the new principal praxis of the kabbalists. In Chapter 5 I discuss the emergence of such commentary and the means by which scholars established their authority as interpreters of the Zohar. Before embarking on that topic, however, I would like to explore the manifestations of the Zohar's authoritative and sacred status, which reaffirmed its value as a cultural asset, influenced the formation of the zoharic collection, and stimulated the growth of its commentarial literature.

CHAPTER FOUR

The Authority of the Zohar

A lion has roared, who can but fear?
Amos 3: 8

THE SYMBOLIC VALUE of the Zohar depended, to a great extent, on its perception as an authoritative source—one that contained binding prescriptions both in kabbalistic doctrine and in Jewish custom and law. Indeed, shortly after the earliest zoharic texts (which already proclaimed R. Shimon's supremacy) began to circulate and the idea of the Zohar as a book emerged, some kabbalists began to present it as a work of great influence.

From the end of the fifteenth century on, and especially in the early sixteenth century, the Zohar's growing authority was evident, particularly among Sephardi sages. Following the expulsion, its elevation to a place of prominence played a pivotal role in the struggle of the elite circle of Spanish exiles to assert themselves in their new places of settlement. The Zohar was soon accepted as a supreme source of authority in the communities where they exerted their influence. With the proliferation of printing, Spanish Jewish culture also made a considerable impact in eastern European communities.[1] In what follows I discuss the various manifestations of the supremacy of the Zohar and the historical and social contexts that led to its recognition in most Jewish communities in the early modern period.

Declarations concerning the exalted status of the Zohar's protagonists, mainly of R. Shimon, are found in the zoharic literature itself. The choice of R. Shimon for the leading role, his comparison to Moses, and the proclamation of his superiority granted the secrets he conveyed paramount importance. His power surpassed that of other sages because God had

[1] On the influence of Spanish culture on that of Ashkenaz by means of printing, see Reiner, 'The Ashkenazi Élite at the Beginning of the Modern Era', 93.

given him permission to reveal those secrets: 'Come and see—human beings are not permitted to utter hidden words and interpret them, except the holy light, R. Shimon, because the Holy One, blessed be He, gave him permission' (Zohar iii. 149*a*).

The emergence of the idea of the Zohar as a book was instantly followed by proclamations of its authority:

'The Enlightened will shine like the splendour of the firmament': these are R. Shimon bar Yohai and his companions, R. Eleazar his son, R. Abba, R. Jose, R. Hiya, R. Isaac, and the rest of the companions, who have shone above like the splendour of the firmament. What does 'like the splendour' mean? When they wrote this work it was agreed above and [it was] named *Sefer hazohar* [Book of Splendour]. (*Tikunei hazohar*, 17*a*)

In some works of the early fourteenth century, zoharic texts are quoted as definitive interpretations of the Torah. The author of *Likutei kabalah* (JTS, New York, MS 1768) juxtaposes a zoharic commentary on Moses' sin at the waters of strife (*mei merivah*), attributed to R. Shimon, with that of Nahmanides, and argues that R. Shimon's interpretation is superior: 'These matters are profound, and they do not agree with the explanation of Nahmanides, of blessed memory. Rather, questions should be asked and [answers should be derived] from the mouth of R. Shimon ben Yohai, of blessed memory.'[2] In his book *Perush sha'arei orah* R. Joseph Angelet states that the zoharic commentary on God's thirteen attributes of mercy is superior to that of Nahmanides and other kabbalists: 'This interpretation follows the method of *Midrash hane'elam* [i.e. the Zohar] in the *Idra*. Even though Nahmanides, of blessed memory, did not explain it in this way, nor did the rest of the kabbalists, we must accept the words of the *tana'im*, the eternal pillars of the world.'[3] Like Angelet, R. Menahem Recanati, too, often quoted zoharic texts as authoritative sources.

As we have seen, the purpose of the proclamations made by the kabbalists outside the Nahmanidean circle regarding the importance of the Zohar was to subvert the Catalan school. Claiming a higher status for the Zohar and for R. Shimon than for Nahmanides and his Torah commentary, these kabbalists collected, edited, and quoted zoharic texts to establish their own cultural power.

[2] *Likutei kabalah*, 105*b*.

[3] Angelet, *Perush sha'arei orah*, 33*b*–34*a*.

The reliance on zoharic texts and the propagation of R. Shimon's as well as the Zohar's authority seldom characterize sources from the second half of the fourteenth or the early fifteenth centuries. Among the few scholars who do quote zoharic texts during this period are R. Menahem Tsiyon and R. Shem Tov ibn Shem Tov. Tsiyon, who was active at the end of the fourteenth century in Germany, Palestine, and Italy, listed the Zohar, *Sefer habahir*, and *Sefer yetsirah* as the principal sources for his commentary on the Torah, referring to them as 'three rows of hewn stones and cedar beams'. However, unlike the kabbalists mentioned above, he never claimed that the Zohar was superior to Nahmanides' commentary. On the contrary, in his own commentary he indicates that Nahmanides' work was his main source: 'The source of the book—its shape and content—are based on the Nahmanidean river bed.'[4] R. Shem Tov ibn Shem Tov, who lived in Spain in the early fifteenth century, often quoted zoharic texts, stating, 'One should follow the kabbalah of R. Shimon ben Yohai.'[5]

The influence of the Zohar grew significantly towards the end of the fifteenth century. As Moshe Idel has argued, proclamations of its importance within the circle of *Sefer hameshiv* indicate that even before the expulsion from Spain the authority of zoharic literature had been established.[6] It was granted similar status by various other circles at the time; a Spanish rabbi, Isaac Arama, concluded a long zoharic quotation (referenced as *Midrash hane'elam*) with the following dramatic statement:

> Lend your ear to the holy sage whose mouth pours forth gems, and it will revive your spirit. Although his themes are deep and old, he pondered and sought out and set in order many true and valuable maxims, to open eyes deprived of light concerning the interpretation of our sacred, profound, and vast Torah, and to free the human mind from the bondage of dark material veils, to be elevated from the bottom to the middle level and from the middle level to the top.[7]

[4] Tsiyon, *Commentary on the Torah*, introduction (Heb.). He mentions other sources as well, such as *Keter shem tov*, *Sefer haḥayim*, *Sha'arei tsedek*, and *Sha'arei orah*.

[5] See Ariel, 'Shem-Tov ibn Shem-Tov's Kabbalistic Critique of Jewish Philosophy', 87. The phrase originally appeared, in slightly different wording, in the Talmud: 'R. Shimon is worthy enough to be relied upon in a time of pressing need' (*Ber.* 9*a*); 'R. Shimon ben Yohai is worthy of being relied upon in his presence as well as in his absence' (*Pes.* 51*b*).

[6] Idel, 'Neglected Writings of the Author of *Kaf haketoret*' (Heb.), 82. Very little is known about the circle of *Sefer hameshiv*, a group of kabbalists that was probably active in Spain before the expulsion.

[7] Arama, *Akedat yitsḥak*, 'Bereshit', gate 7, 1*b*.

In his book *Ḥazut kashah*, Arama wrote in the same context: 'And the godlike R. Shimon ben Yohai delivered us kabbalah signed with his mighty seal.'[8] R. Isaac Mar Hayim, a Spanish kabbalist active in Italy in the late fifteenth century, based his proclamations of R. Shimon's eminence as a kabbalist on the revelations he had been granted by Elijah: 'In this wisdom we should trust R. Shimon more than anyone else since he was regularly visited by Elijah.'[9] Further assertions of the Zohar's authority concerning Jewish customs and laws are included in some responsa attributed to R. Joseph Gikatilla, also written before the expulsion from Spain.

A larger number of statements regarding the Zohar's authority are found in the works of Spanish sages following the expulsion. One such proclamation, which became highly influential, appears in R. Judah Hayat's early sixteenth-century commentary on *Ma'arekhet ha'elohut*, written in Italy:

Blessed and privileged are we to be awarded the Zohar, which our ancestors, whose little finger was thicker than our loins, were not awarded . . . and if one says that its wisdom contains matters alien to reason, it is as the holy, godlike R. Shimon ben Yohai said: 'Not every brain is fit for it, only the holy and wise ones [can], etc.'[10] In any event, we should have total confidence in its words 'because it is not a trifling thing' [Deut. 32: 47], and if it seems a trifle it is because of our own incompetence, and we must truly and wholeheartedly accept their words, and set them as a crown upon our heads and say: 'Even if my heart turns right or left,[11] [I will]

[8] *Ḥazut kashah*, gate 10, printed in Arama's *Akedat yitsḥak*, vi. 19*a* (in my numbering; BH).

[9] Nadav, 'An Epistle of the Kabbalist Isaac Mar Hayim' (Heb.), 455. In his letter Mar Hayim says: 'I wish to copy for your Excellency a text I have found in the Zohar and which has set us free from all perplexity. Had the above rabbi seen it as well as the sage R. Menahem Recanati, of blessed memory, there is no doubt in my mind that neither of them would have held to their opinion. Rather, they would have abandoned the teachings of all the sages they had known, as well as their kabbalah, to pursue the teachings of R. Shimon ben Yohai, of blessed memory, who is considered superior in this wisdom to all the sages of the generation, as we have learnt from his books of secrets' (ibid. 456). He further wrote: 'Therefore, one should move away from it towards the prophetic kabbalah, like that of R. Shimon bar Yohai, for Elijah, may he rest in peace, regularly attended his school' (ibid. 456–8). The tradition that Elijah taught R. Shimon also appears in *Sefer hameshiv*: see Idel, 'Enquiries into the Doctrine of *Sefer hameshiv*' (Heb.), 240. About this tradition in the Lurianic kabbalah see ibid. 241.

[10] Based on *tikun* 69; *Tikunei hazohar*, 116*a*.

[11] This phrase alludes to *Sifrei*, Deut. 17: 11: 'Right and left. Even if they show you left that is right and right that is left, listen to them.'

follow the beliefs of the godlike holy light, the pride of the *tana'im* and the crown of the sages, superior to a prophet, Shimon ben Yohai and his companions'.[12]

Hayat takes R. Ishmael's famous saying regarding the interpretation of the Torah and applies it to the Zohar: 'It is not a trifling matter for you. Sometimes it seems a trifle because you do not know how to expound it.'[13] He states that the words of the Zohar must be followed even if they contradict reason. His somewhat apologetic comment regarding cases in which the zoharic text contradicts reason was probably made in response to the rationalist criticism of some of his contemporaries in Italy.

In his conclusion Hayat alludes to the end of R. Yedayah ben Abraham Bedersi's (Hapenini) book *Beḥinat olam*, first printed in Mantua a few years earlier, in which the author proclaims that the words of Maimonides are the ultimate criteria for truth: 'In the end, whether the heart turns right or left one should follow the words of the last of the geonim by chronology but the first among them by importance, the great master and teacher Maimonides, of blessed memory, to whom none among the sages of Israel can be compared, since the closure of the Talmud.'[14] In contrast to Bedersi, a philosopher living in Provence at the turn of the thirteenth and fourteenth centuries, Hayat sees the Zohar, not Maimonides, as the most reliable source of knowledge. It seems that, in paraphrasing Bedersi's statement and using it to declare the Zohar's authority, Hayat is expressing his polemical stance towards philosophy.

The claim that the Zohar is the criterion for the validity of beliefs and opinions recurs in statements made by other kabbalists in the early sixteenth century. R. Joseph Alashkar, a Spanish exile active in Fez, states, for instance, that, based on what is written in the Zohar and in the works of Nahmanides, he is compelled to accept the doctrine of the transmigration

[12] *Ma'arekhet ha'elohut*, 2*b* (R. Judah Hayat's preface). In the book Hayat emphasizes that the authority of the Zohar exceeds that of *Ma'arekhet ha'elohut*: 'May His Honour the rabbi pardon me. This is a philosophical study, not real knowledge from R. Shimon ben Yohai, of blessed memory, and his companions' (ibid. 159*b*). Elsewhere he writes: 'Now I will gird up my loins to confront the rabbi over this homily and say that I wish I knew who led him to this opinion. For it contradicts most of the kabbalists and the Zohar' (ibid. 165*b*). However, he praises the author of *Ma'arekhet ha'elohut* whenever he agrees with the Zohar: 'Pay attention, brother, to what the rabbi says regarding unification, for his words are concise, proper, and in agreement with the Zohar' (ibid. 206*a*).

[13] *Bereshit rabah* 1: 14.

[14] Bedersi, *Beḥinat olam*, ch. 17, p. 85.

of souls, despite his reservations:

As for the claim that the secret of transmigration is one of the most concealed secrets among the mysteries of the world, had I not feared the companions, I would have followed R. Abraham Hehasid, son of Maimonides, of blessed memory, who argued that it is an alien idea and one should not believe in it . . . it would have been appropriate for me not to take sides or discuss it at all, since I am not worthy of being counted among the decision-makers and should not be caught up in any dispute. I cannot help, however, but speak out and follow the beliefs of the holy light, R. Shimon ben Yohai, of blessed memory, and also those of the great teacher, the high mountain, Nahmanides, of blessed memory, for the reasons mentioned above.[15]

Like Hayat (and probably under his influence), Alashkar bows to the Zohar's authority despite the fact that, from a rationalist point of view, he agrees with R. Abraham Hehasid. In contrast to the fourteenth-century kabbalists who juxtaposed Nahmanides' status with that of the Zohar, Alashkar affirms his commitment to both, and shows them more reverence than the philosophical sources that oppose the idea of transmigration of the soul. His proclamations, like Hayat's, are part of a polemic between the kabbalistic point of view and the rationalist-philosophical one. Although in the above quotation Alashkar seems to equate the weight of the Zohar with that of Nahmanides, in what follows he emphasizes the superiority of the Zohar: 'And even though the aforementioned sages do not believe in transmigration and explain it according to their understanding, we have nothing but the words of the holy light, of blessed memory, who certainly confirms the belief in transmigration.'[16]

A similar point of view, which prohibits any deviation from the words of the Zohar, appears in *Sod hatefilin* by R. Abraham Tsabah, who was probably identical with the exiled Spanish kabbalist and Torah commentator Abraham Saba:

And it is forbidden to deviate from his [R. Shimon's] words because they are the words of the living God, the king of the universe, and they are sweeter than honey and the honeycomb, for he was granted permission from above, which has not been given to any other sage in this world, and the Holy One, blessed be He,

[15] Idel, 'R. Judah Haliwah and His Book *Tsafenat pane'aḥ*' (Heb.), 64*b*–65*a*; ibid., introduction, 54–5.

[16] Ibid. 65*b*.

granted him authority. And his status in comparison to that of other sages is parallel to the status of the prophecy of Moses, our teacher, may he rest in peace, in comparison to that of the rest of the prophets.[17]

Tsabah alludes here to the comparison (in the Zohar and *Tikunei hazohar*) of Moses to R. Shimon, and to the exclusive permission the latter was granted to reveal secrets. Elsewhere he refers to R. Shimon as a lion: 'If the Kedushah [prayer] is recited in Aramaic it does not require [the presence of] ten [men]. This is the opinion of R. Shimon, of blessed memory, the great lion—"A lion has roared, who can but fear?" [Amos 3: 8].'[18] In the responsa attributed to Joseph Gikatilla, written probably in the fifteenth century, the same verse from Amos is used in reference to the Zohar: 'And if that is the Zohar's opinion, "A lion has roared, who can but fear?"'[19] Similar expressions occur in the annotations of R. Moses Khalats to R. Judah Khalats's *Sefer hamusar* (Constantinople, 1536/7).[20] It should be noted that, while Hayat and Alashkar emphasize the primacy of the Zohar in matters of faith and outlook, Tsabah, Khalats, and the responder in the responsa attributed to Gikatilla defer to it in matters of custom and law as well, a subject that I explore later.

Other kabbalists in the sixteenth century followed Hayat's position regarding the mandated authority of the Zohar. R. Solomon Alkabets, in his *Sefer berit halevi*, juxtaposed the zoharic commentary on the words 'law' and 'judgement' with those of R. Joseph Gikatilla and R. David ben Judah Hehasid. Although Alkabets was inclined to agree with the latter's commentary, he argued that it was imperative to accept the Zohar's dictum: 'Nevertheless we will dismiss our opinion and accept what it says because it is supernal.'[21]

[17] Isaac of Acre, *Otsar haḥayim*, Moscow MS, 65*b*–66*a*. Tsabah's *Sod hatefilin* and *Sod hakedushah* (his commentary on the Kedushah) are scattered throughout the manuscript of *Otsar haḥayim*. The beginning of *Sod hakedushah*, for example, appears on pp. 120*b* and 65*a*.

[18] Isaac of Acre, *Otsar haḥayim*, Moscow MS, 65*a*. References to R. Shimon as 'the lion' originated in *Bava metsia* 84*b*, where R. Eleazar, his son, is referred to as 'a lion son of a lion'. The use of the verse 'A lion has roared, who can but fear | the Lord God has spoken who can but prophesy?' to establish authority is found in the Zohar, too, where it says: 'R. Shimon ben Yohai is a lion, and R. Eleazar is a son of a lion, but R. Shimon is not an ordinary lion. Of him it is written: "A lion has roared, who can but fear," etc. And if the upper worlds tremble because of him, we, even more so' (Zohar ii. 15*a*).

[19] See Gikatilla, *Teshuvot*, 59*b*.

[20] *Sefer hamusar*, Constantinople edn., 100; Mantua edn., 46*b*.

[21] Alkabets, *Berit halevi*, 21*a*.

Hayat's claim that one should never deviate from the Zohar, as well as Tsabah's statement that everything written in the Zohar is divine, reappear in *Galya raza*, written by an anonymous kabbalist in 1551/2.[22] The author of that work states that one must rely on R. Shimon's words in the Zohar: 'Since R. Shimon, may he rest in peace, satisfies any intelligent person with solid reasoning to support his words, the majority of the world has followed him and one should not turn right or left because his words are the words of the living God.'[23] The letters of the Italian sage R. Mordecai Dato to R. Ezra of Fano reiterate Hayat's position that the Zohar is the absolute measure of truth within kabbalah: 'We have nothing else but the words of R. Shimon, may he rest in peace, and those of his companions and disciples, and all that is written in the book of life—the Zohar—and by them we dwell within the secrets of kabbalah.'[24] Dato visited the Land of Israel in 1560 and reported that the Safed kabbalists followed the same principle:

> All that the sages of Safed, may it be rebuilt and re-established speedily, and may God protect and preserve them, utter in the principles of the Wisdom of Truth and Justice [i.e. kabbalah] is based on the Zohar. Their words are its words emerging from its splendour; and without it [the Zohar] no one would dare to offer the fruits of his study and the results of his investigations in this wisdom.[25]

Once established as a primary source of truth, by implication the Zohar could contain no contradictions. Indeed, hand in hand with proclamations of its absolute authority, statements were made to that effect. R. Moses Basola, in his ruling in support of the printing of the Zohar, asserts, for instance: 'The Zohar should not be concealed because it is all about the fear of God and it contains no contradictions.'[26] This claim was frequently repeated by sixteenth-century Zohar commentators, who then took enormous pains to resolve the conflicting opinions found within the book.[27]

[22] Regarding the place of origin of *Galya raza* and the identity of its author, see Rachel Elior's introduction to *Galya raza*, ed. Elior, 7–14; Tishby, *Messianism in the Time of the Expulsion* (Heb.), 150–63.

[23] *Galya raza*, ed. Elior, 123.

[24] Benayahu, 'R. Ezra of Fano' (Heb.), 845.

[25] Ibid. 841–2.

[26] Basola's statement was printed in the preface of *Tikunei hazohar* (Mantua edn.).

[27] R. Mordecai Dato writes that the sages of Safed granted the Zohar supreme authority and only used rational considerations to resolve cases in which the Zohar appeared to contradict itself: 'And although their wisdom was profound and their ability to debate was great they did not rely on it in their commentary except in a few cases, in which the statements in the Zohar appear to contradict each other' (Benayahu, 'R. Ezra of Fano' (Heb.), 842).

R. Solomon Alkabets, in his response to a question by R. Joseph Karo, comments on a passage in the Zohar regarding the burial of *tsadikim* in the Land of Israel: 'One should not believe that what is unfit for any author, that is to say, that he contradicts himself and does not follow proper grammar, can be applied to the divine R. Shimon, may he rest in peace.'[28] The argument that the Zohar was free of contradictions was directed at the book's critics and had an apologetic undertone. In *Sefer berit halevi* Alkabets states, for example:

And I have told you already many times that those contradictions in the statements of R. Shimon, may he rest in peace, caused many to go astray and to believe, God forbid, in what one should not believe in. Thus they turned their back on him and did not accept him. Therefore, it is our duty to investigate it thoroughly because everything that the divine one and his companions said has been accepted by the wise and renowned sages, and blessed be He who distinguishes us from those who have gone astray.[29]

One of the first Zohar commentators, R. Simeon Ibn Lavi, expressed similar thoughts in his late sixteenth-century work *Ketem paz*:

And now I come to teach you the way to see the light in what they, may they rest in peace, say, so that it will not occur to you to think that they say one thing on one occasion and something else on another, as those who do not believe in their words think. Indeed, all they say is true and just. And if sometimes you think there is a contradiction in what they say, accept responsibility, for you have not fully understood what they said, and you should ask someone who can explain it to you. And if you cannot find anyone, do not rush to anger.[30]

In R. Hayim Vital's view it is Lurianic kabbalah that holds the key to the resolution of these apparent contradictions:

After all the preambles we have offered, we must make the student of the Zohar aware of the many different and disputed statements it contains, and which [appear to] contradict one another. Without these [i.e. Isaac Luria's] prefaces the resolution [of the apparent contradictions] would elude the student, as it does those who feign wisdom and try to comprehend the Zohar by means of their

[28] Alkabets, *Berit halevi*, 39*b*.

[29] *Sefer berit halevi*, 9*a*. See too Sack, 'Exile and Redemption in Solomon Alkabets's *Berit halevi*' (Heb.), 269 n. 20; Huss, *Sockets of Fine Gold* (Heb.), 52.

[30] *Ketem paz*, i. 8*a*. See also Huss, *Sockets of Fine Gold* (Heb.), 51–2.

human intellect. Their error stems from their inability to distinguish between the different divine spheres to which each statement refers.[31]

The Zohar's authority was not only recognized in explicit proclamations but was also manifested in, and further strengthened by, the proliferation of zoharic commentaries and quotations, as well as rulings on custom and law that were based on its teachings.

Zohar citation became particularly widespread in the first half of the sixteenth century, especially among exiled Sephardi kabbalists, as I have demonstrated. Abraham Saba (Tsabah), whose proclamation of the authority of the Zohar was discussed above, stated in his Torah commentary *Tseror hamor* (Venice, 1514) that the Zohar had been the principal source for his book: 'Now pay attention to what the holy R. Shimon, of blessed memory, wrote, because that is the very foundation, and everything I say in this book revolves around his words and his opinion, which is the true wisdom.'[32]

Similar views were expressed by another Spanish exile, R. Meir Ibn Gabai. In *Tola'at ya'akov*, his commentary on the prayer book, written in Turkey in 1507 and first printed in Constantinople in 1560, he stated:

And the huge tamarisk on which I rely is the book that is famous among the real sages of Israel—a *midrash* by R. Shimon, may he rest in peace, in which he courageously reveals secrets of the Torah, something that no one but he was allowed to do . . . Therefore I study his teachings, infatuated with love of him, and based on his gems I write this book.[33]

Joseph Alashkar, yet another exiled Spanish kabbalist, who settled in North Africa and relied heavily on the Zohar, wrote in the introduction to his book *Tsafenat pane'aḥ*: 'At that time I decided to investigate and explore new and old books of the sages, especially the book of the holy light,

[31] *Sha'ar hahakdamot*, 3.

[32] *Tseror hamor*, 10c (Lev. 14: 35). See also his statement in *Tiferet banim*, printed in the same book, 'Out of all these books I have constructed it and completed it, and founded it on the [words of the] movers of mountains in the Zohar' (*Tseror hamor*, ed. Weichelder, i. 179). See also the colophon in the manuscript quoted by Gross in *Iberian Jewry*, 19: 'I beseech a sage of any kind if lovely fawns he does find here in this book, or a good catch on my hook, know that all I have I took from the Midrash or from the holy R. Shimon's book.'

[33] *Tola'at ya'akov*, 4b.

R. Shimon ben Yohai, infatuated by loving him and overwhelmed by study of his teachings.'[34]

It should be noted that use of the Zohar was not limited to written texts, but was also common in oral homilies—for example in those of R. Joseph Garson, a Spanish exile, whose first sermon after settling in Salonica in 1500 began with a quotation from that revered work.[35]

Recognition of the Zohar as the main source of kabbalistic authority, even if not explicit, characterized most kabbalistic works of the first half of the sixteenth century and many others written later. In the earlier texts it is mainly the frequent quotations that indicate the Zohar's prominence, while in the later period the proliferation of its commentaries attests to this fact (these commentaries will be discussed extensively in the next chapter).

As mentioned above, it was not only in the theological realm that the Zohar's influence became evident, but also in the fields of law and custom. Already at a very early stage of the reception of the Zohar, Moses de León, in his work *Shekel hakodesh*, based himself on a passage he claimed to have found in *Midrash yerushalmi*, and which has a parallel in Zohar 'Ruth', in ruling that the cantor should repeat the words *adonai eloheikhem emet* in order to complete the count of 248 words of the Shema.[36] R. Shem Tov Ibn Gaon recounted in *Migdal oz* that he had changed the order of the Torah passages in his *tefilin* in light of a 'concealed and hidden *midrash*' he had found. He seems to be referring here to the Zohar: 'And a spirit from above aroused us; and we found a concealed and hidden *midrash*; and we needed to change what we held and understood and thought to be the correct

[34] Idel, 'R. Judah Haliwah and His Book *Tsafenat pane'aḥ*' (Heb.), 13*b*. Alashkar states at the end of his book: 'Thus, with God's help, the planned commentary has been completed. . . . I gleaned it one in a town and two in a family, and most of it was taken from the Zohar' (ibid. 228*a*). R. Hayim Obadiah di Bozzolo, a Spanish exile who settled in Salonica, also mentioned the importance of the Zohar in *Be'er mayim ḥayim*, published in 1545/6: 'And in this little work, which focuses on the study of things that improve a man's soul . . . I took long and short ways—gleanings after gleanings; gleaning forgotten sheaf and corner, to graze in gardens, the orchards of the true sages, of blessed memory, and to glean the lilies of R. Shimon, may he rest in peace' (*Be'er mayim ḥayim*, 7*b*).

[35] See Benayahu, 'The Sermons of Joseph ben Meir Garson' (Heb.), 57, 134; Hacker, 'The Immigration of Spanish Jews to the Land of Israel' (Heb.), 52–3.

[36] *Sefer shekel hakodesh*, ed. Mopsik, 84–5, and cf. *Zohar ḥadash*, 78*d*. See also Ta-Shma, '*El melekh ne'eman*: The Development of a Custom' (Heb.), 191–3.

order.'[37] Recanati cites the Zohar in his commentary on the liturgy: 'In addition, our sages said in the Zohar that a man needs to wrap himself in his *talit* before putting on his *tefilin*',[38] and he, too, makes reference to the statement in Zohar 'Ruth' regarding the cantor's repetition of the words *adonai eloheikhem emet*.[39] Along with Recanati and de León, R. David Abudraham also quoted this passage in his commentary on the liturgy, written in Seville in 1340.[40]

Many other examples of reliance on the Zohar regarding laws and customs appear in works from the fifteenth century. We may recall, for example, the Romaniote sage R. Yohanan ben Reuben of Ohrid, who quoted zoharic texts in his commentary on Ahai Gaon's *She'iltot*, and mandated three meals on the sabbath based on the Zohar, arguing that 'he [R. Shimon] is more knowledgeable than we are'.[41] The author of the responsa attributed to R. Joseph Gikatilla, written probably in fifteenth-century Spain,[42] based himself on the Zohar more than once in halakhic questions; and in the sixth responsum, regarding the removal of *tefilin* during *musaf* on Rosh Hodesh, he unequivocally declared the Zohar's authority:

> Certainly we are not involved in this matter, and we have not seen anyone who follows this practice. We have only heard from those who were told by those who follow this custom that it is the opinion [expressed] in the Zohar, on which they rely. And they gave a reason for it, saying that because *musaf* is the secret of the holy spirit and the head *tefilin* is the secret of the matter itself, thus it is removed during *musaf*. And if it is [thus stated] in the Zohar—a lion has roared, who can but fear? And the reason makes sense.[43]

[37] *Migdal oz*, 'Hilkhot tefilin', iii. 5. He might be referring to *Pikudin*, Zohar ii. 43*a*–*b*.

[38] Recanati, *Perush hatefilot*, 40*b*; Zohar iii. 120*b*; Hallamish, *Kabbalah in Liturgy, Halakhah, and Customs* (Heb.), 301.

[39] Recanati, *Perush hatefilot*, 42*a*, 83*b*.

[40] Abudraham, *Perush haberakhot vehatefilot*, 77–8; Ta-Shma, '*El melekh ne'eman*: The Development of a Custom' (Heb.), 188.

[41] Ahai Gaon, *She'iltot derav aḥai gaon*, ed. Mirsky, i. 7, *she'ilta a* (based on Zohar iii. 288*b*); Ta-Shma, 'On Greek Byzantine Rabbinic Literature' (Heb.), 106.

[42] Scholem dates the text to the late 14th or early 15th century; see his 'Responsa Attributed to Joseph Gikatilla' (Heb.), 2. For Benayahu's view that it is of a later period see 'The Dispute between Kabbalah and Halakhah' (Heb.), 63.

[43] Gikatilla, *Teshuvot*, 59*b*. The version printed in Scholem's 'Responsa Attributed to Joseph Gikatilla' (Heb.), 7, is flawed. The errors reappear in Benayahu's 'The Dispute between Kabbalah and Halakhah' (Heb.), 64.

In his discussion of sexual relations in the *sukah*, the same author rules: 'We have heard from true emissaries that according to the Zohar it is forbidden, and if the Zohar forbids, who can allow it?'[44] Interestingly, in neither of the above cases was the author of the responsum familiar with the zoharic source, yet he relied on it. A similar example is R. Isaac Abuhav, who, at the end of the fifteenth century, also granted authority to the Zohar without being personally acquainted with its text, and deferred to it rather than to the major halakhic decisors (*posekim*). The following is his comment on wearing a prayer shawl on the eve of the sabbath and holidays:

And also with regard to the fringed garment, that the person who wraps himself in it stirs up judgment—for that reason, according to the sages of the Zohar, one should never wrap himself in it at night . . . And those *posekim* who allow it do not know the right way . . . And I wonder where those who permit it found an authoritative source on which they can rely. Since the Talmud does not mention it and the Zohar and the kabbalists forbid it, where did they find authorization?[45]

The principle that the Zohar's ruling overrides that of the *posekim* reappears in the works of Spanish sages in the late fifteenth and early sixteenth centuries. In a responsum sent by the rabbinic court in Jerusalem to R. Moses Ashkenazi in 1467, the Zohar is cited as the source for their preference of *yibum* (levirate marriage) over *ḥalitsah* (the removal of the brother-in-law's shoe as part of the law of the levirate), based on the kabbalistic theory of the transmigration of souls. The correspondence was signed by R. Gedalyah ibn Emmanuel, a Spanish sage who probably served as the presiding judge: 'And if it is [based on] kabbalah, a judge cannot reject it, especially after we found this to be the opinion of R. Shimon ben Yohai, the best among the *tana'im*, as well as the opinion of other *tana'im* and *amora'im*.'[46]

A contemporary Spanish rabbi, Joseph ben Tsadik, in his book *Zekher*

[44] Scholem, 'Responsa Attributed to Joseph Gikatilla' (Heb.), 8.

[45] Ibid. 4; Kadosh, 'Kabbalistic Jewish Laws in Responsa' (Heb.), 61. This ruling is not included in the Zohar but Meir Kadosh has found a similar law in *Ma'arekhet ha'elohut*, 133*a*. In his view the attack on halakhists for allowing worshippers to wrap themselves in a *talit* at night was mainly aimed at Jacob ben Asher, author of the *Arba'ah turim*; see 'Kabbalistic Jewish Laws in Responsa' (Heb.), 62–3.

[46] Published by Hacker in 'The Immigration of Spanish Jews to the Land of Israel' (Heb.), 153.

tsadik, cites the Zohar regarding a few halakhic issues, including the number of blessings one is required to recite while putting on *tefilin*.[47] He is also the first to mention, to the best of my knowledge, the prohibition, found in Zohar 'Song of Songs', on donning *tefilin* during the intermediate days of festivals, an issue that played a major role in the history of the recognition of the Zohar's halakhic authority.[48] A further example from the late fifteenth century is the Ashkenazi sage Jacob Landau, who treats the Zohar as a prominent halakhic work in his *Sefer ha'agur*: in section 84 he refers to 'three rulings in the Zohar regarding *tsitsit* and *tefilin* that do not exist in any book of the *posekim* known to us'.[49] From the following comment it is clear that, in his view, the *posekim* should have accepted the position of the Zohar: 'And I, the writer, have found in the Zohar, portion "Pinḥas", that one should not bless over both [the *talit* and the *tefilin*] but make only one blessing . . . and I wonder if those great men who disagree with R. Shimon are aware of this text. Anyway, the custom is to make two blessings.'[50]

R. Isaac Abuhav of Castile, who was exiled from Spain in 1492 and passed away in Portugal a year later, based his opinion on the Zohar more than once in his commentary on *Arba'ah turim*, 'Oraḥ ḥayim'.[51] Citing *Midrash hane'elam*, he mentioned the prohibition on donning *tefilin* during the intermediate days of festivals and added that 'this ruling has already spread to many places'.[52] Like some of the above-mentioned rabbis, he deferred to the Zohar even when relying only on hearsay. For example, with regard to the Torah reading during the synagogue service, he proclaimed: 'I have heard that it is written in *Midrash hane'elam*, which is the Zohar, that only one person should read it. And if indeed [it is true], for I have not seen it written, only heard about it, it should be obeyed.'[53]

The perception of the Zohar as a significant source of law and custom is evident in the writings of several Spanish sages of the exiled generation. R. Joseph Karo recounts that R. Jacob Ibn Habib, one of the greatest halakhic experts who settled in Salonica after the expulsion, was willing to include that work in his halakhic considerations.[54] Karo further cites his

47 *Zekher tsadik*, ed. Shoshanah and Spiegel, 37.
48 Ibid.
49 *Sefer ha'agur hashalem*, 'Hilkhot tefilin', 27–8.
50 Ibid. 36.
51 Rabinowitz, 'Rabbi I. Abuhav's Method of Talmud Commentary' (Heb.), 387–94.
52 Ibid. 389.
53 Ibid. 394.
54 'And our great master, R. Jacob Ibn Habib, wrote that he had heard kabbalists say that, in

uncle, R. Isaac Karo, as stating that the Spanish sages abandoned their custom, based on the ruling of Rabbenu Asher, of donning *tefilin* on the intermediate days of festivals when they became aware that it was prohibited in *Midrash hazohar*.[55] R. Abraham Zacuto acknowledged the authority of the Zohar in his book *Sefer yuḥasin*, which he completed in the first decade of the sixteenth century, and proclaimed: 'it has been established in Israel that anything that does not contradict the Talmud and is not stated explicitly in it, yet is stated explicitly there [in the Zohar], should be accepted.'[56] Zacuto asserts that the Zohar was written by the disciples of R. Shimon's disciples and its authority in halakhic matters stems from the principle of *halakhah kebatra'ei* (the law is according to later generations): 'Therefore the words of the Zohar are more reliable because they are the words of the later sages, who were acquainted with the Mishnah and its rulings as well as the statements of the *amora'im*.'[57] To illustrate his point Zacuto mentions the Zohar's prohibition on replying 'amen' to the blessing 'Ge'al yisra'el'; the requirement of Kiddush at the third meal; the prohibition on donning *tefilin* during the intermediate days of a festival; and the ruling that, when Grace after Meals is recited by one person only, there is no requirement for a cup of wine (which would be the case if several men said grace together).[58]

Abraham Saba (Tsabah) often turned to the Zohar regarding questions of custom and halakhah in his commentary on the liturgy as well as in *Tseror hamor*, his famous Torah commentary.[59] So did R. Meir Ibn Gabai, who, in his commentary *Tola'at ya'akov*, made the following statement on the question of audible prayers:

light of what they had found in the Zohar, it was forbidden to make two blessings. He was shown those articles, and he realized that they did not support such a view, and one kabbalist showed him statements that support the practice of two blessings' (*Beit yosef*, 'Oraḥ ḥayim', 28).

55 Karo, *Responsa*, 385. 56 *Sefer yuḥasin hashalem*, 45. 57 Ibid.

58 Ibid. On the zoharic sources of these rulings see Katz, *Halakhah and Kabbalah* (Heb.), 61–2. It should be noted that in all cases in which Zacuto juxtaposed the opinion of the Zohar with that of Rabbenu Asher (Rosh) (as well as other authorities, the most important being Maimonides), the opinion of the Zohar prevailed.

59 With regard to eating meat after dairy products, for instance, he wrote: 'Although the sages established time spans concerning this matter, R. Shimon, of blessed memory, stated that just as it is forbidden to eat dairy after meat, it is forbidden to eat meat after dairy. The same rule applies to both. Regarding the time span it takes for the food to be digested . . . about six hours, which is the interval between one meal and the next' (Saba, *Tseror hamor*, 20c

This is what I saw in R. Shimon's *midrash*, may he rest in peace, based on which one can prove that, no matter whether in public or not, one should not recite his prayer audibly . . . and in questions such as these, which are not mentioned explicitly in our Talmud, one should rely on the kabbalah of the holy light, R. Shimon, may he rest in peace.[60]

On the subject of reciting Psalm 25 during Tahanun (also known as *nefilat apayim*) in the prayer service, Ibn Gabai's source was, once again, the Zohar:

And there are those who recite other words during *nefilat apayim*, and there are some *posekim* who wrote whatever came into their heads, and they concocted [things] without any reason. In fact, it was ruled that the psalm 'O Lord, I set my hope on you' was assigned to *nefilat apayim*, and we have already stated the reason for it, in accordance with the opinion of the great light, R. Shimon, may he rest in peace, and one should rely on him in cases that are not specified in our Talmud.[61]

The Zohar as a source of custom and law reappears in several works of Spanish exiles written in the first half of the sixteenth century, including the annotations of R. Moses Khalats to *Sefer hamusar* (1537); Hayim Obadiah di Bozzolo's book *Be'er mayim ḥayim* (Salonica, 1546),[62] and *Agudat ezov* by

(Exod. 23: 19)). Saba also relied on the Zohar in the issue of saying *adonai eloheikhem emet*; see *Tseror hamor*, 10*d* (Gen. 5: 32), and 21*b* (Deut. 26: 4).

[60] *Tola'at ya'akov*, 16*b* (based on Zohar ii. 202*a*). Ibn Gabai offered this opinion in contrast to that of Jacob ben Asher in *Arba'ah turim*. A further example of Ibn Gabai's deference to the Zohar is his lengthy citation of Zohar 'Song of Songs' regarding the prohibition on donning *tefilin* during the intermediate days of a festival (*Tola'at ya'akov*, 8*a*–*b*). On the question of tightening the *tefilin* strap he based himself on Zohar 'Pinḥas', iii. 236*b*: 'The holy light, may he rest in peace, wrote that one should bring the *yod* close to the *bayit*' (ibid. 8*a*). With regard to the summoning of Elijah to a circumcision ceremony, he wrote: 'A chair is designated for him and one is required to utter clearly, "This is the chair of Elijah, of blessed memory". And if it is not uttered, he does not come. This is what I saw in Rabbi Shimon's *midrash*' (ibid. 45*b*). Ibn Gabai further ruled, again based on the Zohar, that there is no requirement to recite the Grace after Meals over a cup of wine when fewer than three people are present (ibid. 44*a*). As for the service leader's repetition of the words *barukh adonai hamevorakh le'olam va'ed*, he relied on a statement in Zohar 'Ruth': 'This is what I saw in *Midrash ruth* and it proves that the service leader has to repeat the words *barukh adonai hamevorakh le'olam*' (ibid. 12*b*). He also followed the Zohar in the matter of walking to the synagogue wearing *tsitsit* and *tefilin* (ibid. 8*b*–9*a*).

[61] Ibid. 20*a* (based on Zohar iii. 120*b*). It seems that his words are directed at the author of the *Arba'ah turim*, 'Oraḥ ḥayim', 131: 'And it is a contemporary custom to say: "happy are those who dwell in Your house"; "may the Lord answer you in time of trouble".'

[62] Regarding Grace after Meals, R. Hayim Obadiah asserts: 'Three or more must say

R. Isaac Ha'ezovi.[63] Some rituals that had their roots in the Zohar, such as the late-night liturgy of Shavuot, the recitation of 'Berikh shemeh', and the invitation of *ushpizin* to the *sukah*, took hold in certain circles around the same time, and later gained wide popularity.[64]

grace after a meal and their blessing requires a cup [of wine], as R. Shimon ben Yohai wrote in the Zohar: "No cup for blessing unless there are three"' (*Be'er mayim ḥayim*, 35*b* (based on Zohar ii. 157*b*)). Relying on the same zoharic text, R. Hayim Obadiah goes on to write: 'And while making the blessing one should raise the cup . . . up to his eyes, as it is written in the Zohar: "One needs to look at the cup"' (ibid. 36*a*). Basing himself on Zohar 'Va'etḥanan', iii. 266*a*, di Bozzolo further determined that the name Shadai should be written on the *mezuzah* opposite *vehayah*.

[63] See e.g. R. Isaac's discussion of donning *tefilin* during the intermediate days of a festival, at the end of which he rules as follows: 'Thus, based on the Zohar, it becomes clear to us that one should not don *tefilin* on the intermediate days of a festival' (*Agudat ezov*, 51–2). On the laws of *tefilin* and related matters see ibid. 58–9. R. Isaac presents 'three laws from the Zohar on *tsitsit* and *tefilin* that are not included among any rulings of the halakhists' (without mentioning the source of these rulings—*Sefer ha'agur*).

[64] The nocturnal service of Shavuot is based on a description in Zohar i. 8*a* and iii. 97*b*–98*a*. See also *Tikunei hazohar*, 136*a*; de León, *Sod hashavuot*, 37*b*; David ben Judah Hehasid, *Or zarua*, 72*b*–73*a*. This ritual was revived by members of the circle of R. Solomon Alkabets and R. Joseph Karo even before emigrating to Israel; see Karo, *Magid meisharim*, 18; I. Horowitz, *Shenei luḥot haberit*, i. 30*a* ('Shavuot'). The custom is also mentioned by Khalats in his book *Sefer hamusar* (Constantinople edn.), 127, where he quotes the words of R. David ben Judah Hehasid without mentioning the source; Saba, *Tseror hamor* (Lev. 23: 15), 14*d*; Ha'ezovi, *Agudat ezov*, 214; and an anonymous author's collection of homilies from the early 16th century, Parma, MS 2627 (F. 13543), 35*b*–36*a*. I would like to express my gratitude to Abraham David for introducing me to this source. The night prayer of Shavuot was practised in Safed by the circle of R. Moses Cordovero (see his *Or yakar*, i. 76; xiii. 159) and later by the circle of Isaac Luria (see *Sha'ar hakavanot*, ii. 202–3 and *Sha'ar ma'amrei razal*, 78). R. Simeon Ibn Lavi, who lived in North Africa in the 16th century, also mentioned this custom; see *Ketem paz*, i. 24*a*, 293*a*. For its history see Wilhelm, '*Sidrei tikunim*' (Heb.); Hallamish, *Kabbalah in Liturgy, Halakhah, and Customs* (Heb.), 595–612; Huss, *Sockets of Fine Gold* (Heb.), 16 n. 28. On the basis of Zohar ii. 206*a*, R. Isaac Ha'ezovi recommended the recitation of 'Berikh shemeh' in the morning service (*Agudat ezov*, 166), and so did Moses Cordovero (*Tefilah lemosheh*, gate 6, §10, 136*a*). According to Hayim Vital, Isaac Luria would say the prayer during the morning service on the sabbath (*Sha'ar hakavanot*, ii. 92). Its recitation is first mentioned in the printed version of R. Moses ibn Makhir's *Seder hayom* (p. 22); for a history of 'Berikh shemeh' see Schechter, 'Kabbalistic Interpolations in the Prayer Book', 50–60; Hamburger, *The Roots of Ashkenazi Customs* (Heb.), 156–86. On the summoning of *ushpizin* based on Zohar iii. 103*b*–104*a*, mentioned also in a few sources from the late 13th–early 14th centuries, see de León, *Hanefesh haḥakhamah*, issue 12; David ben Judah Hehasid, *Or zarua*, 90*b*; and the kabbalistic work of R. Hayim ben Samuel, *Ba'al hatserorot* (Bar-Ilan University, Ramat Gan, MS 1039 (previously Moussaieff 64) (F. 22889), 65*a*). In the early 16th century this practice is mentioned by R. Meir Ibn Gabai in *Tola'at ya'akov*, 40*b*, and later by Ha'ezovi in *Agudat ezov*, 252. It was also recom-

Zoharic kabbalah plays an exceptionally important role in the halakhic writings of R. Joseph Karo. In the words of Jacob Katz, 'he absorbed from the Zohar more than any major rabbinic figure before him, and he bestowed more authority on its rulings than any of his predecessors'.[65] Karo relied extensively on the Zohar in his major work *Beit yosef*, which he began writing in 1522, and the first part of which, 'Oraḥ ḥayim', was printed in Venice in 1550. Listing his sources, he states: 'Thus, whoever has this book before him will have at his disposal the Talmud with Rashi's commentary, the *Tosafot*, the Ran [Rabbenu Nisim], the rulings of the Rif [R. Isaac Alfasi] and the Rosh [Rabbenu Asher] . . . and with them the statements of the Zohar.' Israel Ta-Shma has noted:

With regard to the fact that the Zohar is explicitly mentioned among the sources listed in the introduction to *Beit yosef*, one should add that it is a partial list, and important halakhic sources that are frequently used in the body of the book are missing from it; in this context, the inclusion of the Zohar in this list together with classical texts of rabbinic literature makes it even more significant.[66]

Karo often used the Zohar as a supporting source, sometimes to give weight to a recommendation and sometimes to establish mandatory laws.[67] He quoted, for instance, 'novelties absent from the halakhic literature' to support hand-washing with a vessel in the morning (which agrees with R. Solomon ben Adret and negates the ruling of Rabbenu Asher).[68] On the matter of Levites pouring water on the hands of the priests, Karo stated, citing the Zohar: 'this is the custom one should follow'.[69] Regarding the audible recitation of prayers, he said that the words of the Zohar 'should be obeyed' (using the same expression as R. Isaac Abuhav).[70] Concerning walking to the synagogue wearing *tsitsit* and *tefilin* he once again cited the Zohar's opinion:

mended by Moses Cordovero in his commentary on portion 'Emor'; see A. Azulai, *Or haḥamah*, iii. 80*a*. A further recommendation regarding the practice appears in *Heikhal hakodesh* by R. Moses Albaz, written in the second half of the 16th century (74*a*). For the summoning of *ushpizin* in the Zohar and in later sources, see Tishby and Lachower, *The Wisdom of the Zohar*, ii. 520–1; Hallamish, *Kabbalah in Liturgy, Halakhah, and Customs* (Heb.), 323–4.

65 *Halakhah and Kabbalah* (Heb.), 68.

66 *The Revealed in the Concealed* (Heb.), 73.

67 Katz, *Halakhah and Kabbalah* (Heb.), 68; Hallamish, *Kabbalah in Liturgy, Halakhah, and Customs* (Heb.), 166–7.

68 *Beit yosef*, 'Oraḥ ḥayim', 4.

69 Ibid. 128.

70 Ibid. 101 ('Bedek habayit').

The proper order is to make the blessing on the small *talit* [first], then to don the hand and head *tefilin*, and [finally] to go to the synagogue and wrap oneself in the large *talit*; by doing so one fulfils his duty according to R. Shimon ben Yohai, who wrote in Zohar, 'Va'etḥanan', that one should be dressed in *tsitsit* and *tefilin* when leaving home to go to the synagogue.[71]

In reference to the opinion of R. Isaac of Dampierre on spilling semen in vain, Karo wrote: 'Had R. Isaac seen what is written in the Zohar regarding the punishment for letting semen go to waste, one of the gravest sins in the Torah, he would not have written what he wrote.'[72] Based on the Zohar, he further made the following rulings: the leader of the prayer service has to repeat the words *adonai eloheikhem emet* at the end of the Shema (he referred to this as 'a custom of our ancestors that agrees with the Zohar');[73] women should be prevented from going to cemeteries;[74] God's name, Shadai, should be written on the outside of the *mezuzah*, back to back with the word *vehayah*, which is on the inside.[75] He also recommended that, in compliance with the Zohar, synagogues should have twelve windows,[76] and warned against eating meat after cheese in the same meal,[77] as well as against deriving benefit from the sciatic nerve (*gid hanasheh*).[78]

[71] *Beit yosef*, 'Oraḥ ḥayim', 25.

[72] Ibid., 'Even ha'ezer', 25 ('Bedek habayit').

[73] Ibid., 'Oraḥ ḥayim', 61.

[74] Ibid., 'Yoreh de'ah', 359; see Hallamish, *Kabbalah in Liturgy, Halakhah, and Customs* (Heb.), 167.

[75] Ibid., 'Yoreh de'ah', 288. Karo is in disagreement with Rabbenu Asher, who, according to the *Arba'ah turim*, used to write Shadai on the outside, between the portions, based on Zohar 'Va'etḥanan', iii. 266*a*.

[76] In *Beit yosef*, 'Oraḥ ḥayim', 90, he states that 'the number of windows required in a synagogue has not been mentioned in the Talmud nor by the rabbinical authorities. However, based on what is written in Zohar "Pekudei", a synagogue should have twelve windows because of a concealed secret.' Consequently in *Shulḥan arukh* he ruled that 'it is desirable to have twelve windows in a synagogue'.

[77] *Beit yosef*, 'Oraḥ ḥayim', 173, based on Zohar 'Mishpatim', ii. 125*a*.

[78] *Beit yosef*, 'Yoreh de'ah', 65 (based on Zohar 'Vayishlaḥ', i. 170*b*). It should be noted that, in spite of his recommendation in *Beit yosef*, Karo did not rule thus in the *Shulḥan arukh*. On other cases in which his ruling in the *Shulḥan arukh* does not follow the opinion of the Zohar, see Hallamish, *Kabbalah in Liturgy, Halakhah, and Customs* (Heb.), 171–3. The Zohar is also mentioned in *Beit yosef*, 'Oraḥ ḥayim', 27, 32, 56, 240 ('Bedek bayit'), 288, and 568; 'Yoreh de'ah', 197; Hallamish, *Kabbalah in Liturgy, Halakhah, and Customs* (Heb.), 166–7. In 'Oraḥ ḥayim', 182 Karo quotes Zohar 'Ruth' saying that when three people participate in 'grace [after a meal] it requires a cup [of wine]; however, without three it does not require a cup' (*Zohar ḥadash*, 87*c*). He recounts seeing people who were very particular about this distinc-

The most famous ruling that Karo made on the basis of the Zohar is found in his discussion of donning *tefilin* on the intermediate days of a festival. After presenting the sources relevant to the case (including his uncle Isaac Karo's responsum), he quotes at length Zohar 'Song of Songs' (where donning is prohibited),[79] and concludes that since a law concerning this question had not been established in the Talmud one should follow the position of the Zohar: 'Because the laws are not clearly explained in the Talmud, who would dare to disregard the words of R. Shimon, who strictly forbids the donning.'[80] He reiterates this principle in his discussion of whether one should recite *yotser or* when praying alone: 'Although people have always said *kedushat yotser* privately, in my humble opinion one should follow the Zohar since the Talmud did not establish a law, as I write in *siman* 31 on the laws of donning *tefilin* during the intermediate days of a festival.'[81] In these two latter cases, as well as in others, by following the Zohar Karo went against the opinion of Rabbenu Asher and the other rabbinic authorities on whom the *Arba'ah turim* is based.[82] In discussing whether one who is called up to the Torah should read together with the cantor or not, he explicitly declares that the Zohar's opinion is superior to that of the *posekim*:

The Zohar states that only one [person] should read. Since the cantor is the designated reader, the one who is called to the Torah is forbidden to do so, although

tion because they revered the opinion of the Zohar but also that of the halakhic authorities. Therefore they filled the cup even when they were alone, but did not hold it in their hand.

[79] *Zohar ḥadash*, 64*d*–65*a*.

[80] *Beit yosef*, 'Oraḥ ḥayim', 31. Katz, *Halakhah and Kabbalah* (Heb.), 107; as previously mentioned, the first to prohibit the donning of *tefilin* during the intermediate days of a festival was R. Joseph ben Tsadik, who based his opinion on Zohar 'Song of Songs'. The prohibition is mentioned by Isaac Abuhav, Isaac Karo, Abraham Zacuto, Meir Ibn Gabai, and Isaac Ha'ezovi. The opinion of *Midrash hazohar* on this matter is cited by Joseph Alashkar (see Idel, 'Rabbi Judah Haliwah and His Book *Tsafenat pane'aḥ*' (Heb.), 45*b*), and by Moses Cordovero in *Sefer gerushin*, 113. R. David Ibn Zimra wrote, in his responsum concerning this matter: 'Since there is a disagreement, the words of the kabbalah are compelling and one should not don' (*Responsa*, ii. 1*b*).

[81] *Beit yosef*, 'Oraḥ ḥayim', 59 (based on Zohar ii. 132*b*).

[82] As Jacob Katz emphasizes, *Beit yosef*, 'Oraḥ ḥayim', 31 suggests that one should accept the rulings of the Zohar even when they contradict the Jerusalem Talmud, on which Rabbenu Asher based his decision. This is expressed by emphasizing 'our Talmud' (i.e. the Bavli), for it alone is superior to the Zohar; see Katz, *Halakhah and Kabbalah* (Heb.), 69, and compare this to R. Meir Ibn Gabai's statement (quoted above) regarding the authority of 'our Talmud'.

according to the *posekim* he is obliged to read,[83] because without reading his blessing is wasted. Since this question has not been explicitly mentioned in the Talmud we should not forsake the Zohar's ruling because of what the *posekim* say.[84]

As I have shown above, the established principle was that the Zohar could be considered the ultimate authority as long as it did not explicitly contradict the Talmud. This principle, which implies the superiority of the Zohar to the *posekim*, appears in the writings of Abraham Zacuto and Meir Ibn Gabai.[85] In the context of *yibum* or *ḥalitsah*, R. Isaac Karo, R. Joseph Karo's uncle, sets down a similar principle regarding kabbalah in general:

And it is incumbent upon us, as logic dictates, that when the sages of kabbalah make a ruling that contradicts the Talmud, the judge shall rule on the basis of the Talmud that is set before us. But if no law was established in the Talmud, and there is no agreement among the *posekim* as to whose ruling should be followed, and everyone follows his own path, if it was determined in kabbalah to accept [a certain] opinion, the ruling of the kabbalist sage should be followed. I have received [this principle] from my teachers.[86]

[83] He alludes to Jacob ben Asher, author of the *Arba'ah turim*, who states in 'Oraḥ ḥayim', 141: 'My master, Rabbenu Asher's father, of blessed memory, explained . . . and thus they ruled that the service leader will read because he is trained to read; however, the one who is invited to read shall do so quietly along with the service leader, so his blessing is not wasted.'

[84] *Beit yosef*, 'Oraḥ ḥayim', 141 (based on Zohar ii. 201*b*); Katz, *Halakhah and Kabbalah* (Heb.), 69.

[85] Zacuto declared: 'It has been accepted by the people of Israel that a ruling that does not contradict the Talmud and is not explained in the Talmud, but is explained there [in the Zohar], should be followed' (*Sefer yuḥasin hashalem*, 45). In the words of Ibn Gabai, 'In matters that were not explicitly addressed by our Talmud one should rely on the kabbalah of the holy light, R. Shimon, may he rest in peace' (*Tola'at ya'akov*, 16*b*); 'and this is the opinion of the holy light, R. Shimon, may he rest in peace, and we have no one more authoritative than he is concerning matters that are not explicitly addressed in our Talmud' (ibid. 20*a*).

[86] This responsum is incorporated in *Responsa*, 385; see also Katz, *Halakhah and Kabbalah* (Heb.), 57. In contrast to other Spanish scholars who considered the Zohar superior to the halakhic decisors, Isaac Karo generally deferred to the sages of the kabbalah, but the only kabbalistic source he mentioned in his responsum was *Midrash hazohar*. On the other hand, the Sephardi kabbalist and halakhic expert David Ibn Zimra clearly relied on the authority of the *posekim*: 'I have a general and important rule regarding anything written in the Talmud or by one of the *posekim* or any halakhic expert—I accept it even if it is contrary to what is written in books of kabbalah. I do not take heed of what is written in one of those books' (*Responsa*, ii. 20*a*–*b* and ii. 5*a*: 'Whenever one finds [a ruling in] books of kabbalah, follow the Gemara and the *posekim*. However, when there is no contradiction, as in this case, [and the case] is not mentioned in the Gemara or by the *posekim*, I would rely on the words of kabbalah.'

The above survey indicates that deference to the Zohar in matters of kabbalah, halakhah, and custom was widespread among the Spanish exiled elite in the late fifteenth, and especially in the first half of the sixteenth, century. Although the book had enjoyed some degree of authority even earlier, it was during this period that its recognition became unequivocal and significantly more prevalent. This phenomenon was related to the growing influence of kabbalah among the cultural elite of Spanish Jewry in the late fifteenth century.[87] It is unclear what elevated kabbalah to a higher status than philosophy in this period but there is no doubt that the Spanish Jewish theologians' criticism of Aristotelian philosophy contributed to the shift.[88]

Following the fourteenth-century decline of kabbalah there were no active kabbalistic schools that could claim any authority in the sphere of oral tradition. The traditional Nahmanidean chain in Spain had disappeared and other schools (such as the prophetic kabbalah of Abraham Abulafia) failed to gain wide acceptance within the kabbalistic world. In the absence of any prominent figures written sources prevailed, and kabbalah was being studied from texts rather than from teachers. An early fifteenth-century account by Shem Tov ibn Shem Tov illustrates this state of affairs: 'I was searching for a teacher and could not find one until I looked at a few books written by kabbalistic sages and I immersed myself in them for a long time.'[89] Indeed, up until the establishment of the Lurianic school at the end of the sixteenth century, written texts, spearheaded by the Zohar, were the principal sources of authority.

In sum, the Zohar gained authoritative status, particularly among Spanish Jewry, at the turn of the fifteenth and sixteenth centuries. The contemporary elite of other Jewish communities—including sages engaged in kabbalah—were either unacquainted with the Zohar or did not subscribe

[87] See Scholem, *Kabbalah*, 66; Idel, 'Spanish Kabbalah After the Expulsion' (Heb.), 503–4.

[88] Huss, 'On the Status of Kabbalah in Spain' (Heb.), 20 n. 2.

[89] Ariel, 'Shem-Tov ibn Shem-Tov's Kabbalistic Critique of Jewish Philosophy', 19–20; Gottlieb, *Studies in Kabbalistic Literature* (Heb.), 392. Joseph Albo's attack on study of the Zohar and other kabbalistic books without having any oral tradition reflects the new practice of studying kabbalah from books at that time; see Albo, *Sefer ha'ikarim*, 186; Huss, 'On the Status of Kabbalah in Spain' (Heb.), 28.

to its supremacy.[90] It was not until a later period that it became prominent in these communities, due to the influence of Spanish Jewish culture.

Notwithstanding the Zohar's growing importance before the expulsion from Spain, most of the writings in which it is extensively quoted, as well as the majority of statements regarding its authority in religious doctrine and practice, originated after the expulsion. Furthermore, many of the pre-expulsion proclamations are found in the writings of Spanish kabbalists outside Spain.[91] One may infer, therefore, that their reliance on the Zohar as a source of authority was part of their struggle for cultural dominance in the new areas of their settlement.

Multiple factors enabled the Spanish and Portuguese exiles to acquire a dominant position in their new communities. As Joseph Hacker has pointed out, many of them were halakhic experts and religious leaders. They established educational institutions with new teaching methods, and centres for the collection and printing of manuscripts. In Hacker's view it was these factors (or, to use Pierre Bourdieu's terminology, the 'cultural capital' of these sages) that allowed the Iberian immigrants to rise to prominence within the Jewish communities of the Ottoman empire.[92] The Zohar was an important item in the cultural cargo that these elite circles brought with them: access to the zoharic texts, the ability to quote from them, and deference to the Zohar regarding doctrines and religious practices all contributed to the strengthening of the exiles' cultural power.

As I have shown above, the perception of the Zohar as a kabbalistic work originating from the period of the *tana'im* supported the claim for the antiquity of kabbalah and for its superiority over Jewish philosophy. The Spanish exiles proclaimed the Zohar's ancient origins in order to subvert the rationalist schools they encountered during their migration. R. Judah Hayat, for instance, juxtaposed 'philosophical investigation' with the acqui-

[90] On the limited influence of the Zohar on Italian kabbalah in the late 15th and early 16th centuries see Idel, 'Major Currents in Italian Kabbalah', 245 n. 11.

[91] R. Isaac Mar Hayim, for example, asserted the Zohar's authority in a letter to R. Isaac of Pisa, written in Naples, Italy, in 1490/1. Arguing for the preferability of *yibum* over *ḥalitsah*, R. Gedalyah ibn Emmanuel also based his opinion on the Zohar in a responsum he sent from Jerusalem to R. Moses Ashkenazi.

[92] See 'The Intellectual Activities of the Jews of the Ottoman Empire' (Heb.), 569–82, 602–3; id., 'Pride and Despair' (Heb.), 576.

sition of 'true knowledge from Shimon ben Yohai, of blessed memory, and his companions'.[93] R. Joseph Alashkar made his statement regarding the authority of the Zohar within the context of the controversy between kabbalistic and rationalist philosophical principles. Reliance on the Zohar further supported the exiles in their struggle against the non-Spanish kabbalistic schools they encountered.[94] A case in point is R. Isaac Mar Hayim, whose declarations of the Zohar's superiority were directed at kabbalists who employed philosophical principles in their interpretation of kabbalah. Writing to the Italian sage Isaac of Pisa, he advised:

> While investigating these matters do not follow the sages who rely on rational axioms and interpret the kabbalah philosophically. Treat the kabbalah as an axiom and try to make rational reasoning agree with it. If you are unable to do so, you, Your Honour, should know that the intellect has its limits while kabbalah, which has been received from the mouth of a prophet, is superior to the intellect and is able to correct what has been corrupted. Thus, it [reason] should be abandoned in favour of a prophetic kabbalah, such as that of R. Shimon bar Yohai, since Elijah, may he rest in peace, used to reveal himself to him every day in his academy.[95]

As Moshe Idel has shown, Mar Hayim's attack on 'the sages who rely on rational axioms and interpret the kabbalah philosophically' targeted specifically those Italian kabbalists who tried to reconcile kabbalah and philosophy, prominent among them R. Yohanan Alemmano, with whom he often disagreed in his letters.[96] Idel has further argued that Judah Hayat's reliance on the Zohar and his proclamations of the book's authority were also connected to his polemic with the Italian kabbalah, especially that of Alemmano.[97] Hayat wrote his commentary on *Ma'arekhet ha'elohut* in Italy at the beginning of the sixteenth century, and openly declared that his reason for writing the book was the prevalence, in northern Italy, of works combining kabbalah and philosophy, as well as of books by Abulafia. Against the kabbalistic 'canon' of the Italian sages he compiled a list of his own, headed by the Zohar:

93 *Ma'arekhet ha'elohut*, 159*b*.

94 Idel, 'Spanish Kabbalah After the Expulsion' (Heb.), 507–12.

95 Nadav, 'An Epistle of the Kabbalist Isaac Mar Hayim' (Heb.), 458.

96 Idel, 'Essence and Vessels in Kabbalah of the Renaissance Period' (Heb.), 90–1.

97 Idel, 'R. Yohanan Alemanno's Order of Study' (Heb.), 330–1.

And because I have seen in this district many books of kabbalah that confuse the pure mind, I feel the need to warn you about the books which you should avoid, and to bring to your attention those you should peruse. The godly sage, R. Isaac Ibn Latif, of blessed memory . . . who, as far as the wisdom of kabbalah is concerned, has one foot inside and one foot outside, and therefore one can follow part of it but not all of it . . . I have also seen books written by a sage named R. Abraham Abulafia . . . Stay away from him and do not listen to him, because his books are filled with fantasies, falsifications, and fabrications . . . And these are the books you should study: *Sefer yetsirah* . . . and *Sefer habahir* . . . you should wear as a crown over your head. Let not the Zohar cease from your lips; recite it day and night. And the books of R. Joseph Ibn Gikatilla, of blessed memory, and R. Shem Tov de Leon, tie them [as jewellery] around your neck.[98]

On the basis of the above examples we may reasonably assume that the purpose of public declarations of the Zohar's authority, as well as of its numerous quotations in the writings of the Spanish exiles living in Turkey, Greece, Israel, and North Africa, was to establish the exiles' cultural status, and to reject the prevalent philosophical and kabbalistic schools in their new communities. Reliance on the Zohar regarding halakhic matters, and its acceptance as superior to the *posekim*, further contributed to the strengthening of Spanish Jewish cultural dominance. Although presented as tannaitic writings, the zoharic texts written in Castile at the turn of the thirteenth and fourteenth centuries reflect first and foremost the customs, laws, and religious ideals of the medieval Spanish kabbalists.[99] The book thus became a tool for the exiled sages to establish the Iberian customs and laws as authoritative in the communities where they settled.

An example of this can be found in Joseph Karo's discussion of the laws of the recitation of the Shema. Basing himself on the Zohar, Karo reinforced the Spanish custom according to which the leader of the service repeats the words *adonai eloihekhem emet*: 'Since this is the common custom, whoever tries to amend it fails and is reprimanded, and his words are disregarded, and the custom of our ancestors, who followed the Zohar, continues to be followed, [because] they established this custom and were very careful to observe it, since they found it to be true and sound.'[100]

[98] *Ma'arekhet ha'elohut*, 3*b*–4*a*.

[99] See Ta-Shma, *The Revealed in the Concealed* (Heb.), 15.

[100] *Beit yosef*, 'Oraḥ ḥayim', 61.

The practice of quoting from the Zohar and declaring its superiority to rabbinic sources was often connected to a polemic against the position of Rabbenu Asher ben Yehiel (Rosh) and his son, R. Jacob ben Asher (Ba'al Haturim), two prominent Ashkenazi halakhic experts active in Spain in the fourteenth century. Parts of the responsa attributed to Joseph Gikatilla, for example, were based on rulings and customs in the Zohar that contradicted the opinion expressed in Jacob ben Asher's *Arba'ah turim*; and, as Meir Kadosh has argued, 'this kabbalist [the author of the responsa] strove to disseminate zoharic customs and to repress the influence of rulings made by Jacob ben Asher'.[101] In all cases in which Abraham Zacuto follows the halakhic position of the Zohar, his ruling contradicts that of Rabbenu Asher.[102] Declaring the authority of the Zohar regarding the audible recitation of prayers, R. Meir Ibn Gabai explicitly places the opinion expressed in that work above that of Jacob ben Asher:

> This is what I saw in the *midrash* of R. Shimon, may he rest in peace.[103] And based on it one can prove that, no matter whether privately or publicly, one should not make his prayer audible to someone else and should not follow R. Jacob ben Asher, of blessed memory, who wrote that one is allowed to make it audible to the members of his household . . . And in cases which are not stated explicitly in our Talmud, one should rely on the kabbalah of the holy light, R. Shimon, may he rest in peace.[104]

The fact that the Spanish sages used the Zohar to subvert the dominant status of Rabbenu Asher is further evident in the following passage by R. Isaac Karo:

> And after the sages of Spain found a statement in one of the homilies in the Zohar that the commandment to don *tefilin* was not performed during the intermediate days of festivals and that it was forbidden to don them, no one donned them during the intermediate days of festivals. Furthermore, although throughout Spain people had followed the opinion of Rabbenu Asher concerning any law, [both] prohibitions and permissions, and he used to don them [*tefilin*] with a blessing, since they discovered that statement, all the sages in all the communities without exception have stopped donning them.[105]

[101] 'Kabbalistic Jewish Laws in Responsa' (Heb.), 63–4, 66.

[102] Zacuto, *Sefer yuḥasin hashalem*, 45.

[103] Zohar ii. 202*a*.

[104] *Tola'at ya'akov*, 16*b*. The ruling with which he disagrees is in Jacob ben Asher's *Arba'ah turim*, 'Oraḥ ḥayim', 101.

[105] Karo, *Responsa*, 385.

Echoing his uncle's views, Joseph Karo wrote concerning *tefilin*:

And now it has become a custom throughout Spain not to don them during the intermediate days of festivals. And I have heard that they used to don them on those days based on the instructions of Rabbenu Asher, until they found out that R. Shimon had written in a statement that it was forbidden to don them on those days, and since then they have refrained from donning them.[106]

The above quotations reflect how the halakhic authority with which Karo and his Spanish contemporaries invested the Zohar was used to legitimize Spanish customs and laws in their new locales and to subvert the authority of the Ashkenazi halakhists, Rabbenu Asher and his son.[107] The Iberian exiles' employment of the Zohar, however, stirred up some resistance among local scholars, who questioned the supremacy and value of that work. There are several sources (to be discussed in detail in Chapter 7) that voice such a challenge, for example *Beḥinat hadat* by Elijah Del-Medigo, written in Crete at the end of the fifteenth century. Del-Medigo's

[106] *Beit yosef*, 'Oraḥ ḥayim', 31. The authority of the Zohar is juxtaposed many times with the positions of Rabbenu Asher and Jacob ben Asher. In 'Oraḥ ḥayim', 4, Karo quotes from the Zohar 'novel interpretations that are not included in [the writings] of the *posekim*'. He relies on the Zohar in asserting his opinion that one should wash his hands with a vessel in the morning (which agrees with Solomon ben Adret and opposes Rabbenu Asher). In 'Oraḥ ḥayim', 173 Karo's requirement to restrict the eating of meat and poultry after dairy is based on the Zohar. This requirement contradicts the opinion of Jacob ben Asher, who states the following: 'Meat after cheese is allowed immediately by cleaning and washing the mouth and the hands.' In 'Oraḥ ḥayim', 59 Karo rules, again based on the Zohar, that one should not recite *kedushat yotser* by oneself, in contrast to the opinion of Rabbenu Asher, who rules that 'one can recite it by himself'. In 'Oraḥ ḥayim', 141 his opinon that one who is called up to the Torah should not read together with the service leader likewise follows the Zohar and is in disagreement with Jacob ben Asher, who states that 'one who is called to read will read quietly with the service leader'. In 'Yoreh de'ah', 288 Karo rules, as does the Zohar, that the name Shadai must be written on the outside of the *mezuzah* opposite the word *shehayah* inside. This contradicts Rabbenu Asher, who stated that it had to be written on the outside, in the space between the portions, as recorded in the *Arba'ah turim*.

[107] On this point I disagree with Ta-Shma, who argues that Karo's attribution of halakhic authority to the Zohar attested to his desire to be recognized by the Greek-Romaniote communities, because, Ta-Shma claims, they regarded the Zohar as a work of halakhah; see Ta-Shma, *The Revealed in the Concealed* (Heb.), 76–83. The evidence that Ta-Shma provides to support his claims does not seem convincing. As I have shown, the Zohar appears to be used as a source for customs and laws mainly in the writings of Spanish kabbalists. The objection of R. Elijah Mizrahi (the rabbi of the Romaniote community in the early 16th century) to granting the Zohar halakhic authority also disproves Ta-Shma's argument.

attack on the Zohar and kabbalah stemmed from a rationalist Aristotelian point of view and was a reaction to the Zohar's growing influence in Italy and Candia during that period. The writings of Del-Medigo and others are manifestations of mounting criticism of the Zohar in Greece, Italy, and North Africa.[108]

Non-Spanish sages refused to attribute authority to the Zohar in matters of custom and law, especially when it threatened their own practices. In their rejection, however, they did not usually challenge the antiquity or kabbalistic content of the Zohar. For example, R. Elijah Mizrahi, a Romaniote sage and principal rabbi of Constantinople in the late fifteenth and early sixteenth centuries, wrote:

In addition, everything that was not mentioned either in the Babylonian Talmud or the Jerusalem Talmud and was not discussed by the *posekim*, by whom we live and whom we usually trust in all religious matters, even though the kabbalists have explored the matter we cannot impose [their rulings] because all they say is nothing but hints among themselves, the experts in the [field]. But at this time . . . we cannot impose on the people matters that allude to supernal worlds. We have not heard in our time of any of the great and famous kabbalists obligating people to follow the hints given to other kabbalists that allude to the supernal, which the sages in the Talmud and the *posekim* who followed them did not explore.[109]

Those who were reluctant to grant halakhic authority to the Zohar included some Italian sages. R. Azriel Diena, a scholar of French descent and active in the first half of the sixteenth century, did don *tefilin* during the intermediate days of festivals (although without a blessing), and declared:

We should not abandon the words of the *posekim*, for none of the secrets convinced them to follow those profound books, because the wisdom of the heroes

[108] For my survey of Zohar criticism see Ch. 7.

[109] Mizrahi, *Responsa*, 11, no. 1. His disciples, R. Elia Halevi, the rabbi of the Romaniotes, and R. Tam Ibn Yahya, the rabbi of the Castilian exiles, took the same position; see ibid. 12. In a responsum, R. Eliah Halevi addressed the question of donning *tefilin* during the intermediate days of festivals and declared that Rabbenu Asher's position was superior to that of R. Shimon in the Zohar: 'And it is known that the donning of *tefilin* during the intermediate days of festivals is addressed in the Zohar and is forbidden . . . yet we have not found that the *posekim* forbade it based on the words of R. Shimon ben Yohai, and Rabbenu Asher used to don them with a blessing.' However, according to Kadosh, R. Eliah later softened his attitude towards rulings based on kabbalah; see 'Kabbalistic Jewish Laws in Responsa' (Heb.), 130–44. R. Tam Ibn Yahya's statements indicate that there were other Spanish sages who were reluctant to attribute halakhic authority to the Zohar.

mentioned in that book, the Zohar, is unfathomable and no one is able to fully understand what they say and what they mean because they base their words on revelations when they say 'the *tefilin* that God, blessed be He, dons', etc. and we should not interpret their words literally, and we should refrain from interpreting their interpretations, because we might be wrong and we might transgress the positive imperative to don *tefilin*. Thus we should understand and follow the rulings of the *posekim*, who know and understand more than we do and are worthy of being trusted in all situations.[110]

The proposition that the Zohar stood above the *posekim*, particularly Rabbenu Asher, was met with fierce opposition on the part of Ashkenazi sages in eastern Europe, who rejected the ultimate authority granted by Karo to the Zohar. In a responsum concerning the question of whether one stands or sits to don the hand *tefilin*, R. Solomon Luria wrote the following:

You should know, my beloved, that these are neophytes who would like to be part of the kabbalist faction and expounders of secrets, although they have weak eyesight and are unable to gaze into the splendour, and do not know where it comes from and where it goes and what it means. They have found it in the books of R. Shimon, that is all they know. And you, my beloved, should know that all my holy teachers and ancestors, who were the most learned in the world, these were not their customs. They followed the Talmud and the *posekim*. Even if R. Shimon stood before us and shouted that we should change the customs that the early generations practised, no one would pay attention to him, because in most cases halakhah does not agree with him and with what Karo wrote. And the proof is that he wrote great secrets, and amazing warnings, that it was forbidden to recite two separate blessings over the *tefilin* for the head and the arm, but we do not follow him and recite two blessings. He also wrote that one who dons *tefilin* during the intermediate days of a festival deserves death, yet we don *tefilin* and make a blessing over them.[111]

R. Moses Isserles (Rema) was among those who rejected Karo's position regarding the superiority of the Zohar to the *posekim*. On the question of whether one who is called up to the Torah should read with the cantor,

[110] Diena, *Responsa*, ed. Yacov Boksenboim, no. 14, p. 45. The end of the quote echoes *Ber.* 9*a*: 'R. Shimon is worthy of being trusted in times of difficulty.'

[111] S. Luria, *Responsa*, 234, no. 98.

he wrote: 'One should not abandon the rulings of the *posekim*. And even if the Zohar disagrees with them, as mentioned above, one should not follow Beit Yosef [i.e. Karo], who wrote that one should not abandon the Zohar in light of the rulings of the *posekim*.'[112]

Isserles and Solomon Luria (as well as several Ashkenazi sages who followed them), while unwilling to grant precedence to the Zohar above the greatest halakhists, did not oppose kabbalah or deny that book's antiquity and sanctity. Luria, for example, quoted it in his monumental work *Yam shel shelomoh*.[113] Isserles, although reluctant to disseminate the Zohar and kabbalah in print either to the 'masses' or to the uneducated 'people of means', proclaimed that 'the words of the Zohar are words given at Sinai'. He used it as a source to determine customs and laws, and wrote a commentary on it. However, he did not invoke it when it contradicted the customs of Ashkenaz.[114] The refusal of Ashkenazi sages to treat the Zohar as greater than the *posekim* was, thus, likely to have stemmed not from doubts regarding its antiquity or from a discomfort with kabbalah. Rather, those rabbis sought to protect Ashkenazi traditions from the influence of Spanish

[112] In 'Oraḥ ḥayim', 49 Isserles rules, against Karo, that the Zohar has no priority over tractate *Soferim* in the matter of reciting *kedushat yotser* while being alone. 'And since it has been explored in tractate *Soferim* we should not rush to the secrets of the Zohar to contradict it, because the custom has already been established in accordance with it [i.e. tractate *Soferim*].' He also rejects Karo's ruling regarding the donning of *tefilin* on the intermediate days of festivals: 'In all our districts, on the festivals we don and bless, in accordance with [the opinion of] Rabbenu Asher' (*Darkhei mosheh*, 'Oraḥ ḥayim', 31). On the positioning of the name Shadai on the *mezuzah*, he disagrees with the position expressed in *Beit yosef*, 'Yoreh de'ah', 288, and takes the side of Rabbenu Asher: 'And this custom has not been practised thus, but rather according to our teacher [i.e. Rabbenu Asher].' Regarding Karo's warning, based on the Zohar, against deriving benefit from the sciatic nerve ('Yoreh de'ah', 65), he states: 'I have heard that the author of the Zohar is "R. Shimon", who is mentioned in the Talmud, who is R. Shimon ben Yohai, and he disagrees with R. Judah in our Talmud . . . however, if R. Judah [disagrees] with R. Shimon, the law follows R. Judah, according to the *posekim*. And if that is the case the Zohar cannot be used as halakhic evidence.' In 'Oraḥ ḥayim', 294 R. Isserles states that one should not defer to the Zohar's warning not to light a candle until after reciting the benediction over the wine at the end of the sabbath and festivals.

[113] *Yam shel shelomoh*, 'Bava kama', 28*b*, no. 11; Raflad, 'Kabbalistic Remnants in Maharshal's Halakhic Thought' (Heb.), 26. For other works by Luria that reflect his engagement in kabbalah, see ibid. 26–31, and Fram, 'Jewish Law and Social and Economic Realities', 64.

[114] In Chapter 6 I explore Isserles's reluctance to support the circulation of kabbalistic literature (Isserles, *Torat ha'olah*, iii, ch. 4, 3*b*). On his statement that the words of the Zohar were given at Sinai see ibid. ii. 30*a*. On his commentary on the Zohar see Ch. 5.

halakhah, especially from that of Joseph Karo's *Beit yosef* and *Shulḥan arukh*.[115]

Notwithstanding protests at claims of the Zohar's authority (particularly of its superiority to the major decisors), which were raised mainly within the non-Spanish communities of the sixteenth century, in the end it was accepted as the wellspring of kabbalah as well as a significant source of custom and law. Within the Ottoman empire, where Spanish Jews had attained influential status, the Zohar's supremacy was recognized even by those sages who were not of Spanish descent.[116] In Italy, where the book encountered both direct and indirect criticism from the late sixteenth century onwards,[117] it was nevertheless treated by most scholars as an authoritative and sacred text. As I have shown in the previous chapter, from as early as the late fifteenth century Italian sages were involved in the reproduction and distribution of the Zohar, and in the mid-sixteenth century they were a vital force in its printing. The previously mentioned Italian kabbalist R. Mordecai Dato had ruled that the Zohar was the standard by which kabbalistic truth was determined: 'We have nothing else but the words of R. Shimon, may he rest in peace, and of his companions and disciples, and all that is written in the book of life—the Zohar—and by them we dwell within the secrets of kabbalah.'[118]

R. Emmanuel of Benevento, the Italian scholar who was engaged in the printing of the Zohar in Mantua, stated in his introduction to the 1558

[115] Katz, *Exclusiveness and Tolerance* (Heb.), 132. Twersky claims that the purpose of many of Isserles's notes on the *Shulḥan arukh* was to undermine the conclusions of R. Joseph Karo; see Twersky, 'The *Shulḥan arukh*', 150 n. 29, and Fram, 'Jewish Law and Social and Economic Realities', 170.

[116] The Zohar plays a major role in *Tsafenat pane'aḥ*, written by the North African sage R. Judah Haliwah in Safed in 1544/5; see Idel, 'R. Judah Haliwah and His Book *Tsafenat pane'aḥ*' (Heb.), 125. R. Issachar ben Mordecai ibn Susan, the rabbi of the North African community in Safed, relied on the Zohar in halakhic matters; see his book *Tikun yisakhar* (Constantinople, 1563/4), 29*b*, 30*b*. In contrast, R. Hayim Shabetai, an important halakhist in Salonica in the early 17th century, gave precedence to the rabbinic authorities over the Zohar; see Benayahu, *The Position of Rabbi Moses Zacuto and Rabbi Samuel Abuhav* (Heb.), 69 n. 25.

[117] Aspects of Zohar criticism are discussed in Ch. 7 below.

[118] Benayahu, 'R. Ezra of Fano' (Heb.), 845. See also ibid. 842: 'Since what the Zohar states is what the kabbalah states, one should not question them.' See also Ezra of Fano's statement as quoted by Dato: 'We should not question the opinions expressed in the Zohar, [we should] rather implement them, based on the principle "if it is kabbalah we accept it"' (ibid. 844).

edition of *Sefer ma'arekhet ha'elohut* that, in the absence of an authoritative oral tradition, the only criterion for the authenticity of kabbalistic wisdom was its agreement with the Zohar:

And if you say that a person must receive these matters from mouth to mouth, and therefore it is called the wisdom of *kabalah* [receiving], who is that man? A priest son of a priest,[119] who is walking in a field of apples towards us? Who is he to say that he descends from sages and is an expert in this wisdom? How can we trust his dreams and words in the absence of other sources? And how can we recognize and know whether the true wisdom of God is in his mouth, without seeing it written in the true text of R. Shimon, the companions, and their disciples? By means of their words, equal to one hundred witnesses, we are able to see and learn whether that man is wrapped in the light of kabbalah as in a garment and wisdom should be obtained from him, or if he is ignorant and barren and extends the heavens over a void.[120]

Although many were reluctant to attribute halakhic authority to the Zohar,[121] some Italian sages did accept the view that it outweighed the *posekim*.[122] R. Menahem Azaryah da Fano, who was active around the turn of the sixteenth and seventeenth centuries, went even further and extended

[119] Based on Rashi's comment on *Ber.* 28*a*: '*Mazeh ben mazeh*—priest a son of a priest, who pours the water of purification'. [120] *Ma'arekhet ha'elohut*, 'Divrei hamagiha', 4*a*.

[121] See above note. In the early 17th century R. Leon of Modena rejected the halakhic authority of the Zohar as part of his criticism of claims of its antiquity (*Ari nohem*, 65). Modena's arguments are discussed in detail in Ch. 7 below.

[122] R. Elijah Halfan, who was involved in the shaping of the zoharic corpus (see Ch. 3) and in the polemics pertaining to its printing (see Ch. 6), asserted the halakhic authority of the Zohar in a pamphlet he wrote in 1526/7; see Benayahu, *The Position of Rabbi Moses Zacuto and Rabbi Samuel Abuhav* (Heb.), 87–9. In Benayahu's view this pamphlet was written in response to R. Azriel Diena and the Italian sages who refused to grant the Zohar halakhic authority. R. Jacob Israel Finzi, an Italian scholar who opposed the printing of the Zohar (see Ch. 6), also relied on the book in his responsa. It was on the basis of this that he ruled, for example, that one should not don *tefilin* on the intermediate days of festivals, and he accorded greater authority to the Zohar than to the *posekim*. See Kadosh, 'Kabbalistic Jewish Laws in Responsa' (Heb.), 153–65. The Italian kabbalist R. Mordecai Dato recounted what his uncle R. Moses Basola had written in a responsum that had been lost: 'if Rabbenu Asher had seen what R. Shimon wrote he would not have ruled according to R. Akiva' (Benayahu, 'The Dispute between Kabbalah and Halakhah' (Heb.), 90). Benayahu also cites the position of an anonymous Italian rabbi who stated that 'the words of the Yerushalmi have no authority in comparison to R. Shimon's, who was one of the sages of our Talmud' (ibid. 91). In the debate that took place in Cremona in 1680/1 concerning the donning of *tefilin* during the inter-

the principle established by Spanish kabbalists before him. In a responsum on the donning of *tefilin* on the intermediate days of festivals he ruled that one should make an effort to interpret the Talmud in light of the Zohar:

Midrash hane'elam does not contain impossibilities or contingencies, or what is inconceivable or frightening to those who are faint of heart, as someone thought, may God forgive him. And if the Talmud accepts different interpretations and one of them is in accordance with the Zohar, we must lean towards that and follow its instruction . . . and if the Zohar does not agree with one of the commentators or the geonim, yet the Talmud tolerates it, who can but accept it? And if the Zohar does not agree with one of the commentators or the geonim, as long as the Talmud tolerates it, every opinion will be rejected in favour of the Zohar's interpretation. From now on anyone who refuses to listen to the words of Torah and compliments himself by saying that the Zohar did not state it and that it was added by mistake by a student,[123] I call upon him to let the sated satisfy the thirsty.[124]

R. Menahem Azaryah da Fano clearly believed that the Zohar had higher authority and that the Talmud had to be interpreted in its light, not the other way around.[125] There were scholars, however, who disagreed, and in the generations that followed serious conflicts erupted in Italy between

mediate days of festivals, it was an Ashkenazi scholar who refused to disobey the Zohar and accept the compromise suggested by R. Abraham Menahem Hakohen of Porto; see Katz, *Halakhah and Kabbalah* (Heb.), 109; Benayahu, 'The Dispute between Kabbalah and Halakhah' (Heb.), 104–5. On other sages in Italy who ruled in accordance with the Zohar and prohibited the donning of *tefilin* during the intermediate days of festivals, see Benayahu, 98–9, 105.

[123] This is R. Menahem Azaryah da Fano's response to R. Moses Provinciali, mentioned previously.

[124] Da Fano, *Responsa*, 225, no. 101. Katz, *Halakhah and Kabbalah* (Heb.), 110–11; Benayahu, 'The Dispute between Kabbalah and Halakhah' (Heb.), 112–14; Hallamish, *Kabbalah in Liturgy, Halakhah, and Customs* (Heb.), 129.

[125] See Katz, *Halakhah and Kabbalah* (Heb.), 110–11. R. Samuel of Sha'ar Aryeh, the disciple of R. Menahem Azaryah da Fano, adopted the same hermeneutical principle and recommended interpreting the Talmud in light of the Zohar 'even if it is with some difficulty and even more so if it facilitates the explanation of their opinion and intention comfortably, without any difficulty' (Benayahu, 'The Dispute between Kabbalah and Halakhah' (Heb.), 113). R. Emmanuel Hai Ricchi also attributed more authority to the Zohar than to the Talmud and argued that, since R. Shimon had known prophetically what would later be written in the Talmud, one should interpret the Talmud in accordance with his and the Zohar's teaching:

those who argued that *tefilin* should be donned on the intermediate days of festivals and those who opposed it.[126]

The influence of kabbalah in general, and of the Zohar in particular, is noticeable in eastern Europe from the middle of the sixteenth century. In the early seventeenth century zoharic texts were being printed: in 1602/3 the *Zohar ḥadash* in Kraków, and from 1622 to 1624 the Zohar on the Torah in Lublin.[127] Under the influence of Spanish literature, which had penetrated Ashkenazi culture via the Italian printing houses,[128] the Zohar was received by Ashkenazi Jews as one of the most authoritative kabbalistic sources, and it acquired significant influence in the areas of law and custom. While refusing to grant higher status to the Zohar than to the *posekim*, R. Solomon Luria and R. Moses Isserles, the leading Ashkenazi halakhists of the sixteenth century, deferred to it in kabbalistic matters, and did not refrain from quoting it in their halakhic works.

The disciples of Luria and Isserles, R. Moses Matt, author of *Mateh mosheh*, and R. Mordecai Jaffe, author of *Levush malkhut*, who were active at the turn of the sixteenth and seventeenth centuries, also relied on the Zohar in arbitrating questions of custom and law.[129] The first books of conduct, based on the Zohar, were published in eastern Europe at this time —*Mareh kohen* (Kraków, 1588/9) by R. Issachar Baer of Shebershin, a disciple of Isserles, and *Yesh sakhar* (Prague, 1608/9) by R. Issachar Baer of Kremnitz, which is organized according to the *Arba'ah turim* and *Shulḥan*

'One who assumes what the Talmud means to say but the meaning does not agree with his [R. Shimon's opinion] . . . makes a mistake in judgement and does not understand what [the Talmud says]' (*Sefer aderet eliyahu*, 15*a*). See also Katz, *Halakhah and Kabbalah* (Heb.), 118.

126 On R. Hananyah Kazis's opposition to R. Menahem Azaryah da Fano in the early 18th century see Katz, *Halakhah and Kabbalah* (Heb.), 113. Regarding the controversy that broke out in the town of Gorizia in the wake of R. Emmanuel Hai Ricchi's attempt to prevent the public from donning *tefilin* during the intermediate days of festivals, see ibid. 114–17.

127 Elbaum, *Openness and Insularity* (Heb.), 181–222; Fram, 'Jewish Law and Social and Economic Realities', 142–8. To quote Jacob Elbaum, 'there is almost no writer who does not mention the Zohar in his writings' during this period (*Openness and Insularity*, 184 n. 3).

128 On the demise of Ashkenazi literary hegemony over customs and laws in the Middle Ages, see Reiner, 'Changes in the Yeshivot of Poland and Germany' (Heb.), 45. For the impact of the printing press on Ashkenazi Jewry in the 16th century, see Elbaum, *Openness and Insularity* (Heb.), 25–7.

129 Elbaum, *Openness and Insularity* (Heb.), 366–70; Fram, 'Jewish Law and Social and Economic Realities', 156–8.

arukh.[130] It should be noted that these sages, too, rejected the Zohar's rulings when those conflicted with the customs of Ashkenaz.

While most Ashkenazi rabbis denied the Zohar's supremacy over the halakhic authorities,[131] there were eastern European kabbalists who accepted the Spanish principle and granted precedence to the Zohar. For example, R. Benjamin Aaron Slonik, a disciple of Luria and Isserles, agreed with Joseph Karo on this issue, and in *Masat binyamin* (Kraków, 1632/3) he declared the following:

> Here is the Zohar before you, more valuable than all the authors since the completion of the Talmud. If all the authors were on one side of the scale and the Zohar by itself on the other side, it would outweigh them all. Obviously, it is far superior, and as Beit Yosef [i.e. Karo] wrote, we should follow the opinion of the Zohar rather than that of the other authors.[132]

The Zohar thus came to be accepted as a principal source of authority on kabbalistic doctrine, first by the Spanish sages and later in most Jewish communities around the world. Its influence increased, moreover, in the domains of custom and law among Spanish scholars, who considered its authority greater than that of the leading *posekim*. Certain Ashkenazi sages embraced the Spanish position, although the majority considered the Zohar to be subordinate to the legal decisors. Doubts concerning the book's antiquity and authority were raised in some circles, and, as I show in Chapter 7, their criticism was enthusiastically adopted by scholars of the nineteenth-century Jewish Enlightenment. Nonetheless, up until the end of the eighteenth century such criticism did not undermine the Zohar's prominent status, and even today in many Orthodox Jewish circles it is considered one of the most authoritative sources in the realms of kabbalah, custom, and law.[133]

130 See Gries, *Conduct Literature* (Heb.). 76–80; Elbaum, *Openness and Insularity* (Heb.), 186–7.

131 Fram, 'Jewish Law and Social and Economic Realities', 152.

132 *Sefer masat binyamin*, 142, no. 62.

133 The superiority of the Zohar over the rabbinic authorities has generally been accepted by Spanish Sephardi halakhists of recent generations (including R. Isaac Nisim and R. Isaac Brada) and is rejected by their Ashkenazi colleagues (see Hallamish, *Kabbalah in Liturgy, Halakhah, and Customs* (Heb.), 134; Lau, 'Kabbalah' (Heb.), 145). However, the Ashkenazi R. Moshe Feinstein considered the Zohar superior to the decisors, while R. Ovadia Yosef, the Sephardi chief rabbi of Israel, held the opposite view (ibid. 142; Lau, 'Kabbalah in

The formation of the zoharic canon, the distribution of its printed versions, and recognition of its supremacy propelled the writing of commentaries. As these became the predominant genre of kabbalistic literature during the second half of the sixteenth century the question arose as to who should be considered the most authoritative Zohar commentator. Once Isaac Luria was accepted as such, Lurianic kabbalah superseded the Zohar itself, dominating not only matters of doctrine, but also of custom and law.[134] The following chapter examines the emergence of the aforementioned commentaries and the struggle to control the meaning of the Zohar.

R. Ovadyah Yosef's Decrees' (Heb.), 132–51). It should be noted that recently a few collections of zoharic customs and laws have been published, e.g. *Sefer hazohar banigleh* by Moshe Hayim Tiberg and the anonymous *Sefer shulḥan arukh hazohar* (published in 16 volumes); see Hallamish, *Kabbalah in Liturgy, Halakhah, and Customs* (Heb.), 144.

134 Hallamish, *Kabbalah in Liturgy, Halakhah, and Customs* (Heb.), 198. This fact became evident when books of conduct based on Lurianic kabbalah replaced those based on the Zohar (such as *Mareh kohen* and *Yesh sakhar*); see Gries, *Conduct Literature* (Heb.), 78.

CHAPTER FIVE

On the History of Zohar Interpretation

Not all who desire to assume the Name may do so.
Berakhot 8b

As I have shown in the previous chapter, in the first half of the sixteenth century the Zohar's authority became evident in the growing frequency with which it was cited in support of theological views or to settle questions of custom and law. Following the formation and printing of the zoharic canon in the second half of the century, this authority was further manifested in the publication of the first comprehensive Zohar commentaries, and these interpretative works soon developed into a principal genre of kabbalistic literature.

Although partial commentaries had been written before the printing of the Zohar, it was not until the mid-sixteenth century that complete commentaries were published and their production became a major kabbalistic practice. This development took place only during the final stages of, and probably in response to, the canonization process. As I have argued in Chapter 3, before the formulation and printing of the zoharic canon the possession, collection, and redaction of zoharic texts, as well as the ability to quote from that holy book, were sources of cultural power controlled by elite circles of the Iberian exiles. However, once the Zohar was canonized, printed, and widely distributed, the ownership of texts lost its cultural significance. New methods were needed to derive authority from the Zohar's symbolic value, and it was at this moment that the emphasis shifted from the possession of texts to the ability to control their meaning.

Zohar interpretation began more or less simultaneously with the appearance of the first manuscripts, and some of the sections that were ultimately canonized included commentaries on earlier segments.[1] For example, commentaries on parts of *Midrash hane'elam* can be found in the body of the Zohar;[2] *Idra raba* and *Idra zuta* include explications of *Sifra ditseniuta*;[3] and commentaries on earlier zoharic sections form part of *Tikunei hazohar* and *Ra'aya meheimna*, which also contain an explicit hermeneutical reference to *ḥibura kadma'ah* (the early work).[4]

Menahem Recanati was the first kabbalist to quote frequently from the Zohar, often following these quotations with interpretation. In his book *Ta'amei hamitsvot*, furthermore, Recanati mentioned a commentary he had written on the Zohar.[5] Although this work is not in our possession and he never mentioned it elsewhere, Moshe Idel has argued that it may have been incorporated in Recanati's *Perush hatorah*.[6] Zohar interpretations also appear in Joseph Angelet's writings, especially in *Livnat hasapir*: 'Everything that I found difficult in *Midrash hane'elam* I included in this work in order to explain it.'[7] However, despite the major role that explication of the Zohar played in *Livnat hasapir*, the book is primarily a commentary on the Torah and not on the Zohar.[8]

[1] Paraphrases and Hebrew translations of zoharic texts, even before the formulation of the concept of *Sefer hazohar*, had an interpretative character. For example, scholars have identified 'misunderstandings'—i.e. interpretations—in the way Moses de León read zoharic texts: see Scholem, 'Two Booklets by Moses de León' (Heb.), 25; Liebes, 'Zohar and Eros' (Heb.), 100 n. 214; id., '*Shekel hakodesh* by Moses de León' (Heb.), 277; Wolfson, *The Book of the Pomegranate*, 50–5. Commentaries are also embedded in David ben Judah Hehasid's translations of the Zohar; in fact, Moshe Idel has shown that he was the first commentator on the Zohar: see 'Rabbi David ben Judah Hehasid's Translation of the Zohar', pt. 1 (Heb.), 60, 72–3; David ben Judah Hehasid, *Sefer marot hatsovot*, ed. Matt, 16–17.

[2] e.g. in Zohar 'Vayeshev', i. 181*b*–182*a*, which expounds *Midrash hane'elam*, and Zohar 'Ḥayei sarah', i. 126*a*–129*a*. See also Liebes, *Studies in the Zohar*, 196 n. 18.

[3] Liebes, *Studies in the Zohar*, 95–8.

[4] See e.g. segments of *Ra'aya meheimna* printed in Zohar iii. 217*b*, 224*a*, 232*a*, 256*a*.

[5] Recanati, *Sefer ta'amei hamitsvot*, 30*b*, 31*c*, 72*a*, 77*b*, 78*a*.

[6] R. Simhah Bunim Lieberman, the editor of *Sefer ta'amei hamitsvot*, believed that when Recanati referred to his commentary on the Zohar, what he meant was his *Perush hatorah*. See Lieberman's introduction to *Sefer ta'amei hamitsvot*, 13. However, as Moshe Idel has shown, Recanati composed *Perush hatorah* after *Sefer ta'amei hamitsvot* (see Ch. 3), which means that, even before he wrote his *Perush hatefilot* and *Perush hatorah*, he had produced commentaries on segments of the Zohar—hence his reference in *Sefer ta'amei hamitsvot*. He later incorporated those early Zohar commentaries in his *Perush hatorah* and did not mention them as a separate work in his other writings; see Idel, *Menahem Recanati the Kabbalist* (Heb.), 70–1.

[7] *Livnat hasapir* (London MS), 418*a*.

[8] I differ on this point with Idel and Iris Felix, who describe the book as a Zohar commen-

As we have seen, the Zohar did not play a major role in Jewish culture between the mid-fourteenth and late fifteenth centuries. Indeed, it is hard to find exegetical references to its texts from that period: the only kabbalists who regularly quoted, and commented on, the Zohar were R. Menahem Tsiyon and R. Shem Tov ibn Shem Tov. It was not until the end of the fifteenth century, especially after the expulsion from Spain, that commentary on segments of the Zohar became prevalent.

Already before the expulsion, in 1491, R. Isaac Mar Hayim translated and explicated the beginning of *Idra zuta* in a letter sent to R. Isaac of Pisa.[9] The responsa of R. Joseph Elcastil to R. Judah Hayat, written in Spain shortly before the expulsion, also included commentary on zoharic texts.[10] The writings of early sixteenth-century Spanish kabbalists contain many more Zohar commentaries. In the first part of *Ma'amar hayiḥud*, for instance, R. Abraham Halevi explains a section of Zohar 'Bamidbar' iii. 120*a*.[11] At R. Joseph Karo's request, R. Solomon Alkabets wrote a commentary on a zoharic segment concerning the burial of *tsadikim* in the Land of Israel (Zohar i. 21*b*).[12] Zohar exegesis played a major role in Alkabets's other writings, too,[13] as well as in the works of many of his contemporaries,

tary; see Idel, *Menahem Recanati the Kabbalist* (Heb.), 69; Felix, 'Chapters in the Kabbalistic Thought of R. Joseph Angelet' (Heb.), 15.

[9] Greenup, 'A Kabbalistic Epistle by Isaac b. Samuel', 370–4.

[10] Scholem, 'On the Knowledge of Kabbalah in Spain' (Heb.), 171. *Sefer hameshiv*—also written in pre-expulsion Spain according to Idel—contains references to Zohar commentaries (which I further explore below), and the author introduces his own work as a commentary on the obscure parts of the Zohar. See Scholem, 'The Magid of R. Joseph Taitatsak' (Heb.), 78; Idel, 'Neglected Writings of the Author of *Kaf haketoret*' (Heb.), 80. However, as Idel has noted, and in agreement with my point, 'unlike the statements that characterize *Sefer hameshiv* and the works of the anonymous kabbalist [the author of *Kaf haketoret*] regarding the discovery of the books of the Zohar and their interpretation, one cannot find any significant commentary on the secrets of the Zohar in the works produced by the circle we are exploring, and the role zoharic materials play in their spiritual world is also very limited' (ibid. 28).

[11] See Scholem, 'New Investigations Concerning Abraham ben Eli'ezer Halevi' (Heb.), 155–61.

[12] The commentary was printed at the end of Alkabets's *Berit halevi* (40*a*–44*a*). His commentary on a segment of Zohar 'Ruth', included in *Zohar ḥadash*, 89*c*–*d*, was also printed in *Berit halevi*, 44*a*–45*a*.

[13] See Sack, 'Exile and Redemption in Solomon Alkabets's *Berit halevi*' (Heb.), 269. In his commentary, Alkabets applied a method, commonly used in the Talmud and in biblical hermeneutics during the 15th century, whereby one begins a commentary by presenting

including R. Judah Hayat, R. Meir Ibn Gabai, and R. Hayim Obadiah di Bozzolo.

However, it is important to emphasize that during this period and earlier, commentaries on the Zohar were typically incorporated in kabbalistic writings on other topics. With only a few exceptions, such as Recanati's lost work, Alkabets's responsum to Karo, and *Ma'amar hayiḥud* by Abraham Halevi, no work was an exclusive Zohar commentary. As previously mentioned, the first interpretative texts were written in the mid-sixteenth century, and from then on Zohar exegesis became a principal genre of kabbalistic literature.

R. Moses Cordovero's *Perush or yakar* was the first comprehensive commentary on the zoharic corpus. In his *Pardes rimonim*, completed in 1548, he incorporated several zoharic commentaries, and his kabbalistic doctrine was based mainly on exegesis of the Zohar. He started work on *Perush or yakar* while writing *Pardes rimonim*, and continued to perfect it throughout his life. One of the most comprehensive works ever written on the Zohar, Cordovero's commentary includes detailed interpretations of most of the zoharic corpus. Although he created his own zoharic collection based on several manuscripts, he also relied on the printed version of the Zohar, which was published while he was writing his commentary. At the same time, R. Hayim Vital, who studied with Cordovero and later became the main disciple of Isaac Luria, also wrote a Zohar commentary.[14] Luria composed his first exegetical works on the Zohar while still in Egypt, and most

questions and doubts arising from the text. As I will show, R. Moses Cordovero, Isaac Luria, and R. Joseph Ibn Tabul used this method in their commentaries on the Zohar; see Rubin, 'The Zoharic Commentaries of Joseph Ibn Tabul' (Heb.), 377–8, 381. In contrast, R. Hayim Vital and R. Abraham Galante did not apply this method, and R. Abraham Azulai went as far as dropping the questions from those parts of Cordovero's commentary that he quoted in his book *Or haḥamah*; see Huss, *Sockets of Fine Gold* (Heb.), 74–5.

[14] Vital's commentary, which he produced before meeting Luria, is mentioned in *Shivḥei ha'ari*; see Benayahu, *The Biography of Isaac Luria* (Heb.), 162. In *Sefer haḥezyonot* Vital expressed his desire to write a commentary on the Zohar (see *Sefer haḥezyonot*, ed. Aescoly, 50; ed. Faierstein, 78). R. Abraham Azulai included a commentary of Vital's in *Or haḥamah*, an anthology of Zohar commentaries that he edited, and claimed that Vital had written that piece before studying with Luria (*Or haḥamah*, i, introduction, 2*a* [my numbering, BH]). R. Shlomel Dreznitz, in a letter written in 1606/7, also mentioned Vital's text, which he said had been composed 'according to the method and principles of our teacher R. Moses Cordovero, of blessed memory' (J. Delmedigo, *Ta'alumot ḥokhmah*, 43*a*). R. Jacob Tsemah,

of his later writing fell into that genre. While in Safed, he expounded zoharic texts to his disciples, and, according to a kabbalistic tradition, both he and his son died because he had revealed the secrets of the Zohar to them.[15]

Without any doubt, the intensive involvement of the Safed kabbalists in exegesis of the Zohar stemmed from mythical traditions connected to the upper Galilee, Mount Meron in particular, where R. Shimon and his companions are said to have operated, and where R. Shimon and his son are buried. The historical traditions connected to the place inspired a sense of renewal among the kabbalists of Safed.[16] On the basis of the Zohar's descriptions, they tried to replicate the social structure, lifestyle, and activities of R. Shimon's circle. To that end they immersed themselves in the study and interpretation of the Zohar. Borrowing from Brian Stock, who has coined the term 'textual communities', it is possible to classify the kabbalistic circles of sixteenth-century Safed as 'zoharic communities'.[17] The unique characteristics of their commentaries were moulded by the fact that these kabbalists were living in the geographical-mythical space of the Zohar and in close proximity to R. Shimon's burial place.

Not all commentaries of that time were composed in Safed. As mentioned above, Luria himself began writing while in Egypt. R. Simeon Ibn Lavi wrote in Tripoli, Libya,[18] and R. Moses Isserles in Kraków, Poland.[19] At

too, makes reference to a concealed Zohar commentary of Vital, which was probably the same as that mentioned by Azulai (Scholem, 'On the Life and Works of Jacob Tsemah' (Heb.), 192). Those commentaries by Vital which were based on Luria's teachings were included in *Sha'ar ma'amrei rashbi* alongside Luria's handwritten explanations; see Meroz, 'Redemption in Lurianic Teaching' (Heb.), 44.

[15] *Shivḥei ha'ari* states that Vital had recognized Luria's special merits during their first meeting, in which Luria interpreted for him several zoharic texts. See Benayahu, *The Biography of Isaac Luria* (Heb.), 162. On Luria's commentary on *Idra raba*, which he presented to his disciples in Meron, see ibid. 179–81. Regarding the death of his son following his interpretation of Zohar 'Beshalaḥ', ii. 52*b*, see *Sha'ar hakavanot*, ii. 186; Benayahu, *The Biography of Isaac Luria* (Heb.), 197–8. For a description of Luria's death after revealing the secret of *tren ha'orzilin de'ayalta* ('two young roes of a doe', Zohar iii. 55*a*), see Benayahu, *The Biography of Isaac Luria* (Heb.), 200–2.

[16] Liebes, 'Zohar as Renaissance' (Heb.), 10–11; Fine, *Physician of the Soul*, 80.

[17] Stock, *The Implication of Literacy*, 90–1, 522; id., *Listening for the Text*, 23,150. See also Huss, '*Sefer Hazohar* as a Canonical, Sacred and Holy Text', 294.

[18] Ibn Lavi's commentary was later named *Ketem paz*; see Huss, *Sockets of Fine Gold* (Heb.), 10–11.

[19] Benjamin Richler has identified Isserles' commentary in Bodleian, Oxford, MS 1911

the turn of the sixteenth and seventeenth centuries other commentaries appeared in Safed and elsewhere.[20] R. Judah Masud, for example, wrote a translation of, and a commentary on, the Zohar in the late sixteenth century in Egypt.[21] R. Abraham Galante, Cordovero's disciple, produced a

(F. 18844), copied by R. Abraham ben Simeon ben Haida (who probably planned to print it). The commentary was also incorporated into *Sefer aderet eliyahu* by R. Elijah ben Moses Loanz and has been held in Bodleian, Oxford, MS 1829 (F. 18422–18424). Part of this commentary has recently been published by the institute of Sha'arei Ziv; see Richler, 'From the Collections of the Institute of Microfilmed Hebrew Manuscripts' (Heb.); Elbaum, *Openness and Insularity* (Heb.), 148.

[20] Some of the commentaries that were written during that period are not in our possession. R. Aaron Berakhyah of Modena, in his introduction to *Mishḥat hakodesh*, refers to a summary and commentary he had written on the simple meaning of the Zohar; see Tishby, *Studies in Kabbalah* (Heb.), i. 186. Zohar commentaries by R. Menahem Tiktin, a disciple of Isserles, are mentioned in R. Aaron Zelig of Zolkiew's introduction to his book *Amudei sheva*; see Elbaum, *Openness and Insularity* (Heb.), 193. R. Samson of Ostropol often refers to his commentary named *Maḥaneh dan* in his writings. R. Nathan Hannover also mentions a Zohar commentary that was apparently written by R. Samson and which was based on the kabbalah of Luria; see Scholem, *Sabbatai Zevi and the Sabbatian Movement* (Heb.), i. 65; Liebes, 'Jonah ben Amitai as Messiah ben Joseph' (Heb.), 295. In the introduction to his book *Pitḥei yah* (published in Prague, 1608/9), R. Issachar Beer ben Petahyah Moses of Kremnitz makes reference to a comprehensive Zohar commentary that he had written and which he meant to publish; see Kremnitz, *Pitḥei yah*, 1*a*. In the introduction to *Yesh sakhar* (published in the same year) he remarks that, for the time being, he refrains from publishing his Zohar commentary *Yodei binah*. Jacob Elbaum has shown that the approbations of R. Issachar Baer's book *Mekor ḥokhmah* were intended to be included in his commentary on the Zohar (*Openness and Insularity* (Heb.), 188). R. Shlomel Dreznitz recounts that R. Issachar Baer had sent him his Zohar commentary and asked him to share it with the sages of Safed; see J. Delmedigo, *Ta'alumot ḥokhmah*, 41*b*–43*a*. The commentaries of R. Issachar Baer are included in *Amudei sheva* by R. Aaron Zelig of Zolkiew; see Elbaum, *Openness and Insularity* (Heb.), 193 n. 39. Commentaries that seem to be based on those of Issachar Baer are incorporated into *Kanah ḥokhmah kanah binah* by R. Eleazar ben R. Abraham Enokh Altschuler of Prague (Prague, 1609/10–1610/11); see Elbaum, *Openness and Insularity* (Heb.), 197 n. 54.

[21] Masud's book is mentioned by Joseph Sambari in *Sefer divrei yosef*, ed. Shtober, 414. On extant manuscripts of the work (written between 1587 and 1594) see Avivi, 'The Writings of R. Isaac Luria' (Heb.), 98; id., *Ohel shem* (Heb.), 77–88. Another translation of, and commentary on, Zohar 'Bereshit' was produced in Egypt (1575/6) by an unknown author and is part of Jerusalem, MS, 8vo 147. It follows the page order of the Mantua Zohar and consists of summaries and paraphrases of zoharic homilies on Genesis in Hebrew, followed by short commentaries; see Scholem, *Kabbalistic Manuscripts in the Hebrew University* (Heb.), 85. A partial Hebrew translation of the Zohar is in Oxford, MS 1561 (F. 16929), which was copied in 1602/3 by a person named Berakhiel. A translation of portion 'Bereshit' in this manuscript was printed by Obadiah Hedaya under the name *Sefer hazohar hashalem al hatorah* (Jerusalem, 1940/1); see Ch. 8.

commentary named *Sefer yeraḥ yakar*, a synopsis of which was published under the title *Zohorei ḥamah* (Venice, 1654/5).[22] Luria's disciples—R. Joseph Ibn Tabul, R. Joseph Arzin, R. Judah Mishan, and R. Israel Saruk—also composed exegetical works on the Zohar.[23] R. Menahem di Lunzano, a sage who was active in Turkey, Palestine, and Italy, is best known for his book *Omer man*, a commentary on *Idra zuta* and *Sifra ditseniuta*.[24]

In the early seventeenth century two printed works appeared that were composed of summaries of zoharic texts and a commentary on their plain (*peshat*) meaning: *Torat emet* by R. David ben Abraham Shemaryah (Salonica, 1605), and *Mekor ḥokhmah* by R. Issachar Baer of Kremnitz (Prague, 1611). The first anthologies of Zohar commentaries were also produced at this time: *Or haḥamah* by R. Abraham Azulai, written in Hebron before 1624,[25] and *Aderet eliyahu* by Elijah Loanz, which was completed in Friedberg in 1629.[26]

[22] Scholem, *Kabbalistic Manuscripts in the Hebrew University* (Heb.), 102–3; Sack, 'The Commentaries of Abraham Galante' (Heb.), 63.

[23] On the commentaries of Ibn Tabul see Scholem, 'The Document of Association of Luria's Disciples' (Heb.), 154–60; Meroz, 'Redemption in Lurianic Teaching' (Heb.), 83–4; Rubin, 'The Zoharic Commentaries of Joseph Ibn Tabul' (Heb.), 367–84. On Joseph Arzin's exegesis of *Idra raba* and of part of portion 'Va'etḥanan' see Scholem, 'The Document of Association of Luria's Disciples' (Heb.), 144. On Mishan's commentary on *Midrash hane'elam*, *Sitrei torah*, and *Ra'aya meheimna* see ibid. 147–8. On Ibn Saruk's work and his approach to the Zohar, see Meroz, 'Anonymous Commentary on *Idra raba*' (Heb.), 308–9.

[24] *Omer man* was printed in Vilna in 1881/2. Lunzano's *Imrei emet* contains a review of Luria's commentary on *Sifra ditseniuta* and the commentaries of Vital and Ibn Tabul on the *Idra*; see Scholem, 'The Document of Assocation of Luria's Disciples' (Heb.), 158.

[25] Published in Salonica in 1881/2, *Or haḥamah* is based on the exegetical works of Moses Cordovero, Abraham Galante, and Hayim Vital, as well as on a few anonymous commentaries under the title *Gilayon*.

[26] This comprehensive work is found in Bodleian, Oxford, MS 1829 (F. 18422–18424). Its first part has recently been published by the Ziv Institute (Loanz, *Sefer aderet eliyahu*). In his introduction Loanz recounts that he wrote the book in 1619/20–1620/1, and produced a second edition between 1621 and 1626, after having obtained Cordovero's *Or yakar*. In addition to *Or yakar*, *Sefer aderet eliyahu* contains the Zohar commentary of R. Moses Isserles as well as a few Lurianic commentaries. Loanz also wrote a commentary on *Tikunei hazohar* named *Tsafenat pane'aḥ*, which he completed in 1630/1 and which is part of Bodleian, Oxford, MS 1830 (F. 18425). In the early 17th century R. Joseph Hamitz started working on an anthology of exegetical works, *Sefer yodei binah*, which contains the writings of Moses Cordovero, Hayim Vital, Simeon Ibn Lavi, and Isaac Luria. Hamitz's unfinished anthology was eventually completed by R. Moses Zacuto, who incorporated part of it into his book *Or nogah* (Venice, 1657/8).

The intensive engagement in Zohar exegesis attests to the strengthening of that work's canonical status. As Jonathan Z. Smith has argued, the interpretation of canonical texts stems from a need to adjust their authority to new domains and changing circumstances: 'Where there is a canon it is possible to predict the necessary occurrence of a hermeneute, an interpreter whose task it is to continually expand the domain of the closed canon over everything that is known or everything that exists.'[27] There is a link, then, between the perception of the Zohar as a source of authority and the widespread preoccupation with its interpretation—as can be seen, for example, in the work of Recanati and Angelet in the fourteenth century, and in that of Hayat and Alkabets in the sixteenth, who both proclaimed the Zohar's supremacy (see Chapter 4) and incorporated numerous commentaries in their writings.

As I suggested in the previous chapter, the surge of exegetical literature was closely related to the closure of the zoharic canon. We have already seen that, in Smith's view, the link between canonization and interpretation can be explained by the need to extend the authority of a sealed canon to new domains. Similarly, Moshe Halbertal points out in his discussion of the canonization of the Bible that at 'the moment the text was sealed, authority was removed from the writers of the text and transferred to its interpreters'.[28]

Indeed, following the formulation and printing of the zoharic corpus, its explication became a primary kabbalistic activity. All the comprehensive early commentaries were written between 1550 and 1580, the period that saw the distribution of the first printed copies of the Zohar. Cordovero and Ibn Lavi, who pioneered the production of such comprehensive commentaries, began their projects while the first editions of the Zohar were being printed in Mantua and Cremona. Although their interpretations were based on manuscript collections, they were familiar with the printed versions as well. All other kabbalists who produced comprehensive commentaries at that time relied on the printed editions.

Zohar exegesis became a major kabbalistic occupation immediately after the compilation and canonization process was completed, not only

27 'Sacred Persistence', 23; Huss, 'The Anthological Interpretation', 5.

28 *People of the Book*, 19.

because there was a need to apply the Zohar to new situations and conditions, as Smith argues, but because of the cultural power it bestowed on those who were able to understand the text and to publicly demonstrate their comprehension through commentary. As the possession of manuscripts and the ability to quote from them lost their value with the finalizing and printing of the zoharic corpus, cultural authority moved from owners of the texts to those who were able to control their meaning, that is, those who were considered capable of interpreting them.

R. Moses Isserles bemoaned this transition of cultural power and took issue with the 'masses' and laymen who rushed to study kabbalah following the printing of the Zohar and other kabbalistic texts. Ready access to these works led the uneducated to believe that they were able to understand them without guidance and training, Isserles claimed:

Many from the masses rush to study kabbalah because it is a delight to behold, especially the words of the later sages, who explain these matters explicitly in their writings. Even more so at this time, when books of kabbalah are being printed such as the Zohar, Recanati, and *Sha'arei orah*. However, the reader of these books gets the impression that everything has been explained while, in reality, what the books say remains unclear because they have not followed the oral tradition of the truth being passed from the mouth of one kabbalist to another. Furthermore, not only the educated ones [assume that] they understand it, but even *ba'alei batim* ['householders', i.e. laymen] rush to study kabbalah, who do not know right from left and are walking in darkness, unable to explain even Rashi's commentary on a weekly portion. The generation has been orphaned due to their sins, and it has degenerated to a degree that anyone who has found anything in it [in kabbalah], though insignificant, is proudly expounding in public, and sounds like a coin in an empty vessel, and he will be punished for it.[29]

Isserles' comments suggest that as a result of the printing of the Zohar the rabbinic elite had lost, or was afraid of losing, control over kabbalistic knowledge, and that they hoped to regain it by emphasizing the importance of authoritative interpretation. R. Hayim Vital similarly argues in his introduction to *Ets ḥayim* that not everyone is capable of understanding the Zohar:

[29] Isserles, *Torat ha'olah*, iii. 3*b*.

Not everyone who wishes to assume the Name may do so,[30] because the riddles of the Torah and its secrets won't be revealed to human beings by means of their material faculties of understanding but rather through divine emanation from above, by His emissaries and angels, or by the prophet Elijah, as we shall explain at the end of this introduction.[31]

With the establishment of Zohar exegesis as the major genre of kabbalistic literature, hermeneutics became the arena in which the struggle for dominance took place. In the words of Tseviyah Rubin,

> The book rose to a status so pivotal that it is possible to describe the history of kabbalah during those generations as a debate over the interpretation of the Zohar revolving around questions such as: Who is the authoritative commentator on the Zohar and what is the source of his authority, or, which commentaries are legitimate and which should be rejected? The one recognized as a qualified commentator on the Zohar instantly assumed authoritative status.[32]

Indeed, it was often with a view to establishing their own status as authoritative interpreters of the Zohar that early exegetes criticized previous commentaries. For example, R. Simeon Ibn Lavi wrote: 'I have not found among all the books and commentaries on the Zohar, not in the commentary of the sage Menahem Recanati, of blessed memory, and not in any other book, a commentary that interprets this passage from beginning to end. They refer to a small part of the passage and neglect its essence.'[33] Ibn Lavi criticized Recanati's commentary elsewhere as well, but he reserved the harshest language for Judah Hayat:

> And there is no doubt that the path he took is as remote from the hidden meaning of the text as east is from west, because he placed everything in the east and forgot the west . . . and if you study his words you realize that he laboured and compiled a lot of nonsense; he searched and found nothing; and as always he began by exaggerating.[34]

A further negative remark on Hayat's commentary can be found in the writings of R. Moses Cordovero, who states, regarding Zohar 'No'aḥ', 65*a*: 'In spite of its obscure and sublime style, we cannot help but be

30 Based on Mishnah *Ber.* 2: 8.
31 *Ets ḥayim*, i. 15–16.
32 Rubin, 'The Zoharic Works of R. Moses Hayim Luzzatto' (Heb.), 388.
33 *Ketem paz*, i. 50*a*.
34 Ibid. 55*a*.

preoccupied with it as much as possible, because the commentators copied it into their books, especially R. Judah Hayat. Yet he did not explain any of it.'[35] Isaac Luria wrote harsh notes of objection on the folio of Cordovero's commentary on *Sava demishpatim*. His notes were quoted in *Zohar harakia*: 'Isaac says it is a big mistake'; 'Isaac says this interpretation makes no sense'.[36]

Before Lurianic kabbalah was granted canonical status, the commentaries of Luria and his disciples were also weighed and found wanting. For example R. Menahem di Lunzano, an interpreter of the Zohar at the turn of the sixteenth and seventeenth centuries, noted about Luria's commentary on *Sifra ditseniuta*: 'The rabbi, of blessed memory, extended this interpretation and made it too long, and it seems as if he had intended to include the whole Zohar in this commentary, and it is too long and tedious and it confuses the person who studies it.'[37] About Ibn Tabul's commentary on *Idra raba* he remarked: 'I have seen the commentary on parts of *Idra raba* by the sage Joseph Ma'aravi, also known as Ibn Tabul, of blessed memory, and found a few mistakes in it, and decided to reveal them to the reader in order to remove an obstacle from people's path.'[38] He was also critical of R. Hayim Vital's commentary and described it as 'a vacuous and flawed splitting of hairs', adding: 'This sage had not touched, seen, or smelled any of the profound issues at all.'[39]

The description of the meeting between Hayim Vital and Luria clearly reflects how the struggle for cultural power was manifested in the domain of interpretation:

He [Vital] considered himself a greater sage and kabbalist than the Ari [Luria], and was working on a commentary on the Zohar. One day he said to himself, 'Let me go and visit the Ari and see whether he is as he is rumoured to be.' He rose and went to Safed, may it be rebuilt and re-established. As soon as he arrived he went to the Ari to examine his ability to interpret an obscure passage in the Zohar that he [Vital] fully understood. As soon as R. Hayim Vital asked about that passage the Ari conveyed to him the great secrets to which it alluded. And when he heard

[35] *Pardes rimonim*, 38*b*, 63*b*.

[36] Tsemah, *Zohar harakia*, 67*b*, 68*a*, 72*a*–*b*, 79*a*, 82*b*, 87*b*, 91*a*–*b*.

[37] Quoted in Scholem, 'R. Isaac Luria's Authentic Works' (Heb.), 189.

[38] Quoted from di Lunzano's book *Sefat emet* in Scholem, 'The Document of Association of Luria's Disciples' (Heb.), 158.

[39] Ibid. 158–9.

this, he [Vital] was so scared that he almost died. And he questioned him about another passage to see what he would tell him. And he [the Ari] revealed several openings of light, so much so that R. Hayim Vital stood before him as a fox before the lion.[40]

In the end Luria rose to become the authoritative commentator on the Zohar, and his branch of kabbalah, which was based on his exegesis, gained canonical status. Di Lunzano's criticism of Luria's commentary was atypical, and, as Gershom Scholem has noted, one should not wonder why his derogatory piece was sequestered.[41]

Lurianic kabbalah secured its place of prominence within Jewish culture at the beginning of the modern era, following Luria's acceptance as the authoritative Zohar commentator on the one hand, and the rejection of other commentaries, especially that of Cordovero, on the other. As I show below, Luria's kabbalah derived its authoritative status from the supernatural methods that he apparently used in his interpretations.

As previously mentioned, by the early fourteenth century stories were circulating that the divine spirit and supernatural powers—Elijah in particular—had been instrumental in the writing of the Zohar. These traditions, which reappeared at the turn of the fifteenth and sixteenth centuries, contributed to the establishment of the Zohar's authoritative status. With the rise of Zohar exegesis in the second half of the sixteenth century and the shift of authority from the texts themselves to their interpretation, the traditions associated with the texts also shifted from the authors to the commentators. R. Moses Cordovero recounts a supernatural interpretation of a zoharic section that he had obtained while prostrating himself on the grave of R. Shimon and his son: 'And now I will interpret what God has endowed me with on this subject while I was prostrating myself on the grave of R. Shimon and R. Eleazar his son, in Meron, where it was delivered to me by means of Grace and Kindness.'[42] Joseph Karo, too, tried to interpret the Zohar by reaching out to the souls of R. Shimon and his son. But the employment of supernatural means in explicating the Zohar is primarily associated with Isaac Luria. The traditions regarding his transcendental

[40] Benayahu, *The Biography of Isaac Luria* (Heb.), 162.

[41] Scholem, 'The Document of Association of Luria's Disciples' (Heb.), 159.

[42] Cordovero, *Or yakar*, xiii. 175.

abilities played a major role in the establishment of Lurianic kabbalah as the authoritative exegesis of the Zohar. As Yehuda Liebes has shown, there are testimonies in Luria's commentaries that a supernatural *magid* (herald) had revealed himself to him and guided him along the way.[43] R. Hayim Vital relates, for instance, that Luria had to invest enormous effort in the study of the Zohar at the beginning of his career, for which he was rewarded with visits by heralds who supervised him in his studies:

And with regard to his perception, he told me that in the beginning he used to toil a whole week on a single passage of the Zohar in order to understand it, yet they [the *magidim*] would not disclose the meaning to him, because if they had it would not have been considered his own wisdom, and he was expected to attain new insights into that wisdom by means of his own intellect, which had been bestowed upon him at Mount Sinai. Therefore, while he was labouring, they [the heralds] would say to him: 'In such and such case and in such and such passage you explored and truly understood the matter but it still lacks depth.' And sometimes they would say to him: 'You misunderstood the issue', all of it or part of it; and he would go back and study until he fully understood it.[44]

According to the above tradition, at the beginning of his career it took Luria tremendous effort to interpret the Zohar, but after arriving in Safed he easily mastered its many secrets. This ability is emphasized in the description of the first meeting between Luria and Hayim Vital, as well as in hagiographies that circulated in the epistles of Shlomel Dreznitz.

Vital explains that 'all these [difficulties that Luria had experienced] occurred before Elijah revealed himself to him, but after Elijah, of blessed memory, had revealed himself to him he understood and perceived everything, big and small, and all kinds of wisdom'.[45] In the introduction to his book *Ets ḥayim*, Vital recounts:

And then, when he emigrated from Egypt, he placed his hand on me and opened my eyes by means of a few basic principles that had been delivered to him from the heavenly academy and from the Holy One, blessed be He, to revive the surviving remnant in the Land [of Israel], [and] which [he received] from the mouth of Elijah, of blessed memory, who always appeared to him and was permitted to

43 Liebes, 'New Trends in the Research of Kabbalah' (Heb.), 164–5.

44 *Sha'ar ruaḥ hakodesh*, 19.

45 Benayahu, *The Biography of Isaac Luria* (Heb.), 248.

reveal hidden secrets from the *Tikunim* and the Zohar, which have not been revealed since the days of R. Shimon.[46]

Vital draws a parallel between Luria and R. Shimon by means of two allusions: the first is to the permission granted to Elijah and other supernatural forces to divulge secrets to R. Shimon, as stated in *Tikunei hazohar*.[47] The second is to R. Shimon's assertion in the Zohar regarding secrets revealed to him during the Great Assembly that had been hidden since the revelation at Mount Sinai.[48] As we shall see later, other sources also compared Luria to R. Shimon and went so far as to claim that the commentator (Luria) was superior to the author (R. Shimon).

One should note, furthermore, that the story of Elijah's revelation to Luria elevates the latter to a status beyond that of the greatest sage of Safed in that generation, R. Joseph Karo. In a well-known tradition a *magid* had revealed himself to Karo and had spoken through him, yet Karo had hoped to merit the revelation of Elijah, which he considered to be of a higher status. This aspiration was expressed in the *magid*'s promise that he would be given the opportunity to learn secrets from Elijah if he followed his instructions: 'To merit seeing Elijah face to face while being awake you should mortify your soul as I tell you. And he will talk to you mouth to mouth and he will greet you because he will be your master and teacher to teach you all the secrets of the Torah.'[49] In spite of the promises, Elijah did not reveal himself to Karo while being awake, and Karo had to content himself with the revelations of a *magid*. In these traditions Luria assumes a status equal to that of R. Shimon and higher than that of Karo.

Luria, similarly to Cordovero, is said to have obtained the ability to understand the Zohar and its 'author's intention' through a spiritual connection with R. Shimon while prostrating himself on his grave in Meron.[50] As Yehuda Liebes has observed:

[46] *Ets ḥayim*, i. 21. On Elijah's revelation to Luria see Fine, *Physician of the Soul*, 96.

[47] *Tikunei hazohar*, i. 70*a*.

[48] *Zohar* iii. 144*a*.

[49] Karo, *Magid meisharim*, 5 (warnings, amendments, and restrictions); ibid. 13 ('Bereshit'), 44 ('Vayigash'), 69 ('Tetsaveh'), 105 ('Aḥarei mot'). Werblowsky, *Joseph Karo* (Heb.), 251; Fine, *Physician of the Soul*, 97.

[50] According to a well-known tradition, Luria used to visit R. Shimon's grave even before moving to Safed. On one of those visits R. Shimon revealed himself to him:

I saw my master [Luria], of blessed memory, who went there on Lag Ba'omer with his

Subsequently, after immersing himself in the study of the Zohar, Luria was dissatisfied with his achievements, which were limited to sporadic subjects. He aspired to achieve a comprehensive understanding of the Zohar. For that he needed a different kind of *magid*. No one was more appropriate for that role than the author of the Zohar, who, according to Luria, was R. Shimon bar Yohai. It is my opinion that Luria had moved to Safed to prostrate himself on the grave of R. Shimon in Meron, bond with the soul of the author of the Zohar, and thus perceive the wisdom of the book. Indeed, during that time Luria developed a mystical technique that enabled him to connect with the soul of a *tsadik* by prostrating himself on his grave and for that purpose he wrote a special 'unification'.[51]

In 'Unification on the Graves of *Tsadikim*' Luria claims that one can comprehend secrets by prostrating oneself on the *tsadik*'s grave and by clinging to his soul:

And you should focus on bonding your soul to the soul of the *tsadik* during the unification, and when you focus during the unification on the spirit [*ruaḥ*] and the [lower] soul [*nefesh*] of that *tsadik*, they [the spirit and lower soul] will unify with that *tsadik* and you will be awarded the knowledge of all you wish to ask and know.[52]

In a tradition recorded in *Shivḥei ha'ari*,[53] Luria was able to 'perform unifications at the graves of *tsadikim*. He would prostrate himself on their

entire household, and stayed there for the first three days of that week. That was the first time he had come from Egypt. I do not know whether at that time he was skilled and knowledgeable in this amazing wisdom that he obtained later . . . According to the master R. Abraham Halevi, who also went there in the aforementioned year, he [Luria] would go there and recite every day, as part of the 'Tishkon' blessing, 'Lord our God, console the mourners of Zion', etc. and he would also say 'Comfort', etc., and after he finished the Amidah, my master, of blessed memory, told me that he saw, while being awake, R. Shimon, may he rest in peace, standing at his grave. (*Sha'ar hakavanot*, ii. 191)

At the end of another story, about the re-enactment of the Great Assembly by Luria and his disciples, which I will discuss later, after Luria completes his sermon the companions prostrate themselves on the headstone of R. Shimon's grave and recite songs and praises; see Benayahu, *The Biography of Isaac Luria* (Heb.), 179–80.

[51] 'New Trends in the Research of Kabbalah' (Heb.), 165. [52] *Sha'ar ruaḥ hakodesh*, 111.

[53] The hagiographical stories about Luria, known as *Shivḥei ha'ari*, were first circulated in the epistles of R. Shlomel Dreznitz, and were published in 1628/9–1631/2 under the title *Kitvei shevaḥ yakar ugedulat ha'ari* in the book *Ta'alumot ḥokhmah* by Joseph Solomon Delmedigo of Candia Hanau (although the title page says Basilea). Later the stories appeared in R. Naphtali Bacharach's *Emek hamelekh* (Amsterdam, 1647/8) and in *Sefer hakavanot uma'aseh nisim* (Constantinople 1719/20); see Fine, *Physician of the Soul*, 85.

graves while stretching his hands and legs, and bring down the soul, the spirit, and the lower soul of that *tsadik*, revive him and talk to him. And the *tsadik* would reveal to him supreme secrets and mysteries that were explained in the celestial academy.'[54]

As we have seen, attempts to interpret the Zohar by means of communing with the souls of its authors had preceded Luria. One might infer that the interpretation conveyed to Cordovero 'by means of *ḥen vaḥesed*', while prostrating himself on the grave of R. Shimon and his son, was revealed to him by the souls of the protagonists of the Zohar.[55] His disciple R. Abraham Galante quoted an interpretation of a zoharic passage that he had heard from Cordovero at R. Shimon's grave in Meron, the source of which might have been a supernatural revelation, too.[56] The assumption that it is possible to decipher the secrets of the Zohar by connecting with the souls of its authors is evident in the *magid*'s message to Joseph Karo:

> R. Shimon bar Yohai and his son were happy to see you reading the Zohar at their grave and in the nearby village. Therefore you should know that they are happy when you read the Zohar at their grave or in the adjacent village. And if you persist, they will reveal to you supernal secrets, all of which are alluded to in the Zohar. However, people do not recognize them until they are revealed. Then retrospectively they recognize where the allusions occur. This Zohar, which is in your possession, contains many supernal and invaluable secrets, but people are unaware of them. Once [these secrets] are revealed to them they will see them.[57]

While, despite the *magid*'s promise, Karo was not granted the privilege of learning the Zohar's secrets from R. Shimon and his son, this honour was bestowed on Luria, who arrived in Safed five years before Karo's death. The tradition concerning Luria's ability to connect with R. Shimon's spirit is reminiscent of Elijah's revelation to R. Shimon, and portrays him as having a higher prophetic status than Karo.

In addition to the traditions pertaining to Luria's communion with R. Shimon's soul, a comparison is drawn between them in the writings of Luria's disciples, who claim that R. Shimon's soul had transmigrated into their teacher. As I have argued in the first chapter, the development

[54] Benayahu, *The Biography of Isaac Luria* (Heb.), 157.

[55] Cordovero, *Or yakar*, xiii. 175.

[56] Galante, *Kol bokhim*, 54*b*.

[57] Karo, *Magid meisharim*, 48*b* ('Emor').

whereby commentaries assume an authoritative status is often accompanied by a comparison between the status of the commentator and that of the author. Just as R. Shimon was compared to Moses by the compilers of the Zohar, so did Luria's disciples compare their master to R. Shimon.

And indirect comparison of Luria to R. Shimon is discernible in the narrative about Elijah's revelation to Luria, since, according to pervasive traditions in the sixteenth century, R. Shimon had written the Zohar with the help of Elijah. Furthermore, based on the writings of Luria's disciples, he was a spark of R. Shimon's soul:

> On the day that R. Moses Cordovero passed away, when his disciples and the rest of the sages came to visit him, he said to them: 'You should know, masters, that one person will rise up after me and will disclose the wisdom of kabbalah to you. You might think that he disagrees with me but that is not so because everything is one. Since throughout my life the celestial channels have been blocked, I wrote in an esoteric way, based on the *sefirot*. But after I die more channels will be revealed, and that man [i.e. Luria] will explain things based on the aspect of *partsuf*, etc. Thus, since you might think he disagrees with me I am warning you not to oppose him, because that is what his soul received at Mount Sinai, and especially because the spark in his soul is that of R. Shimon, of blessed memory.[58]

In this tradition it is none other than Cordovero who reveals the link between Luria and R. Shimon, and the warning not to oppose him is also presented as if it were Cordovero's will. The choice of Cordovero as the person to endorse Lurianic kabbalah clearly reflects the power struggle between his and Luria's school.[59]

The link between Luria and R. Shimon is emphasized in a central myth of Lurianic kabbalah that identifies five copulations occurring in the divine world, between the male and female *sefirot*. In each of these divine unifica-

[58] Benayahu, *The Biography of Isaac Luria* (Heb.), 58–9. The idea that Luria was a spark from R. Shimon's soul is also suggested in the tradition which states that R. Hayim Vital (the reincarnation of R. Akiva) had taught Luria (the reincarnation of R. Shimon) in a previous transmigration (ibid. 155).

[59] Vital, *Sefer haḥezyonot*, ed. Aescoly, 57; ed. Faierstein, 83–4. Vital recounts that Cordovero, after his death, appeared to him in a dream and told him that Luria's method was 'the inner and the principal one', and that he himself used that method in studying the Zohar. In contrast, the writings of the Italian kabbalist Abraham Yagel present Cordovero as the reincarnation of R. Shimon; see Idel, 'Major Currents in Italian Kabbalah', 253.

tions drops emerge from the divine phallus, Yesod. In the myth the drops are identified with historical figures—Joseph's brothers, the ten martyr rabbis who were executed by the Romans (*aseret harugei malkhut*), the disciples of R. Judah Hanasi, the circle of R. Shimon, and the circle of Luria. The leader of each group is viewed as an aspect of the *sefirah* Yesod.[60] This myth leads to the conclusion that Luria considered himself and his companions to be the reincarnations of R. Shimon and his companions.[61] The same idea is reflected in the famous story about the re-enactment of the Great Assembly by Luria and his disciples:

On one occasion, when the rabbi [Luria] went with the companions to Meron to R. Shimon's grave, he said to the companions: 'Friends, in this place R. Shimon sat with the companions to arrange the Great Assembly [*idra raba*]. The trace of that light still affects this place, since it is a common truth that even after the light disappears it continues to affect that place forever.' Then the rabbi sat in R. Shimon's place and seated R. Hayim Vital in R. Eleazar's place, and the sage R. Jonathan in R. Aba's place, and the sage R. Gedalyah in R. Judah's place, and the sage R. Joseph Mugrabi in R. Yosei's place, and the sage R. Isaac Hakohen in the place of R. Isaac. He went on and seated the rest of the companions where the companions of R. Shimon had sat. He added and said: 'On this day my companion so-and-so was enlightened by the *tana* so-and-so.' Then he studied with the companions the *Idra* and revealed to them secrets and mysteries to which R. Shimon had alluded in the *Idra*.[62]

The story about Luria's staging of the Great Assembly, in which he assumes the role of R. Shimon, highlights the link between the two figures and presents Luria as the authoritative commentator on the Zohar. At the end of the story angels and the souls of *tsadikim* arrive to listen to his commentary on the *Idra*, and R. Shimon and his companions are among them. In this tradition not only does Luria take on R. Shimon's role but he also understands the secrets of the Zohar better than its presumed author.

Before analysing the idea that Luria the commentator is superior to R. Shimon the author, I would like to briefly discuss the link created by Luria's disciples between him and Moses. This link plays an important role

[60] *Sha'ar hagilgulim*, 70*a*, 168–9. Vital, *Sefer haḥezyonot*, ed. Aescoly, 211–20; ed. Faierstein, 185–8.

[61] Liebes, 'Two Young Roes of a Doe' (Heb.), 150.

[62] Benayahu, *The Biography of Isaac Luria* (Heb.), 179–80.

in their portrayal of Luria as greater than R. Shimon and in the canonization of the Lurianic interpretation of the Zohar.

The connection between Luria and Moses is a central element of Lurianic kabbalah in general,[63] and it is related to the link between Luria and R. Shimon. As I have shown in Chapter 1, R. Shimon and Moses are frequently compared in the zoharic literature. In Lurianic kabbalah R. Shimon is described as the reincarnation of Moses.[64] R. Hayim Vital, in his book *Ets ḥayim*, alludes to the connections between the three figures in a passage discussing R. Shimon's statements in *Idra raba* comparing the Great Assembly to the revelation at Mount Sinai, and himself to Moses:

R. Shimon said: 'All the luminaries, the companions who are part of this sacred circle, may the highest of the highest heaven and this holy land, which is supernal among the supernal lands, be my witnesses that I see now what no man has seen since Moses ascended Mount Sinai for the second time, etc. Furthermore, I know that my face is shining and Moses did not know that the skin of his face shone, etc.' [Zohar iii. 132*b*]. And one should not wonder that R. Shimon, one of the last *tana'im*, was granted this special status, since these matters are mysteries of the world and no one is permitted to explain these matters orally, and [they] have been hidden and concealed with us. Hence one should not be surprised by what we shall recount at the end of this introduction regarding the holy sage who has been revealed to us in our time and in this generation. I cannot comment on it but one will understand what he meant in *Sefer hatikunin* regarding 'one generation goes and another comes'. This is Moses, the faithful shepherd, as it is mentioned in *Tikunim*, 69, page 110*a*:[65] 'R. Shimon said: Friends, for sure the Holy One, blessed be He, agrees with us to have the upper world and lower world participate in the composition of this book. Happy is the generation in which it will be revealed, since all of this will be renewed by Moses in the final generation, when the verse "only that shall happen which has happened" [Eccles. 1: 9] will be realized. And his [Moses'] expansion is in every generation and within every *tsadik* and sage who engages himself in Torah up to the total of sixty myriad, and these matters are obscure and concealed.'[66]

The words of the Zohar regarding R. Shimon's exalted status conceal a secret that should not be explained, Vital warns. He hints, however, that this

[63] Fine, *Physician of the Soul*, 321.

[64] *Sha'ar hagilgulim*, 113; Fine, *Physician of the Soul*, 315.

[65] *Tikunei hazohar*, 111*b*–112*a*.

[66] *Ets ḥayim*, i. 16–17.

secret is connected to what he sought to convey at the end of his introduction about 'the holy sage who has been revealed to us in our time'. Obviously this sage is Luria, whose greatness he subsequently describes thus: 'And I, not anyone else, saw with my own eyes awesome things that have not been seen nor heard anywhere since the days of R. Shimon, may he rest in peace, until now.'[67] Vital states that *tikun* 69 of *Tikunei zohar* is the key to understanding the connection between R. Shimon's exalted status described in the Zohar and that of Luria. That *tikun* recounts the transmigration of Moses' soul, based on the verses 'one generation goes, another comes' and 'only that shall happen which has happened' (*mah shehayah hu sheyihyeh*, the acronym of the name Mosheh), and the revelation of the Zohar's secrets by Luria, who is Moses, the messiah of the final generation.

The secret to which Vital alludes is, then, the messianic nature of Luria, the successor of Moses and R. Shimon. Just as R. Shimon's messianic activity consisted in the interpretation and rejuvenation of Moses' Torah by means of the Zohar, the messianic role of Luria, the Moses of the last generation, was to interpret and renew the Zohar.[68] The attribution of a messianic character to Luria's interpretation reappears in Vital's depiction of the revelation of the Zohar in the last generation as part of the messianic process:[69]

> This ancient and concealed wisdom was prohibited from being revealed from the days preceding R. Shimon . . . until now, as he stated, until the last generation, when the king messiah will come. Now is this time, during which our divine and holy teacher R. Isaac di [*sic*] Luria, of blessed memory, by means of the prophetic spirit that inspired him, began to light up our eyes by means of the light of this divine wisdom, which has been concealed from all living beings until an exaltation

[67] Ibid. 18.

[68] Ronit Meroz has pointed out that 'the essence of Luria's messianic mission was to deliver his new wisdom. In so doing, he resembled R. Shimon, whose principal messianic role, according to the Zohar, was to disseminate the new kabbalah' ('Redemption in Lurianic Teaching' (Heb.), 303). One might add that Luria's 'new wisdom' was the interpretation (and renewal) of the Zohar, which is the interpretation (and renewal) of Moses' Torah. On the messianic character of R. Shimon in the Zohar as perceived by later generations, see Liebes, *Studies in the Zohar*, 1–84.

[69] This perception was widespread in the 16th century and became highly influential through its formulation by Judah Hayat in his introduction to *Ma'arekhet ha'elohut* (see Ch. 6 below).

takes place and is supported from below, as our sages of blessed memory have said: 'The upper [worlds] need the active support of the lower [worlds].' And R. Shimon, may he rest in peace, said that there is a need for spiritual awakening to rise from below to assist the coming of the redeemer, may it be soon in our time.[70]

As I have shown in Chapter 1, the authoritative status of a commentary on a canonical text goes hand in hand with the equation of the commentator's status with that of the author, and with his portrayal as superior to the author. Just as R. Shimon was depicted as greater than Moses in the zoharic literature, Luria was portrayed as greater than R. Shimon in the Lurianic literature.

In comparing Luria to Moses and R. Shimon, Vital suggests just that.[71] Although he recognizes the similarities between them, he does not view them as equals. However, he differs with the zoharic view that R. Shimon was equal or even superior to Moses. Quoting the *Idra raba* regarding R. Shimon's exalted status, he states that the Zohar only compares him to Moses in the latter's diminished state, following the sin of the golden calf, and not in his supernal, exalted status upon ascending Mount Sinai for the first time.[72]

'I see now what no one has seen since the time Moses ascended Mount Sinai for the second time, etc.' [Zohar iii. 132*b*]. I have already related to you a long homily concerning the origin and significance of the souls of the ten martyrs. I have explained that R. Shimon and our holy teacher are an aspect of [*sefirat*] Yesod, but there is a difference whether they are the Yesod of Aba or the Yesod of Ze'er Anpin, or the Yesod of Jacob. Moses is also an aspect of Yesod, but he rises through the middle line to [*sefirat*] Da'at. Moses' status at the time of [the giving of] the first tablets, before Israel sinned with the calf, was very high, but when Israel sinned he lost the great light that he possessed, and a thousand particles of light he had

[70] *Sha'ar ruaḥ hakodesh*, 38–9; *Olat hatamid*, 113.

[71] According to Rachel Elior, Joseph Karo, too, had internalized the personae and roles of Moses and R. Shimon; see her 'Joseph Karo' (Heb.), 660 n. 22, 683, 697.

[72] Cordovero, too, emphasized the fact that the Zohar compares the Great Assembly to Moses' second ascent to receive the tablets in the wake of the sin of the golden calf, when the influence of the Torah was weakened and its secrets were concealed: 'The second delivery of the tablets was performed in secrecy, and it consisted of the material aspect of the Torah in its simple meaning, and its spirituality and secrets vanished. Therefore, the Torah's hidden lights, which contain its secrets, were not revealed. Because of their sin with the golden calf the Torah was enshrouded' (*Or yakar*, xxii. 29).

within him were taken away from him. At the time of the second pair of tablets he was given only one particle of the thousand he had previously possessed, and that is the secret of the small *alef* in *vayikra el mosheh*—thousands of particles were taken away from him and he remained with only one particle out of the original thousand particles of light he had had, which the small *alef* denotes. And that is what the scripture conveys: 'but the Lord was wrathful with me on your account' [Deut. 3: 26], because Moses was reduced to a lower status [*katnut*], which is called *ibur*, and lost the great light he had possessed in the beginning. And R. Shimon, may he rest in peace, started from that low level, and then rose during the assembly to the level of Moses when he received the second set of tablets—not to the earlier, higher status of Moses, when he went up Mount Sinai to receive the first set of tablets.[73]

Vital explains that, following the sin of the golden calf, Moses lost the enormous light he had had (a loss hinted at by the small *alef* in the word *vayikra*),[74] and was reduced to a lower level called *katnut* and *ibur*, a state of imperfect perception to which Deuteronomy 3: 26 refers: 'but the Lord was wrathful [*vayitabar*] with me on your account'. Thus, even at his peak during the assembly, R. Shimon could only reach the lower status of Moses (when he received the second set of tablets of the Torah).

In the quote above Vital does not explicitly mention Luria. At the beginning of his discussion, however, he refers to the souls of the ten martyrs within the context of a myth discussed earlier concerning the five supernal copulations, and the drops emerging from Yesod in each act of intercourse. Moses, R. Shimon, and Luria are perceived in this myth as the Yesod aspect of the five supernal copulations. The link between the souls of R. Shimon and Moses is thus part of a link between the three figures, R. Shimon, Moses, and Luria. As I have shown, Vital (in contrast to the Zohar) emphasizes Moses' superiority since R. Shimon, at his highest point, had only reached the former's lowest status. The question then arises, what about Luria's status in relation to R. Shimon? Vital, in his account of meeting Luria a week before the latter's death, offers a comparison between the two:

[73] *Sha'ar ma'amrei rashbi*, 212. See also *Sha'ar hagilgulim*, 123.

[74] Vital's homily is based on (*a*) the difference between the shape of the *alef* in *vayikra el mosheh* in Exod. 24: 16 and the *alef* in *vayikra* in Lev. 1: 1, and (*b*) the homily in Zohar ii. 58*a*: 'from the time of Israel's degradation God, blessed be He, has taken away 5,000 particles from that light'.

And now I will write down what my teacher of blessed memory told me seven days before his passing. And one should know that, from the first time he spoke to me, he instructed me not to disclose his perception and knowledge of the subject matter to any human being since he intended to repair only me, and afterwards others would be repaired through me. And he warned me that if I revealed it great harm would come to him, to me, and to the rest of the world . . . and often my teacher of blessed memory would chastise me for having publicized his genius so widely that students flocked to him, and he no longer had time to teach me. And he used to say to me: 'It is you who caused all of these people to come to me. I am a humble man and in spite of the harm I suffer because of this, I am unable to refuse to see them.' As time went by, he wanted to send all of them away, but they did not want to go and they pleaded with him until he said to them: 'Do you want to bring wrath upon me so that I will return down to the level of *ibur* on your account?'[75]

The comparison between Luria and Moses is clearly implied by Luria's choice of words in Vital's account of the above meeting: 'I am a humble man' alludes to the description of Moses in Numbers 12: 3 as a very humble man, and the reference to '*ibur* on your account' alludes to Deuteronomy 3: 26, where Moses speaks of his punishment on account of Israel following the sin of the golden calf.

On the basis of the above narrative and Vital's commentary on *Idra raba*, Luria feared that, just as Moses had fallen to the status of *ibur* in the wake of the golden calf incident, so would he do so following the companions' demands to have the secrets revealed to them. What Vital claims, then, is that Luria, at his peak, not only reached the exalted status of Moses (before the sin of the golden calf), but thereby superseded the status of R. Shimon.

In his commentary on *Sava demishpatim*, Vital voices his reservations regarding R. Shimon's exaltation more explicitly, and explores the question of why R. Shimon and not someone else was privileged to write the Zohar:

'The son of Yohai knows how to guard his ways, etc.' [Zohar ii. 100*b*]. One should know that some souls of *tsadikim* are like the peripheral light and some are the inner light. And those who possess the peripheral light have the ability to explore the secrets and mysteries of the Torah covertly and clandestinely in order that

[75] *Sha'ar hagilgulim*, 148–9; Vital, *Sefer haḥezyonot*, ed. Aescoly, 188–9.

none but those who merit their understanding will understand. And R. Shimon, may he rest in peace, his soul was of the peripheral light, therefore he had the ability to conceal these secrets and mysteries and to expound them, even publicly, in a way that no one would understand them but those who were worthy of understanding. Therefore he was granted permission to write the Zohar. Permission had not been given to his teachers or to his predecessors to write a book on this wisdom even though they knew this wisdom better than he did. The reason was that they were unable to clothe the words as he did. That is what is meant in 'the son of Yohai knows, etc.' Hence you can appreciate R. Shimon's mastery [of concealment] in the Zohar, which not every human mind is able to understand.[76]

R. Shimon, Vital claims, was privileged to write the Zohar not because of his mastery of kabbalah, but rather because of his ability to write esoterically. Although it is not stated explicitly, one can infer that the status of Luria, a man capable of interpreting the secrets of kabbalah concealed in the Zohar, is higher than that of R. Shimon, who concealed these secrets in his book.

An expression of Luria's superiority to R. Shimon appears in the description of the re-enactment of the Great Assembly by Luria and his disciples. In this story the soul of R. Shimon, together with other elevated souls, comes to listen to Luria's commentary on the secrets of *Idra raba*: 'And while he [Luria] was studying, he said to the companions: "My companions, know that flames of fires surround us. R. Shimon, may he rest in peace, his companions, and the souls of *tsadikim* and other *tana'im*, and the ministering angels have come to hear true Torah from my mouth."'[77] It is possible to infer that R. Shimon appeared at the gathering in order to learn from Luria the meaning of the secrets that were concealed in his own book because he had not fully understood them (this recalls the homily in *Men.* 29*b* on Moses, who comes down to earth to listen to R. Akiva expounding the Torah). Furthermore, according to *Shivḥei ha'ari*, Luria told R. Abraham Halevi that, while sleeping, his soul had studied in the supernal academy 'secrets and mysteries hidden in the Torah that have never been heard nor known even during the time of the *tana'im*'.[78] The idea that secrets were revealed to him that had not been known to the *tana'im* elevates him above the authors of the Zohar.

[76] *Sha'ar ma'amrei rashbi*, 91–2.

[77] Benayahu, *The Biography of Isaac Luria* (Heb.), 179–80.

[78] Ibid. 165.

Luria's portrayal as the exclusive interpreter of the Zohar, who can understand its secrets thanks to his supernatural abilities and spiritual provenance, is related to the depiction of the Zohar as a text so obscure that only a person with outstanding transcendental skills would be able to interpret it. The notion that the Zohar was an esoteric text that required unique abilities to decipher its secrets was not prevalent in the early centuries of its circulation. On the contrary, R. Isaac of Acre noted, in his famous testimony regarding the early distribution of the Zohar, that it included 'wondrous secrets, previously transmitted only orally and not meant to be set in writing, and which are explained in this book so that they can be comprehended by anyone who is able to read a book'.[79] There were kabbalists who noted the difficulty of understanding the Aramaic in it;[80] however, the assumption that the text was inaccessible via conventional intellectual means, and that there was a need to appeal to supernatural forces to understand it, only appeared in the late fifteenth century. In *Sefer hameshiv*, probably written in Spain before the expulsion, God (the narrator) argues that the Zohar was intentionally designed to be an obscure text that would become unfathomable after the passing of R. Shimon, so that no one would be able to understand it unless God himself revealed its secrets.

As for the question you asked me when you saw that my son, the righteous Shimon, had concealed his words in the language of the Bavli [Babylonian Talmud], and not in the concealed language of the Yerushalmi—it was necessary until this time. Now the time has come to reveal them in great detail so as to enable you to understand them . . . Based on my instruction and order, Shimon, my son, intended to conceal that secret; thus he encapsulated it in an allusion that [only] he, his son after him, and a few companions would be able to understand. And when he died, the book and its wisdom and its secrets died with him. And you do not understand it, not you nor those reading it, who are cunning for the sake of evil. And I will take my revenge on whoever reveals its secrets and contents to those who are unworthy.[81]

[79] Zacuto, *Sefer yuḥasin hashalem*, 88–9.

[80] In one of the manuscripts of Angelet's *Perush sha'arei orah* (New York MS, 27*a*) we find: 'R. Shimon's homily is in the tongue of the Yerushalmi, which not many are able to understand.'

[81] Scholem, 'The Magid of R. Joseph Taitatsak' (Heb.), 87–8; Idel, 'Neglected Writings of the Author of *Kaf haketoret*' (Heb.), 80.

A similar idea appears in the words of the *magid* to R. Joseph Karo cited above: 'This Zohar, which is in your possession, contains many supernal and invaluable secrets, but people are unaware of them. However, once [these secrets] are revealed to them they will see them.'[82]

The obscurity of the zoharic text is reiterated and underlined in Hayim Vital's writings. In a passage quoted above he says: 'Hence you can appreciate R. Shimon's mastery of [concealment] in the Zohar, which not every human mind is able to understand.'[83] Elsewhere he writes: 'How would it occur to a human mind to be able to grasp by learning and by reasoning the words of the living God, the words of R. Shimon, may he rest in peace, whose sayings are consuming flames of fire, hidden and locked by a thousand seals?'[84]

Vital's emphasis on the obscurity of the Zohar was directed, without any doubt, at Moses Cordovero, who described the Zohar as an open text:

> This is the reason why it was appropriate to conceal this knowledge, so it would be received from mouth to mouth . . . This was what the sages of Israel used to do until R. Shimon came and immersed himself in this knowledge. He was assisted by heaven, and the gates of wisdom opened before him . . . and he was able to present this wisdom and prevent those who entered it through the gates of [his] books from falling into the pits of mistakes. . . . Nevertheless, he had to obtain permission to write this wisdom in books so it would become a table laid [*shulḥan arukh*[85]] for all, and so that those who desire to assume the Name may come and do so.[86]

Cordovero asserts here that the kabbalah was an esoteric body of knowledge until R. Shimon's time. However, he was given permission to write it down in an accessible language, and the Zohar has thus become an exoteric and open text.[87] Vital, on the other hand, is of the opinion that kabbalah

[82] Karo, *Magid meisharim*, 48*b* ('Emor').

[83] *Sha'ar ma'amrei rashbi*, 91–2.

[84] *Ets ḥayim*, introduction, 17.

[85] This term is reminiscent of Karo's work, which was written and published at that time. On its etymology see Twersky, 'The *Shulḥan arukh*', 141 n. 1.

[86] Cordovero, *Tikunei hazohar im perush or yakar*, i. 15 (the expression is based on Mishnah *Ber*. 2: 8); see also ibid. v. 83.

[87] A typical formulation of the exoteric approach to the Zohar, which presents it as an open text and encourages people 'high and low' to study it publicly, appears in R. Abraham Azulai's introduction to *Or haḥamah*. Azulai (following Cordovero's position in *Or ne'erav*) views the study of the Zohar as something characteristic of the generation of redemption:

was an exoteric wisdom until R. Shimon's time, and has been concealed since: 'And this wisdom used to be revealed by means of revelations until the passing of R. Shimon, may he rest in peace, and from that time on visions have been blocked.'[88] In contrast to Cordovero, who encourages interpretation of the Zohar, Vital argues:

Although it is clear and obvious that this book will sustain the future generations, and this wisdom will be revealed to them, not everyone who desires to assume the Name may do so, because the secrets of the Torah and its mysteries are not revealed to humans by means of earthly studies but through divine emanation that originates from the height of His holiness and is delivered through His messengers and angels, or by the prophet Elijah, as we will explain at the end of this introduction.[89]

Vital clearly aims his words at Cordovero, who asserts that anyone may engage in interpretation of the Zohar. Vital's position, in contrast, is that the ability to explicate that work depends on supernatural guidance; only Luria, assisted by revelations, was able to decipher its secrets. He further claims that the obscure text of the Zohar can only be understood by means of Lurianic principles:

And now, after forwarding all these principles to you we have to warn the person who intends to engage in the Zohar that he will find in it many different statements, disagreements, and contradictions, and without these principles he will be unable to understand them and reconcile them. And he might build on them piles of rags, fettered, speckled, and patched, patch over patch, as is the case with those who pretend to understand the Zohar by means of their human mind.[90]

The words against 'those who pretend to understand the Zohar by means of their human mind' or try to access the secrets of kabbalah 'by means of earthly studies' were undoubtedly addressed to Cordovero, who empha-

And I found it written that the decree not to engage in kabbalah openly had been imposed from above for a limited time, until the year 5250 [1490], and from that time on the time is that of the final generation, and the decree has been lifted and permission has been given to engage in the Zohar. And from the year 5400 (1540) it has been recommended that everyone, high and low alike, should publicly engage in it, as stated in *Ra'ayah meheimna*. (*Or haḥamah*, 'Introduction', i. 1c)

[88] *Ets ḥayim*, introduction, i. 19.

[89] Ibid. 15–16.

[90] *Sha'ar hahakdamot*, second introduction, 3–4; *Ets ḥayim*, i. 42–3.

sized the importance of an intellectual approach to the Zohar and to the secrets of kabbalah.[91] As Isaiah Tishby has shown, elsewhere Vital's vehement criticism of books written by contemporary authors (i.e. *aḥaronim*) and based on intellectual principles[92] was also aimed at Cordovero.[93] In sum, both the emphasis on the obscurity of the zoharic text and the disqualification of any interpretation that did not follow Lurianic kabbalah were an attack, first and foremost, on Cordovero's commentary, in an attempt to establish the monopoly of Luria's interpretation.

Subsequently Luria's commentary did gain recognition as the authoritative exegesis of the Zohar, and other interpretations were gradually rejected, including that of Cordovero, as the superiority of Lurianic commentary came to be accepted not only by Luria's but also by Cordovero's disciples. At the end of the sixteenth century, for instance, R. Menahem Azaryah da Fano, who had played a part in the development and circulation of Cordovero's kabbalah in Italy, acknowledged the supremacy of Lurianic teaching, claiming that it revealed the secret layer of the Zohar, which had not been penetrated by Cordovero.[94] R. Abraham Azulai moved from Fez to Palestine in the early seventeenth century to study Cordovero's *Commentary on the Zohar*, a synopsis of which he included in his anthology of Zohar commentaries, *Or haḥamah*. Notwithstanding, he considered Cordovero's work a lesser study of the Zohar's 'simple meanings' and he, too, accepted the superiority of Luria's commentary. In the introduction to *Or haḥamah* he wrote:

[91] Cordovero states in *Or ne'erav*, 35: 'It is necessary to pursue esoteric matters very carefully, with unusual deliberation and tremendous casuistry, in contrast to those in our generation who crown themselves kabbalists and argue that there is no need for casuistry.' See also ibid. 24, where he says: 'One who studies these books needs to do two things: first, one should read the text superficially many times and make notes for himself to remember the details; [then he should] study it for a second time and analyse it according to his ability.'

[92] *Ets ḥayim*, i. 19–21. The criticism of Cordovero is obvious when Vital talks about the 'latest kabbalists': 'And the astute student is able to absorb and understand most of their [the latest kabbalists'] principles and rules within four or five days. All they do is repeat the same idea in different words, and the only outcome of their principle is that there are ten *sefirot*. Piles upon piles of books have been written on it, when all they say could have been written in two or three pamphlets' (ibid. 19). It is also clear that this statement compares the copious work of Cordovero with the difficulties that Luria experienced in putting his ideas into writing.

[93] Tishby, *Studies in Kabbalah* (Heb.), i. 130 nn. 207, 250.

[94] Ibid. 178–82.

Whenever his [Cordovero's] opinion disagreed with the wisdom of the divine teacher, R. Isaac Ashkenazi [Luria], may he be remembered in the world to come, I deleted it and did not include it. Sometimes, however, even though he had opposed R. Isaac Ashkenazi, may he be remembered in the world to come, I did incorporate it to stimulate the reader and enable him to interpret it easily according to the principles of R. Isaac Ashkenazi.[95]

The spread of Lurianic kabbalah in the seventeenth, and particularly in the eighteenth and nineteenth, centuries facilitated the consolidation of its status as the predominant interpretation of the Zohar.[96] The authority of the Zohar was perceived as dependent on its being understood via Luria's exegesis. The Lurianic kabbalist R. Jacob Tsemah intimates this in the introduction to *Kol baramah*, his commentary on *Idra raba* (Jerusalem, 1643): 'Now, all the homilies of the teacher, may he be remembered in the world to come, prove that he had revealed all the *partsufim* and the *tikunim* by which one can understand the Zohar and learn something from it.'[97] R. Shalom Buzaglo, author of *Mikdash melekh*, the first comprehensive commentary on the Zohar to be printed,[98] makes a similar point in his introduction: 'On the pillars of the Ari, of blessed memory, I have established its foundations, and I have not turned aside from his principles, neither to the right nor to the left.'[99] In the early nineteenth century R. Tsevi Hirsch of Zhidachov proclaimed, in the introduction to his Zohar commentary, *Ateret tsevi*:

Indeed, the Zohar is obscure, sealed and concealed from the human eye, even though the *rishonim*, such as our master and teacher R. Menahem Recanati and his

95 *Or haḥamah*, 'Introduction', i. 2*a*.

96 On its spread in the 17th century see Scholem, *Major Trends in Jewish Mysticism*, 287–8; id., *Sabbatai Zevi and the Sabbatian Movement* (Heb.), i. 52–74. Contrary to Scholem's opinion that the proliferation of Lurianic kabbalah preceded, and played a major role in the emergence and spread of, Sabbatianism, Moshe Idel and Zeev Gries have argued that it only became widely popular as a result of the Sabbatian awakening. See Gries, 'Shaping the Hebrew Conduct Literature' (Heb.), 563, 572; ibid. 82–3, 92; id., 'The Copying and Printing of Kabbalistic Books' (Heb.), 206; Idel, 'One from a Town' (Heb.), 19.

97 Quoted in Scholem, 'On the Life and Works of Jacob Tsemah' (Heb.), 184; see also Idel, 'One from a Town' (Heb.), 13.

98 *Mikdash melekh* was published in Amsterdam in 1740/1. *Hadrat melekh*, Buzaglo's commentary on difficult passages in the Zohar, *Tikunei hazohar*, *Idra raba*, *Idra zuta*, and *Sifra ditseniuta* was published in Amsterdam and London—the first volume in 1765/6 and the second in 1769/70.

99 *Mikdash melekh*, i. 68; Giller, *Reading the Zohar*, 29–30.

companions, and R. Meir Gabai and Judah Hayat, explained a few of its segments; and in particular the holy one, R. Moses Cordovero, who laboured on his own to interpret the Zohar, including all of its allusions. He scrutinized it as if it was the Torah itself. Nonetheless, brothers, one who has not tasted the tree of life or the wisdom of our teacher, the Ari of blessed memory, the depths of the lily of valleys, whose mouth is delicious and all of him is delightful, has not had a taste of the Zohar.[100]

Indeed, there were only a handful of kabbalists who explicitly rejected Luria's approach to the Zohar or disagreed with his interpretation. One such opponent was the above-mentioned R. Menahem Lunzano, who sharply criticized the commentaries of both Luria and his disciples before their general acceptance. Later this became the reason, as Gershom Scholem has pointed out, for the shelving of Lunzano's work.[101] A more moderate criticism was raised by Sabbatian Zohar commentators in the early eighteenth century: R. Abraham Rovigo argued that Luria's commentaries did not help one understand the Zohar. Instead, he extolled the work of his protégé, the Sabbatian seer R. Mordecai Ashkenazi: 'Until now, few could understand it [the Zohar] and it seems that, although the Ari came and wrote what he wrote, he made almost no section of the Zohar comprehensible. And now, by the rules that were given to him [to R. Ashkenazi], one can understand some sections, thank God.'[102]

Criticism of Luria was reiterated by a *magid* (heavenly mentor/angel) to R. Mordecai Ashkenazi: 'We do not have anyone greater than the Ari of blessed memory, yet his words remain obscure although he explained them in great detail, because at that time it was impossible to interpret and to

[100] Eichenstein, *Ateret tsevi*, 3*a*. The grandson of R. Tsevi Hirsch's brother, R. Eliezer Tsevi Safrin, declared the superiority of Luria's interpretation of the Zohar: 'And whoever studies the writings of our master, Isaac Luria, may he be remembered in the world to come, and the text of the holy Zohar with the commentaries that carefully follow Luria's principles . . . this person, by himself, will taste a sweet taste that will make him realize that there is nowhere in the world a wisdom as profound as the wisdom of the secrets of the Torah' (*Damesek eli'ezer*, 3*b*). See also ibid. 4*a*–*b*.

[101] Scholem, 'The Document of Association of Luria's Disciples' (Heb.), 159.

[102] Scholem, *The Dreams of Mordecai Ashkenazi* (Heb.), 24. Scholem shows that Nathan of Gaza expressed the same attitude by saying that no one should read Luria's writings 'because they are obscure and there was no living person who understood his words except R. Hayim Vital, a righteous and holy man of blessed memory' (ibid. 30).

let others understand.'[103] His opinion was consistent with the reservations regarding Lurianic kabbalah in the writings of Sabbatian authors, who thought it was irrelevant to the messianic era.[104]

An independent approach to the interpretation of the Zohar characterizes the commentary of R. Elijah, the Vilna Gaon. Although he employed Lurianic terms and conceptions, he rejected some of Luria's interpretations.[105] As a result he was accused by the hasidim of denouncing the authority and sanctity of Lurianic kabbalah.[106] Although the Gaon's disciple, R. Hayim of Volozhin, denied these accusations, he did acknowledge that his master's interpretations disagreed at first sight with a few of Luria's: 'Although readers might find in this commentary a few minor deviations, a real scholar will be able to settle it so there is no dispute.'[107]

A hasidic tradition that implicitly questions Luria's hermeneutical ability should also be mentioned here. R. Hayim Liebersohn, in *Tseror ha-ḥayim*, recounts a story in which the Ba'al Shem Tov was able to interpret a zoharic text better than Luria and even better than R. Shimon himself:

In a certain place the holy Ba'al Shem Tov met an important person who wished to contact him. On the holy sabbath that important man had dreamt about a text

[103] Scholem, *The Dreams of Mordecai Ashkenazi*, 30–2.

[104] Ibid. 29; Huss, 'Sabbatianism' (Heb.), 57–8. On the Sabbatian commentary on the Zohar see ibid. 64.

[105] Avivi, *The Kabbalah of the Vilna Gaon* (Heb.), 30; Schuchat, 'Lithuanian Kabbalah' (Heb.), 197. The Gaon's reservations regarding Luria's Zohar commentary are another example of the weakening status of Lurianic kabbalah in the late 18th century; see Idel, *Hasidism*, 67–8.

[106] R. Shneur Zalman of Lyady wrote:

> It is clear to us that the righteous Gaon, may his light shine, does not believe that the kabbalah of Isaac Luria in its entirety was received from the mouth of Elijah, of blessed memory. Only a very small part of it was received from Elijah . . . and the rest stems from his great wisdom, and it is not mandatory to believe in it, etc. (*Letters by the Author of the Tanya*, ed. Hilman, 97)

For R. Hayim of Volozhin's reaction to this accusation see his introduction to the commentary of the Vilna Gaon on *Sifra ditseniuta*:

> And whenever I talk about the greatness and holiness of our rabbi's wisdom, may he rest in peace, I remember him, and it makes me sad, and my heart turns into a burning fire when the slander of many illiterate and worthless people in distant districts reaches my ear . . . saying that he does not revere the holy rabbi within whom the sacred spirit of God dwells, R. Isaac Luria of blessed memory.

[107] Ibid.

from the sacred Zohar, for which the holy Ba'al Shem Tov offered [in his dream] a simple interpretation. Since the holy Ari had provided a different interpretation of the same text, they said to each other, 'Let us go and ask R. Shimon.' R. Shimon sided with the Ari. The Ba'al Shem Tov said to R. Shimon, 'You wrote the Zohar by means of the holy spirit. Let us ask Him directly.' In heaven they said, 'The meaning is in accordance with the Ba'al Shem Tov.' This was what the important man dreamt. At the [time] of the third meal he went to the Ba'al Shem Tov and pushed his way through to learn his wisdom, and heard the Ba'al Shem Tov explain this text from the Zohar, and the Ba'al Shem Tov said to him: 'You have already learnt this Zohar tonight.'[108]

An indirect criticism of Luria's Zohar commentary reappears in the writings of the greatest twentieth-century Zohar commentator, R. Judah Ashlag. He, too, uses an original approach in his interpretation of the Zohar, based on Lurianic terms.[109] Ashlag argues that his commentary is superior to all those previously written because the scholars who preceded him neglected to explain the difficult passages, thus their interpretation remains opaque. This criticism, which, to a great extent, recalls that of the aforementioned Sabbatian kabbalist, Mordecai Ashkenazi, is directed, without any doubt, first and foremost at the Lurianic commentaries:

As we can see, all the commentaries on the Zohar that preceded ours did not interpret even 10 per cent of all the difficult sections of the Zohar. And the few [passages] that they did interpret, the interpretation is almost as inexplicable as the Zohar itself. Our generation has been awarded the *Sulam* commentary, which is a complete commentary on the Zohar in its entirety. In addition, it does not leave anything in the Zohar unexplained. Its explications are based on simple logic that the average reader can understand.[110]

Notwithstanding the misgivings, which were few and inexplicit, the authority of the Lurianic Zohar commentary was accepted without objection by almost all kabbalistic circles. This general recognition, however, did

[108] *Tseror haḥayim*, 10*b*; Idel, *Hasidism* (Heb.), 86 n. 73.

[109] Huss, 'Altruistic Communism' (Heb.).

[110] Ashlag, *Matan torah*, 134–5. It is interesting to compare his words to those of Hillel Zeitlin in his letter of 1922 to Simon Rawidowicz: 'The famous Zohar commentators did not explain anything to the simple reader, since their words are more obscure than the words of the Zohar itself' (Rawidowicz (ed.), *Metsudah: Essays and Studies* (Heb.), 38). See also Meir, 'Hillel Zeitlin's Zohar' (Heb.), 143.

not put an end to the production of additional zoharic commentaries in subsequent generations. The fact that Luria had not left a comprehensive commentary allowed later exegetes to engage anew in interpretation of the Zohar and to present their innovative commentaries as further elaborations of, and amendments to, the Lurianic work. For example R. Hayim of Volozhin, in his introduction to the Vilna Gaon's commentary on *Sifra ditseniuta*, emphasizes that Luria had left only a partial commentary on that book:

Although among the writings of our awesome holy teacher, the Ari of blessed memory, one can find *ḥidushim* [novel interpretations], they are nothing but homilies based on his awesome and enormous wisdom. We have not received all of his sacred words on all of it, only a little here and a little there on the beginning of the first and second chapters. Still, we have not received a comprehensive commentary on this sacred text from beginning to end.[111]

According to R. Hayim, the Vilna Gaon himself had argued that 'the Ari of blessed memory had left some room for him in this area'.[112] Unlike the Gaon, R. Judah Ashlag presented his Zohar commentary as the revelation of the secrets of Luria's exegesis that had been concealed up to his day:

In the time of the Ari, of blessed memory, when the time for the completion of the lower vessels was approaching, and the supernal wisdom had been revealed in a concealed way through the divine soul of the Ari, of blessed memory, who was ready to receive this great light, he revealed the principles of the Zohar and the wisdom of kabbalah, so much so that he surpassed all the kabbalists who had preceded him. But since those vessels were not fully complete (because, as it is known, he died in 5332 [1572]), the world was not yet ready for his words to be revealed, and his sacred words were comprehended only by a meritorious chosen few, who were prohibited from revealing them to [the rest of] the world. And now, in our generation, approaching the end of the last two millennia, permission has been given to reveal to the world most of the Ari's words, and to a great extent the words of the Zohar, too. Thus from our generation on, more and more words of the Zohar will be revealed until it is revealed in its entirety according to God's will, may He be blessed.[113]

111 See the introduction to Kremer, *Sifra ditseniuta im be'ur eliyahu mivilna*. 112 Ibid.
113 *Sefer hahakdamot leḥokhmat ha'emet*, 'Introduction to the Zohar', 94.

The general acceptance of the Lurianic commentary as the authoritative interpretation of the Zohar did not completely preclude other hermeneutical methods, such as that of Cordovero.[114] The distinction between esoteric and exoteric layers in zoharic literature facilitated the proliferation of different commentaries independent of Luria's doctrine. R. Hayim Vital, following other Lurianic kabbalists, adopted this distinction and used it to juxtapose Luria's and Cordovero's commentaries, and to proclaim the superiority of the former.[115] In *Sefer haḥezyonot* Vital recounts that Cordovero himself had appeared to him in a dream and responded to the question of how one studied the Zohar in heavenly academies: 'There are two methods, both are true aspects of kabbalah. Although I use the method of the simple meaning for those who are beginners in this wisdom, the method of your teacher is the inner and more profound one. And now, being above, I am using only the method of your teacher.'[116]

R. Menahem Azaryah da Fano, an Italian kabbalist who, until his encounter with Lurianic kabbalah, was an enthusiastic supporter of Cordovero's thought,[117] also adopted this distinction. In his introduction to *Pelaḥ harimon* (a synopsis of Cordovero's great work, *Pardes rimonim*), da Fano differentiates between the Zohar's simple meaning, which applies only to the lower world of *belimah*, and its esoteric layer, which describes the upper levels of the divine world and is interpreted by the Lurianic kabbalah:

And whoever rejects him [i.e. Cordovero] and his wisdom will be rejected by God, because Moses is right and his wisdom is true and based on the simple meaning of

[114] In his articles 'The Showdown between Luria's Kabbalah and that of Cordovero in the Writings of Rambam' and 'The Approach of R. Abraham Azulai to the Kabbalah of Cordovero and Luria' (*Studies in Kabbalah* (Heb.), i. 177–267), Isaiah Tishby has demonstrated that, despite the significant influence of Lurianic kabbalah in the late 16th and early 17th centuries, kabbalists continued to revere Cordovero and distribute his teachings. See also Idel, 'Major Currents in Italian Kabbalah', 252–3.

[115] See Meroz, '*Or haganuz* by R. Abraham Azulai' (Heb.), 316–19; Huss, 'The Anthological Interpretation', 11–13.

[116] *Sefer haḥezyonot*, ed. Aescoly, 57; ed. Faierstein, 83–4. Vital did not explain the difference between Cordovero's interpretation of 'the simple meaning' and Luria's esoteric commentary. However, one may assume that it stems from the difference between the divine systems that the two hermeneutical methods present—ten *sefirot* on the one hand, and the complex divine system of Lurianic kabbalah on the other.

[117] Tishby, *Studies in Kabbalah* (Heb.), i. 178–82.

the Zohar . . . Since he [Cordovero] expounded all his life the world of *belimah*, which we explored in *Sefer yetsirah* . . . and which is part of the wisdom of kabbalah and has been explored by most kabbalists who preceded us . . . The Ari . . . on the other hand, used to expound the principles of the *Idra* and *Sifra ditseniuta*, which explore the *mitkala* [scale] itself and its image in the upper realm.[118]

The distinction between commentaries based on the 'simple meaning', on the one hand, and 'esoteric' interpretations, which were identified with Lurianic commentary, on the other, reinforced Lurianic kabbalah as the supreme kabbalistic method, while simultaneously allowing the development and circulation of alternative Zohar commentaries,[119] including that of Cordovero.[120] Thus, alongside commentaries that expanded, supple-

[118] Da Fano, *Pelaḥ harimon*, 4*a*.

[119] In his book *Or haḥamah*, for instance, R. Abraham Azulai included Zohar commentaries such as Cordovero's *Or yakar* and the writings of Vital and Galante, all of which he defined as explications of the 'simple meaning' of the Zohar: '*Or haḥamah* helps the reader understand the zoharic words, those that are not profound, by shining the bright light of the sun on them to allow all the people, those who understand and those who do not understand, to enjoy them' (introduction to *Or haḥamah*, i. 2*a*). He published a further collection of Lurianic interpretations in his book *Or haganuz*; see Meroz, '*Or haganuz* by R. Abraham Azulai' (Heb.). R. Joseph Hamitz used the distinction between the 'simple meaning' stratum and the esoteric (*sod*) stratum to justify the collection of non-Lurianic Zohar commentaries in his anthology *Yodei binah*. Hamitz lived in Venice before he emigrated to Palestine in 1657/8, where he edited the first part of *Yodei binah*. He incorporated in this anthology commentaries that he had found in Azulai's *Or haḥamah*; segments of Simeon Ibn Lavi's Zohar commentary; Cordovero's annotations to the Zohar; explanations of foreign words found in the Zohar, culled from R. Issachar Baer of Kremnitz's *Imrei binah*; as well as Lurianic interpretations that had come into his hands.

[120] As I have shown above, R. Eliezer Safrin, for instance, accepted the Lurianic interpretation; in the introduction to his commentary on the Zohar he nevertheless explained that his intention was to present the simple meaning of the text:

> I have heard from my master, father, teacher, and rabbi, may he be remembered for the world to come, that he had heard [this] from the holy mouth of our teacher Jacob Isaac ben Motel of Lublin, who in his kindness wished that there was someone in the world to interpret the sacred Zohar according to its simple meaning wherever it was possible. And I myself have also heard from the righteous rabbi, our teacher, the gaon Tsevi of Liska of the land of Hagar, about his desire to see some commentary on the sacred Zohar based on its simple meaning. Hence . . . I took it upon myself, God willing, to do it and interpret [the Zohar] according to its simple meaning wherever the text allows, so that everyone among the holy children of Israel will be able to cling to the words of this sacred Zohar. (*Damesek eli'ezer*, 1*c*)

See also Idel, *Kabbalah: New Perspectives*, 103. Safrin subsequently declares his intention to

mented, and explicated Luria's exegesis, many non-Lurianic interpretations were created and disseminated. This paved the way to the elevation of Zohar commentary as one of the primary genres of kabbalistic literature.

write a Rashi-style commentary on the Zohar: 'Because all I want in this book is for everyone who has a sacred soul to be able to study the holy book of the Zohar as one studies the Talmud with Rashi, may he be blessed in the world to come' (*Damesek eli'ezer*, 1c).

CHAPTER SIX

Revelation versus Concealment in the Reception History of the Zohar

Woe if I reveal and woe if I reveal not.
Zohar iii. 127*b*

THE TENSION between the wish to reveal and publicize the Zohar, on the one hand, and to conceal its content and limit its accessibility, on the other, has characterized the history of that book's reception from its early circulation until today. As we have seen, the zoharic literature was created as a reaction to conservative, esoteric trends that dominated the kabbalistic production field at the end of the thirteenth century. Throughout its history there have been circles that emphasized the exoteric character of the Zohar and have contributed to its circulation while others viewed it as an esoteric text and did their best to limit its proliferation. At times the two inclinations existed side by side within the same circles.

This tension stems from the economic logic inherent in cultural systems. To sustain the value of a cultural product a fine balance must be maintained between its distribution and control of its availability. In other words, value is preserved by balancing supply and demand. To quote Pierre Bourdieu, 'all goods offered tend to lose some of their relative scarcity and their distinctive value as the number of consumers both inclined and able to appropriate them grows. Popularization devalues. *Déclassé* goods no longer give class.'[1] Therefore, although some circulation was necessary to increase the Zohar's value as a sacred and authoritative text, excessive circulation and uncontrolled access threatened to reduce its cultural worth.

Yet it was the perception of the Zohar as incomprehensible to the average human mind that enabled, to a great extent, its distribution to the general public. As I have shown in the first two chapters, the zoharic literature

[1] *Sociology in Question*, 114.

undermined the esoteric approach of Nahmanides' school; Moshe Halbertal argues that 'the Zohar presents a perfect alternative to the concept that the Kabbalah is a closed knowledge'.[2] In the first extant testimony describing the distribution of the Zohar, R. Isaac of Acre recounts his amazement at the exoteric character of that work and at the 'wondrous secrets, previously transmitted only orally and not meant to be set in writing, [which] are explained in this book so that they can be comprehended by anyone who is able to read a book'.[3] His surprise reflects the esoteric position of the Nahmanidean circle, which restricted the documentation of kabbalistic secrets and only allowed their limited and controlled oral dissemination. The distributors of the Zohar, on the other hand, claimed that the texts authored by R. Shimon that were in their possession were accessible and plain to all who could read. This claim validated the exoteric approach to kabbalah, subverted Nahmanides' and Solomon ben Adret's monopolistic authority, and countered their opposition to the written dissemination of kabbalah. The zoharic literature itself treated the revelation of secrets with some ambivalence, which is captured in R. Shimon's famous proclamation at the beginning of *Idra raba*: 'Woe if I reveal and woe if I reveal not' (Zohar iii. 127*b*).

The esotericism of the Zohar versus its exotericism was little discussed before the sixteenth century. From the appearance of the first texts in the late thirteenth century until the end of the fifteenth, the distribution of zoharic literature was more or less confined to Spain. Except for some quotations by early fourteenth-century kabbalists (mainly R. Menahem Recanati and R. Joseph Angelet), very few zoharic passages were included in kabbalistic writings, and only a handful of zoharic manuscripts have been preserved from that time.

Recanati and Angelet, the first to quote extensively from the Zohar, did so without any reservations. At the same time, Angelet instructed his disciples not to share with anyone his book *Livnat hasapir*, which contained a number of zoharic quotations.[4] In the fifteenth century a few kabbalists

[2] *Concealment and Revelation*, 94.

[3] Zacuto, *Sefer yuḥasin hashalem*, 88; Tishby and Lachower, *The Wisdom of the Zohar*, i. 13.

[4] Angelet, *Livnat hasapir* (London MS), 1*b*. He later instructed: 'Therefore this book should be hidden and should not be taught but to an educated elder who is [at least] 40 years

noted the layperson's difficulty understanding the Zohar due to the fact that it was in Aramaic. They did not have any problem with its content, however, or oppose its distribution to the public.[5] In contrast, the anonymous author of *Poke'aḥ ivrim*, written in Spain in the first half of the fifteenth century, stated that he refrained from quoting the secrets embedded in the Zohar because they should not be revealed. The same author was the first to suggest that the Zohar contained both mysteries that had to be concealed and texts that could be revealed: '[There are some] most mysterious matters in the Zohar that should not be written down here because they ought to be concealed, but I will write about those matters that are revealed in the Zohar.'[6] R. Joseph Albo, who lived at the same time, opposed the distribution of the Zohar (and other books of kabbalah) and characterized them as indecipherable to the average human mind:

Therefore it has been established that one is not permitted to use anything the kabbalist sages said based on his own interpretation unless he received it [directly] from the mouth of a master kabbalist, because it is forbidden to make a conjecture that pertains to this wisdom, unless it was transmitted orally from a master to a recipient; and it is impossible to obtain any of the secrets from a written text. That is why it is called *kabalah* [reception] and it is what its name denotes. And I felt obliged to write this because I have seen people going astray by reading the Zohar and other books by kabbalist sages without *kabalah* [i.e. oral instruction], relying only on their personal conjectures. And, in order to prove that they have mastered this great wisdom, they stray beyond their boundaries and employ reason where reason is forbidden. The greatest sage among the late kabbalists, our teacher Nahmanides, of blessed memory, has cautioned against this [practice] and warned that 'words of master kabbalists could not be perceived nor grasped by reason and intelligence but through oral transmission from the mouth of a master to the ear of a recipient kabbalist. A conjecture regarding [these secrets] has no merit and is

old. And our sages, of blessed memory, said that words like honey and milk should be under your tongue.'

[5] Having quoted a zoharic text, R. Menahem Tsiyon explained that he 'needed to quote also Nahmanides, whose words are clearer, since not everyone knows Aramaic' (*Tsefunei tsiyoni*, 61). In the late 15th century R. Isaac Mar Hayim, in his letter to R. Isaac of Pisa, translated into Hebrew the zoharic text on which he had produced a commentary. He explained: 'And since in this country one is not used to reading the Yerushalmi translation [i.e. the Aramaic translation of the Torah], I decided to copy it word for word into Hebrew' (Greenup, 'A Kabbalistic Epistle by Isaac b. Samuel', 370).

[6] *Sefer poke'aḥ ivrim*, 188*a*.

very harmful.' Hence I will teach you this principle—beware and be very careful to protect your soul not to follow them and become ensnared in their traps, because they have abandoned the righteous way to walk along dark paths. They do not know and they do not understand. Those who engage in kabbalah by themselves, without receiving it from a master kabbalist, walk in darkness. (*Sefer ha'ikarim*, 185)

Albo applies to the Zohar Nahmanides' statement in the introduction to his *Commentary on the Torah*. This analogy suggests that the secrets of the Zohar are similar to the secrets of the Torah to which Nahmanides alludes. In this view, then, the Zohar is an esoteric text that can be deciphered only within an orally transmitted hermeneutical system.

A similar perception appears in the late fifteenth-century work *Sefer hameshiv*. In a passage I discussed in the previous chapter God responds to the author's enquiry:

As for the question you asked me when you saw that my son, the righteous Shimon, had concealed his words in the language of the Bavli [Babylonian Talmud] . . . Now the time has come to reveal them in great detail so as to enable you to understand them . . . To reveal this secret to you I will use a comprehensive method by which you will understand the language of the Bavli, which no one else is able to understand. On the basis of my instruction and order, Shimon, my son, intended to conceal that secret; thus he encapsulated it in an allusion that [only] he, his son after him, and a few companions would be able to understand. And when he died, the book and its wisdom and its secrets died with him. And you do not understand it, not you nor those reading it, who are cunning for the sake of evil. And I will take my revenge on whoever reveals its secrets and contents to those who are unworthy.[7]

Like Albo, the author of *Sefer hameshiv* considers the Zohar an obscure text, intentionally written in an esoteric style. But in contrast to Albo he claims that the key to the Zohar had been lost when R. Shimon died, and the only way to obtain access to its secrets was through divine revelation. He presents an ambivalence with regard to the revelation of the Zohar's secrets: on the one hand God threatens to take revenge on those who share his secrets with the unworthy, and on the other hand he says that the time has come to reveal those secrets (at least to the author of *Sefer hameshiv*).

[7] Scholem, 'The Magid of R. Joseph Taitatsak' (Heb.), 77–8. See also Idel, 'Neglected Writings of the Author of *Kaf haketoret*' (Heb.), 80.

The late fifteenth and early sixteenth centuries saw an increase in the circulation of zoharic literature, which was manifested partly in the widespread use of zoharic quotations, especially in Spanish works, as well as in the printing of the first books that contained zoharic material. Many works written in this period justified engagement in study of the Zohar and exposure of its secrets by claiming that the time of redemption was close at hand and the restrictions on the dissemination of kabbalistic knowledge had been lifted. What is more, the study and circulation of the Zohar would hasten the redemption, as seen in *Tikunei hazohar* and *Ra'aya meheimna*, which apparently state that the revelation of the Zohar's secrets and any engagement in it carry messianic implications.[8] This idea appears, for instance, in R. Judah Hayat's introduction to his commentary on *Ma'arekhet ha'elohut*, written around 1500 and printed in Mantua in 1557/8:

Happy are we and good is our share because we have been awarded the Zohar, something that our ancestors, whose little fingers were thicker than our loins, were not awarded, among them R. Hai Gaon, R. Sheshet Gaon, R. Eliezer of Garmisha [Worms], Nahmanides, R. Abraham ben David, R. Solomon ben Adret, and other sages who had not tasted its honey, because in their time it had not been revealed. And it should not make you wonder because for sure it was not revealed until the current generation, in which we live today. And I have found support for this in *Sefer hatikunim*, where it is written: 'Elijah said to R. Shimon: Rabbi, Rabbi, happy are you that this work of yours will sustain some of the celestial beings until it is revealed to the lower ones at the end of days, and because of that "each man will return to his holding and every man will return to his family" [Lev. 25: 10].'[9] Thus it is clear that this work was meant to be concealed, while the inhabitants on high, the angels, enjoy it until the final generation comes and it is revealed to the inhabitants of the earth. And through the merit of those who engage in it and care for it the messiah will come, 'for the knowledge of the Lord shall fill the earth'

[8] *Ra'aya meheimna* states that study of the Zohar, 'the tree of life', will bring about redemption: 'And because Israel will taste from the tree of life, which is the Zohar, it will bring them out of exile, with mercy. And the words "the Lord alone will guide him, no alien god at his side" will come true in their life.' A famous passage in the sixth *tikun* of *Tikunei hazohar*, often quoted in later periods, proclaims: 'And this work of yours will sustain human beings below, when it is revealed below in the final generation at the end of days, and because of it "you shall proclaim liberty throughout the land, etc."'

[9] *Tikunei hazohar*, 23*b*–24*a*.

[Isa. 11: 9]. This will be the principal cause for his coming, thus it [*Sefer hatikunim*] says: 'and because of that "each man will return to his family"'.[10]

A similar conception justifying the Zohar's circulation and encouraging its study appears in *Kaf haketoret*, a work probably written around the same time: 'Because Israel will not be redeemed until they forget all external wisdom, and when the king messiah decides to reveal himself the light from the books of the great luminary R. Shimon ben Yohai and his circle will sustain them. And those who engage in these books draw the power of the Shekhinah down to earth.'[11]

The influence of Hayat's ideas is also apparent in *Avodat hakodesh* (Mantua, 1545), whose author, R. Meir Ibn Gabai, suggests that 'this work will remain concealed and covered, but at the same time it will be enjoyed above until the final generation, when it will be revealed to the earthly inhabitants.'[12] Hayat's words are further paraphrased in *Galya raza*[13] and in *Lev adam*, written by the Italian kabbalist R. Berakhiel Kaufmann.[14] As one of the supporters of the distribution of the Zohar, Kaufmann emphasizes the exoteric nature of that work: 'And we find that R. Shimon explains many things in great detail in the Zohar.'[15]

Hayat and the kabbalists influenced by him not only justified the circulation of the Zohar but went so far as to call for widespread, active participation in its study and circulation. In an anonymous passage quoted by Abraham Azulai in his introduction to *Or haḥamah*, the writer encourages the dissemination of the Zohar. According to Azulai's source, the prohibition against study of the Zohar had expired in 1490. From 1540 on, moreover, it was considered a meritorious deed for 'high and low' to publicly expound on it:

And I have found it written that what was decreed above, that one should not engage in the wisdom of kabbalah publicly, was limited to a certain period, until the end of the year 5250, and from that time on permission was given to the current generation to read it. The decree has been lifted and permission granted to

10 *Ma'arekhet ha'elohut*, Hayat's introduction, 2*a*–*b*.

11 *Sefer kaf haketoret*, 54*a*; Idel, 'Enquiries into the Doctrine of *Sefer hameshiv*' (Heb.), 237.

12 *Avodat hakodesh*, iii. 81*a*.

13 See *Galya raza*, ed. Elior, 64.

14 Tishby, *Studies in Kabbalah* (Heb.), i. 103.

15 Ibid., based on Budapest, MS Kaufmann 218 (F. 14702), 21.

engage in the Zohar. And since the beginning of the year 5300 from the creation of the world, it has become a special *mitsvah* for high and low to engage in it, as it is [stated] in *Ra'aya meheimna*.[16]

The esotericism of the Zohar is seen here not as an inherent quality of the text, but rather as a decree imposed from above for a limited time. Since the temporary restriction had been lifted, engagement in it (and in kabbalah in general) was now permitted to anyone, 'high and low alike'.

While the opinion that the Zohar is an exoteric text is implicit in the writings of Hayat (and other kabbalists who adopted his view), R. Moses Cordovero makes it explicit in his reference to the Zohar as a 'well-laid table' (*shulḥan arukh*) for all:

Since R. Shimon immersed himself in this wisdom and was aided by heaven, and the gates of understanding were opened for him, and he learned from his predecessors and was assisted by the supernal emanation, as he explained, he taught and presented the wisdom in a manner that anyone who uses his books and keeps them close to his heart will certainly avoid falling into the pits of misunderstanding . . . and yet he needed permission to write down this wisdom in books [so that it could] become a well-laid table for all, so that anyone who desires to assume the secret of the Name may come and do so.[17]

As I argued in Chapter 3, until the middle of the sixteenth century the Zohar was circulated mainly through the copying of manuscripts and through quotations embedded in other kabbalistic texts. This circulation was very limited and was controlled by those who possessed the zoharic texts. It was those individuals who determined, to a great extent, the Zohar's scope of readership by being able to decide to whom to sell or deliver the manuscripts that were in their possession. The small number of handwritten collections and the exorbitant expense of their replication significantly restricted the circle of those able to afford a copy of the Zohar. Quotation was an additional measure whereby manuscript owners could control the distribution of zoharic texts. They would select the quotations, limit their scope, and, to a great extent, manipulate their meaning by defining their context and attaching their own interpretations.

[16] Introduction to *Or haḥamah*, i. 1c (my numbering; BH).

[17] Cordovero, *Tikunei hazohar im perush or yakar*, i. 16.

The printing of the zoharic corpus resulted in a remarkable expansion of the Zohar's readership. It had an impact on the methods of its marketing and on its price, and the control over distribution shifted from the editors and copyists of manuscripts to those involved in the publishing and marketing of the printed editions.

The Mantua Zohar was published amidst fierce struggles between those who had initiated its printing and their opponents. The confrontations took place mainly in the town of Pesaro between 1557 and 1558. As mentioned before, the Mantua editions (of *Tikunei hazohar* and the three volumes of the Zohar) were printed by the partners R. Meir ben Ephraim of Padua and Jacob ben Naphtali Hakohen of Gazzulo. In addition to R. Isaac de Lattes, whose ruling in favour of the printing was inserted at the beginning of Zohar 'Bereshit', other rabbis were also recruited for the cause, including R. Moses Basola (who later changed his mind and opposed the publication), R. Moses Provinciali, R. Israel of Ravigo, and R. Moses Bivi. Their supportive rulings were published at the front of *Tikunei hazohar*.

The leaders of those who opposed the printing, R. Jacob Israel Finzi and R. Menahem of Pollino, enlisted R. Meir Katzenellenbogen (Maharam) of Padua and the above-mentioned R. Basola, who had originally supported the printing but later issued a ban on it.[18] The opponents wrote decrees banning the printers and sought to persuade the Mantuan authorities to void their printing permit.

According to Isaiah Sonne, beneath the dispute a social struggle was brewing between itinerant rabbis and their more established colleagues. This dispute followed, Sonne explains, the burning of the Talmud and the banning of halakhic literature by the decree of the Roman inquisition in 1553:

[18] Finzi's ruling stating that 'books of kabbalah should not be published' was written in May 1558, after the printing of *Tikunei hazohar* and before the first volume of the body of the Zohar came out; see Tishby, *Studies in Kabbalah*, i. 114. The ruling was published by Assaf in 'The Controversy over the Printing of Kabbalistic Literature' (Heb.), 4–9. On 29 June 1558 R. Finzi banned the printing again. Basola issued his ban on the same date, as did, possibly, R. David ben Raphael of Tosiniano, R. Meir Katzenellenbogen of Padua, and R. Judah Ortil. These bans were copied with Finzi's ruling into his *Gur aryeh* responsa; see London, Montefiore Library, MS 113 (F. 4627).

The initiative to fill the vacuum that followed the ban on books [the Talmud and later halakhic literature] with books of kabbalah came from a group of professional teachers who, in most cases, were also book merchants. For them the books were a source of income and without them they could not carry on their trade. They were supported by the Hebrew printers, who were looking for a market for their merchandise in the Papal States. Therefore, the majority of the itinerant rabbis, who made their trade mainly from teaching in the Papal States, were in favour of books of kabbalah, especially the Zohar and its *tikunim*, which were intended to replace the Talmud. Rabbis Moses Basola, Isaac Lattes, Emmanuel of Benevento, and others were among these rabbis. However, most of the tenured, official rabbis, such as Meir Katzenellenbogen of Padua, who signed the by-laws of Ferrara in 1554, opposed the distribution of books of kabbalah or at least abstained from supporting the printers.[19]

Isaiah Tishby has vehemently rejected Sonne's 'class theory' (as well as the theory that the burning of the Talmud and the ban on halakhic literature were among the main reasons for the printing of the Zohar).[20] In his view the polemics rested between the opponents of mysticism, who supported a rigid halakhic position, and those who wished to promote spiritual and religious change by spreading the wisdom of kabbalah.[21]

Sonne's class theory is at variance with the fact that both supporters and opponents of the publication of the Zohar belonged to the intellectual elite of northern Italy. At the same time Tishby's alternative, that the struggle fell between kabbalists, who wanted to introduce spiritual changes in Jewish religious life, and the opponents of kabbalah, is not convincing and lacks supporting documentation. Though it is possible that some objected to the printing of the Zohar as part of their general rejection of kabbalah,[22] the information that we have indicates that both supporters and opponents were engaged in kabbalah and recognized the authoritative and sacred status of the Zohar.[23]

[19] Benjamin Nehemiah ben Elnathan, *Mipaulo harevi'i ad pius haḥamishi*, ed. Sonne, 123–4.

[20] Tishby, *Studies in Kabbalah* (Heb.), i. 99, 123–7.

[21] Ibid. 127–30.

[22] This kind of opposition is mentioned by R. Moses Basola in his ruling in favour of the printing of the Zohar, where he talks about 'the young and uneducated one, who is naked and who has never been exposed to any contact with real kabbalah; who has not read nor studied the Zohar, and whose wickedness has led him to remonstrate without any restraint against kabbalah'.

[23] R. Jacob Israel Finzi, who led the opposition against the printing of the Zohar, was

The polemics over the printing of the Zohar, then, did not stem from disagreements between supporters and opponents of kabbalah, nor were they kindled by differences between representatives of different social strata or different kabbalistic trends. Centred in the town of Pesaro, the struggle broke out between representatives of the same social class and ideological orientation,[24] who had opposing interests in distributing the Zohar and controlling kabbalistic knowledge. In the words of Joseph Hacker,

The debate revolved mainly around the question of whether kabbalah should remain an esoteric wisdom, possessed by a few exceptional individuals, or whether it should become public knowledge; whether its secrets and truths should be distributed to the public for any hand to touch and any eye to see, or it should be concealed in manuscripts for the humble and the worthy . . . In other words, should kabbalah turn from an esoteric wisdom into an exoteric one?[25]

Although Sonne's argument regarding the social context of the conflict surrounding the printing of the Zohar is incorrect, one should not deny the link between the burning and banning of halakhic books in 1553 and the printing of the Zohar and other kabbalistic books a few years later. R. Emmanuel of Benevento affirmed this connection by claiming that those who opposed the printing of kabbalistic literature deprived scholars of study material:

And now, since our beloved [Talmud] was taken from us to be burned and consumed by fire, we have been unable to engage in the disputes between Abbaye and Rava. We miss the writings of the *posekim* because they have been locked behind

himself a kabbalist and often relied on that work as well as on other books of kabbalah in his responsa. R. Elijah Halfan, one of the signees of the first ban on the printing, also engaged in kabbalah and accepted the authoritative status of the Zohar, as did R. Moses Basola. R. Meir Katzenellenbogen of Padua, though not involved in kabbalah, did not oppose it; see Tishby, *Studies in Kabbalah* (Heb.), i. 112.

[24] Many of the sages who were involved in the polemics—R. Menahem of Pollino, R. Judah ben Moses de Blanis, R. Isaac de Lattes, R. Abraham ben Meshulam, and R. Jacob Finzi—were among the leaders of Pesaro. The personal element in the dispute comes through in Lattes' words to his father-in-law, R. Abraham ben Meshulam: 'Now a son was born to as important and exalted a man as R. Mordecai of Pollino . . . but I have secretly been told that his father, the master, is upset with you, so is his mother, because you were involved in the printing without consulting any one of them. However, they did not talk to me about it and I pretended not to hear it' (Tishby, *Studies in Kabbalah* (Heb.), i. 311).

[25] 'A New Letter from the Controversy over the Printing of the Zohar' (Heb.), 120.

bars and no one knows how long it will take to redeem them. God, in His mercy, has sent these books to sustain and guide us on a cloudy and misty day. Yet the shepherds came and chased them away, each with a deadly weapon in his hand, to extinguish our embers and to leave us neither name nor remnant on the earth. And even if we survive, those who are teachers by trade have been robbed. What will they do? Which book will they use to realize and understand the glory of God, His majesty and His powerful and heroic acts? [The book of] Boccaccio or chronicles of the [gentile] kings!?[26]

There is no doubt that the printers had a financial interest in the publication of the Zohar,[27] for the burning of the Talmud and the ban on halakhic literature made the printing of kabbalistic books more profitable. Indeed, most of the supporters of printing—R. Emmanuel of Benevento, R. Abraham ben Meshulam, R. Jacob Gazzulo, R. Moses Provinciali, and R. Emmanuel of Corropoli—were involved in the venture, and R. Isaac de Lattes, who had ruled favourably in the matter, was the son-in-law of the editor, R. Abraham ben Meshulam.[28]

The publishers and their supporters were aware of the radical impact the printing press had on the production and marketing of zoharic texts. They were also aware of the shift of control over the dissemination of the Zohar from the owners and scribes of manuscripts to editors, printers, and others engaged in the marketing of the printed books. Indeed, the supporters of the printing expressed their desire to wrest control of the body of kabbalistic knowledge from the manuscript owners in the name of 'democratization of knowledge'.[29] In his ruling in favour of the printing, placed at the front of the Mantua edition of *Tikunei hazohar*, R. Moses Basola

[26] *Ma'arekhet ha'elohut*, 3*b*.

[27] The opponents of printing were aware of this economic motivation. R. Finzi wrote in his ruling: 'Therefore one should not take pride in this deceitful wisdom or claim that he intended to confer on the public the wisdom of kabbalah, because his kabbalah is a tool to make money for his own benefit' (Assaf, 'The Controversy over the Printing of Kabbalistic Literature' (Heb.), 6).

[28] R. Isaac de Lattes was in his father-in-law's printing business and recommended, for instance, that he check the profitability of printing the commentary *Ḥeshek shelomoh* on the *Kuzari*. See Kupfer, 'New Documents Concerning the Polemic over the Printing of the Zohar' (Heb.), 311.

[29] The printing of the Zohar was accompanied by a struggle to seize the manuscripts from the sages and to produce printed editions. R. Finzi recounted how the printers of the Zohar had acquired the manuscripts of R. Elyakim of Macerata through deception:

advocates this principle:

Why should [the Zohar] be kept by the rich and locked amongst their treasures? By virtue of their enormous wealth, they boast of their ability to copy it, although they neither know nor understand it. They walk in darkness. And the poor and lowly wish to be fed from this wisdom and are unable to reach it. Although their heart is that of a lion, capable of exploring secrets and understanding mysteries, they are unable to obtain a handwritten manuscript of the Zohar in its entirety. And those who possess the Zohar hide it and prevent others from using it. Therefore, it is good and appropriate to print it and to provide public access to it. The rich will not be able to withhold food and the poor will not be deprived because they will be able to acquire it inexpensively.

In a similar vein, R. Israel of Ravigo proclaimed in his ruling, which was also printed in the Mantua edition of *Tikunei hazohar*, 'We are permitted to print the Zohar so that the poor will be able to get hold of it, for knowledge will come forth from them.'

In order to justify their enterprise, the initiators of the printing and their supporters argued that not only had the limitations on the distribution of the Zohar been lifted but its dissemination was hastening the redemption or was a sign of messianic times. Thus, for instance, R. Isaac de Lattes asserted in his *pesak* (ruling) in favour of the printing:

By virtue of studying the Zohar our fortunes will be restored and our exile will come to an end, for it is written, '[if] they are worthy'—'I [the Lord] will hasten it',

Therefore this person [R. Emmanuel of Corropoli] should not boast that he received copies of *Sefer hazohar* from the sage, our master, R. Elyakim of Macerata, may the Lord protect and preserve him, because I can testify that our master R. Elyakim did not intend to do it, nor did he deliver anything for the purpose of being printed. Only by deception and fraud did he receive them from his rabbi. (Assaf, 'The Controversy over the Printing of Kabbalistic Literature' (Heb.), 7)

R. Menahem of Pollino also recounted that he had been pressured into delivering the manuscript in his possession:

First of all, you should not be surprised by all the suffering I have endured and the dangers I have faced because of the people who tried to extricate it from me for their own purposes. These high-ranking individuals used force and tried to entrap me, to bring accusations against me, and to punish me physically and monetarily. They took these measures so that every man should wield authority in his home. And, since God's grace has not diminished, He saved me from their trap and they did not succeed. (Kupfer, 'New Documents Concerning the Polemic over the Printing of the Zohar' (Heb.), 312–13)

and as a result Israel will be redeemed and liberty will be proclaimed throughout the land . . . And elsewhere the Zohar announces that in the generation in which the messiah will appear permission will be given to reveal his book and his work.[30]

The messianic justification for the distribution of the Zohar suggests that the zoharic text can be comprehended by the average human intellect. The only reason for the restrictions on its dissemination was that it was forbidden to reveal its contents before the messianic era. R. Emmanuel of Benevento contends, for example, that the Zohar does not deal with any esoteric knowledge the exposure of which is prohibited:

And those who claim that the mysteries of the world should not be revealed out of reverence for God must be able to identify the mysteries of the world that should be concealed, because permission was given to write down those things that are included in the works of these authors, whose books are here with us, and which are not among the mysteries of the world that one should conceal. If everything is concealed and nothing is revealed, the wisdom of the sages will be lost and the knowledge of the learned will be hidden, and men will be 'like the beasts that perish' [Ps. 49: 20] if 'the wisdom of its wise shall fail and the prudence of its prudent shall vanish' [Isa. 29: 14].[31]

A similar approach is seen in the following passage by R. Emmanuel of Corropoli, who writes that the Zohar allows men to know God according to their ability and thus ensures proper religious behaviour:

And the principle on which everything rests is the insertion of a stake in a reliable place to allow a person to know his Creator. The big and the many filled their bellies with the bread and meat of these laws and in the end burned their dishes, as Ahitofel, Do'eg, Elisha Aher [ben Abuyah], and others did. But when a person is privileged to obtain perfect knowledge of his Creator according to his own ability, and he serves God out of awe, then he walks securely along his path and is saved from any harm . . . What do we have that is greater than this sacred book, the Zohar? It explains the ways, removes hurdles from the path, fills the hearts of men with love and fear, teaches and leads us on the path of righteousness to bring us to the 'resting place and the inheritance [that God has given you]' [Deut. 12: 9].[32]

The above passage is R. Emmanuel's response to those who opposed the printing of the Zohar, arguing that the study of kabbalah required pre-

[30] Tishby, *Studies in Kabbalah* (Heb.), i. 89 n. 38.

[31] *Ma'arekhet ha'elohut*, 3*b*.

[32] Introduction to *Sefer hazohar al hatorah* (Mantua), i. 1*b*.

existing mastery of rabbinic knowledge—stuffing the belly with bread and meat.[33] As Isaiah Tishby explains, R. Emmanuel had turned this argument on its head by claiming that it was not mastery of rabbinic knowledge that protected against the dangers of studying kabbalah, but rather, study of the Zohar prevented scholars from veering off the proper path.[34]

Another claim made by supporters of the printing was that the Zohar contained both concealed secrets which only the master kabbalists could understand and segments of simple meaning that were accessible to the less educated, too. This opinion was expressed by R. Moses Basola in his above-mentioned ruling, printed at the front of *Tikunei hazohar*:

> When the Zohar deals with the divine essence and emanation, it uses an obscure language that only a sage who is familiar with the principles of kabbalah can understand. Therefore I contend that the Zohar is good for everyone, because those of lesser knowledge will learn the simple meaning of a few verses according to kabbalah, which is sweeter than honey and honeycomb . . . and when he encounters pure marble stones, he will leap over them like a ram, because they will be like words of a sealed book in his eyes. He will say to himself, I am unable to understand this obscure and sealed text. And those who are very knowledgeable, who have been drinking from the well of fresh water, will drink its words eagerly and wisdom will illuminate their paths.[35]

As previously mentioned, the author of *Poke'aḥ ivrim* distinguished between the exoteric and esoteric elements of the Zohar. Moses Cordovero offered a similar distinction between 'the simple meaning' of the secrets, which he categorized as the 'revealed secrets' of the Zohar, and the 'concealed secrets', that is, the esoteric elements contained in the *Idrot* and in *Tikunei hazohar*.[36] In contrast to *Poke'aḥ ivrim*, whose author refrained from quoting esoteric passages from the Zohar, Basola argued that there was no danger in disseminating the Zohar, including secrets pertaining to the divine world, because those of 'lesser knowledge' who were not masters of kabbalah would not understand the secrets and would skip the obscure passages.

Some among those who opposed the printing raised the concern that it

33 Based on Maimonides, 'Hilkhot yesodei hatorah', 4: 13.

34 Tishby, *Studies in Kabbalah* (Heb.), i. 129 n. 178.

35 *Tikunei hazohar*, Mantua edn.

36 Cordovero, *Tikunei hazohar im perush or yakar*, iii. 148.

would instigate further bans on sacred books by the Christian authorities.[37] However, their primary concern remained the expansion of the Zohar's readership, which threatened their control of the body of kabbalistic knowledge. R. Jacob Israel Finzi prefaced his ruling against the printing of the Zohar and other books of kabbalah by stating:

> I am moved by zeal for the Lord and His holy wisdom, the wisdom of kabbalah, which is being trampled on by a band of thieves, overtaken by legions to be exposed on the streets and in the squares, in front of vain people, as musical instruments are used by the nations. And it [the wisdom] girds on sackcloth to avenge its honour from her Creator. We hold that supernal secrets should not be revealed except to the reapers of the holy field [i.e. the kabbalists].[38]

Finzi feared that printing would render the Zohar readily available to populations that did not satisfy the traditional criteria required for studying esoteric wisdom: 'In addition, following the printing, one might engage in kabbalah by oneself without a companion. Young men, children, and unfit people might engage in it in violation of the decree not to study it without a companion, and [in violation] of the requirement that those who study it must be old enough, humble, and fit.'[39]

In his response to the supporters of printing, Finzi strongly rejects the messianic argument that justifies broad access to the body of kabbalistic knowledge. He primarily targets R. Isaac de Lattes:

> He entertained another foolish idea, that the appearance of this book [the Zohar] indicated the end of days. On the basis of astrology, he claimed that in the two thousandth year of the days of the messiah, this wisdom would become well known, and it would be revealed to everyone, and that the time had come to explain the reasons of its secrets and its hidden mysteries . . . And my response to this is: May the person who calculates the end of days breathe his last . . . and with regard to his claim that in the generation of the messiah it is appropriate to reveal this book, he probably thinks that printing the Zohar will bring about the messiah and that the end of days has come. From his words, one can see his stupidity and his inability to understand anything properly, because when our messiah comes, he will reveal to us the divine secrets that have not yet been revealed to human

[37] R. Jacob Israel Finzi was one of those who voiced such concern; see Assaf, 'The Controversy over the Printing of Kabbalistic Literature' (Heb.), 8. [38] Ibid. 4. [39] Ibid.

beings . . . and the printing of the Zohar will not bring about the end of days, as this fool claims.[40]

R. Moses Basola, who initially supported the printing but later became an opponent, also expressed apprehension that engagement in kabbalah without proper halakhic training might lead to heresy:

One [danger] is that when these books end up in the hands of the public, many among those who might enter the *pardes* [i.e. explore kabbalistic wisdom] have not filled their bellies with meat and wine and have not eaten the bread of Torah. With their limited knowledge and comprehension, they will not learn and they will not understand. They will walk in darkness and use the words of God, God forbid, for heresy.[41]

Basola phrased his opinion by borrowing Maimonides' famous statement (concerning the study of philosophy, not kabbalah): 'One should not walk in the *pardes* unless he has filled his belly with bread and meat, and bread and meat denote the knowledge of all that is prohibited and permitted and other *mitsvot* of this nature.'[42] Finzi, on the other hand, combined Maimonides' requirement pertaining to those who wished to study philosophy (enter the *pardes*)—a complete mastery of the rabbinic curriculum—with Nahmanides' assertion that any engagement in kabbalah had to be based on an authoritative oral tradition. Finzi, like the others, feared the widening of the Zohar's readership beyond the elite circle of halakhic scholars:

By this I do not argue that it is prohibited to put it in writing; all I say is that it should be kept away from uneducated people, as the *rishonim* have done until now. The followers [of zoharic literature] secretly arranged to have it copied [as if it were] more [precious] than silver and gold. They showed it only to those people who had filled their bellies with the six orders of Mishnah, with Scripture, Talmud, and fear of God, and only to those who had learned kabbalah directly from the mouth of another [initiate].[43]

Finzi also feared that in the wake of publication the Zohar would end up not only in the hands of Jews who had no rabbinic training, but also with

[40] Tishby, *Studies in Kabbalah* (Heb.), i. 101–2.
[41] Ibid. 108.
[42] Maimonides, 'Hilkhot yesodei hatorah', 4: 13.
[43] Assaf, 'The Controversy over the Printing of Kabbalistic Literature' (Heb.), 5.

Christians: 'For, God forbid, it might end up in the hands of the nations, who will copy it into their languages to do with it as they please.'[44]

Opponents of the printing expressed the fears of kabbalists of the elite circles who possessed the zoharic manuscripts, and who were concerned that the broadening of access to the body of kabbalistic knowledge would diminish their cultural power and lessen the value of the Zohar. Finzi, in his response to Basola's argument, wished to maintain the status quo and preserve cultural influence in the hands of the manuscript owners by controlling the dissemination of kabbalistic knowledge:

For it should not be revealed to uneducated people, only to those who are learned and within a group; those who guard it in their homes as if it were more [precious] than silver and gold, yet proffer it to anyone. No one, neither rich nor poor, who seeks books of kabbalah and whose home is void of them is denied, for their homes are wide open to sages who engage in it for its own sake. Moreover, as the evidence indicates, several great sages have been engaged in the wisdom of kabbalah until now, and all sages who have sought [the texts] and knew the laws and feared God have been able to obtain it [kabbalistic wisdom], because the tablets and the fragments of the tablets were placed in the ark.[45]

Finzi's words indicate that he feared losing control over the dissemination of zoharic texts more than he opposed the revelation of esoteric secrets. In response to the claim that parts of the Zohar had previously been printed in other works, he wrote:

It will not help anyone to argue that [the books of] Recanati and Nahmanides and other books of kabbalah had already been printed, because my response will be that kabbalistic commentaries such as those of Recanati, Nahmanides, and others

[44] Assaf, 'The Controversy over the Printing of Kabbalistic Literature' (Heb.) 8. R. Moses Basola expressed a similar concern in his ban; however, his fear was that, as the Zohar spread among the Christians, they would not find Jews qualified enough to explain the text to them:

> The third reason is that, if we have numerous books in print, many non-Jews will buy them and ask the sages of Israel to explain the text [to them]. And there will be no one to explain it because the text is ancient and there is no one among us who knows as much as a drop in the sea. The non-Jews will say, only a nation as stupid and evil as this people would lack the knowledge and intellectual ability to understand their own books. They will slander the authors with words that one should not hear, and the name of God will be defiled. (Tishby, *Studies in Kabbalah* (Heb.), i. 161)

[45] Assaf, 'The Controversy over the Printing of Kabbalistic Literature' (Heb.), 7.

do not contain zoharic texts exclusively. They [i.e. the authors] are only supporting their arguments by quoting segments [of the Zohar], and they interpret those quotations according to their proper meaning based on the wisdom [kabbalah] so that no one would falter because of them. The commentary clarifies them. However, to print a whole book of kabbalah, especially one such as the Zohar, *Ma'arekhet ha'elohut*, the *Tikunim*, and other books that contain nothing but kabbalah, to do this great evil would not occur to anyone out of respect for God. It is to the glory of God to conceal a matter [Prov. 25: 2].[46]

That is to say, Finzi opposed the printing of the Zohar and other kabbalistic texts but he did not object to their dissemination in secondary sources through quotations followed by proper interpretation. This allowed those who possessed the primary sources to retain control over the quantity and meaning of the distributed texts.

In spite of the large number of opposing voices, the printing of the Zohar in Mantua was completed and another edition was simultaneously produced in Cremona. This was a significant turning point in the history of the Zohar: not only did it bring about a change in the way it was distributed and marketed, but it also determined, to a great extent, the shape and scope of the book and stimulated the emergence of its commentaries in the second half of the sixteenth century.

The exoteric approach to the Zohar and support for its proliferation appear time and again in the works of kabbalists who wrote commentaries at that time. R. Judah Hayat's claims that the restriction imposed on the circulation of the Zohar had been lifted, and that its revelation and distribution were signs of the coming redemption, are echoed in R. Simeon Ibn Lavi's commentary: 'And because the wisdom of R. Shimon, may he rest in peace, is what sustains the world, Israel will be redeemed when they immerse themselves in it. As he, may he rest in peace, wrote: "At the end of days our Zohar will be revealed because, due to our many sins, it has been forgotten since antiquity."'[47]

R. Moses Cordovero announces in his *Or yakar* commentary that the Zohar will be revealed in the last generation and everyone will possess it: 'It is to say that this work will be concealed from the days of R. Shimon until the final generation of the king messiah, when this work will be revealed

[46] Ibid. 5. [47] *Ketem paz*, i. 12*a*.

and it will be possessed by all [so that they can] immerse themselves in it. Therefore this book was not revealed until our generation, and its revelation is one of the signs of redemption.'[48]

In contrast to Hayat, who speaks about the revelation of the Zohar in the last generation but does not mention its 'discovery' in the early fourteenth century, Cordovero defines three periods in the history of the Zohar: (*a*) from the time it was composed by R. Shimon until the early fourteenth century, a period throughout which the book was concealed and totally unknown; (*b*) from the fourteenth century until his time, in which it remained concealed by a handful of sages; (*c*) from his time on, when the Zohar became well known.

'And when this work will be revealed, etc.'[49] . . . as stated elsewhere, this work was meant to be concealed and hidden from the eyes of the knowledgeable. Thus no one knew how it had been hidden. It had been unknown since antiquity and it was not revealed until about 200 years ago. In antiquity its existence was unknown and its content was unpublished. No writer attested to its existence except the *aḥaronim*, because it had been concealed and hidden from the time it was written until their time, when it was revealed. And even after it was revealed, it was kept hidden by the sages, who did not want its existence to be known until now, when it has been revealed. This indicates that it was mainly intended for the end of the exile, when the Shekhinah reaches an ultimate low, so that it [the Zohar] will support her at the end of our exile, when the sources of light turn completely dark.[50]

The purpose of the publication of the Zohar, Cordovero explains, is to support the Shekhinah in its descent to the utmost depths. The book was written for a theurgical purpose, and its study, which has been stimulated by its proliferation, has a positive influence both on those who engage in it and on the upper worlds:

It has been explained above in previous chapters that when the enslavement and exile of Israel began, following the Temple's second destruction, the Shekhinah accompanied Israel into exile. Therefore R. Shimon and his companions decided to write this book so that by the revelation of the secrets the light of Tiferet would be revealed and Malkhut would derive some pleasure from unification and *tikun*.

[48] *Tikunei hazohar im perush or yakar*, ii. 104.
[49] *Zohar ḥadash*, 94*a*.
[50] Cordovero, *Tikunei hazohar im perush or yakar*, i. 24.

There is also no doubt that, in this generation, when a person engages in this wisdom, he creates great benefits and the Shekhinah rests upon him, especially if his ways are worthy.[51]

The idea that the discovery of the Zohar and engagement in kabbalah marked and hastened the redemption also appeared in the writings of Lurianic scholars. In his introduction to *Ets ḥayim*, R. Hayim Vital wrote the following:

In the sixth *tikun* of *Sefer hatikunim* it says: Many human beings will be sustained below by this work of yours in the final generation at the end of days. And through it 'you shall proclaim release and liberty throughout the land' [Lev. 25: 10]. And elsewhere Elijah, of blessed memory, told R. Shimon: Rabbi, Rabbi, happy are you that this work of yours will sustain some of the celestial beings until it is revealed to the lower ones at the end of days, and because of that 'each man will return to his holding' [Lev. 25: 10], etc. It [the sixth *tikun*] is interpreted to mean that sin has been committed since the days of the first human being until now, and when we repent and re-engage in this wisdom Israel shall be redeemed instantly.[52]

Later he adds: 'And by engaging in this wisdom we hasten redemption, and bring salvation to His powerful presence [Shekhinah] . . . because everything depends on whether or not we engage in this wisdom, and abstinence impedes the building of our Temple, our glory.'[53]

Naturally, the printing of the Zohar broadened its distribution. The Mantua edition mainly targeted the markets of Italy and the Ottoman empire; the Cremona edition became popular in central and eastern Europe.[54] As ever more printed copies of the Zohar, and other kabbalistic works that quoted from it, were circulated, it became a significant factor in Ashkenazi Jewish culture, where it had hardly been known before the second half of the sixteenth century.

While the printing widened the spectrum of the Zohar's readership and extended its distribution into new territories, that readership still consisted mainly of the intellectual elite. Yet R. Moses Isserles complained about the

[51] Ibid. ii. 102. [52] *Ets ḥayim*, i. 9. [53] Ibid. 12–13.

[54] The exact number of copies printed in those editions is unknown. A statement of the convert Sixtus of Siena, who recounted that 2,000 volumes of the Zohar had been saved from being burned in Cremona, might give an indication; see Benayahu, *Hebrew Printing in Cremona* (Heb.), 201 n. 1.

impact the printing of the Zohar and other kabbalistic books had:

Many among the masses rush to study kabbalah because it is a delight to behold, especially the words of the later sages, who explain these matters explicitly in their writings. Even more so in our time, when books of kabbalah, such as the Zohar and *Sha'arei orah* by Recanati, are being printed. And the reader of these books gets the impression that everything has been explained, while in reality what they say remains obscure, because they have not followed the oral tradition of the truth being delivered from the mouth of one kabbalist to another. Furthermore, it is not only the educated who [assume that] they understand it, but even *ba'alei batim* [householders, i.e. laymen] rush to study kabbalah—readers who do not know right from left and are walking in darkness, unable to explain even Rashi's commentary on a weekly portion. The generation has been orphaned due to its sins, and it has degenerated to a degree that anyone who has found anything in it [in kabbalah], however insignificant, is proudly expounding in public, and sounds like a coin in an empty vessel, and he will be punished for it.[55]

It seems, however, that Isserles' complaint (like that of R. Joseph Albo a hundred years earlier) was exaggerated. In his time study of the Zohar was still limited to members of the elite, who could afford to buy the expensive printed works and had the knowledge required to struggle with kabbalistic texts written in Aramaic. Though several Hebrew translations of zoharic literature were produced in the second half of the sixteenth century that would have made these texts more comprehensible to the public, most of these translations were never printed.[56] Similarly, contemporary commentaries that might have contributed to the Zohar's dissemination (although they, too, were aimed at a readership well versed in rabbinic knowledge) remained unprinted during that period.

As we have seen, the claim that the Zohar was an open text worthy of being studied by the public was used to justify its dissemination and publication. However, in the wake of printing several sages reiterated and emphasized the view that the obscurity of the text required proper training and an appropriate hermeneutical method to understand it. In Isserles' view 'the masses' and the laymen who read the printed kabbalistic litera-

[55] *Torat ha'olah*, iii. 3*b*.

[56] On Hebrew translations of the Zohar produced at the time see Huss, 'Translations of the Zohar' (Heb.), 34–6.

ture mistakenly thought that the Zohar was an open, intelligible text. Like Albo, he claimed that in order to understand the Zohar one needed a hermeneutical key, which was only available in the oral kabbalistic tradition: 'any reader who explores them [the kabbalistic texts] thinks that everything in them has been explained, even though what they say remains obscure, because it was not delivered from the mouth of one kabbalist to another'.[57]

The exoteric perception of the Zohar faced opposition within the Lurianic circle as well. In contrast to Cordovero, who presented the Zohar as an open and accessible text written by R. Shimon 'to become a well-laid table for all, and anyone who wishes to assume the secret of the Name may come and do so',[58] R. Hayim Vital argued that 'not everyone who wishes to assume the Name may come and do so, because the secrets of the Torah and its mysteries cannot be revealed to human beings by means of a material intellect'.[59] The hermeneutical key, Vital writes, is embedded in the principles of Lurianic kabbalah:[60]

> And now, after prefacing all these principles, we need to remind the reader who wishes to study the Zohar that he will find in it many kinds of controversial and contradictory elements, and without these principles the reader will be unable to resolve them, because his intellect is incapable of comprehending them. He might build a patched and shabby scaffold, with patches ringed, spotted, and speckled, patch over patch, like those who profess the wisdom of the Zohar through human intellectual exploration.[61]

As Lurianic kabbalah gradually established itself as the authoritative interpretation of the Zohar, the book came to be perceived as an obscure, esoteric text incomprehensible to the rational human intellect. Those who were not experts in Lurianic kabbalah were discouraged from studying it, which might explain why its printing during the seventeenth century was limited. One edition appeared in Lublin, in the publishing house of Tsevi ben Abraham Kalonymus ben Jaffe, in 1623/4. It was based on the Cremona edition, which included the annotations of R. Isaac ben R. Nathan Shapira. In Sulzbach a new edition (also based on the Cremona printing) was produced in 1684 by R. Moses ben Uri Sheraga Bloch with the help of Chris-

[57] *Torat ha'olah*, iii, ch. 4, 3*b*.
[58] *Tikunei hazohar im perush or yakar*, i. 15.
[59] *Ets ḥayim*, i. 15–16.
[60] *Sha'ar ruaḥ hakodesh*, 38–9.
[61] *Sha'ar hahakdamot*, 'Introduction B', 3–4.

tian August, duke of Bavaria, and the famous Christian kabbalist, Christian Knorr von Rosenroth, who wrote a Latin introduction to the book.[62] *Zohar ḥadash*, printed initially in Salonica (1596/7), was reprinted in Kraków (1602/3) by R. Moses Mordecai Margaliyot, and again in Venice (1657/8) by R. Joseph Hamitz and Moses Zacuto, who, for the first time, included Zohar 'Ruth' in their edition. *Tikunei hazohar*, however, was never published in the seventeenth century.

Despite the small number of Zohar editions that appeared in this period, the dissemination of zoharic texts through quotations embedded in printed books continued to be common practice. In addition to books of kabbalah such as *Avodat hakodesh* by R. Meir Ibn Gabai (Kraków, 1576/8), Recanati's *Ta'amei hamitsvot* (Basel, 1580/1), and Cordovero's *Pardes rimonim* (Kraków, 1590/1), zoharic texts also circulated in commentaries as well as in ethical and legal works such as *Mateh mosheh* by R. Moses Matt (1590/1); *Reshit ḥokhmah* by R. Elijah de Vidas (Kraków, 1592–4); *Tseror hamor*, Abraham Saba's Torah commentary (Kraków, 1594/5); *Halevushim* by Mordecai Jaffe (Prague, 1608/9), and many others. While a significant portion of this literature was aimed at the intellectual elite, another part, composed of zoharic segments translated from Aramaic into Hebrew or Yiddish, targeted the broader public. In *Tseror hamor*, Abraham Saba frequently paraphrased zoharic passages in Hebrew. R. Benjamin Slonik quoted from the Zohar in his Yiddish-language *Seder mitsvot nashim* (Kraków, 1577), a work of popular halakhah written for women and laymen that was later translated into Italian.[63] A Yiddish adaptation of a segment of the Zohar describing the palace of righteous women in paradise was printed in *Ma'aseh gadol merabi shimon bar yoḥai* and printed in a volume with *Sefer olam haba* (Hanau, 1620).[64]

The circulation of R. Simeon Ibn Lavi's poem 'Bar yoḥai nimshaḥta ashreikha' contributed greatly to the popularity of the Zohar and to the reverence for R. Shimon. Written in the sixteenth century in North Africa, the

[62] On the printing of the Zohar in Sulzbach see Huss, 'The Text and Context of the Zohar Sulzbach Edition', 117–38.

[63] See Slonik, *Seder mitsvot nashim*, *siman* 73, 138; Fram, 'Jewish Law and Social and Economic Realities', 159 n. 79.

[64] Zfatman-Biller, *Yiddish Narrative Prose* (Heb.), 42. On this story and its various Yiddish versions see Weissler, *Voices of the Matriarchs*, 77–92.

poem was printed for the first time in the early seventeenth century in R. Yehiel Luria Ashkenazi's *Heikhal adonai*. In subsequent decades it was reprinted in several other kabbalistic collections and became highly popular.[65]

In the late sixteenth and throughout the seventeenth century, Hebrew translations of zoharic texts circulated in reference books and anthologies. Indexes to, and collections of tales from, the Zohar were first printed in *Mafte'aḥ hazohar*, written by R. Moses Galante (Venice, 1565/6). Soon after, R. Issachar Baer of Shebershin compiled a book of conduct entitled *Mareh kohen* (Kraków, 1588/9), with indexes and tales from the Zohar.[66] A synopsis of, and commentaries on, the Zohar were published in R. David ben Abraham Shemaryah's *Torat emet* (Salonica, 1604/5). At the same time, R. Issachar Baer of Kremnitz published three books to assist students of the Zohar and to introduce zoharic texts and customs to the broad public: *Yesh sakhar* (Prague, 1608/9) contained laws and codes of conduct from the Zohar; *Imrei binah* (Prague, 1610/11) was a commentary on foreign words in the Zohar, with a complete index and synopsis of zoharic tales;[67] and *Mekor ḥokhmah* (Prague, 1610/11) was a collection of zoharic texts in summary form, translated into Hebrew, and organized according to the biblical order.

Several indexes to the Zohar were published in Kraków in subsequent decades: *Vayizra yitsḥak* by R. Isaac Perls, with a commentary on *Heikhalot* (1632); *Zer zahav* by Barukh ben David, an index to the Zohar and to its *midrashim* (1647); and *Pataḥ einayim* by R. Eliezer ben Menahem Sternburg (1647).[68] Annotations to and interpretations of the Zohar were included by R. Aaron Zelig of Zolkiew in his *Amudei sheva* (Kraków, 1635). Around the same time *Sefer yesha yah* by R. Isaiah ben Eleazar Hayim of Nice was printed in Venice (1637), featuring explanations of foreign words in the Zohar. The book also included 'codes of conduct for meals according to the Zohar', written by the Spanish exile R. Joseph Sheraga. *Me'ulefet*

[65] On the circulation of the poem in the 17th century see Hallamish, *Kabbalah in Liturgy, Halakhah, and Customs* (Heb.), 508–10; Huss, *Sockets of Fine Gold* (Heb.), 14, 23.

[66] The book was published for the second time in Amsterdam (1672/3). Knorr von Rosenroth translated it into Latin and included it in his book *Kabbala denudata*.

[67] The commentaries in *Imrei binah* were incorporated in the Zohar that was printed under the supervision of Knorr von Rosenroth in Sulzbach (1683/4), and in most editions since then.

[68] This index was reprinted in the Sulzbach edition of the Zohar in 1683/4.

sapirim, a popular collection of zoharic sections translated into Hebrew by R. Solomon Algazi, was initially printed in Constantinople in 1660 and was reprinted several times in the eighteenth century.

While the printing of the Zohar allowed unsupervised access to the text, the authors of zoharic anthologies and reference books served as controlling mediators between the text and its readers. They chose sections that they considered fit for a specific readership and which usually included tales, ethical paradigms, and codes of conduct. Furthermore, they often attached to those segments their own interpretations and translations. It was a generally accepted view among compilers of the anthologies that the Zohar, and kabbalistic knowledge in general, was esoteric. They justified the printing and distribution of these anthologies by distinguishing between esoteric and exoteric elements of the Zohar—the same distinction that had previously been made to legitimize the printing of the Zohar. R. Issachar Baer of Shebershin, the author of *Mareh kohen*, notes in the opening pages of his book that the Zohar 'serves as an entryway only for those very few exemplary men of special virtue', but it also contains texts that 'fit everyone and which have been abandoned, for those who wish to come and discern'. He had compiled these accessible sections into a book:

> [The Zohar] includes many additional, enjoyable segments, which are more precious than pearls and sweeter than honey, for the old and the young: simple meanings, allusions, homilies, explanations, awesome warnings pointing out the path one should take in any situation, and the conduct one should adopt in life . . . And since these instructions, which fit everyone, have been gathered, concealed, and captured between the depths of the abyss and the sublime heights of the mysteries of kabbalah . . . I, in my humble mind, thought that it was beneficial to collect and gather these abandoned texts, and to organize them by subject for those who wish to explore them.[69]

R. David ben Abraham Shemaryah, in the introduction to his book *Torat emet*, reiterated and emphasized the esoteric character of the Zohar:

> It is a common truth and well known that not everyone [is capable of accessing] esoteric knowledge and the secrets of the Zohar, only one in a town and two in a family. The greatness, glory, fame, and value of the Zohar are such that it consists

[69] Gries, *Conduct Literature* (Heb.), 72–3.

of difficult statements, it reveals great secrets, as well as pure and clear utterances more desirable than gold and silver, sweeter than honey and the honeycomb. And not everyone merits two tables, and even fewer three—to understand the revealed, the concealed, and the great secrets [*Ber.* 5*b*].[70]

Shemaryah goes on to say, however, that the Zohar also includes an exoteric layer—'clear' and 'straightforward' words—which he summarizes in his book. He describes his collection as 'a synopsis of all the clear segments of the Zohar' and compares it to Alfasi's *Sefer hahalakhot*, to Ibn Habib's *Ein ya'akov*, and to Karo's *Shulḥan arukh*:

And they said to me—arise, write, collect, and copy all the clear passages that are found in the Zohar, and leap over the tall mountains. Set out and learn what R. Jacob Ibn Habib, of blessed memory, sought when he wrote the book *Ein ya'akov*, which is the favourite of all the preachers. Go and see also what the great luminary R. Alfas did. He formulated brief and complex laws, based on his opinion, which are superior to all other rulings. And have you never heard, known, or seen the great rabbi, our teacher R. Joseph Karo, may he be remembered in the world to come, who wrote the *Shulḥan arukh*, short and fit for all the children of Israel because there are not many who are learned enough to read the *Arba'ah turim*? And he was blessed to be read by high and low. Thus, if you set out to write a synopsis of everything that was written and explained in the Zohar for the purpose of the unification of the Holy One, blessed be He, and the Shekhinah, to protect and perform . . . and while listening and contemplating these things I rose to let in my beloved—to collect, compile, and copy all the segments that have been explained and stated in the Zohar, clear and straightforward words in honour of the Holy One, blessed be He, and the Shekhinah.[71]

R. Shemaryah states that, although his target audience is preachers and Torah teachers untrained in Zohar, experts might also benefit from this book. His abridged version of the 'simple texts' of the Zohar was meant to assist the above readers in incorporating these texts into their homilies:

Many have never engaged in the study of the Zohar because they cannot understand its language, and even less its delicious secrets, since [they] are exploring important laws and rulings day and night, incessantly. They have had neither the time nor the leisure to engage in study of the Zohar. And [even] those servants of God who have been learned in the Zohar may find this book helpful because of

[70] *Torat emet*, 1*b*. [71] Ibid.

the annotations that God, the Lord, has put before me. How good and pleasant would this book be for those who preach and teach the Torah every sabbath, so that they could present these simple matters briefly, without lengthy [explanations], a little here and a little there, while leaping over the concealed mountains.[72]

R. Issachar Baer of Kremnitz described his book *Mekor ḥokhmah* as a collection of paraphrases of the 'simple meanings of the Zohar' for the 'world's masses': 'There is no benefit in quoting [zoharic] texts in the original language for several reasons. One of them is that the language of the Zohar in its entirety, as well as its subject matter and things of that nature, are obscure and closed to the world's masses. And there are other reasons as well.'[73]

Another sage, R. Solomon Algazi, explained that his anthology, *Me'ulefet sapirim*, contained zoharic segments interpreted according to their plain meaning: 'And I called it *Me'ulefet sapirim* because they are transparent, for they have been collected from the Zohar according to its plain meaning.'[74]

As is clear from the above examples, the zoharic anthologies were meant for readers beyond the circles of the rabbinic elite. The compilers strove to include texts that reflected 'the simple meaning' of the Zohar. By doing so, those in charge of the preparation and distribution of the anthologies retained control over the omitted esoteric knowledge, magnified the esoteric image of the Zohar, and increased the cultural capital of those who were perceived as masters of that knowledge.

The proliferation of the Zohar was facilitated not only by the publication of anthologies and reference books but also by the integration of zoharic texts into the liturgy. Through prayer services the sacred passages could easily reach a wide public of worshippers. The first zoharic excerpt to be inserted into the liturgy was 'Berikh shemeh demarei alma' (Blessed be the name of the Master of the world), a prayer that, according to Zohar 'Vayakhel' (ii. 206*a*), should be recited when the Torah scroll is being taken out of the ark. Customarily recited in kabbalistic circles of the sixteenth century, 'Berikh shemeh' was first printed (before the Zohar itself) in *Tefilah ledavid*, a collection of prayers compiled by R. David ben Joseph Karko

72 *Torat emet*, 2*a*. 73 *Mekor ḥokhmah*, 1*b*.

74 See the introduction to *Me'ulefet sapirim*.

(Constantinople, 1537/8). Later printings included *Seder hayom* by R. Moses ben Makir (Venice, 1598/9), and the prayer book of Ashkenaz and Poland (Hanau, 1627/8). The prayer is also mentioned in *Ma'adanei leḥem vedivrei ḥamudot* by R. Yom Tov Lipman Heller (Prague, 1627/8). Isaac Luria's custom of reciting 'Berikh shemeh' is noted in *Sefer hakavanot* (Venice, 1620) and in works based on R. Jacob Tsemah's *Nagid umetsaveh*, such as Luria's *Shulḥan arukh* (Prague, 1660) and Solomon Ibn Gabai's *Me'irat einayim* (Constantinople, 1660–70).[75]

Once the Zohar was recognized as an authoritative source of laws and customs, the recitation of 'Berikh shemeh' became commonplace. It was incorporated into the liturgy of most congregations, and is recited to this day just before taking out the Torah scroll for public reading.

Concurrent with the incorporation of 'Berikh shemeh' in the late sixteenth and early seventeenth centuries, other zoharic texts were also enlisted for liturgical purposes—for example 'Pataḥ eliyahu', a collection of kabbalistic principles of faith ostensibly received from the prophet Elijah and originally included in the introduction to *Tikunei hazohar* (17*a*–*b*). It first seems to have appeared in *Ashmoret haboker* (Mantua, 1623/4), a prayer book compiled by the Italian Lurianic kabbalist R. Aaron Berakhyah of Modena for members of the fraternity Me'irei Shahar.[76] The recitation of 'Pataḥ eliyahu' is mentioned again in Nathan Neta Hannover's prayer book *Sha'arei tsiyon* (Prague, 1661/2),[77] and during the eighteenth century the custom spread further, especially in Sephardi communities and later among the hasidim.

In the seventeenth century zoharic texts were also inserted into the night liturgies (*tikunim*) of Shavuot and Hoshana Rabah. The *tikun* for Shavuot was first recited in the sixteenth century by kabbalists who integrated zoharic readings into that night's study schedule based on a description in the Zohar.[78] When the custom spread beyond kabbalistic circles it became ritualized and worshippers were encouraged to recite zoharic

[75] For further sources, written during that period but printed later, in which the recitation of 'Berikh shemeh' is mentioned, see Hamburg, *Sources of a Custom* (Heb.), 159; Frenkel, 'The "Berikh shemeh" Prayer' (Heb.), 564.

[76] See A. Modena, *Ashmoret haboker*, 242.

[77] *Sha'arei tsiyon*, 12*b*.

[78] On the history of *tikun leil shavuot* see Ch. 4. On the history of *tikun leil hoshana raba* see Wilhelm, '*Sidrei tikunim*' (Heb.), 130–43.

segments on the night of Shavuot even without understanding what they meant.

Schedules of study that included readings from the Zohar for the nights of Shavuot and Hoshana Rabah were first printed in a supplement to R. Judah ben David Hakohen's *Tikunei shabat*, published in Kraków in the early seventeenth century. A book entitled *Seder keriah vetikun leleilei ḥag shavuot vehoshana rabah* was printed in Venice in 1648, and the custom of reading *Idra raba* on the night of Shavuot and *Idra zuta* on the night of Hoshana Rabah was mentioned in R. Moses Zacuto's schedule for the night liturgy of these festivals. Zacuto's schedules were printed in R. Nathan Shapira's *Tuv ha'arets* (Venice, 1664/5) and in R. Nathan Neta Hannover's prayer book *Sha'arei tsiyon*. The latter book also recommends reading 'Pataḥ eliyahu' as well as study of the Zohar during the night prayer of 7 Adar (traditionally considered the date of Moses' death). A night liturgy for Shavuot was printed in Venice in 1680. Ascribed to R. Simeon Ibn Lavi, the booklet followed the custom of the Jews of Tripoli and included readings from Zohar 'Emor'.

The ritualistic reading of zoharic excerpts was justified by attributing holiness to the non-semantic elements of the Zohar, that is, by claiming that the sanctity of the text was inherent not only in its content but also in its phonetic and material aspects. It was, therefore, considered beneficial merely to hold the book and read from it even without understanding its meaning.[79] This idea was first proposed by R. Moses Cordovero, who stated that 'even the uttering of the Zohar's language will bestow mental happiness upon a person, for he is serving God as if he were one of the *tsadikim* in the garden of Eden'.[80] In *Shivḥei ha'ari* the story is related of Isaac Luria being approached by a wealthy man from Constantinople who wished to atone for his sins. 'The Rabbi recommended many remedies to him: fasting, taking ritual baths, wearing a sack, and studying ten pages of the Zohar every day—only [uttering] the words without any comprehension.'[81]

[79] As I show below, sanctity was ascribed especially to the Zohar's phonetic aspects. The claim that holiness was embedded in the book's material elements was made in the 18th century and later. See Huss, '*Sefer Hazohar* as a Canonical, Sacred and Holy Text', 295–300.

[80] Cordovero, *Or ne'erav*, 40.

[81] Benayahu, *The Biography of Isaac Luria* (Heb.), 174. *Sha'ar ruaḥ hakodesh* relates that

The view that it was beneficial to read the Zohar without understanding its content reappeared in the works of later Lurianic kabbalists, for example in R. Aaron Berakhyah of Modena's aforementioned prayer book *Ashmoret haboker*:

While the Jerusalem Talmud reflects the power of [*sefirat*] Netsah, which governs the diaspora, and the Babylonian Talmud reflects the power of [*sefirat*] Hod, the language of the Zohar mediates between them, and that is the essence of unification. Therefore, even those who read it [the Zohar] without understanding its profound secrets are unified on high, where holiness dwells, thanks to its sublime and pristine nature. They experience the world to come and attain purity, asceticism, and fear of God, for it purifies their souls, because it [the Zohar] is a fruit of the wisdom in which they engaged while residing under the throne of God before descending to this world.[82]

Expanding the view that reading certain zoharic segments which did not contain secrets was permitted even to those who had not mastered the secrets of kabbalah, R. Aaron Berakhyah spoke of the benefit of reading any zoharic texts, even those that contained secrets, though one might not understand their full meaning. Such ritualistic reading, he claimed, had a theurgical value and benefited the reader's soul. In his book *Ma'avar yabok* (Mantua, 1625/6) he repeated his recommendation:

'One should [first] study [by oral recitation] and subsequently understand it in the world to come' [*Shab.* 63*a*]. 'One should study it even though one does not understand what it says' [*AZ* 19*a*]. It refines those who study it.[83] Anyone who labours and does not merit understanding will merit understanding in the Garden of Eden. Therefore, it is good to study the Zohar, the *tikunim*, *Ra'aya meheimna*, and other [texts] of that kind even for those who do not understand them.[84]

The Lurianic kabbalist R. Meir Poppers also supports the ritual reading of the Zohar in his book *Or tsadikim*: 'If a person is privileged he should

Luria recommended to R. Abraham Halevi that he study the Zohar without paying close attention to its content: 'R. Abraham Halevi, may God protect and preserve him, told me that my teacher told him how to achieve perception/better understanding. He told him to refrain from meaningless conversations, to get up in the middle of the night and weep because of insufficient knowledge, and read the Zohar superficially without deep thinking, forty or fifty pages every day, and read the Zohar many times' (*Sha'ar ruaḥ hakodesh*, 36).

[82] *Ashmoret haboker*, 268*b*.
[83] Based on Zohar i. 69*b*.
[84] A. Modena, *Ma'avar yabok*, 'Siftei renanot', ch. 26, 94*b*.

study the Zohar during the late hours of the night, because by its grace Israel came out of Egypt, an exile similar to night. The one who is not privileged to understand the Zohar should still recite its language because it purifies the soul.'[85] The recommendation to read the Zohar 'even though one does not understand what it says' was repeated in the circle of R. Moses Zacuto, who contributed to the promotion of liturgical reading of the Zohar in the second half of the seventeenth century. Zacuto wrote in his *tikun* for Shavuot: 'One should read the *Idra raba* from portion "Naso" in the Zohar, even if he does not understand what it says, because it is a great and very important *tikun* for the Matronita [Shekhinah] and his soul, as it has been known for several reasons.'[86] In the *tikun* for Hoshana Rabah he states: 'Thus one should read portion 'Ha'azinu' in the Zohar and books of kabbalah in particular, not other texts, even if one does not understand what they mean because the language of the Zohar, especially that of the holy *Idra*, benefits the Shekhinah and the soul more than any other form of Torah study.'[87] The same statement was reprinted in the *tikun* for Shavuot in Hannover's prayer book *Sha'arei tsiyon*.[88]

Zacuto, like Aaron Berakhyah of Modena, considered the reading of the Zohar, even without any comprehension, a ritual of tremendous value, being both a theurgical restoration of the Shekhinah and a beneficial and purifying activity for the reader. As mentioned before, the idea that Zohar study fulfilled a theurgical and eschatological purpose was widespread among kabbalists in the sixteenth century. According to Aaron Berakhyah of Modena and Zacuto, however, the theurgical power of the Zohar stemmed not only from study of its secrets, but also from the recitation of its words. On this view, the phonemes of the Zohar were sacred and their mere utterance was a valuable ritual, which justified and even required widespread dissemination of the Zohar, and at the same time reinforced its esoteric nature. The sanctity of the zoharic phonemes stemmed from the holiness of the Zohar's content, which held the secrets of the divine world and imparted to the phonemes theurgical and eschatological powers. If the mere utterance of zoharic words was so powerful, all the more so was knowledge of its secrets.

[85] *Or tsadikim*, 'Zeman hashkamat haboker', 3*a*. Written in 1643, Poppers's book was first published in Hamburg in 1690.

[86] Shapira, *Tuv ha'arets*, 75*b*.

[87] Ibid. 76*a*.

[88] Hannover, *Sha'arei tsiyon*, 50*b*.

Not only did the idea of the sanctity of the phonemes make the circulation of the Zohar possible to a wider spectrum of the public, but at the same time it reinforced the status of those kabbalists who were considered capable of deciphering the obscure text and understanding its secrets. Most advocates of liturgical reading were Lurianic kabbalists who also claimed to possess the hermeneutical key to the text. Thus the popularization of the Zohar via the practice of ritual reading, together with the justification of the concept that its non-semantic elements carried sanctity, served to elevate the image of Lurianic kabbalah and to buttress the cultural power of the scholars who belonged to that school.

Despite the prevalence of zoharic quotations, the printing of zoharic anthologies and reference books, and the incorporation of zoharic texts into the liturgy, the spread of the Zohar outside scholarly and kabbalistic circles remained quite limited in the seventeenth century. As we have seen, only a few editions of it were published in that period and *Tikunei hazohar* was not printed at all. There were only a handful of anthologies and reference books to support study of the Zohar, and the majority of these works were printed only once. While ritual recitation had begun to make inroads into the liturgy, it was not until the eighteenth century that this practice became widely accepted.

Zohar commentary, the principal kabbalistic literary genre of the second half of the sixteenth century, was limited in the next century to manuscripts, which had a very small circulation. Other than the short commentaries of R. David Shemaryah and R. Issachar Baer of Kremnitz on what they perceived as the plain meaning of the Zohar, only two exegetical works were printed: *Zohorei ḥamah*, a summary of Abraham Galante's *Yereḥ yakar* by R. Moses Zacuto (Venice, 1655), and *Yodei binah*, the beginning of which was written by R. Joseph Hamitz and the rest by Zacuto (Venice, 1658). It should be emphasized that, although these two commentaries were printed by Zacuto, the leading Lurianic kabbalist of the time, neither was based on Luria's thought. This fact demonstrates that while Lurianic kabbalists were promoting the liturgical use of the Zohar and printing commentaries based on its 'simple meaning', they refrained from exposing its esoteric layer, which they identified with Luria's teaching.

A noticeable growth in the Zohar's readership did not begin until the late seventeenth century, and continued throughout the eighteenth. While the late seventeenth century saw the publication of only one edition of the Zohar, fourteen editions appeared in the eighteenth. During the same period eleven editions of *Tikunei hazohar* were published, and three of *Zohar ḥadash*. Several editions of *Idra raba* and *Idra zuta* were printed, some of which included *Sifra ditseniuta*. The number of printed Zohar commentaries also increased significantly;[89] as I show further below, many of these commentaries came from Sabbatian authors. Among those that did not were the comprehensive interpretative works of R. Shalom Buzaglo, Simeon Ibn Lavi's *Ketem paz*, and *Aspaklarya hame'irah* by R. Tsevi Hirsch Horowitz.

Along with the corpus of the Zohar and its commentaries, reference books and anthologies were printed, including R. Solomon Algazi's *Me'ulefet sapirim* (a collection translated into Hebrew), initially published in the seventeenth century and again in various other editions in the eighteenth. Another work that contributed to the popularization of the Zohar was *Ḥok leyisra'el*, a textbook for the public that included excerpts from the Bible, Mishnah, Talmud, and the Zohar, scheduled for daily study. It was first published in Egypt in 1740 and was republished several times.

In the same period zoharic anthologies were printed in Yiddish for the uneducated public, including young people and women.[90] Yiddish ver-

[89] In the mid-18th century the following commentaries were published that are known to us: *Or yisra'el* (Frankfurt an der Oder, 1701/2) by R. Israel ben Aaron Jaffe; *Eshel avraham* (1700/1) by R. Mordecai Ashkenazi; *Ḥemdat tsevi* (Amsterdam, 1700/1), a commentary by R. Tsevi Hotch on *Tikunei hazohar*. Zohar commentaries were included in *Sefer yirah* (Berlin, 1722/3) by R. Leib Priluki; *Sefer ben david* (on *Idra zuta*) by R. Naftali ben David (Amsterdam, 1728/9); and *Ruaḥ david* (on *Idra raba*) by R. David de Medina (Salonica, 1746/7). In the second half of the century two comprehensive commentaries by R. Shalom Buzaglo appeared: *Mikdash melekh* (Amsterdam, 1749/50) and *Hadrat melekh* (Amsterdam, 1765/6, 1769/70). In addition to Buzaglo's writings, the following commentaries were published: *Aspaklarya hame'irah* (1775/6) by R. Tsevi Hirsch Horowitz; *Be'er mayim* (on *Tikunei hazohar)* by R. Isaac ben Yekutiel Zalman of Pollack (Zolkiew, 1777/8); and R. Simeon Ibn Lavi's *Ketem paz* (Livorno, 1794/5).

[90] A single testimony regarding study of the Zohar among women before the 18th century appears in Aaron Berakhyah of Modena's introduction to *Ashmoret haboker*, in which he recounts that his grandmother Fioretta Batsheva (who lived in the 16th century), 'throughout her life did not stop studying Scripture, Mishnah, books of *posekim*, and first and foremost Maimonides. She also looked into the Zohar according to her ability' (*Ashmoret haboker*, 3a). See also Chajes, *Between Worlds*, 218 n. 23. In this context Chajes mentions Johanna, the

sions of zoharic and kabbalistic tales were printed in R. Simeon Akiva Baer ben Joseph's *Ma'aseh adonai*. Targeting uneducated laymen and women,[91] this book was initially published in the late seventeenth century and saw many more printings in the next hundred years. Zoharic tales were published in Yiddish in *Abir ya'akov* (Sulzbach, 1700) by the same author. In 1710/11 a partial Yiddish translation of the Zohar, *Naḥalat tsevi*, was printed for the first time in Frankfurt am Main. The translation was produced by R. Zelig Chotsh and was published by his great-grandson, the Sabbatian scholar Tsevi Chotsh, who had also written a commentary on *Tikunei ha-zohar* entitled *Ḥemdat tsevi* (Amsterdam, 1705/6). Chotsh's translation was reprinted throughout the eighteenth and nineteenth centuries in many editions, some of them under the name *Nofet tsufim*.

The motto Chotsh had chosen for his book was the following telling verse: 'Gather the people—men, women, children, and the strangers in your community—so that they may hear' (Deut. 31: 12). R. Naphtali Hakohen Katz of Frankfurt wrote in support of the book: 'Now he wants to publish simple meanings and morals from the Zohar, which he collected and wrote down in the language of Ashkenaz to benefit the public, the high and the low, the women and the simple.' R. Wolf, head of the rabbinic court of the Dessau community, also pointed out the work's accessibility to all, as well as hinting at its messianic relevance:[92]

> And now, he decided to print those segments from the Zohar that have a simple meaning in every language that women and those whose competence is that of women understand, to [enable them to] grasp the knowledge of God, so that the land shall be filled with knowledge of the Lord, as it is written in the book of the holy Zohar—'when the Messiah comes, even an infant etc.'

Chotsh himself states the following on the title page of his book:

Virgin of Venice, who, Postel relates, revealed the secrets of the Zohar to him (although she knew neither Hebrew nor Aramaic); see Chajes, ibid. On another 16th-century woman, R. Eliezer ben Abraham Eilenburg's grandmother—who was an expert on kabbalah—see Davis, 'A German Jewish Woman Scholar', 101–5 (her grandson, who recounted this fact, did not mention which book of kabbalah she had read).

91 See Weissler, *Voices of the Matriarchs*, 50.

92 On 'women and those whose ability is that of women' see Weissler, *Voices of the Matriarchs*, 38–44.

This book is not for scholars, whose hearts resemble a huge hall and who are able to ascend by means of a ladder. Here [in this book] I use a method fit for women; I close my eyes and ignore all the concealed matters, targeting those among the masses who have the ability to comprehend but lack the means to possess the Zohar. [I am] also addressing those who own it [the Zohar] but are unable to distinguish between holy and holy, to observe and to interpret, to search and leap like a lonely bird from one roof to the other to find the thing he seeks and moral instructions. And the secrets should be left alone.

As I have previously shown, the argument that the zoharic corpus included a layer of 'simple meaning' was already used in the seventeenth century to justify the printing of anthologies of the Zohar's proverbs, morals, anecdotes, and customs. However, one must emphasize that *Naḥalat tsevi* contained significantly more zoharic material than the previous anthologies and, unlike them, was not organized by subject matter, but rather according to the portions of the Zohar. In addition to the claim that the texts incorporated in *Naḥalat tsevi* belonged to the simple layer of the Zohar, R. Naphtali Hakohen Katz added a further argument in support of the Yiddish edition:

If [one thought that] I intended to prevent the printing [of the book] in the language of Ashkenaz because the words of the Zohar are sacred . . . like sparks of fire coming out of the mouth of Shimon ben Yohai, his companions, and his disciples, and therefore it is inappropriate [to let] everyone look at them . . . the opposite is true. Is it not the case that R. Shimon himself wrote it in a foreign tongue, the tongue of the Targum [Aramaic] that everyone used to speak? Even if he had other reasons and more profound explanations for writing it in the language of the Targum, as is often the case in revealed and concealed books, he was not bothered [by the possibility] that women and simple people might read it.

This argument leads to the conclusion that the Zohar in its entirety was written as an exoteric text. Therefore one should not prevent its circulation, but rather support it by translating the book into the vernacular.

The dissemination of the Zohar among the broad public, including women and the young, was carried out not only by literary means, but also by oral instruction. In Italy during the 1730s, R. Solomon Aviad Sar-Shalom Basilea recounted teaching kabbalah and Zohar to children and laymen. He welcomed the growing interest of students in the Zohar, and in his book

Emunat ḥakhamim criticized R. Jacob Francis's poem, written seventy years earlier, against the dissemination of the holy book. The poem in question was printed by R. Solomon Morpurgo at the end of *Ets hada'at*, his commentary on R. Yedayah Bedersi's *Beḥinat olam*. Although Basilea rejected Francis's claim that even schoolchildren were engaged in kabbalah, his denial reveals his support for such practice:

> First he said that schoolchildren were engaged in kabbalah, which is a lie because it has never happened. They are taught only the clear, simply formulated parts of *Reshit ḥokhmah* which lead to fear of God, and simple passages from the Zohar. The only difference between those and *Midrash rabah* is the language [in which they are written]. These studies train them to zealously fulfil [their] religious duties.[93]

Not only does Basilea not hide his support for teaching schoolchildren zoharic texts defined as *peshat*, he also defends the unrestricted study of the Zohar by laymen and the common folk:

> In addition, he slanders and spreads lies about the students of the Zohar, saying that they use foul language, all of which is nothing but lies and falsehood . . . and he refers to uneducated and common people who, despite their shortcomings and urges, do not cease to make time for Torah study and read the Mishnah and the Zohar. What is wrong with that? Even with regard to idolatry, which is a serious sin, our rabbis of blessed memory said, 'May they abandon Me but keep my Torah', since through their engagement in it [the Torah], its light would lead them back to the right path.[94]

Taking a different stance, R. Moses Hagiz, in his *Mishnat ḥakhamim*, expressed reservations regarding the translation of the Zohar into the vernacular and its being taught to the young and to women:

> In ancient times there would not be even one among the elders and the leaders of a town, [let alone] two in a family, who would possess the Zohar. Now, any irresponsible, vain, and ignorant youth grasps the Zohar in his hands and boasts publicly that he knows it well enough to expound, annotate, and translate it from one language to another. They sit and read it to women and children in foreign languages. And I am surprised that the leaders of this generation do not prevent it, especially those in this large city of sages and writers . . . How is it possible that

[93] *Sefer emunat ḥakhamim*, 31*a*. [94] Ibid. 31*a*–*b*.

they allow the study of this holy Zohar publicly and openly, and [if that is not enough] in the vernacular?[95]

It seems that this criticism was directed at the Sabbatians, who were actively engaged in the dissemination of the Zohar among the uneducated. The practice of teaching the Zohar to women and the young in Sabbatian circles, and especially among the Frankists, is evident in sources from the eighteenth century.

It is in this period that the incorporation of zoharic segments into the liturgy becomes widespread, together with the study and ritualized reading of the Zohar on festivals. 'Berikh shemeh' (which, as we have seen, had been recited earlier in certain circles) gets regular mention in books of law and custom, and is found in many prayer books printed in the eighteenth century, as well as in the influential *Ḥemdat yamim* (Smyrna, 1731/2). The latter work was probably written by a group of Sabbatians affiliated to R. Jonah Ashkenazi's prominent publishing house in Smyrna.[96] *Ḥemdat yamim* also mentions the custom of reciting 'Pataḥ eliyahu', which originated in kabbalistic circles in the seventeenth century; in fact, its recitation is recommended before each prayer (a practice attributed to R. Moses Cordovero).[97] The same work further recommends the reading of a passage from Zohar 'Vayakhel' (ii. 207*b*) before Kiddush on the sabbath,[98] as well as one from *Ra'aya meheimena* (iii. 98*b*) before sounding the *shofar* on Rosh Hashanah.[99] Both of these customs were later incorporated into the Sephardi and hasidic liturgies.

The practice of reciting zoharic sections on the eve of Shavuot, Hoshana Rabah, and 7 Adar as well as on other Jewish festivals gained significant momentum in the eighteenth century. *Tikunim* containing readings from the Zohar spread substantially. The first printed references to readings for the seventh day of Passover appeared in the prayer book entitled *Sha'arei raḥamim* by the Sabbatian sage R. Judah ben R. Joseph Perets (Venice, 1709/10), and in a *tikun* for the seventh day of Passover (Amsterdam, 1724/5). The reading of the Zohar on the night of Lag Ba'omer (the thirty-third day of the *omer* period connecting Passover and Shavuot) also originated in the early eighteenth century, while the custom of reading on

[95] *Mishnat ḥakhamim*, 5; see Rapoport-Albert, *Women and the Messianic Heresy of Sabbatai Zevi*, 143–4. [96] *Ḥemdat yamim*, i. 77*b*. [97] Ibid. iv. 39*a*. [98] Ibid. i. 53*a*. [99] Ibid. iv. 36*a*.

the eve of a circumcision was first noted in *Shomer haberit* (Amsterdam, 1718/19), published by R. Solomon Ailion. Most of the *tikunim* printed in the eighteenth century for the eve of a circumcision contained zoharic segments.[100] R. Simeon Frankfurt incorporated zoharic texts in his book *Sefer haḥayim* (Amsterdam, 1702/3), to be studied at the bedside of a dying person.[101]

Ḥemdat yamim contributed to the spread of the study of zoharic excerpts and of ritualized reading by recommending these activities for the above festivals and for the eve of Rosh Hodesh, the days of *shovavim*,[102] Tu Bishevat, and Sukkot.[103] Many *tikunim* printed since then have followed the order of zoharic readings established in that work.[104]

Moreover, some eighteenth-century editions of the Zohar itself were published specifically for the purpose of ritual reading. R. Jonah Ashkenazi, the printer of *Tikunei hazohar* (Orta-Koi, 1719), recommended reading the book from the first day of the month of Elul to Yom Kippur to 'repair the soul'. R. Jonah divided the texts of *Tikunei hazohar* into forty segments corresponding to the number of days between 1 Elul and Yom Kippur.[105] An edition of *Idra raba* (Venice, 1701) was designed, according to its editor, to be read over the grave of the prophet Samuel on the anniversary of his death, 28 Iyar. *Idra raba* and *Idra zuta*, included in the Constantinople edition of *Ne'edar bakodesh* (1736), were to be read on the eves of Shavuot and

[100] On the history of customs performed on the eve of a circumcision see E. Horowitz, 'The Eve of the Circumcision'.

[101] See Bar-Levav, 'The Concept of Death in the *Book of Life*' (Heb.), 348.

[102] *Shovavim* is an abbreviation of six (of the eight) Torah portions read during the months of Tevet and Shevat.

[103] On Zohar study on the eve of a new month (Yom Kippur Katan) see *Ḥemdat yamim*, ii. 8*d*–10*b*. For the history of the night liturgy on the eve of a new month, see Hallamish, *Kabbalah in Liturgy, Halakhah, and Customs* (Heb.), 537–66. On study of the Zohar during the *shovavim* period (see n. 103 above), see *Ḥemdat yamim*, ii. 100*a*–*b*, 102. For a history of the night liturgy of the *shovavim* period see Hallamish, *Kabbalah in Liturgy, Halakhah, and Customs* (Heb.), 567–94. On reading from the Zohar on 15 Shevat (Tu Bishvat), a custom that was established by the authors of *Ḥemdat yamim*, see *Ḥemdat yamim*, ii. 109*a*–*b*. *Peri ets hadar* (Salonica, 1752/3) was written based on the description of the order of study in *Ḥemdat yamim*. For the history of the Tu Bishvat *seder* see Ya'ari, 'History of the New Year of Trees' (Heb.); Huss, 'The New Year of the Tree' (Heb.). On study during Sukkot see *Ḥemdat yamim*, iii. 85*a*–86*a*.

[104] Ya'ari, '*Tikunim* and Prayers According to *Sefer ḥemdat yamim*' (Heb.).

[105] It is possible that this custom is a Jewish equivalent of the Muslim practice of reading the Koran during Ramadan.

Hoshana Rabah, respectively. In his introduction to the Amsterdam edition of *Zohar ḥadash*, which he published in 1701, R. Isaac ben Abraham of Neustadt recommended reading that book between Rosh Hashanah and Hoshana Rabah. On the title page of this edition a 'quotation' is printed, in which the Zohar itself addresses its readers:

To you, O man, I call [Prov. 8: 4]! Righteous followers of faith, come forth[106] and study my wise words, even those who may not fully understand those words. Since reading aids, refines, and pleases the soul, make time for study, even of a single page, especially on the sabbath, while attaining your supernal souls. Therefore go forth and purchase me; for the one who acquires [me] obtains wisdom. How much better to get wisdom than gold, as it is more precious than the silver of this world [Prov. 16: 16]. Thus do not pursue silver and wealth, for God will provide [the best].

The above quotation clearly indicates that the attribution of value to the ritual reading of zoharic texts, even in the absence of comprehension, served to promote the dissemination and marketing of the book. Some authors went so far as advising readers to obtain two copies—as seen, for example, in *Or hayashar* (Amsterdam, 1708/9): 'If possible, one should have two copies of the Zohar: one to study and one to recite. And one should study first. In my calculation it takes thirty-five nights to go over twenty-five small pages in the Mantua edition.'[107]

The designation of Lag Ba'omer to commemorate R. Shimon's passing and to celebrate the Zohar attests to the book's growing influence and centrality in Jewish culture from the eighteenth century on.[108] Based on a practice established by Luria, the pilgrimage on Lag Ba'omer to R. Shimon's grave in Meron is first noted by R. Hayim Vital and has been customary since the late seventeenth century.[109] The call for those who are unable to visit R. Shimon's grave to celebrate Lag Ba'omer in his memory was first mentioned in R. Emmanuel Hai Ricchi's book *Mishnat ḥasidim* (Amsterdam, 1726/7). He warns, 'To avoid punishment, one should be careful not to mourn the destruction at all on this day; on the contrary, one is required to be happy in celebration of R. Shimon. And those who live in the Land of

[106] Based on Isa. 26: 2.

[107] Poppers, *Or hayashar*, 10a.

[108] Huss, 'Sacred Space, Sacred Time, and Sacred Book' (Heb.), 250–6.

[109] *Sha'ar hakavanot*, ii. 191.

Israel should go and celebrate over his grave and have a great feast there.'[110] *Ḥemdat yamim* recommends study of the Zohar, especially *Idra zuta*, on Lag Ba'omer, as well as participation in festivities in R. Shimon's memory. The same book was the first to record the tradition that this date marked the anniversary of R. Shimon's death: 'We found it written in the books of the ancients that the thirty-third day of the *omer* is the day R. Shimon, may he rest in peace, left this world. It is customary to study the secrets of his wisdom and *Idra zuta* on that night, and to rejoice on that festival. Happy are those who do.'[111]

The night service of Lag Ba'omer was originally prepared by R. Isaac ben Abraham de Segura and was printed by his son R. Samuel. Serving as a prototype for all future editions, de Segura's collection contained the poem 'Bar yoḥai, nimshaḥta ashrekha'; 'Pataḥ eliyahu' from *Tikunei hazohar*; segments from the Zohar on R. Shimon's personality, and *Idra zuta*—these readings were to form the core of the festival's liturgy. The compilation has frequently been published (sometimes with additions) under the titles *Tikun leil lag ba'omer* and *Hilula rabah*.[112]

The impressive growth, from the late seventeenth century on, in the printing of zoharic literature and commentaries, as well as in the number of those studying and reciting the Zohar, raises the possibility of a link between these phenomena and Sabbatianism, similar to the influence that Sabbatianism had on the dissemination of Lurianic kabbalah, as demonstrated in the research of Moshe Idel and Zeev Gries.[113] The eighteenth-century expansion of the Zohar's circulation can partly be explained by the growth of the print industry and of the number of literate Jews during that period, as the number of printed books increased three- or fourfold.[114] However, although the proliferation of printed editions of the Zohar fits into this trend, it does not explain sufficiently the large number of these editions.

110 *Mishnat ḥasidim*, 107.

111 *Ḥemdat yamim*, iii. 38*d*. The establishment of Lag Ba'omer as the date on which R. Shimon died is first mentioned by R. Meir Poppers in his adaptation of Vital's *Peri ets ḥayim*, which was written in the early 17th century (but was not printed until 1781/2); see *Peri ets ḥayim*, 530.

112 Hallamish, 'The Bar Yohai Poem' (Heb.), 372–5.

113 Gries, 'The Shaping of Hebrew Conduct Literature' (Heb.), 563, 572; id., 'The Copying and Printing of Kabbalistic Books' (Heb.), 206; Idel, 'One from a Town' (Heb.), 19.

114 Gries, *The Book in the Jewish World*, 16.

It seems likely that the Sabbatian ideology—which regarded the Zohar as the principal text of the days of redemption—and some of its influential adherents, including well-known rabbis, kabbalists, and printers, played an important role in the dissemination of the Zohar and its penetration into ever-widening circles of Jewish society beyond the intellectual elite. The fact that many Sabbatians were involved in this activity did not go unnoticed by their opponents, who were incited to reassert their demand to limit access to the sacred book.

As Abraham Elkayam has stated, it is difficult to overestimate the importance of the Zohar within the Sabbatian movement:

The Zohar played a major role in the mythology, liturgy, conduct, and ideology of the Sabbatian movement and its later forms—from Sabbatai Zevi, who (according to R. Moses Pinheiro) 'never studied kabbalah other than the Zohar and *Sefer hakanah*', up to the followers of Jacob Frank, who were called Zoharites. The Sabbatians wrote commentary on the Zohar, some of them in the Zohar's own language. Indeed, the conceptual language of the Sabbatians, who called themselves 'believers' and their wisdom 'the secret of belief', drew from the language of the Zohar. No one disputes the fact that the Zohar played a major role in the shaping of the Sabbatian movement throughout its history.[115]

The narrative in which Elijah told Sabbatai Zevi to study the Zohar day and night,[116] and another which says that the Sultan put the Zohar on Sabbatai Zevi's lap at his conversion ceremony, attest to the importance of that work in Sabbatian thought.[117] Nathan of Gaza and other Sabbatians perceived it to be part of the sacred canon alongside the Bible and the Talmud; its authority was, in fact, considered higher than that of the Talmud in matters of eschatology. Nathan of Gaza formulated this idea in a text entitled 'This is from our teacher and master R. Nathan about the king messiah':

We must reiterate what Maimonides, of blessed memory, said in the 'Epistle to Yemen': 'Details pertaining to the king messiah will remain unknown to us until

[115] 'The Holy Zohar of Sabbatai Zevi' (Heb.), 345–7.

[116] Elijah's instruction to Sabbatai Zevi was written in a note at the beginning of the Toronto, MS Friedberg 5-015 (F. 70561). According to Elkayam, Sabbatai Zevi himself used to own this manuscript; see 'The Holy Zohar of Sabbatai Zevi' (Heb.), 347.

[117] This is related in a Spanish Sabbatian poem that was written during the time of Sabbatai Zevi; see *Romansero sefaradi*, ed. Attias (Heb.), 177–8.

he comes, because we do not comprehend what the sages of blessed memory have said.' Nevertheless anyone who desires to explore this matter thoroughly will be greatly assisted by understanding the gist of what he [Maimonides] conveyed based on statements made by our sages of blessed memory, especially in the Zohar. Since there is nothing in the Talmud that contradicts it explicitly, we must follow the Zohar and rule according to it. . . . In order not to mislead anyone, God forbid, matters concerning the king messiah were not explicitly revealed in the Talmud. They were hidden in the Zohar, which was concealed. It stated that these matters would not be revealed until the advent of the messiah. In addition, it says that several books of legends, in which these matters were revealed, would be found in the king messiah's generation. The Zohar mentions several times that 'the last generation will be sustained by your [R. Shimon's] book'. Therefore we should use the Zohar as a source for these matters. If there is anything in the Talmud that contradicts it, it will be settled with God's help.[118]

Similarly, the *magid* (angelic messenger) of the Sabbatian seer R. Mordecai Ashkenazi valued the Zohar (and *Sefer hakanah*) more than the talmudic sages: 'If anything contradicts the words of our teachers of blessed memory, one should know that I do not say them from my own mind, but that they are clearly proved in the Zohar and the *tikunim* and even more so in *Sefer hakanah*.'[119] The attribution of greater authority to the Zohar than to the Talmud resulted in the preference for studying the Zohar over other works in the Jewish canon. In the words of Nathan of Gaza, 'when a person studies the Zohar, he is as worthy as someone who reads Scripture, Mishnah, Talmud, and everything else.'[120] He was also quoted as saying that 'they should stop splitting hairs over laws for it is better to study the Zohar, *tikunim*, and homilies'.[121]

In the passage cited above, Nathan of Gaza suggests that the Zohar is superior to the Talmud because of the messianic information concealed within it and which was confirmed by the appearance of Sabbatai Zevi. Exploiting the idea that the secrets of the Zohar would be revealed upon the coming of the messiah (that is to say, in Sabbatai Zevi's age), he explains that at the time of redemption not only will the external constraints on the dissemination of the Zohar become null and void, but the obscurity of

[118] See Scholem, *Studies and Texts Concerning the History of Sabbatianism* (Heb.), 241.

[119] Quoted by Scholem in *The Dreams of Mordecai Ashkenazi* (Heb.), 29.

[120] Ibid. 294.

[121] Freimann, *Writings Related to Sabbatai Zevi and His Followers* (Heb.), 96.

the texts will be clarified in light of the messianic events. Basing himself on Maimonides, who argued that messianic matters would not be revealed until the messiah comes, Nathan claims that in the days of the final redemption the Zohar will be converted from an esoteric text into an exoteric one. This idea is also formulated in his 'Epistle on Conversion':

> Although we do not find allusions to [messianic events] in the simple meaning of the Torah, we have already encountered the perplexing words of our sages regarding these matters, and we were unable to understand anything they said. As the great luminary of blessed memory, Maimonides, has stated: 'Their words will not be understood until it happens [redemption comes] with God's help.'[122]

On the basis of the rest of the epistle, which relies mainly on zoharic texts, it seems clear that when Nathan refers to the 'words of our sages' he means primarily the Zohar.

The Sabbatian exegesis of the Zohar was largely determined by the view that one could understand the meaning of the text in light of the current events related to Sabbatai Zevi, his personality, and his faith. Elkayam emphasizes the 'renaissance' approach of the Sabbatian ideologists to the Zohar:

> From the beginning of the second century (when they believed the Zohar was written) until the seventeenth century, the divine secret of faith of the Zohar's author was forgotten. Many days had passed and Israel was unaware of the mystery of divinity that had been concealed within the Zohar. That is to say, upon the death of R. Shimon and his companions the Zohar died with them. Thus it is impossible to talk about any continuous engagement in the secrets of the Zohar.[123]

This new outlook, which presents a criticism—direct or indirect—of earlier approaches to the interpretation of the Zohar, including that of Luria, finds expression in the tradition according to which '[Sabbatai Zevi] disclosed the secret of divinity as we know it to him [R. Moses Pinheiro] and showed him how simple the Zohar was although no one had understood it [up until his time]'.[124] The criticism of the Lurianic interpretation for being unable to clarify sufficiently the secrets of the Zohar, especially the eschato-

[122] Sasportas, *Tsitsat novel tsevi*, ed. Tishby, 260.
[123] Elkayam, 'The Secret of Faith in Nathan of Gaza's Writings' (Heb.), 63.
[124] Benayahu, *The Sabbatian Movement in Greece* (Heb.), 487–8.

logical information contained within it, augmented the Sabbatians' claim that Lurianic kabbalah was irrelevant in the messianic age.[125] In the words of Gershom Scholem,

> the crisis of the Lurianic kabbalah started at the initial phase of the [Sabbatian] movement and continued until the days of the last Frankists . . . Therefore it is not surprising that the Lurianic system itself was shaken by the idea that when the true end of days arrives the secrets of the Zohar, unknown even to Luria, will be fully and truly revealed.[126]

Acquiring dominant status in most kabbalistic circles in the seventeenth century, the Lurianic kabbalah presented a highly complex system of supernal entities and divine worlds as the hermeneutical key to the Zohar. The Sabbatian interpretation, at the same time, was based on current messianic events, the character of Sabbatai Zevi, and the secret of his faith.[127] The Sabbatian sense of Jewish revival and the subversion of Lurianic exegesis, together with the belief that contemporary eschatological developments could explain the Zohar, brought about an eruption of creative Zohar interpretations.[128] As Abraham Michael Cardozo proclaims,

> The duty of a kabbalist used to be to pass on the secrets only to people of special merit and not to anyone else. Now, however, everyone who understands the Zohar or the sayings of our teachers, of blessed memory, who discuss God's divinity, is obligated to interpret it openly, and elaborate on it as much as possible. This is not considered a sin [any more], rather a virtue . . . therefore, it is incumbent upon me to offer water to the thirsty.[129]

The efforts made by the first generation of Sabbatian leaders to disseminate the Zohar can be explained partly by the importance of that work in Sabbatianism, and partly by their belief that it shed light on both Sabbatai Zevi's messianic mission and the secret of his faith. A trend emerged to include the Zohar in study syllabuses and rituals, as is apparent in the conduct manuals compiled by Nathan of Gaza. R. Shemayah de Mayo, one of the copyists of Nathan's manuals, states at the beginning of his manuscript:

125 Scholem, *The Dreams of Mordecai Ashkenazi* (Heb.), 46–8.
126 Ibid. 29.
127 Elkayam, 'The Holy Zohar of Sabbatai Zevi' (Heb.), 362.
128 Elkayam, 'The Secret of Faith in Nathan of Gaza's Writings' (Heb.), 65.
129 Quoted in Benayahu, *The Sabbatian Movement in Greece* (Heb.), 182.

'Before anything else, one should allot time to study the Zohar.'[130] According to R. Elijah Mojajon's testimony, Nathan used to study the Zohar every day:

This was the order in which the Rabbi used to study: at the beginning of the day he used to study a biblical verse, then Midrash, then Talmud, and then Zohar. When he got up to study before sunrise, he studied in reverse order: first Zohar, then Talmud, then Midrash, and then a biblical verse, denoting the four worlds of ABIA [*atsilut, beriah, yetsirah, asiyah*], that is, emanation, creation, formation, and action.[131]

This is to say that the Zohar, which corresponds to the world of emanation, is more exalted than other canonical texts, which correspond to the worlds of creation, formation, and action. *The Conducts of Nathan of Gaza* reiterates Nathan's view that study of the Zohar is superior to that of other canonical texts: 'The order of daily study included Scripture, Mishnah, Talmud, Midrash, and, above all, the holy book of the Zohar. And if he [Nathan] had no time, he would study [only] the Zohar.'[132] The text further recommends the memorization and recitation of a number of zoharic works: 'It is beneficial to recite by heart the five chapters of *Sifra ditseniuta*, *Sefer yetsirah*, and the two *Idrot*. This is what "happy is the man who comes hither with his study in his hand" [*Pes*. 50*a*] meant, he said. It is recommended that one read these [texts] regularly, that is to say, once every day.'[133]

Adherents of Sabbatianism were involved in most activities pertaining to the dissemination of the Zohar in the eighteenth century. The book's proliferation served their cause, especially after the movement went underground, because it enabled them to promote the messianic idea without explicitly proclaiming their belief that Sabbatai Zevi was the messiah. Sabbatian scholars were engaged, for example, in the printing of the Zohar: a new edition of *Tikunei hazohar* was published by R. Tsevi Chotsh (Amsterdam, 1705/6),[134] with his commentary *Ḥemdat tsevi*, which contained obvious Sabbatian references. Two editions of *Tikunei hazohar* and an edition of Zohar on the Torah were published by the printing house of R. Jonah ben Jacob Ashkenazi, who was active in Constantinople, Orta-Koi, and Smyrna. This printing house, in which the aforementioned *Ḥemdat yamim*

[130] 'The Sabbatian Movement in Greece' (Heb.), 277. [131] Ibid. 285. [132] Ibid. 282.
[133] Ibid. [134] The first edition of *Tikunei hazohar* was printed in the 16th century.

was printed and probably also written, was an important centre of Sabbatian activity. Sabbatians were also involved in publishing the Zohar in the printing house of R. Solomon Props in Amsterdam.

Except in the edition of *Tikunei hazohar* that included Chotsh's commentary, no explicit Sabbatian elements appeared in other Zohar editions printed in the first half of the eighteenth century. Nevertheless the messianic argument, which had been used to justify the distribution and printing of the book in the sixteenth century and was often repeated by the first generation of Sabbatians, reappeared in some eighteenth-century editions. The double claim that it was permissible to disseminate the Zohar in the messianic age, on the one hand, and that engagement in the Zohar would accelerate redemption on the other, had special meaning for the Sabbatians, who believed that the messianic process had already started, and who eagerly anticipated the reappearance of Sabbatai Zevi.

Many of the Zohar commentaries printed in that period were authored by Sabbatians. *Eshel avraham* (Fürth, 1701), for instance, was written by R. Mordecai Ashkenazi, a Sabbatian preacher in R. Abraham Rovigo's circle.[135] A year later, in Frankfurt an der Oder, R. Israel ben Aaron Jaffe's *Or yisra'el* appeared. A collection of Zohar commentaries, the book contained several Sabbatian allusions. In Salonica two commentaries were published in 1747: *Ruaḥ david* on *Idra raba*, and *Nishmat david* on the Song of Songs, both composed by the Sabbatian R. David de Medina. Sabbatian motifs can be detected in both of these works.

As we have seen, Sabbatian Zohar exegesis stemmed directly from the conviction that the limitations on the dissemination of kabbalistic knowledge had been lifted and that the current eschatological events had clarified the secrets of the Zohar. R. Mordecai Ashkenazi, in his aforementioned commentary *Eshel avraham*, made reference to a famous passage in *Tikunei hazohar* and suggested that it was an allusion to the disclosure of the Zohar at the end of days, which he claimed had arrived with the advent of Sabbatai Zevi:

Its [the Zohar's] intention is that 'it [Zohar] will be known'. As it has already been said: 'Israel will taste of the Tree of Life, which is this book of the Zohar, and by it

135 Liebes, *The Secret of the Sabbatian Faith* (Heb.), 153–4.

they will get out of exile mercifully', meaning that it will be disclosed to them, as mentioned above. This could not happen but in the last generation and at the end of days, as Elijah told R. Shimon [in the Zohar].[136]

In light of the revelations of the messianic era the Zohar was now readily comprehensible: 'Without any doubt, by means of the principles that are suggested here, at the beginning of the book, pertaining to the *sefirot*, anyone can study and understand the Zohar and the *tikunim* in less than three months, better than others have understood it after several years.'[137] This statement probably expresses criticism of the complexity and difficulty of the Lurianic interpretation of the Zohar. Similar criticism is expressed by R. Abraham Rovigo in reference to R. Mordecai Ashkenazi's Zohar commentary: 'Up to now, almost no one could go through it [the Zohar]. It seems that although the Ari wrote what he wrote, one could understand almost nothing of the Zohar from what he wrote. Now, through the principles that he [R. Ashkenazi] has applied to it, thank God, one can understand a significant number of passages.'[138]

The opinion that interpretation of the Zohar could propel the messianic process influenced the dissemination of that book as early as the sixteenth century. The same idea underlay the eighteenth-century Sabbatian commentaries, for example that of R. Baer Perlhafter, who states, in his apocalyptic chapters recounting the words of the angelic messenger that spoke through him: 'The last redemption depends on this sea that is the Torah. One needs to split this great sea by interpreting the Zohar, by reciting it, and by copying *Sifra ditseniuta*, which has been revealed in the generation of the messiah.'[139]

Sabbatian scholars stood at the forefront of the dissemination of the Zohar to large segments of the public, including women. As mentioned above, R. Tsevi Chotsh published a Yiddish translation which openly targeted an uneducated readership and women. The Dönmeh community of Sabbatian converts to Islam translated the book into Judaeo-Spanish, most probably for the same purpose.[140] Further evidence concerning the teach-

[136] *Eshel avraham*, 3*b*.

[137] Ibid. 6*b*.

[138] Scholem, *The Dreams of Mordecai Ashkenazi* (Heb.), 24.

[139] Scholem, *Studies in Sabbatianism* (Heb.), 545.

[140] See Benayahu, *The Sabbatian Movement in Greece* (Heb.), 182, 271 n. 46. A translation of

ing of the Zohar to women and the young within the Sabbatian movement, and especially among the Frankists, appears in other sources.[141] The phenomenon of making the Zohar accessible to women should be evaluated not only as part of the Sabbatian strategy to disseminate the venerated book, but also, as Ada Rapoport-Albert has suggested, in the context of the egalitarian trend that blurred the distinction between the genders and which characterized Sabbatianism.[142] One can assume that R. Moses Hagiz's criticism, cited above, of teaching the Zohar to women and the young in the vernacular was directed at the Sabbatians.

Sabbatian circles seem to have played a major role in the promotion of customs relating to the study and ritual recitation of the Zohar, which, as we have seen earlier, gained tremendous popularity in the course of the eighteenth century. In the footsteps of Nathan of Gaza, who recommended the daily reading of the Zohar and the memorization and ritualistic reading of the *Idrot* and *Sifra ditseniuta*, R. Judah ben Joseph Perets printed *Kirei mo'ed* (Venice, 1706/7), a collection of zoharic segments to be recited during dinner on various occasions. He also published a prayer book entitled *Sha'arei raḥamim* (Venice, 1709/10), which included zoharic passages to be read in the night liturgy of the seventh day of Passover. Yet another example is the aforementioned *Ḥemdat yamim*, which contains numerous Sabbatian elements, including three poems by Nathan of Gaza. Serving as the basis for a large number of eighteenth-century prayer books and *tikunim*, this work motivated many to study and recite the Zohar during festivals.[143]

The distribution of the Zohar, the burgeoning of its readership, and the involvement of Sabbatians in this process incited rabbinic elite circles, especially in eastern Europe, to voice their disapproval of the Zohar's widespread circulation and its perception as an exoteric text. In an attempt

some zoharic portions can be found in Harvard, Cambridge, MS 79, which was copied in the 18th century by Moses Tsuri Asa'el, a member of the Dönmeh. See Fenton, 'A New Collection of Sabbatian Poems' (Heb.), 331 n. 7.

141 See Rapoport-Albert, *Women and the Messianic Heresy of Sabbatai Zevi*, 141–56.

142 Ibid. 151.

143 On *Ḥemdat yamim* and the question of its authorship see Tishby, *Paths of Faith and Heresy* (Heb.), 108–68; id., *Studies in Kabbalah* (Heb.), ii. 339–418; Barnai, *The Jews in the Land of Israel* (Heb.), 77–84; id., 'On the History of the Sabbatian Movement' (Heb.), 64–7.

to limit access to the book, they repeatedly emphasized its obscurity. Complaints about the dissemination of the Zohar and of Luria's writings among the uneducated had, in fact, first appeared in the seventeenth century, before the emergence of Sabbatianism.[144] R. Jacob Frances, who later became known for his opposition to the new movement, raised objections to the popularization of the Zohar and kabbalah in a pamphlet entitled *Ashrei hagoy*, which he wrote in the early 1660s (that is, before Sabbatai Zevi appeared on stage):

> Lend your ear and weep, dust with ashes, and listen
> It calls for tears.
> The boisterous kabbalah calls out
> In marketplaces, everywhere.
> The infant's hand immersed in secrets
> The young still smelling of his birth
>
> . . . .
>
> Who would believe it? Indeed it happened,
> The Zohar's awesome language in a careless mouth—
> Obscenities, mockery, and deceit.
> All source of filth [in their mouth]
> All disgrace
> Those fit, grasp a boat and paddle;
> Look out and search for the Tree of Life.[145]

In the late seventeenth century the Ashkenazi sage R. Yair Bacharach expressed reservations with regard to engagement in the Zohar, repeatedly underlining its obscurity. In contrast to Frances, Bacharach, who had enthusiastically welcomed the Sabbatian movement at the onset,[146] did not refer to the popularization of the book, but rather to difficulties of its interpretation, echoing the Lurianic view that it was inaccessible to human understanding:

[144] For example, in his preface to *Mekor ḥayim* (Amsterdam, 1754/5), R. Hayim Hakohen of Haleb vehemently opposed the printing of the book *Emek hamelekh*. See Liebes, 'Towards a Study of the Author of *Emek hamelekh*' (Heb.), 102.

[145] Nave, *The Poems of Jacob Frances* (Heb.), 404.

[146] On Bacharach's Sabbatian involvement see Scholem, *Sabbatai Zevi and the Sabbatian Movement* (Heb.), ii. 456.

It is true that I have wondered from a young age about the books written by the later authors [*aḥaronim*] who quoted passages from the Zohar, *Sefer yetsirah*, *Ra'aya meheimna*, and the *tikunim*—all enigmatic writings. They argue about it [the text], they examine the language minutely, word by word, and explain it according to their own rationale, although these are most weighty affairs. Who allowed the human mind to contrive by reason . . . These late authors wish to explain the Zohar's statements, which are concealed and mysterious and sometimes seem to be contradictory. How is the human intellect able to judge, especially in the last generation, [and] to find meaning based on logic and reasoning?[147]

Unlike Hayim Vital, who argues that the only way to understand the Zohar is by obtaining the proper hermeneutical key embedded in Lurianic kabbalah, Bacharach contends that Luria's teaching is incomprehensible to the human mind: 'Directly from the upper worlds these words were delivered to the divine Ari and his young disciples, who received them from him, mouth to mouth. Yet we, through studying them, are unable to find anything comprehensible in them except the plain meaning of the words.'[148] Since the esoteric layer of the Zohar is closed and concealed, Bacharach warns that people should limit their exploration to the plain meaning and to ethical lessons: 'We should not delve into the mysteries but learn the plain meaning of Scripture according to the apparent teachings of the Zohar. We should learn from the ethical admonitions how to follow righteous ways and God will forgive us.'

During the eighteenth century many more scholars voiced reservations about the distribution of the Zohar, most of which were related to the struggle against Sabbatianism. As previously mentioned, R. Moses Hagiz complained in his book *Mishnat ḥakhamim* (Wansbeck, 1732/3) about the proliferation and public teaching of the Zohar: 'One should not wonder that I blame the leaders of the generation for not preventing it, especially those in a large city of sages and writers . . . How is it possible that they allow the study of the holy Zohar in large public groups, openly, and, even worse than this, in the vernacular?'[149] The rabbis of Frankfurt issued a ban on the printing of R. Moses Hayim Luzzatto's books in 1735, expressing therein their wish to put an end to the publication of kabbalistic works in order to prevent their distribution to the 'masses':

[147] *Sefer she'elot uteshuvot*, no. 210.
[148] Ibid.
[149] *Mishnat ḥakhamim*, 56*b*.

In any case, it is justified not to print any book of kabbalah, not even the writings of the Ari of blessed memory, so as to prevent their distribution to the masses, who do not know or understand anything [written] in them; the honour of God is in concealment. As for us, we will do anything in our power to prevent it. And, together with the rest of the rabbinic leadership of this generation, we will place a ban on printing any book of kabbalah.[150]

The most famous and influential act taken against the popularization of kabbalah was the ban issued by the prominent sages of the *kloiz* in Brody in 1757 as part of their struggle against Frankism. Reiterating R. Hayim Vital's statement (based on *Ber.* 8*b*) that 'Not all who desire to assume the Name may do so', they stipulated that in order to study kabbalistic texts one had to be at least 30 years old and had to have mastered in-depth halakhic knowledge:

Furthermore, we see the need to erect a fence and to call out to those who [attempt to] break through and ascend to the Lord; who try to discern the divine chariot and feel obliged to leave behind the study of Talmud and rabbinic rulings and set forth to collect sparks of light among the secrets of the wisdom before being able to read God's Torah or examine carefully the simple meaning [of Scripture] and Talmud. Yet they intend to come to the caves of the tenfold secrets. They have caused this hindrance. Due to their limited intellect, they destroy the [protective] fences of the Torah and its laws, and seize study and worship and make mockery of them. They ascribe nonsense that they invented to the Zohar and the writings of the Ari, of blessed memory. They offer conceits to replace and corrupt the texts. Therefore, by the power of the oaths that are written above, we decree that it is forbidden for anyone to study those texts, God forbid, even the writings that are known to be authored by the Ari. Thus it is absolutely prohibited for anyone to study the books [of the Ari] until he reaches the age of 40. [As for] the Zohar, the book of *Shomer emunim*, and *Pardes rimonim* by R. Moses Cordovero, of blessed memory, a single law applies to all of them—only those 30 years old and above are allowed to study them, provided that they are printed and not handwritten. The person who insolently transgresses these words will be treated as one of the heretics, the wicked, and the hypocrites. Even if one reaches his fortieth year, not all who desire to assume the Name may do so, only those who have filled their belly with Shas [the Talmud] and *posekim*.[151]

150 Ginzburg, *R. Moses Hayim Luzzatto and His Contemporaries* (Heb.), 286.

151 Quoted in Ya'ari, *Studies in Hebrew Booklore* (Heb.), 452–3. See also Bałaban, *The History of the Frankist Movement*, 125–7.

Announced as part of the struggle against the Frankist movement, the ban reflects not only the awareness among the sages of Brody of the connection between Sabbatianism-Frankism and the dissemination of the Zohar, but also the fear of the rabbinic elite that the spread of kabbalah would undermine the authority of rabbinic sources and the status of those who had mastered them. In the words of Elhanan Reiner:

The engagement of members of the *kloiz* in kabbalah reflected the traditional view that assigned the study of kabbalah and practice of its customs to the select few who had previously 'filled their belly with Shas and *posekim*'. It is to say that scholarship preceded piety. This requirement restricted access to the kabbalah to those who had achieved some command of canonical literature and naturally to those who could study esoteric wisdom. It reserved this field for a limited, select group that was part of the traditional rabbinic elite.[152]

Other rabbinic leaders expressed a similar position; for instance R. Ezekiel Landau, the highly influential author of the responsa *Noda biyehudah* (Prague, 1775/6), who had been a member of the Brody *kloiz* in his youth, called for a limitation of kabbalistic study in light of the Sabbatian popularization of the Zohar:

Those who engage openly in the Zohar and in books of kabbalah upset me very much because they nonchalantly cast off the yoke of Torah. They study the Zohar and they succeed neither in this nor in that. As a result, the Torah is being forgotten by Israel. Moreover, in our generation the heretics from the sect of Sabbatai Zevi, may his bones be worn out, have multiplied. It is, therefore, appropriate to constrain study of the Zohar and of books of kabbalah.[153]

The physician R. Judah Leib Hurwitz, an early member of the Jewish Enlightenment, also linked the proliferation of kabbalah to Sabbatianism, and complained about popular engagement in it:

Since the kabbalists' sect has grown, idolatry has spread and excellence has diminished. Anyone who is completely ignorant in the wisdom of kabbalah is being presented as an expert on the Zohar; one lacking any spirit of life is being perceived as having eaten from the Tree of Life; one whose heart is full of filth is being introduced as having read *Sefer hagilgulim*; and one who is incapable of studying a page of Talmud is being presented as reading the book of *Heikhalot*.[154]

152 'Wealth, Social Status and Torah Study' (Heb.), 324.

153 *Noda biyehudah*, 10: 74.

154 *Tsel hama'alot*, epigram 269.

The call to limit the study of the Zohar also found its advocates among the early hasidim. R. Barukh of Kosov, a member of the circle of the Magid of Mezerich (who was in contact with members of the Brody *kloiz*), stated in the opening section of his book *Amud ha'avodah*:

These heretics hold several principles that constitute heresy. They rely on the words of the Zohar and the *tikunim* . . . At the beginning of their studies people should distance themselves from the Zohar until they become advanced in the holy writings of the Ari, may he be remembered in the world to come . . . and they should refrain from immersing themselves in the Zohar at the beginning of their studies, because it is an obscure and proscribed book that might lead them astray by its words . . . Study of the Zohar should thus be minimized.[155]

Like the sages of Brody, R. Barukh was concerned about the Frankists' reliance on the Zohar. However, in contrast (and perhaps in response) to the Brody scholars, who limited the study of Lurianic kabbalah far more than study of the Zohar, R. Barukh argued that one should mainly avoid the latter. Unlike his colleagues, he did not see prior knowledge of the rabbinic canon as a prerequisite; however, he did require mastery of Lurianic kabbalah. It seems that his reservation stemmed mainly from his opposition to the Sabbatian interpretation of the Zohar, which subverted the authoritative status of the Lurianic interpretation.

The popularization of the Zohar and the Sabbatian involvement in that process led to the attempt to limit its study not only by reviving claims of its esoteric nature but also by questioning its antiquity and authority. Dissatisfied with existing efforts to limit the distribution of the Zohar, R. Jacob Emden, a relentless combatant against Sabbatianism, presented a comprehensive criticism of the book's literary unity and antiquity in his *Mitpaḥat sefarim* (1768). He concluded his analysis by asserting that the Zohar's definitive status should be rejected.

The ban of the rabbis of Brody, one of the most important centres of Jewish learning in that period, together with the reservations expressed by other prominent sages, ultimately succeeded in limiting popular involvement in kabbalah. As a result, the general perception of the Zohar as an esoteric text was strengthened.[156] Nevertheless, alongside those who

155 *Amud ha'avodah*, 1.

156 In contrast to the centrality of the Zohar and of kabbalah in the thought of the Vilna

sought to limit its distribution or stressed its inaccessibility, there were others, especially among the hasidim, who continued to present it as an exoteric text and called for its dissemination. For instance R. Phineas Koretz, one of the first hasidic masters, was known for promoting intensive study of the Zohar.[157] Popular engagement in kabbalah also held special status among the hasidim of Komarno, whose rabbis wrote several Zohar commentaries. R. Isaac Safrin of Komarno, in his commentary on the Mishnah, *Notser ḥesed*, stated the following:

A man of Israel depends on the Zohar and on the writings of our masters. He should study in holiness, joy, happiness, fear, and love, each one according to his ability and holiness, since all of Israel are holy, etc. Had my people in this wicked generation, when heresy is gaining power, listened to me, they would have explored the Zohar and the *tikunim* even with a 9-year-old child. Their fear of sinning would prevail over their wisdom and they would be sustained.[158]

The nineteenth and twentieth centuries saw the publication of several new editions of the Zohar, its commentaries, and its translations into Hebrew and other languages by scholars who supported its wide circulation. Notable among these is the work of R. Judah Ashlag (1884–1954), who translated most of the zoharic corpus into Hebrew and supplemented it with a comprehensive commentary. Since the 1980s a widespread movement for the popularization of the Zohar has emerged, partly among Ashlag's disciples. As in previous periods, their activity has stirred criticism in rabbinic circles that oppose the Zohar's circulation, especially among secular Jews and non-Jews.[159]

The confrontation between advocates and opponents of the dissemination of the Zohar surveyed in this chapter took place among circles that unanimously recognized its authority and sacred status; the point on which they differed was whether it was to be perceived as an esoteric or exoteric text. This debate formed an essential part of the struggle for the cultural

Gaon and his disciples, engagement in these subjects did not play a major role in Lithuanian circles in the second half of the 19th or in the 20th century. See Nadler, *The Faith of the Mithnagdim*, 29–49; Magid, *Hasidism on the Margin*, 12.

[157] See Heschel, 'Annals of Pinhas of Koretz' (Heb.), 215–16, 236.

[158] *Notser ḥesed*, 4: 6. On the importance of engagement in the Zohar among the hasidim of Izhbitza-Radzin, see Magid, *Hasidism on the Margin*, 12.

[159] See Meir, 'The Revealed and the Revealed within the Concealed' (Heb.).

power gained through access to that sacred work and through control of kabbalistic knowledge. However, as a result of Jacob Emden's novel challenge to the Zohar's authority, and especially in the wake of criticism among scholars of the Jewish Enlightenment, the Zohar lost its canonical status and positive symbolic value in modern, westernized Jewish society. Criticism of its holiness and authority, alongside attempts to ascribe to it new historical, literary, and national values, will be explored in the coming chapters.

CHAPTER SEVEN

The History of Zohar Criticism

If you wish to be strangled, suspend yourself from a mighty tree.
Pesaḥim 112*a*

THE OPPOSITION provoked by the first printings of the Zohar intensified in the course the eighteenth century, due partly to the book's growing readership and to the Sabbatian involvement in its dissemination. In addition to those who raised objections to its proliferation, some contested its authority, sanctity, and antiquity, or questioned its attribution to R. Shimon. In the late eighteenth and nineteenth centuries these views, which had not garnered much support in their own time, were enthusiastically adopted by the maskilim (adherents of the Haskalah, or Jewish Enlightenment) in eastern and western Europe. While basing themselves on these earlier claims against the Zohar, the maskilim employed new methods—satire and historical-philological research.

Criticism of kabbalah in general and of the Zohar in particular played a major role in the maskilic opposition to traditional Judaism, especially hasidism. It was an important tool of their self-definition as representatives of 'enlightened Jewry' and distinct from other contemporary Jewish groups. Although more sympathetic approaches also emerged during the nineteenth and twentieth centuries, the Enlightenment viewpoint had a definitive influence on the way kabbalah and the Zohar were perceived by Jewish circles that adopted modern European values.

This chapter explores the evolution of the claims raised against the Zohar, and the mechanism whereby those claims were preserved and reused by scholars in later periods. I start my survey with a look at early Zohar criticism, from the appearance of the first texts to the eighteenth century, and then move on to examine the rejection of the Zohar during the Enlightenment.

The claim that the Zohar was an ancient text written by R. Shimon was challenged as soon as the first zoharic texts began circulating and the concept of *Sefer hazohar* emerged. This is evident from R. Isaac of Acre's famous statement quoted by Abraham Zacuto in *Sefer yuḥasin*:

Some say that R. Shimon never wrote this book but that this R. Moses de León knew the Holy Name and by means of His power wrote these wonderful words and, in order to sell them for a good price and much gold, he suspended himself from a mighty tree and said: 'From the book that R. Shimon, his son R. Eleazar, and his companions wrote I am copying these words.'[1]

Further to this anonymous claim, R. Isaac of Acre quoted R. David de Pancorbo, who lived in the same city as de León, as saying: 'Have no doubt that this Zohar was never in the possession of this R. Moses and it never existed. But R. Moses was a master of the Holy Name and whatever he wrote in this book he wrote through its power.' De Pancorbo apparently based his statement on what de León's wife had told the wife of R. Joseph de Avila after her husband's death:

Thus and more may God do to me, if my husband ever possessed this book. He wrote it out of his head and his heart, out of his knowledge and his mind. And when I saw him writing without anything before him I would say to him: 'Why do you tell [everyone] that you are copying from a book when you have no book, and you write out of your own head? Would it not be more appropriate for you to say that the work was your own brainchild to gain more respect by it?' And he would reply and say: 'If I told them my secret and that I am writing out of my own head, they would pay no heed to my words and would not pay me any money for them, because they would say that I had made it all up. But, as it is, when they hear that I am copying from the book of the Zohar, which R. Shimon wrote under the influence of the Holy Spirit, they pay for them [i.e. my words] a lot of money, as you can see.'[2]

Although R. Isaac of Acre's faith in R. Shimon's authorship was left unshaken by all this evidence, he did claim that some zoharic texts that were written in Hebrew were forged (he was possibly referring to certain parts of *Midrash hane'elam*). Zacuto paraphrased R. Isaac's statement in the

[1] *Sefer yuḥasin hashalem*, 88; Tishby and Lachower, *The Wisdom of the Zohar*, i. 13–14.

[2] Zacuto, *Sefer yuḥasin hashalem*, 88; Tishby and Lachower, *The Wisdom of the Zohar*, i. 14–15.

following words:

He [R. Isaac] went to Spain to investigate how the book of the Zohar, written by R. Shimon and R. Eleazar in the cave, came to be discovered in his time. Happy are those who have merited its truth; in its light may they see light. He said 'its truth' because part of it was forged by the forger. And he said that he had been taught that one should believe whatever is written in the Jerusalemite tongue [Aramaic] for those were the words of R. Shimon, but as to what was written in the holy tongue [Hebrew], they were not his words, but the words of the forger; for the real book was written entirely in the Jerusalemite tongue.[3]

Though R. Isaac rejected claims of Moses de León's authorship, he nevertheless recorded those claims, and Zacuto, in turn, quoted them in *Sefer yuḥasin*. Together with R. David de Pancorbo's account of the admission by de León's wife that her husband had written the Zohar, R. Isaac's testimony became the cornerstone of criticism in later generations.

As I suggested in the opening chapters, zoharic literature posed a challenge to the predominant position of Nahmanides and his circle. The question arises: did Nahmanides' disciples level a criticism against the Zohar in retaliation? Although *Sefer hazohar* as such was never mentioned by R. Solomon ben Adret or his disciples, this does not mean that they were unfamiliar with zoharic literature. Scholars have suggested that it may have been a deliberate oversight on their part. In the words of Amos Goldreich, 'R. Solomon ben Adret's attitude towards the Zohar was probably an unfavourable disregard.' Moshe Halbertal has argued that R. Shem Tov Ibn Gaon, a disciple of R. Solomon ben Adret and a follower of the Nahmanidean tradition, issued his warning against pseudepigraphic books specifically with the Zohar in mind.[4] As Joseph Dan has pointed out, R. Shem Tov did not include the Zohar in his list of reliable ancient works.[5] Yet none of the above-mentioned scholars voiced an explicit criticism of the Zohar. Upon examining the mode of distribution of zoharic literature in the fourteenth century, it seems plausible that contemporary kabbalists' disregard of the Zohar did not imply criticism at all, since many of them may not have been familiar with the concept of *Sefer hazohar* in the first place.

[3] Zacuto, *Sefer yuḥasin hashalem*, 88; Tishby and Lachower, *The Wisdom of the Zohar*, i. 13.

[4] Halbertal, *By Way of Truth* (Heb.), 325.

[5] Dan, 'The Worms Epistle' (Heb.), 136.

Evidence of actual criticism of the Zohar is recorded, albeit in an indirect form, in Joseph Angelet's book *Livnat hasapir*, written in the early fourteenth century. After interpreting a zoharic passage (Zohar i. 193*a*), Angelet makes the following statement: 'Until He comes and rains righteousness this is what one should say to stop the liars who spread slander on *Midrash hane'elam*: "All its words are straightforward to the intelligent men, and right to those who have attained knowledge" [Prov. 8: 9].'[6] It seems that Angelet was responding to a challenge to the Zohar's content and not to its antiquity. The criticism might have been raised by disciples of Nahmanides and R. Solomon ben Adret, with whom he was affiliated.

Objection to the Zohar appears in R. Joseph Ibn Wakar's *Shorshei hakabalah*, written in Toledo in the 1340s. In his book Ibn Wakar presents a list of authoritative sources regarding kabbalistic matters: 'The works on which one should rely concerning this wisdom are the legends of the Talmud, the *midrashim Sifra*, *Sifrei*, *Sefer habahir*, and *Pirkei derabi eli'ezer*, and whatever exists from the works of . . . R. Moses ben Nahman and R. Todros Halevi Abulafia, of blessed memory.'[7] At the same time, he warns not to 'trust anyone who disagrees [with the books mentioned above]. The Zohar includes many mistakes, one must stay away from them not to be misled.'[8] From the context, the 'mistakes' to which Ibn Wakar refers are the viewpoints that disagree with the sources he classifies as 'reliable'. His criticism seems to reflect a conservative approach with a double goal: to preserve the authoritative status of the earlier kabbalistic sources, headed by the writings of Nahmanides and his disciples, and to undermine anything that questions their authority, mainly the Zohar. Although Ibn Wakar's book had a significant circulation it was never printed, and his criticism of the Zohar was rarely used by critics of later generations.

R. Avigdor Kara, who was active in Prague in the late fourteenth century, records further opposition to the Zohar in his book on the contemporaneous adversaries of kabbalah: 'These are some of their arguments: *Sefer yetsirah* teaches halakhah that does not follow the Torah; and those considering *Sefer habahir* have not seen a bright light in the skies; and any exalted arrogant person is pursuing the Zohar.'[9] In contrast to Ibn Wakar's

[6] *Livnat hasapir*, 50c.
[7] Quoted in Fenton, 'The Origins of Kabbalah' (Heb.), 186.
[8] Ibid.
[9] See Kupfer, 'Concerning the Cultural Image of German Jewry' (Heb.), 123.

statement, the rejection mentioned by Kara of kabbalah's canonical texts —*Sefer yetsirah*, *Sefer habahir*, and the Zohar—is absolute. It is impossible to determine on the basis of the above quotation who was behind this criticism; as far as we know, the Zohar did not circulate in Ashkenaz in that period. It is possible that the criticism recounted by Kara was directed mainly at R. Menahem Tsiyon's Torah commentary, written in Ashkenaz at the end of the fourteenth century, and which relied, to a large extent, on zoharic literature.[10]

A substantiated refutation of the antiquity of the Zohar and its authority appeared for the first time in R. Elijah Del-Medigo's work *Beḥinat hadat* (Crete, 1491).[11] Del-Medigo's opposition to kabbalah stemmed from his Aristotelian world-view: he rejected as heresy the conception that the *sefirot* were the essence of God,[12] together with the idea that the purpose of the commandments was to repair the upper worlds, which he claimed was a 'harmful fantasy'.[13] With regard to the antiquity and supremacy of the Zohar, Del-Medigo dismissed the claim that it was an ancient book written by R. Shimon,[14] and he was the first to put forward the following historical arguments: (*a*) the lack of any reference to the Zohar in the Talmud as well as its recent discovery suggested that the book belonged to a later period; (*b*) the references to figures who lived after R. Shimon further undermined its claim to antiquity.

Those opposing this opinion argue that kabbalists who claim that the words found in the book called the Zohar are those of R. Shimon ben Yohai are wrong. And it is obvious for many reasons: first, if R. Shimon had written it, a *beraita* or a legend from it would have been cited in the Talmud, as the *Sifrei* and other talmudic

[10] As I have mentioned above, the anonymous criticism quoted by Kara was aimed at *Sefer yetsirah*, *Sefer habahir*, and *Sefer hazohar*; indeed, R. Menahem Tsiyon, in the introduction to his Torah commentary *Sefer tsiyoni*, presented these three works as his main sources: '*Bahir* and Zohar and *Sefer yetsirah*, three courses of hewn stones and cedar beams'.

[11] This work first appeared as part of *Ta'alumot ḥokhmah*, published by Joseph Solomon Delmedigo (Basel, 1628–9) and later reprinted by Isaac Samuel Reggio (Vienna, 1833).

[12] *Beḥinat hadat*, ed. Ross, 91.

[13] Ibid. 99–101.

[14] Del-Medigo claimed to be citing the arguments of other adversaries of kabbalah. According to Isaiah Tishby and Jacob Joshua Ross, he indeed based himself on sources that were readily to hand. See Tishby and Lachower, *The Wisdom of the Zohar*, i. 31; Del-Medigo, *Beḥinat hadat*, ed. Ross, 41–3. Idel, however, doubts the existence of these sources; see *Kabbalah: New Perspectives*, 3.

works were—and no such citation is to be found. Moreover, the people mentioned in this book lived many years after R. Shimon ben Yohai, as is clear to anyone who knows their names from the Talmud. Thus it is absolutely impossible that R. Shimon ben Yohai was the author of this book. They also claim that our nation was unaware of this book until about 300 years ago. Furthermore, if R. Shimon ben Yohai was the authoritative sage among the kabbalists and knew the secrets of the laws and their true meaning it would have been appropriate for the halakhah to follow him—and it did not.[15]

Moshe Idel believes that Del-Medigo's challenge to the antiquity of the Zohar was connected to his identification of kabbalah with Platonism, which he vehemently opposed.[16] Being aware of the influence of the Jewish Neoplatonic school of the eleventh and twelfth centuries on kabbalah in general and on the Zohar in particular, he came to the conclusion that the book could not have been written more than 300 years before his own time. It should be emphasized that Del-Medigo was unfamiliar with R. Isaac of Acre's aforementioned testimony.

Idel further notes the influence on Del-Medigo's outlook of the critical approach of the Italian humanists with whom he had associated while living there. Their rejection of the antiquity of pseudo-Dionysian writings in light of the Neoplatonic trends discernible in those texts contributed to Del-Medigo's rejection of the antiquity of the Zohar on the same grounds.[17]

Del-Medigo's criticism had little impact in the sixteenth century, and although his book was printed a hundred years later as part of R. Joseph Solomon Delmedigo's *Ta'alumot ḥokhmah*, its impact and circulation were minimal until the Enlightenment (when it was printed for a second time by Isaac Samuel Reggio). It seems likely, as Jacob Ross has argued, that the main cause of its limited distribution was Del-Medigo's rejection of kabbalah and the Zohar.[18]

Indirect evidence indicates that additional arguments were levelled against the Zohar in the sixteenth century as part of a general criticism of kabbalah. A distressed R. Solomon Alkabets recounted, for example, that

[15] *Beḥinat hadat*, ed. Ross, 91.

[16] See *Kabbalah: New Perspectives*, 3–4. See also Hames, 'Elia del Medigo', 224–5.

[17] Idel, *Kabbalah: New Perspectives*, 21.

[18] See Ross's introduction to Del-Medigo, *Beḥinat hadat*, ed. Ross, 60.

people were turning their backs on the Zohar because of the seeming contradictions in it: 'These [seeming] contradictions in R. Shimon's statements, may he rest in peace, caused many to lose their faith and believe that which, with God's help, one should never believe.'[19] According to Jordan Penkower, the antiquity of certain zoharic sections is indirectly questioned in the writings of R. Elijah Bahur. Bahur based his criticism on the Zohar's references to the cantillation (*te'amim*) and vocalization (*nikud*), of biblical texts, which were much later in origin.[20]

Some printers also raised questions regarding the authenticity of the Zohar. R. Jacob ben Naphtali Hakohen of Gazula, for instance, asks at the back of the first edition of *Tikunei hazohar*:

> Out of whose belly did the Zohar emerge that until this day no one knows where it was found? Neither in the schools of France nor in those of Spain was its name ever mentioned. And who knows whether or not at this time there are people with pure hearts and pure reason and unblemished ideas who construed, out of their hearts, those plain meanings and homilies?

In the second half of the sixteenth century, in North Africa, R. Simeon Ibn Lavi spoke of those who rejected the words of the Zohar and pointed out its inconsistency—philosophers who accused kabbalah in general and the Zohar in particular of conceiving of God as corporeal.[21] However, it should be emphasized that, except for the evidence found in *Beḥinat hadat*, we do not know of a single instance of direct criticism of the Zohar from that period. Although its printing and circulation stirred up objections, these mainly concerned its dissemination to the general public rather than its ancient or sacred character. Interestingly, although the supporters of printing acknowledged the questionable antiquity and authenticity of the Zohar, these arguments are nowhere to be found in the writings of those who opposed the printing and which are in our possession today. As I have shown in Chapter 4, the attribution of higher halakhic authority to the Zohar than to the rabbinic decisors met with some opposition among non-Sephardi sages, especially in Ashkenaz. However, even they did not question the antiquity and sanctity of that book. Although there were those

[19] *Berit halevi*, 9*a*.

[20] Penkower, 'A Renewed Enquiry into *Masoret hamasoret*' (Heb.), 35, 49.

[21] Ibn Lavi, *Ketem paz*, i. 78*a*, 90*b*. Huss, *Sockets of Fine Gold* (Heb.), 8, 52.

who wondered whether some or all of the Zohar was written after R. Shimon's time,[22] or noted that it had not been known in previous generations,[23] these claims were not made in objection to its status.

Despite limited criticism of the Zohar in the sixteenth century, earlier charges were often reiterated, making them available to future genera-

[22] R. Abraham Adrotil, for example, argued that the book of the *Tikunim* was written by R. Shimon himself whereas the Zohar was composed by his contemporaries or even later; see Scholem, '*Sefer avnei zikaron*' (Heb.), 265. R. Abraham Zacuto believed that the Zohar was written in the generations that followed R. Shimon; however, in his view this fact confirmed the halakhic authority of the Zohar:

> And thus the Zohar illuminates the whole world and is called *Midrash vayehi or*, which is one of the secrets of Torah and kabbalah. It was named after him [R. Shimon], although he did not write it, because his disciples, and his son, and the disciples of his disciples wrote it based on what they had received from him, just as we say that the Mishnah and *Sifra* and *Sifrei* and *Tosefta* are all based on [the teachings of] R. Akiva, although these books were written more than sixty years after his death. Thus the words of the Zohar are more authentic, because they convey the statements of the last [sages] who were involved in the Mishnah and the rulings of *halakhot* and the statements of the *mora'im* [*sic*] who were there. (*Sefer yuḥasin hashalem*, 45)

In R. Abraham Galante's view, the Zohar was written by the geonim, who edited sayings that had been recorded by R. Shimon's disciples. See Azulai, *Or haḥamah*, i. 159*a*, where Galante's text is printed. See also R. Abraham Azulai's introduction to *Or haḥamah*, where he follows Zacuto and Galante in claiming that the Zohar was written before *Ra'aya meheimna*. R. Azaryah dei Rossi, in his book *Me'or einayim* (Mantua, 1573–5), pointed out supplements which he claimed had been added to the Zohar, and he raised questions about the references to *amora'im* in *Midrash hane'elam* (*Me'or einayim*, 232).

[23] R. Judah Hayat, in his introduction to the commentary on *Ma'arekhet ha'elohut*, argued that

> R. Hai Gaon and R. Sheshet Gaon and R. Eliezer of Worms and Nahmanides and the Rabad and the Rashba and other sages besides them did not have the opportunity to taste its [the Zohar's] sweetness because in their time it had not been discovered. It should not surprise you because for sure it had not been discovered until this most recent generation, in which we live today. (*Ma'arakhet ha'elohut*, 2*a*)

R. Abraham Zacuto asserted that 'this book was discovered after [the days of] Nahmanides and the Rosh, who had not seen it' (*Sefer yuḥasin hashalem*, 45). Similarly, R. Gedalyah Ibn Yahya wrote that 'it had not been revealed during the time of Maimonides and the Rosh' (*Shalshelet hakabalah*, 70*a*). R. Moses Cordovero noted, 'And it must be the case that Nahmanides could not have possessed it, let alone those who preceded him' (*Tikunei hazohar im perush or yakar*, ii. 100). R. Simeon Ibn Lavi claimed that Nahmanides 'did not see the Zohar because it had not been revealed during his lifetime, and what proves this is that he did not mention it by name as he mentioned *Sefer habahir*' (*Ketem paz*, i. 19*a*). These sages, as well as others, resolved the contradiction between assumptions of the Zohar's antiquity and aware-

tions. As we have seen, the words of R. Isaac of Acre in his lost book *Divrei hayamim*, which contained challenges to the antiquity of the Zohar, have come down to us in R. Abraham Zacuto's *Sefer yuḥasin*. Via Zacuto's mediation other sixteenth-century sages became cognizant of R. Isaac's testimony. Although these rabbis, like R. Isaac himself, never questioned the authenticity of the Zohar, they contributed to the preservation and circulation of the sceptics' arguments. R. Moses Cordovero, for example, made reference to R. Isaac's statement in the following remark: 'It was investigated long ago, during the time of R. Moses de León and during the time of R. Isaac of Acre, the author of *Me'irat einayim*.'[24] R. Gedalyah Ibn Yahya quoted R. Isaac in his book *Shalshelet hakabalah* (Venice, 1586) and dismissed his claim by saying, 'I believe that it is nothing but vanity. The truth is that R. Shimon and his sacred companions said those things and many others.'[25] R. Azaryah dei Rossi, who also rejected the attribution of the Zohar to R. Moses de León (while at the same time expressing doubts regarding R. Shimon's authorship), relied on the same book by Zacuto in his work *Imrei binah*: 'And here in *Sefer yuḥasin* . . . written in the name of the Dayan of Acre, are lies pertaining to a few words of truth; that is to say that R. Moses, who is mentioned above, with the power of a holy Name fabricated [words] which he inserted [into the text] and spread a great deal of nonsense to make a lot of money.'[26]

As the above examples attest, although Zacuto and the sages quoting him refused to challenge the antiquity of the Zohar, it was in their writings that R. Isaac's testimony was preserved. In later editions of *Sefer yuḥasin* that source was omitted, but the attempts to censor it did not succeed, and it remained the cornerstone on which the rejection of the Zohar rested in subsequent generations.

In the early seventeenth century Christian Hebraists, too, began to question the authenticity of the Zohar. Their criticism, Matt Goldish

ness of its much later emergence by employing traditions pertaining to the concealment of the Zohar and its miraculous revelation. See e.g. Cordovero, *Tikunei hazohar im perush or yakar*, ii. 104; A. Azulai, introduction to *Or haḥamah*, i. See also the legend quoted by R. Hayim Joseph David Azulai, attributed to R. Moses Zacuto, in *Shem hagedolim* (see under 'Zohar').

[24] *Tikunei hazohar im perush or yakar*, ii. 104.

[25] *Shalshelet hakabalah*, 71.

[26] *Me'or einayim*, 233.

claims, often targeted the Christian kabbalists, for whom the Zohar was an ancient text containing Christian truths.[27] Discussing the antiquity of the vowel system in a letter written to Johannes Buxtorf in 1606, Joseph Scaliger claimed that the Zohar was written after the Talmud.[28] Buxtorf, on the other hand, argued that the book's references to the vocalization system might prove that system's antiquity—although, based on Zacuto's *Sefer yuḥasin*, he did raise doubts regarding R. Shimon's authorship.[29]

Another claim against the antiquity of the Zohar appeared in *Arcanum punctationis revelatum*, a book by the French Protestant scholar Ludovicus Cappellus, published anonymously in 1624. Cappellus, who set out to refute Buxtorf's arguments regarding the ancient origins of the vowel system, noted that the Zohar's reference to vocalization proved that the book belonged to a later period. He stated as further evidence that it is never mentioned in the Talmud or even in later sources.[30] A similar argument appeared, it will be recalled, in Elijah Del-Medigo's *Beḥinat hadat*, and later in the criticism of R. Judah Aryeh of Modena, which I discuss below. Although Jewish sceptics in the seventeenth century did not mention Christian criticism of the Zohar's antiquity, it may have influenced them directly or indirectly.

As I have shown in previous chapters, the influence of the Zohar continued to increase in the seventeenth and eighteenth centuries throughout the Jewish world. As it gained canonical status in most communities, the voice of its critics remained subdued, and only a handful of polemical works set out to question or negate its authenticity and authority.

[27] In the review that follows I rely on Goldish's unpublished article 'Preliminary Thoughts on Kabbalah Criticism'. I am grateful to him for allowing me to use a copy of his article.

[28] His letter is quoted by Secret in *Le Zohar chez les kabbalistes chrétiens*, 100; see also ibid. 35 n. 1; Burnett, *From Christian Hebraism to Jewish Studies*, 211.

[29] Buxtorf, *Tiberias, sive, Commentarius Masorethicus*, 75, 79–80; Burnett, *From Christian Hebraism to Jewish Studies*, 227, 233. Buxtorf expressed his doubts regarding the antiquity of the Zohar already in 1630; see Secret, *Le Zohar chez les kabbalistes chrétiens*, 100; Burnett, *From Christian Hebraism to Jewish Studies*, 227. In a letter to Scaliger (1607), Buxtorf pointed out that, according to *Sefer yuḥasin*, it was not R. Shimon himself who had written the Zohar, but his disciples. See Burnett, 212–31, 233 n. 144.

[30] The statement is quoted in Secret, *Le Zohar chez les kabbalistes chrétiens*, 101. Cappellus also relied on Ibn Yahya's argument that it was not R. Shimon himself but his disciples and the disciples of his disciples who wrote the Zohar.

In 1629 Del-Medigo's *Beḥinat hadat* was printed for the first time as part of *Ta'alumot ḥokhmah* by R. Joseph Delmedigo (Yashar of Candia), a distant relative of his. Although Yashar, in his other work *Matsref leḥokhmah* (printed in the same collection), rejected the arguments against the antiquity of the Zohar, at the same time he made note of the statement of R. Isaac of Acre and of other claims that shed doubt on the book's origins. Like those before him, by merely recording these points he contributed to the perpetuation of Zohar criticism.[31]

Yashar may well have had a hidden agenda: notwithstanding his claim to have written his book in defence of kabbalah at the request of his patron, he instructed his readers 'never to assume that one can grasp the true opinion of an author based on his book'.[32] Judah Aryeh (Leon) of Modena, his contemporary and friend, noted that Yashar's arguments against the charges in *Beḥinat hadat* were weak, and their real intention was to subvert both kabbalah and the Zohar: 'While pretending to respond to the opinion of the rabbi, his relative, the author of *Beḥinat hadat*, he [Yashar] is hitting the kabbalists on their heads harder than he [Del-Medigo] did.'[33]

R. Jacob Halevi, Judah Modena's son-in-law, also examined the challenges to the Zohar in his book *Naḥalat ya'akov*,[34] and refuted them at the end of the work. While he did not mention who the critics were, from Modena's book *Ari nohem* it is apparent that Halevi was in dispute with his own father-in-law.[35]

[31] See J. Delmedigo, *Matsref leḥokhmah*, 21*b*–22*a*.

[32] Ibid. 20*a*. See Ruderman, *Jewish Thought and Scientific Discovery*, 125. It should be mentioned that an explicit criticism of the antiquity of the Zohar appeared in *Mikhtav aḥuz*, which was discovered in the 19th century and was attributed to Yashar of Candia. See Barzilay, *Yoseph Shlomo Delmedigo*, 99–100; Ruderman, *Jewish Thought and Scientific Discovery*, 141–3. However, as David Ruderman has shown (ibid. 143–6), there were good reasons to doubt the authenticity of this letter.

[33] L. Modena, *Ari nohem*, 61. See also ibid. 38; Ruderman, *Jewish Thought and Scientific Discovery*, 125.

[34] See Hallamish, 'On the Controversy Concerning Kabbalah in Italy' (Heb.), 181.

[35] See L. Modena, *Ari nohem*, 57; see also ibid. 2; Hallamish, 'On the Controversy Concerning Kabbalah in Italy' (Heb.), 182 n. 20. Talya Fishman has suggested that Modena had put his objections to the Zohar into writing before he wrote *Ari nohem*, and the source of the challenges mentioned by R. Jacob Halevi was a lost pamphlet. See Fishman, *Shaking the Pillars of Exile*, 170–1. Fishman thinks it is possible that the criticism of kabbalah in the book *Kol*

Indeed, *Ari nohem* contains all the arguments that were listed by Halevi.[36] Based on the debate between Modena and his son-in-law, and written for his student R. Joseph Hamitz, it was the first work dedicated entirely to kabbalah criticism. Modena dismissed the kabbalists' claim that their system constituted an ancient tradition. Although focusing mainly on the antiquity of the Zohar, he also questioned the ancient origins of *Sefer habahir* and *Sefer yetsirah*.[37]

Modena built his main argument on the anachronisms in the Zohar. Like Del-Medigo, he noted that many of the sages mentioned in the book lived after R. Shimon.[38] He found other anachronisms as well, such as the reference to the prayers 'Nishmat kol ḥai' and 'Keter yitenu lekha'.[39] Some of his arguments were of a historical nature: he contended, for instance, that had R. Shimon written the Zohar, he would not have done so in Aramaic, which was the vernacular, but rather in Hebrew.[40] He pointed out phrases and puns that were written in the style of the Castilian sages,[41] and he repeated Del-Medigo's argument that if R. Shimon had been the most eminent of kabbalists, halakhah would have been established according to him.[42] Like Yashar of Candia, he highlighted the contradictions between the Zohar and the Talmud,[43] and concluded that the author of the Zohar could not have been a halakhic expert, which R. Shimon

sakhal is also based on a lost work. In the words of Hallamish, the debate between Modena and his son-in-law starts 'orally, continues in the pamphlet of the son-in-law, and ends in the work *Ari nohem*' ('On the Controversy Concerning Kabbalah in Italy' (Heb.), 182).

[36] See Cohen, *The Autobiography of a Seventeenth-Century Venetian Rabbi*, 153; Idel, 'Differing Conceptions of Kabbalah', 153 n. 72. For a recent discussion of Modena's criticism of the Zohar see Dweck, *The Scandal of Kabbalah*, 61–100.

[37] *Ari nohem*, 54–6.

[38] See Hallamish, 'On the Controversy Concerning Kabbalah in Italy' (Heb.), 197; L. Modena, *Ari nohem*, 67.

[39] Hallamish, 'On the Controversy Concerning Kabbalah in Italy' (Heb.), 198; L. Modena, *Ari nohem*, 67. Modena raises the possibility that the Zohar's references to vocalization and cantillation also attest to its later composition: 'They explore the characters because, as you know, there are many opinions concerning the vowels and the tropes among recent scholars, whether the vowels and tropes preceded Ezra or not, and there are those who think they appeared a long time after him' (*Ari nohem*, 31).

[40] See Hallamish, 'On the Controversy Concerning Kabbalah in Italy' (Heb.), 195; for more details see L. Modena, *Ari nohem*, 68.

[41] *Ari nohem*, 68–9.

[42] Hallamish, 'On the Controversy Concerning Kabbalah in Italy' (Heb.), 194; L. Modena, *Ari nohem*, 60–1.

[43] *Ari nohem*, 68.

was.[44] Modena further cited expressions in the Zohar that glorified R. Shimon and which he thought could not have been written by R. Shimon or by his companions:

And it is inconceivable that, had R. Shimon written the Zohar or had it been written during his lifetime, he himself would have written or would have allowed someone else to write these things about him, such as 'the great light', 'happy is the generation he lived in', and more praises of this kind; and not only did the angels come out to greet him but even 'the faithful shepherd [i.e. Moses] stood up and prostrated himself before R. Shimon'.[45]

Relying on evidence that pointed to the Zohar's late appearance, Modena showed that kabbalah in general, and the Zohar in particular, had been unknown in antiquity.[46] He quoted at length, for instance, the statement of R. Isaac of Acre recorded in *Sefer yuḥasin*,[47] and concluded that the Zohar was 'a recent work that had not been handed down; it was composed neither by R. Shimon nor by his disciples; and it [is] nothing but an invention of one of the late authors, written no earlier than the last 350 years'.[48]

As previously mentioned, R. Elijah Del-Medigo, under the influence of the critical approach of Christian humanism, based his own refutation on historical considerations and anachronisms found in the Zohar. The method of focusing on historical and philological considerations was further developed by Modena; he, too, was probably influenced by the humanistic critical approach, especially that of Scaliger, who had challenged the authenticity of the Hermetic corpus and of the Sibylline oracles.[49]

At the same time as he rejected the kabbalistic content and antiquity of the Zohar, Modena praised its stylistic, literary, and hermeneutical aspects:

[44] See ibid. 61, 65, where Modena points out contradictions between the Zohar and the *posekim* concerning halakhic questions and rejects the position that the opinion expressed in the Zohar should take precedence.

[45] Ibid. 66–7.

[46] Hallamish, 'On the Controversy Concerning Kabbalah in Italy' (Heb.), 196; L. Modena, *Ari nohem*, 36–46.

[47] *Ari nohem*, 69–71; Hallamish, 'On the Controversy Concerning Kabbalah in Italy' (Heb.), 193.

[48] Hallamish, 'On the Controversy Concerning Kabbalah in Italy' (Heb.), 56–7, 69, 74.

[49] See Goldish, 'Preliminary Thoughts on Kabbalah Criticism'. Idel has pointed out the similarity between Modena's criticism of the Zohar and the widespread rejection of the antiquity of the Hermetic corpus in his time ('Differing Conceptions of Kabbalah', 174 n. 74).

The book itself (as you have heard me say many times) is amiable, desirable, valuable, and glorious. It is noble in all its approaches, which follow the Torah, including all its commentaries on the Torah according to its simple meaning, its homilies, and its allusions. It is its style to have everything done in a proper, complete, and beautiful order. And its language is pleasing, and it weaves a narrative that draws [the reader] into the subject matter. And never has there been anything as arousing for those who are sleeping, and as stimulating for those who are indifferent, drawing them into the service of God.[50]

Modena subsequently argues that the aforementioned aesthetic traits further confirm the Zohar's later date:

Something else indicates that it is the work of a more recent author, who suspended himself from a mighty tree and stitched together an exquisite work of colourful embroidery. He found a clever way to prevent the reader from rushing through the difficult riddles and secrets, bundles upon bundles, for he mixed within them simple meanings of verses that are easy to understand and are sweeter than honey, as the simple meanings offered by the Castilian sages are . . . which truly please the ears of the listeners. How beautiful and how pleasant they are! Therefore, I am praising and glorifying this work, the Zohar, for it is better than any work written by our people in the last 300 years.[51]

The fact that Modena denied the Zohar's antiquity and rejected its kabbalistic content but at the same time admired its aesthetic aspects foreshadowed modern approaches, which I explore in the next chapter. His opposition to all things kabbalistic was an essential feature of his general outlook in his late works, and grew out of the philosophy of Maimonides.[52]

Moshe Idel has shown that negation of the antiquity of kabbalah in general, and of the Zohar in particular, was, in part, a means of attacking Christian kabbalists, who perceived kabbalah as a tradition that had preceded the Talmud and contained Christian principles.[53] Nonetheless, one should bear in mind that Modena meant his criticism for the Jewish public, and only included Christian kabbalah[54] in order to point out the dangers arising from the proliferation of kabbalah.[55] He was careful not to attribute

[50] *Ari nohem*, 57–8.

[51] Ibid. 68–9.

[52] See Idel, 'Differing Conceptions of Kabbalah', 174.

[53] Ibid. 166, 174.

[54] See *Ari nohem*, 9, 44, 95–7.

[55] He vehemently attacked the printing of kabbalistic literature, which enabled Christians and converts to study and appropriate kabbalistic ideas; see ibid. 9, 93, 96.

Christian ideas to the Jewish kabbalists 'because I know that none of this was the intention of those who are involved in it, God forbid'. Immediately following this statement, however, he lists kabbalistic phrases that allow Christian interpretations.[56]

In the first chapter of *Ari nohem* Modena explicitly states the motives for writing his book: first, Cordovero's claim that belief in the *sefirot* was the essence of the Jewish faith; second, R. Meir Ibn Gabai's declaration that belief in kabbalah was necessary for achieving perfection of the soul; and third, R. Shem Tov ibn Shem Tov's and Ibn Gabai's criticism of Maimonides.[57] In his autobiography *Ḥayei yehudah*, Modena reiterates that he had written his book in response to the kabbalists' criticism of Maimonides: 'About six months earlier I completed a treatise against the kabbalah. I entitled it *Ari nohem* [The Roaring Lion] because of my great anger at one of those [kabbalists] who had spoken wrongly in his books against the great luminaries of Israel, especially the Eagle, Maimonides, of blessed memory.'[58] Refuting both the kabbalists' criticism of Maimonides' philosophy and the contention that theirs was an authentic Jewish tradition, he argues that kabbalah only emerged after Maimonides and under the influence of Greek philosophies:

And now come and hear once more how far-fetched is the claim that this is the tradition [*kabalah*] received from the prophets. And therefore a person with a mind capable of understanding what is in front of him will realize that these are foreign offspring, the vain ideas of Greek philosophy that entered the ears of some of our more recent sages, who renamed and arranged them according to their ideas, and referred to them as supreme holiness and the secrets of divinity . . . However, it is clear that they are contemporary, probably from Spain, where some of the sages, shortly after the period of the great teacher Maimonides, of blessed memory, developed an interest in the study of philosophy. They discovered similarities between [Jewish teachings and] the ideas of the great philosophers of antiquity,

[56] Ibid. 96. He also added that he was refraining from studying kabbalah because, in his polemics with converts, he realized the similarity between their claims and those of kabbalah: 'One of the reasons why I refrain from this study stems from what I have learned from my polemics with converts since my early years—its principles and methods are similar to theirs' (ibid. 95).

[57] Ibid. 3–6.

[58] Quoted in Cohen, *The Autobiography of a Seventeenth-Century Venetian Rabbi*, 153.

especially the wisdom of Plato, who came closer than all his peers to the opinions of our sages, and his riddles came closest to their homilies. They arranged these studies and findings according to a superficial understanding of *Sefer yetsirah*, which had not had the same intention . . . And they spun and weaved and stretched this study, and named it the wisdom of kabbalah. They suspended themselves from a mighty tree—R. Shimon, may he rest in peace—so they could claim that this was the prophets' kabbalah.[59]

Modena's criticism of the Zohar, then, seems to have been triggered by the important role that book played in endowing the kabbalah with an air of authority and antiquity. By attacking the Zohar he sought to combat the growing influence in Italy of the Safed school: 'In our time and our days, the books of the teacher Cordovero of blessed memory were published . . . and then the words of the Ari of blessed memory were discovered', he wrote.[60] Cordovero's kabbalah had, indeed, acquired enormous influence in Italy in the late sixteenth century,[61] as had Luria's.[62] As I pointed out in previous chapters, the kabbalah of both scholars was built upon the Zohar and its commentaries. Modena's arguments were thus intended to undermine the new kabbalistic systems that were gaining momentum in Italy, and to which even his close associates were drawn, namely, his son-in-law R. Jacob Halevi and his disciple R. Joseph Hamitz.[63] *Ari nohem* was further meant as an attack on Yashar of Candia and his kabbalistic work *Matsref*

[59] *Ari nohem*, 52–4.

[60] Ibid. 48.

[61] Information concerning R. Moses Cordovero's kabbalah arrived in Italy through R. Mordecai Dato and his uncle R. Moses Basola, who lived in Safed during the 1560s. The most prominent among the kabbalists in Italy in the late 16th and early 17th centuries, R. Menahem Azaryah da Fano, recounted that Cordovero himself had sent him a copy of his book *Pardes rimonim* (*Pelaḥ harimon*, 2*b*). R. Menahem Azaryah assisted Cordovero's son R. Gedalyah Cordovero in printing the works of his father, *Perush seder avodat yom hakipurim* (Venice, 1586/7), *Or ne'erav* (Venice, 1586/7), and *Tomer devorah* (Venice, 1588/9). *Pelaḥ harimon*, R. Menahem Azaryah's synopsis of *Pardes rimonim*, was printed in Venice in 1599/1600, and R. Samuel Gallico's synopsis *Asis rimonim* appeared in Mantua in 1622/3. Cordovero's kabbalah was distributed through the mediation of Elijah de Vidas's *Reshit ḥokhmah*, printed in Venice in 1578/9 and again in 1592/3.

[62] R. Israel Saruk, whom Modena had met as a young man (see L. Modena, *Ari nohem*, 81), taught the sages of Italy Lurianic kabbalah according to his own system in the last decade of the 16th century. As Joseph Avivi has shown, other Lurianic texts had reached R. Menahem Azaryah's circle even before ('The Writings of R. Isaac Luria' (Heb.), 80).

[63] Ibid. 1–2, 57. Idel, 'Differing Conceptions of Kabbalah', 154.

leḥokhmah (1628/9), which included, among other things, the epistles of R. Shlomel of Dresnitz emphasizing the strong link between the Zohar and Luria's thought.[64]

Modena was probably not the only scholar to oppose the kabbalah or the Zohar in his generation.[65] After him R. Jacob Frances continued the battle, denying both kabbalistic doctrines and the antiquity of the Zohar. To quote R. Solomon Aviad Sar-Shalom Basilea, Frances 'did not believe in the mysteries of the Torah as we have them. He used to say: "A kabbalist pursues vanity and becomes vain." He denied the Zohar and taught others that R. Shimon did not write it, and that the book was a forged work.'[66] Criticism against the Zohar was also raised in Amsterdam at that time, probably among former crypto-Jews. Our source for this is R. Jacob ben Aaron Sasportas, who recounted that people who had ridiculed kabbalah and the Zohar changed their attitude only when they started believing in Sabbatai Zevi.[67]

Evidence that the polemic of *Sefer yuḥasin* and *Ari nohem* was well known to, and utilized by, early eighteenth-century critics is found in the introduction to *Ḥoker umekubal* by R. Moses Hayim Luzzatto (Ramhal). Written in refutation of Modena's claims in *Ari nohem*,[68] Luzzatto's work was an attack on sages who did not take the wisdom of kabbalah seriously, 'so much so that they deny the principle that the Holy Zohar was written by R. Shimon, may he be remembered in the world to come, and his companions'.[69] Furthermore, in a letter to R. Isaiah Basan written in 1734,

[64] See Adelman, 'Success and Failure in the Seventeenth Century Ghetto of Venice', ii. 796–801; Ruderman, *Jewish Thought and Scientific Discovery*, 123–4.

[65] R. Menahem Azaryah da Fano recounted, for example, that R. Moses Provençal, who rejected the authority of the Zohar regarding the prohibition on donning *tefilin* during the intermediate days of festivals, 'often blustered against the Zohar in casual conversation' (*Responsa*, 67*b*, no. 108). We also know that R. David Farrar, a former crypto-Jew from Amsterdam, was opposed to kabbalah.

[66] Basilea, *Emunat ḥakhamim*, 31*a*.

[67] *Tsitsat novel tsevi*, ed. Tishby, 56–7. Goldish believes it is possible that Sasportas meant R. Benjamin Musaphia (and perhaps also Barukh Spinoza and Juan de Prado); see Goldish, 'Rabbi Jacob Sasportas, Defender of Torah Authority', 45.

[68] See Ginzburg, *R. Moses Hayim Luzzatto and His Contemporaries* (Heb.), 256–7, 268, 344, 352–3.

[69] See Tishby, *Studies in Kabbalah* (Heb.), iii. 652; Avivi, 'R. Moses Hayim Luzzatto's *Ma'amar havikuaḥ*' (Heb.), 52.

Luzzatto recounted a polemic among Christians in which one of the participants relied on Modena's book in claiming that kabbalah was vanity.[70]

All of the above demonstrates that some criticism existed against the Zohar; yet, as a rule, public opposition was rare in Jewish circles before the end of the eighteenth century. *Ari nohem* was not printed until the nineteenth century; *Beḥinat hadat*, originally published by Yashar of Candia, was only reprinted in 1833; *Sefer yuḥasin* appeared several times, but only in the censored version of the Kraków edition. This limited criticism between the sixteenth and late eighteenth centuries attests to the centrality of kabbalah in Jewish culture and to the canonical status of the Zohar during that period.

In Christian circles, on the other hand, attacks on kabbalah and the Zohar intensified at the turn of the seventeenth and eighteenth centuries. As previously mentioned, Johannes Buxtorf, Joseph Scaliger, and Ludovicus Cappellus had expressed doubts regarding the book's antiquity already in the early seventeenth century. In 1669 a detailed and well-received criticism appeared in Jean Morin's book *Exercitationes biblicae: de hebraei graecique textus sinceritae*. Quoting evidence from Zacuto's *Sefer yuḥasin* and from Gedalyah Ibn Yahya's *Shalshelet hakabalah*, Morin denied the Zohar's antiquity on the basis of the anachronisms in it, especially the references to the vowel system.[71]

Other objections were expressed in response to Christian Knorr von Rosenroth's influential book *Kabbala denudata* (published in 1679 and 1684), which contained translations of numerous passages from the Zohar and other kabbalistic texts. In contrast to Christian kabbalists, who believed in the antiquity of kabbalah and treated it as the ancient source of Greek

70 See Ginzburg, *R. Moses Hayim Luzzatto and His Contemporaries* (Heb.), 255.

71 Morin, *Exercitationes biblicae*, ii. 358–70. Secret, *Le Zohar chez les kabbalistes chrétiens*, 101–2; id., *Les Kabbalistes chrétiens de la Renaissance*, 335–6. Regarding the possibility that Morin was acquainted with Modena's complaints in *Ari nohem*, see Secret, *Le Zohar chez les kabbalistes chrétiens*, 99 n. 2. From R. Samuel Abuhav's letter to R. Moses Zacuto it appears that Modena shared his rejection of the antiquity of the Zohar with a Christian scholar: 'And I was already told here by a gentile official of this town that while he was there, the previously mentioned sage [i.e. Modena] shared his negative view about the wisdom of kabbalah with him' (Benayahu, *The Position of Rabbi Moses Zacuto and Rabbi Samuel Abuhav* (Heb.), 41). In his letter to R. Isaiah Basan in 1734/5, Luzzatto recounted the reliance of Christian sages of a later period on Modena's arguments (Ginzburg, *R. Moses Hayim Luzzatto and His Contemporaries* (Heb.), 255).

philosophical systems, its critics argued that it was a late phenomenon based on Greek philosophy or oriental religions. Matt Goldish has described this criticism as blending into the new intellectual trends of the time, such as the emergent biblical criticism, modern scientific thinking, and the Enlightenment.[72]

It was within the framework of this general criticism of kabbalah that some Christian scholars challenged the Zohar's antiquity.[73] The French Huguenot Jacques Basnage, in his book *History of the Jews*,[74] argued that the Zohar was indeed based on R. Shimon's work but that Moses de León had added many forgeries to it:

R. Moses, born in the kingdom of Lyon, was a sage, but he was poor. Although he was invited to manage a synagogue, his wages were insufficient to support his large family. To provide for his family he decided to deceive the rabbis. They had in their possession a few pamphlets of the Zohar, a work attributed to R. Shimon. When Moses de León saw that small segments of it had been distributed and highly revered, he imitated the style, replaced the missing parts [with his own additions], and sold it as if it were the complete work. His machinations succeeded. He sold many copies of the book and was able to make ends meet. However, a few stylistic differences between the ancient sage and the contemporary rabbi aroused attention and as a result he suffered humiliation and shame.[75]

72 Goldish, 'Preliminary Thoughts on Kabbalah Criticism'. Goldish connects the criticism of kabbalah in this period to the intellectual crisis in European thought that, according to Paul Hazard, occurred between 1680 and 1715. Hazard described this occurrence in his well-known book *La Crise de la conscience européenne*.

73 Goldish, in his study 'Preliminary Thoughts on Kabbalah Criticism', has named some other scholars who could be counted among the critics of kabbalah during this period: Henry Moore, whose anti-kabbalistic writings were included in *Kabbala denudata*, was close to the circle of von Rosenroth. For Moore's criticism of kabbalah see Coudert, *The Impact of the Kabbalah in the Seventeenth Century*, 233–6. Johann Georg Wachter argued in his book *Der Spinozismus im Jüdenthumb* (Amsterdam, 1699) that Spinoza's heresy stemmed from kabbalistic ideas; see Goldish, *Judaism in the Theology of Sir Isaac Newton*, 144 n. 14. Goldish also mentions Johann Buddeus, who believed in the antiquity of the Zohar but claimed there was a link between kabbalah and Gnosticism, an argument shared by Sir Isaac Newton (see *Judaism in the Theology of Sir Isaac Newton*, 144). Although Newton opposed kabbalah, he did not question the attribution of the Zohar to R. Shimon (ibid. 146).

74 The French original, *L'Histoire et la religion des Juifs*, was printed in Rotterdam in 1706, and an English translation (*History of the Jews from Jesus Christ to the Present Time*) appeared in London in 1708.

75 *L'Histoire et la religion des Juifs*, v. 1775–6 (vii. 664 in the English edn.); see also Abrams, 'Critical and Post-Critical Textual Scholarship', 61.

Christian criticism of kabbalah and the Zohar did not resonate among Jews at the time. However, enlightened Jewish circles at the turn of the eighteenth and nineteenth centuries were acquainted with the aforementioned works, especially with Basnage's book on Jewish history, and adopted some of their arguments.[76] During the second half of the eighteenth century, even before the representatives of the Jewish Enlightenment launched their offensive, questions were raised within rabbinic circles as to the Zohar's antiquity and coherence. Before addressing the antagonistic attitude of the maskilim, let me first turn to the criticism of these rabbinic scholars, with special focus on R. Jacob Emden's *Mitpaḥat sefarim*.

As I mentioned in the previous chapter, the dissemination of the Zohar beyond the rabbinic elite, and the Sabbatian involvement in its popularization, elicited counter-reactions and demands to limit the public's engagement in it. However, these calls did not include any challenges to the Zohar's kabbalistic content or antiquity. There were, nonetheless, rabbis who voiced such criticism: in Altona R. Jacob Emden, famed for his zealous struggle against Sabbatianism, printed his book *Mitpaḥat sefarim* in 1768. The work discusses the Zohar's complexity, the fact that some of its sections are older than others, and the errors in the published corpus.[77]

Emden opens his book with the testimony of R. Isaac of Acre known from *Sefer yuḥasin*.[78] Although he takes issue with R. Isaac on a number of points, he admits that his words contain some truth, and concludes that parts of the zoharic corpus were, indeed, written by Moses de León, 'who

[76] For Mendelssohn's and his circle's acquaintance with Basnage's book, and the unsuccessful initiative to translate it into Hebrew, see Feiner, *Haskalah and History* (Heb.), 39, 44; Raz-Krakotzkin, 'The National Narration of Exile' (Heb.), 22–3. For the use of Basnage's book by representatives of the Galician Enlightenment in the early 19th century, see Feiner, *Haskalah and History* (Heb.), 173, 183. For evidence that R. Nahman Krochmal had read Basnage's book see Rawidowicz, *Nahman Krochmal's Works* (Heb.), 28. On the use made by the 19th-century maskilim of Johann Christoph Wolf's work, see Kilcher, *Die Sprachtheorie der Kabbala*, 218. On the fact that Solomon Munk relied on Jean Morin for the dating and final editing of the Zohar, see Munk, *Mélanges de philosophie juive et arabe*, 275; Secret, *Le Zohar chez les kabbalistes chrétiens*, 99 n. 2.

[77] In his book *Edut beya'akov*, which was printed about thirteen years before *Mitpaḥat sefarim*, Emden had already voiced his doubts regarding the antiquity of the Zohar: 'The Zohar was not transcribed by the *tana* R. Shimon at all . . . but by the disciples of his disciples. They wrote it, collected it, and compiled it . . . nevertheless, it should be considered as if it had been written by R. Shimon himself' (*Edut beya'akov*, 21).

[78] *Mitpaḥat sefarim*, 7.

considered it his privilege to suspend himself from a mighty tree'.[79] Emden points out that contradictions exist between the zoharic tenets and the Talmud,[80] that the references to *amora'im* are anachronistic, and that amoraic statements are misattributed to *tana'im*.[81] He also presents some philological arguments not mentioned by earlier critics, according to which the zoharic texts were written in a later period than had been claimed. Emden was the first to show that the source of the word *ash noga*, meaning synagogue, which appears in *Tikunei hazohar* and *Ra'aya meheimna*, was the Iberian word *esnoga*,[82] and that the Zohar contained references to Islam.[83] He explored the influence of Sephardi sources on zoharic texts, including the writings of R. Samuel Hanagid and the *Kuzari*.[84] He also pointed out expressions characteristic of the philosophical language of the Middle Ages, as well as references to the vocalization and cantillation systems of the Torah,[85] and highlighted some mistakes concerning the topography of the Land of Israel.[86] He objected to some Zohar homilies that seemed to him exaggerated and baseless.[87] Like R. Judah of Modena, he disapproved of the glorification of R. Shimon and resented statements such as 'Who is the face of the Lord God? R. Shimon bar Yohai' (Zohar ii. 38*a*), which he considered arrogant and blasphemous.[88]

In his discussion of the Zohar, Emden mainly relied on the arguments of others before him, but he employed a more comprehensive, methodological approach. Having studied European languages, and being interested in contemporary intellectual trends, he was probably acquainted with the Protestant criticism of biblical sources,[89] which may well have influenced his own philological and historical challenge.

As we have seen, some of Emden's arguments had originally been made by R. Elijah Del-Medigo and R. Judah of Modena. However, in contrast to them, Emden did not come to the conclusion that the Zohar as a whole was a later text; rather, he distinguished between different sections

[79] Ibid. 7–8. [80] See e.g. ibid. 14–16, 24. [81] See e.g. ibid. 21, 25, 29–30, 36–7.
[82] Ibid. 8–9. [83] Ibid. 15, 22. [84] Ibid. 9–11.
[85] Ibid. 34. See Penkower, 'S. D. Luzzatto, Vowels and Accents, and the Date of the Zohar', 127 n. 168. [86] *Mitpaḥat sefarim*, 22–3. [87] See e.g. ibid. 25–7. [88] Ibid. 22.
[89] In Emden's autobiography *Megilat sefer*, he mentions his knowledge of German, Dutch, and Latin, as well as foreign literature he had read.

and placed each of them in a different period.[90] In his view the zoharic corpus comprised three main elements or books: the first and most ancient one was what modern scholarship calls the body of the Zohar. This part was written during the period of the *amora'im*, Emden claimed, and it might include traditions from R. Shimon's time,[91] as well as later texts written in the amoraic, the savoraic, or the geonic period, by a person whose name was also R. Shimon bar Yohai.[92] Forgeries from subsequent generations had been interwoven into these texts by copyists, he noted.[93]

The second book of the zoharic corpus contained *Tikunei hazohar* and *Ra'aya meheimna* (Emden was the first to discover the link between the two)[94] as well as *Ma'amerei hapikudin*. These texts, Emden argued, had been composed by a Spanish sage in the late thirteenth century,[95] which opened the possibility of R. Moses de León's authorship or that of the prophet of Avila, who is mentioned in the responsa of R. Solomon ben Adret.[96] Emden did not suggest that this section was a forgery, but rather that it had been produced with the assistance of *magidim*, celestial heralds. The errors found in the Zohar proved, he explained, that *magidim*, too, could make mistakes, and that further corruptions had found their way into the text through the additions of copyists and scribes.

The third main zoharic unit in Emden's classification was *Midrash hane'elam*. This book, he contended, was a ludicrous imitation of the previous two sections, and he identified it as the 'forged Zohar' mentioned by R. Isaac of Acre.[97]

In contrast to Del-Medigo and Modena, who dismissed the kabbalistic content of the Zohar from a rationalist and anti-kabbalistic point of view, Emden (who, incidentally, also questioned the attribution of the *Guide of the Perplexed* to Maimonides) stated: 'I consider anyone who denies the true wisdom of the kabbalah a heretic and a complete Epicurean.' The original parts of the Zohar, he asserted, contained ancient, sacred, and authoritative traditions: 'This is what I claim with regard to the author of the original Zohar . . . for his words are surely the Holy of Holies. Words that are the secrets of the world are under his tongue.'[98] He did not fully dismiss the

[90] Emden, *Mitpaḥat sefarim*, 39, 104–5. [91] Ibid. 39. [92] Ibid.
[93] Ibid. 39, 104. [94] Ibid. 12, 37, 39. [95] Ibid. 39.
[96] Ibid. 12, 37–8, 94. [97] Ibid. 6, 39–40. [98] Ibid. 37.

doctrines of *Ra'aya meheimna* and *Tikunei hazohar* either, since, as we have seen, he considered them to have been written with the assistance of *magidim*.[99] He continued to cite zoharic texts in the second part of his *Mitpaḥat sefarim*, and accepted the Zohar's authority in halakhic questions.[100]

However, Emden emphasized that mistakes had been made even in the ancient part of the Zohar, as in all of its other sections. He thus called for 'a careful examination and serious study' to establish whether there was 'straw and slop mixed up in it, as you know that foreign hands had tampered with it, at least in some of its parts'.[101] The printed versions of his own time presented even more problems due to the text's greater complexity and the many additional errors that had been introduced into it; his conclusion was therefore that one should not rely on the printed zoharic corpus: 'From now on, an Israelite who is loyal to his God should know that he is not obligated to believe anything that is found in the printed version of the Zohar.'[102] He nevertheless believed that a thorough editing of the book could remove the corrupted additions and establish a sacred, reliable text.

In short, Emden did not call for outright rejection of the Zohar, but rather for its re-editing to purge it of later additions and corruptions. To that end—the production of an authoritative version—he advised readers to use his own annotations and his *Mitpaḥat sefarim*: 'Therefore, I did not labour in vain to purge its scraps, dregs, and dross, and to establish it as pure flour; and I annotated it in its entirety in my book until it shone like the light of the dawn, like the very sky, for purity.'[103] He hoped to make his corrections widely available: 'If God will be with me and strengthen my hands, I will publish my annotations for the world, and my corrections to the Zohar with some commentary.'[104]

Emden explicitly stated that his motive for discussing the unity and antiquity of the zoharic corpus was his struggle against the Sabbatians, who 'based all their evils on the Zohar, *Ra'aya meheimna*, and *Tikunei hazohar*'.[105] Therefore he decided, despite his concerns about blemishing the holiness of the Zohar, to express his opinions and doubts in writing:

In reality I did it despite my inclination, because I had to, and it is for this reason that I did not question it publicly until now; it was locked in my heart for forty

[99] Ibid. 94. [100] Ibid. 56. [101] Ibid. 37, 39. [102] Ibid. 105.
[103] Ibid. 40. [104] Ibid. 104. [105] Ibid. 1.

years. I controlled my spirit and I did not want to release it until now, when I am forced by the duty to guard the truth. My fear is that this last generation will whitewash the wrongdoers by means of the Zohar, a process they have already begun.[106]

Emden was particularly upset by the fact that the Sabbatians based their beliefs on interpretations of the Zohar. Their commentary, he claimed, perplexed even expert kabbalists of his time.[107] Like other sages, he realized that the Sabbatians had successfully used the cultural power of the Zohar to strengthen their position by producing their own commentary, which, as I have shown, subverted the monopoly of the Lurianic interpretation. Other contemporaries of Emden tackled this problem in a variety of ways: they expressed support for the Lurianic interpretation, emphasized the esoteric character of the Zohar's text, and tried to limit the public's engagement with it. Emden, upon witnessing the failure of Lurianic kabbalists to prevent the spread of the Sabbatian commentary, chose to fight it by criticizing the Zohar's textual unity and antiquity. Looking at it from this perspective, his project seems to have been an attempt to regain control of the Zohar's cultural supremacy by re-editing its text and defining its final version and scope, rather than by writing a new commentary on it.

The purpose of Emden's criticism was not only to subvert Sabbatianism but also to put an end to the popularization of the Zohar among wide sections of the Jewish public. It was in this context that he mentioned, with great disapproval, the involvement of the first hasidim of Podolia in Zohar study:

Now any mindless fool who does not have any knowledge of what is required and what is prohibited, who is unable to discern, who has no understanding or knowledge of even the Scriptures, Talmud, or Mishnah, who is unskilled in the holy tongue and has no insight, is engaging in study of the Zohar without being able to distinguish between good and evil. For sure, he is even unable to read the straightforward words of the Zohar, other books of kabbalah, and books that deal with revealed issues, because he does not know Hebrew. And although he may mumble in Aramaic, he does not know what he mumbles.[108] I am staggered by what I hear,

[106] Emden, *Mitpaḥat sefarim*, 1.

[107] Ibid.

[108] Based on *Sotah* 22*a*. Emden makes an ironic reference to the concept of the importance of the ritualistic reading of the Zohar 'even though one does not understand what one says'.

that recently a new cult of such hasidim has been established in Volhynia Podolia, and that some of them have come to this country and all they do is engage in the Zohar and other books of kabbalah.[109]

The popularization of the Zohar, Emden contended, resulted in the neglect of halakhah and of careful performance of the commandments, on the one hand, and in the strengthening of Sabbatianism on the other:

I have already uttered judgments against those who study the Zohar exclusively and abandon the study of *mitsvot* and the way they should be performed . . . and although it is written in *Sefer hatikunim* that by this book [i.e. the Zohar] they will be redeemed from exile and on its account you shall proclaim liberty, statements like these have moved the hearts of the children of Israel away from service and [have caused them] to abandon the Talmud and the books of the *posekim*, the laws and the rulings, and they do not care to know what the proper conduct is. All they are interested in is the Zohar and nothing else. As a matter of fact, they are hindering the coming of the end of days. Several misfortunes have occurred due to our many sins. It [i.e. exclusive engagement in the Zohar] has brought about licentiousness, heaven forbid, and a promiscuous way of life. By doing so, the new, cursed sect of Sabbatai Zevi, may the name of the wicked rot, is gaining power.[110]

What triggered Emden's attack was not the Sabbatian turn to the Zohar as such, but rather its broad dissemination and the public's engagement in it. He particularly disapproved of studying the Zohar from books alone, without a teacher or previous mastery of halakhic literature.[111] He feared that immersion in the Zohar and in kabbalah would lessen the importance of halakhic studies and undermine the status of the rabbinic elite, whose power depended on the overriding authority of the law. From this point of view, Emden's *Mitpaḥat sefarim* aligned with the trend, reflected in other eighteenth-century works, to protect rabbinic authority and 'faith in the sages' (*emunat ḥakhamim*).[112]

109 *Mitpaḥat sefarim*, 78. For a summary of the opinions of scholars as to whether his words were aimed at the circle of the Ba'al Shem Tov or at other hasidic groups, see Friedlander, *Hebrew Satire and Polemics in Europe* (Heb.), 109–10.

110 Emden, *Mitpaḥat sefarim*, 104.

111 Ibid. 77, 105.

112 See Rosenberg, 'Emunat Hakhamim', 285–341; Carlebach, *The Pursuit of Heresy*, 260–1. On Emden's struggle for the independence of spiritual leadership, and on his criticism of the dependence of contemporary rabbis on community leaders, see Dothan, 'R. Jacob Emden and his Generation' (Heb.), 115.

Indeed, the second part of *Mitpaḥat sefarim* is dedicated to the discussion of one such work, *Emunat ḥakhamim* by R. Solomon Aviad Sar-Shalom Basilea, who had, as Emden put it, preceded him 'in the struggle to protect the standing of our true kabbalah and the Zohar, and we both had the same goal'.[113] However, while Basilea did not object to the proliferation of the Zohar or deny its antiquity, Emden, who lived a generation later, saw the danger the rabbinic elite might face as a result of the popularization of kabbalah. He therefore concluded his book by warning readers not to abandon the study of traditional rabbinic literature for the pursuit of metaphysical knowledge:

From now on, an Israelite who is loyal to his God should know that he is not obligated to believe anything that is found in the printed version of the Zohar or is included in the writings and copies made in the name of the Ari . . . in the end, even if my heart turns right to follow the words of kabbalists, or if it turns left towards external books, scholars, and their riddles, I must not seek what is above, and that which is concealed from me I must not pursue. Do not rely on your intellect and do not think yourself to be wise like Bedersi at the end of the book *Beḥinat olam*.[114] . . . Rather, believe in what your ancestors believed in ('ask your father and he will tell you', etc.; 'follow the first generation', etc.) and [follow] the teachers and the authors of the Mishnah . . . and do not abandon the words of the Talmud, which were established by *tana'im* and *amora'im*. Do not stray from your path and stray neither right nor left from anything they teach you.[115]

Emden's aim in criticizing the Zohar, then, was to limit its influence lest it subvert the authority of halakhic literature and undermine the status of the rabbinic elite. In this he was close to other sages of the eighteenth century.[116] But whereas his colleagues restricted engagement in the Zohar by emphasizing its esoteric character and by tightening the requirements for kabbalistic study, Emden instead questioned the unity of the zoharic corpus, criticized its printed versions, and called for a new edition of the Zohar based on his annotations.

Emden's arguments elicited little response in his own time. Hayim Joseph David Azulai (Hida) was acquainted with *Mitpaḥat sefarim* but dismissed it, stating that Emden had 'feigned' criticism of the Zohar in order

113 Emden, *Mitpaḥat sefarim*, 49.

114 See *Beḥinat olam*, ch. 17, p. 85.

115 *Mitpaḥat sefarim*, 105–6.

116 See Katz, *Halakhah in Straits* (Heb.), 94.

to fight Sabbatianism.[117] R. Isaac Satanow, one of the first maskilim in Berlin, wrote a short refutation of a few of Emden's arguments under the title *She'elot uteshuvot mitpaḥat sefarim*, but whether he indeed meant to reject his claims is unclear. In the early nineteenth century the Hungarian R. Moses Kunitz published a comprehensive refutation of *Mitpaḥat sefarim* in his *Sefer ben yoḥai*.[118] Later in the century several maskilim who denied the antiquity of the Zohar engaged in disputes with Kunitz.

In addition to the maskilim in Germany and Galicia, who enthusiastically adopted Emden's arguments in their own attack on the Zohar, several Orthodox rabbis also accepted his claims. R. Moses Sofer (Hatam Sofer), for example, implied that he agreed with Emden's position regarding the writing of the Zohar: 'In the book *Mitpaḥat sefarim*, written by our teacher R. Jacob ben Tsevi, something important was said by the prophet of blessed memory regarding this matter, and those who see it will be amazed, and a word to the wise is sufficient.'[119]

Another scholar to base himself on Emden's criticism was Eleazar Fleckeles, a disciple of Rabbi Ezekiel Landau, who inherited Landau's post as chief rabbi of Prague after the latter's death. Fleckeles, like Emden, pointed out the link between Sabbatianism and study of the Zohar, opposed the book's circulation and widespread study,[120] and welcomed the decrees of the Habsburg emperor Joseph II and his successor Leopold II prohibiting the import of books of kabbalah.[121] In response to the activity of the Frankists in Prague, Fleckeles openly denied the sanctity of the Zohar. In a letter composed in 1806 and printed in *Sefer teshuvah me'ahavah* (Prague, 1808/9), he dealt with the question of whether or not it was permissible to take an oath on the Zohar. Since, in his opinion, the book was based on human reason, he abrogated its sacred status:

There is no need to respond to the person who wished to concoct something new and to make an Israelite swear on the Zohar. Since, as we have explained, by

[117] H. Azulai, *Shem hagedolim*, 'Zohar' entry, 15*b*.

[118] See *Sefer ben yoḥai*, 62*b*–149*a*.

[119] *Ḥatam sofer*, 20*a*.

[120] In his book of homilies (Prague, 1699/1700), Fleckeles mentions that study of the Zohar (especially by women) was the custom of the Frankists of his time (*Kuntres ahavat david*, 6*b*, 18*a*, 25*b*, 27*a*).

[121] Ibid., introduction; see also Werses, *Haskalah and Sabbatianism* (Heb.), 66.

changing the custom one must be sensitive to the corrosive effect on the oath itself and that it will make a mockery of that person [the oath-taker] in the eyes of the witnesses. They [will ask]: 'Who is this mindless Israelite simpleton, whose oath is false according to the Laws of Moses, servant of God? He relies on the wisdom of the Zohar, which is based on human reason.'[122]

He then goes on to challenge the Zohar's authenticity in the following powerful statement:

I hereby swear by the Lord's Torah that forgeries and several corruptions that were inserted into the Zohar have been found in it. One page of the Babylonian Talmud containing disputes between Abaye and Rava is more sacred than the whole book of the Zohar . . . the Zohar was not mentioned by anyone throughout the previous generations, not while awake and not in a dream . . . none of them knew anything or saw any evidence of it until about 300 years ago. [Some people] spoke up and declared that they had discovered it . . . and I do not mean, God forbid, to find faults and imperfections with the honourable *tana*, the divine R. Shimon bar Yohai, since he was one of the supernal, righteous men; however, what I do say is that R. Shimon's seal and signature is not upon it. Anyone who has any brain will agree because several *tana'im* and *amora'im* who are mentioned [in the book] lived many years after R. Shimon. I have discussed it at length elsewhere, relying on authors and books, as it had been explained in *Sefer mitpaḥat* by the gaon, our teacher Yabets [Emden], of blessed memory, may he abide in paradise, who decreed that hands had tampered with it and suspected [it had been] the sage Rabbi Moses de León.[123]

In pointing out the anachronisms in the Zohar and the fact that it was never mentioned in ancient sources, Fleckeles was repeating Emden's arguments. But whereas Emden had found positive aspects in the book and believed that its ancient parts were based on R. Shimon's doctrines, Fleckeles discredited it as a forgery by arguing that the entire work was of more recent origin.

Fleckeles' fierce denunciation of the Zohar was unusual in traditional circles, which typically chose to ignore Emden's controversial views. Fleckeles' above letter also seems to have gone largely unnoticed, and it was strategically omitted from the second, 1912 edition of *Sefer teshuvah me'ahavah*. It is nevertheless possible that Emden's and Fleckeles' criticism

[122] *Teshuvah me'ahavah*, i. 13*c*. [123] Ibid. 13*c*–*d*.

contributed to the reluctance of some traditional circles in nineteenth-century eastern and central Europe to engage in Zohar study.

As mentioned above, the early maskilim were quick to adopt Emden's arguments against the antiquity and authority of the Zohar: Moses Mendelssohn was acquainted with *Mitpaḥat sefarim* and agreed with Emden's points. In the introduction to his Torah commentary *Or linetivah* (Berlin, 1783), Mendelssohn cautions against reliance on *Sefer habahir* and the Zohar regarding the antiquity of the biblical vocalization and cantillation systems:

> [These] books do not provide compelling proof because they were never approved by the whole diaspora as were the Mishnah and the Talmud, and it is possible that, through time, the lengthy exile, and the wandering, things were absorbed in them that had not come from the original authors and are only ascribed to them, as the Gaon, our teacher Yabets [Emden], of blessed memory, may he abide in paradise, demonstrated in the book *Mitpaḥat sefarim* and supported it with many clear proofs that cannot be refuted.[124]

His reservations notwithstanding, Mendelssohn did quote the Zohar and other kabbalistic works from time to time,[125] and he never totally invalidated claims of the Zohar's antiquity. The reason he warned against indiscriminate reliance on it was the additions that had been inserted into it over time. A similar disinclination to acknowledge the authority of the Zohar, although less explicit, appears in the writings of the moderate maskil Naphtali Hertz Wessely. In a letter printed by Fleckeles, Wessely responds to the accusation that he did not believe in the Zohar or Lurianic kabbalah, and that in this he followed his teacher R. Jonathan Eybeschutz, according to whom one was not required to accept kabbalah.[126] In his defence Wessely stated that he highly respected kabbalah and that he did rely on the Zohar and other kabbalistic works in his writings.[127]

Like Emden, then, Mendelssohn and Wessely did not reject the kabbalistic content of the Zohar, but were reluctant to acknowledge its overriding authority. However, in contrast to Emden, who engaged in kabbalah and accepted its principles, the *Weltanschauung* of the early maskilim was not in any way shaped by kabbalistic ideas. This difference was pointed out and

124 *Or linetivah*, 13. 125 See Horwitz, *Multi-Faceted Judaism* (Heb.), 14, 40.

126 Fleckeles, *Kuntres ahavat david* (unnumbered page).

127 Wessely, *Divrei shalom ve'emet*, 53*a*.

emphasized by Jacob Katz:

Indeed, the attitude of Mendelssohn to kabbalah is different to that of Rabbi Jacob Emden. The latter, although seeking to purge kabbalistic tradition of its errors and to put a stop to its defilement, did not invalidate its authority or the meaning of its concepts. He continued to perceive it . . . as an ancient tradition that holds the authentic key to the secrets of the Divinity and the Torah. Mendelssohn regarded kabbalah as nothing but a blurred branch of religious philosophy that, after removing its mystical cloak, permits us to elicit certain seeds of thought from it.[128]

Katz's source for Mendelssohn's position was Friedrich Nicholai's report of a lecture on kabbalah that the latter had presented to the non-Jewish intelligentsia.[129] Nicholai's testimony suggests that Mendelssohn saw kabbalah as consisting of a grain of philosophical truth covered with a mantle of metaphors, the outcome of an exaggerated, oriental imagination and an insufficient philosophical vocabulary in Hebrew.[130] As Moshe Idel has noted, the reference to kabbalists as 'orientalischen Philosophen' echoed the label 'philosophia orientalis antique' in the Latin title of R. Isaac Satanow's book *Imrei binah*.[131]

Other scholars within Mendelssohn's circle took a similar position towards kabbalah and the Zohar. Idel has pointed out the similarity between Mendelssohn's perception of kabbalah and that of Salomon Maimon. Both regarded kabbalah as a source of real and valid philosophical, psychological, and scientific knowledge conveyed through parables and allegories whose original meaning had been forgotten.[132] Maimon, like Mendelssohn, rejected the antiquity of the Zohar and further proposed the rather unusual theory that its author was a French kabbalist by the name of R. Moses de Lyon.[133]

An implied denial of the antiquity of the Zohar is detectable in the writings of R. Isaac Satanow.[134] His aforementioned pamphlet *She'elot uteshuvot*

[128] *Halakhah in Straits* (Heb.), 95.

[129] Ibid. 99 n. 80; Idel, *Hasidism*, 81.

[130] Quoted in Horwitz, *Multi-Faceted Judaism* (Heb.), 19. See also Idel, *Hasidism*, 81.

[131] *Hasidism*, 81 n. 52.

[132] Ibid. 75–6.

[133] See Maimon, *Salomon Maimons Lebensgeschichte*, 107.

[134] Satanow arrived in Berlin from Podolia at the age of 40. He was the head of the publishing press of the maskilim until 1788, when he was replaced by Isaac Eichel, but he continued to work there as a printer. About his life see Feiner, *The Jewish Enlightenment* (Heb.), 276; Berson, 'Isaac Satanow', 3–20.

mitpaḥat sefarim, written in response to Emden's treatise, was printed as an appendix to his pseudepigraphic work *Ḥibura tinyana* in 1783. Allegedly the purpose of this pamphlet was to refute Emden's arguments; however, in the fabricated endorsement of the book Satanow accepted, in the name of the fictitious endorser 'R. Joseph, head of the Holy Congregation of Frankfurt an der Oder', Emden's assertion that the Zohar contains pseudepigraphic segments, by which he justified his own pseudepigraphic writing:

However, it is possible that the publisher himself [i.e. Satanow] wrote this book, because I know the person and his thoughts. He belongs to those who steal words; however, he is different from them. While they steal words of others and attribute them to themselves, he is stealing from himself and attributing it to others. And it has already been permitted [by our sages] of blessed memory, who said, 'if you wish to be strangled, suspend yourself from a mighty tree' . . . and even in the old book of the Zohar things were said in the name of people who had not said them, as the Gaon Yabets [Emden], of blessed memory, [wrote] in his book *Mitpaḥat sefarim*.[135]

Later, in his commentary on *Kuzari* (Berlin, 1795), Satanow explicitly agreed with Emden's position regarding the genesis of the Zohar and claimed that he had additional information to prove it.[136] But notwithstanding his awareness of the pseudepigraphic character of the book, he proceeded to proclaim his respect for it:

Ultimately every sage will realize that the words of the Zohar are honest and truthful in and of themselves, stimulating and arousing fear and love in the hearts of those who study it. There is no room for this kind of consternation, because any intelligent person who is trying to promote himself will use various devices to persuade his listeners in concert with the power of his language.[137]

Evidently, Satanow did not find fault with the pseudepigraphic style of the Zohar (or with his own), and considered it a legitimate literary device. This position is reminiscent of that of R. Judah Aryeh of Modena, who also praised the literary qualities of the Zohar while denying its antiquity. However, Satanow's approach to it, and to kabbalah in general, is ambiguous.[138] He was clearly well acquainted with kabbalistic literature and was also

[135] Satanow, *Ḥibura tinyana*, 1.
[136] Satanow, *Sefer hakuzari*, 1*a*, 25*b*, 88.
[137] Ibid. 26*a*.
[138] Berson, 'Isaac Satanow', 151.

involved in the printing of Lurianic works.[139] In his writings he expressed appreciation for the Zohar and kabbalah.[140] The purpose of *Imrei binah* (another pseudepigraphic work of his, printed in Berlin in 1784) was to prove the correlation between philosophy and kabbalah. At the same time, his labelling of the latter as 'philosophia orientalis antique' in that book illustrates the kinship between his and Mendelssohn's approach, as Moshe Idel has shown. He viewed kabbalah as allegorical literature alluding to rational content,[141] and argued that its study was contingent upon scientific knowledge—a position that was close to Solomon Maimon's.[142]

Satanow, in brief, did not reject kabbalah but called for its rational, allegorical interpretation. While denying the antiquity of the Zohar, he justified its pseudepigraphic style and acknowledged its value. However, the thin pseudepigraphic veil of *Ḥibura tinyana*, the transparent allusions to the real identity of its author, and the justification of pseudepigraphy via a fictitious approbation, as well as Satanow's ambiguous attitude to Emden's criticism—all of these carry a touch of irony and point to the complexity of his approach. *Ḥibura tinyana* may thus be considered a precursor to the satirical pseudo-zoharic writings of the maskilim that will be discussed below.

Further reservations concerning the study of kabbalah, especially its teaching to adolescents, were expressed by the Italian maskil R. Elijah Morpurgo in a letter to the heads of Hevrat Hinukh Ne'arim (Society for the Education of Adolescents) in Berlin, which was published in *Hame'asef* in 1786.[143] Basing himself on Rabbi Jacob Frances's poem denouncing the proliferation of kabbalah and the Sabbatians' role in it, Morpurgo referred to study of the Zohar as a 'sore evil'. Yet he refrained from criticizing the content of kabbalah, and presented his suggestions in the framework of an attempt to reform adolescent education in the spirit of the Enlightenment.

Although the early maskilim levelled some criticism against the kabbalah and the Zohar, it was not their major concern and they refrained

139 Friedberg, *History of Hebrew Typography* (Heb.), 74 n. 1.

140 Satanow, *Imrei binah*, 4, 12, 14, 17, and 20.

141 Satanow, *Zemirot asaf*, v. 5, 5*b*–6*a*.

142 Ibid. 6*a*. For Maimon's view that a comprehensive knowledge of science, psychology, and philosophy is a prerequisite for a proper study of kabbalah, see Idel, *Hasidism*, 38–41.

143 Morpurgo, 'Mikhtav me'eliyahu', repr. in Assaf, *Sources for the History of Jewish Education* (Heb.), ii. 222–33.

from directly challenging the content of the Zohar. Even those who accepted Emden's arguments and opposed the dissemination of the book were willing to identify some ancient elements of value in it. Opposition to the kabbalah in general, and to the Zohar in particular, became prevalent among Jewish scholars in the 1790s and continued throughout the nineteenth century. During this period maskilim reverted to the philological and historical arguments that had been raised in previous generations against the literary unity and antiquity of the Zohar, while at the same time introducing some new critical devices—satire and parody.

As I pointed out above, an ironic attitude towards the Zohar was perceptible even earlier, in Satanow's *Ḥibura tinyana*; but the first openly satirical work was Saul Levine-Berlin's epistle *Ketav yosher*, which was printed anonymously in Berlin in 1794. A fierce attack on the contemporary traditional rabbinic establishment, *Ketav yosher* mocks Wessely's moderate position in *Divrei shalom ve'emet*, and reaches its climax when the fictive 'author' realizes that Wessely's work is a disguised kabbalistic piece. By means of the kabbalistic 'interpretation' that Levine-Berlin offers for Wessely's text, he ridicules the kabbalists' hermeneutical system and its Lurianic concepts. Although he writes ironically about the Zohar,[144] its rejection is not his focal point—ridiculing kabbalah is. *Ketav yosher* can be seen as the cornerstone of the Enlightenment's radical criticism of the rabbinic establishment of the time.

Siḥah be'erets haḥayim, a play by Aaron Wolfson of Halle, was also a satire on kabbalah, serialized without attribution in *Hame'asef* between 1794 and 1796. Although the play criticizes traditional Judaism in general, its focus is on the Zohar. Written in the style of conversations among the dead that was prevalent in European literature in the seventeenth and eighteenth centuries, *Siḥah be'erets haḥayim* is a polemic between the souls of Maimonides, Peloni (an anonymous character), and Moses Mendelssohn. Peloni, a ludicrous east European rabbi, relies on the sages of kabbalah and on the Zohar in his arguments. Maimonides, who is unfamiliar with the kabbalistic sources, 'says to himself: "a sacred and pure Zohar? What kind of book is it? Who produced it? I have heard nothing about it! And who are these sages of kabbalah? Who are these people who give themselves high

[144] See Friedlander, *Studies in Hebrew Satire in Germany* (Heb.), 105.

and pompous titles?'"[145] In a footnote to these words, Wolfson refers to R. David Gans's *Tsemaḥ david* and asserts that the Zohar was completely unknown in Maimonides' time.[146] In response to attacks on the published instalments of *Siḥah be'erets haḥayim*, he expands his arguments against the antiquity of the Zohar, basing himself on several sources including Mendelssohn's introduction to *Or linetivah* and his letters to R. Jacob Emden; *Novelot ḥokhmah* by Yashar of Candia, and Emden's *Mitpaḥat sefarim*.[147]

Contrary to earlier critics, Wolfson focused his attack not on the Zohar's questionable antiquity but rather on its content and its use of anthropomorphic imagery. His polemic was conveyed in the satirical exchange between Peloni and Maimonides, in which Peloni quotes a zoharic statement (iii. 241*b*) that describes God as eating and drinking in order to prove God's corporeality:

PELONI: Did you hear these words? Now you can see that describing His actions is not according to the way of imagination, since Elijah and R. Shimon attested to it explicitly.

MAIMONIDES (angrily): You must be possessed by an evil spirit to say these terrible things about God. Go away lest . . .

PELONI: Pray my lord, do not put the blame of sin upon me, because I have not said anything out of my own will, since these words have been written in the holy book by kabbalist sages.

MAIMONIDES: Who are they and what are the names of those kabbalist sages? I do not know them, neither did my ancestors know anything about them. And also the name of the book you mentioned is unknown and it never existed. Does anyone know who wrote it? This nonsense must have been written by you and people like you!

PELONI: Pray, my lord, by God, the *tana* R. Shimon ben Yohai wrote this book, and started it with the word *berish* [beginning], denoting the acronym for Rabbi Shimon ben Yohai.

MAIMONIDES: Shame on you. This sage would never have uttered senseless words such as these. He would never refer to himself arrogantly as master of

145 *Siḥah be'erets haḥayim*, 146.

146 Ibid. In *Tsemaḥ david* (ed. Breuer), 93, Gans quotes *Sefer yuḥasin*, according to which the Zohar was discovered after Nahmanides' time.

147 *Siḥah be'erets haḥayim*, 342.

the truth . . . It must be someone from your native land and from your father's house who wrote this book, since arrogance is their style.[148]

In a note containing his translation of the zoharic passage quoted by Peloni, Wolfson adds that there are many others like it, and expresses concern over the negative impression such statements might make on non-Jews: 'Who among us would not be embarrassed and whose face would not turn white to read this segment and others like it (since there are numerous stories like it in the Zohar), and even more so when they are exposed to the sages of the world?'[149] In his response to questions allegedly raised by one R. Dov Berl of Vienna (but probably written by Wolfson himself[150]) concerning *Siḥah be'erets haḥayim* he reiterates his discomfort with the anthropomorphism that he sees expressed in the Zohar.[151]

Wolfson ridicules not only the Zohar's claim of antiquity and its anthropomorphisms, but also the sanctity attributed to it. Mocking Peloni's behaviour before his recitation of the zoharic quotation, he writes:

PELONI: (whispers and wipes his hands with a cloth)

MAIMONIDES: What is this?

PELONI: I wiped my hands to purify them, because the study of this sacred book requires diligent adherence to the laws of purity, and I prayed a silent prayer; a prayer established to precede the study of this pure book, to weaken the power of the Sitra Ahra and to prevent it from asserting control over me.[152]

In the eyes of radical critics such as Levine-Berlin and Wolfson, faith in kabbalah in general, and veneration of the Zohar in particular, were part of the negative image of traditional Judaism, especially as practised in eastern Europe. Peloni probably represents R. Raphael Ziskind Kohen, one of Mendelssohn's opponents.[153] He is depicted in the play as an east European rabbi whose theological beliefs are false, whose language is stammering, and whose behaviour is inappropriate. Peloni is the antithesis of the enlightened Jew personified by Maimonides and Mendelssohn. The juxtaposition of the backward rabbi and the two prominent philosophers reflects the dichotomy between rational, enlightened contemporary Jews

148 Ibid. 148–50.
149 Ibid. 149.
150 See Feiner, *The Jewish Enlightenment* (Heb.), 392.
151 *Siḥah be'erets haḥayim*, 339–44.
152 Ibid. 148.
153 Ibid. 56.

and a traditional east European Jewry entrapped in kabbalah and superstition.

Rejection of all things kabbalistic played an important role in Levine-Berlin's and Wolfson's depiction of enlightened Judaism. In contrast to the first generation of maskilim, who had voiced their criticism in a circumspect manner and were willing to acknowledge an element of philosophy in kabbalistic writings, their rejection is unequivocal. Although Wolfson seemingly restrained his criticism of the Zohar in his response to the alleged attack of R. Dov Berl of Vienna,[154] he used that opportunity to put forward further arguments against the book's antiquity and content.[155] The radical tone of *Siḥah be'erets haḥayim* provoked several angry responses and caused further deterioration in the relations between the maskilim and their opponents. Objections even emerged from moderate maskilim affiliated to *Hame'asef*.[156]

More reserved was the criticism levelled by Prague's enlightened Jewry in the early nineteenth century. Opposition to the dissemination of the Zohar and to Frankist involvement in it appeared in *Siḥah bein shenat* [5]560 *uvein shenat* [5]561, written by R. Barukh ben Jonah Jeiteles and published anonymously.[157] Alluding to R. Jacob Emden's denial of the Zohar's antiquity and unity, Jeiteles added his own refutation of some zoharic ideas that he claimed contradicted 'reason and faith'.[158] Peter Beer, one of Prague's maskilim, dedicated a lengthy discussion to kabbalah in the second volume of his book *Lehren und Meinungen aller bestandenen und noch bestehenden religiosen Sekten der Juden und der Geheimlehre oder Kabbala*.[159] Although he had no real sympathy for kabbalah, he refrained from condemning its adherents. Notwithstanding his belief that kabbalah stemmed from ancient sources such as Philo of Alexandria and the Neoplatonic philosophy of ancient Egypt, he accepted Emden's argument in *Mitpaḥat sefarim* that the Zohar was written in a much later period, and rejected Kunitz's claims of its antiquity.[160]

154 *Siḥah be'erets haḥayim*, 347.

155 Ibid.

156 See Friedlander, *Studies in Hebrew Satire* (Heb.), 124; Tsamriyon, *Hame'asef: The First Modern Hebrew Periodical* (Heb.), 212; Pelli, *Kinds of Genre in Haskalah Literature* (Heb.), 52–3.

157 Kestenberg-Gladstein, 'Who Was the Author of the *Siḥah*?' (Heb.).

158 Jeiteles, *Siḥah*, 11–12 n. 6.

159 See Hecht, 'An Intellectual Biography of the Maskil Peter Beer' (Heb.), 331.

160 Beer, *Lehren und Meinungen*, ii. 29–34.

Intensive and more aggressive attacks on kabbalah and the Zohar were launched by several maskilim in eastern Europe (especially Galicia) in the same period. The context for their criticism was their battle against hasidism, and satire was their primary weapon. In the 1790s the Polish scholar R. Menahem Mendel Lefin, 'the father of the Galician Enlightenment', had already expressed deep disdain for kabbalah and the Zohar in his initiative for the reformation of Polish Jewry. He submitted his programme to a committee of the Sejm charged with Jewish affairs, and it was published anonymously in French in 1792. Like Wolfson, but much more explicitly, Lefin identified two trends in Judaism—one enlightened and rational, represented by the Talmud and Maimonides; the other obscure and retrograde, the epitome of which was the Zohar. He blamed that book for the backward condition of Polish Jewry (particularly in Ukraine and Podolia) and for their lack of proper education. He also believed that the Zohar had contributed to the rise of hasidism, which he vigorously fought.[161] Adopting the negative Christian portrayal of the Jewish condition, he accepted the accusations levelled against rabbinic Judaism. Since the Zohar was responsible for destructive trends among the Jews as well as for their inferior circumstances, he recommended censuring it along with its commentaries, and promoted the circulation of Emden's *Mitpaḥat sefarim*. He also suggested bestowing a prize upon anyone who wrote a piece exposing irrationality not only in the Zohar but also in other mystical works, such as the Zend Avesta and the writings of Emmanuel Swedenborg.[162] It should be emphasized, though, that Lefin's work (written in French) was not aimed at a Jewish readership. In *Likutei kelalim* (which remained unpublished in manuscript form) he formulated in Hebrew his suggestions for ameliorating the condition of the Jews. There he took a milder position against engagement in kabbalah.[163]

Criticism of the Zohar reappears in Lefin's introduction to *Elon moreh*, his partial translation of the *Guide of the Perplexed* (printed posthumously).

[161] See Gelber, 'Mendel Lefin Satanover' (Heb.), 271–5; Sinkoff, 'Strategy and Ruse in the Haskalah of Mendel Lefin', 97–8; Wodziński, *Haskalah and Hasidism in the Kingdom of Poland*, 22–7.

[162] See Sinkoff, 'Tradition and Transition', 77 n. 54.

[163] See Gelber, 'Mendel Lefin Satanover' (Heb.), 287–301; Sinkoff, 'Tradition and Transition', 23–36, 84.

In it he attacks the sacred status of the Zohar, its claim to antiquity, and the festivities related to R. Shimon on Lag Ba'omer.[164] His discussion focuses primarily on the sexual symbolism in the book, as well as in the writings of Luria, which, he asserts, formed the basis of the heretical acts of the Sabbatians and Frankists. Juxtaposing Maimonides' philosophy with kabbalah, he writes:

> And behold, abomination never crossed the lips of the teacher [Maimonides], of blessed memory, let alone foul language or detestation. However, in the days of Sabbatai Zevi and [Jacob] Frank, may their memory be erased, people's souls were corrupted. They [the false messiahs] used the zoharic text and the Ari's writings to lead the people to perform acts of sexual perversion and other abominations against God.[165]

Here, for the first time, the claim appears that the Zohar led to sexual perversion. As I demonstrate below, this accusation was to play an important role in the Zohar criticism of the nineteenth century.

Like the radical German maskilim, Lefin and other east European authors made parody and satire their weapons of choice in attacking the Zohar, kabbalah, and hasidism. To that end Lefin wrote a satirical work entitled *Maḥkimat peti* (which was lost).[166] At the turn of the eighteenth and nineteenth centuries, Tobias Feder, Lefin's colleague, wrote parodies for Purim in a pseudo-zoharic language mocking the Zohar (*Zohar ḥadash lepurim*), *Tikunei hazohar* (*Kilusa de'eliyahu*), and the *Idrot* (*Idra kadisha leleil purim*).[167] One might think that these works could be associated with the humorous Purim genre referred to as *masekhta purim*, which emerged in the fourteenth century.[168] However, in spite of the resemblance of Feder's works to the Purim parodies, his imitation of the zoharic style was a novel feature and served to repudiate the Zohar's sanctity. Although he did not directly criticize its antiquity or kabbalistic content, the homilies praising dancing and drunkenness in the name of fictitious sages such as R. Shikhra (ale) and R. Tsintsena (bottle) were clearly meant as sarcastic caricatures of the Zohar's language and protagonists. Feder's *Idra kadisha leleil purim*

164 Lefin, *Elon moreh*, 6.

165 Ibid. 7–8.

166 Werses, *Trends and Forms in Haskalah Literature* (Heb.), 319–21.

167 Davidson, *Parody in Jewish Literature*, 57–9; *Words of the Righteous*, ed. Meir, 88 n. 183.

168 Davidson, *Parody in Jewish Literature*, 19–26, 30–1, 44–7, 115–34, 140–7, 172–99.

starts as follows:

On the great day of Purim, R. Farfale [noodles] and R. Gargale [chicken neck] were walking sadly because they did not have any wine to get drunk on the fifteenth [of Adar]. And we have been taught: One who does not get drunk on that night is worthy of being buried by his mother. R. Gargale picked up some dirt, smelled it, and said: 'As a matter of fact, we are not far from a certain place. I remember that when I was young I used to follow R. Nafha Saba [old flatulence] on walks and get drunk regularly, because that was what he would do all his life—get drunk. From morning to night his lips used to praise the good wine that was available there named Garzvalka.[169]

Parodic imitation of the Zohar's style also appears in an untitled play written anonymously by Jacob Samuel Bick, Lefin and Feder's friend.[170] This play targets hasidism, not the Zohar itself. In it the hasidim use zoharic language during a ludicrous ceremony in which they bestow the title of *tsadik* on a rich man.

The above works, which were the first to ridicule the Zohar's language, were not printed until much later, and were followed by others. Joseph Perl directed his famous satirical work *Megaleh temirin* (Vienna, 1819) at hasidism but refrained from any explicit attacks on the Zohar. However, in the addendum to *Über das Wesen der Sekte Chassidim* (1816) he did describe the Zohar ironically.[171] On the basis of that addendum, the censor of Vienna prepared a list of kabbalistic and hasidic books that had to be found and confiscated, including the Zohar.[172] Perl also included ironic allusions to the Zohar in his adaptation of Isaac Baer Levinsohn's parody *Megaleh sod*, which he inserted into his *Divrei tsadikim* (Vienna, 1830).[173]

The Zohar was harshly criticized by the Galician scholar Samson Halevi Bloch in a letter written to Perl in 1817. In it Bloch presented a satirical homily, seasoned with kabbalistic-zoharic terms, justifying homosexual intercourse (of which two hasidic Jews were accused at the time): 'Since they master esoteric wisdom, most *tsadikim* practise forbidden forms of intercourse without considering them a sin.'[174]

[169] Feder, 'New Zohar for Purim' (Heb.), 11.

[170] The play was published in Sadan, *Humoristic Visions* (Heb.), 99–108.

[171] *Über das Wesen der Sekte Chassidim*, 159.

[172] Ibid. 13.

[173] See *Words of the Righteous*, ed. Meir, 57–8.

[174] See S. Katz, 'Epistles of Maskilim Disparaging Hasidim' (Heb.), 275.

In a letter to Jacob Samuel Bick (1821) Bloch cites the zoharic homily on the verse 'O Lord! I have learned of Your renown; I am awed, O Lord, by your deeds' (Hab. 3: 2), which states, 'once bitten by a dog, one shakes merely on hearing its voice' (Zohar ii. 45*a*). Bloch refers ironically to the Zohar's exegesis of the verse as a 'pure and pleasant' phrase, denies the book's antiquity, and accuses it of anthropomorphism:

Did you see or hear in the above books a phrase as pure and pleasant as this one? If you are a man of good taste and knowledge, say whether there are sublime anthropomorphisms like this one among the vanities of the Gentiles. And why, my son, are you still erring on the side of the Gentiles, and caressing foreign books more than that holy book? With closed eyes you can trust Yabets Gaon [Emden]—this awesome book did not drop out of the belly of that *tana*.[175]

It should be emphasized that Bloch wrote these and other, similar words of criticism in letters that were never published.

The Galician scholar Judah Leib Mises wove a ruthless and detailed polemic into his satire *Kinat ha'emet*. In contrast to the aforementioned works, which remained unpublished in the authors' lifetime, this one was published by the author himself (Vienna, 1828). A parody of hasidism, *Kinat ha'emet* is of the same genre as Wolfson's *Siḥah be'erets haḥayim* and several other works of the Haskalah. It is a dialogue between the soul of Maimonides and that of R. Solomon Helmah, the author of *Merkavah hamishneh*, a well-known commentary on Maimonides' *Mishneh torah*. Mises puts in Helmah's mouth the accusation that kabbalah and the Zohar are responsible for the Jews' inability to recover from their 'moral disease':

One finds an additional grievous evil in them, an old leprosy that clings to their souls and undermines the attempts of the wise to heal their minds and improve their behaviour. This grievous evil is caused by the numerous vanities lodged in their minds based on the wisdom of kabbalah. It stems also from their strong belief in the sacredness of the Zohar.[176]

Mises' polemic is more aggressive than that of previous maskilim, exposing in harsh words the 'swindler' R. Moses de León:

This book was written by one of the swindlers, who wrote books of vanity and wickedness to establish his reputation in Israel or to make a huge profit, since he

175 Bloch, 'Letter' (Heb.), 257.

176 *Kinat ha'emet*, 134.

was aware that, if people knew he wrote it, his own writing would not gain him recognition. Thus he suspended himself from a mighty tree and said in public: 'This is a recently discovered book, precious and distinguished, by an anonymous companion who lived in ancient times and was famous among the people of Israel. And from that time until now this work was concealed from the eyes of man, and the early generations were not privileged to see it or to learn its secrets. But now, at the time of redemption, during which all the mysteries of the Torah will be revealed, we have been privileged, by the grace of God, to reveal it to the generations of the end of days—and [we have been permitted] to publish this work so that Israel will know the truth.' Many are the swindlers who have forged books under names of famous [people], and they filled them with content that the original authors had never dared to consider, and certainly had never written down. One of these swindlers, whose name is R. Moses de León, wrote this book in Aramaic at the beginning of the sixth millennium, in the name of the *tana* R. Shimon ben Yohai. He did it on purpose, either [because he wanted] the masses to believe that it had been written at a time when the children of Israel could speak and read that language properly, and [to believe] it was a very old book, or he wanted the book to be like a sealed book for most people, which might attract them to it even more.[177]

Mises rejects altogether the content of the Zohar and does not find anything of value in it. Based on imagination and not reason, he asserts, its words are stolen from other writers, and it expounds the Torah incorrectly:

Most of the fabrications of this man rest on nothingness and are baseless. His opinions are rooted in his imagination, and he has no real knowledge of these matters. He failed to examine his statements rationally, as a writer should. He wrote it to be discovered so he could mislead the people and incite them with the endless wonders he told them. He did not refrain from stealing many ideas of the sages of Israel, and those ideas are the only good ones [he had]. Oftentimes he uses ambiguous language. He has filled his book with spirits and demons, and his interpretations of the Torah are misleading. This book wrought upon the children of Israel innumerable negative outcomes because it introduced many [undesirable] customs.[178]

Mises, in the name of Helmah, called for writings critical of kabbalah, especially of the Zohar (something Lefin had previously suggested):

[177] Ibid. [178] Ibid.

'Before anything else, any enlightened person among our people should write books against books of kabbalah, the new and the old, especially against the Zohar, and prove, based on reason and the Torah, that everything they claim is vanity and lies, nonsense and heresy.'[179] In the name of Maimonides he disparaged earlier critics of the Zohar, arguing that it was insufficient to prove Moses de León's authorship, and demanded the exposure of the book's pagan sources:

The sages you have mentioned used the wrong methods. It is insufficient to show, and to inform the children of Israel, that R. Moses de León fabricated all of the Zohar in the name of R. Shimon. It requires proof with clear evidence that most of the principal ideas included in the Zohar and in all the other kabbalistic writings, from the earliest to the most recent works, are lies and vanity. Many of them derive from idolatrous, vain beliefs that the children of Jacob had absorbed from the people of Egypt, Canaan, Chaldea, India, Persia, Medea, and Greece. One should demonstrate that the Gentiles with whom they mingled and socialized when they followed other gods, as well as those who converted to Judaism, were the source of these vanities.[180]

Mises goes on to develop a theory of how pagan sources had influenced kabbalah in general, and the Zohar in particular. The concepts of *sefirot* and *tsimtsum* and the belief in demons and spirits had originated, he argues, in Gnosticism, Zoroastrianism, and Hellenistic philosophy.[181] In his annotations to *Kinat ha'emet*, he expands his criticism and quotes R. Isaac of Acre's statement in *Sefer yuḥasin*, as well as the arguments of Judah of Modena and Jacob Emden.[182] In addition, he is the first to cite some blunt and satirical passages from *Mikhtav aḥuz*, a work attributed to Yashar of Candia,[183] which David Ruderman has shown to be a forgery of a letter written by Yashar.[184]

A more complex and rather positive approach to kabbalah is reflected in the works of R. Nahman Krochmal, one of the most prominent philosophers of the Galician Haskalah.[185] In his book *Moreh nevukhei hazeman*, pub-

[179] *Kinat ha'emet*, 134. [180] Ibid. [181] Ibid. 138–51. [182] Ibid. [183] Ibid. 175.

[184] About this letter and its peregrinations see Ruderman, *Jewish Thought and Scientific Discovery*, 144–6. Ruderman has concluded that the letter was forged by the Karaitic scholar Abraham Firkovich or someone in his circle in the early 19th century.

[185] See Biale, 'The Kabbala in Nachman Krochmal's Philosophy of History', 85–97.

lished posthumously in 1851, Krochmal described kabbalah as an ancient wisdom that had arrived in Europe from the East and had degenerated over time. In contrast to contemporary scholars who perceived it as the obverse of philosophy, he, in agreement with the early maskilim, viewed it as a philosophical system that had originated in the Second Temple period. The first phase of its evolution, which he viewed positively, lasted from the time of the Babylonian geonim until the death of Nahmanides. It was followed by a period of decline, which reached its nadir in Sabbatianism and hasidism.[186] Denying the Zohar's antiquity,[187] Krochmal, like the German maskilim, dated it to this later period of deterioration.

Similar criticism of the Zohar is expressed indirectly by Krochmal's fellow scholar, Solomon Judah Rapoport, in his biography of R. Hai Gaon, published in the periodical *Bikurei ha'itim* in 1829. Rapoport argued that, although Hai Gaon himself had engaged in kabbalah, in his time it had not been polluted 'by impurities and additions of oriental and Sephardi secrets':[188]

> Any intelligent reader who studies the words of the ancient sages of kabbalah, such as R. Hai [Gaon] and those after him up until the days of Nahmanides, and compares them to the *aḥaronim* [later rabbis] will find significant differences between them. [That person] will witness how pure water flowing from a clear and clean source of marble stones and drawn by degrees becomes murky, lacking clarity and splendour, especially after *notarikon* and *gematria* are mixed in it. It is impossible to explain here what happened to it in 1292/3, but with God's help it will be explored at length somewhere else.[189]

Rapoport, like Krochmal, distinguishes between ancient kabbalah, that is, up to the end of the Nahmanidean area, and kabbalah from that time on. The reference to the year 1293 and the ironic phrase 'lacking clarity and splendour [*zohar*]' are obvious allusions to the Zohar and to statements made in *Sefer yuḥasin* regarding the appearance of the book in Moses de León's possession at that time.[190] Rapoport writes that the Zohar, which he believes was written in Spain in the late thirteenth century, was to blame for the corruption of ancient, rationalist kabbalah. He responds in the

186 *Moreh nevukhei hazeman*, 225, 238.

187 Ibid. 222.

188 Rapoport, 'Annals of Hai Gaon' (Heb.), 81.

189 Ibid. 90 n. 17.

190 See Zacuto, *Sefer yuḥasin hashalem*, 222.

following harsh terms to criticism levelled against him:

What I said about R. Moses de León I did not hide and I will not hide . . . because all of R. Moses Kunitz's evidence to prove the antiquity of the Zohar is vacuous. I will say unequivocally that those who are able to recognize the forgery in this book and are trying to support this falsehood and to uphold it in the eyes of the people hate religion and hate the people. They feel no remorse for tarnishing its splendour and diminishing its honour.[191]

Rapoport's criticism of Kunitz's *Sefer ben yoḥai* was published posthumously in 1872 under the title *Naḥalat yehudah*. In this book Rapoport lists R. Jacob Emden's arguments and refutes Kunitz's claims against them. However, unlike Emden, he does not believe that the Zohar contains even a kernel of antiquity, but asserts that it was written by Moses de León in its entirety:

Because he felt it urgent to relieve us from suffering the strangeness and awkwardness of the Zohar, the Gaon [Jacob Emden] wrote that it would be better to accept some of it in order to sustain the sacred crown on its brow . . . The Gaon, of blessed memory, he too tried in vain to accept its strange and awkward [statements] when the evidence before us proves that all of it was fabricated by the latest of the late authors [de León].[192]

Privately Rapoport did not mince his words about the sexual 'abominations' in the Zohar. In a letter sent to Samuel David Luzzatto in 1833, he complained about the 'many profanities and crude metaphors that are harsh on a pure and delicate ear', and for which, he said, the book should be concealed in 'a prison'.[193]

Opposition to kabbalah and the Zohar also appears in the writings of R. Isaac Baer Levinsohn, 'the father of Russian Haskalah'. In his anti-hasidic satire *Megaleh sod* (1820), written in support of Joseph Perl's *Megaleh temirin*, Levinsohn included a parody of the Zohar, which Perl adapted and incorporated into his *Divrei tsadikim* (Vienna, 1830).[194] In his work Levinsohn assigns an ironic quotation from the fictitious book *Sifra derazin*

[191] Rapoport, 'Epistle 11' (Heb.), 163. The criticism to which he was responding had been published anonymously in the periodical *Kerem ḥemed*, 6 (1841).

[192] *Naḥalat yehudah*, 32.

[193] See Graber, *Igerot shir*, 6.

[194] About the history of these two works see *Words of the Righteous* (Heb.), ed. Meir, 87.

to R. Enoch the Hasid, who prophesies against Obadiah ben Petahyah (i.e. Perl) and his book *Megaleh temirin*.[195]

In *Te'udah beyisra'el*, printed in 1828, Levinsohn rejected Kunitz's claims of the Zohar's antiquity.[196] He reiterated his criticism of kabbalah and the Zohar in *Beit yehudah*, published in 1839, where he entertained the idea of reprinting Emden's *Mitpaḥat sefarim* with additions and corrections of his own.[197] He wrote yet another pamphlet disputing the Zohar's antiquity, part of which he published at the end of his book *Shoreshei levanon* in 1841.[198] Like Krochmal, he distinguished between authentic, ancient kabbalah and the new one that had been degenerating since the days of the Zohar.[199] Together with Lefin and Perl, Levinsohn tried to prevent the printing of kabbalistic and hasidic books.[200]

Let us now turn to the views of the Italian maskilim of the period, many of whom sharply criticized the Zohar and kabbalah and promoted the printing of books by earlier Italian scholars who had opposed the Zohar. As I mentioned above, in the late eighteenth century R. Elijah Morpurgo had already voiced his disapproval of the proliferation of copies of the book and expressed interest in Emden's *Mitpaḥat sefarim*. R. Isaac Samuel Reggio of Gorizia, one of the founders of the Italian rabbinical academy, initially had a positive attitude towards kabbalah, so much so that he sent Kunitz a letter praising his book *Ben yoḥai*.[201] Later, however, he changed sides and published Elijah Del-Medigo's *Beḥinat hadat* (Vienna, 1833). In his comments on the book he added arguments of his own refuting the antiquity of the Zohar.[202] He also intended to print *Ari nohem*; in the end it was published, with Reggio's comments, by Julius Fürst in 1840.[203]

Reggio's friend R. Samuel David Luzzatto, who maintained close relations with the Galician maskilim, was another prominent Italian scholar who raised objections to the Zohar.[204] In his autobiography, Luzzatto recounts having realized very early that, because of its references to the Torah's vocalization and cantillation systems, the work could not have been

195 Ibid. 196 Levinsohn, *Te'udah beyisra'el*, 150. 197 *Beit yehudah*, 282–3.

198 *Shorshei levanon*, 239–46.

199 See *Words of the Righteous* (Heb.), ed. Meir, 43–5, especially n. 81. 200 Ibid. 45 n. 84.

201 Reggio, *Beḥinat hadat*, 113. 202 Ibid. 43–5, 108–15.

203 See Leibowitz's introduction to Leon of Modena's *Ari nohem*, 34.

204 See Feiner, *Haskalah and History* (Heb.), 176.

written by R. Shimon.[205] He fiercely criticized kabbalah and the Zohar in his work *Vikuaḥ al ḥokhmat hakabalah ve'al kadmut sefer hazohar vekadmut hanekudot vehate'amim*.[206] Along with others, Luzzatto, too, based his refutation on R. Isaac of Acre's testimony, on previous historical and philological challenges to the authenticity of the Zohar, and on his own new philological discoveries, which identified errors in the Aramaic of the book.[207] One of his principal arguments for rejecting the antiquity of the Zohar—its references to vocalization and cantillation—was given special emphasis by being embedded in the title of his work. In contrast to Emden and his followers, Luzzatto dismissed the possibility that the Zohar contained ancient sections, and contended that it had been forged in its entirety.[208] He condemned it for the abandonment of literal (*peshat*) Torah commentary and for bringing '500 years of darkness and obscurity' to Israel.[209] His book is written as a debate between the 'author', who apparently believes in the antiquity of the Zohar and accepts its authority, and the 'guest', a Polish Jew who remonstrates with him. Luzzatto uses the literary device of irony in his portrayal of the 'author', who is eventually led by the 'guest' to question the validity of kabbalah and the Zohar. In his introduction to the French version of the book, Luzzatto stated that his main objective was theological rather than scholarly, and that his criticism was directed at the hasidim, 'the enemies of culture', who blindly accepted the sanctity and authority of the Zohar.[210]

German Jewish historians and maskilim were no less involved in presenting refutations of the Zohar's antiquity. Leopold Zunz, in his book *Gottesdienstlichen Vorträge der Juden* (1832), asserted that the Zohar was written around 1300 and contained late material.[211] Listing the sources that pro-

[205] See Penkower, 'S. D. Luzzatto, Vowels and Accents, and the Date of the Zohar', 82–4.

[206] See Goetschel, 'Samuel David Luzzatto: Ein antikabbalistischer Romantiker', 68–9. Luzzatto's book was written in 1825 and published in Gorizia in 1852; its title translates as *Polemic against the Wisdom of Kabbalah and against the Antiquity of the Zohar and of the Punctuation System*.

[207] *Vikuaḥ al ḥokhmat hakabalah*, 110–24. See also Penkower, 'S. D. Luzzatto, Vowels and Accents, and the Date of the Zohar', 113–14.

[208] *Vikuaḥ al ḥokhmat hakabalah*, 112–13, 118.

[209] Ibid. 121.

[210] See Luzzatto's introduction to the French edition of *Vikuaḥ al ḥokhmat hakabalah*, 3–4.

[211] See the Hebrew edition of Zunz's work: *Jewish Sermons* (Heb.), 191.

vided evidence for his claims he mentioned *Mitpaḥat sefarim*, *Beḥinat hadat*, and *Ari nohem*; the strongest proofs, however, remained concealed with himself and with Solomon Rapoport, he claimed.[212]

The historian Isaac Marcus Jost did not question the antiquity of kabbalah in general, but he regarded it as an 'oriental figment of the imagination'[213]—an idea which had first appeared, it will be recalled, among the early German maskilim. In his book *Geschichte der Israeliten seit der Zeit der Maccabaer bis auf unsere Tage*, published in nine volumes between 1820 and 1828, Jost briefly discusses the Zohar. He rejects its antiquity and, basing himself on Emden's *Mitpaḥat sefarim*, goes on to refute Moses Kunitz's arguments in *Ben yoḥai*.[214]

Towards the end of his life Jost developed a more complex attitude towards kabbalah.[215] In the third volume of his book *Geschichte des Judenthums und seiner Sekten*, he wrote that the appearance of the Zohar was an important event in the history of Judaism. Although he did not change his mind regarding its dating, he asserted that its authors should not be accused of forgery since, in spite of being written much later than claimed, the work did contain ancient perceptions.[216]

Later on in the century the interest in kabbalah, and particularly in the Zohar, became widespread among Jewish historians and maskilim in central Europe, especially in Germany. Strong opposition to the Zohar at this time coexisted with a more recent, sympathetic approach influenced by the Romantic movement. The French Jewish scholar Adolphe Franck suggested, in his book *La Kabbale, ou la philosophie religieuse des hébreux* (1843), that the Zohar indeed contained ancient traditions from R. Shimon's time. In response, David Heymann Joël published a book entitled *Midrash ha-Zohar: Die Religionsphilosophie des Sohar und ihr Verhältnis zur allgemeinen jüdischen Theologie*, in which he rejected Franck's claim regarding the kabbalah's Chaldean and Persian origins, as well as the Zohar's antiquity.

Meyer Heinrich Landauer, another scholar who was sympathetic towards kabbalah, assumed that the Zohar reflected ancient traditions that

212 Ibid. 508 n. 217.
213 *Geschichte der Israeliten*, xii. 424–6 (note to Book 24).
214 Ibid. iv. 52; iv. 229 (note to Book 13); ix. 167 (bibliography, see 'Zohar').
215 See Michael, *I. M. Jost* (Heb.), 191–3.
216 *Geschichte des Judenthums*, iii. 74.

preceded Christianity.[217] Later he retracted his opinion and suggested instead that its author was Abraham Abulafia.[218]

Adolf Jellinek, who translated Adolphe Franck's book into German, rejected Landauer's theory and concluded, in his book *Moses ben Schem-Tob de Leon und sein Verhältnis zum Sohar* (Leipzig, 1851), that de León was the principal author of the Zohar. Jellinek, who, as we shall see in the next chapter, was nevertheless sympathetic to kabbalah, constructed his argument on three pillars: (*a*) R. Isaac of Acre's testimony; (*b*) the noticeable influence of thirteenth-century kabbalistic books on the Zohar, and (*c*) a comparison between de León's *Shekel hakodesh* and the Zohar.[219]

The Hungarian scholar Ignaz Stern, in research that he published serially in the periodical *Ben Chananja* between 1858 and 1862, discussed the complexity of the zoharic text and asserted that it had some ancient layers.[220] Solomon Munk, the French orientalist, similarly believed that, despite its late compilation, the Zohar contained ancient traditions and homilies.[221]

In contrast to the aforementioned historians, whose criticism of kabbalah and the Zohar was moderate, the attack of Heinrich Graetz, the leading Jewish historian of the time, was fierce and unequivocal. In the seventh volume of his monumental work *Geschichte der Juden* (Leipzig, 1863),[222] Graetz repudiated kabbalah and contended that the zoharic corpus as a whole was a forgery of R. Moses de León (including *Tikunei hazohar* and *Ra'aya meheimna*).[223] Like R. Judah of Modena and R. Jacob Emden, he was bothered by the Zohar's glorification of R. Shimon's image, especially in statements such as 'who is "the face of the Lord, God" [Exod. 34: 23]? That is R. Shimon bar Yohai' (Zohar ii. 38*a*).[224] True, the book occasionally offered 'a faint suggestion of an idea', he conceded, but these evaporated instantly in 'feverish fancies or dissolve in childish silliness'.[225] The Zohar, or rather, Moses de León, distorted the meaning of Scripture and 'twists the sense of the words',[226] and 'carps at and criticizes the Talmud and its method'.[227]

217 Landauer, *Wesen und Form des Pentateuchs*, 87.

218 Landauer, 'Vorläufiger Bericht', 345.

219 *Moses ben Schem-Tob de Leon*, 41–5, 72–4.

220 See Tishby and Lachower, *The Wisdom of the Zohar*, i. 48.

221 Munk, *Mélanges de philosophie juive et arabe*, 275–6.

222 *Geschichte der Juden*, vii. 231–49, 487–507; see also ibid. iv. 11–25.

223 Ibid. vii. 231–7, 497; iv. 11–12.

224 Ibid. vii. 236; iv. 14.

225 Ibid. vii. 238.

226 Ibid. vii. 239.

227 Ibid. vii. 244.

Its contents promulgated a false doctrine which was not only absurd 'but sometimes even appears blasphemous and immoral'.[228] Like the maskilim who preceded him, Graetz was disgusted by the erotic language of the Zohar and claimed that it was the prime cause of the emergence of Sabbatianism: 'Through its constant use of coarse expressions, often verging on the sensual, in contradistinction to the chaste, purified Jewish literary style, the Zohar sowed the seeds of unclean desires, and later on produced a sect that laid aside all regard for decency.'[229] Graetz's polemic was a novel mixture of historical and philological arguments,[230] as well as harsh language and irony reminiscent of the satire employed by the east European maskilim before him.

Abraham Geiger, a leader of the German Reform movement, also expressed fierce opposition to the Zohar. In the 1840s he published *Mikhtav aḥuz*, a work attributed to Yashar of Candia, in which the author attacks both kabbalah and the Zohar.[231] In the third volume of his book *Das Judenthum und seine Geschichte* he claims that the dissemination of the Zohar marked the nadir of the history of Judaism: 'At a time when the power of free thinking almost fell asleep, this book attained dangerous dominance in scope and level of corruption.'[232] A negative attitude towards kabbalah and the Zohar also characterized the position of Moritz Steinschneider, the father of Jewish bibliography.[233]

Historical criticism of the antiquity of the Zohar and the employment of parody and satire to attack its adherents persisted throughout the nineteenth century among east European maskilim. Abraham Baer Gottlober dedicated four chapters to criticizing the Zohar in his *History of Kabbalah and Hasidism* (Zhitomir, 1869).[234] Relying on the objections of Graetz, Judah of Modena, and Jacob Emden, he launched a fierce assault on the book:

> [The Zohar] destroyed the fortresses of the intellect and 'built the shrines of Topheth in the valley of Ben Hinnom' [Jer. 7: 31]. It opened the doors of She'ol and

228 Ibid. vii. 239.
229 Ibid. vii. 249.
230 Ibid. vii. 487–507.
231 See *Mikhtav aḥuz*, printed in Geiger, *Melo ḥofnayim*.
232 *Das Judenthum und seine Geschichte*, iii. 77. See also Michael, *Historical Jewish Writing* (Heb.), 291.
233 Steinschneider, *Polemische und apologetische Literatur*, 360.
234 *The History of Kabbalah and Hasidism* (Heb.), 78–116.

Abaddon and released from there demons, spirits, and angels of destruction to gain dominion over the earth and to fill the earth with superstition and vanity that true believers of previous generations could not even imagine. It planted vanity and maliciousness in the hearts of those who studied it, and hid Judaism from view.[235]

Peretz Smolenskin, editor of the periodical *Hashaḥar*, expressed emphatic opposition to the Zohar in his article 'Time to Plant', stating that 'the way of kabbalah according to the Zohar and its wisdom constitutes a complete antithesis to the faith of Israel and its Torah'.[236] In the same piece he accused the Zohar of deliberately leading astray the children of Israel:

> Since the Zohar set out to blind the eyes, this book and its sources and foundations, all of them together, are alien to Israel. Its intention is solely to seduce the hearts of Israel [to follow] a new belief. It camouflages its face and sometimes uses talmudic words like those who roll like raging billows to trap souls by spreading lies to mislead the people.[237]

Further satires and Zohar parodies that were published at the time included *Zohar ḥadash*, written in zoharic language by the scholar Senior Sachs. Sachs claimed that it had been composed by a certain Judah Leib Katz Nathan, to attack the reformers in Germany.[238] In 1867 a work praising the Enlightenment and opposing hasidism was written, again in a zoharic style, by Tobias Shapira.[239] Entitled 'Questions of Rav Hasida and the Solutions of Rav Petahyah',[240] Shapira's satirical piece was published in *Hamelits*, the periodical of the Russian maskilim. In 1877 Aaron Samuel Lieberman put out a collection of articles written in a pseudo-zoharic language. His pieces appeared in the 'Erev rav' section of *Ha'emet*, the first Hebrew socialist newspaper.[241]

An acerbic parody of hasidim in general, and of Habad in particular,

[235] *The History of Kabbalah and Hasidism* (Heb.), 114.

[236] 'Time to Plant' (Heb.), 101.

[237] Ibid. 100.

[238] *Zohar ḥadash* was published in Sachs's *Kanfei yonah*, 21–2; see also Davidson, *Parody in Jewish Literature*, 78, 235; *Words of the Righteous*, ed. Meir, 88 n. 183.

[239] See Davidson, *Parody in Jewish Literature*, 244.

[240] The title's Rabbi Petahyah is an allusion to R. Obadiah ben Petahyah, 'the author' of Joseph Perl's *Megaleh temirin*.

[241] The articles were published a second time by Zwi Kroll in his book *Ha'emet: The First Socialist Periodical* (Heb.), 31–2. Yet another work in zoharic language, *Idra kadisha*, was intended for the fourth issue of *Ha'emet* but was not published there in the end; it did appear,

was Leib Friedland's *Sefer hatikun: 370 Halakhic Amendments to the Bylaws of the Association Tson Kodashim*. In the introduction the hasidic 'author' R. Leibshe quotes 'zoharic' segments advocating drunkenness, reminiscent of Feder's aforementioned Purim parodies.[242] The late nineteenth century also saw the printing of earlier, hitherto unpublished zoharic satires. Feder's Purim parodies, for instance, appeared in the third volume of the periodical *Otsar hasifrut* in 1890, and Samson Bloch's letter to Jacob Samuel Bick, which included a satire of the Zohar, was published in the fourth volume in 1892.

The above survey indicates the importance that nineteenth-century maskilim attributed to criticism of the Zohar. As we have seen, they employed different literary tools in their opposition, including polemic and satire, the latter being especially popular among east European maskilim. Further attacks were launched in historical publications, and, towards the end of the nineteenth century, several books were dedicated to the Zohar and the question of its authorship. The maskilim relied to a great extent on earlier critical works, especially Elijah Del-Medigo's *Beḥinat hadat*, Judah of Modena's *Ari nohem*, and Jacob Emden's *Mitpaḥat sefarim*; oftentimes they were also involved in printing these books. Isaac Samuel Reggio, for instance, besides reprinting *Beḥinat hadat*, prepared Modena's *Ari nohem* for its first ever publication.[243] Samson Halevi Bloch and Samuel Rosenthal of Pest were involved in another edition of *Ari nohem*, which was eventually printed in Leipzig in 1840.[244] Maskilim often took part in the circulation and printing of *Mitpaḥat sefarim*; originally published by Emden himself in 1768, this work was seen as an important weapon in the struggle against hasidism, and in 1792 Menahem Mendel Lefin had already suggested its

though, in Berkowitz's *Aaron Samuel Lieberman* (Heb.), 83–5. See also Davidson, *Parody in Jewish Literature*, 257; *Words of the Righteous*, ed. Meir, 88 n. 183. In contrast to other scholars, who wrote in pseudo-zoharic language with the intention of mocking kabbalah and hasidism, Lieberman used it as a means to spread his socialist ideas and to conceal them from the eyes of the authorities. See Berkowitz, *Aaron Samuel Lieberman*, 86. In the same period Michael Levi Rodkinson (Frumkin), the publisher of the periodical *Kol*, wrote a polemical article in pseudo-zoharic language for the journal. See Malachi, *View from a Distance* (Heb.), 67 n. 130; Meir, 'Michael Levi Rodkinson' (Heb.).

242 *Sefer hatikun*, 2, 2*b*–3*b*.

243 Del-Medigo, *Beḥinat hadat*, ed. Reggio, 103.

244 See Letteris, *Memoirs* (Heb.), 109; see also the introduction to Modena's *Ari nohem*, 21, 24.

circulation to help improve the conditions of east European Jewry. Levinsohn, in his book *Beit yehudah*, expressed his desire to publish the same work with his own annotations and supplements. The book was finally reprinted in 1870 in Lviv (Lemberg).[245] One should also mention Abraham Geiger's reprinting of *Mikhtav aḥuz* (attributed to Yashar of Candia) in *Melo ḥofnayim* (1840).

While most maskilim rejected the Zohar and its authoritative status by literary means, there were some who also participated in political attempts to prevent the dissemination of the Zohar and other kabbalistic books, and were willing to collaborate with the authorities to that end. Lefin, in a French programme presented to the Polish Sejm, called for a prohibition on printing such works. In 1816 Joseph Perl submitted his work *Über das Wesen der Sekte Chassidim* to the governor of Galicia; it was from this document that the censor of Vienna copied the list of books to be banned, including the Zohar. Levinsohn, at the same time, was making efforts to put an end to the publication of kabbalistic books in Russia.

Maskilim of different ideological orientations—moderate and radical, writers and historians, Reform and traditional rabbis—voiced their objections to the Zohar throughout Europe. Although there were some who approved of the book, as the above examples show, its criticism was generally characteristic of the Haskalah movement and played an important role in the construction of the enlightened Jewish identity.

Unlike in earlier periods, when such attacks were marginal and had a very limited effect, in the nineteenth century opposition became widespread and to a great extent successful in bringing about the rejection of the Zohar by movements that based themselves on Enlightenment values. These movements, which gained cultural prominence in the Jewish centres of Europe, the United States, and Israel in the twentieth century, no longer recognized the canonical status of the Zohar. From the late eighteenth century to the end of the nineteenth, more and more Jewish circles in eastern and western Europe adopted the ideology of the Enlightenment, including its foundational dichotomies between 'light' and 'darkness', progress and backwardness, rationalism and mysticism, West and East. Frequently,

[245] About the printing of Emden's *Mitpaḥat sefarim* and other works of his by Michal Wolf see Werses, *Haskalah and Sabbatianism* (Heb.), 61–2; Ettinger, 'The Emden–Eibeschuetz Controversy' (Heb.), 345–6.

Jews and Judaism were perceived in Enlightenment thinking as 'Asian' and 'oriental', bearing the pejorative image of the East as decadent and primitive. Those who wished to integrate into European society were required to dissociate themselves from the 'oriental' elements of their culture.[246] The maskilim who participated in the discourse largely accepted this negative image of contemporary Judaism. They worked not only towards adopting the values of the Enlightenment and incorporating them into Jewish culture, but also towards rejecting elements in Judaism that were perceived as contradicting those values. The renunciation of traditional Jewish practices, texts, and customs was central to the new, enlightened Jewish identity. Among the elements to be rejected were, first and foremost, kabbalah and the Zohar.

The maskilim viewed kabbalah and its adherents, especially the hasidim, as the antithesis of enlightened Judaism and its values. In their polemic they presented both kabbalah and hasidism as false beliefs based on ignorance and which had led to the backwardness of contemporary Jewry. Eventually kabbalah was perceived not only as contrary to the Enlightenment but also as alien to Judaism.

Adherence to canonical texts and traditional bodies of knowledge is a core determinant of a community's self-identity. It supports the links between members of the community as well as their awareness of continuity. In a similar manner, rejection of canonical texts and traditional bodies of knowledge can assist in the development of a new communal identity. Those who adopt this new identity will emphasize the distinction between themselves and other communities, which remain loyal to these texts.

By rejecting kabbalah and the Zohar the maskilim were able to define the difference between themselves and the traditional Judaism of their time, especially hasidism, and at the same time maintain their ties to other Jewish traditions and canonical texts. This rejection was an essential step towards the formation of modern Jewish identity, with its imagined tradition centred around the Bible, talmudic Judaism, and medieval Jewish philosophy, and whose present manifestation was the Jewish Enlightenment. The canonical texts that the maskilim considered authentic elements of the Jewish tradition were described and interpreted by them in the light of

[246] See Raz-Krakotzkin, 'Orientalism, Jewish Studies, and Israeli Society' (Heb.), 40–1.

novel, enlightened values. They juxtaposed against this venerable tradition the bleak picture of a failing Judaism that commenced with kabbalah and the Zohar and evolved through Lurianic kabbalah, Sabbatianism, and hasidism. In this depiction kabbalah was a negative, exogenous element that penetrated Judaism, perverted its positive values, and prevented Jews from adopting contemporary, enlightened mores. Criticism of kabbalah and the Zohar played such a crucial role in the struggle against hasidism, and in the attempt to reform the hasidim, due to the centrality of the Zohar within that movement. Objection to the authoritative and sacred status of the Zohar entailed the renunciation of all kabbalistic traditions that had grown out of it, especially the Lurianic kabbalah, which was heavily based on the interpretation of the Zohar.

We may apply Barbara Herrnstein Smith's model of the canonization of literary texts in our analysis of the de-canonization of the Zohar. Similar to the endurance identified by Smith in the canonical status of a text, endurance and cumulative effect can also be discerned in the history of the criticism and rejection of the Zohar. The book was an easy target for the maskilim partly because of its problematic features—such as the evidence concerning its late composition, its anachronisms, and its erotic language—but also because of the existence of earlier criticism. The fact that its antiquity had been questioned before the Enlightenment, and that its critics had included well-known and authoritative rabbinic figures (such as Judah of Modena and Jacob Emden), was emphasized and exploited by the maskilim, who often quoted the arguments of these scholars and promoted their books.

Even though opposition to kabbalah and the Zohar played an important role in the discourse of nineteenth-century Haskalah, it nearly vanished in the twentieth century. In that period hardly any polemical works were written, with two exceptions: Ephraim Deinard's *Alatah*, which, according to its cover page, sets out to prove that 'the Zohar was forged; it was not [written] by R. Shimon; kabbalah is idolatrous, and God does not approve its ways';[247] and R. Yihya Kafih's *Sefer milḥamot hashem*, a vehement attack on kabbalah and the Zohar.[248]

[247] For Deinard's criticism of the Zohar see pp. 1–29, 46–7.

[248] In 1913/14 R. Kafih expressed his opposition to kabbalah for the first time in the

Parodies of the Zohar, which were written mainly by east European maskilim in the early nineteenth century and which gained popularity by the end of the century, completely disappeared in the twentieth century. Not only was it impossible to write such parodies without profound knowledge of zoharic literature, it was equally difficult to read them or understand their irony without a command of the language of the Zohar. This kind of parody could only be written, and become popular, in a society in which, on the one hand, the Zohar maintained its cultural centrality and, on the other hand, there were those who rejected its sanctity. Indeed, this scenario typified the Jewish society of nineteenth-century eastern Europe, and the dynamic interactions between maskilim and traditional Jewry at the time. The disappearance of zoharic parodies in the twentieth century (and even earlier among German maskilim) illustrates the growing cultural gap between traditional circles, which were acquainted with the Zohar and accepted its holiness, and the 'enlightened' Jews, who rejected the Zohar but were no longer able to parody it or to enjoy reading such parodies, its language and conceptual world having become alien to them.

The polemics surrounding the Zohar disappeared due to the prevalence of Enlightenment and secular values in modern Jewish culture, especially after the Second World War and following the establishment of the State of Israel. Those circles that continued to recognize its authority and sanctity (especially the ultra-Orthodox of east European descent and Jewish immigrants from Islamic countries) were marginalized in the large Jewish cultural centres of the United States and Israel. The evanescence of the dispute is further related to the emergence of a more positive approach to kabbalah and the Zohar at the turn of the last century in the wake of Romanticism and the rise of Jewish nationalism, as I have noted above. This new approach suggested different readings of the Zohar, which will be discussed in the next chapter.

pamphlet *Amal ure'ut ruaḥ*. In 1931, after the publication of *Sefer milḥamot hashem*, he put out the pamphlet *Sefer da'at elohim*, in response to Hillel Zeitlin's arguments in support of the Zohar; see Meir, 'Wrestling with the Esoteric' (Heb.).

CHAPTER EIGHT

The Recanonization of the Zohar in the Modern Era

If one turns to the writings of the great kabbalists one seldom fails to be torn between alternate admiration and disgust.

Scholem, *Major Trends in Jewish Mysticism*, 36

As the Zohar lost its status of sanctity and authority within maskilic circles, its positive symbolic value was preserved in the communities that rejected modern European culture (or were exposed to it to a lesser degree). Yet even within these communities, especially in eastern Europe, engagement in kabbalah in general, and study of the Zohar in particular, were restricted. These restrictions stemmed partially from the opposition of earlier scholars to the free dissemination of the Zohar (see Chapter 6), and possibly from the arguments of the maskilim against the work itself (see Chapter 7).

Meanwhile, calls for a positive re-evaluation of the Zohar and kabbalah were sounded in Jewish circles that adopted Romantic, neo-Romantic, and nationalistic ideologies at the turn of the century. The endeavour of these circles to reappraise the Zohar as a literary, philosophical, and 'mystical' text, and to grant it a central place in modern Jewish culture, succeeded to a certain extent. The reason they met with limited success was that their recanonization attempt was rooted in a modern perspective that had an ambivalent view of kabbalah, and of traditional Jewish communities which continued to maintain kabbalistic and hasidic traditions. The ambivalent recanonization of the Zohar was fused, as it were, with 'admiration and disgust'—expressions used by Martin Buber and Gershom Scholem—determining, at least until recently, the attitude towards kabbalah and the Zohar within modern Jewish and Israeli cultures.

As I pointed out in the previous chapter, notwithstanding the fierce criticism of nineteenth-century maskilim several Jewish philosophers and scholars in western Europe related favourably to the kabbalah and the Zohar. A fine example of this sympathetic approach is Adolphe Franck, a French Jewish scholar of law and philosophy, who, in his book *La Kabbale, ou la philosophie religieuse des hébreux*,[1] dedicates several chapters to the examination of the Zohar's antiquity, description of its hermeneutical system, and analysis of its religious doctrine. Franck argued that the Zohar was, indeed, based on R. Shimon's teachings, which had initially been transmitted orally, then transcribed, and finally redacted in the thirteenth century. The Zohar and *Sefer yetsirah* merited preservation, he asserted, because of their historical value:

These two books are the product of several generations. Whatever the value of the doctrines contained in them, they will always be worthy of preservation as a monument to the long and patient effort of intellectual freedom in the heart of a people at a time when religious despotism made the most use of its power. But this is not the only claim to our interest. As we have already said, and as we shall soon be convinced, the system they contain is, in itself, by reason of its origin and of the influence it exercised, a very important factor in the history of human thought.[2]

A similar opinion is voiced by other scholars of the period. Meyer Heinrich Landauer, who expressed great interest in kabbalah, argued in support of the antiquity of the Zohar in his book *Wesen und Form des Pentateuchs*, printed in Stuttgart in 1838, before the publication of Franck's work. Although Landauer later reviewed his position and attributed the Zohar to R. Abraham Abulafia, he did not alter his profound appreciation for the book or lose interest in it.[3] Some scholars, including Solomon Munk and Ignaz Stern, adopted Franck's view that the Zohar contained ancient strata despite its late compilation.[4]

In 1849, in response to Franck's book, David Heymann Joël published *Midrash ha-Zohar*, , in which he repudiated Franck's argument regarding the

[1] Franck's book was published in Paris in 1843 and was translated into German by Adolf Jellinek a year later. On Franck's attitude to kabbalah see Hanegraaff, 'The Beginnings of Occultist Kabbalah'.

[2] Franck, *Die Kabbalah*, 120.

[3] See Goodman-Thau, 'Meyer Heinrich Hirsch Landauer', 249–75.

[4] Munk, *Mélanges de philosophie juive et arabe*, 276; Stern, 'Versuch einer umständlichen Analyse des Sohar', 1–5.

foreign influence on kabbalah and contended that the Zohar expressed genuine Jewish theology of the Middle Ages.[5] Adolf Jellinek, who translated Franck's book into German, examined the claim that Moses de León was the author of the Zohar and confirmed its accuracy in his 1851 book *Moses ben Schem-Tob de Leon und sein Verhältnis zum Sohar*. Although Jellinek's research supported those who rejected the Zohar, including Graetz, his own attitude was much more sympathetic. His professed intention was 'to stimulate more interest in the most significant field of the history of philosophy and theology . . . There are among the kabbalists some whose consistent and profound thought surpasses many rationalists of the school of Moses ben Maimon.'[6]

Although the historian Isaac Marcus Jost expressed contempt for the kabbalah in his first book (Berlin, 1820–8) and rejected the antiquity of the Zohar, at the end of his life he changed his views. As mentioned in Chapter 7, in his book *Geschichte des Judenthums und seiner Sekten* (Leipzig, 1857–9) he describes the appearance of the Zohar as 'an important event in the history of religion'. It contains, he asserts, the 'essence of the Torah', a profound enquiry that constitutes a counterweight to the 'sterile' talmudic tradition.[7] R. Elijah Benamozegh, an Italian Jewish scholar of North African descent, also looked favourably on the Zohar and dedicated two of his books, *Eimat mafgia* (1855) and *Ta'am lashed* (1863), to the refutation of arguments against its antiquity. Although Benamozegh held a more traditional viewpoint than the aforementioned scholars,[8] he too was influenced by Romanticism.

Whereas the criticism and decanonization of the Zohar were influenced by Enlightenment values, the impact of the Romantic movement was clearly discernible in the more positive attitudes towards kabbalah and

[5] See Fenton, 'La Cabbale et l'académie', 221–2.

[6] Jellinek, *Beiträge zur Geschichte der Kabbala*, 5–7.

[7] Jost, *Geschichte des Judenthums*, iii. 74–8.

[8] Benamozegh studied kabbalah with his uncle, the kabbalist R. Judah Kuriat. At the age of 16 he wrote an introduction to a collection of kabbalistic writings, *Maor vashemesh*, which was published by his uncle in Livorno (1839). Benamozegh was one of the printers of the Livorno Zohar (1851/2), and he added to this edition his own notes as well as those of R. Moses Kunitz in *Sefer ben yoḥai*. He was also involved in the printing of the second edition of the Livorno Zohar (1858/9); see Guetta, 'Un Kabbaliste à l'heure du progrès', 415–36; Idel, 'On Kabbalah in Elijah Benamozegh's Thought' (Heb.).

the Zohar that emerged during the nineteenth century. A reaction to the Enlightenment, the Romantic movement adopted the Enlightenment's juxtaposition of reason with emotion and imagination, rationalism with mysticism, modernity with the Middle Ages, and the West with the East. However, it rejected the positive appraisal of reason and modernity and their evaluation as 'enlightened'; rather, it preferred the 'obscure' elements the Enlightenment had rejected. Emotion, imagination, mysticism, and the East garnered a favourable response. Within this framework non-Jewish philosophers, too, expressed interest in Christian and Jewish kabbalah: for example the German theosophical philosopher Franz Molitor, who was close to Friedrich Schelling and Franz von Bader, devoted his life to the study of Judaism and kabbalah and was the most prominent representative of this trend. His book *Philosophie der Geschichte oder über die Tradition* was published in four volumes between 1827 and 1853. Under the influence of Romanticism some Jewish thinkers became acquainted with, and influenced by, Molitor's work and his positive attitude towards kabbalah.[9] They glorified the vivid imagination, emotional richness, and profound mysticism of both kabbalah and the Zohar, and emphasized their historical importance. Yet even this sympathetic approach was ambivalent; Adolphe Franck, for example, wrote the following:

> Under the modest form of a commentary on the Pentateuch, it [i.e. the Zohar] touches, with absolute independence, upon all questions of a spiritual nature, and at times it rises to the height of doctrines which the strongest intellect may be proud of even in our day. But it is very far from always maintaining the same heights. Very often it sinks to a language, to sentiments, and to ideas which betray the lowest degree of ignorance and superstition.[10]

This ambivalence is embedded in the Romantic position, which embraced and opposed the values of Enlightenment at the same time. The Romantics revered and glamorized pre-modern and oriental traditions as long as they remained within their original geographical and historical framework—that is, outside nineteenth-century Europe. This attitude was reflected in Jellinek's response to Franck's statement that kabbalah was 'the heart and

[9] About Molitor and his influence on Scholem see Biale, *Gershom Scholem: Kabbalah and Counter-History*, 31–2; Schulte, '"Die Buchstaben haben . . . ihre Wurzeln oben"'; Raz-Krakotzkin, 'The National Narration of Exile' (Heb.), 143.

[10] Franck, *Die Kabbalah*, 87.

life' of Judaism.[11] He contended that this was true regarding ancient Judaism, up to the canonization of the Talmud, but for contemporary Judaism, kabbalah was a 'foreign and external element'.[12] Indeed, most of the Jewish philosophers mentioned above dedicated historical and philological studies to the Zohar and underlined its historical, literary, and metaphysical value, but did not participate either in its dissemination or in the integration of kabbalistic themes into contemporary Jewish culture.

Esoteric movements of the *fin de siècle* in France, England, the United States, Germany, Russia, and other countries turned with great interest to kabbalah in general and to the Zohar in particular. Drawing their information mainly from Christian kabbalistic literature, the modern occultists wrote enthusiastically on the subject and translated zoharic texts into European languages. Samuel Liddell MacGregor Mathers, who was affiliated to the Theosophical Society in England and was among the founders of the Hermetic Order of the Golden Dawn (of which he later became the leader), published an English translation of zoharic texts under the name *The Kabbalah Unveiled* in 1887, relying on Christian Knorr von Rosenroth's seventeenth-century Latin translations of the Zohar in *Kabbala denudata*.[13] Another member of the Golden Dawn, the English scholar Arthur Edward Waite, published a book called *The Secret Doctrine in Israel: A Study of the Zohar and Its Connections* (London, 1913).[14] Translations of zoharic texts were published in 1888 in Philadelphia by the scholar and Freemason Isaac Myer. Unlike Mathers (and the French occultists) he did not use von Rosenroth's text, but translated the original source.[15] The French ex-Catholic priest and occultist Eliphas Lévi (born Alphonse Louis Constant) translated *Idra raba* into French. Based on von Rosenroth's *Kabbala denudata*, his work was printed posthumously under the title *Le Livre des splendeurs* (Paris, 1894). A year later Henri Chateau, a member of L'Ordre Kabbalistique de la

[11] Franck, *Die Kabbalah*, 302.

[12] Ibid. 283.

[13] About Knorr von Rosenroth's translation of the Zohar and its influence on European culture see Huss, 'Translations of the Zohar', 41–4 (Heb.).

[14] Waite's first work to discuss the Zohar was *The Doctrine and Literature of the Kabbalah* (1902). He later incorporated *The Secret Doctrine in Israel* in another book of his, *The Holy Kabbalah* (London, 1929).

[15] Among other things, Myer translated the beginning of *Idra raba* under the title 'An Ancient Lodge of Initiates'; see his *Qabbalah*, 440–3. The book also contains Myer's other Zohar translations; see pp. 335–438.

Rose-Croix, published the French translation of all zoharic sections that were included in *Kabbala denudata*. A translation of *Sifra ditseniuta* by Albert Jounet, a Christian socialist and member of the French Theosophical Society, was printed under the title *La Clef du Zohar* (Paris, 1909).[16] The first comprehensive translation of the Zohar into French (and indeed into any European language), was produced by Jean de Pauly and printed in Paris between 1906 and 1912. In contrast to the partial translations mentioned above, de Pauly's work was based on the Aramaic source. It was translated from a Christian perspective and contained Christological interpolations added to the text. Although de Pauly presented himself as an Albanian nobleman, he seems to have been none other than the notorious Jewish convert Paulus Meyer.[17]

The above-mentioned authors accepted the antiquity of the Zohar and believed that it contained vestiges of an ancient wisdom, the *philosophia perennis*, and the original axioms of ancient Christianity.[18] They emphasized the universal aspect of kabbalah and the Zohar and found them consanguine with the mystical religious wisdom of other cultures. Isaac Myer, for example, saw a link between kabbalah, the Zohar, and the ancient Asian 'wisdom religion':

> The Qabbalah of the Hebrews is undoubtedly of great antiquity, a reminiscence of an ancient 'Wisdom Religion' of Asia, for we find its doctrines, in germ, in the ancient Buddhist, Sanskrit, Zen, and Chinese books, also examples of its peculiar exegesis in the occult book, Genesis, and in Jeremiah. The present text-book of the Qabbalah is the Sepher ha-Zohar, Book of Illumination, or Splendor.[19]

Eliphas Lévi believed that the kabbalah had been known to Jesus and the apostle John but not to Paul, who had only speculated about its existence.[20] He claimed that the Zohar contained the secrets of the universal revelation that Judaism had announced to the world—secrets that were

[16] See Godwin, *The Beginnings of Theosophy in France*, 9, 20.

[17] See Scholem, *From Berlin to Jerusalem*, 116–17; Bourel, 'Notes sur la première traduction française du Zohar', 121–9. De Pauly's translation was received very positively upon its publication, and it served as the basis for several 20th-century French anthologies of zoharic texts. In 1970 it was published a second time in its entirety in Paris.

[18] See e.g. Mathers, *The Kabbalah Unveiled*, 2; Lévi, *Le Livre des splendeurs*, 2.

[19] *Qabbalah*, 439.

[20] Lévi, *Le Livre des splendeurs*, 2.

shared by the Freemasons, pure Gnostics, Templars, and other occult movements:

The publication of this work [the Zohar] will clarify the Catholic priests' implacable hatred of the Freemasons' Order. [The Freemasons] belong to the reformed Judaism that adopted the thought of Jesus and that of his most distinguished apostle, John, whose kabbalistic revelation has always been the gospel of occult Christianity and of the unblemished Gnostic schools. The Johannites, the Templars who are not idolaters, and the distinguished trainees of the Masons' secret order are affiliated with these schools. It [the Zohar] holds the keys to the future, since the secrets of the single, universal revelation had been concealed within early Judaism, perhaps the only religion among all other religions that preached its doctrine to the world.[21]

Albert Jounet, whose book was written from a Christian occult point of view, dated the Zohar to the thirteenth century and asserted that it contained ancient doctrines that agreed both with esoteric Christianity and with Eastern religions: 'But the doctrines that the Zohar teaches are connected to those of Hebrew mystical works that were [written] prior to the thirteenth century in accordance with esoteric Christianity and the ancient doctrines that are preserved in Egyptian, Assyrian, Chaldean, Persian, Chinese, Hindu, Celtic, and Greek mysticism.'[22]

Despite their interest in, and enchantment with, kabbalah and the Zohar, some of the authors mentioned above expressed an ambivalent attitude towards both. Eliphas Lévi described the Zohar as obscure and marvellous (*ténébreux et merveilleux*);[23] Jounet argued that, like other oriental books, it was chaotic and lacked logical coherence;[24] Waite wrote that it was 'one of the most attractive curiosities of the human mind, full of greatness and littleness, of sublimity and folly'.[25] In his introduction to de Pauly's Zohar translation, Émile Lafuma compared the book to a gigantic river at whose source (the ancient Judaeo-Christian tradition) the waters are pure, but whose waters have become polluted by errant traditions over time.[26]

At the same time there was an upsurge of interest in kabbalah, hasidism, and the Zohar among Jewish intellectuals in western and eastern

[21] Lévi, *Le Livre des splendeurs*, 3–4.

[22] *La Clef du Zohar*, 1.

[23] *Le Livre des splendeurs*, 2.

[24] *La Clef du Zohar*, 2.

[25] *The Doctrine and Literature of the Kabbalah*, 489–90; see also ibid. 201.

[26] *Sepher ha-Zohar*, trans. de Pauly, iii. 5.

Europe, including Micah Joseph Berdichevsky, Samuel Abba Horodezky, Martin Buber, Hayim Nahman Bialik, and Hillel Zeitlin. The young Gershom Scholem, who was later to establish the academic discipline of kabbalistic studies, was part of the same trend. These scholars approached kabbalah and the Zohar from a neo-Romantic and orientalist perspective, and with a Jewish nationalist and Zionist outlook.

Like those in the previous generation, Jewish intellectuals at the turn of the century were particularly interested in the historical, literary, and metaphysical traits of the Zohar. Those who leaned towards mysticism, occultism, and neo-Romanticism focused on its religious and metaphysical aspects, while others stressed its historical importance as a national asset. Many combined Zionist ideology with an attraction to mysticism and the occult. Paul Mendes-Flohr, in his study 'Fin de Siècle Orientalism, the Ostjuden, and the Aesthetics of Jewish Self-Affirmation', demonstrates this fusion, especially in Buber's work. Within this context one should also mention Ernst Müller, who translated zoharic texts into German and later wrote a book on the history of Jewish mysticism. A member of the Zionist student movement in Prague, he was also a follower of Rudolf Steiner's anthroposophy.[27] Another scholar whose thought was characterized by the integration of Zionism and mysticism was Naphtali Hertz Imber, author of the Zionist anthem 'Hatikvah', who was, at the same time, interested in kabbalah and was affiliated to theosophical and Western occult circles.[28] The link between these two trends stemmed from a Jewish orientalist perspective, which regarded both the Zionist project and the study of kabbalah as a reconnection with Judaism's Eastern roots.

Fin-de-siècle authors often used Romantic and expressionist language in their descriptions of the Zohar; Mendele Mokher Sefarim, for example, compared it to a pillar of fire that lit up the darkness of the Middle Ages:

> The Zohar is as sacred as Mount Sinai, a mountain of God that emanates flames of fire, love, and sublime feelings of affinity. There, heaven and earth, the Children of God and the Children of Man, the inhabitants of heaven and the inhabitants of the earth, all together indulge in love, joy, and gratitude, and utter 'halleluyah'—

[27] See Huss, 'Translations of the Zohar' (Heb.), 67.

[28] See Kabakoff, *Master of Hope*, 179; Huss, 'Translations of the Zohar' (Heb.), 65–6; id., 'Forward to the East'.

the Zohar is the pillar of the fire of love that the Children of Israel saw for the first time in the darkness of the Middle Ages.[29]

In his article 'A Key to the Zohar', Hillel Zeitlin uses a similar language, with a strong emphasis on the mystical and religious value of the Zohar:

What is the Zohar? The Zohar is a sublime, divine soul that descended suddenly from the world of emanation down to earth in order to be revealed to the eyes of man in millions of lights and shadows, colours and hues. God, blessed be He, picked one precious stone from his crown and threw it down, and the stone shattered and scattered, sowing myriads of sparks, elating, rejoicing, and delighting in myriads of shapes and shades that emerged from eternity to illuminate all the dark corners and to satisfy all that craves and yearns for light; and to sustain and warm everything that had been killed by the chill of science and the darkness of ignorance, and the blindness, and the burden of nature, and the malice and the hardship, and the cruelty of mankind. The Zohar was revealed to the people of Israel and to the entire world through visions, parables, tales, and flashing words, piercing thoughts, the heights of heaven, the depths of the abyss, the glory of the stars, the language of divine heights, the murmur of eternal trees, the depth of the forest thicket.[30]

Many considered the Zohar the expression of the vital, mystical spirit of Judaism in contrast to halakhah and philosophy. Simon Bernfeld, an eastern European scholar active in Berlin in the late nineteenth century, writes as follows:

Subsequently we realized that Israel was not harmed by the Zohar; on the contrary—it helped, to a great extent, to unchain the fetters of a Judaism constrained by the syllogism of Aristotle and the hair-splitting of the Talmuds . . . this book is a bone of our bones and flesh of our flesh. It is the fruit of the spirit of the people of Israel, and they have no reason to be ashamed of it.[31]

Samuel Abba Horodezky, like Bernfeld, perceived the Zohar as a manifestation of deliverance from the fetters of both halakhah and Jewish philosophy. In his article 'Kabbalah',[32] he described the book as a reflection of

[29] *Emek habakhah* (Heb.), 87–8.

[30] *Hatekufah* (1920), 314. Similar expressive language is used by Samuel Tsevi Setzer: 'The glorious and fundamental book, the Zohar, the deep and vast mystical ocean the waves of which rise to the heights of human imagination and break in the ether into shards of colours and hues that leave the eye insatiate' (*Selected Writings* (Heb.), 113).

[31] *Da'at elohim*, 398–9.

[32] The article was published in the Hebrew-language paper *Netivot* in 1913.

the vibrant spirit of Judaism in exile, the opposite of rabbinic Judaism:

The Zohar revived Judaism. It blew life into the letters and words of the Torah, and it imbued Scripture, long petrified by the rabbinate, with vitality. It added sanctity to its holiness, added more spirituality to its spirituality . . . The Zohar echoes Jewish prophecy. The Zohar is the prophecy of the exile. It surpasses aggadah, the offspring of prophecy. It is more profound, more sublime, more mysterious, more religious than aggadah . . . The Zohar is the focal point of the religious and spiritual life of the people of Israel and it radiates waves of light around it.

The writer and historian Azriel Nathan Frenk emphasized, in his *Sefer agadot hazohar*, the importance of the Zohar as a national text:

This is how the Zohar showered the people of our nation; it was absorbed in our blood, our souls, our spirit, and hearts; it planted in us tenderness and innocence, compassion and forgiveness, yearning for greatness, glory, and grandeur. It ridiculed the suffering in exile and in this world; it scorned the obstacles and hurdles in our lives which characterize our people and are rarely found among the nations. The Zohar planted all these [traits] in the hearts of those who studied it, and they disseminated it among all the people of our nation that they led.[33]

The English Jewish scholar and theosophist Joshua Abelson, in his introduction to the 1931 English translation of the Zohar, depicted kabbalah in general, and the Zohar in particular, as the mystical spirit that bestowed life on rabbinic Judaism:

Indeed herein may be said to lie the undying service which the Cabbalism has rendered Judaism, whether as creed or as life. A too literal interpretation of the words of Scripture giving Judaism the appearance of being nothing more than an ordered legalism, an apotheosis of the 'letter which killeth', a formal and petrified system of external commands bereft of all spirit and denying all freedom of the individual—these have been, and are still in some quarters, the blemishes and shortcomings cast in the teeth of Rabbinic Judaism. The supreme rebutter of such taunts and objections is Cabbalah. The arid field of Rabbinism was always kept well watered and fresh by the living streams of Cabbalistic lore.[34]

The trend of renewed appreciation for kabbalah brought with it novel attempts to prove the antiquity of the Zohar. Zeitlin tried to do so in two

33 *The Legends of the Zohar* (Heb.), i. 12.

34 *The Zohar*, trans. Simon et al., i. 14.

articles, 'The Antiquity of Mystery in Israel' and 'A Key to the Zohar'.[35] The Zohar is based, he asserts, on the oral teachings of R. Shimon and his disciples, which were written down and interpreted in a later period, with R. Moses de León eventually editing and adapting them:

Thus the Zohar developed in the following way: R. Shimon bar Yohai, his companions, and his disciples delivered to those who came after them abstracts of the secrets of divinity in the language they spoke . . . those who later wrote commentaries on these abstracts combined them [i.e. their commentaries] with the abstracts and created from them a single corpus. They tried to write the commentary in the style of the abstracts . . . R. Moses [de León] collected and gleaned with amazing diligence all of the previously mentioned pamphlets, but he was not only the collector and redactor; he influenced them by his own thoughts, by which he further developed the great, sacred ideas which he had discovered.[36]

It was not uncommon for philosophers and scholars of the time to believe that the Zohar, even if edited in the thirteenth century, was based on ancient sources. Simon Dubnow, in his *History of the Jews*, argued thus:

The original and, partly, beautiful apocalyptic style of the Zohar—if one also bears in mind its Aramaic language along with the system of the old midrashim—testifies to the fact that the chief contents of the book belong to the East, not to the West. It seems plausible that upon his arrival in Palestine in 1267, Ramban, who was somewhat of a Kabbalist, took to assembling copies of old midrashim, and transmitting them to Spain. . . . Copies of those fragments circulated for a while in the circles of the 'hallowed.' And later, Moses de Leon assembled and edited them in the language of the originals—in Aramaic—at the same time interposing ideas of the new Kabbala into the texts.[37]

Abelson took a similar position and wrote, in his aforementioned introduction to the Zohar: 'From the survey of the subject, one is drawn irresistibly to the conclusion that the Zohar, so far from being a homogeneous work, is a compilation of materials drawn from many strata of Jewish and non-Jewish mystical thought over many centuries.'[38] At the beginning of his career Gershom Scholem also opposed the attribution of the Zohar to

[35] See Zeitlin, *Befardes haḥasidut vehakabalah*, 53–102, 104–44.
[36] Ibid. 142–3.
[37] *History of the Jews*, iii. 133 (see id., *Weltgeschichte des jüdischen Volkes*, v. 152).
[38] *The Zohar*, trans. Simon et al., i. 10.

R. Moses de León and raised the possibility that it indeed contained ancient traditions.

Within the context of the re-evaluation of kabbalah, scholars of the period strove to foster the Zohar and assimilate it into the cultural milieu, especially through the compilation of anthologies of zoharic texts translated into Hebrew, Yiddish, German, and English.[39] Imber (who recounted the plan of Reform rabbi Solomon Schindler and George Ayers, president of the Theosophical Society in Boston, to raise funds to enable him to translate the Zohar[40]) included zoharic texts in his book *Treasures of Two Worlds*, published posthumously in Los Angeles in 1910.[41] Translations of zoharic sections formed part of Erich Bischoff's book *Die Elemente der Kabbalah* (Berlin, 1913).[42] Ernst Müller and Samuel Hugo Bergman put out German translations of several zoharic texts at the back of *Vom Judentum*, the organ of the Zionist student organization of Prague.[43] Between 1913 and 1920 several of Müller's Zohar translations appeared in the periodical *Der Jude*;[44] in 1920 he published a book on the Zohar containing his translations,[45] and in 1932 an anthology of zoharic texts in German.[46]

In 1920 another anthology appeared in Berlin, translated into German in a neo-Romantic spirit by Jacob (Jankew) Seidman,[47] who was affiliated to Zionist circles.[48] Scholem, in a critical review article, accused the author of

[39] In the first half of the 19th century R. Elyakim Milzahagi translated the Zohar into Hebrew but his translation was lost; see Tishby and Lachower, *The Wisdom of the Zohar*, i. 102. Segments of zoharic texts in French were included in a book by Michael Weill, the first French chief rabbi of the Jews in Algeria. See Weill, *La Morale du judaïsme*, ii. 60–114; Fenton, 'La Cabbale et l'académie', 223. For a comprehensive survey of all translations of the Zohar into various languages in this period, see Huss, 'Translations of the Zohar' (Heb.).

[40] Imber related this plan in an article in the kabbalistic periodical *Uriel*. The article was republished by Kabakoff in *Master of Hope*, 181; see also ibid. 16 and Huss, 'Forward to the East', 404.

[41] *Treasures of Two Worlds*, 76–110; Huss, 'Forward to the East', 406.

[42] *Die Elemente der Kabbalah*, i. 80–137. According to Christian Ginsburg, the Jewish scholar Ignaz Stern translated, but never published, *Sifra ditseniuta*, *Idra raba*, and *Idra zuta* into German; see C. Ginsburg, *The Kabbalah*, 230.

[43] *Vom Judentum* (1913), 274–84.

[44] See Meir, 'Hillel Zeitlin's Zohar' (Heb.), 147 n. 114. Lappin, *Der Jude*, 362 n. 78.

[45] Müller, *Der Sohar und seine Lehre*. An expanded version of the book was published in Vienna and in Leipzig in 1923 and again in Zurich in 1959 (with Bergman's introduction).

[46] Müller, *Der Sohar: Das Heilige Buch*.

[47] Seidman, *Aus dem heiligen Buch Sohar*.

[48] Seidman was married to Sigmund Freud's niece, the illustrator and children's writer known as Tom (Martha) Freud-Seidman. He committed suicide in 1929 due to financial hardship following his failed attempt to establish a publishing house. On the relationship between

having produced an obscure translation in the style of German expressionism under the influence of Buber and the Bar Kokhba circle.[49] In the years 1923–4 a two-volume Hebrew anthology, Azriel Nathan Frenk's aforementioned *Sefer agadot hazohar*, appeared in Warsaw. The eastern European scholar Samuel Tsevi Setzer published zoharic texts translated into Yiddish, and later into Hebrew, in the same period.[50]

The second part of Zeitlin's 'Key to the Zohar', comprising a selection of zoharic segments organized and interpreted by topic (human body, human soul, worlds, and divinity), was published in 1921. This work anticipated in many ways Isaiah Tishby and Fischel Lachower's major anthology, *The Wisdom of the Zohar*, printed in 1949.[51] As part of the objectives of the Dvir publishing house, in 1922 Hayim Nahman Bialik proposed a comprehensive plan to publish kabbalistic works including 'the Zohar with *Zohar ḥadash* and *Tikunim*, etc., with an introduction, translation of the Aramaic portions, and explications of difficult words'.[52] At the same time Zeitlin started the project of translating the Zohar into Hebrew, initiated by the Ayanot publishing house; according to Simon Rawidowicz, the editor of Ayanot at the time (and originator of the idea), the company considered the undertaking 'a special national responsibility'.[53] Eventually this translation did not materialize; only the introduction was published, in 1943

Scholem and Tom Freud (before her marriage to Seidman) see Scholem, *From Berlin to Jerusalem*, 124–5. On the relationship between Seidman and Bialik, and his involvement in the Ofir publishing house, see Ginsburg, 'Demise of Sigmund Freud's Seduction Theory'.

[49] See Biale, *Gershom Scholem: Kabbalah and Counter-History*, 73; Kilcher, 'Figuren des Endes', 170–1.

[50] Setzer's Yiddish translations appeared under the title 'Fun Zohar' in the periodical *Das Wort*, 1–4 (1921–4). In 1946 he published zoharic texts translated into Hebrew in *The Yearbook of the Jews of America*, 24–5, and in 1954 these excerpts reappeared in *Hadoar*, 38–9. His translations were reprinted posthumously; see Setzer, *Selected Writings* (Heb.), 17–110. See also Scholem, *Bibliographia*, 144; Meir, 'Hillel Zeitlin's Zohar' (Heb.), 138–9 n. 80.

[51] Bearing the Hebrew title *Mishnat hazohar*, the first volume of the book was published by Mosad Bialik in 1949, the second in 1961, and its abridged version, by Sifriyat Dorot, in 1968. It was translated into English by David Goldstein and published by the Littman Library of Jewish Civilization in 1989 under the title *The Wisdom of the Zohar*.

[52] See Meir, 'Hillel Zeitlin's Zohar' (Heb.), 124. In 1913 Bialik suggested translating kabbalistic works from Aramaic into Hebrew within the framework of the project of 'ingathering'.

[53] See Zeitlin, 'Annotated Translation of the Introduction to the Zohar' (Heb.), 36. Meir, 'Hillel Zeitlin's Zohar' (Heb.), 130.

in the periodical *Metsudah*, by Rawidowicz, after Zeitlin had perished in a transport to Treblinka.[54] The Soncino Press published a comprehensive English edition of the Zohar (London, 1931) prepared by Jewish scholars Maurice Simon, Harris Sperling, and Paul P. Lavertoff, and with an introduction by Joshua Abelson.[55]

Doubtless galvanized by the interest that the Zohar had stimulated among maskilim and Zionists, Jews in traditional circles also worked towards its translation and dissemination. In the early twentieth century R. Judah Yudl Rosenberg began a project of translating the Zohar into Hebrew, which he continued over many years in Warsaw, Łódź, and Montreal. The first volume was printed in Warsaw in 1906 under the title *Sha'arei zohar torah*. His complete translation appeared later, between 1924 and 1930, and was entitled *Zohar torah al ḥamishah ḥumshei torah*.[56] An earlier translation of Zohar 'Bereshit', attributed to Berakhiel Kaufmann, was published by R. Obadiah Hadaya of the Beth El Yeshiva in 1946.[57] In the 1940s R. Judah Ashlag started work on a Hebrew edition of the Zohar, and the project was completed just before his death in 1954.[58]

Scholem and his disciples exhibited little interest in the dissemination of the Zohar or its inclusion in contemporary culture. Nevertheless in 1949 Scholem himself published, in collaboration with Sherry Abel, a small collection of zoharic segments translated into English.[59] In the same year Mosad Bialik printed the first volume of Lachower and Tishby's *Wisdom of the Zohar*, a comprehensive anthology of zoharic texts in Hebrew translation, with commentary, including detailed introductions and discussions of the Zohar and its core topics. This project had been the initiative of Samuel Abba Horodezky and Fischel Lachower, and the book was

[54] See Zeitlin, 'Annotated Translation of the Introduction to the Zohar' (Heb.), 40–81. Zeitlin also wrote works in Aramaic, which were printed at the beginning of his book *Sifran shel yeḥidim*, 9–16.

[55] *The Zohar*, trans. Simon et al.

[56] Rosenberg, *Sha'arei zohar torah*; id., *Zohar torah* (New York and Montreal edns.); id., *Hazohar hakadosh*, on Psalms, Song of Songs, Proverbs, and Ecclesiastes. Rosenberg, moreover, printed stories on the protagonists of the Zohar in Hebrew and in Yiddish (*Niflaot hazohar*). On his Zohar translations see Meir, 'Hillel Zeitlin's Zohar' (Heb.), 14 n. 104.

[57] See Meir, 'Hillel Zeitlin's Zohar' (Heb.), 150 n. 127.

[58] See Gottlieb, *The Ladder* (Heb.), 162–9.

[59] *Zohar, the Book of Splendor: Basic Readings*. Scholem also translated the beginning of Zohar 'Bereshit' into German; see his *Die Geheimnisse der Schöpfung*.

published by Lachower and Isaiah Tishby,[60] the latter completing the work after the former's death.

Like the occult circles of the *fin de siècle* or the nineteenth-century Jewish scholars who had called for a re-evaluation of the Zohar from a Romantic perspective, the next generation of Jewish thinkers expressed an ambivalent attitude towards kabbalah, and particularly the Zohar, while advocating its recanonization. Most of the intellectuals mentioned above were drawn to kabbalah because of its metaphysical, literary, and historical merits, but they did not attribute any authority or sanctity to the Zohar (except Zeitlin, whose vision included a more profound commitment to kabbalah). Their attraction to it and to other kabbalistic works was, in fact, coupled with disdain. As Buber stated in his article 'Jewish Mysticism',

> And if, indeed, the power of Jewish mysticism stems from a fundamental trait of the people who created it, the people's destiny has also left its impression on it. The wandering and the suffering of the people repeatedly produced the same vibrations of despair in the Jewish soul, which sometimes released a flash of ecstasy. At the same time, it [the suffering] also prevented the shaping of the perfect expression of the ecstasy. It dragged the people along until they adulterated the necessary and experiential with the unnecessary and accidental. Since [they] felt that the pain interfered with [their] ability to express themselves, [they] engaged in continuous prattle on alien topics. In this way, works like the Zohar were written that incite admiration and disgust. Between clumsy anthropomorphisms that do not improve with allegorical interpretation, and barren, colourless discussions that are presented in an opaque and pretentious language, insights into the hidden depths of the soul and revelations of finite secrets shine through again and again.[61]

Buber was not the only one with an ambivalent appreciation for the Zohar. Dubnow, for example, labelled it 'a wondrous book . . . a mixture of metaphysics and mystical delusional ideas'.[62] Abelson characterized it as

[60] See Gries, 'On Tishby's Contribution to the Study of the Zohar' (Heb.), 21; Meir, 'Hillel Zeitlin's Zohar' (Heb.), 154–5.

[61] Buber's article served as the introduction to his 1906 book *Die Geschichten des Rabbi Nachman*; see p. 8. The harsh criticisms of the Zohar were omitted from the English translation; see *The Tales of Rabbi Nachman*, 5.

[62] Dubnow, *Weltgeschichte des jüdischen Volkes*, v. 15: 'diese seltsame Buch . . . ein Gemisch von Metaphysik und mystischen Wahnideen'.

'a veritable storehouse of anachronisms, incongruities, and surprises'.[63] Ambivalence towards the Zohar can be detected even in the words of Zeitlin, who strove for the religious revival of kabbalah. In his article 'A Key to the Zohar', quoted above, he wrote:

The Zohar—a mixture of the deep of the deepest truisms and fantasies, straight and crooked lines, straight and misleading paths, fit, perfect, and clear sketches and alien and strange ones, the strength of a lion and the weakness of a child, the sound of cascading waters and the whisper of a spring, pits of darkness and caves of mysteries, brevity, clarity, and acuity of eternal wisdom and prolonged discussions that continue endlessly, infiltrating one another and interweaving as in a long and complex dream . . . according to its content and its richness, the Zohar is all—divinity; and in its appearance it is sometimes a mélange and a mist.[64]

The scholarly perspective of Gershom Scholem, who became the leading authority in the study of Jewish mysticism and established kabbalah research as an academic discipline, took shape within the framework of neo-Romanticism, nationalism, and orientalism that I have described above.[65] Scholem did not deny the impact that Buber's writings on hasidism had had on him; he mentioned it in his autobiographical book *From Berlin to Jerusalem*: 'The lasting impression which Buber's first two volumes on Hasidism made on me surely played a part as well. Still wholly written in the style of the Vienna School of the *Jugendstil* [the German version of *art nouveau*, *c*.1895–1905] they drew attention to this area in romantic transfiguration and flowery metaphors.'[66]

Zeitlin's writing likewise had a major influence on the young Scholem, who translated the former's essay 'Shekhinah' into German in 1916.[67] In that period, while living in Bern, he read Horodezky's Hebrew writings on hasidism and met him in person.[68] The enormous impression that the Christian theosophist Franz Molitor's work made on him is also notable, as is his interest in occult societies that engaged in kabbalah. In his youth Scholem met members of the Oskar Goldberg circle and the writer Gustav Meyrink,[69] and he was familiar with the writings of theosophists and

[63] *The Zohar*, trans. Simon et al., i. 12.
[64] 'A Key to the Zohar' (Heb.), 314.
[65] See Huss, 'Ask No Questions', 146–7.
[66] *From Berlin to Jerusalem*, 112–13.
[67] See Scholem, *Explications and Implications* (Heb.), 45–6; Meir, 'Hillel Zeitlin's Zohar' (Heb.), 132.
[68] See Scholem, *From Berlin to Jerusalem*, 113.
[69] On their meeting see Scholem, *From Berlin to Jerusalem*, 132–5, 146–9.

occultists including Madame Blavatsky, Eliphas Lévi, Papus, S. L. MacGregor Mathers, and Arthur E. Waite.[70] Despite his strong reservations regarding the approach of these occultists to kabbalah,[71] he acknowledged Waite's 'real insights into the world of Kabbalism' and compared them to those of Molitor.[72] In a private letter he even expressed a degree of appreciation for Madame Blavatsky.[73]

Scholem's involvement in the study of kabbalah was connected first and foremost to Zionist ideology, which he had adopted in his youth in Germany. In a 1974 interview with Muki Tsur he explained: 'I wanted to enter the world of kabbalah via my thinking and belief in Zionism as something vital, as a renewal of a declining nation . . . I was intrigued by the question: does halakhic Judaism have enough stamina to survive? Is halakhah with-

[70] At the time Scholem kept a number of books in his library that were written by members of theosophical and occult groups. Many of these books he included in the bibliography on kabbalistic literature that he printed in 1927. See Burmistrov, 'Gershom Scholem und das Okkulte'; Kilcher, 'Figuren des Endes', 162–8; Huss, 'Authorized Guardians'. In 1931 Scholem published a 'Review of A. E. Waite's *The Holy Kabbalah*' and a review of Vulliaud's translation of the Zohar ('Vulliauds Übersetzung des Sifra Dizeniuta').

[71] He characterized Goldberg as a schizophrenic and pseudo-kabbalist (*Walter Benjamin: The Story of a Friendship*, 95–8), and 'praised' Gustav Meyrink's 'talent for mystical charlatanism' (*From Berlin to Jerusalem*, 133). He considered Eliphas Lévi's works *charlatanrie* (ibid. 134), and the writings of Aleister Crowley 'highly coloured humbug' (*Major Trends in Jewish Mysticism*, 2). He labelled Madame Blavatsky's Theosophical Society 'pseudo-religion'.

[72] See Scholem, *Major Trends in Jewish Mysticism*, 2; id., 'Review of A. E. Waite's *The Holy Kabbalah*', 638. Scholem wrote that Waite's *The Doctrine and Literature of the Kabbalah* and *The Secret Doctrine in Israel* 'are among the best books written on kabbalah, from a theosophical point of view' (*Bibliograpia Kabbalistica*, 158). Nevertheless he vehemently criticized Waite in his review of *The Holy Kabbalah*, and, in a note he made inside his copy of the book, he called it a 'lying and deceitful' work (Burmistrov, 'Gershom Scholem und das Okkulte', 26).

[73] In a letter to Joseph Blau in 1944, Scholem wrote:

> You are certainly too harsh on Madame Blavatsky. It is surely too much to say that the meaning of cabala has been forgotten in the *Secret Doctrine*. After all, the Lady has made a very thorough study of Knorr von Rosenroth in his English adaptation, and of Franck's 'Cabale Juive'. She certainly knew more about kabbalism than most of the other people you mention . . . I think it might be rather interesting to investigate the kabbalistic ideas in their theosophical development. There is, of course, a lot of humbug and swindle, but, at least in Blavatsky's writings there is something more. (*Briefe*, 294)

See also his discussion of the origins of the *Book of Dzyan*, mentioned in Blavatsky's writings, in *Major Trends in Jewish Mysticism*, 398–9 n. 2.

out mysticism possible? Did it have enough vitality of its own to survive for 2,000 years without degenerating?'[74]

Like other intellectuals and scholars who were engaged in hasidism and kabbalah before him, Scholem considered mysticism the life force in Judaism as opposed to the decadence and ossifying power of the rabbinic tradition. As Amnon Raz-Krakotzkin puts it,

> Scholem viewed the mystical element as a vital and revolutionary component of Jewish history, the component containing the essence needed for its vibrant and dynamic existence. Its presence enabled a dialectical development and, he argues, it prevented Judaism from a spiritual degeneration that would have occurred if its only stimulus had been the rabbinic source. Kabbalah, in Scholem's view, is the element that truly reveals Jewish continuity . . . kabbalah reveals a historical continuity because by having only superficial contact with 'external' culture, it [i.e. external culture] did not affect its essential strata . . . He considered the concealed history, the history of the mystical trend, the real Jewish history—the history the revival of which was the condition for the national spiritual renaissance as he saw it.[75]

Although it was with the influence of neo-Romantic trends that Scholem engaged in the study of kabbalah, he criticized from the beginning the neo-Romantic enthusiasm for Jewish mysticism and the attempts to describe kabbalah in German expressionistic terms.[76] He rejected Buber's, Zeitlin's, and Horodezky's approach, claiming it was emotional and not scholarly enough,[77] and juxtaposed it with meticulous research, which he regarded as the only legitimate method for disclosing the significance of kabbalah. He saw value in the mystical and metaphysical content of kabbalistic texts but argued, unlike his neo-Romantic predecessors, that the only way to grasp this mystical and metaphysical depth was through historical-philological research. In this respect his scholarship is an integration of the historical-philological method of the nineteenth century, Wissenschaft des Judentums, and the Romantic nationalistic approaches of

[74] Scholem, *Explications and Implications* (Heb.), 26–7.

[75] 'The National Narration of Exile' (Heb.), 129.

[76] See Biale, *Gershom Scholem: Kabbalah and Counter-History*, 73–4, 88.

[77] For Scholem's criticism of Buber, especially of his understanding of hasidism, see *Explications and Implications* (Heb.), i. 361–82, ii. 363–413.

the turn of the century. He clarified his position in a letter to Solomon Zalman Schocken:

Certainly, history may seem to be fundamentally an illusion, but an illusion without which in temporal reality no insight into the essence of things is possible. For today's man, that mystical totality of 'truth' (*des systems*), whose existence disappears particularly when it is projected into historical time, can only become visible in the purest way in the legitimate discipline of commentary and in the singular mirror of philological criticism.[78]

A neo-Romantic perspective, Zionist ideology, and the application of historical-philological methods were the three main factors, then, that shaped Scholem's approach to the Zohar. On the basis of historical and philological arguments, he rejected the authorship of Moses de León in his famous 1926 article 'Did Moses de León Write the Zohar?' In so doing, he attempted to refute claims that the Zohar was a forgery, and to point out the possibility that, indeed, it contained ancient sources:

The conclusion of this careful examination of R. Isaac of Acre's statement, the analysis of Moses de León's literary work on the Zohar, and the theories that Moses de León is the author of the Zohar are insubstantial and do not hold water (or, to be more precise, one has to assume that they will not hold water in the future) as far as facts are concerned . . . in any event, we are permitted to argue that we have no grounds to presume positively that R. Moses was a forger. Thus the whole question regarding the Zohar's appearance, its organization and redaction, and its actual relationship to R. Moses de León will be reopened. Indeed, a new, systematic study is needed of the development of kabbalah in its entirety to provide a conclusive answer to the following questions: how did the Zohar come into being? How was it compiled? Did Moses de León compile midrashic sources from unknown periods that were in his possession, and while arranging them did he add to them something of his own? How did the vestiges of ancient generations come into his hands and into the hands of earlier Castilian kabbalists?[79]

Later in his life Scholem retracted his claim and accepted most of Graetz's contention that the Zohar had been written in the thirteenth century by

[78] The letter, 'A Candid Word about the True Motives of My Kabbalistic Studies' (1937), was published in Biale, *Gershom Scholem: Kabbalah and Counter-History*; for the quote see p. 76.

[79] 'Did Moses de León Write the Zohar?' (Heb.), 28–9; Biale, *Gershom Scholem: Kabbalah and Counter-History*, 117–18.

Moses de León.[80] He formulated this position in great detail in the first chapter of the two that deal with the Zohar in his classic *Major Trends in Jewish Mysticism*,[81] which was based on his 1938 lectures at the Jewish Theological Seminary in New York. Although he accepted as accurate the claim of the Zohar's late composition and its attribution to de León, for him—unlike for Graetz and other scholars—this did not diminish its value; he described it as one of the most unique books in Jewish literature and in mystical literature in general. He concluded the chapter by saying:

> Pseudepigraphy is far removed from forgery . . . The Quest for Truth knows of adventures that are all its own, and in a vast number of cases has arrayed itself in pseudepigraphic garb. The further a man progresses along his own road in this Quest for Truth, the more he might be convinced that his own road must have already been trodden by others, ages before him. To the streak of adventurousness which was in Moses de León, no less than to his genius, we owe one of the most remarkable works of Jewish literature and of the literature of mysticism in general.[82]

Scholem asserts that the pseudepigraphic style of writing neither nullifies nor diminishes the value of the Zohar. Rather, it is a legitimate part of the 'adventure' of the 'Quest for Truth'. As David Biale has argued: 'Scholem then accepted Graetz's accusation of pseudepigraphy, but made it a virtue, since pseudepigraphy became a means for legitimizing a creative work as part of a hidden tradition. The authority of tradition is recognized, but the freedom of literary creativity is preserved.'[83]

Despite his high esteem for the Zohar (the only subject that is treated at such length in *Major Trends in Jewish Mysticism*) and admiration for the 'genius' of the author, Scholem shared the ambivalent attitude of many modern thinkers. He described the spirituality of the Zohar's author as being

> centered as it were in a more archaic layer of the mind. Again and again one is struck by the simultaneous presence of crudely primitive modes of thought and feeling, and of ideas whose profound contemplative mysticism is transparent . . . a

[80] Scholem first expressed this view in the introduction to his *Die Geheimnisse der Schöpfung* in 1935 (for an English translation see id., *Zohar, the Book of Splendor*, 13–21).

[81] See pp. 156–204.

[82] Ibid. 204.

[83] *Gershom Scholem: Kabbalah and Counter-History*, 119.

very remarkable personality in whom, as in many mystics, profound and naïve modes of thought existed side by side.[84]

He expressed a similarly ambivalent appreciation for the Zohar's style: 'It is true that the style shows a great many variations; it runs all the way from serene beauty to labored tortuousness, from inflated rhetoric to the most paltry simplicity, and from excessive verbosity to laconic and enigmatic brevity.'[85] In the introduction to *Major Trends in Jewish Mysticism*, in a language reminiscent of Buber's, he speaks about the 'admiration and disgust' that kabbalistic writings provoke:

It would be idle to deny that Kabbalistic thought lost much of its magnificence where it was forced to descend from the pinnacles of theoretical speculation to the plane of ordinary thinking and acting. The dangers which myth and magic present to the religious consciousness, including that of the mystic, are clearly reflected in the development of Kabbalism. If one turns to the writings of the great kabbalists one seldom fails to be torn between alternate admiration and disgust.[86]

The historical-philological research of Scholem and his followers produced impressive results; however, they made no attempt to integrate their achievements into the contemporary culture. Tishby and Lachower were the first, in their aforementioned work *Wisdom of the Zohar*, to present the findings of Zohar scholarship to a wider readership. In his introduction to the first edition, Tishby stated that the objective of the book was 'to open these hidden riches to the Hebrew reader'.[87] Tishby was Scholem's student and *The Wisdom of the Zohar* mostly reflects the latter's position. However, the initiators of this monumental project had been Lachower and Horodezky, who were not Scholem's disciples, and had more interest in integrating the Zohar into contemporary culture.[88] One should emphasize that the purpose of the anthology was to 'present the teaching of the Zohar and its literary character in an ordered and concentrated form',[89] and not to offer the Israeli reader a comprehensive translation. In this sense, *The Wisdom*

[84] *Major Trends in Jewish Mysticism*, 175. [85] Ibid. 163. [86] Ibid. 36.
[87] *The Wisdom of the Zohar*, i, p. xxv.
[88] Ibid.; Gries, 'On Tishby's Contribution to the Study of the Zohar' (Heb.), 21.
[89] Tishby and Lachower, *The Wisdom of the Zohar*, i, p. xxv.

of the Zohar is a supplement to Bialik's 'ingathering project'—an attempt to collect and edit the classics of Jewish literature in the spirit of secular Zionism.[90]

Engagement with the Zohar in the second half of the twentieth century was limited to very small circles: on the one hand to academics in Israel and throughout the world who, until recently, adopted Scholem's approach without reservation; and, on the other, to a few kabbalistic yeshivas where the Zohar was studied (and, in the case of R. Judah Ashlag, interpreted and translated). The dominant Israeli culture, in its revival of traditional Hebrew sources (especially those related to the Land of Israel), did not express great interest in a medieval text that had originated in Spain and was written in Aramaic. The new disregard for kabbalah and the Zohar played a role in the marginalization of traditional groups that believed in the sacredness and authority of that work—east European Orthodox Jews and immigrants from Muslim countries.[91] Notwithstanding the interest of academic circles, the Zohar did not have a significant presence either in modern Israeli culture or in Jewish communities of the diaspora. The Reform, Conservative, and Modern Orthodox movements, which had become defining elements of Jewish cultural and religious life, also lacked any real interest in the Zohar.

Following the emergence of global post-modernist trends and the New Age movement a significant change took place, and kabbalah and the Zohar (as well as other traditions and cultural products that modern Western society had rejected) regained favour with the public.[92] In recent years various groups have undertaken the dissemination of the Zohar by publishing commentaries as well as translations into Hebrew and other languages, offering classes to the public, and holding ritual readings. The new kabbalistic groups include the Kabbalah Centre, the Bnei Baruch Institute, the Jewish Renewal movement, traditional hasidic groups including Habad, and kabbalistic yeshivas such as Nehar Shalom and Ahavat Shalom. These organizations have initiated large projects dedicated to the promulgation of the Zohar: the Kabbalah Centre has, for example, launched the 'Global

[90] For Bialik's 'ingathering project' and his intention to include the Hebrew translation of the Zohar in it, see Meir, 'Hillel Zeitlin's Zohar' (Heb.), 120–4.

[91] See Huss, 'Ask No Questions', 65.

[92] See Huss, 'The New Age of Kabbalah'.

Zohar Project',[93] while other groups set up websites devoted to the study and dissemination of the Zohar, such as Zohar Leyisra'el and Mifal Hazohar Ha'olami.[94] Some of the classes they offer are open to the general public and are streamed live over the internet.[95] In addition, the Zohar, with R. Judah Ashlag's *Hasulam* commentary, has been distributed (sometimes free of charge) by Ashlag's disciples, mainly by the Kabbalah Centre and Bnei Baruch.[96] Earlier commentaries, such as those of R. Moses Zacuto, R. Elijah ben Moses Luntz, and R. Shalom Buzaglo,[97] have recently been reprinted and new, comprehensive anthologies of commentaries have been published. These include *Sefer tiferet tsevi*, edited by R. Mordecai Spielman, Yehiel Bar Lev's *Sefer hazohar im be'ur yedid nefesh*, and *Sefer matok midevash*, edited by Daniel Frisch.[98] The last two collections contain a Hebrew translation of the Zohar, as does Ashlag's *Hasulam*. A further Hebrew translation (presented alongside the vocalized original text) was printed in 1993 by the Yerid Hasefarim publishing house.[99] R. David Shalom Basri of Yeshivat Ahavat Shalom published *Tales from the Zohar*, an anthology of zoharic legends in Hebrew, a decade earlier.[100]

The Zohar has recently been translated into a number of other languages: Basri's *Tales from the Zohar*, for example, has come out in English, French, and Spanish, and another anthology has been published in Eng-

[93] See Myers, *Kabbalah and the Spiritual Quest*, 128–9; Meir, 'The Revealed and the Revealed within the Concealed' (Heb.), 186–8; <http://www.kabbalah.co.il/zohar/zohar.asp>.

[94] See <www.zohar-israel.com>, <http://ha-zohar.net/index.htm>.

[95] Lessons are now available at <http://hazohar.net>, <http://www.kabbalahmedia.info>, the website of Bnei Baruch <http://www.zohar.com>, and the website of the Kabbalah Centre. Basri's lessons are accessible at <http://hashem1.net>.

[96] The Zohar with the *Hasulam* commentary (and its translation into English) is for sale on the website of the Kabbalah Centre, and it can be downloaded for free from the website of Bnei Baruch, <www.kabbalah.info>.

[97] Zacuto, *The Remez Commentary on the Zohar*; Loanz, *Sefer aderet eliyahu*; Buzaglo, *Sefer mikdash melekh*.

[98] See also Frisch (ed.), *Sefer tikunei hazohar im perush matok midevash*, *Sefer zohar ḥadash ve'alav ḥoneh perush matok midevash*.

[99] The team of translators was headed by Solomon Kohen, and the book includes a detailed introduction by R. Judah Edri.

[100] The book came out in three volumes. In 1992/3 another two volumes were published: Basri, *Tales from Zohar ḥadash* (Heb.).

lish by Moshe Miller of Habad.[101] The Kabbalah Centre, as mentioned above, has prepared a comprehensive English edition with the *Hasulam* commentary.[102]

Kabbalistic motifs, including zoharic ones, have found their way into popular culture:[103] for example the Israeli band Shotei Hanevuah have composed a song entitled 'Kol galgal', with lyrics from the Zohar (translated by Ashlag).[104] Kabbalistic circles (such as Yeshivat Nehar Shalom) have been active in promoting ritual readings of the Zohar, independent of any understanding of the text.[105] Together with these traditional customs (which were discussed in Chapter 6) the Kabbalah Centre has introduced a practice called 'scanning', which is another way of connecting to the non-semantic, sacred elements of the book, and which enables people who are unable to read Hebrew to perform a ritual reading. The website of the Kabbalah Centre describes the practice in the following words:

> As you begin your spiritual work with the Zohar, simply scanning the pages allows you to pass over the words and letters—opens a direct connection to the divine spark hidden within each of us. The more you bring the Zohar into your life, the stronger your connection to the Light becomes. The kabbalists tell us that just being in the presence of the volumes creates an impenetrable shield of spiritual protection against the forces of chaos and negativity in the world. Scanning the letters is a hugely beneficial next step, and one that anyone can take at any time. The power is always there, for all humanity. And it is here for you right now.[106]

[101] See Miller, *Zohar: Selections Translated and Annotated*.

[102] The translation was produced by Michael Berg, son of the leader of the Kabbalah Centre, Philip Berg. This 2003 edition includes the translation of the zoharic texts, a partial translation of Ashlag's *Hasulam* commentary, and the Zohar in the Aramaic original, punctuated, and divided into units following Ashlag's division. The book contains long introductions by Philip and Michael Berg. See Meir, 'The Revealed and the Revealed within the Concealed' (Heb.); Huss, 'Translations of the Zohar' (Heb.), 88–91.

[103] The most famous example is the integration of kabbalistic motifs in pop star Madonna's songs, video clips, and children's books; see Huss, '"Die Another Day"' (Heb.).

[104] The song is on their 2004 album *Meḥapsim et dorot*. The words of the song were taken from the *Tosefta* section in Zohar 'Vayeḥi', i. 233*b*. Other kabbalistic motifs (most of which are based on the doctrine of the Kabbalah Centre) also appear on this album as well as on their previous CD, which came out in 2000.

[105] The printing of the punctuated Aramaic original next to the Hebrew translation in the Yerid Sefarim edition was also geared towards such ritual recitation of the Zohar.

[106] See <http://cdn1.kabbalah.com/files/scanchart12_13_eng.pdf>.

Within the framework of activities geared towards dissemination of the Zohar, contemporary kabbalists have repeatedly declared its authority and sacredness (which extends to its non-semantic aspects), and have advanced arguments for its antiquity. They have justified Zohar study in light of the well-known claim that engagement in it hastens redemption. Based on the statements of hasidic scholars and earlier rabbinic authorities, these ideas reappear in the introduction to many of the books previously mentioned, as well as in contemporary publications such as the pamphlet *Mi ha'ish heḥafets ḥayim*, Daniel Frisch's *Sha'arei zohar*,[107] and *Ma'alot ha-zohar*, published by the Global Zohar Project (Mifal Hazohar Ha'olami).[108] Several contemporary kabbalists fuse these traditional concepts with those found in New Age movements, and emphasize the universal character of the Zohar, similar to esoteric circles at the turn of the last century. For example the late Philip Berg, founder of the Kabbalah Centre, has referred to the Zohar as the Holy Grail—a Christian term that gained tremendous popularity following the release of the bestseller, *The Da Vinci Code*. Berg linked the dissemination of the Zohar among the general public to the arrival of the New Age of Aquarius:

> The entire world will come to understand that the holy Zohar, which ushered in the second revelation, was intended for all humankind . . . The critical moment of change would arrive in conjunction with the Aquarian Age . . . The Aquarian influence will be a subtle force that will permit the gradual spread of the Holy Grail until it becomes an integral force of humankind.[109]

In recent years attitudes towards the Zohar, and to kabbalah in general, have shifted within academic circles, one of the most crucial changes being the repudiation of Scholem's assumptions regarding the Zohar's compilation. Yehuda Liebes, in his article 'How the Zohar Was Written',[110] has denied the textual unity of the Zohar and its attribution to R. Moses de León, suggesting instead the possibility that 'the Zohar is a collective work of a group engaged in kabbalah that shared a common heritage and ancient texts'.[111] The same assumption underlies the studies of Ronit Meroz,

107 See pp. 108–37.

108 See <http://www.ha-zohar.info>.

109 *The Zohar, by Rav Shimon bar Yochai*, ed. Berg, i. 25–8.

110 The article first appeared in 1989, and an abridged version was published in Liebes, *Studies in the Zohar*, 85–138.

111 Ibid. 88.

who has been engaged in recent years in a comprehensive study of zoharic literature.[112]

Academic scholars have translated the Zohar into English and French: in the 1980s and 1990s Charles Mopsik was working on a French translation but, sadly, this project was cut short by his premature death.[113] Daniel Matt began publishing his English translation of the Zohar in 2004, and has produced nine volumes to date.[114] These two translations are based on historical-philological research that embraces, to a great extent, Scholem's assumptions pertaining to the authorship and dating of the Zohar. Nevertheless, they diverge from Scholem's views regarding the book's distribution and its place in modern culture. This is reflected, first and foremost, in the translators' choice to prepare a complete edition of the Zohar and not a mere anthology of translated texts. Although both of these scholars have employed academic methods and presented a modern, annotated study, they do not consider the Zohar to be of primary importance in a historical sense. Rather, they deem it a cultural resource that carries spiritual significance for the modern reader.

Scholem's ambivalent approach to the text of the Zohar—one of 'admiration and disgust'—was also apparent in his presumption that Jewish mystical ideas, even if they had had significance and merit in their historical context, had lost their relevance for the modern individual. The translations of Mopsik and Matt, in contrast, reflect a sympathetic view and their authors express mostly admiration for the Zohar, calling to mind the neo-Romantic attitude of a hundred years ago. This unequivocally positive approach, which is connected to contemporary spiritual trends,[115] is clearly articulated in Matt's introduction:

The Zohar's teachings are profound and intense . . . follow the words to what lies beyond and within; open the gates of imagination . . . above all, don't reduce anything you encounter in these pages to something you already know. Beware of

[112] Meroz has published her findings in several articles in recent years, e.g. 'Ezekiel's Chariot—an Unknown Zoharic Commentary' (Heb.); '"And I Was Not There?!"' (Heb.), as well as in her forthcoming book *Headwaters of the Zohar*.

[113] *Le Zohar: Genèse*; *Le Zohar: Livre de Ruth*; *Le Zohar: Cantique des cantiques*; *Le Zohar: Lamentations*.

[114] *The Zohar: Pritzker Edition*, trans. Matt.

[115] Huss, 'The New Age of Kabbalah'.

trying to find 'the essence' of a particular teaching . . . here, essence is inadequate unless it stimulates you to explore ever deeper layers and to question your assumptions about tradition, God and self.[116]

A similar view is expressed by the Israeli kabbalah scholar Melila Hellner-Eshed in her book *A River Flows from Eden*: 'The Zohar is a spiritually inspired work of the highest order, and to my mind the world it describes is neither closed nor lost nor confined to the Middle Ages. I experience its insights as a living invitation to a special religious consciousness as well as to exegetical, cultural, and religious creativity.'[117]

The decline of the grand narratives of modernity in general, and the waning impact of socialist-secular Zionism within Israeli culture in particular; the increasing power of the ultra-Orthodox and Mizrahi communities, which had been marginalized within Israeli society; the growing influence of the culture of the New Age and the attraction of spiritual alternatives—all of these have stimulated interest in kabbalah and the Zohar in contemporary culture, both in Israel, in diaspora Jewish communities, and in the Western world in general. As a result many groups now engage in the study, commentary, and dissemination of the Zohar and compete for control of the cultural capital it represents. The application of new methods of study and circulation has expanded its accessibility. The traditional conceptions of the Zohar's stature and sanctity have been augmented with the emergence of new definitions of its symbolic value. All of these changes mark the beginning of a new chapter in the history of the Zohar.

[116] *The Zohar: Pritzker Edition*, trans. Matt, i. 25–8.

[117] *A River flows from Eden*, 9.

Bibliography

Manuscript Sources

F = microfilm number at the Institute of Microfilmed Hebrew Manuscripts, Jerusalem

Berlin, Staatsbibliothek

MS Or. Qu. 833 (F. 1754): Moses ben Shem Tov de León, *Mishkan ha'edut*

Budapest, Magyar Tudományos Akadémia

MS Kaufmann 218 (F. 14702)

MS Kaufmann A 179 (F. 4513)

MS Kaufmann A 180 (F. 12650)

Cambridge, University Library

MS Add. 389 (F. 16307)

MS Add. 521.1 (F. 16813)

MS Add. 523 (F. 16815)

MS Add. 1023 (F. 17030)

MS Add. 1196 (F. 17061)

MS Dd.3.3 (F. 15914)

MS Dd.4.2.1 (F. 15917)

MS Dd.10.14.5 (F. 15927)

Cambridge, Mass., Harvard University

MS 79

El Escorial, Biblioteca de San Lorenzo de El Escorial

MS G-3-14, 16 (F. 8840)

Florence, Biblioteca Medicea Laurenziana

MS Plut. II 18 (F. 17663)

MS Plut. II 41 (F. 17803): *Khaf dalet sodot*

MS Plut. II 48 (F. 17809)

Jerusalem, National Library of Israel

MS 8vo 147

Leiden, Universiteitsbibliotheek

MS 4762 (F. 17370): Shemayah ben Isaac Halevi, *Tseror haḥayim*

London, British Library

MS Add. 17745 (Margoliouth cat. no. 762) (F. 4952)

MS Add. 26929 (Margoliouth cat. no. 771/1) (F. 5454): David ben Judah Hehasid, *Or zarua*

MS Add. 26929 (Margoliouth cat. no. 771/4) (F. 5454): *Perush eser hasefirot*

MS Add. 27000 (Margoliouth cat. no. 767) (F. 5663): Joseph Angelet, *Livnat hasapir*

MS Add. 27003 (Margoliouth cat. no. 768) (F. 5660)

MS Or. 10527 (F. 7889)

MS Or. 10763 (F. 8078)

London, Montefiore Library

MS 113 (F. 4627)

Lyons, Bibliothèque Municipale

MS 10 (F. 5604)

MS 11 (F. 5605)

MS 12 (F. 5606)

Mantua, Comunità Israelitica

MS 129 (F. 2257)

Milan, Biblioteca Ambrosiana

MS O 81 Sup. (F. 12917)

MS O 100 Sup. (cat. no. 58) (F. 14601)

MS P 12 Sup. (F. 14595)

Modena, Biblioteca Estense

MS cat. no. 12 (F. 27777)

Moscow, Russian State Library

MS Guenzburg 83 (F. 6763)

MS Guenzburg 130 (F. 6810)

MS Guenzburg 293 (F. 47618)

MS Guenzburg 607 (F. 4192): Abraham Ibn Askirah, *Yesod olam*

MS Guenzburg 1062 (formerly 775) (F. 4194): Isaac of Acre, *Otsar haḥayim*

Munich, Bayerische Staatsbibliothek

MS hebr. 12 (F. 23107)

MS hebr. 20 (F. 23110)

MS hebr. 47 (F. 82674)

MS hebr. 203 (F. 12917)
MS hebr. 217 (F. 23122)
MS hebr. 218 (F. 31425)

New York, Jewish Theological Seminary

MS 1578 (F. 10676)
MS 1644 (F. 10742): Joseph Angelet, *Perush sha'arei orah*
MS 1674 (F. 10772): Isaac of Acre, *Otsar haḥayim*
MS 1737 (F. 10835): Joseph ben Abraham Gikatilla, *Teshuvot gikatila*
MS 1768 (F. 10866): *Likutei kabalah*
MS 1918 (F. 11016)
MS 1927 (F. 11025)
MS 1929 (F. 11027)
MS 1930 (F. 11028)
MS 2069 (F. 11167)
MS 2076 (F. 11174)
MS 2203 (F. 11301): *Perush eser hasefirot*

Oxford, Bodleian Library

MS 1561 (F. 16929)
MS 1829 (F. 18422–18424)
MS 1830 (F. 18425)
MS 1911 (F. 18844)
MS 2350 (F. 21414)
MS 2512 (F. 22226)
MS Heb. C. 53 (F. 21204)
MS Mich. 23 (F. 18073): Shemayah ben Isaac Halevi, *Tseror haḥayim*

Paris, Bibliothèque Nationale

MSS Héb. 778–9 (F. 12560)
MS Héb. 781 (F. 12562)
MS Héb. 783 (F. 12564)
MS Héb. 784 (F. 12565)
MS Héb. 791 (F. 12623)
MS Héb. 796 (F. 12628)
MS Heb. 817 (F. 12842): *Sefer hane'elam*
MS Héb. 845 (F. 14474): *Sefer kaf haketoret*

Parma, Biblioteca Palatina

MS Parm. 351 (F. 27566)

MS Parm. 2572 (F. 13534): *Sefer poke'aḥ ivrim*

MS Parm. 2627 (F. 13543)

MS Parm. 2718 (F. 13654)

MS Parm. 2774 (F. 13623)

Ramat Gan, Bar-Ilan University

MS 1039 (previously Moussaieff 64) (F. 22889)

Sassoon MS 27 (F. 9126)

Toronto, University of Toronto

MS Friedberg 5-015 (F. 70561)

Vatican, Biblioteca Apostolica

MS ebr. 68 (F. 185)

MS ebr. 204 (F. 262)

MS ebr. 206 (F. 264)

MS ebr. 207 (F. 265–6)

MS ebr. 208 (F. 267)

MS ebr. 210 (F. 269)

MS ebr. 213 (F. 272)

MS ebr. 428 (F. 501): Moses ben Shem Tov de León, *Sod hashevuot*

MS ebr. 504 (F. 589)

MS ebr. 606 (F. 8671)

MS Neofiti 22 (F. 630)

MS Neofiti 24 (F. 632)

MS Neofiti 25 (F. 633)

Warsaw, Żydowski Instytut Historyczny

MS 198 (F. 30159)

Works Cited

ABRAHAM BEN ELI'EZER HALEVI, *Ma'amar mashra ketarin*, introduction by G. Scholem, revised by Malachi Beit-Arié (Jerusalem, 1977).

ABRAMS, DANIEL, 'Critical and Post-Critical Textual Scholarship', *Kabbalah: Journal for the Study of Jewish Mystical Texts*, 1 (1996), 17–71.

—— *Kabbalistic Manuscripts and Textual Theory: Methodologies of Textual Scholarship and Editorial Practice in the Study of Jewish Mysticism* (Los Angeles, 2013).

——'Knowing the Maiden Without Eyes: Reading the Sexual Reconstruction of the Jewish Mystic in a Zoharic Parable', *Da'at*, 50–2 (2003), 487–511.

——'Orality in the Kabbalistic School of Nahmanides: Preserving and Interpreting Esoteric Traditions and Texts', *Jewish Studies Quarterly*, 2 (1995), 85–102.

——*R. Asher ben David: His Complete Works and Studies in his Kabbalistic Thought* [R. asher ben david: kol ketavav ve'iyunim bekabalato] (Los Angeles, 1996).

——'When Was the Introduction to the Zohar Written, and When Were the Copies of the Introduction of the Mantua Printed Edition Modified?' (Heb.), *Asufot*, 8 (1994), 211–26.

——'The Zohar as a Book: On the Assumptions and Expectations of Kabbalists and Modern Scholarship' (Heb.), *Kabbalah: Journal for the Study of Jewish Mystical Texts*, 12 (2004), 201–32.

ABUDRAHAM, DAVID BEN JOSEPH, *Abudraham hashalem: perush haberakhot vehatefilot* (Jerusalem, 1963).

ABULAFIA, ABRAHAM, *Sefer imrei shefer*, ed. Amnon Gros (Jerusalem, 1999).

ABULAFIA, TODROS BEN JOSEPH HALEVI, *Otsar hakavod* (Warsaw, 1808; repr. Jerusalem, 1987).

——*Sha'ar harazim*, ed. Michal Kushnir-Oron (Jerusalem, 1989).

ABULAFIA, TODROS BEN JUDAH HALEVI, *Gan hameshalim vehaḥidot*, ed. David Yellin, vol. i (Jerusalem, 1932).

ADELMAN, HOWARD E., 'Success and Failure in the Seventeenth Century Ghetto of Venice: The Life and Thought of Leon Modena' (Ph.D. diss., 2 vols., Brandeis University, 1985).

AHAI GAON, *She'iltot derav aḥai gaon*, ed. Samuel Kalman Mirsky, 5 vols. (Jerusalem, 1960–73).

AHITUV, YOSEF, 'Changes in the Religious Leadership' (Heb.), in Avraham Sagi and Zeev Safrai (eds.), *Between Authority and Autonomy in Jewish Tradition* [Bein samkhut le'otonomyah bemasoret yisra'el] (Tel Aviv, 1997), 56–83.

——*On the Border of Change* [Al gevul hatemurah] (Jerusalem, 1995).

ALASHKAR, JOSEPH BEN MOSES, *Sefer tsafenat pane'aḥ*, introd. Moshe Idel (Jerusalem, 1991).

ALBAZ, MOSES BEN MAIMON, *Heikhal hakodesh* (Amsterdam, 1653; repr. Brooklyn, 1988).

ALBO, JOSEPH, *Sefer ha'ikarim* (Warsaw, 1877; repr. Jerusalem, 1960).

ALGAZI, SOLOMON BEN ABRAHAM, *Me'ulefet sapirim* (Constantinople, 1660).

ALKABETS, SOLOMON BEN MOSES HALEVI, *Sefer berit halevi* (Lemberg, 1863).

ALMALIKH, ABRAHAM BEN JUDAH, *Likutei shikheḥah ufe'ah* (Ferrara, 1555).

AL-NAKAWA, ISRAEL IBN JOSEPH, *Sefer menorat hamaor*, ed. Hyman Enelow, 6 vols. (New York, 1929–32).

ALTMANN, ALEXANDER, 'Beyond the Border of Philosophy: The Image of the Kabbalist Rabbi Elia Hayim Genazzano' (Heb.), in Moshe Idel, Zeev Harvey, and Eliezer Schweid (eds.), *Shlomo Pines Jubilee Volume* [Sefer hayovel lishelomoh pines], vol. i (Jerusalem, 1988), 61–101.

—— 'Moses de León's *Or zarua*' (Heb.), *Kovets al yad*, 9 (1980), 219–93.

AMRAM, DAVID, *The Makers of Hebrew Books in Italy* (London, 1988).

ANGELET, JOSEPH, *Livnat hasapir*, London, British Library, MS Add. 27000 (Margoliouth cat. no. 767) (F. 5663).

—— *Livnat hasapir: A Commentary on Midrash hane'elam and an Addition to the Book of the Zohar* [Livnat hasapir: perush midrash hane'elam vetosefta lesefer hazohar, ḥibero david ben yehudah heḥasid] (Jerusalem, 1913; repr. 1971).

—— *Perush sha'arei orah*, New York, Jewish Theological Seminary, MS 1644 (F. 10742).

ANIJAR, GIL, 'Jewish Mysticism Alterable and Unalterable: On Orienting Kabbalah Studies and the Zohar of Christian Spain', *Jewish Social Studies*, 3 (1996), 89–157.

ARAMA, ISAAC BEN MOSES, *Sefer akedat yitsḥak al ḥamishah ḥumshei torah*, 6 vols. (1974).

ARIEL, DAVID S., 'Shem-Tov ibn Shem-Tov's Kabbalistic Critique of Jewish Philosophy in the Commentary on the *Sefirot*: Study and Text' (Ph.D. diss., Brandeis University, 1982).

ASHKENAZI, MORDECAI BEN JUDAH LEIB, *Eshel avraham* (Fürth, 1701).

ASHLAG, JUDAH HALEVI, *Matan torah* (Jerusalem, 1982).

—— *Sefer hahakdamot leḥokhmat ha'emet* (Benei Berak, 1996).

ASSAF, SIMHAH, 'The Controversy over the Printing of Kabbalistic Literature' (Heb.), *Sinai*, 5 (1939–40), 1–9.

—— (ed.), *Sources for the History of Jewish Education* [Mekorot letoledot haḥinukh beyisra'el], 4 vols., vols. i and ii (Tel Aviv, 1954).

AVIVI, JOSEPH, *Binyan ari'el: Introduction to the Homilies of Rabbi Isaac Luria* [Binyan ari'el: mevo derushei ha'elohi rabi yitsḥak lurya] (Jerusalem, 1987).

—— *The Kabbalah of the Vilna Gaon* [Kabalat hagra] (Jerusalem, 1993).

—— *Ohel shem: The List of Manuscripts in the Collection of Rabbi Solomon Musayef* [Ohel shem: reshimat kitvei hayad asher be'osef rabi shelomoh musayef] (Jerusalem, 1992).

—— 'R. Moses Hayim Luzzatto's *Ma'amar havikuaḥ*' (Heb.), *Hama'ayan*, 16 (1975), 49–58.

—— 'The Writings of Rabbi Isaac Luria in Italy Before 1620' (Heb.), *Alei sefer*, 11 (1984), 91–134.

AZRIEL OF GERONA, *Perush ha'agadot*, ed. Isaiah Tishby, 2nd edn. (Jerusalem, 1983).

AZULAI, ABRAHAM BEN MORDEKHAI, *Or haḥamah*, 3 vols. (Peremyshliany, 1896–8; repr. Jerusalem, 1981).

AZULAI, HAYIM JOSEPH DAVID, *Moreh be'etsba* (Livorno, 1786).

—— *Shem hagedolim* (Warsaw, 1876).

BACHARACH, NAPHTALI BEN JACOB ELHANAN, *Emek hamelekh* (Amsterdam, 1648; repr. Jerusalem, 1994).

BACHARACH, YAIR HAYIM, *Sefer she'elot uteshuvot ḥavot ya'ir* (Lemberg, 1896; repr. Jerusalem, 1968).

BAER, YITZHAK, *History of the Jews in Christian Spain* [Toledot hayehudim bisefarad hanotserit] (Tel Aviv, 1986).

—— *Studies and Essays in the History of the Jewish People* [Meḥkarim umasot], 2 vols. (Jerusalem, 1985).

BAHYA BEN ASHER, *Commentary on the Torah* [Be'ur al hatorah], ed. Charles Ber Chavel (Jerusalem, 1982).

BAŁABAN, MAJER, *The History of the Frankist Movement* [Letoledot hatenuah hafrankit], 2 vols. (Tel Aviv, 1934).

BAR-LEVAV, AVRIEL, 'The Concept of Death in the *Book of Life* by Rabbi Shimon Frankfurt' [Tefisat hamavet besefer haḥayim lerabi shimon frankfurt] (Ph.D. diss., Hebrew University of Jerusalem, 1997).

BARNAI, JACOB, *The Jews in the Land of Israel in the 18th Century* [Yehudei erets yisra'el bame'ah ha-18] (Jerusalem, 1982).

—— 'On the History of the Sabbatian Movement and its Place in the Life of the Jews in the Ottoman Empire' (Heb.), *Pe'amim*, 3 (1979), 59–71.

BARUCHSON, SHIFRA, *Books and Readers: The Reading Culture of Italian Jews at the End of the Renaissance* [Sefarim vekore'im: tarbut hakeriah shel yehudei italyah beshilhei harenesans] (Ramat Gan, 1993).

BARZILAY, ISAAC, *Yoseph Shlomo Delmedigo (Yashar of Candia): His Life, Works and Times* (Leiden, 1974).

BASILEA, SOLOMON AVIAD SAR-SHALOM, *Sefer emunat ḥakhamim* (Mantua, 1730; repr. Tel Aviv, 1970).

BASNAGE, JACQUES, *L'Histoire et la religion des Juifs depuis Jésus-Christ jusqu'à présent*, 5 vols. (Rotterdam, 1706–7); English edn.: *History of the Jews from Jesus Christ to the Present Time*, trans. and ed. Thomas Taylor (London, 1708).

BASRI, DAVID SHALOM, *Histoires du Zohar* (Jerusalem, 1993).

—— *Tales from the Zohar* [Ma'asiyot hazohar], 3 vols. (Jerusalem, 1981–9).

—— *Tales from Zohar ḥadash* [Ma'asiyot zohar ḥadash], 2 vols. (Jerusalem, 1992).

BEDERSI, YEDAYAH BEN ABRAHAM, *Beḥinat olam* (Jerusalem, 1954).

BEER, PETER, *Lehren und Meinungen aller bestandenen und noch bestehenden religiosen Sekten der Juden und der Geheimlehre oder Kabbala*, 2 vols. (Brün, 1822–3).

BEIT-ARIÉ, MALACHI, COLETTE SIRAT, and MORDEKHAI GLATZER, *Collection of Medieval Hebrew Manuscripts* [Otsar kitvei-yad ivriyim miyemei habeinayim], vols. ii and iii (Jerusalem, 1979, 1986).

BENAYAHU, MEIR, 'The Ashkenazi Community of Jerusalem 1687–1747' (Heb.), *Sefunot*, 2 (1958), 128–89.

—— *The Biography of Isaac Luria* [Toledot ha'ari] (Jerusalem, 1967).

—— 'Books Composed and Books Edited by Rabbi Moses Hagiz' (Heb.), *Alei sefer*, 2 (1976), 121–62.

—— 'The Dispute between Kabbalah and Halakhah' (Heb.), *Da'at*, 5 (1980), 61–115.

—— *Hebrew Printing in Cremona* [Hadefus ha'ivri bikrimonah] (Jerusalem, 1971).

—— *The Position of Rabbi Moses Zacuto and Rabbi Samuel Abuhav in the Controversies among the Portuguese Converts Who Returned to Judaism* [Emdatam shel rabi mosheh zakut verabi shemu'el abuhav bapulmusim shenitoreru bekerev anusei portugal sheshavu layahadut] (Tel Aviv, 1993), 29–44.

—— 'Rabbi Ezra of Fano: A Sage, a Kabbalist, and a Leader' (Heb.), in S. Israeli, N. Lamm, and Y. Raphael (eds.), *Jubilee Volume in Honor of Our Learned Rabbi Joseph B. Soloveitchik* [Sefer hayovel likhevod morenu hagaon rabi yosef dov halevi soloveitchik] (Jerusalem, 1984), 786–854.

—— *The Sabbatian Movement in Greece* [Hatenuah hashabeta'it beyavan], Sefunot 14 (Jerusalem, 1977).

—— 'The Sermons of Rabbi Joseph ben Meir Garson as a Historical Source Regarding the Expulsion from Spain and the Spanish Exiles in the Ottoman Empire' (Heb.), *Mikha'el*, 7 (1981), 42–205.

BENJAMIN NEHEMIAH BEN ELNATHAN, *Mipaulo harevi'i ad pius haḥamishi*, ed. Isaiah Sonne (Jerusalem, 1954).

Berit menuḥah (Warsaw, 1884).

BERKOWITZ, MICHAEL, *The Writings of Aaron Samuel Lieberman* [Kitvei aharon shemu'el liberman] (Tel Aviv, 1928).

BERNFELD, SIMON, *Da'at elohim* (Warsaw, 1899).

BERSON, NEHAMA, 'Isaac Satanow, the Man and His Work: A Study in the Berlin Haskalah' (Ph.D. diss., Columbia University, 1975).

BIALE, DAVID, *Gershom Scholem: Kabbalah and Counter-History* (Cambridge, Mass., 1979).

—— 'The Kabbala in Nachman Krochmal's Philosophy of History', *Journal of Jewish Studies*, 32 (1981), 85–97.

BIBAGO, ABRAHAM, *Derekh emunah* (Constantinople, 1532; repr. Jerusalem, 1970); ed. Chava Fraenkel-Goldschmidt (Jerusalem, 1978).

BISCHOFF, ERICH, *Die Elemente der Kabbalah*, 2 vols. (Berlin, 1913).

BLAU, JOSEPH L., *The Christian Interpretation of the Kabbalah in the Renaissance* (Port Washington, 1965).

BLOCH, SAMSON HALEVI, 'Letter' (Heb.), *Otsar hasifrut*, 4 (1892), 254–8.

BONFIL, ROBERT (REUBEN), *The Rabbinate in Italy during the Renaissance* [Harabanut be'italyah bitekufat harenesans] (Jerusalem, 1979).

BOURDIEU, PIERRE, *The Field of Cultural Production*, ed. Randal Johnson (New York, 1993).

—— 'The Forms of Capital', in John G. Richardson (ed.), *Handbook of Theory and Research for the Sociology of Education* (New York, 1986), 241–58.

—— *Sociology in Question*, trans. Richard Nice (London, 1993).

BOUREL, DOMINIQUE, 'Notes sur la première traduction française du Zohar', in Motzkin Mattern and Simon Sandbank (eds.), *Jüdisches Denken in einer Welt ohne Gott. Festschrift für Stéphane Mosès* (Berlin, 2001), 121–9.

BUBER, MARTIN, *Die Geschichten des Rabbi Nachman* (Leipzig, 1920).

BURMISTROV, KONSTANTIN, 'Gershom Scholem und das Okkulte', *Gnostika*, 33 (2006), 23–34.

BURNETT, STEPHEN G., *From Christian Hebraism to Jewish Studies: Johannes Buxtorf (1564–1629) and Hebrew Learning in the Seventeenth Century* (Leiden, 1996).

BUSI, GIULIO, *Mantua and the Kabbalah* (Milan, 2001).

BUXTORF, JOHANNES, *Tiberias, sive, Commentarius Masorethicus* (Basel, 1665).

BUZAGLO, SHALOM, *Sefer mikdash melekh hashalem*, 5 vols. (Jerusalem, 1995–2000).

CARLEBACH, ELISHEVA, *The Pursuit of Heresy* (New York, 1990).

CHAJES, JEFFREY HOWARD, *Between Worlds: Dybbuks, Exorcists, and Early Modern Judaism* (Philadelphia, 2003).

CHATEAU, HENRI, *Le Zohar: La Kabbale dévoilée* (Paris, 1895).

COHEN, MARK R., *The Autobiography of a Seventeenth-Century Venetian Rabbi: Leon Modena's Life of Judah* (Princeton, NJ, 1988).

CORDOVERO, MOSES BEN JACOB, *Or yakar letikunei hazohar* (Jerusalem, 1972–5).
——*Sefer gerushin* (Jerusalem, 1962).
——*Sefer hazohar im perush or yakar*, 22 vols. (Jerusalem, 1962–95).
——*Sefer or ne'erav* (Jerusalem, 1990).
——*Sefer pardes rimonim* (Jerusalem, 1962).
——*Sidur tefilah keminhag sefarad im perush tefilah lemosheh* (Peremyshliany [Przemyśl], 1892).

COUDERT, ALLISON P., *The Impact of the Kabbalah in the Seventeenth Century: The Life and Thought of Francis Mercury von Helmont (1614–1698)* (Leiden, 1999).

DA FANO, MENAHEM AZARYAH, *Pelaḥ harimon* (Venice, 1600).
——*Responsa* [Sefer she'elot uteshuvot] (Dyhernfürth, 1788).

DAN, JOSEPH, 'The Worms Epistle and the Pseudepigraphy Problem in Early Kabbalah' (Heb.), in Joseph Dan and Joseph R. Hacker (eds.), *Studies in Jewish Mysticism Presented to Isaiah Tishby on his Seventy-Fifth Birthday* [Meḥkarim bekabalah mugashim liyeshayah tishbi bimelot lo shivim veḥamesh shanim], Jerusalem Studies in Jewish Thought 3/1–2 (Jerusalem, 1984), 111–38.

DANZIG, NEIL, 'The Geonic Responsa *Sha'arei teshuvah* and *Responsa from Heaven*' (Heb.), *Tarbiz*, 58 (1988), 21–48.

DAVID, ABRAHAM, 'The Historical Significance of the "Elders" in the Words of Obadiah of Bertinoro' (Heb.), in B. Z. Kedar (ed.), *Jerusalem in the Middle Ages: Selected Papers* [Perakim betoledot yerushalayim] (Jerusalem, 1979).
——*Immigration and Settlement in the Land of Israel in the Sixteenth Century* [Aliyah vehityashvut be'erets yisra'el bame'ah hashesh-esreh] (Jerusalem, 1993).
——*Two Chronicles from the Generation of the Spanish Exile* [Shetei khronikot ivriyot midor gerush sefarad], introd. Abraham David (Jerusalem, 1979).

DAVID BEN JUDAH HEHASID, *Or zarua*, London, British Library, MS Add. 26929 (Margoliouth cat. no. 771/1) (F. 5454).
——*Sefer marot hatsovot*, ed. Daniel Chanan Matt (Chico, Calif., 1982).

DAVIDSON, ISRAEL, *Parody in Jewish Literature* (New York, 1907).

DAVIS, JOSEPH M., 'A German Jewish Woman Scholar in the Early 16th Century', in Rela Mintz Geffen and Marsha Bryan Edelman (eds.), *Freedom and Responsibility: Exploring the Challenges of Jewish Community* (Hoboken, NJ, 1999), 101–9.

DE LEÓN, MOSES BEN SHEM TOV, *Commentary on Ezekiel's Chariot* [Perush hamerkavah], ed. Asi Farber-Ginat (Los Angeles, 1998).
—— *Mishkan ha'edut*, Berlin, Staatsbibliothek, MS Or. Qu. 833 (F. 1754).

—— *Sefer hanefesh haḥakhamah* (Basel, 1608).

—— *Sefer shekel hakodesh*, ed. Charles Mopsik (Los Angeles, 1996).

—— *Sod hashevuot*, Vatican, Biblioteca Apostolica, MS ebr. 428 (F. 501).

DE LONZANO, MENAHEM BEN JUDAH, *Derekh ḥayim* (Constantinople [1570–3?]).

—— *Shetei yadot* (Venice, 1618).

DEI ROSSI, AZARYAH, *Me'or einayim* (Vilna, 1867).

DEINARD, EPHRAIM, *Alatah* [Darkness] (New Orleans, 1927).

DEL-MEDIGO, ELIJAH, *Beḥinat hadat*, ed. Isaac Samuel Reggio (Vienna, 1833; repr. Jerusalem, 1970).

—— *Beḥinat hadat*, ed. Jacob Joshua Ross (Tel Aviv, 1984).

DELMEDIGO, JOSEPH SOLOMON, *Matsref leḥokhmah* (Basel, 1529).

—— *Ta'alumot ḥokhmah* (Basel, 1529–31).

DI BOZZOLO, HAYIM OBADIAH, *Be'er mayim ḥayim* (Salonica, 1546).

DIENA, AZRIEL, *Responsa* [She'elot uteshuvot], ed. Yacov Boksenboim (Tel Aviv, 1977).

DOTHAN, SHMUEL, 'Rabbi Jacob Emden and his Generation' (Heb.), *Hebrew Union College Annual*, 47 (1976), 105–24.

DUBNOW, SIMON, *History of the Jews* (New York, 1969).

—— *Weltgeschichte des jüdischen Volkes: Von seinen Unfängen bis zur Gegenwart*, 10 vols. (Berlin, 1925–9).

DURAN, SHIMON BEN TSEMAH, *Sefer hatashbets*, 4 vols. (Lemberg, 1891; repr. Tel Aviv, 1959).

DWECK, YAACOB, *The Scandal of Kabbalah: Leon Modena, Jewish Mysticism, Early Modern Venice* (Princeton, NJ, 2011).

EICHENSTEIN, TSEVI HIRSCH BEN ISAAC OF ZHIDACHOV, *Ateret tsevi* (Lemberg, 1871–2).

ELBAUM, JACOB, *Openness and Insularity* [Petiḥut vehistagerut] (Jerusalem, 1990).

ELIOR, RACHEL, 'Joseph Karo and Israel Ba'al Shem Tov: Mystical Metamorphosis, Kabbalistic Inspiration, and Spiritual Internalization' (Heb.), *Tarbiz*, 65 (1996), 671–709.

ELKAYAM, ABRAHAM, 'The Holy Zohar of Sabbatai Zevi' (Heb.), *Kabbalah: Journal for the Study of Jewish Mystical Texts*, 3 (1998), 343–87.

—— 'The Secret of Faith in Nathan of Gaza's Writings' [Sod ha'emunah bekhitvei natan ha'azati] (Ph.D. diss., Hebrew University of Jerusalem, 1993).

EMDEN, JACOB, *Edut beya'akov* (Altona, 1756).

—— *Megilat sefer*, ed. Abraham Bick (Sha'uli) (Jerusalem, 1979).

EMDEN, JACOB, *Mitpaḥat sefarim* (Lemberg, 1870; repr. Jerusalem, 1970).

—— *Sefer leḥem mishamayim vesefer mishneh leḥem al zera'im umo'ed* (Jerusalem, 1978).

EMMANUEL BEN YEKUTIEL OF BENEVENTO, *Livyat ḥen* (Mantua, 1658).

ETKES, IMMANUEL, 'Regarding the Precursors of the Haskalah in Eastern Europe' (Heb.), in id. (ed.), *Religion and Life: The Haskalah Movement in Eastern Europe* [Hada'at vehaḥayim: tenuat hahaskalah bemizraḥ eiropah] (Jerusalem, 1993), 95–104.

ETTINGER, SHMUEL, 'The Emden–Eibeschuetz Controversy in Light of Jewish Historiography' (Heb.), *Kabbalah: Journal for the Study of Jewish Mystical Texts*, 9 (2003), 329–92.

EVEN-SHEMUEL, JUDAH, *Midreshei ge'ulah* (Jerusalem, 1944).

EVEN-ZOHAR, ITAMAR, 'Polysystem Theory', *Poetics Today*, 11/1 (1990), 9–26.

FARBER-GINAT, ASI, 'The Concept of the Merkavah in Thirteenth-Century Jewish Esotericism: *Sod ha'egoz* and Its Development' [Tefisat hamerkavah betorat hasod bame'ah hashelosh-esreh] (Ph.D. diss., 2 vols., Hebrew University of Jerusalem, 1986).

—— 'A New Fragment from Rabbi Joseph Gikatilla's Preface to *Sefer ginat egoz*' (Heb.), *Jerusalem Studies in Jewish Thought*, 1 (1981), 158–76.

—— 'On the Sources of Rabbi Moses de León's Early Kabbalistic System' (Heb.), in Joseph Dan and Joseph R. Hacker (eds.), *Studies in Jewish Mysticism Presented to Isaiah Tishby on his Seventy-Fifth Birthday* [Meḥkarim bekabalah mugashim liyeshayah tishbi bimelot lo shivim veḥamesh shanim], Jerusalem Studies in Jewish Thought 3/1–2 (Jerusalem, 1984), 67–96.

FEDER, TOBIAS, 'New Zohar for Purim' (Heb.), *Otsar hasifrut*, 3 (1889–90), 5–15 (satire and humour section).

FEINER, SHMUEL, *Haskalah and History: The Emergence of a Modern Jewish Historical Consciousness* [Haskalah vehistoryah: toledoteiha shel hakarat-avar yehudit modernit] (Jerusalem, 1995); English edn. published by the Littman Library of Jewish Civilization, 2002.

—— *The Jewish Enlightenment* [Mahapekhat hane'orut: tenuat hahaskalah hayehudit bame'ah hashemoneh-esreh] (Jerusalem, 2002).

FELIX, IRIS, 'Chapters in the Kabbalistic Thought of Rabbi Joseph Angelet' [Perakim bahaguto hakabalit shel harav yosef angelet] (MA thesis, Hebrew University of Jerusalem, 1991).

FENTON, PAUL B., 'La Cabbale et l'académie', *Pardes*, 19–20 (1994), 216–38.

—— 'A New Collection of Sabbatian Poems' (Heb.), in Rachel Elior (ed.), *The Sabbatian Movement and its Aftermath: Messianism, Sabbatianism and Frank-*

ism [Haḥalom veshivro: hatenuah hashabeta'it usheluḥoteiha: meshiḥiyut, shabeta'ut, ufrankizm], Jerusalem Studies in Jewish Thought 16–17, 2 vols. (Jerusalem, 2001), i. 329–51.

—— 'The Origins of Kabbalah' (Heb.), *Kabbalah: Journal for the Study of Jewish Mystical Texts*, 4 (1999), 141–254.

FINE, LAWRENCE, *Physician of the Soul, Healer of the Cosmos: Isaac Luria and His Kabbalistic Fellowship* (Stanford, 2003).

FISHMAN, TALYA, *Shaking the Pillars of Exile: An Early Modern Jewish Critique of Rabbinic Culture* (Stanford, 1997).

FLATTO, SHARON, 'Prague's Rabbinic Culture: The Concealed and the Revealed in Ezekiel Landau's Writings' (Ph.D. diss., Yale University, 2000).

FLECKELES, ELEAZAR BEN DAVID, *Kuntres ahavat david* (Prague, 1800).

—— *Teshuvah me'ahavah: sefer she'elot uteshuvot maharaf*, 3 vols. (Prague, 1809–21).

FRAM, EDWARD, 'Jewish Law and Social and Economic Realities in Sixteenth and Seventeenth Century Poland' (Ph.D. diss., Columbia University, 1991).

FRANCK, ADOLPHE, *La Kabbale, ou la philosophie religieuse des hébreux* (Paris, 1843); German edn.: *Die Kabbalah, oder die Religions Philosophie der Hebräer*, trans. A. Jellinek (Leipzig, 1844). English edn.: *The Kabbalah: The Religious Philosophy of the Jews*, trans. I. Sossnitz (New York, 1926).

FREIMANN, AARON, *Writings Related to Sabbatai Zevi and His Followers* [Inyenei shabetai tsevi] (Berlin, 1912).

FRENK, AZRIEL NATHAN, *Sefer agadot hazohar*, 2 vols. (Warsaw, 1923–4).

FRENKEL, YITSHAK, 'The "Berikh shemeh" Prayer' (Heb.), *Yeshurun*, 2 (1997), 559–80.

FRIEDBERG, BERNHARD HAYIM DOV, *History of Hebrew Typography of the Following Cities in Central Europe* [Toledot hadefus ha'ivri be'arim ha'eleh shebe'eiropah hatikhonah] (Antwerp, 1935).

FRIEDLAND, LEIB, *Sefer hatikun* (Chernivtsi, 1881).

FRIEDLANDER, YEHUDA, *Hebrew Satire and Polemics in Europe from the Eighteenth to Twentieth Centuries* [Bein halakhah lehaskalah] (Ramat Gan, 2004).

FRIEDLANDER, YEHUDA, *Studies in Hebrew Satire in Germany, 1790–1797* [Perakim basatirah ha'ivrit beshilhei hame'ah hashemoneh-esreh begermanyah] (Tel Aviv, 1989).

FRIMER, NORMAN, and DOV SCHWARTZ, *The Life and Thought of Shem Tov Ibn Shaprut* [Hagut betsel ha'eimah: demuto, ketavav vehaguto shel rabi shem tov ibn shaprut] (Jerusalem, 1992).

FRISCH, DANIEL, *Sha'arei zohar* (Jerusalem, 2005).

GALANTE, ABRAHAM BEN MORDECAI, *Kol bokhim* (Venice, 1689).

Galya raza. Critical Edition Based on Manuscripts, with an Introduction, Different Versions and References [Hotsa'ah bikortit al-pi kitvei yad im mavo, ḥilufei nusḥaot umarei mekomot], ed. Rachel Elior (Jerusalem, 1981).

GANS, DAVID BEN SOLOMON, *Tsemaḥ david*, ed. Mordechai Breuer (Jerusalem, 1983).

GARB, JONATHAN, 'The Understandable Resurgence of Mysticism Today' (Heb.), in Avi Sagi and Nahem Ilan (eds.), *Jewish Culture in the Eye of the Storm: Festschrift in Honour of Yosef Ahituv* [Tarbut yehudit be'ein hase'arah: sefer yovel limelot shivim shanah leyosef aḥituv] (Tel Aviv, 2002), 172–99.

GEIGER, ABRAHAM, *Das Judenthum und seine Geschichte*, 3 vols. (Breslau, 1871).

—— *Melo ḥofnayim* (Berlin, 1840).

GELBER, NATHAN MICHAEL, 'Mendel Lefin Satanover and the Proposals He Presented to the Polish Great Sejm to Improve the Polish Jews' Way of Life 1788–1792' (Heb.), in Samuel Belkin (ed.), *The Abraham Weiss Jubilee Volume* [Sefer yovel likhevod harav dr avraham weiss] (New York, 1964), 271–305.

GENAZZANO, ELIJAH HAYIM BEN BENJAMIN OF, *Igeret ḥamudot*, ed. A. W. Greenup (London, 1912).

GIKATILLA, JOSEPH BEN ABRAHAM, *Commentary on Ezekiel's Chariot* [Perush hamerkavah], ed. Asi Farber-Ginat (Los Angeles, 1998).

—— *Sha'arei orah*, ed. Yosef Ben Shlomo (Jerusalem, 1971).

—— *Teshuvot gikatila* [responsa], New York, Jewish Theological Seminary, MS 1737 (F. 10835).

GILLER, PINHAS, *The Enlightened Will Shine: Symbolization and Theurgy in the Later Strata of the Zohar* (Albany, NY, 1993).

—— *Reading the Zohar: The Sacred Text of Kabbalah* (Oxford, 2001).

GINSBURG, CHRISTIAN D., *The Kabbalah* (London, 1955).

GINSBURG, LAWRENCE M., 'Demise of Sigmund Freud's Seduction Theory', *International Forum of Psychoanalysis*, 12/4 (2003), 268–9.

GINZBURG, SIMON (ed.), *R. Moses Hayim Luzzatto and His Contemporaries: Collected Letters and Documents* [R. mosheh ḥayim lutsato uvenei doro: osef igerot ute'udot] (Tel Aviv, 1937).

GLATZER, MORDEKHAI, CHARLES BERLIN, and RODNEY G. DENNIS, *Hebrew Manuscripts in the Houghton Library of the Harvard College Library* (Cambridge, Mass., 1975).

GODWIN, JOSCELYN, *The Beginnings of Theosophy in France* (London, 1989).

—— *The Theosophical Enlightenment* (New York, 1994).

GOETSCHEL, ROLAND, 'The Conception of Prophecy in the Works of Rabbi Moses de León and Rabbi Joseph Gikatilla' (Heb.), in Joseph Dan (ed.), *The Age of the Zohar: Proceedings of the Third International Conference on the History of Jewish Mysticism* [Sefer hazohar vedoro: divrei hakenes habeinle'umi hashelishi letoledot hamistikah hayehudit], Jerusalem Studies in Jewish Thought 8 (Jerusalem, 1989), 217–37.

—— 'Samuel David Luzzatto: Ein antikabbalistischer Romantiker', in Eveline Goodman-Thau, Gert Mattenklott, and Christoph Schulte (eds.), *Kabbala und die Literatur der Romantik: Zwischen Magie und Trope* (Tübingen, 1999), 67–80.

GOLDISH, MATT, *Judaism in the Theology of Sir Isaac Newton* (Dordrecht, 1998).

—— 'Preliminary Thoughts on Kabbalah Criticism' (unpublished paper).

—— 'Rabbi Jacob Sasportas, Defender of Torah Authority in an Age of Change' (MA thesis, Hebrew University of Jerusalem, 1991).

GOLDREICH, AMOS, 'Examinations of the Self-Image of the Author of *Tikunei hazohar*' (Heb.), in Michal Oron and Amos Goldreich (eds.), *Masuot: Studies in Kabbalistic Literature and Jewish Philosophy, in Memory of Professor Ephraim Gottlieb* [Masuot: meḥkarim besifrut hakabalah uvemaḥshevet yisra'el mukdashim lezikhro shel prof. efrayim gottlieb] (Jerusalem, 1994), 459–96.

—— 'An Iberian Phrase in an Unknown Fragment of the Author of *Tikunei hazohar*' (Heb.), in Joseph Dan (ed.), *The Age of the Zohar: Proceedings of the Third International Conference on the History of Jewish Mysticism* [Sefer hazohar vedoro: divrei hakenes habeinle'umi hashelishi letoledot hamistikah hayehudit], Jerusalem Studies in Jewish Thought 8 (Jerusalem, 1989), 89–121.

—— '*Sefer hagavul* by Rabbi David ben Judah Hehasid' [Sefer hagevul lerabi david ben yehudah heḥasid] (MA thesis, Tel Aviv University, 1972).

—— '*Sefer me'irat einayim* by Rabbi Isaac of Acre: A Critical Edition' [Sefer me'irat einayim lerabi yitsḥak demin ako: mahadurah mada'it] (Ph.D. diss., Hebrew University of Jerusalem, 1981).

GOODMAN-THAU, EVELINE, 'Meyer Heinrich Hirsch Landauer: Eine Brücke zwischen Kabbalah und aufgeklärten Judentum', in Eveline Goodman-Thau, Gert Mattenklot, and Christoph Schulte (eds.), *Kabbala und die Literatur der Romantik: Zwischen Magie und Trope* (Tübingen, 1999), 249–75.

GOTTLIEB, ABRAHAM MORDECAI, *The Ladder* [Hasulam] (Jerusalem, 1997).

GOTTLIEB, EPHRAIM, *Kabbalah in the Writings of Rabbenu Bahya ben Asher* [Hakabalah bekhitvei rabenu baḥya ben asher] (Jerusalem, 1970).

GOTTLIEB, EPHRAIM, *Studies in Kabbalistic Literature* [Meḥkarim besifrut hakabalah], ed. Joseph Hacker (Tel Aviv, 1976).

——(ed.), *The Hebrew Writings of the Author of* Tikunei hazohar *and* Ra'aya meheimna [Haketavim ha'ivriyim shel ba'al tikunei hazohar vera'aya meheimna], introd. Moshe Idel (Jerusalem, 2002).

GOTTLOBER, ABRAHAM BAER, *The History of Kabbalah and Hasidism* [Toledot hakabalah vehaḥasidut] (Zhitomir, 1869).

GRABER, ISAAC SHALTIEL (ed.), *Igerot shir* (Peremyshliany, 1885).

GRAETZ, HEINRICH, *Geschichte der Juden*, 9 vols. (Leipzig, 1863); trans. Bella Löwy as *The History of the Jews* (London, 1904).

GREEN, ARTHUR, *A Guide to the Zohar* (Stanford, 2004).

——'Rabbi Isaac Ibn Sahula's Commentary on the Song of Songs' (Heb.), in Joseph Dan (ed.), *The Beginnings of Jewish Mysticism in Medieval Europe: Proceedings of the Second International Conference on the History of Jewish Mysticism* [Reshit hamistikah hayehudit be'eiropah: divrei hakenes habeinle'umi hasheni letoledot hamistikah hayehudit], Jerusalem Studies in Jewish Thought 6 (Jerusalem, 1987), 393–491.

GREENUP, ALBERT WILLIAM, 'A Kabbalistic Epistle by Isaac b. Samuel b. Ḥayyim Sephardi', *Jewish Quarterly Review*, 21 (1930–1), 365–75.

GRIES, ZEEV, *The Book in the Jewish World, 1700–1900* (Oxford, 2007).

——*Conduct Literature (Regimen Vitae): Its History and Place in the Life of Beshtian Hasidim* [Sifrut hahanhagot: toledoteiha umekomah beḥayei ḥasidav shel habesht] (Jerusalem, 1990).

——'The Copying and Printing of Kabbalistic Books as a Source for the Study of Kabbalah' (Heb.), *Maḥanayim*, 6 (1993), 204–11.

——'The Image of the Jewish Publishing Editor at the End of the Middle Ages' (Heb.), *Igeret ha'akademyah hayisra'elit lemada'im*, 11 (1992), 7–11.

——'On Tishby's Contribution to the Study of the Zohar and on the Polemics Concerning the Zohar and Its Reception in the Sixteenth Century' (Heb.), *Davar* (25 Nov. 1994), 21.

——'Shaping the Hebrew Conduct Literature at the End of the Sixteenth and Seventeenth Centuries and its Historical Significance' (Heb.), *Tarbiz*, 56 (1987), 521–87.

GROSS, ABRAHAM, *Iberian Jewry from Twilight to Dawn: The World of Rabbi Abraham Saba* (Leiden, 1995).

——'Rabbi Abraham Saba's Abbreviated Messianic Commentary on Haggai and Zechariah', *Studies in Medieval Jewish History and Literature*, 2 (1984), 389–401.

GRUENWALD, ITHAMAR, 'The Speculum and the Technique of Prophetic and Apocalyptic Vision' (Heb.), *Beit mikra*, 15 (1970), 95–7.

GUETTA, ALESSANDRO, 'Un Kabbaliste à l'heure du progrès: Le Cas d'Elie Benamozegh', *Revue de l'histoire des religions*, 208 (1991), 415–36.

HACKER, JOSEPH, 'The History of the Study of Kabbalah and Its Dissemination in Salonica in the Sixteenth Century' (Heb.), in Rachel Elior and Peter Schäfer (eds.), *Creation and Recreation in Jewish Thought: Festschrift in Honor of Joseph Dan on his Seventieth Birthday* [Al beriah ve'al yetsirah bamaḥashavah hayehudit: sefer hayovel likhevodo shel yosef dan bimelot lo shivim shanah] (Tübingen, 2005), 163–80.

—— 'The Immigration of Spanish Jews to the Land of Israel and Their Attachment to It between 1391 and 1492' (Heb.), *Shalem*, 1 (1974), 138–47.

—— 'The Intellectual Activities of the Jews of the Ottoman Empire' (Heb.), *Tarbiz*, 53 (1994), 570–603.

—— 'A New Letter from the Controversy over the Printing of the Zohar in Italy' (Heb.), in Michal Oron and Amos Goldreich (eds.), *Masuot: Studies in Kabbalistic Literature and Jewish Philosophy, in Memory of Professor Ephraim Gottlieb* [Masuot: meḥkarim besifrut hakabalah uvemaḥshevet yisra'el mukdashim lezikhro shel prof. efrayim gottlieb] (Jerusalem, 1994), 120–30.

—— 'On the Spiritual Image of Spanish Jews at the End of the Fifteenth Century' (Heb.), *Sefunot*, 17 (1983), 21–95.

—— 'Pride and Despair: The Polarity in the Spiritual and Social Experience of the Spanish and Portuguese Exiles in the Ottoman Empire' (Heb.), in Robert Bonfil, Menahem Ben-Sasson, and Joseph Hacker (eds.), *Culture and Society in Medieval Jewish History: Festschrift in Memory of H. H. Ben-Sasson* [Tarbut veḥevrah betoledot yisra'el biyemei habeinayim: kovets ma'amarim lezikhro shel ḥayim hilel ben-sason] (Jerusalem, 1989), 541–86.

HA'EZOVI, ISAAC BEN SOLOMON, *Agudat ezov*, ed. Ya'ir Ben Shalom (Netanyah, 1995).

HAGIZ, MOSES, *Mishnat ḥakhamim* (Wandsbeck, 1733).

HALBERTAL, MOSHE, *By Way of Truth: Nahmanides and the Creation of a Tradition* [Al derekh ha'emet: haramban viyetsiratah shel masoret] (Jerusalem, 2006).

—— *Concealment and Revelation* (Princeton, NJ, 2007).

—— *People of the Book: Canon, Meaning and Authority* (Cambridge, Mass., 1997).

HALEVI, ISAAC, *see* SHEMAYAH BEN ISAAC HALEVI

HALLAMISH, MOSHE, 'The Bar Yohai Poem' (Heb.), in Joseph Dan (ed.), *The Age of the Zohar: Proceedings of the Third International Conference on the History of Jewish Mysticism* [Sefer hazohar vedoro: divrei hakenes habeinle'umi hashelishi letoledot hamistikah hayehudit], Jerusalem Studies in Jewish Thought 8 (Jerusalem, 1989), 257–386.

HALLAMISH, MOSHE, *Kabbalah in Liturgy, Halakhah, and Customs* [Hakabalah batefilah, ba-halakhah uvaminhag] (Ramat Gan, 2000).

—— 'On the Controversy Concerning Kabbalah in Italy at the Beginning of the Seventeenth Century' (Heb.), *Bar-ilan*, 22–3 (1987), 179–204.

HAMBURGER, BENJAMIN SOLOMON, *The Roots of Ashkenazi Customs* [Shorshei minhagei ashkenaz] (Benei Berak, 1995).

HAMES, HARVEY, 'Elia del Medigo: An Archetype of the Halachic Man?', *Tradition*, 56 (2001), 213–27.

—— 'Elijah and a Shepherd: The Authority of Revelation', *Studia Lulliana*, 34 (1994), 93–102.

HANEGRAAFF, WOUTER J., 'The Beginnings of Occultist Kabbalah: Adolphe Franck and Eliphas Lévi', in Boaz Huss, Marco Pasi, and Kocku von Stuckrad (eds.), *Kabbalah and Modernity: Interpretations, Transformations, Adaptations* (Leiden, 2010), 107–28.

HANNOVER, NATHAN NATA, *Sha'arei tsiyon* (Amsterdam, 1671).

HARAN, MENAHEM, *The Biblical Canon: Its Consolidation Until the End of the Second Temple Period and Its Restructuring Until the End of the Middle Ages* [Ha'asufah hamikra'it: tahalikhei hagibush ad sof yemei bayit sheni veshinuyei hatsurah ad motsa'ei yemei habeinayim] (Jerusalem, 1996).

HAZARD, PAUL, *La Crise de la conscience européenne* (Paris, 1935).

HECHT, LOUISE, 'An Intellectual Biography of the Maskil Peter Beer (1758–1838)' (Ph.D. diss., Hebrew University of Jerusalem, 2002).

HELLER-WILENSKY, SARAH, *The Philosophy of Isaac Arama* [Rabi yitsḥak arama umishnato hafilosofit] (Jerusalem, 1956).

HELLNER-ESHED, MELILA, *A River Flows from Eden: The Language of Mystical Experience in the Zohar* (Stanford, 2009).

Ḥemdat yamim, 4 vols. (Venice, 1763; repr. Jerusalem, 1970).

HESCHEL, ABRAHAM JOSHUA, 'Annals of Rabbi Pinhas of Koretz' (Heb.), in *Alei ayin: The Salman Schocken Jubilee Volume* [Alei ayin: minḥat devarim lishelomoh zalman shoken aḥarei mele'ut lo shivim shanah] (Jerusalem, 1948–52), 213–44.

—— *Heavenly Torah: As Refracted through the Generations*, 2 vols. (London, 1965).

HOLZMAN, GITIT, 'The Introduction to Rabbi Samuel Zarza's *Mikhlal yofi*' (Heb.), *Sinai*, 109 (1991), 16–47.

HORODEZKY, SAMUEL ABBA, 'Kabbalah' (Heb.), *Netivot*, 1 (1913), 53–7.

HOROWITZ, ELLIOT, 'The Eve of the Circumcision: A Chapter in the History of Jewish Nightlife', in David B. Ruderman (ed.), *Essential Papers on Jewish Culture in Renaissance and Baroque Italy* (New York, 1992), 554–88.

HOROWITZ, ISAIAH BEN ABRAHAM HALEVI, *Shenei luḥot haberit*, 2 vols. (Jerusalem, 1975).

HOROWITZ, TSEVI HIRSCH BEN JOSHUA MOSES, *Aspaklarya hame'irah* (Fürth, 1776).

HORWITZ, RIVKA, *Multi-faceted Judaism* [Yahadut rabat panim: sifrut vehagut] (Jerusalem, 2002).

HURWITZ, JUDAH BEN MORDECAI HALEVI, *Tsel hama'alot* (Königsberg, 1765).

HUSS, BOAZ, 'Altruistic Communism: The Modernist Kabbalah of Rabbi Yehudah Ashlag' (Heb.), *Iyunim bitekumat yisra'el*, 16 (2006), 109–30.

—— 'The Anthological Interpretation: The Emergence of Anthologies of Zohar Commentaries in the Seventeenth Century', *Prooftexts*, 19 (1999), 1–19.

—— 'Ask No Questions: Gershom Scholem and the Study of Contemporary Jewish Mysticism', *Modern Judaism*, 25/2 (2005), 141–58.

—— 'Authorized Guardians: The Polemics of Academic Scholars of Jewish Mysticism against Kabbalah Practitioners', in Olav Hammer and Kocku von Stuckrad (eds.), *Polemical Encounters: Esoteric Discourse and Its Others* (Leiden, 2007), 81–103.

—— 'Dictionary of Foreign Words in the Zohar: A Critical Edition' (Heb.), *Kabbalah: Journal for the Study of Jewish Mystical Texts*, 1 (1996), 167–204.

—— '"Die Another Day": Madonna and Postmodern Kabbalah' (Heb.), *Zemanim*, 81 (2005), 4–11.

—— 'Forward to the East: Naphtali Hertz Imber's Perception of Kabbalah', *Journal of Modern Jewish Studies*, 12 (2013), 398–418.

—— 'Imitating the Zohar: Compositions, Poems, and Parodies Written in Zoharic Aramaic' (Heb.), in Maren R. Niehoff, Ronit Meroz, and Jonathan Garb (eds.), *And This Is for Yehuda: Studies Presented to Our Friend, Professor Yehuda Liebes, on the Occasion of His Sixty-Fifth Birthday* [Vezot liyehudah: kovets ma'amarim hamukdash leḥavrenu, prof. yehudah liebes, leregel yom huladeto hashishim veḥamishah] (Jerusalem, 2012), 359–80.

—— 'Martin Buber's Introduction to the Stories of Rabbi Nahman and the Genealogy of Jewish Mysticism' (Heb.), in Uri Ehrlich, Howard Kreisel, and Daniel J. Blidstein (eds.), *By the Well: Studies in Jewish Philosophy and Halakhic Thought Presented to Gerald J. Blidstein* [Al pi habe'er: meḥkarim behagut yehudit uvemaḥshevet yisra'el, mugashim leya'akov blidstein] (Be'er Sheva, 2008), 97–113.

HUSS, BOAZ, 'The New Age of Kabbalah: Contemporary Kabbalah, the New Age and Postmodern Spirituality', *Journal of Modern Jewish Studies*, 6 (2007), 107–25.

—— 'The New Age of Kabbalah Research' (Heb.), review of Ron Margolin, *The Human Temple*, Melila Hellner-Eshed, *A River Issues Forth from Eden*, and Jonathan Garb, *Manifestations of Power in Jewish Mysticism*, *Theory and Criticism*, 27 (2005), 246–53.

—— 'The New Year of the Tree, that is, Sabbatai Zevi' (Heb.), *Haaretz*, 'Culture and Literature' section (28 Jan. 2005).

—— 'NiSAN, the Wife of the Infinite: The Mystical Hermeneutics of Rabbi Isaac of Acre', *Kabbalah: Journal for the Study of Jewish Mystical Texts*, 5 (2000), 155–81.

—— 'On the Status of Kabbalah in Spain after the Persecutions of 1391: *Sefer poke'aḥ ivrim*' (Heb.), *Pe'amim*, 56 (1993), 20–32.

—— 'Sabbatianism and the Reception of the Zohar' (Heb.), in Rachel Elior (ed.), *The Sabbatian Movement and its Aftermath: Messianism, Sabbatianism and Frankism* [Haḥalom veshivro: hatenuah hashabeta'it usheluḥoteiha: meshiḥiyut, shabeta'ut, ufrankizm], Jerusalem Studies in Jewish Thought 16–17, 2 vols. (Jerusalem, 2001), i. 53–71.

—— 'Sacred Space, Sacred Time and Sacred Book: The Impact of *Sefer hazohar* on the Pilgrimage to Meron and Lag Ba'omer Celebrations' (Heb.), *Kabbalah: Journal for the Study of Jewish Mystical Texts*, 7 (2002), 237–56.

—— '*Sefer Hazohar* as a Canonical, Sacred and Holy Text: Changing Perspectives of the Book of Splendor between the Thirteenth and Eighteenth Centuries', *Journal of Jewish Thought and Philosophy*, 7 (1998), 257–307.

—— '*Sefer poke'aḥ ivrim*: New Information about the History of Kabbalistic Literature' (Heb.), *Tarbiz*, 61 (1992), 489–504.

—— *Sockets of Fine Gold: The Kabbalah of R. Simeon Ibn Lavi* [Al adnei faz: hakabalah shel r. shimon ibn lavi] (Jerusalem, 2000).

—— 'The Text and Context of the Zohar Sulzbach Edition', in Chanita Goodblatt and Howard Kreisel (eds.), *Tradition, Heterodoxy and Religious Culture: Judaism and Christianity in the Early Modern Period* (Be'er Sheva, 2006), 117–38.

—— 'Text und Kontext des Sulzbacher "Zohar" von 1684', *Morgen-Glantz: Zeitschrift der Christian Knorr von Rosenroth-Gesellschaft*, 16 (2006), 135–59.

—— 'Translations of the Zohar' (Heb.), in Ronit Meroz (ed.), *New Developments in Zohar Studies* [Ḥidushei zohar: meḥkarim ḥadashim besifrut hazohar], Te'udah 21–2 (Tel Aviv, 2007), 33–110.

IBN ASKIRAH, ABRAHAM, *Yesod olam* [The Foundation of the World], Moscow, Russian State Library, MS Guenzburg 607 (F. 4192).

IBN GABAI, MEIR, *Avodat hakodesh* (Jerusalem, 1954).

—— *Derekh emunah* (Berlin, 1850).

—— *Tola'at ya'akov* (Jerusalem, 1963).

IBN GAON, SHEM TOV BEN ABRAHAM, *Badei ha'aron umigdal ḥananel*, ed. David Shemuel Levinger (Jerusalem, 1979).

IBN LAVI, SIMEON, *Ketem paz* (Livorno, 1895; Jerba, 1940; repr. Jerusalem, 1981).

IBN MAKHIR, MOSES, *Seder hayom* (Venice, 1599).

IBN SHEM TOV, SHEM TOV, *Sefer ha'emunot* (Ferrara, 1658).

IBN SHUAIB, JOSHUA, *The Sermons of Rabbi Joshua Ibn Shuaib* [Derashot rabi yitsḥak ibn shu'aib], ed. Ze'ev Metsger, 2 vols. (Jerusalem, 1992).

—— *Sermons on the Torah* [Derashot al hatorah] (Kraków, 1573).

IBN SUSAN, ISSACHAR BEN MORDECAI, *Tikun yisakar* (Constantinople, 1564).

IBN TSADIK, JOSEPH, *Zekher tsadik: seder ḥag hapesaḥ*, ed. Avraham Shoshana and Shemuel Ya'akov Spiegel (Jerusalem, 1994).

IBN YAHYA, GEDALYAH, *Shalshelet hakabalah* (Jerusalem, 1962).

IBN YAHYA, TAM, *Responsa* [She'elot uteshuvot ohalei tam] (Venice, 1622; repr. Jerusalem, 1990).

IBN ZIMRA, DAVID BEN SOLOMON, *Responsa* [She'elot uteshuvot haradbaz] (New York, 1967).

IDEL, MOSHE, 'Abraham Abulafia's Works and Doctrine' [Kitvei rabi avraham abulafyah umishnato] (Ph.D. diss., Hebrew University of Jerusalem, 1976).

—— 'Abulafia on the Jewish Messiah and Jesus', *Immanuel*, 11 (1980), 64–80.

—— 'Anonymous Commentary on the Pentateuch from the Circle of Rabbi Solomon ibn Adret' (Heb.), *Mikha'el*, 11 (1989), 9–21.

—— 'The Concept of the Torah in Heikhalot Literature and its Metamorphoses in Kabbalah' (Heb.), *Jerusalem Studies in Jewish Thought*, 1 (1981), 23–84.

—— 'Differing Conceptions of Kabbalah in the Early Seventeenth Century', in Isadore Twersky and Bernard Septimus (eds.), *Jewish Thought in the Seventeenth Century* (Cambridge, Mass., 1987), 137–200.

—— 'Enquiries into the Doctrine of *Sefer hameshiv*' (Heb.), *Sefunot*, NS 2 (1983), 185–266.

—— 'Essence and Vessels in Kabbalah of the Renaissance Period' (Heb.), *Italyah*, 3 (1982), 89–110.

—— 'From Hiding to Printing an Esoteric Lore Between Rabbi Isaac Sagi Nahor and Rabbi Isaac Luria', unpublished manuscript (2005).

—— *Hasidism: Between Ecstasy and Magic* (New York, 1995).

IDEL, MOSHE, 'Jewish Thought in Medieval Spain' (Heb.), in Haim Beinart (ed.), *Moreshet Sepharad: The Sephardi Legacy* [Moreshet sefarad] (Jerusalem, 1992), 207–23.

—— 'Kabbalah and Elites in Thirteenth-Century Spain', *Mediterranean Historical Review*, 9 (1994), 5–19.

—— *Kabbalah: New Perspectives* (New Haven, 1988).

—— 'The Kabbalah's "Window of Opportunities", 1270–1290', in Ezra Fleischer, Gerald D. Blidstein, C. Horowitz, and Bernard Septimus (eds.), *Me'ah She'arim: Studies in Medieval Jewish Spiritual Life in Memory of Isadore Twersky* (Jerusalem, 2001), 171–208.

—— 'The Magical and Neoplatonic Interpretations of the Kabbalah in the Renaissance', in David Ruderman (ed.), *Essential Papers on Jewish Culture in Renaissance and Baroque Italy* (New York, 1992), 107–69.

—— 'Maimonides and Kabbalah', in Isadore Twersky (ed.), *Studies in Maimonides* (Cambridge, Mass., 1990), 31–81.

—— 'Major Currents in Italian Kabbalah between 1560 and 1600', *Italia Judaica*, 2 (1986), 243–62.

—— *Menahem Recanati the Kabbalist* [R. menaḥem recanati hamekubal] (Jerusalem, 1998).

—— 'Moses Gaster on Jewish Mysticism and the Book of the Zohar' (Heb.), in Ronit Meroz (ed.), *New Developments in Zohar Studies* [Ḥidushei zohar: meḥkarim ḥadashim besifrut hazohar], Te'udah 21–2 (Tel Aviv, 2007), 111–27.

—— *The Mystical Experience in Abraham Abulafia* (Albany, NY, 1988).

—— 'Neglected Writings of the Author of *Kaf haketoret*' (Heb.), *Pe'amim*, 53 (1993), 75–89.

—— 'On the History of the Interdiction against the Study of Kabbalah before the Age of 40', *Association for Jewish Studies Review*, 5 (1980), Hebrew section, 1–20.

—— 'On Kabbalah in Elijah Benamozegh's Thought' (Heb.), *Pe'amim*, 43 (1998), 87–97.

—— 'On the Medieval Development of an Ancient Technique for Prophetic Vision' (Heb.), *Sinai*, 86 (1980), 1–7.

—— 'On Symbolic Self-Interpretations in Thirteenth-Century Jewish Writing', *Hebrew University Studies in Literature and the Arts*, 16 (1988), 90–6.

—— 'One from a Town, Two from a Clan: The Diffusion of Lurianic Kabbalah and Sabbatianism. A Re-examination' (Heb.), *Jewish History*, 7/2 (1993), 79–104.

——'PaRDeS: Some Reflections on Kabbalistic Hermeneutics', in John J. Collins and Michael Fishbane (eds.), *Death, Ecstasy, and Other Worldly Journeys* (Albany, NY, 1995), 249–68.

——'Patterns of Redeeming Activity in the Middle Ages' (Heb.), in Zvi Baras (ed.), *Messianism and Eschatology* (Jerusalem, 1983), 253–80.

——'Rabbi David ben Judah Hehasid's Translation of the Book of the Zohar and His Interpretation of the Alfa Beita' (Heb.), *Alei sefer*, 8 (1980), 60–73; 9 (1981), 84–98.

——'Rabbi Isaac Sagi Nahor's Mystical Intention in the *Shemoneh esreh*' (Heb.), in Michal Oron and Amos Goldreich (eds.), *Masuot: Studies in Kabbalistic Literature and Jewish Philosophy, in Memory of Professor Ephraim Gottlieb* [Masuot: meḥkarim besifrut hakabalah uvemaḥshevet yisra'el mukdashim lezikhro shel prof. efrayim gottlieb] (Jerusalem, 1994), 25–52.

——'Rabbi Judah Haliwah and His Book *Tsafenat pane'aḥ*' (Heb.), *Shalem*, 4 (1984), 119–48.

——'Rabbi Moses ben Nahman: Kabbalah, Halakhah, and Spiritual Leadership' (Heb.), *Tarbiz*, 64 (1995), 535–80.

——'Rabbi Yohanan Alemanno's Order of Study' (Heb.), *Tarbiz*, 48 (1979), 303–31.

——Review of Robert Bonfil, *The Rabbinate in Italy during the Renaissance Period* (Heb.), *Pe'amim*, 4 (1980), 100–2.

——'The Sefirot above the Sefirot' (Heb.), *Tarbiz*, 51 (1982), 239–80.

——'Spanish Kabbalah after the Expulsion' (Heb.), in Haim Beinart (ed.), *Moreshet Sepharad: The Sephardi Legacy* [Moreshet sefarad] (Jerusalem, 1992), 503–12.

——'Transmission in Thirteenth-Century Kabbalah', in Ya'akov Elman and Israel Gershoni (eds.), *Transmitting Jewish Traditions: Orality, Textuality, and Cultural Diffusion* (New Haven, 2000), 138–65.

——'We Have No Kabbalistic Tradition on This', in Isadore Twersky (ed.), *Rabbi Moses Nahmanides: Explorations in His Religious and Literary Virtuosity* (Cambridge, Mass., 1983), 51–73.

IMBER, NAPHTALI HERTZ, *Treasures of Two Worlds: Unpublished Legends and Traditions of the Jewish Nation* (Los Angeles, 1910).

ISAAC OF ACRE, *Otsar haḥayim*, Moscow, Russian State Library, MS Guenzburg 1062 (formerly 775) (F. 4194).

——*Otsar haḥayim*, New York, Jewish Theological Seminary, MS 1674 (F. 10772).

ISSERLES, MOSES BEN ISRAEL, *Responsa* [She'elot uteshuvot harama], ed. Asher Ziv (Jerusalem, 1970).

ISSERLES, MOSES BEN ISRAEL, *Torat ha'olah* (Lemberg, 1858; repr. Tel Aviv, 1991).

JAFFE, ISRAEL BEN AARON, *Or yisra'el* (Frankfurt an der Oder, 1702).

JEITELES, BARUKH, *Siḥah bein shenat [5]560 uvein shenat [5]561* (Prague, 1800).

JELLINEK, ADOLF, *Beiträge zur Geschichte der Kabbala*, 2 vols. in 1 (Leipzig, 1852).

—— *Moses ben Schem-Tob de Leon und sein Verhältnis zum Sohar* (Leipzig, 1851).

—— (ed.), *Beit hamidrash*, 2 vols. (Jerusalem, 1967).

JOËL, DAVID HEYMANN, *Midrash ha-Zohar: Die Religionsphilosophie des Sohar und ihr Verhältnis zur allgemeinen jüdischen Theologie* (Leipzig, 1849).

JOST, ISAAC MARCUS, *Geschichte der Israeliten seit der Zeit der Maccabaer bis auf unsere Tage*, 9 vols. (Berlin, 1820–8).

—— *Geschichte des Judenthums und seiner Secten*, 3 vols. (Leipzig, 1857–9).

JOUNET, ALBERT, *La Clef du Zohar* (Paris, 1909).

KABAKOFF, JACOB (ed.), *Master of Hope: Selected Writings of Naphtali Herz Imber* (London, 1985).

KADDARI, MENAHEM ZEVI, *The Grammar of the Aramaic of the Zohar* [Dikduk halashon ha'aramit shel hazohar] (Jerusalem, 1971).

KADOSH, MEIR, 'Kabbalistic Jewish Laws in Responsa from the Thirteenth Century to the Early Years of the Seventeenth Century' [Hapesikah hakabalit besifrut hashe'elot uteshuvot: mehame'ah ha-13 ve'ad reshit hame'ah ha-17] (Ph.D. diss., Bar-Ilan University, 2004).

KAFIH, YIHYA BEN SHELOMOH, *Amal ure'ut ruaḥ veḥaramot uteshuvatam: me'oraot yerushalayim 5406 veteiman (tsan'a) bishenat 5672* (Tel Aviv, 1914).

—— *Sefer da'at elohim: bikoret emet tori'it* (Jerusalem, 1931).

—— *Sefer milḥamot hashem* (Jerusalem, 1931).

KARO, JOSEPH BEN EPHRAIM, *Responsa* [She'elot uteshuvot beit yosef] (Jerusalem, 1950).

—— *Sefer magid meisharim* (Amsterdam, 1768).

KATZ, JACOB, *Exclusiveness and Tolerance* [Bein yehudim legoyim] (Jerusalem, 1977).

—— *Halakhah and Kabbalah* [Halakhah vekabalah] (Jerusalem, 1986).

—— *Halakhah in Straits: Obstacles to Orthodoxy at its Inception* [Halakhah bemeitsar] (Jerusalem, 1992).

KATZ, SIMHAH, 'Epistles of Maskilim Disparaging Hasidim' (Heb.), *Moznayim*, 10 (1940), 266–76.

KAZUM, AZIZA, 'Western Culture, Ethnic and Social Closure: The Background of Ethnic Inequality in Israel' (Heb.), *Sotsiologyah yisra'elit*, 1/2 (1999), 385–428.

KESTENBERG-GLADSTEIN, RUTH, 'Who Was the Author of the *Siḥah bein shenat [5]560 uvein shenat [5]561?*' (Heb.), *Kiryat sefer*, 40 (1965), 569–70.

Khaf dalet sodot , Florence, Laurenziana, MS Plut. II. 41 (F. 17803).

KHALATS, JUDAH BEN SOLOMON, *Zeh hasefer hamefo'ar, nikra sefer hamusar* (Constantinople, 1537).

KIENER, RONALD, 'The Vicissitudes of Abulafia in Contemporary Scholarship', in *Gershom Scholem's 'Major Trends in Jewish Mysticism': 50 Years After* (Tübingen, 1993), 145–59.

KILCHER, ANDREAS B., 'Figuren des Endes: Historie und Aktualität der Kabbala bei Gershom Scholem', in Stéphane Mosès and Sigrid Weigel (eds.), *Gershom Scholem: Literatur und Rhetorik* (Cologne, 2000), 153–99.

—— *Die Sprachtheorie der Kabbala als ästhetisches Paradigma: Die Konstruktion einer ästhetischen Kabbala seit der Frühen Neuzeit* (Stuttgart, 1998).

KLAUSNER, JOSEPH, *A History of Modern Hebrew Literature* [Hahistoryah shel hasifrut ha'ivrit haḥadashah], 3 vols. (Jerusalem, 1930).

KOCH, KATHARINA, *Franz Joseph Molitor und die jüdische Tradition: Studien zu den kabbalistischen Quellen der 'Philosophie der Geschichte'* (Berlin, 2006).

KORNBLATT, JUDITH DEUTSCH, 'Solov'ev's Androgynous Sophia and the Jewish Kabbalah', *Slavic Review*, 50 (1991), 487–96.

KOSOV, BARUKH BEN AVRAHAM OF, *Amud ha'avodah* (Chernivtsi, 1863).

KREMER, ELIJAH BEN SOLOMON ZALMAN [GRA], *Sifra ditseniuta im be'ur eliyahu mivilna* (Vilna, 1882).

KREMNITZ, ISSACHAR BAER BEN PETAHYAH MOSES, *Imrei binah* (Prague, 1611).

—— *Mekor ḥokhmah* (Prague, 1611).

—— *Pitḥei yah* (Prague, 1609).

—— *Sefer yesh sakhar* (Prague, 1609).

KROCHMAL, NAHMAN, *Moreh nevukhei hazeman* (Lemberg, 1863).

KROLL, ZWI, *Ha'emet: The First Socialist Periodical in Hebrew* [Ha'emet: ha'iton hasotsyalisti harishon be'ivrit], ed. Aaron Samuel Liebermann (Tel Aviv, 1938).

KUNITZ, MOSES, *Sefer ben yoḥai* (Vienna, 1815).

KUPFER, EPHRAIM, 'Concerning the Cultural Image of German Jewry and Its Rabbis in the Fourteenth and Fifteenth Centuries' (Heb.), *Tarbiz*, 42 (1973), 385–423.

—— 'New Documents Concerning the Polemic over the Printing of the Zohar' (Heb.), *Mikha'el*, 1 (1972), 302–18.

KURIAT, JUDAH, *Maor vashemesh* (Livorno, 1839).

LANDAU, EZEKIEL BEN JUDAH, *Noda biyehudah* (Jerusalem, 1960–1).

LANDAU, JACOB BEN JUDAH, *Sefer ha'agur hashalem*, ed. Moshe Hershler (Jerusalem, 1960).

LANDAUER, MEYER HEINRICH, 'Vorläufiger Bericht über meine Entdeckung in Ansehung des Sohar', *Literaturblatt des Orients*, 6 (1845), 322–7, 341–5, 380–4, 417–22, 471–5, 488–92, 507–10, 525–8, 542–4, 556–8, 570–4, 587–92, 709–13, 748–50.

—— *Wesen und Form des Pentateuchs* (Tübingen, 1838).

LAPPIN, ELEONORE, *Der Jude: 1916–1928* (Tübingen, 2000).

LAU, BINYAMIN, 'Kabbalah in Rabbi Ovadyah Yosef's Decrees' (Heb.), *Da'at*, 55 (2005), 131–51.

LAZAROFF, ALLAN, *The Theology of Abraham Bibago* (Tuscaloosa, Ala., 1981).

LEFIN, MENAHEM MENDEL, *Elon moreh* (Odessa, 1867).

LETTERIS, MEÏR [MAX], *Memoirs* [Zikaron basefer] (Vienna, 1869).

Letters of Jewish Teachers in Renaissance Italy (1555–1591) [Igerot melamedim: italyah [5]315–[5]351], ed. Yacov Boksenboim (Tel Aviv, 1985).

LÉVI, ELIPHAS, *Le Livre des splendeurs* (Paris, 1894); trans. as *The Book of Splendours* (Wellingborough, 1973).

LEVINE, HILLEL, 'Between Hasidism and Haskalah: On a Disguised Anti-Hasidic Polemic' (Heb.), in Immanuel Etkes and Joseph Salmon (eds.), *Chapters in the History of Jewish Society in the Middle Ages and the New Era* [Perakim betoledot haḥevrah hayehudit biyemei habeinayim uva'et haḥadashah] (Jerusalem, 1980), 182–91.

LEVINSOHN, ISAAC BAER, *Beit yehudah* (Vilna, 1839).

—— *Shorshei levanon* (Vilna, 1841).

—— *Te'udah beyisra'el* (Vilna, 1828).

LIEBERMAN, CHAIM, *Ohel raḥel*, 2 vols. (New York, 1980).

LIEBERSOHN, HAYIM, *Tseror haḥayim* (Biłgoraj, 1913).

LIEBES, YEHUDA, *Elisha's Sin: The Four Who Entered the Pardes* [Ḥeto shel elisha: arba'ah shenikhnesu lapardes] (Jerusalem, 1986).

—— 'God's Attributes' (Heb.), *Tarbiz*, 70 (2000), 51–74.

—— 'Hebrew and Aramaic as Languages of the Zohar', *Aramaic Studies*, 4/1 (2006), 35–52.

—— 'How the Zohar Was Written' (Heb.), in Joseph Dan (ed.), *The Age of the Zohar: Proceedings of the Third International Conference on the History of Jewish Mysticism* [Sefer hazohar vedoro: divrei hakenes habeinle'umi hashelishi letoledot hamistikah hayehudit], Jerusalem Studies in Jewish Thought 8 (Jerusalem, 1989), 1–71.

—— 'Jonah ben Amitai as Messiah ben Joseph' (Heb.), in Joseph Dan and Joseph R. Hacker (eds.), *Studies in Jewish Mysticism Presented to Isaiah Tishby on his Seventy-Fifth Birthday* [Meḥkarim bekabalah mugashim liyeshayah tishbi bimelot lo shivim veḥamesh shanim], Jerusalem Studies in Jewish Thought 3/1–2 (Jerusalem, 1984), 269–311.

—— 'The Messiah of the Zohar' (Heb.), in S. Re'em (ed.), *The Messianic Idea in Jewish Thought* [Hara'ayon hameshiḥi beyisra'el] (Jerusalem, 1982), 87–236.

—— 'New Trends in the Research of Kabbalah' (Heb.), *Pe'amim*, 50 (1992), 150–70.

—— *The Secret of the Sabbatian Faith* [Sod ha'emunah hashabeta'it] (Jerusalem, 1995).

—— 'Sections of a Zohar Lexicon' [Perakim bemilon sefer hazohar] (Ph.D. diss., Hebrew University of Jerusalem, 1976).

—— '*Shekel hakodesh* by Moses de León, prepared for publication by Charles Mopsik' (Heb.), *Kabbalah: Journal for the Study of Jewish Mystical Texts*, 2 (1997), 271–85.

—— *Studies in Jewish Myth and Jewish Messianism* (Albany, NY, 1993).

—— *Studies in the Zohar* (Albany, NY, 1993).

—— 'Towards a Study of the Author of *Emek hamelekh*: His Personality, Writings and Kabbalah' (Heb.), *Jerusalem Studies in Jewish Thought*, 11 (1993), 101–37.

—— 'Two Young Roes of a Doe: The Secret Sermon of Rabbi Isaac Luria before His Death' (Heb.), in Rachel Elior and Yehuda Liebes (eds.), *Lurianic Kabbalah: Proceedings of the Fourth International Conference on the History of Jewish Mysticism* [Kabalat ha'ari: divrei hakenes habeinle'umi harevi'i letoledot hamistikah hayehudit], Jerusalem Studies in Jewish Thought 10 (Jerusalem, 1992), 113–69.

—— 'The Use of Words in the Zohar' (Heb.), in *In Memory of Ephraim Gottlieb* [Rabi efrayim gottlieb] (Jerusalem, 1975), 17–18.

—— 'Zohar and Eros' (Heb.), *Alpayim*, 9 (1994), 67–119.

—— 'The Zohar as a Halakhic Book' (Heb.), *Tarbiz*, 64 (1995), 581–605.

—— 'The Zohar's Relation to the Land of Israel' (Heb.), in Warren Zeev Harvey (ed.), *Zion and Zionism amongst the Jews of Spain and the Orient* [Tsiyon vet-siyonut bekerev yehudei sefarad vehamizraḥ] (Jerusalem, 2002), 31–44.

—— 'Zohar as Renaissance' (Heb.), *Da'at*, 46 (2001), 5–11.

—— 'Zohar and *Tikunei zohar*: From Renaissance to Revolution' (Heb.), in Ronit Meroz (ed.), *New Developments in Zohar Studies* [Ḥidushei zohar: meḥkarim ḥadashim besifrut hazohar], Te'udah 21–2 (Tel Aviv, 2007), 251–302.

Likutei kabalah, New York, Jewish Theological Seminary, MS 1768 (F. 10866).

LOANZ, ELIJAH BEN MOSES, *Sefer aderet eliyahu* (Jerusalem, 1998).

LURIA, DAVID BEN JUDAH, *Kadmut sefer hazohar* (Benei Berak, 1985).

LURIA, SOLOMON BEN YEHIEL, *Responsa* [Sefer she'elot uteshuvot maharshal] (Jerusalem, 1969).

—— *Yam shel shelomoh* (New York, 1968).

LUZZATTO, SAMUEL DAVID, *Vikuaḥ al ḥokhmat hakabalah ve'al kadmut sefer hazohar vekadmut hanekudot vehate'amim* (Gorizia, 1852).

LUZZATTO, SIMON BEN ISAAC SIMHAH, *Ma'amar al yehudei venetsyah*, ed. Aaron Zeev Aescoly, trans. from Italian by Dan Lates (Jerusalem, 1951).

Ma'arekhet ha'elohut im perush haḥayat (Mantua, 1558; repr. Jerusalem, 1963).

MACK, HANANEL, 'The Image of Pharaoh, King of Egypt, and the Status of the Jews in the Kingdom of Aragon-Catalonia in the Eyes of Ramban' (Heb.), *Sefunot*, 7/22 (1999), 33–47.

MAGID, SHAUL, *Hasidism on the Margin* (Madison, Wis., 2003).

MAHLER, RAPHAEL, *Hasidism and the Jewish Enlightenment in Galicia and the Congress Kingdom of Poland in the First Half of the Nineteenth Century* [Haḥasidut vehahaskalah begalitsyah uvepolin hakongresa'it bemaḥatsit hame'ah hatesha-esreh] (Merhavia, 1961).

MAIMON, SALOMON, *Salomon Maimons Lebensgeschichte*, ed. Zwi Batscha (Frankfurt am Main, 1984).

MALACHI, ELIEZER RAPHAEL, *View from a Distance: Selected Articles on Erets Yisra'el* [Mineged tireh: asupah mima'amrei e. r. malakhi, be'inyenei erets yisra'el] (Jerusalem, 2001).

MALACHI, TSEVI, *Pleasant Words* [Beno'am siaḥ] (Tel Aviv, 1983).

MARGOLIN, RON, *The Human Temple: Religious Interiorization and the Structuring of Inner Life in Early Hasidism* [Mikdash adam: hahafnamah hadatit ve'itsuv ḥayei hadat hapenimiyim bereshit haḥasidut] (Jerusalem, 2005).

MATHERS, SAMUEL LIDDELL MACGREGOR, *The Kabbalah Unveiled* (New York, 1907).

MATT, DANIEL, '*Matnita dilan*: A Technique of Innovation in the Zohar' (Heb.), in Joseph Dan (ed.), *The Age of the Zohar: Proceedings of the Third International Conference on the History of Jewish Mysticism* [Sefer hazohar vedoro: divrei hakenes habeinle'umi hashelishi letoledot hamistikah hayehudit], Jerusalem Studies in Jewish Thought 8 (Jerusalem, 1989), 123–45.

MEIR, JONATAN, 'Hillel Zeitlin's Zohar: The History of a Translation and Commentary Project' (Heb.), *Kabbalah: Journal for the Study of Jewish Mystical Texts*, 10 (2004), 119–57.

——'Michael Levi Rodkinson: Between Hasidism and Haskalah' (Heb.), *Kabbalah: Journal for the Study of Jewish Mystical Texts*, 18 (2008), 229–86.

——*Rabbi Nahman of Bratslav: World Weariness and Longing for the Messiah: Two Essays by Hillel Zeitlin* [Rabi naḥman mibratslav, tsa'ar ha'olam vekhisufei mashiaḥ: shetei masot me'et hilel zeitlin] (Jerusalem, 2006).

——'The Revealed and the Revealed within the Concealed: On the Opposition to the "Followers" of Rabbi Yehudah Ashlag and the Dissemination of Esoteric Literature' (Heb.), *Kabbalah: Journal for the Study of Jewish Mystical Texts*, 16 (2007), 151–258.

——'Stations in the Life of Michael Levi Rodkinson: Prolegomena to a Biography' (Heb.), *Gal-ed*, 22 (2010), 13–44.

——'Wrestling with the Esoteric: Hillel Zeitlin, Yehudah Ashlag, and Kabbalah in the Land of Israel' (Heb.), in Ephraim Meir and Haviva Pedaya (eds.), *Judaism: Topics, Fragments, Faces, Identities: Jubilee Volume in Honor of Professor Rivka Horwitz* [Yahadut: sugyot, keta'im, panim, zehuyot: sefer rivkah] (Be'er Sheva, 2007), 585–647.

Mekhilta derabi yishma'el, ed. Hayim Shaul Horovitz and Israel Abraham Rabin (Jerusalem, 1970).

MENASSEH BEN ISRAEL, *Nishmat ḥayim* (Stettin, 1861; repr. Jerusalem, 1968).

MENDELE MOKHER SEFARIM, *Emek habakhah* (Tel Aviv, 1957).

MENDELSSOHN, MOSES, *Or linetivah* (Berlin, 1783; repr. Bat-Yam, 1967).

MENDES-FLOHR, PAUL, 'Fin de Siècle Orientalism, the Ostjuden, and the Aesthetics of Jewish Self-Affirmation', in id., *Divided Passions: Jewish Intellectuals and the Experience of Modernity* (Detroit, 1991).

MERHAVYAH, KHEN-MELEKH, 'Two Quotes from *Midrash hane'elam* in a Latin Manuscript' (Heb.), *Kiryat sefer*, 23 (1968), 560–8.

MEROZ, RONIT, '"And I Was Not There?!": The Complaints of Rabbi Shimon bar Yohai According to an Unknown Zoharic Story' (Heb.), *Tarbiz*, 71 (2002), 163–93.

——'Anonymous Commentary on *Idra raba* by a Member of the Saruk School' (Heb.), in Rachel Elior and Joseph Dan (eds.), *Rivka Schatz Uffenheimer Memorial Volume* [Kolot rabim: sefer hazikaron lerivkah shats-ufenheimer], Jerusalem Studies in Jewish Thought 12–13, 2 vols. (Jerusalem, 1996), i. 307–78.

——'Der Aufbau des Buches Zohar', *Pardes*, 11 (2005), 16–36.

——'Ezekiel's Chariot—An Unknown Zoharic Commentary' (Heb.), *Te'udah*, 16–17 (2001), 567–616.

MEROZ, RONIT, *Headwaters of the Zohar* [Yuvelei zohar] (forthcoming).

——'The Middle Eastern Origins of the Kabbalah', *Journal for the Study of Sephardic and Mizrahi Jewry* (Feb. 2007), 39–56.

——'*Or haganuz* by Rabbi Abraham Azulai' (Heb.), *Kiryat sefer*, 60 (1985), 310–24.

——'The Path of Silence: An Unknown Story from a Zoharic Manuscript', *European Journal of Jewish Studies*, 1/2 (2008), 319–42.

——'Rabbi Joseph Angelet and his "Zoharic Writings"' (Heb.), in ead. (ed.), *New Developments in Zohar Studies* [Ḥidushei zohar: meḥkarim ḥadashim besifrut hazohar], Te'udah 21–2 (Tel Aviv, 2007), 303–404.

——'Redemption in Lurianic Teaching' [Ge'ulah betorat ha'ari] (Ph.D. diss., Hebrew University of Jerusalem, 1988).

——'The Writing of the Zoharic *Sitrei torah*: Rabbi Jacob Shats and His Co-writers' (Heb.), *Kabbalah: Journal for the Study of Jewish Mystical Texts*, 22 (2011), 253–81.

——'Zoharic Narratives and Their Adaptations', *Hispania Judaica Bulletin*, 3 (2000), 3–63.

——and JUDITH WEISS, 'The Source of Guillaume Postel's 1553 Zohar Latin Translation', *Renaissance Studies*, 28/4 (2014), 1–14.

MICHAEL, REUVEN, *Historical Jewish Writing* [Haketivah hahistorit hayehudit] (Jerusalem, 1993).

——*I. M. Jost: Founder of Modern Jewish Historiography* [I. m. jost: avi hahistoryografyah hayehudit hamodernit] (Jerusalem, 1982).

Midrash hane'elam: ruth, ed. Daniel Abrams (Jerusalem, 1992).

Midrash tanḥuma, ed. Solomon Buber, 2 vols. (Vilna, 1885).

Midrash vayikra rabah: Published According to a Manuscript and Genizah Fragments [Midrash vayikra rabah: yotse la'or al pi ketav yad useridei hagenizah], ed. Mordecai Margalioth, 3 vols. (Jerusalem, 1953).

MILLER, MOSHE, *Zohar: Selections Translated and Annotated* (Morristown, NJ, 2000).

MISES, JUDAH LEIB, 'Epistle 2' (Heb.), *Kerem ḥemed*, 1 (1833), 129–34.

——*Kinat ha'emet* [Zeal for Truth] (Vienna, 1828).

MIZRAHI, ELIJAH BEN AVRAHAM, *Responsa* [Sefer she'elot uteshuvot] (Jerusalem, 1938).

MODENA, AARON BERAHYAH BEN MOSES, *Ashmoret haboker* (Mantua, 1624).

——*Ma'avar yabok* (Mantua, 1626).

MODENA, LEON [JUDAH ARYEH], *Ari nohem*, ed. Nehemiah Samuel Leibowitz (Jerusalem, 1929).

—— *Beḥinat hakabalah*, ed. Isaac Samuel Reggio (Gorizia, 1852; repr. Jerusalem, 1968).

—— *Responsa* [She'elot uteshuvot ziknei yehudah], ed. Shlomo Simonsohn (Jerusalem, 1956).

MOPSIK, CHARLES, *Moïse de Léon: Le Siècle du sanctuaire* (Lagrasse, 1996).

MORIN, JEAN, *Exercitationes biblicae: de hebraei graecique textus sinceritate*, 2 vols. (Paris, 1669).

MORPURGO, ELIA, 'Mikhtav me'eliyahu', *Hame'asef*, 4 (1786), 66–78.

MÜLLER, ERNST, *Der Sohar: Das heilige Buch der Kabbalah, nach dem Urtext* (Vienna, 1932).

—— *Der Sohar und seine Lehre: Einführung in die Kabbalah* (Zurich, 1959).

—— *Der Sohar und seine Lehre: Einleitung in die Gedankenwelt der Kabbalah* (Vienna, 1920).

MUNK, SOLOMON, *Mélanges de philosophie juive et arabe* (Paris, 1859).

MYER, ISAAC, *Qabbalah: The Philosophical Writings of Solomon ben Yehudah Ibn Gebirol* (Philadelphia, 1888).

MYERS, JODY, *Kabbalah and the Spiritual Quest: The Kabbalah Centre in America* (Westport, Conn., 2007).

NADAV, YAEL, 'An Epistle of the Kabbalist Rabbi Isaac Mar Hayim Concerning the Doctrine of "Supernal Lights"' (Heb.), *Tarbiz*, 26 (1957), 440–58.

—— 'A Kabbalistic Treatise by Rabbi Solomon Ayllion' (Heb.), *Sefunot*, 3–4 (1960), 301–48.

NADLER, ALLAN, *The Faith of the Mithnagdim: Rabbinic Response to Hasidic Rapture* (Baltimore, 1997).

NAHMANIDES [MOSES BEN NAHMAN], *Collected Works* [Kitvei rabenu mosheh ben naḥman], ed. Charles Ber Chavel, 2 vols. (Jerusalem, 1963–4).

—— *Commentary on the Torah* [Perushei hatorah lerabenu mosheh ben naḥman], ed. Charles Ber Chavel, 2 vols. (Jerusalem, 1959–60).

NATHAN BEN YEHIEL OF ROME, *Arukh hashalem*, ed. Alexander Kohut, 8 vols. (Tel Aviv, 1970).

NAVE, PENINAH (ed.), *The Poems of Jacob Frances* [Kol shirei ya'akov frances] (Jerusalem, 1999).

Olat hatamid, *see* VITAL

O'MALLEY, JOHN W., *Giles of Viterbo on Church and Reform* (Leiden, 1968).

ORON, MICHAL, '*Midrash hane'elam*: Old and New' (Heb.), *Kabbalah: Journal for the Study of Jewish Mystical Texts*, 22 (2010), 109–48.

—— 'The *Peliah* and the *Kanah*: Kabbalistic Principles Contained within Them, Social and Religious Criticism, and Literary Composition' [Ha'peliah' veha'kanah': yesodot hakabalah shebahem, emdatam hadatit ḥevratit vederekh itsuvam hasifrutit] (Ph.D. diss., Hebrew University of Jerusalem, 1980).

ORON, MICHAL, 'Three Interpretations of *Ma'aseh bereshit* and Their Implications in the Research of the Zohar' (Heb.), *Da'at*, 50–2 (2003), 183–99.

PEDAYA, HAVIVA, *Nahmanides: Cyclical Time and Holy Text* [Haramban, hitalut: zeman maḥzori vetekst kadosh] (Tel Aviv, 2003).

PELLI, MOSHE, *Kinds of Genre in Haskalah Literature: Types and Topics* [Sugot vesugiyot besiporet hahaskalah ha'ivrit] (Tel Aviv, 1999).

PENKOWER, JORDAN S., 'A Renewed Enquiry into *Masoret hamasoret* of Elijah Levita: Lateness of Vocalization and Criticism of the Zohar' (Heb.), *Italyah*, 8 (1989), 7–73.

—— 'S. D. Luzzatto, Vowels and Accents, and the Date of the Zohar', in R. Bonfil, I. Gottlieb, and H. Kasher (eds.), *Samuel David Luzzatto: The Bicentennial of His Birth* (Jerusalem, 2004), 80–130.

PERL, JOSEPH, *Über das Wesen der Sekte Chassidim*, ed. Avraham Rubinstein; Heb. title: *Al mahut kat haḥasidim*; German manuscript with introduction and annotations in Hebrew (Jerusalem, 1977).

PERLES, JOSEPH, *Beiträge zur Geschichte der hebräischen und aramäischen Studien* (Munich, 1884).

Perush eser hasefirot, London, British Library, MS Add. 26929 (Margoliouth cat. no. 771/4) (F. 5454).

Pesikta derav kahana, ed. Bernard Mandelbaum, 2 vols. (New York, 1962).

Pesikta rabati, ed. Meir Ish Shalom [Friedmann] (Tel Aviv, 1963).

PIEKARZ, MENDEL, *The Beginning of Hasidism* [Biyemei tsemiḥat haḥasidut] (Jerusalem, 1978).

Pirkei derabi eli'ezer (Warsaw, 1852; repr. Jerusalem, 1970).

POLKAR [POLGAR], ISAAC, *Ezer hadat*, rev. Ya'akov Levinger (Tel Aviv, 1984).

POPPERS, MEIR BEN JUDAH LEIB, *Or hayashar* (Amsterdam, 1709).

—— *Or tsadikim* (Hamburg, 1690).

RABINOWITZ, HOSEA, 'Rabbi I. Abuhav's Method of Talmud Commentary' [Rabbi i. abuhav veshitato befarshanut hatalmud] (Ph.D. diss., Bar-Ilan University, 1992).

RAFLAD, MEIR, 'Kabbalistic Remnants in Maharshal's Halakhic Thought' (Heb.), *Da'at*, 36 (1996), 17–33.

RAPOPORT, SOLOMON JUDAH LOEB, 'Annals of Rabbi Hai Gaon' (Heb.), *Bikurei ha'itim*, 10 (1830), 79–95.

——'Epistle 11' (Heb.), *Kerem ḥemed*, 6 (1841), 159–78.

——*Naḥalat yehudah* (Lemberg, 1873).

RAPOPORT-ALBERT, ADA, *Women and the Messianic Heresy of Sabbatai Zevi 1666–1816* (Oxford, 2011).

RAWIDOWICZ, SIMON (ed.), *Nahman Krochmal's Works* (Heb.) (Waltham, Mass., 1961).

——(ed.), *Metsudah: Essays and Studies*, 1 (Heb.) (London, 1943).

RAZ-KRAKOTZKIN, AMNON, 'Between "Berit Shalom" and the Temple' (Heb.), *Theory and Criticism*, 20 (2002), 87–112.

——*The Censor, the Editor, and the Text: The Catholic Church and the Shaping of the Jewish Canon in the Sixteenth Century* [Hatsenzor, ha'orekh vehatekst: ha-tsenzurah hakatolit vehadefus ha'ivri bame'ah hashesh-esreh] (Jerusalem, 2005).

——'The National Narration of Exile' [Yitsugah hale'umi shel hagalut: hahistoryografyah hatsiyonit viyehudei yemei habeinayim] (Ph.D. diss., Tel Aviv University, 1996).

——'Orientalism, Jewish Studies, and Israeli Society: A Few Considerations' (Heb.), *Jama'ah*, 3/1 (1999), 34–61.

RECANATI, MENAHEM, *Perush hatorah* (Jerusalem, 1961).

——*Perush hatefilot* (Basel, 1581).

——*Sefer ta'amei hamitsvot*, ed. Simhah Bunim Lieberman (London, 1963).

REIF, STEFAN C., *Hebrew Manuscripts at Cambridge University Library* (Cambridge, 1997).

REINER, ELCHANAN, 'The Ashkenazi Élite at the Beginning of the Modern Era: Manuscript versus Printed Book', *Polin*, 10 (1997), 85–98.

——'Changes in the Yeshivot of Poland and Germany during the Sixteenth and Seventeenth Centuries and the Debate over Pilpul' (Heb.), in Israel Bartal (ed.), *Studies in Jewish Culture in Honour of Chone Shmeruk* [Keminhag ashkenaz upolin: sefer yovel leḥone shemeruk] (Jerusalem, 1993), 44–80.

——'Wealth, Social Status, and Torah Study: The Kloiz in the Jewish Society of Eastern Europe in the Seventeenth and Eighteenth Centuries' (Heb.), *Zion*, 58 (1993), 287–328.

RICCHI, EMMANUEL HAI BEN AVRAHAM, *Sefer mishnat ḥasidim* (Amsterdam, 1627).

——*Zeh sefer aderet eliyahu* (Livorno, 1742).

RICHLER, BENJAMIN, 'From the Collections of the Institute of Microfilmed Hebrew Manuscripts of the Jewish National and University Library in Jerusalem' (Heb.), *Kiryat sefer*, 58 (1983), 196–7.

ROBINSON, IRA, 'Abraham ben Eli'ezer Halevi: Kabbalist and Messianic Visionary of the Early Sixteenth Century' (Ph.D. diss., Harvard University, 1980).

Romansero sefaradi, ed. Moshe Attias (Jerusalem, 1955).

ROSENBERG, JUDAH YUDL, *Hazohar hakadosh* (Biłgoraj, 1929/30).

——*Niflaot hazohar* (Montreal, 1927).

——*Sha'arei zohar torah* (Warsaw, 1906).

——*Zohar torah al ḥamishah ḥumshei torah*, vols. i and ii (Montreal, 1924); vols. iii–v (New York, 1924–5); repr. as *Zohar torah*, 5 vols. (New York, 1955).

ROSENBERG, SHALOM, 'Emunat Hakhamim', in Isadore Twersky and Bernard Septimus (eds.), *Jewish Thought in the Seventeenth Century* (Cambridge, Mass., 1987), 285–341.

ROTH, CECIL, *The Jews in the Renaissance* (Philadelphia, 1959).

RUBIN, TSEVIYAH, *Citations from the Zohar in Rabbi Menahem Recanati's Commentary on the Torah* [Muvaot misefer hazohar baperush al hatorah lerabi menaḥem rekanati] (Jerusalem, 1992).

——'R. Moses Hayim Luzzatto and His Writings on the Zohar' [R. mosheh ḥayim lutsato: ḥiburim uferushim] (Ph.D. diss., Hebrew University of Jerusalem, 1997).

——'The Zohar Project: Goals and Achievements' (Heb.), *Kiryat sefer*, 68 (1998), 167–74.

——'The Zoharic Commentaries of Joseph Ibn Tabul' (Heb.), in Rachel Elior and Yehuda Liebes (eds.), *Lurianic Kabbalah: Proceedings of the Fourth International Conference on the History of Jewish Mysticism* [Kabalat ha'ari: divrei hakenes habeinle'umi harevi'i letoledot hamistikah hayehudit], Jerusalem Studies in Jewish Thought 10 (Jerusalem, 1992), 363–88.

——'The Zoharic Works of Rabbi Moses Hayim Luzzatto and his Messianic Conception' (Heb.), in Joseph Dan (ed.), *The Age of the Zohar: Proceedings of the Third International Conference on the History of Jewish Mysticism* [Sefer hazohar vedoro: divrei hakenes habeinle'umi hashelishi letoledot hamistikah hayehudit], Jerusalem Studies in Jewish Thought 8 (Jerusalem, 1989), 387–412.

RUDERMAN, DAVID B., *Jewish Thought and Scientific Discovery in Early Modern Europe* (Jerusalem, 2003).

SABA, ABRAHAM BEN JACOB, *Perush tseror hamor*, rev. Ya'akov Meir Weichelder, 2 vols. (Benei Berak, 1990).

——*Tseror hamor* (Warsaw, 1880; repr. Tel Aviv, 1975).

SACERDOTE, GUSTAVO, *Catalogo dei Codici Ebraici della Biblioteca Casanatense* (Florence, 1897).

SACHS, SENIOR, *Kanfei yonah* (Berlin, 1858; repr. Jerusalem, 1970).

SACK, BRACHA, 'The Commentaries of Abraham Galante' (Heb.), *Misgav Yerushalayim Studies in Jewish Literature* (1987), 61–86.

——'Exile and Redemption in Rabbi Solomon Alkabets's *Berit halevi*' (Heb.), *Eshel be'er sheva*, 2 (1980), 265–86.

——*The Kabbalah of Rabbi Moses Cordovero* [Besha'arei hakabalah shel rabi mosheh kordovero] (Be'er Sheva, 1995).

——'The Mystical Theology of Solomon Alkabez' (Ph.D. diss., Brandeis University, 1977).

SADAN, DOV, *Humoristic Visions* [Ḥezyonei hitul] (Tel Aviv, 1954).

SAFRIN, ELIEZER TSEVI, *Damesek eli'ezer* (Jerusalem, 1972).

SAFRIN, ISAAC JUDAH YEHIEL, *Notser ḥesed* (Jerusalem, 1912).

SAMBARI, JOSEPH BEN ISAAC, *Sefer divrei yosef*, ed. Shimon Shtober (Jerusalem, 1994).

SASPORTAS, JACOB, *Tsitsat novel tsevi*, ed. Isaiah Tishby (Jerusalem, 1954).

SATANOW, ISAAC, *Ḥibura tinyana* (Berlin, 1783).

——*Imrei binah* (Berlin, 1784).

——*Sefer hakuzari*, with commentary (Berlin, 1795).

——*Zemirot asaf* (Berlin, 1793).

SCHECHTER, ABRAHAM ISRAEL, 'Kabbalistic Interpolations in the Prayer Book', in id., *Lectures on Jewish Liturgy* (Philadelphia, 1933).

SCHOLEM, GERSHOM, *Bibliographia Kabbalistica* (Leipzig, 1927).

——*Briefe*, i: *1914–1947*, ed. Itta Shedletzky (Munich, 1994).

——Considérations sur l'histoire des débuts de la kabbala chrétienne', in Gershom Scholem et al. (eds.), *Kabbalistes chrétiens* (Paris, 1979), 19–46.

——'Did Moses de León Write the Zohar?' (Heb.), *Mada'ei hayahadut*, 1 (1926), 16–29.

——'The Document of Association of Luria's Disciples' (Heb.), *Zion*, 5 (1940), 133–60.

——*The Dreams of Rabbi Mordecai Ashkenazi, a Follower of Sabbatai Zevi* [Ḥalomotav shel hashabeta'i rabi mordekhai ashkenazi] (Jerusalem, 1938).

——*Elements of the Kabbalah and Its Symbolism* (Jerusalem, 1976).

——*Explications and Implications: Writings on Jewish Heritage and Renaissance* [Devarim bego: pirkei morashah uteḥiyah], 2 vols. (Tel Aviv, 1975–6).

——'The First Quotation of *Midrash hane'elam*' (Heb.), *Tarbiz*, 3 (1932), 181–3.

——*From Berlin to Jerusalem: Memories of My Youth* (New York, 1980).

—— *Die Geheimnisse der Schöpfung* (Berlin, 1935).

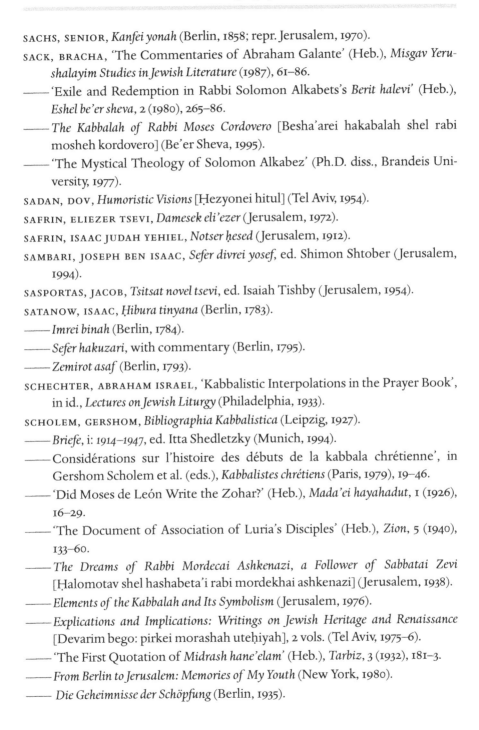

SCHOLEM, GERSHOM, 'Israel Sarug, Luria's Disciple?' (Heb.), *Zion*, 5 (1940), 214–43.

—— *Kabbalah* (Jerusalem, 1977).

—— 'The Kabbalah of Rabbi Isaac ben Solomon ben Sahula and Sefer Hazohar' (Heb.), *Kiryat sefer*, 6 (1929–30), 109–18.

—— 'The Kabbalist Rabbi Abraham ben Eli'ezer Halevi' (Heb.), *Kiryat sefer*, 2 (1925), 101–41, 269–73.

—— *Kabbalistic Manuscripts in the Hebrew University* [Kitvei yad bekabalah] (Jerusalem, 1930).

—— 'A Letter to Rivka Schatz Uffenheimer' (Heb.), *Yediot genazim*, 8(14) (1983), 345–6.

—— 'The Magid of Rabbi Joseph Taitatsak and the Revelations Attributed to Him' (Heb.), *Sefunot*, 11 (1971–7), 69–112.

—— *Major Trends in Jewish Mysticism* (New York, 1988).

—— 'Nahmanides' Real Commentary on *Sefer yetsirah*', *Kiryat sefer*, 6 (1929–30), 385–419.

—— 'New Investigations Concerning Abraham ben Eli'ezer Halevi' (Heb.), *Kiryat sefer*, 7 (1930–1), 149–65.

—— 'On Knowledge of Kabbalah in Spain on the Eve of Expulsion' (Heb.), *Tarbiz*, 24 (1955), 167–206.

—— 'On the Life and Works of the Kabbalist Rabbi Jacob Tsemah' (Heb.), *Kiryat sefer*, 26 (1950), 184–94.

—— *Origins of the Kabbalah* (Princeton, NJ, 1987).

—— 'Rabbi David ben Judah Hehasid, the Grandson of Nahmanides' (Heb.), *Kiryat sefer*, 4 (1928), 302–27.

—— 'Rabbi Isaac Luria's Authentic Works' (Heb.), *Kiryat sefer*, 19 (1942–5), 184–99.

—— 'The Remnants of Rabbi Shem Tov Ibn Gaon's Book on the Foundations of the *Sefirot* Doctrine' (Heb.), *Kiryat sefer*, 8 (1932), 397–408, 534–52; 9 (1933), 126–33.

—— 'Responsa Attributed to Joseph Gikatilla' (Heb.), in *Festschrift dr. Jakob Freimann zum 70. Geburtstag* (Berlin, 1937), 1–8.

—— Review of A. E. Waite, *The Holy Kabbalah*, *Orientalistische Literaturzeitung*, 7 (1931), 633–8.

—— *Sabbatai Zevi and the Sabbatian Movement in His Lifetime* [Shabetai tsevi vehatenuah hashabeta'it biyemei ḥayav], 2 vols. (Tel Aviv, 1974).

—— '*Sefer avnei zikaron*' (Heb.), *Kiryat sefer*, 6 (1929–30), 259–76.

—— *Studies in Sabbatianism* [Meḥkerei shabta'ut], ed. Yehuda Liebes (Tel Aviv, 1991).

—— *Studies and Texts Concerning the History of Sabbatianism and Its Metamorphoses* [Meḥkarim umekorot letoledot hashabeta'ut vegilguleiha] (Jerusalem, 1974).

—— 'Two Booklets by Rabbi Moses de León' (Heb.), *Kovets al yad*, 8 (1976), 325–84.

—— 'Vulliauds Übersetzung des Sifra Dizeniuta aus dem Sohar und andere neuere Literatur zur Geschichte der Kabbala', *Monatsschrift für Geschichte und Wissenschaft des Judentums*, 75 (1931), 347–62, 444–55.

—— *Walter Benjamin: The Story of a Friendship* (Philadelphia, 1981).

—— *Zohar, the Book of Splendor: Basic Readings from the Kabbalah* (New York, 1949).

SCHUCHAT, RAPHAEL, 'Lithuanian Kabbalah as an Independent Trend of Kabbalistic Literature' (Heb.), *Kabbalah*, 10 (2004), 181–206.

SCHULTE, CHRISTOPH, '"Die Buchstaben haben . . . ihre Wurzeln oben": Scholem und Molitor', in Eveline Goodman-Thau, Gert Mattenklot, and Christoph Schulte (eds.), *Kabbala und die Literatur der Romantik: Zwischen Magie und Trope* (Tübingen, 1999), 143–64.

SECRET, FRANÇOIS, *Les Kabbalistes chrétiens de la Renaissance* (Paris, 1964).

—— *Le Zohar chez les kabbalistes chrétiens de la Renaissance* (Paris, 1964).

Seder eliyahu raba veseder eliyahu zuta, ed. Meir Ish Shalom [Friedmann] (Jerusalem, 1960).

Seder keriah vetikun leleilei ḥag shavuot vehoshana rabah (Venice, 1648).

SED-RAJNA, GABRIELLE, 'Manuscrits du *Tiqquney ha-Zohar*', *Revue des Études Juives*, 129 (1970), 161–78.

Sefer habahir: An Edition Based on the Earliest Manuscripts [Sefer habahir: al pi kitvei hayad hakedumim], ed. Daniel Abrams (Los Angeles, 1994).

Sefer habahir: hanikra midrasho shel r. neḥunya ben hakanah, ed. Reuben Margaliot (Jerusalem, 1951).

Sefer hane'elam, Paris, Bibliothèque Nationale, MS Heb. 817 (F. 12842).

Sefer hazohar (Cremona 1559).

Sefer hazohar, ed. Reuben Margaliot, 3 vols. (Jerusalem, 1984).

Sefer hazohar al ḥamishah ḥumshei torah, 9 vols. (Jerusalem, 1994).

Sefer hazohar hashalem al hatorah, ed. Obadiah Hadaya (Petah Tikvah, 1946).

Sefer hazohar al hatorah, 3 vols. (Mantua, 1558–60).

Sefer kaf haketoret, Paris, Bibliothèque Nationale, MS 845 (F. 14474).

Sefer matok midevash: vehu perush hazohar, 6 vols., ed. Daniel Frisch (Jerusalem, 1986–90).

Sefer poke'aḥ ivrim, Parma, Biblioteca Palatina, MS Parm. 2572 (F. 13534).

Sefer shushan sodot: hameyuḥas le'eḥad mitalmidei haramban (Petah Tikvah, 1995).

Sefer tikunei hazohar (Mantua, 1658).

Sefer tikunei hazohar, ed. Reuben Margaliot (Jerusalem, 1978).

Sefer tikunei hazohar im perush matok midevash, ed. Daniel Frisch (Jerusalem, 1991).

Sefer zohar ḥadash ve'alav ḥoneh perush matok midevash, ed. Daniel Frisch (Jerusalem, 2000).

SEGAL, ALAN FRANKLIN, *Two Powers in Heaven* (Leiden, 1977).

SEIDMAN, JACOB [JANKEW], *Aus dem heiligen Buch Sohar des Rabbi Schimon ben Jochai* (Berlin, 1932).

Sepher ha-Zohar (Le Livre de la splendeur): Doctrine ésotérique des Israélites, trans. and annot. Jean de Pauly, 6 vols. (Paris, 1906–12).

SEPTIMUS, BERNARD, 'Hasidism and Power in Thirteenth-Century Catalonia', in Isadore Twersky (ed.), *Studies in Medieval Jewish History and Literature* (Cambridge, Mass., 1979), 197–230.

The Sermons of Rabbi Isaac Karo [Derashot rabi yitsḥak karo], ed. Shaul Regev (Ramat Gan, 1996).

SETZER, SAMUEL TSEVI, *Selected Writings* [Ketavim nivḥarim: meḥkarim umasot] (Tel Aviv, 1966).

Sha'ar hagilgulim, see VITAL

Sha'ar hahakdamot, see VITAL

Sha'ar hakavanot, see VITAL

Sha'ar hapesukim, see VITAL

Sha'ar ma'amrei rashbi, see VITAL

Sha'ar ma'amrei razal, see VITAL

Sha'ar ruaḥ hakodesh, see VITAL

SHAPIRA, NATHAN BEN REUVEN DAVID, *Sefer tuv ha'arets* (Venice, 1655).

SHAPIRA, TOBIAS, 'Questions of Rav Hasida and the Solutions of Rav Petahyah' (Heb.), *Hamelits*, 7/48 (19 Dec. 1867), 358–61.

SHEFFY, RAKEFET, 'The Concept of Canonicity in Polysystem Theory', *Poetics Today*, 11 (1990), 511–22.

SHEMARYAH, DAVID BEN ABRAHAM, *Torat emet* (Salonica, 1605).

SHEMAYAH [SHEMAYAHU] BEN ISAAC HALEVI, *Tseror haḥayim*, Leiden, Universiteitsbibliotheek, MS Cod. Or. 4762 (F. 17370).

—— *Tseror haḥayim*, Oxford, Bodleian Library, MS Mich. 23 (F. 18073).

—— *Tseror haḥayim*: A Critical Edition [Tseror haḥayim: mahadurah bikortit], rev. Raphael Cohen (Jerusalem, 2000).

Shivḥei habesht, ed. A. Rubinstein (Jerusalem, 1991).

SHMERUK, CHONE, *Yiddish Literature in Poland* [Sifrut yidish bepolin: meḥkarim ve'iyunim historiyim] (Jerusalem, 1981).

SHNER, MOSHE, 'Chaos, Sinai Tradition and the Formation of New Leadership' (Heb.), *Tura*, 3 (1994), 98–112.

SHNEUR ZALMAN OF LYADY, *Letters by the Author of the Tanya and His Contemporaries* [Igerot ba'al hatanya uvenei doro], ed. David Tsevi Hilman (Jerusalem, 1953).

Sifrei devei rav: maḥberet rishonah. Sifrei al sefer bamidbar vesifrei zuta, ed. Hayim Shaul Horovitz (Jerusalem, 1966).

SIMHONI, YA'AKOV NAPHTALI, 'The New Kabbalah Literature in Ashkenaz' (Heb.), *Hatekufah*, 8 (1921), 508–16.

SIMONSOHN, SHLOMO, *History of the Jews in the Duchy of Mantua* [Toledot hayehudim bedukasut mantovah], 2 vols. (Jerusalem, 1965).

SINKOFF, NANCY, 'Strategy and Ruse in the Haskalah of Mendel Lefin of Satanow', in Shmuel Feiner and David Sorkin (eds.), *New Perspectives on the Haskalah* (London, 2001), 86–102.

—— 'Tradition and Transition: Mendel Lefin of Satanow and the Beginnings of the Jewish Enlightenment in Eastern Europe, 1749–1826' (Ph.D. diss., Columbia University, 1996).

SLONIK, BENJAMIN AARON BEN ABRAHAM, *Seder mitsvot nashim* (Kraków, 1577).

—— *Sefer masat binyamin* (Vilna, 1894; repr. Jerusalem, 1968).

SMITH, BARBARA HERRNSTEIN, *Contingencies of Value: Alternative Perspectives for Critical Theory* (Cambridge, Mass., 1988).

SMITH, GARY, '"Die Zauberjuden": Walter Benjamin, Gershom Scholem, and Other German-Jewish Esoterics between the World Wars', *Journal of Jewish Thought and Philosophy*, 4 (1995), 227–43.

SMITH, JONATHAN Z., 'Sacred Persistence: Toward a Redescription of Canon', in William S. Green (ed.), *Approaches to Ancient Judaism*, vol. i (Missoula, 1978), 11–28.

SMITH, WILFRED CANTWELL, *What Is Scripture?* (London, 1993).

SMOLENSKIN, PERETZ, 'Time to Plant' (Heb.), *Hashaḥar*, 8 (1877), 97–105.

SOFER, MOSES, *Ḥatam sofer*, 'Oraḥ ḥayim', i (Vienna, 1895; repr. Jerusalem, 1970).

SPIELMAN, MORDECAI BEN TSEVI, *Sefer tiferet tsevi al sefer hazohar*, 6 vols. (Brooklyn, 1981–2003).

STEINSCHNEIDER, MORITZ, *Polemische und apologetische Literatur in arabischer Sprache* (Leipzig, 1877).

STERN, IGNAZ, 'Versuch einer umständlichen Analyse des Sohar', *Ben Chananja*, 1–5 (1858–62).

STOCK, BRIAN, *The Implication of Literacy* (Princeton, NJ, 1983).

—— *Listening for the Text: On the Uses of the Past* (Baltimore, 1990).

STRACK, HERMANN LEBERECHT, *Talmud Babylonicum Codicis Hebraici Monacensis 95* (Leiden, 1912).

SUNDBERG, ALBERT C., 'Towards a Revised History of the New Testament', *Studia Evangelica*, 4 (1968), 452–61.

The Tales of Rabbi Nachman, adapted by Martin Buber; trans. from the German by Maurice Friedman (New York, 1956).

TAMAR, DAVID, *Studies in the History of the Jews in the Land of Israel and Italy* [Meḥkarim betoledot hayehudim be'erets yisra'el uve'italyah] (Jerusalem, 1970).

TA-SHMA, ISRAEL M., '*El melekh ne'eman*: The Development of a Custom' (Heb.), *Tarbiz*, 39 (1969), 184–94.

—— 'On Greek Byzantine Rabbinic Literature of the Fourteenth Century' (Heb.), *Tarbiz*, 62 (1992), 101–14.

—— 'Responsa from Heaven' (Heb.), *Tarbiz*, 57 (1997), 51–66.

—— *The Revealed in the Concealed* [Hanigleh shebanistar] (Tel Aviv, 1995).

—— 'Where Was *Sefer alilot devarim* Written?' (Heb.), *Alei sefer*, 3 (1977), 44–53.

TIBERG, MOSHE HAYIM, *Sefer hazohar banigleh* (Tel Aviv, 1989).

TISHBY, ISAIAH, *Messianism in the Time of the Expulsion from Spain and Portugal* [Meshiḥiyut bedor gerushei sefarad uportugal] (Jerusalem, 1985).

—— *Paths of Faith and Heresy* [Netivei emunah uminut] (Jerusalem, 1982).

—— *Studies in Kabbalah and Its Branches* [Ḥikrei hakabalah usheluḥoteiha], 3 vols. (Jerusalem, 1982–3).

—— and FISCHEL LACHOWER (eds.), *The Wisdom of the Zohar: An Anthology of Texts*, trans. David Goldstein, 3 vols. (Oxford, 1989).

TSAMRIYON, TSEMAH, *Hame'asef: The First Modern Hebrew Periodical* [Hame'asef: ketav ha'et hamoderni harishon be'ivrit] (Tel Aviv, 1988).

TSEMAH, JACOB BEN HAYIM, *Zohar harakia* (Sighet, 1875).

TSIYON, MENAHEM, *Sefer tsefunei tsiyoni* (Brooklyn, 1985).

—— *Sefer tsiyoni* (Lemberg, 1882).

TWERSKY, ISADORE, 'The *Shulḥan arukh*: Enduring Code of Jewish Law', *Judaism*, 16 (1967), 141–58.

VITAL, HAYIM BEN JOSEPH, *Sefer haḥezyonot*, ed. Aaron Zeev Aescoly (Jerusalem, 1954).

—— *Sefer haḥezyonot: yomano shel rabi ḥayim vital*, ed. Morris Faierstein, rev. edn. (Jerusalem, 2006).

—— *Works of the Ari* [Kol kitvei ha'ari], 15 vols. (Jerusalem, 1988): vol. v: *Sha'ar hahakdamot*; vol. vi: *Sha'ar ma'amrei rashbi—Sha'ar ma'amrei razal*; vol. vii:

Sha'ar hapesukim; vols. viii–ix: *Sha'ar hakavanot*; vol. x: *Sha'ar ruaḥ hakodesh —Sha'ar hagilgulim*; vol. xii: *Olat hatamid*; vol. xiv: *Peri ets ḥayim*.

Vom Judentum: Ein Sammelbuch (Leipzig, 1913).

VULLIAUD, PAUL, *Traduction intégrale du Siphra Di-Tzeniutha: Le Livre du secret* (Paris, 1930).

WAITE, ARTHUR EDWARD, *The Doctrine and Literature of the Kabbalah* (London, 1902).

—— *The Holy Kabbalah* (London, 1929).

—— *The Secret Doctrine in Israel: A Study of the Zohar and Its Connections* (London, 1913).

WEILL, MICHAEL A., *La Morale du judaïsme*, 2 vols. (Paris, 1875).

WEISS, JOSEPH G., 'A Contemporary Poem on the Appearance of the Zohar', *Journal of Jewish Studies*, 8 (1957), 219–21.

WEISS, JUDITH, 'Guillaume Postel's Introduction to His First Latin Translation and Commentary on the Book of the Zohar' (Heb.), in Maren R. Niehoff, Ronit Meroz, and Jonathan Garb (eds.), *And This Is for Yehuda: Studies Presented to Our Friend, Professor Yehuda Liebes, on the Occasion of his Sixty-Fifth Birthday* [Vezot liyehudah: kovets ma'amarim hamukdash leḥavrenu, prof. yehudah liebes, leregel yom huladeto hashishim veḥamishah] (Jerusalem 2012), 254–80.

WEISSLER, CHAVA, *Voices of the Matriarchs* (Boston, 1998).

WERBLOWSKY, TSEVI, *Joseph Karo: Lawyer and Mystic* [R. yosef karo: ba'al halakhah umekubal] (Jerusalem, 1996).

—— 'Prayers at the Tomb of the Prophet Samuel' (Heb.), *Sefunot*, 8 (1964), 237–54.

WERSES, SAMUEL, *Haskalah and Sabbatianism: The Story of a Controversy* [Haskalah veshabeta'ut: toledotav shel ma'avak] (Jerusalem, 1988).

—— 'Isaac Satanow and His *Mishlei asaf*', *Tarbiz*, 32 (1963), 370–92.

—— *Trends and Forms in Haskalah Literature* [Megamot vetsurot besifrut hahaskalah] (Jerusalem, 1990).

WESSELY, NAPHTALI HERTZ, *Divrei shalom ve'emet* (Berlin, 1785).

—— 'Ma'amar ḥikur din', *Hame'asef*, 4 (1884), 97–111, 145–65.

WIJNHOVEN, JOCHANAN, '*Sefer hamishkal*: Text and Study' (Ph.D. diss., Brandeis University, 1964).

WILHELM, YA-AKOV D., '*Sidrei tikunim*' (Heb.), in *Alei ayin: The Salman Schocken Jubilee Volume* [Alei ayin: minḥat devarim lishelomoh zalman shoken aḥarei mele'ut lo shivim shanah] (Jerusalem, 1948–52), 125–46.

WIRSZUBSKI, CHAIM, *Between the Lines: Kabbalah, Christian Kabbalah, and Sabbatianism* [Bein hashitin: kabalah, kabalah notserit, shabeta'ut], ed. Moshe Idel (Jerusalem, 1989).

—— *Pico della Mirandola's Encounter with Jewish Mysticism* (Jerusalem, 1989).

WODZIŃSKI, MARCIN, *Haskalah and Hasidism in the Kingdom of Poland: A History of Conflict* (Oxford, 2005).

WOLFSON, AARON, *Siḥah be'erets haḥayim*, *Hame'asef*, 7 (1794–5), 54–67, 120–53, 203–28, 279–380.

WOLFSON, ELLIOT R., 'Beautiful Maiden without Eyes: *Peshat* and *Sod* in Zoharic Hermeneutics', in Michael Fishbane (ed.), *Midrashic Imagination* (Albany, NY, 1993), 155–203.

—— 'Beyond the Spoken Word: Oral Tradition and Written Transmission in Medieval Jewish Mysticism', in Ya'akov Elman and Israel Gershoni (eds.), *Transmitting Jewish Traditions: Orality, Textuality, and Cultural Diffusion* (New Haven, 2000), 166–224.

—— *The Book of the Pomegranate: Moses De Leon's* Sefer harimon (Atlanta, 1988).

—— 'By Way of Truth: Aspects of Nahmanides' Kabbalistic Hermeneutic', *Association for Jewish Studies Review*, 14 (1989), 103–78.

—— 'Hai Gaon's Letter and Commentary on *Aleynu*: Further Evidence of Moses de Leon's Pseudepigraphic Activity', *Jewish Quarterly Review*, 81 (1991), 365–409.

—— The Hermeneutics of Visionary Experience: Revelation and Interpretation in the Zohar', *Religion*, 18 (1988), 311–45.

—— *Through a Speculum that Shines: Vision and Imagination in Medival Jewish Mysticism* (Princeton, NJ, 1994).

Words of the Righteous: An Anti-Hasidic Satire by Joseph Perl and Isaac Baer Levinsohn [Gilgulav shel megaleh sod: kuntres divrei tsadikim lerival veyosef perl], ed. and introd. Jonatan Meir (Los Angeles, 2004).

YA'ARI, AVRAHAM, 'History of the New Year of Trees' (Heb.), *Maḥanayim*, 42 (1960), 15–24.

—— *Studies in Hebrew Booklore* [Meḥkerei sefer] (Jerusalem, 1958).

—— 'Three Generations of Printers in Constantinople: Yonah ben Jacob Ashkenazi, His Sons, and His Grandsons' (Heb.), *Kiryat sefer*, 14 (1937), 238–54.

—— '*Tikunim* and Prayers According to *Sefer ḥemdat yamim*' (Heb.), *Kiryat sefer*, 38 (1963), 97–112, 247–62, 380–400.

YISRA'ELI, ODED, *The Interpretation of Secrets and the Secrets of Interpretation: Midrashic and Hermeneutic Strategies in Sava demishpatim of the Zohar* [Parshanut hasod vesod haparshanut: megamot midrashiyot vehermenoitiyot be'sava demishpatim' shebazohar] (Los Angeles, 2005).

YUVAL, YISRA'EL, *Scholars in Their Time: The Religious Leadership of German Jewry in the Late Middle Ages* [Ḥakhamim bedoram: hamanhigut haruḥanit shel yehudei germanyah beshilhei yemei habeinayim] (Jerusalem, 1988).

ZACUTO, ABRAHAM BEN SAMUEL, *Sefer yuḥasin hashalem*, ed. Herschell [Tsevi] Filipowski (Jerusalem, 1962).

ZACUTO, MOSES BEN MORDECAI, *The Remez Commentary on the Holy Zohar* [Sefer perush haremez lazohar hakadosh], 6 vols. (Moshav Bithah, 1998–2006).

ZEITLIN, HILLEL, 'Annotated Translation of the Introduction to the Zohar' (Heb.), *Hametsudah*, 1 (1943), 36–81.

—— 'The Antiquity of Mystery in Israel' (Heb.), *Hatekufah*, 5 (1920), 280–322.

—— *Befardes haḥasidut vehakabalah* (Tel Aviv, 1965).

—— 'A Key to the Zohar' (Heb.), *Hatekufah*, 6 (1920), 314–32; 7 (1920), 353–68; 9 (1921), 265–330.

—— *Sifran shel yeḥidim: ketavim mekubatsim* (Jerusalem, 1979).

ZFATMAN-BILLER, SARA, *Yiddish Narrative Prose from Its Beginnings to 'Shivḥei habesht' (1504–1814)* [Hasiporet beyidish: mereshitah ad 'shivḥei habesht' (1504–1814)] (Jerusalem, 1985).

Le Zohar: Cantique des cantiques, trans. Charles Mopsik (Paris, 1999).

Le Zohar: Genèse, 4 vols., trans. Charles Mopsik (Paris, 1981–94).

Le Zohar: Lamentations, trans. Charles Mopsik (Paris, 2000).

Le Zohar: Livre de Ruth, trans. Charles Mopsik (Paris, 1987).

The Zohar, trans. Maurice Simon, Harry Sperling, and Paul Lavertoff, 5 vols. (London, 1931–4).

Zohar: The Book of Enlightenment, trans. and introd. Daniel Matt (Ramsey, NJ, 1983).

The Zohar: Pritzker Edition, trans. and commentary Daniel C. Matt, vols. i–iii (Stanford, Calif., 2004–6).

The Zohar, by Rav Shimon bar Yochai, from the Book of Avraham, with the Sulam Commentary by Rav Yehuda Ashlag, ed. and comp. by Michael Berg, 23 vols. (New York, 2003).

The Zohar with the Yedid nefesh *Commentary* [Sefer hazohar im be'ur yedid nefesh], commentary Yehiel Avraham Bar Lev, 14 vols. (Petah Tikvah, 1992–9).

Zohar ḥadash, ed. Reuben Margaliot (Jerusalem, 1978).

Zohar ḥadash umidrash hane'elam (Salonica, 1597).

ZUNZ, LEOPOLD, *Jewish Sermons and Their Historical Development* [Haderashot beyisra'el vehishtalshelutan hahistorit] (Jerusalem, 1974).

ZWELLING, JEREMY, 'Joseph of Hamadan's *Sefer tashak*: Critical Text Edition with Introduction' (Ph.D. diss., Brandeis University, 1975).

Index

Moses Bivi 191
Moses of Kiev 77–8
Moses de León, *see* de León, Moses
Moses ibn Makhir 211
Moses Matt 145, 206
Moses Pinheiro 224, 226
Müller, Ernst 301, 305
Munk, Solomon 258 n. 76, 286, 295
Myer, Frederick Isaac 298, 299
mysticism:
 and halakhah 310–11
 and Romanticism 290, 294, 297, 299–302, 308, 309, 319

N

Nahmanides (Moses ben Nahman; Ramban):
 and Castilian kabbalists 31–2, 34, 59–62, 67, 200, 242
 commentary on the Torah 12, 59–60, 64, 67, 114, 187
 conservatism 11–13, 32–4, 60, 63–6, 185
 and criticism of Zohar 241–2
 dominance 7, 11, 31, 36, 59–61, 64–5, 67, 241
 and oral tradition 11–12, 32, 63–6, 133, 199, 304
 and primary elite 11–12, 57, 59
 revelation from Moses 63
 and Shimon bar Yohai 12–13, 17–18, 60–2, 113, 116–17
 works: *Sha'ar hagemul* 17, 32–3
Naphtali Hakohen Katz of Frankfurt 217–18
Naphtali ben Joseph Ashkenazi 105
Nathan of Gaza 177 n. 102, 224–6, 227–8, 231
nationalism, Jewish 9, 293, 294, 301, 303, 309, 311–12
Neoplatonism, Jewish 244, 274
neo-Romanticism 301, 305, 309, 311–12, 319
New Age movement, and kabbalah 315–16, 318, 320
Newton, Isaac 257 n. 73
Nicholai, Friedrich 268
Nisim, Isaac 146 n. 133
North Africa:
 and criticism of Zohar 139
 and interpretation of Zohar 152
 and kabbalah manuscripts 86–7, 93, 96, 97–8, 105
 and Spanish kabbalists 85, 87, 89, 116, 121, 206–7

O

Obadiah ben Petahyah 283, 288 n. 240
occultism 298–301, 308, 309–10
oral tradition:
 and kabbalah 11–12, 32, 63–6, 133, 143, 156, 186–7, 199
 and Zohar 65–6, 109–10, 172, 185–7, 204–5, 295
orientalism, and kabbalah 297–8, 300–1, 309
Ottoman empire, and Spanish exiles 134, 136, 142

P

paganism, and kabbalah 280
Palestine:
 kabbalists in 48, 73, 85, 88, 102, 119, 175, 182 n. 119
 and Zohar manuscripts 82, 101–2, 105
Papus (Gérard Encausse) 310
Parnas, Isaiah Gershoni (Franciscus) 93–4, 98
parody, and criticism of Zohar 2, 271, 276, 278–80, 282, 287–9, 292–3
'Pataḥeliyahu' 211–12, 220, 223
Pedaya, Haviva 32
Penkower, Jordan S. 245
Perl, Joseph 277, 282, 288 n. 240, 290
Perlhafter, Baer 230
Perls, Isaac 207
Perush eser hasefirot 51 n. 63
Pesikta rabati 25
philology, and authenticity of Zohar 251, 259, 284, 287, 298, 311–12, 314, 319
philosophy:
 and kabbalah 133, 134–6, 139, 253–4, 256–7, 268, 270, 274, 276, 280–1, 296–7
 see also Maimonides; Neoplatonism; Platonism
Pico della Mirandola, Giovanni 77 n. 41
Pikudin 68, 89, 104
Pirkei derabi eli'ezer 27
Platonism, and kabbalah 244, 253–4
Poli, Judah 105
Polkar, Isaac 109 n. 160
Poppers, Meir 213–14

T

Printed and bound by CPI Group (UK) Ltd, Croydon, CR0 4YY
09/06/2025
14685945-0004